PRINCETON SEMIN

in American Religion and C

PRINCETON SEMINARY
in American Religion and Culture

James H. Moorhead

WILLIAM B. EERDMANS PUBLISHING COMPANY
GRAND RAPIDS, MICHIGAN / CAMBRIDGE, U.K.

Published 2012 by

Wm. B. Eerdmans Publishing Co.

2140 Oak Industrial Drive N.E., Grand Rapids, Michigan 49505 /
P.O. Box 163, Cambridge CB3 9PU U.K.

Printed in the United States of America

18 17 16 15 14 13 12   7 6 5 4 3 2 1

Library of Congress Cataloging-in-Publication Data

Moorhead, James H.

Princeton Seminary in American religion and culture / James H. Moorhead.

p.   cm.

ISBN 978-0-8028-6752-0 (cloth: alk. paper)

1. Princeton Theological Seminary — History.

· 2. United States — Church history.   I. Title.

BV4070.P76M66   2012

230.07´35174965 — dc23

2012009864

www.eerdmans.com

In memory of

THOMAS WILLIAM GILLESPIE,

president, pastor, and friend to the Princeton Seminary community

from 1983 to 2004

Contents

Contents

Acknowledgments and a
Brief Note on the Method of This Study

T HE TWO centuries of Princeton Seminary's life could yield many histories. To investigate and narrate them all would require at least a lifetime of patient study, and even then the goal would most likely elude the researcher. Lefferts A. Loetscher, a fine historian who taught for thirty-three years at Princeton, devoted a significant portion of his career to exploring the seminary's history and continued the effort during the seven years of his all-too-brief retirement. His meticulous labors produced an excellent work, published posthumously; but its scope — a study of Archibald Alexander — fell considerably short of what Loetscher had once hoped to cover. When conducting a preliminary survey of the mountains of relevant sources before starting to write this book, I was overcome by a sinking feeling — an existential appreciation of the reason Loetscher got no further than he did and an anxiety that perhaps anyone who attempted a history from 1812 to the present would likewise miss the target.

Recognizing the impossibility of reading every document or of adequately covering every aspect of the seminary's history, I opted for a more focused inquiry and decided on the questions I wanted most to answer and the issues I wished chiefly to illuminate. In his perceptive study of pre–Civil War theological education, Glenn T. Miller posed a problem that resonated with my own interests: What, he asked, were "the aims and purposes of early nineteenth-century theological education" and how were "those ideals incarnated in particular schools"? Miller stated succinctly part of what I hoped to answer. What did successive generations of leaders at Princeton, from the founders to the present, want to accomplish? What convictions, theological and otherwise, shaped their perception of their work, the church, and the world? I also wanted to avoid a narrowly focused institutional history in favor of a narrative placing the seminary's vision and goals within the larger ecology of American religion, culture, and society — hence the title of the book, *Princeton Seminary in American Religion and Culture.*[1]

In constructing the narrative, I have not attempted to discuss every professor or every facet of the seminary's life. Undoubtedly some who read these pages will rue the failure to mention certain favorite professors or will bemoan the relatively brief treatment that others have received. Because of the focus of my work, other important matters receive relatively light treatment: for example, student life at Princeton, the seminary's contributions to the church and world through its alumni, the growth of the school's physical plant, the development of its music program, and the process by which the endowment of the seminary was raised. Readers may have other topics that they would add to the list. Thus this book makes no claim to offer a complete or definitive history of Princeton Seminary. It is, to reiterate the point already made, a narrative tracing the school's sense of mission, its basic values, and the way these interacted with — and sometimes against — the religion and culture of the time.

A book begins long before pen is set to paper or fingers to keyboard. This volume has perhaps its most distant origins in a visit I made to Princeton Seminary in 1966. My pastor, Donald R. Davis (Princeton B.D., 1959), was commuting on Mondays to his alma mater as he studied for the Th.M. degree. Knowing my ambitions for a theological education, he invited me to spend a day of my freshman spring break accompanying him on one of his Monday trips. I sat in on a class or two, prowled the campus, explored the bookstore, and talked with Don about the school on our long car ride back. After that visit, my intention to pursue a divinity degree at Princeton never seriously wavered. My studies at Westminster College in New Wilmington, Pennsylvania, also pushed me toward things Presbyterian. As a history major, I wrote a senior thesis on Presbyterian attitudes toward missions and imperialism around the year 1900 and received valuable counsel from Professors Delber McKee, Arthur Jensen, Harry Swanhart, and Norman Adams. Then in the fall of 1968,

---

1. Glenn T. Miller, *Piety and Intellect: The Aims and Purposes of Ante-Bellum Theological Education* (Atlanta: Scholars Press, 1990), 1.

when I matriculated at Princeton Seminary, I took Lefferts Loetscher's class on American Presbyterianism, was thoroughly hooked on the subject, and thereafter squeezed as many of his courses into my schedule as the curriculum permitted. Lefferts Loetscher introduced me to the history of Princeton Seminary. His own career at the school, combined with that of his father, Frederick, spanned nearly a third of the institution's life. At Lefferts's suggestion, a couple of my seminar papers became initial forays into Princeton's history. Writing this book has reminded me how profoundly his knowledge and insights have contributed to my own. Another formative influence came after my graduation from the seminary and during a Ph.D. program at Yale. Sydney Ahlstrom, my doctoral advisor, exemplified intellectual curiosity as well as an astonishing breadth of knowledge about an endless number of topics — or so it seemed to awed graduate students. Sydney pressed us to find our own scholarly voices but always insisted that whoever we studied be portrayed as embodied persons, set in the fullest possible context of their times and places. When I showed him an essay I was preparing for publication — it dealt with a nineteenth-century Princeton Seminary professor — Sydney offered one sentence of advice: "Make him less of a wraith."

Since joining the faculty of Princeton Seminary as professor of American church history in 1984, work with various colleagues has also contributed to my understanding of the seminary's history. For two decades — first with Jane Dempsey Douglass and, then after her retirement, with James C. Deming — I have co-taught a course entitled "Presbyterian History and Theology." Having to interpret to successive generations of seminarians the Presbyterian experience, including Princeton Seminary's role in that experience, has sharpened my perceptions of the school. In 1997, Professor John W. Stewart and I organized a conference on the life and work of Charles Hodge. Over numerous breakfasts and lunches, we hammered out the program and then afterwards assembled the essays into a book. Those essays — along with Jack's considerable knowledge of Hodge — forced me to take a fresh and much deeper look at the nineteenth-century theologian.

Professional opportunities beyond Princeton have also enriched the perspective brought to these pages. Since 1996, it has been my privilege to serve as one of two senior editors of *The Journal of Presbyterian History* in partnership with Fred Heuser, director of the Presbyterian Historical Society in Philadelphia. In March 1994, at Pittsburgh Theological Seminary, I delivered the annual David Schaff Lectures, my topic being

"Theological Education in Historical Perspective." Many of the ideas expressed in those lectures, previously unpublished, have now found their way into this book.

But none of these prior influences would have led to *Princeton Seminary in American Religion and Culture* without a request from the seminary's sixth president, Iain R. Torrance, that I undertake a one-volume history as part of the school's bicentennial celebration. Iain has proved to be an ideal facilitator. Although he commissioned the project on behalf of the seminary and offered valuable comments on the manuscript, he in no way tried to censor, restrict, or influence the interpretations advanced herein. He left the planning and execution of the project entirely in my hands. When the manuscript took longer to complete than he or I had anticipated, he graciously made more leave time available. He also provided resources to speed the transformation of the manuscript into a book. I am grateful for his encouragement, support, and friendship throughout the process. I am also grateful to history colleagues for reshuffling departmental responsibilities in order to accommodate my delayed return to the classroom.

During the writing of this history, Aaron Sizer and Jason Bruner performed impeccable service as research assistants. My queries were almost always answered within a few days by a flood of relevant information assembled by Aaron and Jason. Kenneth W. Henke, the seminary's Reference Archivist *extraordinaire,* was an invaluable resource; and to Ken I am especially indebted for assembling the pictures out of which the illustrations for this book have been selected. In years past, William O. Harris, then Librarian for Archives and Special Collections, often regaled me with bits of Princetoniana that also contributed to this book. Conversations over my time as a Princeton Seminary professor with Karlfried Froehlich, Daniel Migliore, Charles West, James Lapsley, and the late Edward A. Dowey Jr. offered insights about Princeton during the presidencies of John Mackay and James McCord. Dan went an extra mile by reading and commenting on the entire manuscript of this book, which, despite his preference for hard copy, he gallantly read from the computer screen. In the fall of 2011, the Frederick Neumann Lecture delivered at Princeton Seminary by Professors Freda Gardner (emerita) and Katherine Doob Sakenfeld on the experience of the first cohort of women students and faculty at Princeton Seminary was also invaluable. To my colleagues Richard Osmer and Gordon Mikoski I am indebted for their willingness to share with me in manuscript form their subsequently published book *With Piety and Learning: The History of Practical Theology at Princeton Theological Seminary.* It has been an invaluable resource. Conversation with John M. Metzger, the grandson of John A. Mackay, provided insight into the third president of the seminary; and Metzger's biography of Mackay — *The Hand and the Road* — has been indispensable. Unfortunately the volume on Émile Cailliet by Abigail Rian Evans and Clemens Bartollas (with the aid of Gordon Graham and Kenneth Henke) came into my hands too late for its insights to be incorporated in this book.

One of the pleasures of writing this history was the opportunity to compare notes with Paul C. Gutjahr, who was then completing his excellent biography *Charles Hodge: Guardian of American Orthodoxy.* Paul's research trips to Princeton became the occasion for sharing our findings about the seminary in the nineteenth century, and I learned much from him.

Eerdmans has expedited the publication of this book in a manner at once professional and congenial. I am especially grateful to Jon Pott, Jenny Hoffman, and David Bratt.

My debt to my family is of a different order. Although some authors maintain a balanced rhythm of work and leisure while completing a major project, I am surely not one of them. As my wife and now grown children know all too well, my manner of work at such times approaches the obsessive-compulsive. Without their love, support — and tolerance — I could not have completed this book. So thank you indeed to my wife Cynthia, our sons Evan and Stefan, our daughter Olivia, and our daughter-in-law Dana. I love you all.

While researching and writing this book, I frequently saw the seminary's former president, Thomas W. Gillespie, at church or ran into him elsewhere in Princeton. Almost invariably, Tom asked with his usual cheerfulness and interest how the history was going, and I looked forward to handing him a copy of the finished product. In late 2011, Tom's unexpected and deeply lamented death foreclosed that possibility, and I am left with the poor substitute of dedicating this volume to his memory.

Princeton: August 12, 1812

O N AUGUST 12, 1812, a few weeks after the United States had entered into its second war against Great Britain, a group of Presbyterian leaders gathered in Princeton, New Jersey, to mark the formation of their denomination's first theological seminary and to inaugurate the school's first professor, Archibald Alexander. Princeton Seminary was following the example of Andover Theological Seminary, founded four years earlier. It established a three-year post-collegiate program of theological study. Previously in North America ministers received their basic education in a college — or in an academy where instruction was at a level that we would peg as somewhere between high school and college. Ministerial candidates pursued further instruction in an informal way, either by remaining at their colleges or academies for a time and reading divinity with a tutor or by studying in the field with a minister engaged in preaching and pastoral care. When Princeton opted for the Andover model, it settled on what would become the dominant model of American theological education for the next two centuries.

One of the chief reasons for the departure from the old pattern was that it did not seem to be producing enough clergy. Dr. Samuel Miller of New York City, who preached the sermon at Alexander's inauguration, lamented "the alarming necessities of the church" and called upon fellow Christians to behold the sad spectacle of "several hundred vacant congregations earnestly desiring spiritual teachers but unable to obtain them."[1]

---

1. [Samuel Miller, Archibald Alexander, and Philip Milledoler,] *The Sermon Delivered at the Inauguration of the Rev. Archibald Alexander, D.D. as Professor of Didactic and Po-*

For Miller, however, theological education involved far more than turning out clergy in sufficient numbers. The primary concern, he told his Princeton audience, was the duty of the church to train up for its congregations "an able and faithful ministry." Of the traits essential to a good minister, Miller first named piety. A pastor should be "a regenerated man," one exhibiting "a living faith in that Saviour whom he preaches to others." Yet religious devotion by itself would not prove adequate for effective ministry. The clergy also needed to be men of learning. Miller realized that in his day many religious groups, especially those enjoying great appeal among the masses, saw no need for advanced training. Noting that "the gospel was first preached by fishermen and tax-gatherers," they reasoned that "fervent piety and plain sense" sufficed for preachers. Miller demurred, insisting that "the apostles were *not* an illiterate ministry." Taught by Christ himself or by revelation from the Holy Spirit, they were "the soundest and best informed divines that ever adorned the Christian church." But now, "the age of inspiration and of miracle . . . [being] long since past," ministers needed to study diligently to acquire that which had been given in a different fashion to the apostles.[2]

And what did Miller wish future ministers to study? As those for whom the Bible was the ultimate authority, they ought to become thoroughly versed in the Scriptures, including the original languages in which they were written. To aid in interpretation, clergy should also have familiarity with the history of the Bible's peoples, their customs, and the geography of the places where they lived. They needed to know the history of the church and of the world at large. Ministers should, of course, study the various branches of theology and the ways of applying its insights to particular cases. From an immersion in moral philosophy, they would derive "an important auxiliary in studying man, his constitution, the powers and exercises of his depraved and sanctified nature, and his duties thence arising." Rounding out this education, ministers "must add a respectable share of knowledge in general grammar, in logic, metaphysics, natural philosophy, mathematical science, geography, natural history, and polite literature." Miller envisioned an ambitious, comprehensive education for clergy — a breadth and depth necessary if they were to be ready to offer

---

lemic Theology in the Theological Seminary of the Presbyterian Church in the United States of America, to Which Are Added the Professor's Inaugural Address and the Charge to the Professor and Students (New York: Whiting and Watson, 1812), 53.

2. *The Sermon*, 12, 21, 22.

cogent defense of the gospel in an age when many wrongly used learning to assault orthodox faith.[3]

For Miller the stakes in having "an able and faithful ministry" were for both time and eternity. "It may be said without exaggeration," he remarked, "that every interest of man is involved in this blessing." The spiritual needs of the church as well as the salvation and growth in grace of individual believers depended upon a faithful and competent ministry. But so, too, did the welfare of the social order. The faithful preaching of the gospel contributed to "the regularity, peace, polish, and strength of civil society."[4]

In his inaugural address as professor of polemic and didactic theology, Alexander provided an instance of what a pious and learned theological education meant. Framing his discourse as a response to Jesus' command "Search the scriptures" (John 5:39), the new professor offered a wide-ranging argument for the reliability of the Bible. He believed it particularly important "to prove that the scriptures have suffered no material injury from the fraud of designing men or from the carelessness of transcribers." That possibility, Alexander averred, had been thoroughly investigated by "learned men" who, "with unparalleled diligence, employed their whole lives in the collation of manuscripts and noting every, even the smallest, variation in their readings." The result of that meticulous scholarship had been to show that all the variants discovered "do not materially affect one important fact or doctrine." "It is true," he allowed, "a few important texts in our received copies have by this critical process been rendered suspicious; but this has been more than compensated by the certainty which has been stamped on the great body of scripture by having been subjected to this severe scrutiny."[5]

Then, having established to his satisfaction that the current Bible accurately reflects the original, Alexander tackled the deeper issue of authority. How does one know that the Bible, even if it is an accurate transcription of the original, was inspired by God? Alexander believed the accounts of biblical miracles "will indubitably prove that those persons by whom they were performed must have been sent and assisted of God." Likewise, the Bible's authority was confirmed by the fact that it recorded

3. *The Sermon,* 25, 26. In listing the desirable courses, Miller was citing what the General Assembly of the Presbyterian Church had prescribed in setting up the seminary.
4. *The Sermon,* 9.
5. *The Sermon,* 67.

Preface

far in advance accurate "predictions of events which no human sagacity could have foreseen." Then, too, the "sublimely excellent" teachings of the Bible corresponded so well to the human condition that they self-evidently attested their divine origin. Or one could point to the social, cultural, and moral impact of the biblical message over the centuries. "The beneficial effect of Christianity on those nations which have received it," Alexander contended,

> is a striking fact and furnishes a strong argument in favour of the authenticity and inspiration of the Scriptures. Under their benign influence, war has become less sanguinary and ferocious; justice has been more equally distributed; the poor have been more generally instructed, and their wants supplied; asylums have been provided for the unfortunate and distressed; the female character has been exalted to its proper standard in society. . . . In short, the whole fabric of society has been meliorated; and real civilization promoted by Christianity wherever it has been received.[6]

Assured that the text of the Bible was reliable and confident that God inspired it, one still needed to know how to interpret it. Alexander rejected the Roman Catholic notion that tradition was a necessary supplement to Scripture, for this assumption "takes away all fixedness and certainty which a written revelation was intended and calculated to give to religion." Equally unacceptable were ideas that persons' rational faculty would allow them to override portions of Scripture they deemed unreasonable, that readers themselves could possess an inspiration comparable to that of the writers of the Bible, or that discerning interpreters might uncover layers of mystical meaning hidden under the surface of Scripture. Here Alexander saw the same threat he feared in Roman Catholic veneration of tradition: "a direct tendency to overthrow all certainty in divine revelation" — the creation of an interpretive world where the Bible became so malleable that "every man makes it out according to the liveliness of his own imagination." The only safeguard against this danger lay in interpretation that hewed closely to the "grammatical and literal sense of the biblical text." In order to become proficient in such interpretation, the student of divinity needed to know the original biblical languages and would benefit also by studying other related ancient lan-

6. *The Sermon,* 69, 70, 71, 72.

xvii

guages. But Alexander went further: *All* learning was of value to the clergyman. "Indeed, to speak the truth," he wrote:

> there is scarcely any science or branch of knowledge which may not be made subservient to theology. . . . The state of learning in the world requires the advocate of the Bible to attend to many things which may not in themselves be absolutely necessary. He must maintain his standard as a man of learning. He must be able to converse on the various topics of learning with literary men; otherwise the due respect will not be paid to him; and his sacred office may suffer contempt in consequence of his appearing to be ignorant of what is expected all learned men should be acquainted with.[7]

After this hymn to scholarship, Alexander ended his inaugural on a different note. "A proud and self-sufficient person," he warned, ". . . is continually prone to fall into pernicious error whilst the humble man occupies a station from which truth may be viewed to advantage." Without a lively sense of "divine illumination" acquired through unceasing prayer and devotion, the study of divinity "would be a mere dry system of speculation, of ethics and ceremonies." With that illumination, theological study acquired "its life, its soul." Despite the centrality of solid learning to theological preparation for ministry, "the word of God," Alexander acknowledged, ". . . is on a plan too vast, too sublime, too profound, to be measured by the feeble intellect of man."[8]

There remained one more major item in the day's solemn observance. After Miller's sermon and Alexander's inaugural address, the Rev. Philip Milledoler rose to give the charge to the new professor and to the students on behalf of the seminary's board of directors. (Since these three addresses take up more than one hundred pages of text, one suspects that perhaps a few heads had begun to nod on that August day by the time Milledoler spoke.) Echoing the previous speakers, Milledoler asserted forcefully: "We want a learned ministry. Whatever mischief has been done to the world by philosophy, falsely so called, we are persuaded that true learning has never injured the church and never will. . . . It has been said that ignorance is the mother of devotion; that aphorism we ut-

7. *The Sermon*, 73, 78, 84-85.
8. *The Sermon*, 92, 95.

terly and indignantly reject." But this learning was to be placed in the service, not of a generic Christianity, but of a particular denomination's heritage. Or, in Milledoler's words:

> Strongly attached to the doctrines of the reformation contained in her standards [the Westminster Confession of Faith and the Larger and Shorter Catechisms], jealous of innovation, and anxious to transmit the truth as it is in Jesus inviolate to posterity, the Presbyterian Church will expect, and permit me to add, Sir, after the signal mark of her confidence reposed in you, will have a right to expect that her doctrines, and especially her distinguishing doctrines, will be taught in this school without adding to or taking aught from them in any wise or under any pretext whatsoever.

Milledoler feared that even the "surrender [of] truths deemed of minor importance" would be to start down the proverbial slippery slope "till all is gone that is worth contending for."[9]

Echoing through these addresses were major themes that would long characterize Princeton Seminary's life and identity. Most fundamental was the assumption that religious experience and scholarly knowledge needed to go together. All of the speakers endorsed the Plan of the Seminary, which said that the school's aim "is to unite, in those who shall sustain the ministerial office, religion and literature; that piety of the heart which is the fruit only of the renewing and sanctifying grace of God, with solid learning; believing that religion without learning, or learning without religion, in the ministers of the Gospel, must ultimately prove injurious to the church." At the heart of solid learning was thorough knowledge of the Bible. Thus Alexander exerted great pains to prove the reliability of Scripture and establish its authority. The important role he and Miller gave to teaching the original languages in which the Bible was written — and, ideally, cognate ancient languages as well — attested the centrality of Scripture. Alexander's choice of the inaugural text "Search the scriptures" served as a reminder that every aspect of theological education — whether systematic theology, history, practical theology, or church government — ultimately found its warrant in the Bible. Whatever else the Princetonians were, they first and foremost saw themselves as expositors of God's Word. But they were never simply men

9. *The Sermon*, 108, 113, 114.

of one book, even a sacred book. Scholars of many books and subjects, they hoped to train their students broadly and believed, as Alexander put it, "there is scarcely any science or branch of knowledge which may not be made subservient to theology." This reverence for learning derived from traditional Protestant sources, but also took on a new edge under the influence of the Enlightenment, especially the Scottish Common Sense philosophy that had profoundly shaped both Alexander and Miller. Despite awareness that knowledge had sometimes been put to uses contrary to faith, they ultimately shared the Enlightenment's confidence in the power of the human intellect. Thus Alexander ticked off arguments for the authority of the Bible certain that no sane man could resist their logical force. Accompanying that confidence in reason was an assumption that the gospel they were training young men to preach was in the process of reshaping culture and society. To put it simply, Christianity was riding a wave of progress as it ameliorated the lot of the poor, elevated the status of women, and reduced the horrors of war. Thus the founding of Princeton brought together a confluence of multiple commitments and assumptions — an emphasis upon religious experience, a faith in solid learning and the Enlightenment, and an optimism that these forces together were improving the human lot. Yet at Princeton, it was assumed, these ideas would not flow undisciplined into heterodoxy nor even into some form of orthodoxy as yet unimagined. Sound teaching would keep these currents within the bounds of the Reformed tradition as defined by the Westminster Standards; and those standards, Milledoler noted, "will be taught in this school without adding to or taking aught from them in any wise or under any pretext whatsoever."

The subsequent history of the seminary would in part be a narrative of the way in which these varying commitments played themselves out or how, like the design in a kaleidoscope, they shifted into different patterns. It would not be a trouble-free story, for the various loyalties sometimes fit together awkwardly. For example, which would be the dominant Princeton outlook toward the power of the human intellect: the confident assertions of Alexander that any person of common sense would perceive the proofs of the Bible's veracity or the humbler epistemological note that he sounded at the end of his inaugural — namely, that God's ways were "too vast, too sublime, too profound, to be measured by the feeble intellect of man"? In what manner would religious experience and doctrinal truth be brought into harmony? For all their stress upon the importance of religious experience, Princeton's founders seemed fearful of allowing it too much freedom lest experience become a subjectivism in which truth is no more than what "every man makes out according to the liveliness of his own imagination." Or again: Would a straightforward examination of the "grammatical and literal sense of the biblical text" and rigorous theological reflections always yield conclusions fully in accord with the Westminster Standards? Similarly, could there be any movement, latitude, or progress in the interpretation of those standards or were all future generations at the seminary to be held to the strict constructionist position of Milledoler — a stance deeming even minor departures from Westminster to be dangerous?

The addresses of August 12, 1812, also revealed assumptions about the role that the seminary's founders expected the school and the clergy it trained to play within American religion and society. The seminary would provide for Presbyterianism a unifying influence. Taught a common theological curriculum and establishing friendships that would continue throughout their careers, seminarians would go forth from Princeton, as Miller envisioned them, "a holy phalanx united in the same great views of doctrine and discipline." The seminary would be an antidote to a "heterogeneous, divided, and distracted ministry." Or as the Plan of the Seminary put it, the institution would "promote harmony and unity of sentiment among the ministers of our Church." That hope was credible because, for the moment, the denomination had no other theological seminary — hence the school's official title, The Theological Seminary of the Presbyterian Church in the United States of America. The addresses also assumed that Princeton would be preparing those who would hold a learned office, honored for its contributions to larger society as well as the church. The ministry, to use Miller's words again, promoted "the peace, polish, and strength of civil society." Alexander implied the same thing when he suggested that the preaching of the gospel exercised a "benign influence" over public and private life wherever it was heard. He did not envision for the clergy an overt role of advocacy in matters social and political, but rather saw ministers as indirect agents of secular improvements that would come as almost silent by-products of the religious function. In succeeding decades, alternate realities — hints of which the discerning might already read in 1812 — would test those assumptions. A surge of populist sentiment in the young republic caused many to question whether the ministry was or should be a learned office, seminaries multiplied, and theological squabbles frayed unity. Moral controversies over slavery and other questions belied the hope of clergy exerting an indirect and noncontroversial "benign influence" upon the secular order or even of keeping peace among themselves.[10]

Thus August 12, 1812, foreshadowed many of the issues that would define the life and identity of Princeton Seminary in the decades ahead. Succeeding chapters will elaborate these matters. But first we must turn to the seminary's prelude. What were the events that brought the Presbyterian Church to the particular vision of theological education that Miller, Alexander, and Milledoler set forth? How and why had the Presbyterian Church chosen this new model of theological education — the post-undergraduate seminary — to prepare its clergy? In what ways did that model perpetuate older commitments or advance new ones?

10. *The Sermon,* 39.

CHAPTER ONE

The Founding of Princeton Seminary

I N STRESSING a learned ministry, the founders of Princeton Seminary continued a traditional ideal. One of the chief purposes of the founding of the first North American colleges was to produce a well-educated clergy. An anonymous pamphlet published on behalf of Harvard College seven years after its founding in 1636 described the school's purpose thus: "After God had carried us safe to New England, and we had builded our houses, provided necessaries for our livelihood, reared convenient places for God's worship, and settled the civil government, one of the next things we longed for and looked after was to advance learning, dreading to leave an illiterate ministry to the Churches, when our present ministers shall lie in the dust." The founders of Yale College in 1701 claimed as their mandate "the glorious public design of our now blessed fathers in their removal from Europe . . . to propagate in this wilderness, the blessed Reformed Protestant religion, in the purity of its order and worship." The charter of the College of William and Mary in 1693 indicated that the first goal of the institution was "that the church of Virginia may be furnished with a seminary of ministers of the gospel, and that the youth may be piously educated in good letters and manners, and that the Christian faith may be propagated among the Western Indians, . . . [we do] make, found, and establish a certain place of universal study, or perpetual college of divinity, philosophy, languages, and other good arts and sciences."[1]

1. Edwin Oviatt, *The Beginnings of Yale, 1701-1726* (New Haven: Yale University Press, 1916), 198; *History of the College of William and Mary from Its Foundation, 1693, to 1870* (Balti-

Colleges, Academies, and Theological Education

Despite the use of the word "seminary" in William and Mary's charter, none of these schools fitted what today is generally meant by that term — a post-collegiate institution designed for the education of the ministry. They were colleges designed to provide a broad education, as the charter put it, in "other good arts and sciences" as well as in divinity. Thus of 776 Harvard alumni from 1642 to 1689, only slightly more than 46 percent entered the ministry. The remainder assumed careers such as physician, magistrate, teacher, merchant, and gentleman farmer. This outcome was intentional. For example, the founders of Yale declared that their institution was designed "for the educating and instructing of youth in good literature, arts, and sciences that so by the blessing of Almighty God they may be the better fitted for public employment both in church and civil state." The scope of the standard curriculum testified to the comprehensive goal of the founders. Students pursued a common course of study, emphasizing ancient languages, logic, natural philosophy (physics and astronomy), mathematics, metaphysics, rhetoric, and theology. In short, colonial Protestants founded liberal arts colleges, not theological seminaries, for the training of ministers.

This setting was appropriate for theological education because it was suffused with religious purpose. While divinity constituted only one subject among many, in another sense it framed all the others. "Every student," said the laws of Yale, "shall consider the main end of his study ... to know God in Jesus Christ and answerably to lead a godly sober life." The language at Harvard was similar. Each scholar was urged to remember that the chief purpose of his studies was "to know God and Jesus Christ which is eternal life ..., and therefore to lay Christ in the bottom, as the only foundation of all sound knowledge and learning." Often instructors taught the various courses so that biblical and religious material intruded. For example, early lectures on natural philosophy at Yale managed to include a section on angels. This was scarcely surprising, for

---

more: John Murphy and Co., 1870), 3. Also useful in framing my thoughts about colonial and pre–Civil War theological education are James W. Fraser, *Schooling the Preachers: The Development of Theological Education in the United States, 1740-1875* (Lanham, MD: University Press of America, 1988); Glenn T. Miller, *Piety and Intellect: The Aims and Purposes of Antebellum Theological Education* (Atlanta: Scholars Press, 1990); and Richard Warch, *School of the Prophets: Yale College, 1701-1740* (New Haven: Yale University Press, 1973). The spelling and punctuation of quotations in this chapter have generally been modernized.

the overwhelming majority of instructors — and presidents — in these schools were clergy.

The college was also a fitting site for theological education because of the role the clergy occupied within society. The earliest American colleges arose in colonies — Massachusetts, Virginia, and Connecticut — where state-established churches existed, and both secular rulers and ministers were understood as leaders of a Christian society subject to the will of God. Or as Puritan minister John Cotton put it, the magistrate was the left hand of God and the minister his right. With church and state in close cooperation, it was assumed that all leaders — whether clergy, magistrates, or others — needed to have a common fund of knowledge and conviction in order to fulfill their roles in the public realm. This conception of education rested on an elitist assumption that the clergy along with the magistrates and other gentleman were, in Richard D. Brown's words, "gatekeepers who were broadly responsible for screening the passage of information and its diffusion to the public at large."[2]

Presbyterians encountered more obstacles to putting such a vision into operation than the Congregationalists in New England or the Anglicans in Virginia. By the late seventeenth century, immigrants from Scotland and some of English Puritan origin had begun to form Presbyterian congregations, and the first presbytery was organized in Philadelphia in 1706. Between approximately 1720 and the eve of the American Revolution, more than one hundred thousand, perhaps as many as two hundred thousand, Ulster Scots or Scots-Irish dramatically increased the denomination's strength. Most Presbyterians settled initially in the middle colonies — New York, New Jersey, Pennsylvania, Delaware, and Maryland. Significantly, each of these colonies lacked an establishment of religion, except for New York, whose lower counties had a very weak establishment. For reasons of either necessity or principle, they shunned the state establishment of churches and enjoyed the highest degree of religious pluralism anywhere within Britain's American dominions. Thus Presbyterians could not turn to the state support that Anglicans could claim in the founding of William and Mary in Virginia or that New England Congregationalists possessed with the creation of Harvard or Yale.

---

2. Richard D. Brown, *Knowledge Is Power: The Diffusion of Information in Early America, 1700-1865* (New York: Oxford University Press, 1989), 21. Cotton's description is taken from E. Brooks Holifield, *God's Ambassadors: A History of the Christian Clergy in America* (Grand Rapids: Eerdmans, 2007), 48.

Nor did Presbyterian settlement patterns lend themselves to the creation of schools. Unlike New England, where colonists congregated in towns where it was easier to form and sustain institutions, many Presbyterians — especially the Ulster Scots — seldom tarried in the eastern ports where they disembarked but dispersed to the backcountry. As Patrick Griffin observes, "after sailing to America, they bypassed eastern cosmopolitan towns and cities to settle on the frontier. Poor and mobile, they scratched a precarious existence out of the woods beyond the reach of the law and polite society."[3]

Yet, remarkably, Presbyterians did overcome these roadblocks and created schools. In many ways, the Ulster Scots were well prepared to do so. When their forebears had emigrated from Scotland to the northern portions of Ireland, some as early as the reign of England's James I (1603-1625) and others in greater numbers after the troubles of the English Civil War and the restoration of the monarchy in 1660, they brought with them a sense of the intimate connection between faith and education. Characteristic of the Scottish Reformation was the aim of the *First Book of Discipline* (1560) to place a school for basics in every parish, a grammar school in every town, and a college teaching Greek, Latin, logic, and rhetoric in larger communities. The *Discipline* proposed the reform and strengthening of the universities at St. Andrews, Glasgow, and Aberdeen in order to provide the highest level of learning for the professions, including the ministry. Although these reforms initially failed during the political turmoil of the mid-sixteenth century, the ideal was not lost; and by the early eighteenth century the Scottish universities were among the most innovative in Europe. The Scots who immigrated to Ireland also faced great difficulties in realizing the educational ideal. As dissenters in a place where the Anglican church was established, they were not allowed to teach above the grammar school level and were not permitted to receive university degrees. Yet they did not give up on the ideal of providing education for their clergy and people. What emerged were Presbyterian-run academies that, in Elizabeth Nybakken's words, sought "to become invisible to local authorities. They operated in semi-secret and left no paper trail that might incriminate them." After 1715, regulation eased, and the

---

3. For different estimates of the size of the Ulster Scots migration, see Patrick Griffin, *The People with No Name: Ireland's Ulster Scots, America's Scots Irish, and the Creation of a British Atlantic World, 1689-1764* (Princeton: Princeton University Press, 2001), 1, 3; and Edwin Scott Gaustad and Philip L. Barlow, *New Historical Atlas of Religion in America* (New York: Oxford University Press, 2001), 38-41.

academies could work more openly. Although the lack of records makes it difficult to know the precise nature of their curricula, the academies appear to have taught Greek, Latin, and philosophy. Students who wished to enter the ministry either studied further with a Presbyterian minister or went to Scotland for training in one of the universities. The often furtive academies testified to the determination of the Ulster Scots to maintain their ideals of education even in adversity.[4]

Awakening, Enlightenment, and Theological Education

Presbyterians exhibited the same tenacity in establishing academies when they migrated to North America. Of these, the best known was the school begun by William Tennent Sr., in Bucks County, Pennsylvania, sometime after his arrival there in 1727. About the time he built a rude structure in 1735 to house his academy, the school became a center of debate between New Side and Old Side Presbyterians. Old Side detractors of Tennent's "Log College" objected to its alleged educational deficiencies and scorned its graduates' overzealous promotion of revival. In 1738, the synod — then the highest judicatory in American Presbyterianism — ruled that candidates for ordination who did not have a degree from a college in New England or Europe had to be examined by a special commission. This thinly veiled attempt to limit the influence of the Log College was one of the signs of a mounting tension within Presbyterianism, leading in 1741, at the height of the Great Awakening, to the division of the Old and New Sides into separate denominations.

The Log College was not the only model for the Presbyterian academy in America. The Old Side had its own counterpart in the school founded by Francis Alison in New London, Pennsylvania, in 1737. Here, with the aid of assistants, he provided education through the college level. After Alison departed to new labors in Philadelphia, his school moved across the border into Maryland and subsequently to Newark, Delaware. (Alison's school eventually evolved into the present-day University of Delaware.) The academies that he, Tennent, and others estab-

---

4. Elizabeth Nybakken, "In the Irish Tradition: Pre-Revolutionary Academies in America," *History of Education Quarterly* 37 (Summer 1997): 163-83; Douglas Sloan, *The Scottish Enlightenment and the American College Ideal* (New York: Teachers College Press, Columbia University, 1971); Griffin, *People with No Name.*

lished among North American Presbyterians proved to be fruitful proto-
types. Historian Douglas Sloan has counted over sixty such institutions
founded before the end of the eighteenth century. The level of instruction in these schools varied from basic to collegiate, and some quickly
vanished while others matured into colleges. Especially in the middle Atlantic and the South, they provided education not only for clergy but also
for other professionals. The academy model pioneered under adverse
circumstances in Ireland proved remarkably adaptable in America.

The debate over the Log College was part of a larger crisis triggered
by the Great Awakening. In various places and among Protestants of different traditions, religious revivals had broken out periodically for decades. Instances included the numerous "harvests" of souls gathered
into the Congregational Church in Northampton, Massachusetts, during
the sixty-year pastorate (1669-1729) of the formidable Solomon Stoddard
or the religious excitement generated by his grandson and successor,
Jonathan Edwards, when he preached a series of sermons on justification by faith in the mid-1730s. In central New Jersey a decade earlier, the
Dutch Reformed pastor Theodore Frelinghuysen, educated in the traditions of European Pietism, awakened several congregations along the
Raritan River. After 1726 he had a sympathetic neighboring colleague in
the person of the local Presbyterian pastor, Gilbert Tennent, who had
been trained for the ministry by his father, William. Influenced both by
the Scots-Irish piety of his father and by Frelinghuysen's brand of continental Pietism, Tennent thundered at the complacence of the unconverted and preached the terrors of the law to arouse the unregenerate to
seek spiritual rebirth through God's free grace. When the young Anglican
preacher George Whitefield toured the colonies, traveling from Georgia
to New England beginning in 1739, he helped to assemble the various local revivals into a larger movement. To do so, Whitefield relied partly on
the force of his evangelistic message, partly on a powerful voice and skill
as a speaker, but also on a talent for self-promotion. He used correspondence and newsprint to build anticipation of his evangelistic prowess
before he arrived in a community. His meetings frequently drew crowds
so large that they had to meet in the fields. As the Awakening swelled,
some of its adherents swooned with emotional passion or attacked as
unconverted those clergy who dared to question the revivals. Under the
influence of the Spirit, women, children, or black slaves sometimes
shared their spiritual testimonies, speaking out publicly in a world in
which they were expected to be subordinate or silent. The Great Awak-

ening, in short, was exceedingly controversial. Its defenders would long remember it as a time when revivals demonstrated God's mighty work, and its detractors as a moment when multitudes were "seriously, soberly, and solemnly out of their wits."[5]

One of the issues in contention was education. Around the movement's fringes, some of the more radical revivalists led a dramatic assault against ungodly learning. At New London, Connecticut, in 1742, James Davenport led a crowd in the public burning of books, many of which were volumes deemed impious. Although most defenders of the Awakening repudiated Davenport's action, he had expressed in dramatic, if extreme, fashion the anxiety that many felt toward the colleges. Isaac Backus, a Baptist revivalist in New England, warned "that in our colleges many learn corrupt principles"; and George Whitefield himself said of Harvard and Yale: "Their light is become darkness." The revivalists did not oppose learning per se — in fact, as noted above, they founded numerous academies and colleges — but they did insist that the studies in existing institutions often did more harm than good to the cause of true religion. Unless those training for the ministry exhibited a piety wrought by the regenerating influences of the Holy Spirit, their learning was worse than useless. Failing to understand this truth, the colleges turned out worldlings rather than children of God.[6]

The opponents of the revival often missed the nuances of the argument. Dismissing Awakeners as "enthusiasts" (a term indicating those who believed in direct revelation and roughly equivalent to "fanatics" today), they accused revivalists of repudiating sound knowledge. "For GOD's sake, brethren," asked the Rev. John Hancock of Braintree, Massachusetts,

> what would have become of the Christian religion long ago, had it not been for the wise and learned defenders of it against its ablest adversaries? . . . And indeed the revival of learning, since the glori-

5. For an overview of the Awakening, see Thomas S. Kidd, *The Great Awakening: The Roots of Evangelical Christianity in Colonial America* (New Haven: Yale University Press, 2007). See also Frank Lambert, *"Pedlar in Divinity": George Whitefield and the Transatlantic Revivals, 1737-1770* (Princeton: Princeton University Press, 2002).

6. Backus quoted in Douglas Sloan, ed., *The Great Awakening and American Education* (New York: Teachers College Press, 1973), 122; [George Whitefield,] *A Continuation of the Reverend Mr. Whitefield's Journal from a Few Days after His Return to Georgia to His Arrival in Falmouth* (London: W. Strahan, 1741), 55.

ous reformation, has been a great elucidation and establishment of the truths of our holy religion: So that the enemies of good literature are enemies to the true interest of Christianity, whether they know it or not.

Given Protestants' historic alliance with learning and the colleges, Hancock and others like him struck a telling blow against the Awakening, at least in its more radical forms.[7]

The Awakeners, however, could also appeal to the tradition. Especially in the Puritan manifestations so formative of early America, earlier Protestantism had never univocally endorsed the clerical pursuit of learning. As devotionally minded people, the Puritan divines valued learning only insofar as it functioned as a tool in service to experiential piety. "If a man be not guided by the Spirit," Puritan Thomas Granger averred in 1621,

> his observations are but superstitious, and false rules, his readings erroneous, yea, though he hath read all books, and hath not root or seed in himself, he is but in a maze tossed to and fro, hearing and seeing as in a dream: In a word, he wants wisdom, he hath no learning.[8]

Early American schools had sought to entwine godliness and learning. The Great Awakening raised anew the question as to how that should be accomplished.

The rise of the Enlightenment underscored the importance of that question. By the beginning of the 1700s, a new intellectual mood was appearing. Among its many examples were the scientific works of Sir Isaac Newton, the philosophic writings of John Locke, and the new moral philosophy typified by Lord Shaftesbury and Francis Hutcheson. "In the broadest sense," Ned C. Landsman rightly observes, "the Enlightenment can be identified with a particular version of a progressive view of history that emerged during the seventeenth and eighteenth centuries, one in which progress represented not the movement toward an otherworldly paradise but rather cumulative advances in intellectual, cultural, technological, and even moral affairs on earth." Educationally, this

---

7. Hancock quoted in Sloan, *Great Awakening*, 106.

8. Granger quoted in John Morgan, *Godly Learning: Puritan Attitudes toward Reason, Learning, and Education* (Cambridge: Cambridge University Press, 1986), 76.

outlook appeared in exposure to new books with new ideas. By the 1680s and '90s, for example, the tutors at Harvard were permitting much greater latitude in the choice of books. They recommended Anglican authors who challenged the assumptions of New England's Congregational way, and in response the more traditional Increase Mather, then Harvard's commuting president, thundered that the college might become a "Degenerate Plant." Yale witnessed a similar development several decades later. In 1722, the rector Timothy Cutler and several tutors defected to Anglicanism outright and were forced to resign. The Great Apostasy, as it was known, constituted a dual threat to the New England churches. To adhere to Anglicanism was to refute the congregational polity that was the hallmark of the New England religious establishments. It was also to render oneself suspect of harboring a vaguely defined Arminianism at variance with the tenets of the Reformed faith.[9]

The dilemma both Harvard and Yale faced derived partly from the Enlightenment spirit of open-minded toleration encouraging students to read widely. Yet that was but the tip of the iceberg, for some subjects of instruction had acquired a new content and method that promoted less overtly theological ways of understanding the world. For example, by 1740 natural philosophy, now thoroughly informed by Newton, had become experimental and investigative, focusing more directly upon phenomena and natural laws than upon the One who made them. Under the influence of authors such as Lord Shaftesbury and Francis Hutcheson, ethics or moral philosophy separated itself partially from theology. "As in the preceding theological era," Norman Fiering has written, "God's will was the final source of moral truth and obligation, but in the era of moral philosophy His will was to be uncovered indirectly, through the book of nature. The superhuman standpoint no longer overtly predominated, although it was constantly implicit." The new learning, one must again emphasize, did not repudiate Christian faith. In fact, many individuals by the late eighteenth century were pursuing self-improvement — in Landsman's phrase, "cumulative advances in intellectual, cultural, technological, and even moral affairs on earth" — along lines that might be considered simultaneously evangelical and enlightened.[10]

9. Ned C. Landsman, *From Colonials to Provincials: American Thought and Culture, 1680-1760* (Ithaca: Cornell University Press, 2000 [1997]), 60.

10. Norman Fiering, *Moral Philosophy at Seventeenth-Century Harvard: A Discipline in*

The College of New Jersey

In this context, Presbyterians took an important step in fulfilling their educational mission. As early as 1739, the Presbyterian Synod had called for the establishment of a school where ministers could be trained, but the division of that body into New and Old Sides in 1741 put the project on hold. In 1746, the New Side Presbytery of New York took the initiative in the formation of the College of New Jersey; and Jonathan Dickinson, pastor of the Presbyterian Church in Elizabeth Town, New Jersey, became its first president. Located briefly in Dickinson's home, the school moved for a time to Newark after his death in 1747 and eventually relocated to Princeton in 1756. This new school, the College of New Jersey, continued the legacy of the Log College. Several men closely associated with the Log College — Samuel Blair, Samuel Finley, and two of William Tennent's sons (William Jr. and Gilbert) — were initially on the board of trustees. The first five presidents of the school also demonstrated its strongly New Side and pro-Awakening bent. Dickinson, a son of Connecticut Congregationalism and a graduate of Yale, affiliated with the Presbyterians a few years after assuming the pastorate in Elizabeth Town. He combined his Puritan heritage with a moderate revivalism. Initially he had held back from full identification with the New Side at the time of the separation and tried to play the mediator, but his revivalist sympathies and the Old Side inflexibility brought him to join the New Side. In his successor, Aaron Burr, father of the infamous politician of the same name, the college turned to another Connecticut minister deeply shaped by the Great Awakening. Upon his death in 1757, the trustees called Jonathan Edwards from his labors in Stockbridge, Massachusetts. Burr's father-in-law and the most eminent theologian of the revival, Edwards served for only a couple of months until he succumbed to a bad reaction to a smallpox vaccination. His successor, Samuel Davies, had promoted revival among the Presbyterians of Virginia and was a product of Fagg's Manor, one of the academies created in the image of the Log College. His abbreviated tenure of only nineteenth months was followed by the somewhat longer service (five years) of Samuel Finley, who had been

---

Transition (Chapel Hill: University of North Carolina Press, 1981), 302. For a good example of the way in which evangelical faith and the pursuit of enlightenment might merge, see John Fea, *The Way of Improvement Leads Home: Philip Vickers Fithian and the Rural Enlightenment in Early America* (Philadelphia: University of Pennsylvania Press, 2008).

born in County Armaugh, Ireland, immigrated to the colonies in his late teens, and most likely received his education at the Log College. From this enumeration of the college's first five leaders, one sees — in addition to the speedy rate of presidential mortality — two streams that flowed together to shape the school: a New England Puritan heritage as mediated through evangelical revivalism and a Scots-Irish piety in the Log College tradition. (Of course, there was also a larger Scots-Irish element in Presbyterianism that was Old Side and resistant to the newer evangelical expressions.)[11]

Yet the College of New Jersey was more than a New Side revival–oriented academy. Unlike its predecessors, the college had a charter from the colonial governor and a board of trustees, and it granted degrees. Moreover, the college was the first to be chartered in a colony without an established church and with considerable religious pluralism. Even though the majority of the trustees were Presbyterian and all the school's presidents likewise, no legal stipulation required this affiliation. The charter did not speak explicitly of preparing clergy, and there was no sectarian test for the student body. As one historian has remarked, "in the religiously heterodox middle colonies, it would have been suicidal to announce that Princeton would welcome only Presbyterian students." President Aaron Burr put the best face on this situation when he declared:

> Though our great intention was to erect a seminary for educating ministers of the gospel, that we might have a sufficient number of pious and well qualified men to supply the demands of our churches and propagate the kingdom of the redeemer among those who have hitherto lived in darkness and ignorance, yet we hope that it will be a means of training up men that will be useful in the other learned professions — ornaments of the state as well as the church. Therefore we propose to make the plan of education as extensive as our circumstances will admit.

---

11. Elijah R. Craven, "The Log College of Neshaminy and Princeton University," *Journal of the Presbyterian Historical Society* 1 (June 1902): 308-14; Sloan, *Scottish Enlightenment*, 58-64. For a classic analysis stressing the polarity between a conservative Scots-Irish group and revivalistically oriented New Englanders, see Leonard J. Trinterud, *The Forming of an American Tradition: A Re-examination of Colonial Presbyterianism* (Philadelphia: Westminster Press, 1949).

At one level, Burr's rhetoric testified to the traditional view of the college as a place for the education of all leaders in society, and his language about producing "ornaments of the state as well as the church" echoed time-honored assumptions about the unity among church, state, and university. Yet, in stepping back from specific language about preparing a godly ministry, the college's charter acknowledged, if only faintly, that perhaps the older assumptions were no longer fully applicable. The Presbyterian founders of the College of New Jersey were inching into a world of new social, cultural, and religious realities.[12]

But despite the concessions made to those realities, the school retained a decidedly New Side Presbyterian cast, and it remained the training ground for a substantial portion of the Presbyterian clergy. With the death of Samuel Finley in 1766, the school stood at a crossroads. The enthusiasms of the revival had lessened, New Side Presbyterians had rejected the more extreme forms of awakening, and their most talented leaders lay buried in the Princeton cemetery. In 1758, the Old and New Sides had reunited. Though some have characterized the reconciliation as a "union without love," Presbyterians were attempting to move beyond old divisions. What would this mean for the College of New Jersey? When the question of Finley's successor came up, the issue had to be faced squarely. Former Old Sides made a bid for control of the institution by proposing an Old Side president and at least one faculty member. The trustees sidestepped the proposal by offering the presidency to someone identified with neither the Old or New Side. They turned to a Scottish minister by the name of John Witherspoon (1723-1794), who, after an initial refusal, accepted and took up his duties in Princeton in 1768.[13]

12. Howard Miller, *The Revolutionary College: American Presbyterian Higher Education, 1707-1837* (New York: New York University Press, 1976), 67; William L. Broderick, "Pulpit, Physics, and Politics: The Curriculum of the College of New Jersey, 1746-1794," *William and Mary Quarterly*, 3rd ser., 6 (January 1949): 42-68; Burr quoted in Broderick, 56-57. For a fascinating discussion of the difficulties the founders had in gaining a secure charter in religiously heterogeneous New Jersey, consult Bryan F. Le Beau, *Jonathan Dickinson and the Formative Years of American Presbyterianism* (Lexington: University of Kentucky Press, 1997), 172-84.

13. The phrase "union without love" is from a chapter in Trinterud, *Forming of an American Tradition*, 144-65.

John Witherspoon

Witherspoon had made his reputation as a champion of the Popular party in its struggles against the Moderates in the Church of Scotland. The Moderates, without rejecting the church's doctrinal standards, favored a tolerant, urbane stance and eschewed theological controversy. Stressing ethics as the heart of Christianity, they believed that the gospel went hand in glove with intellectual progress and gentility. They were particularly strong in the universities, counted among their ranks many men of letters, and were among the chief promoters of the Enlightenment in Scotland. Moderates increasingly supported the use of patronage — a traditional practice by which a local land owner or noble had the right to present a minister to a church. Patronage had come under attack by those who favored a consistent Presbyterian polity whereby the congregation, with the approval of presbytery, called a pastor. Abolished and revived multiple times during the political and religious upheavals of the late seventeenth and early eighteenth centuries, patronage had again been restored in 1712. Moderates reconciled themselves to the practice in part because they found it a useful tool to install ministers of their own persuasion in churches that otherwise would not call them. Against the Moderates, the Popular party insisted on the right of each congregation to call its own pastor. Although those committed to this position did not always agree theologically, a significant portion — probably a majority — of the Popular party adhered to traditional Calvinist views and were sympathetic to the evangelical revivals of the eighteenth century.[14]

Witherspoon satirized the Moderates in *Ecclesiastical Characteristics, or the Arcana of Church Polity* (1753). Purporting to be maxims by those of that persuasion and studded with allusions to its principal authors, the pamphlet offered as the first principle of Moderatism that "all ecclesiastical persons . . . that are suspected of heresy are to be esteemed men of great genius, vast learning, and uncommon worth." Another was that a "moderate man . . . [should] never speak of the Confession of Faith but with a sneer . . . and [should] make the word orthodoxy a term of contempt and reproach." Moreover, a good minister should preach not tradi-

---

14. Richard B. Sher, *Church and University in the Scottish Enlightenment: The Moderate Literati of Edinburgh* (Princeton: Princeton University Press, 1985). For a treatment stressing the complexities within the Popular party, see John R. McIntosh, *Church and Theology in Enlightenment Scotland: The Popular Party, 1740-1800* (East Linton: Tuckwell Press, 1998).

tional doctrines but only "social duties," and "his authorities must be drawn from heathen writers, none, or as few as possible from Scripture." The creed of a Moderate involved a confession of the "divinity" of Lord Shaftesbury and the "perpetual duration" of Francis Hutcheson's writings. No doubt such sentiments made Witherspoon seem theologically sound to the predominantly New Side trustees who called him to Princeton. Yet he was not so extreme as to reject the new learning, the point of his satire being that he had mastered that learning himself and could turn it against any who would employ it to subvert orthodoxy.[15]

Witherspoon took vigorous charge in Princeton, raised admission requirements, and embarked upon fund-raising tours from New England to Virginia. Within his first year alone, he more than doubled the endowment. The number of students rose to an average of twenty-five per year in the last half decade before the Revolutionary War. Witherspoon also put Princeton on the map politically. He gave ardent support to colonial resistance to Great Britain, made the school a hotbed of revolutionary and republican fervor, and was the only clergyman to sign the Declaration of Independence. Educationally, he increased the study of the natural sciences, of rhetoric, and of moral philosophy and made lectures the key method of instruction. Under his leadership, the school became the most truly national of America's colleges in its constituency. While Yale and Harvard, for example, drew students overwhelmingly from New England and while William and Mary served chiefly Virginia, the College of New Jersey drew students from New England, the mid-Atlantic states, and the South. Although the training of clergy remained a major goal of Witherspoon, the percentage of Princeton graduates seeking ordination fell during the Revolutionary years to 21 percent, and after the war near the close of Witherspoon's tenure the percentage dropped to 13 percent. At the same time, the school was turning out an extraordinary range of other leaders for the young nation: six representatives to the Continental Congress, a major architect of the U.S. Constitution and a future American president (James Madison), twenty senators, and twenty-three members of the House of Representatives. Nassau Hall also produced important contributors to literature in Philip Freneau and Hugh Henry Brackenridge.[16]

15. John Witherspoon, *The Works of the Rev. John Witherspoon, D.D., LL.D.*, 2nd ed., 4 vols. (Philadelphia: William W. Woodward, 1802), 3:211, 216, 219, 234.

16. Mark A. Noll, *Princeton and the Republic: The Search for a Christian Enlightenment*

Despite the declining numbers of clergy produced at the college and his own political activities notwithstanding, Witherspoon had by no means given up on the church. He continued to be an active minister, preaching on traditional topics and offering religious instruction to students. A major force within the Presbyterian Church, he was a leading player in the creation of the denomination's General Assembly. The breadth of his influence was attested by the fact that at the first meeting of that body in 1789 ninety-seven of the 188 clergy commissioners were graduates of the College of New Jersey and over half of these were Witherspoon's former students. It was not that Witherspoon or the trustees had ceased to care about piety or commitment to traditional Christian doctrines of the Reformed faith. These they continued to affirm and to make a crucial part of education in Princeton, but within a new framework or context.[17]

The central place that Witherspoon gave to moral philosophy illustrated the new context. In his *Ecclesiastical Characteristics,* he had not seemed to do so. In fact he sharply criticized the new moral philosophy and its apparent indifference to traditional theological concerns. In particular he lampooned Francis Hutcheson, but once in America Witherspoon himself borrowed heavily from Hutcheson in constructing his own lectures on moral philosophy. Hutcheson had grounded morality in a universal sentiment and thereby suggested that an empirical science of ethics was possible through the study of human consciousness. Witherspoon adopted these assumptions. "It must be admitted," he averred, "that a sense of moral good and evil is as really a principle of our nature as the gross external or reflex senses. . . . It is the law which our Maker has written upon our hearts and both intimates and enforces duty previous to all reasoning." In a later lecture, he conceded that writers on moral philosophy often disagreed with one another more than those who dealt with natural science, but he held out the hope that "perhaps a time may come when men, treating moral philosophy as Newton and his successors have done natural, may arrive at greater precision." In

---

in the Era of Samuel Stanhope Smith (Princeton: Princeton University Press, 1989), 28-58; Broderick, "Pulpit, Physics, and Politics," 67, 68.

17. Elwyn A. Smith, *The Presbyterian Ministry in American Culture: A Study in Changing Concepts, 1700-1900* (Philadelphia: Westminster Press, 1962), 92. For an account of his life and thought emphasizing the centrality of religious commitment and practice, see L. Gordon Tait, *The Piety of John Witherspoon: Piety, Pulpit, and Public Forum* (Louisville: Geneva Press, 2001).

an age enamored of the triumphs of Newton and of other scientific discoveries, this was a seductive vision. Moral philosophers might aspire to an empirical science of morality. Through meticulous investigation of human consciousness, they might arrive at an exactness and objectivity comparable to that yielded by study of the physical universe. The implication was that the moral philosopher could begin with a study of human nature, not of divine revelation. Witherspoon, of course, had no intention of repudiating revelation — he frequently stressed its thorough congruence with that which could be learned from the study of human consciousness. Yet he was illustrating what Norman Fiering, as previously noted, has described as a central feature of the new moral philosophy: God's "will was to be uncovered indirectly, through the book of nature. The superhuman standpoint no longer overtly predominated."[18]

More particularly, Witherspoon was contributing to the triumph in America of a philosophic outlook known as Scottish Realism or the Common Sense philosophy. In its characteristic form developed by Thomas Reid — for example, in *Inquiry into the Human Mind, on the Principles of Common Sense* (1764) — this school stressed observation as the foundation of knowledge and had a profound admiration of inductive or Baconian science. Yet love of the scientific method did not lead these thinkers into the skepticism sometimes associated with empiricism, for they believed that consciousness itself contained common sense principles that no sane person could doubt. These principles included the reality of the external world and of humanity's moral intuitions and its sense of a god who had created the cosmos. These intuitions were, for the common sense philosophers, as self-evident as the reality of the physical cosmos that Newton and others had investigated and were as capable of the same systematic exploration. These thinkers strongly eschewed abstruse speculation and wished philosophy — whether natural or moral — confined to the observation, cataloguing, and analysis of facts. Although Witherspoon was directly influenced more by the ethical theories of Hutcheson than by the later more developed common sense realism of Thomas Reid, the Princeton president nevertheless anticipated Reid's basic conclusions, and he set the College of New Jersey down that philosophic path. One of his first acts after coming to the school was to purge from its teaching what he saw as philosophic idealism drawn from

---

18. Witherspoon, *Works,* 3:379, 470; Fiering, *Moral Philosophy at Seventeenth-Century Harvard,* 302.

Bishop Berkeley. Henceforth Princeton, both the college and later the seminary, would tread the safe path of Common Sense Realism, as would most American schools for decades to come.[19]

Witherspoon was not a thinker of the first rank. A practical man whether in the pulpit, the classroom, or the public arena, he was not at his best in parsing the nuances of ideas. According to one of his students and an early biographer, Witherspoon derived his power from the fact that he had "more of the quality called *presence* — a quality powerfully felt, but not to be described — than any other individual" whom the writer had met, "Washington alone excepted." With that presence, he gave forceful embodiment to ideals widely held in the late eighteenth century. "Witherspoon did nothing less," Mark Noll has aptly remarked, "than draw the Princeton circle into the main currents of developments for American society and Western learning. Through his efforts the college became a highly regarded nursery for the republican principles of the new nation. And it became a leader in promoting scientific learning. It did so, moreover, without seeming to abandon the configuration of purposes that had governed the school since its inception." In other words, Witherspoon embraced the new science, the Enlightenment as embodied in Common Sense Realism, American patriotism, republican values, and the evangelical rendition of Calvinism. Whether at the end of the day all of these commitments would cohere remained to be seen.[20]

Samuel Stanhope Smith and Demands for Reform

The first serious hints that they might not hold together easily came during the presidency of Witherspoon's successor and son-in-law, Samuel Stanhope Smith. Trained by his New Side father in the latter's academy in Pequea, Pennsylvania, the precocious lad entered the junior class at the College of New Jersey at the age of 16. After graduation, he tutored in his father's academy, returned to Princeton to study theology with

19. See, for example, Sydney E. Ahlstrom, "The Scottish Philosophy and American Theology," *Church History* 24 (September 1955): 257-72; Theodore Dwight Bozeman, *Protestants in an Age of Science: The Baconian Ideal and Antebellum Religious Thought* (Chapel Hill: University of North Carolina Press, 1977); Mark A. Noll, *America's God: From Jonathan Edwards to Abraham Lincoln* (New York: Oxford University Press, 2002).

20. Noll, *Princeton and the Republic,* 54.

Witherspoon, then served as a missionary and pastor before becoming president of Prince Edward Academy (today's Hampden-Sydney College). In 1779, he came back to Princeton as professor of moral philosophy, steadily took on additional duties in the school, and succeeded Witherspoon as president in 1795. Smith pursued Witherspoon's vision for the college with perhaps more consistency — certainly with greater precision and finesse — than the blunt Scot had managed. Smith impressed many as a model of solid learning, urbanity, and good taste. In particular, he won kudos for his *Essay on the Causes of the Variety of Complexion and Figure in the Human Species* (1787). At a time when some were questioning the common origins of all humanity, Smith provided a learned argument that different climates and social customs had over time accentuated minor physical differences to produce the separate races of humanity. By stressing the single origin of humanity, Smith was perceived by many as a vindicator of the biblical account of creation. He expanded instruction in science at the college. In his lectures on moral philosophy, he drew upon the mature Common Sense philosophy to present a system more finely polished than his predecessor's. Yet he did not forsake his clerical and theological responsibilities any more than Witherspoon had. For example, he lectured to students on theology and structured the addresses after the Westminster Confession. Although he sometimes softened the asperities of Westminster, he affirmed the central tenets of the confession and made clear his continued adherence to the Reformed tradition. The Presbyterian General Assembly recognized his leadership in the denomination by electing him moderator in 1808. Smith had, of course, carried Princeton's instructional program further down the road toward emphasis upon science, belles-lettres, and gentility than his predecessor had, but he still clearly stood within the heritage that Witherspoon had established. Why then did Smith encounter from trustees much covert opposition and criticism while his father-in-law had won general support and praise?[21]

The answer lay partly in the misfortune of Smith to stand at Princeton's helm when the college faced serious difficulties. In 1802 a fire gutted Nassau Hall. Smith wrote to a correspondent that, despite the absence of "direct proof," the fire was probably "communicated [caused] by design."

---

21. Noll, *Princeton and the Republic,* 54; Samuel Holt Monk, "Samuel Stanhope Smith: Friend of Rational Liberty," in *The Lives of Eighteen from Princeton,* ed. Willard Thorpe (Princeton: Princeton University Press, 1946).

When the trustees met they likewise presumed that Nassau Hall "was intentionally set on fire" and proceeded to suspend seven students. A successful fund-raising effort by Smith to rebuild the edifice as well as an increase in student enrollment surmounted the immediate crisis. But five years later open student revolt broke out. In late March 1807, the faculty suspended three students for infractions such as insulting townsfolk, carousing, and cursing a tutor. Responding to these sanctions, more than 150 students signed a petition asserting that the faculty had acted unjustly and with improper haste. The school authorities, as one of the trustees put the matter in a public meeting with the student body, argued that the petition itself was evidence of a conspiracy "to control the government of the college." When angry, jeering students stomped out, the faculty regarded them as part of the illicit conspiracy, took down their names, and promptly suspended them — 126 in all. Some of the rebels smashed doors and windows, armed themselves with clubs and stones, and prepared to defend themselves against local militia who had been summoned to eject the rioters. Fearing violence, the faculty sent the militia away, and several days later the trustees ordered the school closed until the start of the summer session. In the wake of the student riot, the number of students dropped by nearly half, and in succeeding years the continuing dip in enrollment forced the school to reduce the number of faculty.

The dilemma facing the college was part of a larger crisis within the nation. Smith's tenure as Princeton's leader coincided with major rethinking of the young republic's basic assumptions and values. For example, national unity frayed when two political parties emerged in the 1790s: the Federalists led by figures such as John Adams and the Democratic Republicans led by Thomas Jefferson. Federalists favored stronger central government, wished to promote commerce and banking, and believed that the masses owed deference to men of property and standing. By contrast, Jeffersonians stressed the rights of individual states, saw independent farmers rather than bankers or merchants as key to the nation's prosperity, and wanted common people to exercise the same rights as their so-called "betters" in society. The debates about domestic policy were bitter enough, but differences over foreign policy introduced additional rancor. When the French Revolution began in 1789, most Americans sympathized with the revolutionaries and saw their struggle as a continuation of the same cause of liberty for which the United States had recently waged a war of independence. By the mid-1790s, however, the revolution in France had turned radical, and the guillotine was devouring not only the leaders of the ancien régime but even those revolutionaries deemed insufficiently committed to the cause. Perceiving the Christian churches as enemies, French leaders embarked upon a campaign of "de-Christianization." As the revolution took this turn, American attitudes toward it became sharply divided. Democratic Republicans tended to maintain their enthusiasm while Federalists were increasingly aghast at the disorder, violence, and religious unbelief. At the same time a militant form of Deism typified by Ethan Allen's *Reason the Only Oracle of Man* (1784) and Thomas Paine's *The Age of Reason* (1794) gained notoriety in the United States with harsh attacks on orthodox Christianity, the Bible, and the divinity of Christ. Paine epitomized the sharpness of the critique when he declared: "The most detestable wickedness, the most horrid cruelties, and the greatest miseries that have afflicted the human race have had their origin in this thing called revelation, or revealed religion." Since Paine and company criticized Federalist conservatism and endorsed Democratic Republican ideals, Federalist clergy, who were especially numerous among New England Congregationalists and also many middle-states Presbyterians, easily tarred their political opponents with the brush of religious infidelity. Despite his general public silence on his religious views, Jefferson's heterodoxy was widely suspected and lent credibility to Federalist charges that Republicans were unbelievers. By the end of the 1790s, then, the two parties had created hostile caricatures of one another. Federalists saw Jeffersonians leading the country to anarchy, mob rule, and anti-Christian views. For their part, the Democratic Republican followers of Jefferson viewed their opponents as enemies of liberty — aristocrats — who did not really believe in the principles of the American Revolution and would undo them if they could. After Jefferson won the presidency from Adams in 1801, the Federalist party never again elected a chief executive, and Federalism gradually faded away. For the Princeton community, largely Federalist in sympathy and now on the losing side in the political contest, these developments called for a rethinking of how the parts of Witherspoon's vision — the embrace of science and the Enlightenment, commitment to the American republic, and loyalty to the Calvinist tradition — could be kept together.[22]

22. Thomas Paine, *The Age of Reason,* ed. Philip S. Foner (Secaucus, NJ: Citadel Press, 1948 [1794]), 182. Gary B. Nash, "The American Clergy and the French Revolution," *William*

To those in Princeton the events in the country and in the school seemed closely linked. In the same letter in which Smith suggested that the fire of 1802 had been deliberately set, he also added that the fire was "one effect of those irreligious and demoralizing principles which are tearing the bands of society asunder & threatening in the end to over-turn our country." In other words, a spirit of revolt in the college itself was a direct product of the irreligion and Jeffersonian anarchy threatening the nation at large. Unfortunately for Smith, important figures on the board of trustees eventually concluded that he had not done enough to suppress those "irreligious and demoralizing principles" at the college. Believing that he had lost control of the situation, they sought new leadership. Smith had weakened himself in the estimation of some by es-pousing views of questionable soundness: for example, a suggestion that polygamy was not against natural law (although he added that the New Testament opposed it), and a sermon containing passing comments that seemed to underplay the gravity of original sin. But undoubtedly the continuing emphasis in the curriculum upon science and belles-lettres and the serious decline in the number of college graduates entering the ministry were factors of at least equal importance in undermining Smith's position. The numbers going on to theological education had dipped below 10 percent in the several years before the student revolt of 1807. Smith's effort to remedy that problem with the appointment of Henry Kollock as professor of theology in 1803 failed. Attracting few students, Kollock resigned in 1806. The appointment itself was arguably ill-advised and at best poorly handled. A protégé of Smith, Kollock seemed to one faction of the board of trustees too young and the manner of his appointment too hasty. The doubters favored calling the more seasoned Ashbel Green, a Philadelphia pastor who had been a student, tutor, and now trustee at the college and who had acted as interim president when Smith went on his fund-raising tour after the 1802 fire. Although Green himself had brushed aside an overture with regard to the theology position, he nevertheless took offense at Kollock's appointment.

When a major turnover on the board of trustees occurred in 1807-1808, Green's alienation from Smith proved dangerous to the president.

and Mary Quarterly, 3rd ser., 22 (July 1965): 392-412. For a helpful overview of the contro-versies over Deism, see the introduction by the editor in Kerry S. Walters, ed., *The Ameri-can Deists: Voices of Reason and Dissent in the Early Republic* (Lawrence: University Press of Kansas, 1992), 1-50.

The new majority turned more to their ministerial members — men such as Green — for leadership. They created in 1810 a board of visitors to oversee discipline at the school. The trustees had placed the president and faculty on a short leash, and in July 1812 they prepared to shorten the leash further. They authorized the appointment of a vice president whose primary function, under the supervision of the board, would be to maintain discipline in the school. With his powers about to be curtailed, and following the negotiation of what today would be called a severance package, Smith resigned on August 14. The trustees then named Ashbel Green as the new president. Green introduced the study of the Bible into the curriculum, added William Paley on natural theology, and returned Witherspoon's lectures to the course of study. He markedly tightened discipline, encouraged the organization of student religious voluntary societies, witnessed in 1814 and '15 a religious revival on campus, and saw an increased number of the school's graduates — a quarter — enter the ministry. Eventually student riots disrupted Green's tenure, and in 1822 disenchanted trustees engineered his resignation just as they had his predecessor's. Yet Green's administration marked a significant course correction for the college. Without repudiating the school's commitment to the Enlightenment, to republicanism, patriotism, and public service, the school sought to promote these goals indirectly. It chose to emphasize distinctly religious means, such as the promotion of revivals, the mobilization of voluntary societies, and the professional training of clergy. To achieve this last goal, a new institution, separate from the college, was founded.

The Endeavor to Create a Presbyterian Seminary

As Ashbel Green promoted the reform of the College of New Jersey, he was simultaneously one of several prominent Presbyterians encouraging the creation of a theological seminary. As early as January 1800, he wrote a private letter to Edward Dorr Griffin, pastor in Newark, New Jersey, suggesting a theological school independent of the college. In private correspondence over the next several years, he also broached two other vaguely defined possibilities for Presbyterian theological education: a divinity school at the College of New Jersey or an internship program in which young ministers would serve churches in rural areas. It is interesting to speculate on what would have happened had either of the latter two plans been fleshed out and adopted. The former might have led to the creation of a university-based divinity school such as the ones that emerged at Harvard and Yale; the latter would possibly have tended toward the kind of parish-based apprentice education that some of Jonathan Edwards's disciples — commonly called adherents of the New Divinity — underwent, through which more than 450 men entered the ministry, most of them in western Massachusetts or Connecticut, between 1750 and 1825. (Among them was Green's correspondent Griffin.)[23]

In 1805, Samuel Miller, then a pastor in New York City, wrote to Green about his concern for the establishment of a theological school. As he would do seven years later in his address at Archibald Alexander's inaugural, he noted the dearth of Presbyterian pastors: "We have, if I do not mistake, a melancholy prospect, indeed, with respect to a supply of ministers for our churches. Cannot the General Assembly, at their next sessions, commence some plan of operation for supplying this deficiency?" He saw two possibilities: "either to establish a theological school in some central part of our bounds; or direct more of our attention to extend the plan and increase the energy of the Princeton establishment [the College of New Jersey]." But he quickly added: "On the latter part of the alternative many doubts occur to me." Miller had joined those disaffected with Smith's regime. In the same letter Miller also noted the necessity of combating the increasingly "arrogant claims and high church principles" of the Episcopalians in New York. Inadequate numbers of clergy, dissatisfaction with the College of New Jersey, and a realization that Presbyterians needed to hold their own in denominational competition — all of these concerns prompted Miller to encourage Green to offer a proposal on the subject of theological education at the coming General Assembly. Green did so. At the Assembly in May he made a stirring appeal to the Assembly for more ministers; but aside from encouraging better financial support for the clergy and greater diligence by presbyteries in seeking out appropriate candidates for ordination and in directing them to appropriate places of instruction, he offered no specific proposals.[24]

Soon Presbyterians had the example of another denomination to emulate. In 1805, a rising liberal party in New England Congregational-

---

23. David W. Kling, "New Divinity Schools of the Prophets, 1750-1825: A Case Study in Ministerial Education," *History of Education Quarterly* 37 (Summer 1997): 185-206.

24. Samuel Miller, *The Life of Samuel Miller, D.D., LL.D.*, 2 vols. (Philadelphia: Claxton, Remsen and Haffelfinger, 1869), 1:191, 192.

ism — a party then becoming overtly Unitarian — secured the election of one of its own as the professor of divinity at Harvard. The following year a liberal was elected to the presidency of the college. Trinitarian Congregationalists, themselves divided into two factions, managed to come together to sign an agreement in May 1808 to create an orthodox seminary at Andover, Massachusetts, to stand as a bulwark against liberal religion. Samuel Miller was in correspondence with Jedidiah Morse, one of the chief movers in organizing the new seminary, and the example of the Congregationalist effort appears to have goaded Presbyterians in the same direction.[25]

In the same month that the Andover agreement was sealed, Archibald Alexander, the outgoing moderator of the Presbyterian General Assembly, preached an opening sermon to the judicatory in which he urged greater exertions on behalf of theological education. Taking a swipe at existing schools and, by implication, at Samuel Stanhope Smith, Alexander "doubted whether the system of education pursued in our colleges and universities is the best adapted to prepare a young man for the work of the ministry. The great extension of the physical sciences, and the taste and fashion of the age, have given such a shape and direction to the academical course, that I confess, it appears to me to be little adapted to introduce a youth to the study of the sacred Scriptures." Alexander looked for a time when "every Presbytery, or at least every Synod, shall have under its direction a seminary established for the single purpose of educating youth for the ministry." In 1809, the Philadelphia Presbytery, at the urging of Ashbel Green, overtured the General Assembly to establish a theological school. The Assembly's response was to poll all the presbyteries to see which of three alternatives they preferred: a single school for the entire denomination, two schools situated "in such places as may best accommodate the northern and southern divisions of the Church," or a school in each of the four synods.[26]

Reported to the 1810 Assembly, the responses of the thirty-six presbyteries were inconclusive. Ten favored a single national seminary, ten wished a school in each synod, and one desired two seminaries (one in the north and the other in the south). Six presbyteries thought the pres-

25. John H. Giltner, "The Fragmentation of New England Congregationalism and the Founding of Andover Seminary," *Journal of Religious Thought* 20, no. 1 (1964): 27-42; Miller, *Life of Samuel Miller*, 1:229-33.

26. James W. Alexander, *The Life of Archibald Alexander, D.D.* (New York: Charles Scribner, 1854), 314-15.

ent moment inopportune to launch any ventures, and nine presbyteries failed to respond. Samuel Miller was appointed chair of a seven-member committee to evaluate the responses and report to the Assembly. With considerable interpretative license, Miller's committee turned the results into a clear mandate for a single national seminary. "As several of the objections" to that plan, the committee reported, "are founded entirely on misconception . . . it seems fairly to follow that there is a greater amount of presbyterial suffrage in favor of a single school, than of any other plan." (Apparently some presbyteries feared that a seminary would assume their historic prerogative to decide who should or should not be ordained.) The committee recommended an immediate "attempt to establish a seminary" that would eventually have "at least three professors, who shall be elected by, and hold their offices during the pleasure of, the General Assembly." These professors would give instruction "in Divinity, Oriental and Biblical Literature, and Ecclesiastical History and Church Government, and on such other subjects as may be deemed necessary." The Assembly approved the proposal but made clear that the new institution would in no way usurp the right of the presbyteries to license and ordain candidates for the ministry. It appointed Ashbel Green to chair a committee of seven, including Miller and Alexander, to draw up a plan for the theological school.

As the Assembly and its representatives worked out the details over the next two years, several issues had to be resolved: (1) Would the seminary's curriculum concentrate solely on postgraduate studies in theology, Scripture, church history, and the practice of ministry or would it also include liberal arts at the collegiate level? (2) Where would the school be located? (3) If it resided in Princeton, what relationship would it sustain to the college? With regard to curriculum, the original plan drafted by Green called for the establishment of a "theological academy" allied to the seminary, and the description of the academy — though somewhat vague — made clear that such an institution might become a serious rival to the College of New Jersey. Perhaps fear of this possibility lay behind the invitation from the trustees to locate the seminary in Princeton and organize it under the aegis of the CNJ charter.

When the General Assembly of 1811 received both the draft of the proposed plan for the seminary and the invitation from the college, it kept its options open. It appointed a committee headed by Archibald Alexander to negotiate with the college and postponed action upon the recommendation of the Green committee to establish a satellite academy. Except for the proposal for an academy and a recommendation concerning the library, the Assembly approved with minor additions the remainder of the plan. The Assembly action also seemed to leave open the possibility of an organic union of the seminary with the college but avoided final commitment. Even the matter of location remained unresolved because the committee received authority to consider spots other than Princeton between "the rivers Raritan and Potomac." During the next round of negotiations, the trustees of the college chose Ashbel Green himself to represent the school in its talks with the Assembly's representatives! Not surprisingly, matters proceeded swiftly and to the seminary's advantage. Within weeks an agreement was hammered out. The seminary was to be located in Princeton, the General Assembly would retain full control of the new institution, the seminary could use college facilities while its own were being constructed, and it could even build on college land. Richard Stockton, a wealthy college trustee living in Princeton, made the last item unnecessary by donating several acres of his own property to the theological seminary. When the General Assembly approved this agreement in 1812, it quietly dropped the notion of creating an academy that would compete with the college. The Assembly proceeded to the election of a thirty-member board of directors, which the following month chose Ashbel Green as its president. Green would hold the position until his death in 1848. Before adjourning, the Assembly elected Archibald Alexander to serve as professor of didactic and polemical theology; and, as previously mentioned, he was inaugurated on August 12. As a coda to the long drama that had led to the creation of the seminary and the installation of its first professor, the Smith regime ended two days later. The trustees then elected Ashbel Green president of the College of New Jersey. The long campaigns to reform the college and to create a new school for theological education had both triumphed simultaneously.

Although the seminary was to be separate from the college and would not follow the divinity school route that Harvard and Yale later pursued, the full implications of the decision were not immediately apparent. For the moment, the two schools shared not only a common outlook but common personnel. Green was president simultaneously of the college and of the seminary's board of directors. In fact, nine of the seminary's board of directors also sat on the college's board of trustees. To a considerable degree, the sense of congruence between the two institutions would last until the late nineteenth century.

What should one make of the decision to create the seminary? "Historically considered," Mark Noll has suggested, "the establishment of Princeton resulted from the actions of desperate men, men who thought their society was undergoing a crisis of unprecedented magnitude requiring nothing less than unprecedented solutions." There is much to commend that reading. Americans had entered a strange new world whose impact on the churches seemed uncertain. The rancorous political debates and the formation of political parties in the 1790s, the movement away from classical republicanism toward a more expansive democratic rhetoric, the attacks on revealed religion by men such as Thomas Paine — all of these were sources of anxiety. At the same time, the frontier beckoned settlers westward at an astonishing rate, and in those newly settled areas denominations such as the Methodists and Baptists seemed to be having more success than Presbyterians in planting churches and providing clergy. Yet it would be a mistake to suggest that the founders in Princeton were simply acting out of fear. While they had grave anxieties, they also found much to gladden the heart. Numerically, Presbyterians remained one of the largest churches in the nation. They were also well positioned to exert influence in the young republic. New England excepted, they constituted a national church. Also, Presbyterians were, by education and positions of influence, excellently situated to help form the new nation's character. Out of that dialectic of fear and hope the founders of Princeton Theological Seminary launched their experiment.[27]

27. Noll, "Founding of Princeton Seminary," *Westminster Theological Journal* 42, no. 1 (Fall 1979): 85.

Chapter Two

Archibald Alexander and Samuel Miller

I N ITS FIRST years, the seminary was the lengthened shadow of two men who had led the movement to create a theological seminary. They were products of two very different worlds. Archibald Alexander came from the Shenandoah Valley and counted rural Virginia as home even after he had gone elsewhere. Approximately the first thirty-five years of his life were shaped by that environment; he told tales of it to his children, cherished his connections to it, and visited it frequently after he had gone to live in Philadelphia and then Princeton. Samuel Miller, though reared in rural Delaware as the son of a preacher who also farmed, nevertheless seemed less a man of the country than of the city. He went to the University of Pennsylvania at the age of 19; at age 23 he was called to a pastorate in Manhattan. Unlike Alexander, who maintained his ties to Virginia, Miller went back to Delaware infrequently. He quickly and easily felt at home in the more cosmopolitan life of the city. The manner of the two was also quite different. Although Alexander observed the proprieties of city life, he initially exhibited a somewhat rustic quality. Throughout his life, people commented on the spontaneity of the man. By contrast, Miller was usually described as methodical and urbane. Frequently observers attached the adjective "bland" to describe him, by which they meant not insipid or lukewarm, as we often use the term, but instead suave or pleasing. Yet these two very different men, by all the surviving evidence, got along harmoniously and served together without serious difficulty for nearly forty years. Their partnership established the basic shape and tone of Princeton Seminary for decades to come.

Archibald Alexander

Archibald Alexander was a third-generation product of the Scots-Irish immigration that swelled Presbyterian ranks in the eighteenth century. His grandfather Archibald — called Ersbell by contemporaries of Scottish descent — and two brothers arrived in Pennsylvania from Londonderry about 1736. He lived near what is now Norristown and there, under the preaching of New Side Presbyterian John Rowland, was deeply affected by the Great Awakening. Within a couple of years, Alexander moved his family down the Shenandoah Valley of Virginia and established a farm near Lexington. Ersbell's son William married Ann Reid, daughter of a family that owned considerable land; and Archibald Alexander was born in 1772, the third of William and Ann's nine children. In addition to farming, the Alexanders ran a store. They eventually built a house in the heart of Lexington — the center of town being a prized location and an indicator of elevated social status. By comparison to the Tidewater gentry, the family occupied middling status; but by the standards of the Valley, they had become people of substance.[1]

A commitment to education and Presbyterian identity characterized the family. Shaped by a New Side piety, Ersbell helped to build a church meetinghouse and provided basic schooling "to such of the neighbouring youth as would resort to him at night." Although William had fewer educational opportunities than his father, Archibald recalled him as having "a considerable fund of knowledge" and as knowing "the whole Larger Catechism" and "almost all Watts's Psalms and Hymns." As for William's religious zeal, the family remembered it as less than "the Christian eminence" of Ersbell, but William did serve as a Presbyterian elder. He exercised selectivity in bestowing the benefit of advanced education on his sons. (Given prevailing gender roles, the daughters of William and Ann were not even considered for this privilege.) When Archibald was 10, he later recalled, "my father having determined to give a liberal education to one of his sons, selected me, saying to me that learning was to be my estate." His chief instructor was the Rev. William Graham, a Pennsylvania native and graduate of the College of New Jersey. In 1775, Graham was called, upon the recommendation of Samuel Stanhope Smith, by the

---

1. Lefferts A. Loetscher, *Facing the Enlightenment and Pietism: Archibald Alexander and the Founding of Princeton Theological Seminary* (Westport, CT: Greenwood Press, 1983), 3-6.

Presbytery of Hanover in Virginia to "establish a school for the rearing of young men for the ministry." Eventually chartered as Liberty Hall in 1782, the school was explicitly patterned on the Princeton model. "The course which we followed," Alexander noted years later, "was that which prevailed at Princeton under Dr. Witherspoon. We had the same textbooks, and even transcribed his lectures on moral philosophy and criticism." "Most of those who entered the holy ministry in the Valley of Virginia," he noted, "pursued their preparatory studies under his direction." Yet, as in most of the academies founded by Presbyterians in the eighteenth century, the instruction was not simply for the ministry. Beginning at a secondary level of education, the academy took young men up through the collegiate level, preparing them for a variety of later professions of which the ministry was one option. Those who wished to enter the ministry often stayed on longer than did others for additional study with Graham.[2]

For Alexander, the additional study did not happen until other events had intervened. As he was preparing for final examinations at the academy at the age of 17, he later recorded, "my father returned from a journey to Fredericksburg, and informed me that he had made an engagement for me to be a tutor in the family of General Posey, of the Wilderness, twelve miles west of Fredericksburg." Given the timing of his father's decision, it is little wonder that even decades later Alexander still recalled him "as very peremptory in his orders." Just as William had told him, apparently without consultation, seven years earlier that he was to be the one in the family for whom learning would be his "estate," his father informed him with equal directness when it was time to move on. Alexander had to travel more than a hundred miles to join the household of Thomas Posey, a Revolutionary War veteran. The household, Alexander later said, was "somewhat decayed in wealth" but had "maintained much of the style which belonged to old Virginia families." His responsibility was to educate several children of the family — a task that often had him only one lesson preparation ahead of his pupils. At Greenwood, the Posey estate, he availed himself of the library to broaden his knowledge; and there he encountered a religious world beyond the Scots-Irish Presbyterianism of his youth. Mrs. Tyler, a woman of genteel origins who had apparently fallen into straitened circumstances and who resided

---

2. Loetscher, *Facing the Enlightenment and Pietism*, 5-14. Donald Robert Come, "The Influence of Princeton on Higher Education in the South before 1825," *William and Mary Quarterly*, 3rd ser., 2 (October 1945): 359-96.

with the Poseys, introduced him to that wider world. A former Anglican turned Baptist, she shared her faith with the young tutor and thereby helped precipitate a religious crisis for him.[3]

In the aftermath of the Great Awakening, Baptists surged into Virginia. A few Regular Baptists resided there prior to this time, but the great influx of Baptists into Virginia came in the 1760s and later as the so-called Separate Baptists entered the colony. The Separate Baptists had originally spun off from New England Congregationalism in the aftermath of the Great Awakening. Shubal Stearns and Daniel Marshall had taken the movement to the Carolinas in the 1750s, and by the following decade it began making significant inroads into Virginia. Theologically, the differences between the two groups of Baptists were relatively small. The chief difference was the revivalistic zeal of the Separates, their emphasis upon dramatic conversions sometimes experienced amid outbursts of emotion, and their apparent contempt for the marks of distinction honored in Virginia society. As one of their most perceptive students has observed, the Separate Baptists exhibited in pre-Revolutionary Virginia a countercultural quality as "these men, calling each other brothers, who believed that the only authority in their church was the meeting of those in fellowship together, conducted their affairs on a footing of equality in sharp contrast to the explicit preoccupation with rank and precedence that characterized the world from which they had been called." Because of their implicit rebuke to the existing order, Baptists were on occasion subjected to violence, sometimes promoted by persons in authority. For example, Jack Waller, one of the Separates' preachers, was interrupted at the opening of worship one Sunday in 1771 when the local Anglican minister, the sheriff, and some others rode up to the meeting, pulled Waller down from where he was speaking, beat him against the ground, dragged him some distance, and then gave him twenty lashes with a horsewhip. By the time Alexander was exposed to the Baptists in the late 1780s, the violence against them had abated and the Regulars and Separates had reached a degree of union. Yet the Separates had not lost all of their countercultural edge, as Archibald Alexander discovered.[4]

3. James W. Alexander, *The Life of Archibald Alexander, D.D.* (New York: Charles Scribner, 1854), 15, 24, 35, 38; John Thornton Posey, *General Thomas Posey: Son of the American Revolution* (East Lansing: Michigan State University Press, 1992).

4. Rhys Isaac, "Evangelical Revolt: The Nature of the Baptists' Challenge to the Traditional Order in Virginia, 1765 to 1775," *William and Mary Quarterly*, 3rd ser., 31 (July 1974): 346-68; the quotation is on 354, the account of Waller's beating on 346-47.

His Baptist mentor, Mrs. Tyler, though not a Separate herself, took the teenage tutor to one of the group's services since there were no Regular Baptists close to the Posey estate. Alexander's recollection of the event was not flattering. The preacher, he said, was "a stout, corpulent man, who when he preached in warm weather, took off his coat and neck cloth, threw open his collar, and generally became so earnest that before he was done he was black in the face." The minister also took verbal swipes at the learned, and within his audience were instances of "leaping, contortions, swooning, and convulsions." "Mrs. Tyler was mortified at these exhibitions," Alexander's biographer reported. Wishing that her young friend could hear her minister, a Regular Baptist, she persuaded Alexander to travel across the Rappahannock River to attend services. Although the preacher was more restrained and took at least "a fling at learning," he did not make much impression on Alexander.[5]

Yet these encounters raised an important issue for him. A Baptist millwright named Waller — brother to the Jack Waller who years earlier had been beaten during Sunday service — was doing work on the Posey plantation and put a question to Alexander directly.

> [O]ne day he unexpectedly turned to me and asked me whether I believed that before a man could enter the kingdom of heaven he must be born again. I knew not what to say, for I had for some time been puzzled about the new birth. However, I answered in the affirmative. He then asked whether I had experienced the new birth. I hesitated and said, "Not that I knew of." "Ah," said he, "if you had ever experienced this change, you would know something about it!" Here the conversation ended; but it led me to think more seriously whether there were any such change. It seemed to be in the Bible; but I thought there must be some method of explaining it away; for among the Presbyterians I had never heard of any one who had experienced the new birth, nor could I recollect ever to have heard it mentioned.

Perhaps Alexander exaggerated or perhaps the memories of his own grandfather's indebtedness to New Side revivalism had dimmed, but clearly his encounter with the Baptists pressed the matter upon him with new intensity and urgency. The new birth became a subject of table

---

5. Alexander, *Life of Archibald Alexander,* 39, 40.

talk in the Posey household, especially at Sunday meals after Mrs. Tyler had withdrawn, the others perhaps waiting to speak candidly lest they offend her Baptist sensibilities. Posey expressed disbelief in "such miraculous change," and Major William Jones, a neighbor, hinted "that religion was a disease of weak and superstitious minds." By contrast, Mrs. Posey and Mrs. Jones defended the Baptists.[6]

Mrs. Tyler helped Alexander take the first steps out of religious perplexity. A great admirer of John Flavel, the seventeenth-century English Presbyterian, she sometimes asked her young friend to read aloud from his works. It should come as no surprise that Flavel appealed to her, for the Baptists had grown out of the same dissenting religious movement in Great Britain that had produced Presbyterianism and Congregationalism; and the vast majority of American Baptists in her time remained strongly Calvinistic in theology. Since Flavel represented the tradition in which Alexander had been reared, his works carried weight with the young man, who perused them to discover what they had to say about regeneration. During his year as a tutor, Alexander went home to Lexington once and heard William Graham preach on Isaiah 64:6, "For all our righteousnesses are as filthy rags." The sermon, he recalled, stressed "the utter insignificancy of our own works, and our need for a better righteousness than our own." From Flavel and from his own mentor, Alexander was discovering that there was indeed a Presbyterian theological teaching about the new birth.[7]

If the Baptists posed one challenge to Alexander, religious skeptics offered another. His Sunday table companion, Major Jones, spoke for many when he declared "that religion was a disease of weak and superstitious minds." Alexander realized that Jones's views were not idiosyncratic and "that many intelligent men in the country rejected revelation." Among the gentry of Virginia — Alexander was encountering the lower edge of that group when he resided with the Poseys — it was fashionable to read Voltaire, Hume, and others who flirted with religious doubt or Deism. "So ignorant was I," Alexander later wrote of this period of his life, "that I did not know that any book had ever been written in defense of Christianity." When he went through a trunk of books sent from home, his eye thus fell with especial interest upon a volume by Soame Jenyns, *A View of the Internal Evidence of the Christian Religion* (1776). The idea that

6. Alexander, *Life of Archibald Alexander,* 40-41.
7. Alexander, *Life of Archibald Alexander,* 42.

Christianity might be rationally defended exhilarated Alexander. "I was rejoiced; and as all the family had gone to church, I sat down and began to read. At every step conviction flashed across my mind, with such bright and overwhelming evidence, that when I ceased to read, the room had the appearance of being illuminated."[8]

After a year at the Poseys, the tutor returned home, his mind still agitated by religious concerns. Revival had broken out in Prince Edward County east of Lexington, and William Graham had been invited to come over the Blue Ridge and add his preaching to the evangelistic efforts. He took Alexander and another man with him. There amid the revivals Alexander's emotions alternated wildly. He knew moments of joy when he felt assurance and times when he "rolled on the ground in anguish of spirit, bewailing my [spiritual] insensibility." He also experienced a period of stoic resignation as he concluded that he was probably numbered among the damned:

> My mind was calm and my thoughts deliberate, and when I came to this result I was nowise agitated, but began to contemplate the justice of God in my condemnation. It was evident to me that as a righteous Governor he could not do otherwise than condemn me to hell; and I could not but approve the sentence of my own condemnation.

These emotional fluctuations appear to have subsided after a conversation with James Mitchell, one of the Presbyterian pastors in the area. Alexander confided a fear that his religious convictions fell short of the intensity required for salvation. Mitchell dismissed the doubts with a succinct reply: that "no certain degree of conviction was prescribed; that the only purpose which conviction could answer was to show us our need of Christ, 'and this,' added he, 'you have.' He then represented Christ as an Advocate before the throne of God, ready to undertake my cause, and able to save to the uttermost all that come unto God by him." From these assurances came "a joyful hope" to the troubled man. Surveying the emotional upheavals of this period of Alexander's life, Lefferts Loetscher has observed: "It seems that a more stable state of mind came

---

8. Alexander, *Life of Archibald Alexander,* 43; Loetscher, *Facing the Enlightenment and Pietism,* 21-23; Henry F. May, *The Enlightenment in America* (New York: Oxford University Press, 1976), 133-39.

to him only as he abandoned such agonizing introspection and gave himself to a faith that was more objective and did not seek continual psychological confirmation."[9]

Alexander's religious life was shaped by a piety that made a virtue of learning. At crucial moments in his spiritual crisis, books played an important role: for example, John Flavel's works, Soame Jenyns's *Internal Evidences,* a volume of George Whitefield's sermons, the writings of the English dissenting minister Philip Doddridge. True piety for Alexander was piety informed by sound learning. That learning came chiefly from writers in the Puritan-Presbyterian tradition of the seventeenth century or from their religious descendants in the eighteenth. Thus it is not surprising that his spiritual experience bore the marks often associated with Puritanism: intense self-examination, a sense of utter sinfulness, and an awareness that salvation was entirely the work of a gracious God in Christ. So, too, his oscillations from anxiety to hope and from fear to elation — then back and forth many times — were notable characteristics of that tradition. Alexander's story illustrates that the religious excitement of the Great Awakening and its aftermath did not simply produce a generic evangelicalism. Despite the common experience of new birth in which Methodists, Baptists, Presbyterians, and others rejoiced, the fruits of revival were being shaped into different denominational patterns. For Alexander, that pattern was decidedly Presbyterian.[10]

Once Alexander had reached a measure of religious peace, he turned to the question of a career and decided, with trepidation, to pursue the ministry. He approached William Graham about supervising his theological education, expecting that he would be given a number of volumes to read. To his surprise, Graham replied: "If you mean ever to be a theologian, you must come at it not by reading but by thinking." Alexander was

9. Alexander, *Life of Archibald Alexander,* 61, 63, 64; Loetscher, *Facing the Enlightenment and Pietism,* 64.

10. For an account of the way in which revivals were shaped into different denominational patterns, see Philip N. Mulder, *A Controversial Spirit: Evangelical Awakenings in the South* (New York: Oxford University Press, 2002). On the Puritan morphology of conversion, see Patricia Caldwell, *The Puritan Conversion Narrative: The Beginnings of American Expression* (Cambridge: Cambridge University Press, 1983); Charles Lloyd Cohen, *God's Caress: The Psychology of Puritan Religious Experience* (New York: Oxford University Press, 1986); Edmund S. Morgan, *Visible Saints: The History of a Puritan Idea* (New York: New York University Press, 1963); Norman Pettit, *The Heart Prepared: Grace and Conversion in Puritan Spiritual Life,* 2nd ed. (Middletown, CT: Wesleyan University Press, 1989).

initially discouraged by this advice, but later claimed that "it did me more good than any directions or counsels I ever received. It threw me on my own resources, and led me to feel the necessity of disciplining my own thoughts and searching into the principles of things." Graham, he explained further, encouraged him "to think for myself, and form my own opinions from the Bible." Of course, Alexander did read theological works, and of these he later noted the writings of Swiss Reformed theologian Francis Turretin, Puritan John Owen, and Jonathan Edwards's works on the will, original sin, and the religious affections, as well as John Bates's *Harmony of the Divine Attributes,* the last named representing an instance of late-seventeenth-century English nonconformity. On Saturdays, Graham's theological students — initially only Alexander and one other person but eventually numbering a half dozen — gathered to report on their reading and to engage in debate.[11]

Alexander in future years manifested ambivalence about his studies with Graham. On the one hand, he continued to regard his teacher as an "instrument employed by Providence" to further his education. On the other, Alexander also contrasted him unfavorably with other mentors. For example, he wrote appreciatively of an older minister who, when he spent time with him as a young preacher, listened "patiently and candidly" — a manner unlike that of Graham, who "was very dogmatical, treated with contempt all opinions which he rejected, and was impatient of contradiction." Perhaps Alexander was reacting to an issue deeper than his teacher's temperament — an issue at which he hinted in noting that Graham "was not much read in books" and in observing that he pursued "the philosophy of mind" primarily "by paying close attention to the exercises of his own mind." Graham was following one possible trajectory that might be drawn from the Common Sense philosophy he had learned from Witherspoon. If it were indeed possible to have an empirical science of moral philosophy by examining the sentiments and principles that God had planted in human consciousness, what else did the Christian need when interpreting the Bible than a careful scrutiny of "the exercises of his own mind"? Other authorities and tradition might be ignored. In fairness to Graham, we must quickly add that he stayed within the bounds of then accepted orthodoxy, and yet in his mode of defending orthodoxy "he departed considerably," Alexander observed, "from the common track." Even when supporting accepted truth, there

11. Alexander, *Life of Archibald Alexander,* 83.

was too much of the opinionated free spirit in Graham to allow him to do so in the customary fashion. His unwillingness to accept usual constraints showed especially in his politics. Except for his defense of slavery, Graham opposed concentrated power. An ardent supporter of the American Revolution, he later concluded that the federal constitution proposed in 1787 gave too much dominion to the central government, and he opposed the compact. Similarly, in 1794 when state militias were called into the service of the national government to put down the so-called Whiskey Rebellion — that is, the resistance of backwoods farmers to paying the federal excise tax on whiskey — Graham used a church meeting to attack the military suppression of the rebellion. At the time of his death, he was planning to establish a utopian community on the banks of the Ohio River. Alexander, moderate by temperament, respectful of tradition, and not inclined to be politically outspoken, may well have found Graham a bit too strident and idiosyncratic for his taste.[12]

At Graham's behest, Alexander was sent as a ruling elder commissioner to the Presbyterian General Assembly in 1791. There in Philadelphia a rather self-conscious 19-year-old saw for the first time leading figures of American Presbyterianism such as John Witherspoon and Samuel Stanhope Smith. That fall Alexander's presbytery licensed him as a probationer for the gospel ministry, and for the next several years he itinerated through Virginia's Southside and in adjacent North Carolina counties as he preached in many out-of-the-way places, sometimes outdoors. In 1794 he was ordained to serve the churches at Briery and Cub Creek in the Southside. In 1797, he accepted the invitation of the trustees of Hampden-Sydney College to serve as president, despite the fact that the school was teetering on the brink of extinction. Like many other contemporary leaders of colleges or academies, he continued preaching and pastoral work as well. The surviving records from these years depict a young minister learning to prepare sermons on horseback, tending to stare at the floor while preaching, but nevertheless winning widespread approval for his energy and cogency in the pulpit. He continued to struggle with questions of faith. Baptists again produced uncertainty for him, this time over the validity of infant baptism. For a season, he suspended

---

12. William B. Sprague, *Annals of the American Pulpit*, vol. 3 (New York: Robert Carter and Brothers, 1857), 365-70. On Graham's political views, consult David W. Robson, "'An Important Question Answered': William Graham's Defense of Slavery in Post-Revolutionary Virginia," *William and Mary Quarterly*, 3rd ser., 37 (October 1980): 644-52.

baptizing children until he had satisfied his qualms on the legitimacy of the practice. Likewise, he continued to encounter religious skepticism. Thomas Paine's *The Age of Reason* was widely read, and Alexander reported that "most of our educated and professional young men became Deists or worse. Young lawyers openly reviled religion." In part because he had to defend Presbyterian practice against other Christian groups and because Christianity itself was under assault from nonbelievers, his desire to learn acquired urgency even before he took on responsibilities at Hampden-Sydney. In a world where books were scarce and expensive, he bought the volumes he could. Among his significant early purchases were works by Thomas Reid and Dugald Stewart — evidence of the continuing importance of Scottish moral philosophy in his intellectual development and of the role it would play in framing his subsequent defenses of Christianity.[13]

By 1801 Alexander was tired after several bouts with illness. Hoping that an extended trip through New England might restore his health and expand his horizons, he resigned his pastoral charges and the presidency of Hampden-Sydney. His presbytery appointed him commissioner to the General Assembly; so the first portion of the trip assumed official status. In Philadelphia, the General Assembly, responding to an invitation from Connecticut Congregationalists to establish greater cooperation between the two bodies, made a set of specific proposals and appointed Alexander along with two others to present them to the General Association meeting shortly afterward in Litchfield, Connecticut.

This so-called Plan of Union outlined principles whereby the denominations could work together in the creation of churches in the "new settlements" produced by the nation's westward expansion. The plan allowed congregations composed of members of one denomination to call a minister of the other. The Plan of Union was not simply a policy decision imposed from the top down. It formalized and ratified cooperative efforts already under way in particular communities, especially in the state of New York. The originators of the plan, while blurring denominational distinctions, did not envision their obliteration. Assuming that parallel Congregational and Presbyterian structures would continue to exist in the same territory, the creators of the plan sought to coordinate efforts so that together the two denominations might more efficiently

13. For discussion of the events in this paragraph and the next, see Alexander, *Life of Archibald Alexander,* 82-271.

serve the expanding populations of the nation's western regions. Alexander and his colleagues had a successful mission to Litchfield; the General Association approved their proposal without debate.[14]

The plan seemed eminently logical since Congregationalism and Presbyterianism were variants of a common theological tradition. Despite their differences in polity, the two groups both adhered to the theological tradition represented by the Westminster Confession of Faith and had often maintained cordial and relaxed relationships in the eighteenth century. The careers of the early presidents of the College of New Jersey illustrate the point. Jonathan Dickinson, Aaron Burr, and Jonathan Edwards were all children of Connecticut Congregationalism and of Yale College who transferred to the Presbyterian denomination. To be sure, theological innovations had begun to emerge in New England as a group of ministers who were considered the disciples of Jonathan Edwards sought to improve and refine the doctrines of their master. Their leading figures included Samuel Hopkins (1721-1803), Joseph Bellamy (1719-1790), and Nathanael Emmons (1745-1840). Their movement, often called the New Divinity or sometimes Hopkinsianism, was an effort to render the Calvinist or Reformed position more consistent or coherent and thus more defensible in the age of Enlightenment. The New Divinity became a formidable power in northwestern Connecticut and western Massachusetts, and, in a time of close cooperation between Congregationalists and Presbyterians, the theology made its appearance among the latter as well. Although its adherents believed the New Divinity to be a preservation and restatement of orthodox Calvinism, opponents within both Congregationalism and Presbyterianism charged otherwise. But in 1801, most Presbyterians, even if they sometimes grumbled about the New Divinity, regarded the innovations as lying within the range of legitimate toleration. Alexander appears to have accepted that consensus. In carrying the General Assembly's overture to Litchfield, he signaled openness to New England Congregationalism. In fact, he was traveling to New England to get to know its religious leaders and their views better.[15]

His trip through New England was something of a grand tour. From Litchfield, he went to Hartford and to New London and then, leaving

14. Robert Hastings Nichols, *Presbyterianism in New York State: A History of the Synod and Its Predecessors*, ed. James Hastings Nichols (Philadelphia: Westminster Press, 1963), 70-83.

15. For further discussion of the New England theologians and their impact on Presbyterianism and Princeton Seminary, see Chapter Five.

Connecticut, on to Newport, Rhode Island, and thence to Boston, "the grand object of his curiosity," his son later recalled. After stops in the shipping towns of Ipswich and Newburyport north of Boston, he swung through New Hampshire to Dartmouth College, then descended the Connecticut River Valley, stopping in Northampton, Massachusetts, where Jonathan Edwards had once occupied the pulpit. During this circle through New England, he preached in numerous pulpits and, to his surprise, frequently won effusive praise. He met two major figures of the New Divinity — Samuel Hopkins and Nathaniel Emmons. Although his visit with the elderly Hopkins did not lead to any extended discussion, Alexander preached in his church and carried away a memory of a dedicated minister who "showed a childlike simplicity and entire submission to the will of God." For Emmons, with whom he stayed for a few days, Alexander formed a deep respect despite their "very different theological opinions." Perhaps it was not surprising that he was open to Hopkins and Emmons, for the young Virginia minister considered himself "quite a follower of Edwards." In the Boston area, he met Jedidiah Morse, a clergyman who in 1805 would found the *Panoplist* to defend Trinitarian faith against Unitarianism and who would play a major role in the formation of Andover Seminary in 1808. On either ends of the New England trip, Alexander's stays in Philadelphia, Princeton, and New York City gave him the chance to deepen his acquaintance with major figures in the Presbyterian Church.

When he returned to Virginia, Hampden-Sydney College had not filled the position of president and tendered it again to Alexander, who accepted. He resumed his duties in May 1802, as his son later reported, with "a confidence which had been wanting in his earlier efforts." The self-assurance reflected the experience of the previous year. Through his travels, he had met many of the leading ministers and theologians of the Congregational and Presbyterian communities and learned that, despite differences, he liked and respected them. What's more, as he preached in their pulpits or discussed theology with them, he could hold his own and win their respect. The 30-year-old Alexander also took an important personal step testifying that he had found his identity and place in life; on April 5, a month before returning to Hampden-Sydney, he married Janetta Waddel, daughter of a prominent Presbyterian pastor in Virginia.[16]

Alexander's second tenure at the college was relatively brief. After

16. Alexander, *Life of Archibald Alexander,* 272.

turning down an invitation to visit Third Presbyterian Church (also called "Old Pine") in Philadelphia, he decided subsequently to accept the invitation. He did so at a time when the Hampden-Sydney students "were in a state of much turbulence and insubordination" and when he had apparently wearied of the role of academic leader. His actions bore the marks of one eager to make a move, for he did not inform any of his friends of the decision to explore the possibilities of a call to Philadelphia. After he preached at "Old Pine" for two Sundays, the congregation called him unanimously. He then went back to Virginia and requested his presbytery to approve the call and dismiss him. By the beginning of 1807 he and his family had arrived in Philadelphia in preparation for his formal reception by presbytery and installation as pastor in April.[17]

In Philadelphia, Alexander found himself at the epicenter of American Presbyterianism in one of the premier cities of the United States. The first American presbytery was organized there in 1706, and the port served as the major point of debarkation for the great Scots-Irish immigration that swelled Presbyterian ranks in the eighteenth century. During the quarter century after the denomination's General Assembly first organized in 1789, more than twenty of its annual meetings took place in Philadelphia. Within the city itself, Presbyterians along with Quakers and Episcopalians constituted the leading religious groups. Although the Pine Street Church did not draw the city's most elite classes — Alexander described his congregation as "plain and unceremonious" people "with few exceptions . . . [being] of the middling classes" — the congregation had a solid respectability. To serve as a Presbyterian pastor in this setting almost inevitably entailed recognition as a leader of the denomination, and that putative claim was reinforced by Philadelphia's role as a cultural and economic hub of the new nation. For Alexander, recognition of eminence came within weeks of his installation at Pine Street. The 1807 General Assembly elected him moderator. Little more than a decade after his ordination to serve rural congregations in the Southside of Virginia, he had become one of the Presbyterian Church's foremost leaders.[18]

The move to Philadelphia also gives a glimpse of Alexander's involvement with slavery. As a native Virginian, Alexander was familiar with the peculiar institution; and like many Southerners who came of age during the Revolution and its immediate aftermath, he recognized in

17. Alexander, *Life of Archibald Alexander,* 276.
18. Alexander, *Life of Archibald Alexander,* 280.

theory its incongruity with the liberty Americans touted. In 1794 he preached a sermon praising the United States as a land "where the rights of men are so well secured. To this there is but one exception, which distorts the political features of our country." Yet he quickly added that this was a matter "with which it is not my business to meddle." Indeed, Alexander routinely accommodated himself to the institution. The Briery church where he had ministered owned slaves at various times and quite likely during his tenure. His accommodation to slavery also involved his own household. At the time he moved to Pennsylvania, his family owned at least one female slave — a woman named Daphne — who had attended Janetta Alexander since her childhood. Under the gradual emancipation laws adopted by Pennsylvania in 1780, those in bondage at the time of the act's passage would remain so and children of slaves born subsequently would, after a period of service, be freed. Slaves brought into Pennsylvania from other states would, if their owners remained more than six months, become free. Although the Alexanders apparently did not formally emancipate Daphne when they went to Philadelphia, she and they recognized her changed legal status when she accompanied them.[19]

The Alexanders' subsequent relationship with Daphne — or at least the family's memory of it — is illuminating. As told by Alexander's son more than a half century later, the salient facts were these: Daphne's husband, John Boatman, had remained in Virginia as a slave, presumably owned by a family other than Alexander's. When members of Philadelphia's Society of Friends learned of her separation from her spouse, they raised money to purchase his freedom, and he joined her. For a time, Alexander "kept them both as hired servants upon wages." Realizing that he could earn more elsewhere, Boatman — remembered by the Alexanders as "a brawny and ill-favored black" — became a coachman for the governor of Pennsylvania. Likewise his wife "learned to entertain more lofty thoughts" and "she soon left her kind protectors and set up for herself." Then the husband went astray, deserted his wife, and ended up in prison. She fell ill, could no longer work, and had to enter an almshouse. When two of Janetta Alexander's sisters visited her there and proposed

19. Alexander, *Life of Archibald Alexander,* 280-82. The Pennsylvania laws on slavery and the erosion of the institution in Pennsylvania in the decades just before Alexander's residence there are treated in Gary B. Nash and Jean R. Soderlund, *Freedom by Degrees: Emancipation in Pennsylvania and Its Aftermath* (New York: Oxford University Press, 1991). Loetscher, *Facing the Enlightenment and Pietism,* 53.

that she return to the service of the Waddel family in Virginia, she readily agreed. Archibald Alexander, now living in Princeton, told her that this meant she would have to go back to slavery. She acquiesced, recalling "the quiet and ease which she [had] enjoyed under a nominal bondage." Or so the story was remembered by the Alexander family; how it appeared to Daphne, one suspects, may well have been different. Yet whatever the facts of the case, the episode reveals much about Alexander's view of slavery. Despite his distaste for the institution in the abstract, he was willing to own slaves, believed himself their "kind protector," and seemed sure that blacks who entertained "lofty thoughts" and struck out on their own risked harm to themselves. As his later writings would reveal, his hope for the eventual end of slavery was leavened by a fear that its premature demise would injure black and white alike.[20]

At Third Presbyterian, Alexander found himself in a setting that alternately seemed to distress and please him. He was upset to discover that "there is much less religious knowledge among the bulk of the people here than in the country. Multitudes grow up with very little knowledge of the doctrines of religion." But he set about remedying this with "plain preaching," and he helped organize what he called an "Evangelical Society." Its purpose was to recruit volunteers who would go out among the children of the poor and to talk with their parents about religion and to "read the Scriptures and other good books." Later, after Alexander had left Philadelphia, the society merged into larger Sunday school and city missions activities. One of the activities of the Evangelical Society in which Alexander was deeply interested was the formation of a Presbyterian church among the city's African Americans. Within several blocks of "Old Pine" stood Richard Allen's Bethel congregation, the "mother church" of what would become the African Methodist Episcopal denomination; and perhaps this proximity encouraged Alexander to dream of establishing a Presbyterian presence among African Americans. He had the opportunity to pursue the matter through the General Assembly when a Tennessee presbytery recommended the licensure of a black candidate, John Gloucester, in 1807. Since Gloucester was a slave, the permission of his owner was required; and Alexander was instrumental in persuading the owner to allow Gloucester to labor in Philadelphia. Eventually Alexander, Ashbel Green, and a group of other Presbyterian leaders in the city persuaded the owner to free Gloucester altogether so that

20. Alexander, *Life of Archibald Alexander,* 280-82.

he could labor as a free man. From Gloucester's initial street evangelism emerged the First African Presbyterian Church in Philadelphia.

In addition to his ministerial labors, Alexander pursued an aggressive program of self-education made possible by the resources available in Philadelphia. He visited the booksellers and accumulated volumes of Latin theology and delved into the theological writings of the Reformation and post-Reformation eras. Taking advantage of the presence of a Jewish community, he took lessons in Hebrew. In the process, Alexander was acquiring knowledge that he would soon put to use in Princeton.[21]

Samuel Miller

While the ancestors of Archibald Alexander were part of the large Scots-Irish influx of the eighteenth century, Samuel Miller's lineage represented other strands of American Presbyterianism. His grandfather, John Miller, came directly from Scotland in 1710 and settled in Boston, where he wed Mary Bass, a descendant of *Mayflower* immigrant John Alden. Like many of Presbyterian origin who came to heavily Congregationalist New England, Miller affiliated with a church of that persuasion. Though he reportedly had "a good knowledge of the Latin language," he did not enter any of the classic professions. Instead, he ran a sugar refinery and distillery. Of his three children — all sons — his namesake John, born in 1722, chose to study for the ministry. The younger John Miller did not go to college but acquired sufficient prior education to read divinity with a Boston minister. Licensed to preach in 1748 by a council of Boston Congregational clergy, he visited Delaware and Maryland and received a call in March 1749 from two Presbyterian churches in what is today Smyrna, Delaware, just north of Dover. The churches presented the call, not to the local Presbyterian authorities, but rather to the Boston council of clergy that had licensed Miller and requested that body to ordain him. Perhaps their decision reflected the churches' unwillingness to take sides during this time of internal Presbyterian schism by approaching either the Old or the New Side presbytery. Miller himself apparently did not affiliate with either group until approximately a year before their

---

21. Alexander, *Life of Archibald Alexander,* 283, 299; William T. Catto, *A Semi-Centenary Discourse Delivered in the First African Presbyterian Church, Philadelphia* (Philadelphia: Joseph M. Wilson, 1857), 25-26.

1758 reunion, when he joined an Old Side presbytery. As told by his grandson more than a century later, Miller's hesitation to choose indicated that he was "a lover of peace, and drawn both ways by kindly associations and amiable feelings." The fact that Miller could be ordained by the Congregationalists to serve a Presbyterian church — and then not join a presbytery for nearly a decade — also illustrated the porous boundary between Presbyterianism and Congregationalism as well as the relative looseness of ecclesiastical structures at the time.[22]

For over forty years, John Miller labored in this rural pastorate. Poorly paid, he had to supplement his income by farming the one hundred plus acres on which he lived in order to support his wife, Margaret Millington, and their nine children. Yet he nevertheless accumulated a substantial library, received an honorary master's degree, educated his sons in the classical languages, and was able to send four of them to the University of Pennsylvania and a fifth to the academy in Newark, Delaware, founded by Francis Alison. A respected figure in Presbyterian circles — he served as moderator of his presbytery — he also counted among his friends John Dickinson, a leading political figure in both Delaware and Pennsylvania and author of the *Letters from a Farmer in Pennsylvania* (1767-68), which enunciated colonial grievances against Great Britain in the years before the Revolution.[23]

Samuel, born in 1769, received the usual paternal instruction in Greek and Latin but initially had scant enthusiasm for it. He later confessed that for roughly his first eighteen years, he pursued these studies "with little zeal, owing to an expectation and a desire of . . . entering a counting-house with a future view to merchandise as a profession." His love of learning and his religious commitment appear to have kindled at approximately the same time. He described the matter thus:

> it pleased God, in a remarkable manner . . . to excite in me a desire
> for the acquisition of knowledge; though without any settled pur-
> pose as to a future profession. After this change of feeling and of
> purpose respecting a classical education, I was, for some months,
> under great perplexity and embarrassment, how to pursue and

---

22. Samuel Miller, *The Life of Samuel Miller, D.D., LL.D.*, 2 vols. (Philadelphia: Claxton, Remsen and Haffelfinger, 1869), 1:13-27; quotation on 22. It should be noted that the author of the volume was the son of the subject of the book.

23. Miller, *The Life of Samuel Miller*, 1:13-27.

complete my education in a better manner than I could possibly do under the tuition of an aged and infirm parent. During this anxiety, I was brought under very serious impressions of religion, which I hope soon after issued in a cordial acceptance of the Saviour as my hope and life. Early in the Spring of 1788, I made a profession of religion in the church of Dover, under my father's pastoral care.

Not only did Miller link his commitment to learning and his religious awakening; he made the latter seem almost automatic. Perhaps he himself wondered if it had been too easy, for he immediately added: "I have often looked back on that step . . . with much solicitude as to the question, whether it was founded on a saving acquaintance with Christ or not. I can only say that I had a hope in Christ, which, though afterwards and often painfully interrupted, was then steady and comfortable." Theologically Miller interpreted salvation in the same manner as did Archibald Alexander: it was solely the free gift of God in Christ to the undeserving sinner. Yet in Miller that awareness appears to have prompted less turmoil, fewer dramatic psychological fluctuations, than it did in his future Princeton colleague. Even when Miller confessed in a prayer written in his diary several years after his initial awakening that he deserved "to be cut off from every hope, and banished from thy presence and glory forever," he immediately added: "But blessed be thy name, that thou hast contrived a way for our recovery from this fallen state. Blessed be thy name, that those who come unto thee, through Jesus Christ, thou wilt in no wise cast out." It is difficult to imagine the youthful Miller experiencing the anxiety that prompted the young Alexander to roll on the ground in anguish of spirit.[24]

Having made a religious commitment and having found a new enthusiasm for learning, Miller went off to study at the University of Pennsylvania in 1788. He boarded with his sister and brother-in-law and began attending Ashbel Green's church. From Delaware, his father worried about the cost of his son's education. When "Sammy" planned a trip to Princeton, John Miller grumbled that his son "has neither time nor money to spend on any such jaunt." But "Sammy" was not using his time frivolously. After a year at the school, he received "first honor" in the class and was asked to give a commencement oration in Latin. At the

---

24. Miller, *The Life of Samuel Miller*, 1:33, 51-52.

same ceremony, his older brother Edward was awarded the degree "Doctor of Physic" (i.e., medicine).[25]

By August of 1789, Samuel had resolved to study for the ministry. He commenced under his father's tutelage, and by June 1791 passed the first portion of his examinations before the presbytery. In late July, John Miller died. Within the next several months, Samuel completed his examinations, was licensed to preach, and was given permission to continue his theological studies with Charles Nisbet, the first principal (president) of Dickinson College in Carlisle, Pennsylvania. From the fall of 1791 to the beginning of March 1792, Miller resided in Carlisle. Nisbet, who had been in the United States for only six years, had previously served as a minister of the Church of Scotland. Like Witherspoon before him, he was a leader in the Popular or evangelical party and had gained a reputation for considerable learning. Moreover, the fact that he had spoken favorably of American grievances during the Revolution added to his appeal to the trustees of the young college. Perhaps Miller was drawn to Nisbet not only by his reputation but also by the fact that his father's good friend John Dickinson was one of the chief benefactors of the school in Carlisle and the person for whom it was named.[26]

Just as Alexander deemed William Graham an instrument of Providence in his education, Miller later expressed the same regard for Nisbet. He did not get to hear the principal's lectures on divinity, which were given only once and then abandoned because of the press of other teaching and administrative duties. Instead, Miller's time with his mentor was more in the nature of an intellectually invigorating tutorial. Speaking of the encounters in the third person, he explained how pupil and teacher met most evenings in the principal's home. "And on whatever subject he [Miller] might desire information, whether in Theology or Literature, ancient or modern, he had but to propose the topic and suggest queries, to draw forth everything that he wished." Nor were these exchanges one-sided performances; they were genuine conversations. Miller believed that "no man on this side of the Atlantic ever brought into the social circle, such diversified and ample stores of erudition." His time with Nisbet convinced him that the learned person is not a *"mere devourer of books,"* but also one who has grown accustomed to "the mingling of reading with close thought; to independent inquiry.... Without these adjuncts to read-

25. Miller, *The Life of Samuel Miller,* 1:36, 41.
26. Miller, *The Life of Samuel Miller,* 1:43-60.

ing, there is little hope of forming that robust mental structure . . . which so eminently characterized men formed in the middle ages, by travel, by oral communication, and by personal conflict." Miller's admiration for Nisbet was somewhat remarkable because the two had rather different cultural and political assumptions. As partisan division grew in the years ahead, the Dickinson leader moved toward strongly Federalist views in his disgust with the French Revolution and his disenchantment with the vulgar excesses of American democracy; Miller in the 1790s defended the French Revolution and the democratic republicanism of Thomas Jefferson. Yet Nisbet and his former student maintained a friendly respect and correspondence. From the principal, Miller had gained an exciting glimpse of what the give-and-take of ideas, the acquisition of knowledge across a broad front, might mean. He had caught a vision of a cosmopolitan community of learning — what some have called a "republic of letters" — that would shape his thinking profoundly.[27]

But before he could put that vision into effect, Samuel Miller had first to receive a call to a church. After leaving Carlisle, he went to Long Island as a possible candidate for a pulpit, and along the way he stopped in New York City to visit John Rodgers, a former minister in Delaware and good friend of his father. In the city, Rodgers and John McKnight served as the collegiate pastors of two united congregations. Rodgers persuaded Miller to stay a fortnight and to preach multiple times. The licentiate clearly impressed his hearers, and by April the congregations wanted to explore the possibility of adding Miller as a third pastor. (Technically, the two congregations — the Brick Church and the church on Wall Street — were one congregation, First Presbyterian, served by the two co-pastors; in 1796, a third congregation on Rutgers Street was organized and added to the collegiate arrangement.) At the same time that the New Yorkers were showing interest in him, the church his father had served in the Dover area for over four decades indicated that it wished to call Miller. His presbytery "put [the call] into the hands of Mr. Miller for consideration" and at the same time gave him permission to visit "the Presbyterian congregations in New York at their earnest request." The return visit went well, the united congregations formally called him, and in November he accepted. On January 3, 1793, he arrived

27. Samuel Miller, *Memoir of the Rev. Charles Nisbet, D.D.* (New York: Robert Carter, 1840), 211, 214. On Nisbet also see Charles Coleman Sellers, *Dickinson College: A History* (Middletown, CT: Wesleyan University Press, 1973), 77-135.

in New York City, a lad of 23, to begin his pastoral labors. It is not surprising that many called him "the boy minister."[28]

The New York City to which Miller moved in 1793 was far from the colossal center of commerce, population, and culture that contemporary Americans know — in fact, it had fewer than fifty thousand inhabitants, who lived on the lower tip of Manhattan. But during the 1790s the city's international trade surged dramatically, and New York surpassed Philadelphia as the nation's major port of entry. The city experienced a swelling of cultural life during the decade. As historians Edwin Burrows and Mike Wallace note, "would-be New York philosophes — primarily youthful merchants and professionals who aspired to be men of letters as well as men of affairs — began to create associations to incubate a worthy municipal culture." These included groups that gathered to discuss literature, philosophy, scientific discoveries, and politics. New Yorkers also came together to improve the lives of their fellow citizens in organizations such as the Society for the Promotion of Agriculture, Arts, and Manufactures. Religiously, New York was pluralistic. In addition to the Presbyterians and Associate Presbyterians, other Protestants in the city included Episcopalians, Dutch Reformed, German Reformed, Baptists, Lutherans, and Moravians. Small Catholic and Jewish congregations had also established a presence. After the formal legal end in 1777 of Anglican establishment in the state's four lower counties (including New York City), the religious communities of Manhattan enjoyed an era of good feelings and modest cooperation. To be sure, Protestants continued to harbor traditional suspicions of Catholics, but there were none of the major outbreaks of anti-Catholicism that would occur in the nineteenth century. The Jewish community, in part because of its ardent support of the Revolution, was well regarded. Protestants collaborated informally, as when Trinity (Episcopal) allowed Brick Presbyterian to use its facilities while the latter was renovating its building, or when Trinity provided land where the Presbyterians could build manses for their clergy. Protestants worked together more formally through the New York Society for Promoting Christian Knowledge and Piety (1794), which had members from seven denominations, and which distributed Bibles and tracts and supported missionary enterprise. William Linn, a Dutch Reformed pastor, provided a theological rationale for cooperation. In an era pregnant with both the promise of democratic revolutions and the

---

28. Miller, *The Life of Samuel Miller*, 1:80-87.

peril of infidelity, it was vital that believers address "the want of union among the followers of Christ." Concord among Christians "would remove a great stumbling block out of the way of infidels," and he believed a day of unity was coming when all denominations would find common ground "not on the doctrines of men" but by adherence "to the lively oracles of God." Another form of unity was offered by the Masonic movement, ten of whose lodges were organized in the city between 1784 and 1801. One of the great appeals of freemasonry in the post-Revolutionary world was that it proposed to recognize the worth of all men, unite them in benevolent brotherhood across all lines of division, and thereby promote the ideals of the young republic. As De Witt Clinton, then mayor of New York City and later the state's governor, said in June 1806 upon his installation as Grand Master of Masons throughout the state: Masonry "inculcates the natural equality of mankind: it declares that all brethren are upon a level: it admits of no rank except the priority of merit, and its only aristocracy is the nobility of virtue." To sum up, the New York City of the 1790s was a place of increasingly expansive and cosmopolitan hopes, whether in matters of economics, culture, or religion.[29]

Samuel Miller quickly established his place in this milieu. Although his pastoral responsibilities of necessity occupied most of his time, he engaged in a variety of civic and intellectual enterprises. He was invited to address the Tammany Society on the Fourth of July following his move to the city. That organization was not yet the political machine it would become in the following century, but it was already identified with the emerging Democratic Republicans. During his first year in the city, Miller also joined one of the city's Masonic lodges and affiliated with the New York Manumission Society. The society, founded in 1785, encouraged the gradual emancipation of slaves — *gradual* being the operative word, for many of the founders of the society themselves continued to

29. Edwin G. Burrows and Mike Wallace, *Gotham: A History of New York City to 1898* (New York: Oxford University Press, 1999), 374; William Linn, *Discourses on the Signs of the Times* (New York: Thomas Greenleaf, 1794), 20, 21; De Witt Clinton, *Address Delivered by the Most Worshipful the Hon. DeWitt Clinton, Esq., to the Grand Lodge of the State of New York* (New York: Southwick and Hardcastle, 1806), 11. On the city's religious situation in the post-Revolutionary era, see Richard W. Pointer, *Protestant Pluralism and the New York Experience: A Study of Eighteenth-Century Religious Diversity* (Bloomington and Indianapolis: Indiana University Press, 1988), 121-40. Steven C. Bullock, "A Pure and Sublime System: The Appeal of Post-Revolutionary Freemasonry," *Journal of the Early Republic* 9 (Autumn 1989): 359-73.

own slaves. When New York State finally passed a law for ending slavery in 1799, the statute adopted a slow and measured approach: all who were born into bondage after July 4 of that year would in theory be free but were bound to the service of their mother's master until the ages of 25 for women and 28 for men. In addition to these organizations, Miller also became part of the Friendly Club of New York City, called by historian Henry May "perhaps the most brilliant of all the organizations of earnest and enlightened young men." Although its exact origins are disputed, the club probably began in 1793 or '94. Miller and his brother Edward — the latter had moved to New York in 1796 and was living with Samuel — did not join the club until about 1798. The Millers were associating with a group of young men who would make their mark in a variety of fields: Elihu Hubbard Smith and Samuel Latham Mitchill, physicians, who along with Edward Miller founded the nation's first medical journal; Charles Brockden Brown, a novelist now regarded by critics as one of the most significant writers in the early republic; and James Kent, who would acquire renown as a jurist. A Democratic Republican, Samuel Miller was in a minority in the largely Federalist club and was the only minister in a group many of whose members tended toward some form of religious heterodoxy.[30]

The members of the Friendly Club met regularly in each other's homes during the winter months. Conversation was at the heart of these evening gatherings — not, its members hoped, conversation on trivial subjects or talk for the sake of mere amusement. They envisioned conversation as the occasion for collective and individual self-improvement as men with superior knowledge engaged in analytical and candid discourse about topics of significance. Usually the host read a passage from a book or article or novel as the point of departure. According to the diary of Elihu Smith — our chief source for what transpired in these meetings — the conversation might stay on the passage read, but it usually turned to the ideas and works of other figures. The range of topics and people discussed was large. In one *soirée* alone, Smith noted that the conversation touched, among many others, on Shakespeare, the contemporary English radical William Godwin, John Locke, Adam Smith,

30. Burrows and Wallace, *Gotham,* 285-87; Graham Russell Hodges, *Root and Branch: African Americans in New York and East Jersey, 1613-1863* (Chapel Hill: University of North Carolina Press, 1999), 166-67; Henry F. May, *The Enlightenment in America* (New York: Oxford University Press, 1976), 233; Bryan Waterman, *Republic of Intellect: The Friendly Club and the Making of American Literature* (Baltimore: Johns Hopkins University Press, 2007).

and Jonathan Edwards. Such wide-ranging discussion could become superficial or gossipy, and when it did, Smith's diary expressed irritation. These men did not agree on all matters, but full agreement was not their goal. Through the sharing of information and by the smack of idea against idea, they assumed that knowledge would be sharpened and intellectual progress would occur. In the Friendly Club, Samuel Miller found people among whom he might pursue what he had admired so greatly in his time with Charles Nisbet in Carlisle. Here was a community of vigorous intellectual exchange where each participant might become more than a *"mere devourer of books,"* where he might enjoy "the mingling of reading with close thought," and where one might hope to form "that robust mental structure" in the give-and-take of "oral communication, and by personal conflict."[31]

Miller's published addresses of the 1790s reveal a man in tune with the ferment of the era. In a Fourth of July address to the Tammany Society in 1793, he showed an exuberant faith in the march of democracy and a conviction that Christianity itself propelled this forward movement. The gospel, he asserted, "tends to quench every extravagant thirst for power; to beat down every high thought, that exalteth itself against the general good; and to render men contented with those rights which the God of nature gave them." Looking at the French Revolution in light of scriptural prophecies that a time was coming "when there shall be nothing to hurt or destroy in all the holy mountain of God," he argued that the "convulsive struggles" in Europe were hastening "this heavenly era." Addressing fellow New York Masons in 1795, Miller commended the order's basic principles as those which the Bible "recognizes and inculcates. They are such as the blessed Redeemer perpetually dropped from his hallowed lips." He applauded the cosmopolitanism of freemasonry, which encouraged a love and respect for every human being "of whatever kindred, or people, or nation, or tongue." While admitting that the movement appealed to non-Christians as well as to Christians, he insisted that nothing in the ideals and teaching of Masonry contradicted Christianity. In an address to the Manumission Society in 1797, he appealed to the fundamental principle of the American Revolution — that "all men are born free and equal" — and applied it to chattel slavery. Who could doubt that the "enslaving, or continuing to hold in slavery, those who have forfeited their liberty by no

31. James E. Cronin, "Elihu Hubbard Smith and the New York Friendly Club, 1795-1798," *PMLA* 64 (June 1949): 471-79; Waterman, *Republic of Intellect.*

crime, is contrary to the dictates both of justice and humanity"? Miller also insisted that the Bible led to the same conclusion:

> The divine system, in which we profess to believe, teaches us that God has made of one blood all nations of men that dwell on the face of the whole earth. It teaches us, that of whatever kindred or people, we are all children of the same common Father. . . . It teaches us that we should do to all men whatever we, in like circumstances, would that they should do unto us. It teaches us, in a word, that love to man and a constant pursuit of human happiness is the sum of all social duty.

These principles, Miller believed, "forbid every species of domination, excepting that which is founded on consent, or which the welfare of society requires." While acknowledging that Christ and the apostles did not "in so many words prohibit the practice of slavery," Miller went on to claim that "they taught principles and doctrines utterly abhorrent from such a practice." In light of Miller's subsequent views, his biblical interpretation in 1797 is noteworthy, for it bore some resemblance to what some more strident abolitionists would argue after 1830. He made the biblical case for antislavery, not on the basis of specific prohibitions in Scripture, but on the grounds of principles — for example, the Golden Rule and a common heavenly Father of all humanity — that he believed inevitably led to opposition to slavery. Yet Miller was not a nineteenth-century abolitionist born several decades early. He was, like the Manumission Society he addressed, committed to the slow elimination of slavery. He believed immediate emancipation involved "greater mischief than the original disorder designed to be cured." Certain that sending forth prematurely liberated slaves "into society, with all the ignorance, habits, and vices of their degraded education . . . would probably produce effects more unhappy than any one is able to calculate or conceive," Miller hoped for "emancipation in a gradual manner."[32]

32. Samuel Miller, *A Sermon Preached in New York, July 4th 1793, Being the Anniversary of the Independence of the United States at the Request of the Tammany Society* (New York: Thomas Greenleaf, 1793), 22, 29, 30; Miller, *A Discourse Delivered in the New Presbyterian Church, New York, before the Grand Lodge of the State of New York* (New York: F. Childs, 1795), 23, 24; Miller, *A Discourse Delivered April 12, 1797, at the Request and before the New York Society for Promoting the Manumission of Slaves* (New York: T. and J. Swords, 1797), 9, 11, 17-18, 22, 30.

Nothing better illustrated the breadth of Miller's interests than a work that evolved from a sermon he preached on January 1, 1801, discussing the achievements of the century just ending. Encouraged by the reception of the address, he expanded it into *A Brief Retrospect of the Eighteenth Century,* which came off the presses in January 1804. The title was a misnomer, for the "brief" survey ran to over a thousand pages in two volumes. The scope of the work was astonishing, providing in the words of the extended subtitle "a sketch of the revolutions and improvements in science, arts, and literature." The author requested numerous correspondents to furnish information, and his own brother Edward largely wrote the section on medicine. Miller modestly acknowledged his indebtedness to others and readily admitted that no one should suppose "that the author has attentively read all the works concerning which he delivers opinions. Some of them he never saw, and has ventured to give their character entirely on the authority of those whom he considers better judges than himself." In his first volume Miller dealt chiefly with discoveries and developments in the physical sciences: for example, electricity, astronomy, chemistry, zoology, botany, geology, anatomy and medicine, geography, mathematics, navigation, agriculture, mechanical inventions, and arts such as painting, sculpture, and architecture. In the second volume, he turned to developments in what we would call philosophy, literature, and history. He began the survey with the observation that while "the physical sciences have received great improvements during the century under consideration, it is feared the same cannot, with truth, be said respecting the science of the human mind." Yet he did reserve great praise for John Locke's work on epistemology because of Locke's ability to write "on such abstract subjects with simplicity and perspicuity." He also singled out for approbation the Scottish Common Sense philosophers, who represented "the most important accession which the philosophy of mind has received since the time of Mr. Locke." Thomas Reid's *Inquiry into the Human Mind on the Principles of Common Sense* (1764) was a work, Miller insisted, "which no one . . . can peruse without profound respect for the author." He saw Reid and others of his school as appealing "from the delusive principles and shocking conclusions" of skeptics "to the Common Sense of mankind, as a tribunal paramount to all the subtleties of philosophy." By contrast, Miller judged the alternate epistemology of Immanuel Kant to be "obscure and scarcely intelligible." In rejecting Kantian views for Scottish Realism, Miller was joining the majority of American thinkers — a choice with important ramifications for future theological reflection.[33]

Yet, despite his biases, Miller insisted that much could be learned even from those with faulty theology or flawed character. At the outset of *A Brief Retrospect,* he observed:

> justice is due all men. A man who is a bad Christian may be a very excellent mathematician, astronomer, or chemist; and one who denies and blasphemes the Saviour may write profoundly and instructively on some branches of science highly interesting to mankind. It is proper to commiserate the mistakes of such persons, to abhor their blasphemy, and to warn men against their fatal delusions; but it is surely difficult to see either the justice or utility of withholding from them that praise of genius or of learning to which they are fairly entitled.[34]

Miller's *Brief Retrospect* was ultimately an ambivalent work. Its breadth of learning, its unbridled curiosity about virtually every subject under the sun, and its willingness to find truth even in heterodox places clearly marked it as a product of the Enlightenment. Indeed, one historian has with some justice called it "a major American contribution to the Enlightenment" and "a monument to one of the most ambitious attempts to write intellectual history ever undertaken by an American scholar." Yet Miller by 1804 was also increasingly uncomfortable with radical manifestations of the Enlightenment and eager to see the movement rendered subservient to Christian orthodoxy. Miller's concluding chapter exemplifies his ambivalence. In summarizing the eighteenth century, he noted that "almost every department of knowledge" has been marked by "monuments of enterprise, discovery, and improvement . . . so numerous as to stand without parallel in the history of the human mind." At the heart of this improvement was a spirit of free inquiry. "Never . . . ," Miller remarked, "was the human mind, all things considered, so much unshackled in its inquiries." This freedom "has contributed greatly to enlarge the bounds of literature, science, and general improvement." "But,"

33. Samuel Miller, *A Brief Retrospect of the Eighteenth Century,* 2 vols. (New York: T. and J. Swords, 1803), 1:xi; 2:1, 4, 11. The official publication date was 1803 despite the work's appearance in January 1804.

34. Miller, *Brief Retrospect,* 1:xii-xiii.

he quickly added, "this spirit of inquiry, like every thing else in the hands of man, has been perverted and abused . . . and, in the midst of zeal for demolishing old errors, the most sacred principles of virtue and happiness have been rejected or forgotten." And what lesson should one draw from this mixed legacy? In the last paragraph of his text, he admonished those who would be the "philosophers of the nineteenth century":

> Behold how much has been done by patient inquiry, by accurate experiment, and by careful analysis and induction; but how little by fanciful speculation, by the dreams of hypothesis, by vain boasting, or by waging war against Nature's God! Learn to distinguish that philosophy which is the friend of truth, the handmaid of virtue, the humble interpreter of Jehovah's works, and the ornament of rational minds, from the *ignis fatuus* which shines but to deceive, and allures but to destroy.

In that final paragraph Miller succinctly outlined what would be the dominant approach at Princeton Seminary — and in most of antebellum higher education — toward the Enlightenment and its legacy. Undue speculation or hypothesis was dangerous; true intellectual progress occurred through the patient accumulation of facts; and these, when analyzed in the right spirit, made the scientist or philosopher "a humble interpreter" of God's works. Here was a prescription for assimilating and taming the Enlightenment.[35]

It is not that Miller had suddenly discovered a commitment to orthodoxy. He had always sounded a distinctly Christian note in his public addresses whether to the Tammany Society, the Masonic Lodge, or the Manumission Society. But in *A Brief Retrospect*, one senses a greater defensiveness, a deeper preoccupation with policing the boundaries of faith against the incursions of irreligion and skepticism. The transformation was not absolute, for Miller remained throughout his life a man of broad interests, but henceforth his published works would have much more to say about the defense of Christianity or would be more preoccupied with exclusively theological or ecclesiastical themes.

His political views also gradually changed during these years. In 1800

---

35. "A Sketch of the Revolutions and Improvements in Science, Arts and Literature in America," reprinted from Miller, *Brief Retrospect*, with intro. and notes by L. H. Butterfield, *William and Mary Quarterly*, 3rd ser., 10 (October 1953): 579; Miller, *Brief Retrospect*, 2:442.

he ardently supported Jefferson's bid for the presidency and took the extraordinary step, for a clergyman at least, of suggesting that the candidate be judged on political views, not religious commitment. "Because Mr. Jefferson is suspected of Deism," Miller wrote to a friend, "are we to raise a hue and cry against him, as if he ought to be instantly deprived of his citizenship?" Even if the charges were true, Miller claimed, "I had much rather have Mr. Jefferson for President, than an aristocratic Christian." Around the time Jefferson's administration ended in 1809, Miller's support cooled, and during the former president's remaining years (he died in 1826) Miller "lost all confidence in him as a genuine patriot, or even as an honest man." With the publishing of Jefferson's posthumous writings, any lingering respect "was exchanged for contempt and abhorrence." "I renounce," Miller went on to say, "and wish unsaid, everything that I ever said or wrote in his favor." Yet even before 1809, Miller's enthusiasm for Jeffersonian views had started to wane. The pastor, who in 1793 hailed the promise of the French Revolution, by 1805 condemned France, "one of the most enlightened nations of Europe," for "dethroning and decapitating a mild and gentle king" and then within a dozen years yielding "to the will of a despotic usurper." Miller was not merely rethinking specific political views; he was moving toward the conclusion that clergy needed to have a much lower profile with regard to partisan politics. "I was wrong," he later concluded, "in suffering myself to be so warmly and actively engaged in politics as I was during that period. . . . I fear I did an amount of injury to my ministry, which could by no means have been counterbalanced by my usefulness as a politician."[36]

As Miller turned more exclusively to that ministry, he took on the role of denominational defender and controversialist. A key figure who inadvertently pushed him in that direction was John Henry Hobart, a fellow student at the University of Pennsylvania from 1788 to 1789 and a graduate of the College of New Jersey in 1793. Hobart had whetted his loyalties to the Episcopal Church in disputes with Calvinists in Samuel Stanhope Smith's Princeton and brought those convictions to Manhattan when he became an assistant minister in 1801 at Trinity Church, probably the most influential Episcopal congregation in the nation. Hobart refused to participate in the then increasingly common interdenominational voluntary societies such as those for Bible distribution, helped organize separate Episcopal ones, and set forth a high church vi-

---

36. Miller, *The Life of Samuel Miller*, 1:131, 132.

sion for his denomination. He saw himself as a defender of the apostolic order of the church; his Presbyterian neighbor Samuel Miller, in a letter to Ashbel Green in March 1805, portrayed the matter differently. The Episcopalians, he wrote, had been trying to revive "the high-toned doctrines of [William] Laud," Charles I's Archbishop of Canterbury, who had become for subsequent generations of those in the Puritan or Presbyterian tradition a symbol of the dangers of Anglicanism. The specific threat that Miller perceived in Hobart and the high church party was their claim that valid ordination required the laying on of hands by a bishop who stood in the line of apostolic succession. If this claim were true, Miller and clergy of all other denominations were in effect defrocked, and the congregations they served were not true churches. A war of letters in the Albany *Centinel* ensued over the views of Hobart, his allies, and their critics. Samuel Miller figured prominently among the critics.[37]

Miller's first round of letters appeared as a book in 1807. Through close analysis of biblical passages, he argued that the New Testament did not recognize "ranks" among the clergy and that it did not authorize an office of bishop higher than that of other duly ordained ministers. Following standard Presbyterian argument, he contended that the New Testament passages employing the title "bishop" *(episkopos)* used it synonymously with the term "elder" *(presbyteros)*. "Bishop," in a word, was one of multiple designations given to ministers of the gospel and implied no superiority of status or power. Miller also marshaled facts from the first two centuries of church history to demonstrate that there was no evidence that the episcopal office, as commonly understood by subsequent generations, yet existed and that it gradually crept in by the third and fourth centuries as a corruption of the biblical pattern.[38]

Miller vigorously defended Presbyterian practice, but he did so in a way that attempted to respect other Protestant groups. His purpose

---

37. Miller, *The Life of Samuel Miller,* 1:192. For an excellent account of these controversies with emphasis upon the Episcopal developments, see Robert Bruce Mullin, *Episcopal Vision/American Reality: High Church Theology and Social Thought in Evangelical America* (New Haven: Yale University Press, 1986), 26-59.

38. Samuel Miller, *Letters Concerning the Constitution and Order of the Christian Ministry,* 2nd ed. (Philadelphia: C. Sherman and Co., 1830); this edition includes the 1807 letters and an 1809 addition; Miller later wrote a second volume reiterating and refining his arguments in response to further Episcopal criticisms of his position; see *A Continuation of Letters Concerning the Constitution and Order of the Christian Ministry* (New York: Williams and Whiting, 1809).

was not, he insisted, "to disturb the convictions or feelings" of others or "to make proselytes." He desired to reassure those of his *own* denomination that they were "connected with a Church as nearly conformed to apostolic and primitive order as any on earth." In a word, Miller sought to protect his own sheep, not to steal from another flock. Or to change the metaphor, his approach was designed both to guard his own turf and to preserve amicable relations with other Christian groups — a useful strategy in pluralistic New York. A deeper question lurked behind this strategy and his controversy with Hobart: How ought the various groups of Christians — Methodists, Episcopalians, Presbyterians, Lutherans, Congregationalists, and many others — understand themselves vis-à-vis one another? To what extent could they recognize each other as legitimate expressions of that which they all confessed: the one holy, catholic or universal church? Miller offered an implicit answer to that question when, after noting that it was important to determine what Scripture taught about the offices of the church, he quickly put the issue in perspective:

> the names and powers of Christ's ministers, and the form of government adopted in his Church, . . . are yet to be numbered among the externals of religion. . . . The scriptures speak to us frequently respecting the outward organization of the Church; but they speak to us with much more fervent and solemn emphasis on that faith, which unites the soul to Jesus Christ; that repentance which is unto life; and that holiness of temper and practice, without which no man can see the Lord. . . . "Every believer in Jesus," says an eminent Episcopalian, "who is a partaker of the grace of God, in truth is a member of the true Church, to whatever particular denomination he may belong."

Especially in a world where "bold and impious infidelity abounds," it was essential "to unite in exhibiting our common Christianity to mankind in her meekest, loveliest, and most attractive form!"[39]

Miller's observations rested upon a notion of denominationalism that is largely taken for granted today but has actually been common only in the last several centuries. The concept, often more a tacit working ar-

39. Miller, *Letters Concerning the Constitution and Order of the Christian Ministry,* 3, 13, 224, 225.

rangement than a fully formed theory, assumes that Christians may adhere to separate "churches" with differing theologies, practices, and polities while recognizing that all are part of a greater entity: namely, *the* church. Denominationalism offered a way of coming to terms with religious fragmentation in the wake of the Reformation. It held especial relevance in the pluralistic religious world of the early American republic, where all but two states had ended religious establishments and where the holdouts would shortly follow suit: Connecticut in 1817 and Massachusetts in 1833. In this environment, acceptance of denominationalism permitted each group to cultivate its own field, to cooperate with others as it wished, and to maintain amity with them. In effect, Hobart was refusing to grant theological legitimacy to the reality of pluralism; Miller was not only accepting that reality as an empirical fact but also seeking to accommodate it theologically. His position allowed him to support voluntary societies and also the so-called Plan of Union with the Congregationalists that he, as a commissioner to the General Assembly in 1801, had endorsed. It also permitted him to bow to the prudential concern that "exhibiting our common Christianity" was perhaps essential at a time when "bold and impious infidelity abounds."[40]

He had not, however, foreclosed the possibility of disputation among Christian denominations. In his *Letters,* he argued vigorously for the Presbyterian conception of the ministry and mercilessly exposed what he deemed the shortcomings of the Episcopal view. In fact, he insisted that each denomination, when it encountered what it believed to be errors, had an obligation "to expose and refute them." Contentions of this sort, if carried on in a civil and meek spirit, would serve the cause of truth. Out of candid debate would emerge a deeper knowledge of the truth and bring to pass the fulfillment of the prophecy of Isaiah: "Many shall run to and fro, and knowledge shall be increased." Miller's views could, in short, lead to tolerance and cooperation but also to a rigorous patrolling of denominational boundaries. In the years to come, he would exhibit both tendencies.[41]

During the first decade of the nineteenth century, Samuel Miller redirected his professional energies and found a new focus in his vocation as a minister. At the outset of those ten years, he envisioned intellectual projects across a wide range of subjects — a breadth manifested in his

40. Miller, *The Life of Samuel Miller,* 1:139.
41. Miller, *Letters Concerning the Constitution and Order of the Christian Ministry,* 21.

Brief Retrospect. He initially intended to write additional volumes to that already lengthy work and had in mind a history of New York as well. In preparation for the latter venture he had gotten his friend De Witt Clinton, at the time a member of the legislature, to introduce a bill allowing Miller free access to the official sources he would need to write the history. Neither of these undertakings came to fruition, for Miller turned his literary energies to more specifically theological and religious topics. Also, he and his two co-pastors at the United Presbyterian Churches encountered difficulties in maintaining as one congregation three different groups of people, each with its own house of worship. After considerable effort and some controversy, he succeeded in ending the collegiate arrangement and creating three formally separate congregations. In addition to these local responsibilities, Miller was elected moderator of the General Assembly in 1806 and the same year joined the board of trustees of the College of New Jersey. As a trustee, he allied himself with those engaged in the coup that deposed Samuel Stanhope Smith in favor of Ashbel Green. As noted in the previous chapter, he and Green were also among the chief movers in the creation of Princeton Seminary. Changes in Miller's personal life likewise diminished the time he had to pursue his wider interests. During the first eight years in New York, he was a bachelor, a life he shared with his unmarried brother Edward after the latter moved to the city and the two took up residence together. In October 1801, however, Samuel Miller married Sarah Sergeant, a daughter of the recently deceased Attorney General of Pennsylvania. A year after their marriage, the first of their ten children was born.

When Miller was elected the second professor at the seminary in 1813, he prepared for his new position under a cloud of grief. A little more than a year before, both his 7-year-old son Edward and the man for whom the little boy was named — Samuel's brother Edward — died. The full impact of these losses must remain a matter of speculation, but Miller's biographer hints at some tantalizing possibilities. More than sixty years later, in evaluating the relationship of the two brothers, Samuel Miller Jr. called the death of Edward "one of the sorest bereavements" of his father's life, and offered the following intriguing description of their relationship: Edward's "very warm and decided" political partisanship may have encouraged Samuel to "participate in party strife . . . far too much for a minister of the gospel." For his part, Samuel may have failed Edward, too. "The clerical brother, had he shewn more decisively . . . that he was determined not to know anything save Jesus Christ and him crucified, would have exerted upon the physician a much more effectual religious influence." The concern about more "effectual religious influence" derived from the fact that Edward never made a profession of religious faith. Samuel Miller may well have blamed himself for this lack because he had failed to set a proper example by not concentrating his energies more exclusively upon his ministerial calling. In any event, the man who moved to Princeton in 1813 to take up a professorship had a far more focused vision of his vocation than the boy minister who had come to New York City twenty years earlier.[42]

---

42. Miller, *Life of Samuel Miller,* 1:322, 323.

CHAPTER THREE

Learning and Piety

W HEN Archibald Alexander and, a year later, Samuel Miller set themselves to the task of creating a three-year course of study, they did so within the mandate established by the General Assembly. It was not, however, as if they were subjecting themselves to someone else's ideas. They along with Ashbel Green, chair of the seminary's board of directors, had served on the committee that drafted the Plan. The Plan did not prescribe specific courses that the curriculum had to include, for it recognized that these would vary according to "the views and habits of the teachers" and should be subject to revision "as experience may suggest improvements." What the Plan did specify were "the attainments which must be made" by the students. Biblical knowledge and its proper interpretation came first: the student "must be well skilled in the original languages of the Holy Scripture" and competent "to explain the principal difficulties which arise in the perusal of the Scriptures." In order to understand the Scriptures properly, the student also needed to demonstrate familiarity with the ancient history, customs, and geography that formed the context of the Bible. In addition to thorough grounding in the Scriptures, the student "must have read and digested the principal arguments and writings relative to . . . the deistical controversy" and thereby "be qualified to become a defender of the Christian faith." He must also be able to defend "the doctrines of the Confession of Faith and Catechisms" and provide "abundant quotations of Scripture texts" in support of the teachings of the Westminster Standards. Preparation in theology needed to include "Natural, Didactic, Polemic, and Casuistic Theology." The seminarian would acquire "considerable acquaintance with general history and chronology, and a particular acquaintance with the history of the Christian church." The student "must have read a considerable number of the best practical writers on the subject of religion." He needed to demonstrate an ability to give popular lectures and sermons, and to that end would have to compose at least two lectures and four sermons to the satisfaction of the professors. Then, too, "he must have carefully studied the duties of the pastoral care." Finally, a Princeton seminarian would learn "the form of church government authorized by the Scriptures." To assess how well students reached these goals, those who stayed for the entire three years of instruction — it was not required to do so — would be examined, and those who performed adequately would receive a certificate.[1]

The Plan also provided that "when the Seminary shall be completely organized, there shall not be less than three professors, one of Didactic and Polemical Divinity; one of Oriental and Biblical Literature; and one of Ecclesiastical History and Church Government." The professor of didactic and polemical divinity was designated the presiding officer of the faculty. Although departments as understood today did not exist in the seminary's early years, one sees in the Plan and in the professorships the rudiments of the fourfold division of theological education that was later systematized in departments of Bible, theology, history, and practical theology.[2]

The Plan suggested an intriguing dialectic between Bible and theology. Based on its priority in the list of desired student "attainments," not to mention Presbyterian commitment to the Reformation principle *sola scriptura,* the study of the Bible was to be the foundation of education at Princeton. The emphasis on mastery of Hebrew and Greek as well as the stress on the geography, history, and customs of the biblical era underscored this commitment. Yet, at the same time, a *de facto* precedence was given to theology. The Plan itself suggested a preference when it named the professor of didactic and polemical divinity, not the professor of oriental and biblical literature, as the faculty's presiding officer. In keeping with this preference, the General Assembly in its first appointment elected Alexander to the professorship of theology, not of Bible. (Of course, since he initially operated a one-man educational enterprise, he

---

1. *Plan of the Theological Seminary of the Presbyterian Church in the United States of America* (Elizabethtown, NJ: Isaac A. Kolloch, 1816), 14, 15.

2. *Plan of the Theological Seminary,* 10-11.

had to teach broadly.) The central role of theology — indeed, the central role of Reformed theology and that of a particular stamp — was underscored by the vow required of each professor upon installation:

> In the presence of God and of the directors of this Seminary, I do solemnly, and *ex animo* adopt, receive, and subscribe the Confession of Faith and Catechisms of the Presbyterian Church in the United States of America, as my faith; or, as a summary and just exhibition of that system of doctrine and religious belief which is contained in holy Scripture, and therein revealed by God to man for his salvation: and in the same manner I profess to receive the Form of Government of said Church, as most agreeable to the inspired oracles. I do solemnly promise and engage, not to inculcate, teach, or insinuate any thing which shall appear to me to contradict or contravene, either directly or impliedly, any thing taught in the said Confession of Faith, Catechisms, or Form of Government, while I shall continue a professor in this Seminary.

From the perspective of the seminary founders, there was no conflict between the theological oath and the primacy of the Bible, for they operated from the assumption that Westminster provided "a summary and just exhibition of that . . . which is contained in holy Scripture."[3]

The Plan's treatment of theology was suggestive in yet another respect. Before the document mentioned branches of theology — natural, didactic, and polemical — it addressed Deism first. Each seminary student "must have read and digested the principal arguments and writings relative to . . . the deistical controversy" and thereby "be qualified to become a defender of the Christian faith." This emphasis reflected the experience of church leaders such as Alexander, Green, and Miller. Having come to intellectual maturity at a time when Deism was fashionable and appeared the major threat to Christian orthodoxy, they deemed it essential to educate ministers who could deal with this challenge. The irony was that the great day of American Deism had already passed when the first Princeton seminarians gathered to study with Alexander, and the nineteenth century would bring new intellectual challenges.[4]

The 1822 pamphlet *A Brief Account of the Rise, Progress, and Present*

---

3. *Plan of the Theological Seminary*, 11.
4. *Plan of the Theological Seminary*, 14.

State of the Theological Seminary of the Presbyterian Church in the United States at Princeton, something analogous to today's catalogue, described the program created to carry out the Plan. The first year emphasized biblical study and ancient languages, presumably Hebrew, since students were expected to have learned Greek by the time they left college. Also included were sacred chronology and geography, these subjects being "passed over in a rapid and general manner as preliminary" to an examination of Jewish antiquities and oriental customs. In the first year seminarians also grappled with biblical criticism. By "biblical criticism" the Princeton professors did not mean what was later called higher criticism, but rather the establishing of "the true text" of Scripture in distinction from apocryphal writings and how that text, once determined, should be interpreted. In the second year, students continued language study one day a week and added didactic — that is, systematic — theology and church history. The third year brought the conclusion of didactic theology and church history but also introduced the student to polemic theology, in which religious movements and ideas deemed erroneous were examined and refuted. In the final year, students also heard a series of lectures on the composition of sermons and pastoral care. By the time the 1838 version of the document appeared, the curriculum retained much of the same basic structure with a few significant additions and minor clarifications. The emphasis in the first year remained heavily upon the Bible, but with the explicit statement that Hebrew and exegesis would be studied. Added to the first year, however, were mental and moral science as well as evidences of revealed and natural religion. The middle year now included missionary instruction. The senior year remained substantially the same as in the earlier catalogue.[5]

The curriculum stuck to the order implied by the Plan, especially in the 1822 rendition. Courses followed a chronological progression from Bible, to theology and church history, and finally to the ways in which this knowledge would be put in service to the church through preaching and the giving of pastoral care. That sequence was to some extent altered in the 1838 version by including in the first year the study of moral

---

5. *A Brief Account of the Rise, Progress, and Present State of the Theological Seminary of the Presbyterian Church in the United States at Princeton* (Philadelphia: A. Finley, 1822), 45, 46; *A Brief History of the Theological Seminary of the Presbyterian Church at Princeton, New Jersey* (Princeton: John Bogart, 1838), 36. See also Archibald Alexander, *The Canon of the Old and New Testaments Ascertained; Or, the Bible Complete without the Apocrypha and Unwritten Traditions* (New York: G. and C. Carvill, 1826).

philosophy and the evidences of religion. Yet the decision to make this addition reflected another aspect of the Plan: its concern that each seminarian "be qualified to become a defender of the Christian faith." Forged in the conflict over Deism, the desire for a stout apologetic on behalf of the faith led, as E. Brooks Holifield has argued, to "an unprecedented degree of interest in the Christian evidences.... What emerged was a stronger sense among theologians that Christianity had to prove itself as rational in the way that men and women of 'common sense' understood rationality."[6]

Archibald Alexander and Christianity as a Rational Religion

Archibald Alexander's career at Princeton offered a prime example of this preoccupation. His first book, *A Brief Outline of the Evidences of the Christian Religion* (1825), grew out of a sermon he had preached at the college in 1823 as a refutation of a band of religious skeptics within the student body. In the work Alexander argued for the rationality of Christian revelation as contained in Scripture. Attested by miracle and by fulfilled prophecy, the Bible bore the stamp of empirical verification so that any reasonable person, believer or not, could be convinced of its authenticity. Biblical revelation also presented internal evidence of its divine origin. Unlike the external proofs of miracles performed and predictions accomplished, the internal evidence had to do with the "moral fitness and beauty" of the biblical message, "in its adaptation of the truth to the constitution of the human mind, in its astonishing power of penetrating the conscience." Alexander set forth his understanding of conscience most succinctly in *Outlines of Moral Science*. Although his last book — it was posthumously published in 1854 — *Outlines of Moral Science* represented the themes and ideas "in mental and moral science" that he had for decades shared with first-year seminarians "as a transition from college work." In this brief volume, he made audacious claims, at least for a Calvinist, about the unaided power of the conscience. He attributed to "the intuitive perceptions of conscience" an independence of "every doctrine of theology, even the greatest." "There are," he went on to argue, "certain self-evident truths, which are intuitively perceived by every one

6. E. Brooks Holifield, *Theology in America: Christian Thought from the Age of the Puritans to the Civil War* (New Haven: Yale University Press, 2003), 273.

who has the exercise of reason, as soon as they are presented to the mind." Expanding on the point, he underscored the universality of the moral sense, independent of culture and social setting:

> In cases of flagrant injustice or ingratitude, all men of every coun-
> try and of every age, agree in their judgment of their moral evil.
> There is, in regard to such actions, no more difference in the judg-
> ment of men, than respecting the colour of grass, or the taste of
> honey. If any man does not perceive grass to be green, or honey to
> be sweet, we do not thence conclude that men's bodily senses are
> not similarly constituted, but that the organs of the individual
> who does not see and taste as other men do, are defective, or de-
> praved by disease.

In Alexander's emphasis upon the autonomy of reason and the universality of self-evident principles, one sees the influence of Thomas Reid and
the Common Sense philosophy. One can also understand why historian
Sydney E. Ahlstrom once commented that anyone reading Alexander's
Outlines of Moral Science and "unaware that its author was one of the nation's most inflexible champions of Old School Calvinism would assume
on reading this book by itself, that it was written, perhaps, by some mild
English Latitudinarian."[7]

Yet despite his views of moral philosophy, Alexander was anything
but a mild latitudinarian. The *Outlines of Moral Science* closed with the
observation: "It is evident from the slightest view of the character of man
in all ages and countries, that he has lost his primeval integrity, that the
whole race have by some means fallen into the dark gulf of sin and misery. This, reason teaches; but how to escape from this wretched condition, she teaches not." Alexander's goal — through arguments from evidences, external or internal, and from the self-evident perceptions of the
conscience — was to prepare the way for a systematic exploration of
Christian truth as manifested in the Reformed tradition. As a text to introduce his students to this subject, he chose Francis Turretin's *Institutio
Theologiae Elencticae* (1679-1685) or, in English, *Institutes of Elenctic Theology.* Descendant of Italian *émigrés* who had fled the inquisition and set-

---

7. Archibald Alexander, *Outlines of Moral Science* (New York: Charles Scribner, 1854),
12, 13, 20, 40; Sydney E. Ahlstrom, "The Scottish Philosophy and American Theology,"
Church History 24 (September 1955): 266.

tled in Geneva, Turretin (1623-1687) served for a time as pastor of an Italian congregation in the city and after 1652 as theology professor at the Geneva Academy. He became one of the major voices of Reformed thought; and his elenctic theology — that is, a theology designed to refute erroneous views — used the methods and categories of late medieval scholasticism, often rejected or ignored by the first generation of Protestant reformers. Turretin saw himself as using those methods to systematize and defend the legacy of Calvin, not to repudiate or alter it. How well he and other Protestant "scholastics" succeeded in their endeavor has been a matter of dispute among historians of theology. Some have seen Turretin's work as unduly speculative and arid — a declension from the christocentric dynamism of Calvin's thought. Others insist that Turretin merely preserved the Calvinist tradition in a new institutional context and reconnected it with older forms of theological discourse. Despite their differences, all interpreters would agree that the theology of Turretin was highly technical, its arguments often complex and difficult. In choosing the *Institutio,* Alexander was not unmindful of the problems. The work, his son recalled, "was ponderous, scholastic and in a dead language"; but believing that wrestling with "this athletic sinewy reasoner" had helped him, the Princeton professor assigned Turretin to his students. Alexander dissented from him at points, and his own style of presenting theological topics diverged dramatically from that of the Genevan. Alexander's lectures, as remembered by some students, lacked the architectonic complexity of the scholastic. He often cut to the heart of a matter in a memorable way. William M. Paxton, class of 1848, recalled how "Dr. Alexander would take the . . . subject, and strike it with a javelin, and let the light through it. His aim was to make one point, and nail it fast."[8]

8. Alexander, *Outlines of Moral Science,* 272; James W. Alexander, *The Life of Archibald Alexander, D.D.* (New York: Charles Scribner, 1854), 368; William M. Paxton, Theodore L. Cuyler, and William C. Cattell, *The Alexander Memorial* (New York: Anson D. F. Randolph, 1879), 13-14. For examples of differing assessments of Turretin and scholasticism, see, for example, John W. Beardslee III, ed. and trans., *Reformed Dogmatics: J. Wollebius, G. Voetius, and F. Turretin* (New York: Oxford University Press, 1965), and Richard A. Muller, *After Calvin: Studies in the Development of a Theological Tradition* (New York: Oxford University Press, 2003). An English translation of Turretin's work may be found in Francis Turretin, *Institutes of Elenctic Theology,* 3 vols. trans. George Musgrave Giger and ed. James T. Dennison Jr. (Phillipsburg, NJ: Presbyterian and Reformed Publishing, 1992-1994).

Samuel Miller, Ecclesiastical History,
Church Government, and Practical Theology

Samuel Miller's portfolio included church history and church government, though in the seminary of his era those responsibilities were not
sharply demarcated from normative theology. In fact, while Alexander's
title specified polemical theology as his peculiar domain, Miller was often the sharper controversialist. In many of his works, one sees the historian using his craft primarily as a defense of endangered orthodoxy. For
example, he wrote *Letters on Unitarianism* (1821) to a Presbyterian congregation in Baltimore. Two years earlier, at the ordination of Jared
Sparks to serve the Unitarian congregation in that city, William Ellery
Channing had delivered a powerful sermon generally regarded as the
most succinct and compelling manifesto of the fledgling denomination.
The threat to orthodoxy seemed great, not only because of the power of
Channing's discourse, but also because of its location. With a foot in Baltimore, a major mid-Atlantic port, Unitarianism appeared to be moving
beyond its origins in maritime Massachusetts and to be poised to spread
more widely. Accordingly, Trinitarian Congregationalists — out of which
body the Unitarians had come — quickly renewed their pamphlet war
against the movement. When Miller joined the attack in 1821, he was
coming to the aid of a former student whose ordination sermon he had
preached in Baltimore several years earlier. Not surprisingly, Miller's argument began with careful arguments from the Bible, but it also included a substantial case on the basis of church history. He surveyed
church fathers such as Clement of Alexandria, Cyprian, Tertullian, and
Athanasius as well as figures from the Reformation era. Miller's appeal to
history was designed to demonstrate how isolated Unitarianism was
from the totality of the Christian tradition. In making his argument, he
managed inadvertently to land himself in a collateral controversy with
one of his Trinitarian allies, Moses Stuart, who was a biblical scholar at
Andover Seminary. Stuart feared that Miller had weakened the orthodox
position by tying it to the notion of the eternal generation of the Son
from the Father — a doctrine that Stuart claimed he had never once
heard "seriously avowed and defended" in New England. In fact, he
thought that virtually all contemporary New England clergy were
"united in rejecting it, or at least in regarding it as unimportant." Miller
replied to Stuart at great length, again drawing extensively on arguments
from church history as well as from the Bible. Although he did not doubt

Stuart's orthodoxy, Miller feared that questioning the eternal Sonship — a view assumed by the Christian tradition and embodied in many of its great creeds — would ultimately contribute to heterodoxy. Or, as Miller put the matter, "I consider you as a sincere Trinitarian, and as a truly pious Christian. . . . I go farther; and hesitate not to say, that I entertain the same opinion of the great body of my fathers and brethren in New England, who agree with you in this doctrine. I believe them to be faithful ministers, daily doing good, and leading souls to glory. Yet, with my views of the subject, I cannot but tremble for the next generation." In short, he saw New England's departure from the idea of the Son's eternal generation as the first step on a slippery slope away from orthodoxy.[9]

As professor of church government, Miller took particular interest in the distinctive features of Presbyterian polity. His most notable contribution was his study of the biblical and historical role of the ruling elder. Miller first published a sermon on the topic in 1811 and continued to revise and augment his treatment of the subject. In addition to copious arguments from Scripture and history to show the divine mandate for the office, Miller devoted considerable space to the reasons for its importance. Foremost among these was his conviction that discipline was essential to the welfare of the church. Or, in his words, it was necessary

> that there be a constant and faithful inspection of all the members and families of the Church; that the negligent be admonished; the wanderers be reclaimed; that scandals be removed; that irregularities be corrected; that differences be reconciled; and every proper measure adopted to bind the whole body together by the ties of Christian purity and charity.

In fact, in some passages Miller suggested that discipline was an essential mark of the church. "Without wholesome discipline for removing of-

9. Samuel Miller, *Letters on Unitarianism; Addressed to the Members of the First Presbyterian Church in the City of Baltimore* (Trenton, NJ: George Sherman, 1821), esp. 111-90; Moses Stuart, *Letters on the Eternal Generation of the Son of God, Addressed to the Rev. Samuel Miller* (Andover, MA: Flagg and Gould, 1822), 5; Samuel Miller, *Letters on the Eternal Sonship of Christ* (Philadelphia: Woodward, 1822), 290. For a careful exposition of Miller's dispute with Stuart, see Bruce M. Stephens, "Samuel Miller (1769-1850): Apologist for Orthodoxy," *Princeton Seminary Bulletin* 67 (1975): 33-47. The sermon by Channing that prompted much of this discussion is thoughtfully excerpted and introduced in Sydney E. Ahlstrom and Jonathan S. Carey, eds., *An American Reformation: A Documentary History of Unitarian Christianity* (Middletown, CT: Wesleyan University Press, 1985), 90-117.

fenses and excluding the corrupt and profane," he explained, "there may be an assembly; but there cannot be a church."[10]

The question, then, concerned the manner in which discipline was to be properly exercised. Even if it were feasible to bestow the responsibility upon the pastor alone, Miller thought it wrong to entrust him with the task. Since ministers "shared the same frailties and imperfections of other men," one could not trust them to perform the task unchecked. When the Christian community did allow this to happen in the post-apostolic era, the result was "first prelacy and afterwards popery, which has so long enslaved the church." "Ecclesiastical tyranny" should be no more acceptable than political. On the other hand, those churches that allowed the "whole body" of the congregation to exercise discipline were equally in error. As a group, Miller insisted, "they have neither the knowledge, the wisdom, nor the prudence necessary for the purpose." The idea that "every weak, childish, and indiscreet individual" who happened to qualify for church membership should also participate in discipline was "preposterous." The office of ruling elder stood between the extremes of ecclesiastical tyranny and unbridled democracy. A body of ruling elders — chosen by the congregation for their prudence, piety, and soundness in the faith — would establish a golden mean between one-person rule and complete egalitarianism. But who should be eligible for the office, how long should they serve, and who in the congregation should be qualified as their electors? Miller advocated restriction of the office to men and favored service for life unless ill health, inappropriate behavior, or some other necessity dictated otherwise. As to those who should be allowed to vote, Miller recognized a "diversity of opinion" within the Presbyterian Church. All agreed that males in "full communion" were eligible as electors. Many, though not without opposition, would extend the privilege to all baptized members, and some would allow "female heads of families . . . not represented by some qualified male relative . . . to vote in the choice of ruling elders as is generally the case in the choice of a pastor." Without making a specific proposal, Miller suggested that the franchise in the election of ruling elders should be narrower than in the ballot for a pastor. When a new pastor was called to a church, the presbytery needed to approve the choice and could thus check an unwise con-

10. Samuel Miller, *An Essay on the Warrant, Nature, and Duties of the Office of Ruling Elder in the Presbyterian Church,* 3rd ed. (Philadelphia: Presbyterian Board of Education, 1840), 174-75.

gregational decision. But the presbytery did not have to approve the choice of ruling elders; therefore, there was a greater imperative to have wise restrictions on those who served as their electors. Thus, through a careful process of screening the choice of elders, Miller believed the church could be properly governed by a select group who would neither play the tyrant nor serve as mouthpiece for popular opinion. To use a political analogy, Miller was preparing his ministerial students to participate in a style of church governance closer to the classical republicanism favored by many of America's revolutionary founders than to the expansive vision of democracy increasingly common in early-nineteenth-century America.[11]

Another significant part of Miller's responsibility was to lecture to students in their third year on preaching and pastoral care, thus providing a transition into their future work. His *Letters on Clerical Manners and Habits* (1827) offers a sense of what he thought appropriate practice for a minister. The shaping of clerical character began with proper deportment in seminary. Miller warned against students who lounged indolently in class, who came in late, who whispered to their peers, or who appeared in the lecture hall "in a slovenly dress" as if "in that kind of *dishabille* which might have been expected if they had five minutes before quitted their beds." He also criticized students who, if they had already been licensed to preach by their presbyteries, missed classes because they had unwisely overcommitted themselves to pulpit assignments. Miller's vision of proper seminarians was captured in his description of punctual, highly organized young men moving about from their rooms to chapel, lectures, or meals with "no running, noisy walking, whistling, singing, loud talking or boisterous laughter." (The fact that Miller felt constrained to warn against excessive noise, tardiness, unkempt appearance, or slouching in class suggests that such vices were not unheard of among his students.) His ideal of the seminary was an almost monastic community of young men whose ordered lives revolved about study and worship. The monastic comparison is apt, for Miller took for granted that students would not be married, so that they could give themselves

11. Miller, *Warrant, Nature, and Duties,* 178, 180, 264, 265. See Belden Curnow Lane, "Democracy and the Ruling Eldership: Samuel Miller's Response to Tensions between Clerical Power and Lay Activity in Early Nineteenth Century America" (Ph.D. Dissertation, Princeton Theological Seminary, 1976); Lane, "Presbyterian Republicanism: Samuel Miller's Answer to Lay-Clerical Tensions," *Journal of Presbyterian History* 56 (Winter 1978): 311-24.

without distraction to their preparation for ministry. To be sure, he also assumed that ultimately most ministers would — and should — marry, but not until they had a call to a post and the prospect of being able to support a wife and family.[12]

Once in the pastorate, the former seminarian needed to manifest a similar singleness of purpose and discipline. For example, in conducting worship, the pastor should start punctually — "wait for no one." He must enter the sanctuary in a manner "grave, dignified, and yet perfectly simple and unaffected." It was never appropriate to go into the place of worship with "hurried steps, or in a light, airy manner; looking over the house . . . as if in search of an acquaintance." During worship the minister should read Scripture, pray, and preach in a voice never "abrupt, harsh, or loud; but studiously gentle and reverential." After the service, he should retire "gravely, silently, and alone." Miller's notion of ministerial decorum did not include hearty handshakes with departing parishioners. Miller also encouraged the minister to undertake systematic visitation of his flock. When in conversation with his people, a wise pastor showed interest in them and their families but never allowed talk to dwell unduly upon mere superficiality, gossip, or worldly topics. As minister, his duty was to engage them tactfully but unashamedly on matters of religion. Miller took issue with those who fulfilled this duty "chiefly in tender and solemn exhortation" because they believed "that the grand object aimed at ought to be to impress the conscience and the heart, rather than to impart doctrinal knowledge." While admitting that pastoral care did not mean that the minister should "perplex" souls "with the metaphysical refinements of theology," he was adamant that basic theological facts about the plan of salvation did need to be communicated. "Neither the conscience nor the heart," he declared, "can ever be suitably impressed but through the medium of truth." He also warned against giving those worried about their spiritual condition too speedy a relief from distress. "Be not too ready to speak peace," he counseled, "or to administer consolation to those who are in a serious, anxious state of mind." Behind that advice lay the Anglo-American tradition that saw the task of the minister to skillfully guide the troubled soul through the morphology of conversion.[13]

Although much of the advice on the cure of souls tendered in the *Let-*

12. Samuel Miller, *Letters on Clerical Manners and Habits; Addressed to a Student in the Theological Seminary at Princeton, New Jersey* (New York: G. & C. Carvill, 1827), 197, 257.

13. Miller, *Clerical Manners*, 137, 138, 153, 154, 276, 279, 285.

ters on Clerical Manners and Habits identifies it as a work in pastoral theology written in the tradition of William Baxter's *The Reformed Pastor* (1656), Miller's volume also stood in another genre. In the late eighteenth and early nineteenth centuries, there was a vogue in writings about manners, stressing the habits and practices that designated their possessors as persons of gentility. Perhaps the best known of these was Lord Chesterfield's *Letters to His Son* (1774), which enjoyed immense publishing success both in the United Kingdom and in America. Originally associated with the aristocracy or gentry, notions of gentility and refinement were adopted — and adapted — by larger segments of society, including what we would today call the middle class. In many of the popular "courtesy books," genteel conduct entailed a respect for rank and a restraint of the body and its functions so that "in company the body was to be presented and conceived of as immaculate, devoid of every form of filth and baseness." The courtesy books also contained an emphasis on a respect for the feelings of others — a principle that, in the words of Richard L. Bushman, "resembled in spirit the second, bodily restraint." "Both assumed," Bushman explains, "that polite society consisted of sensitive beings who might suffer irritation and offense if treated wrongly. Delicate sensibilities would draw back in revulsion at a mouth agape in a yawn or upon contact with a spoon that someone else had touched." Rank, however, posed a greater problem. Americans, living in a republican society that manifested ambivalence about notions of hierarchy and aristocracy, found the issue problematic and in need of reinterpretation as they embraced the ideals of gentility and refinement.[14]

The *Letters on Clerical Manners and Habits* represented Miller's effort to portray the minister as a "Christian gentleman." He distinguished Christian gentility from "the hollow, insincere system of artificial manners" that qualified a person "to make a distinguished figure in a ballroom, or at the levee of a great man, and which manifest that he has studied Chesterfield more than his Bible." Miller's goal was "to recommend those manners which become the Christian gentleman; which naturally flow from the meekness, gentleness, purity, and benevolence of our holy

---

14. Richard L. Bushman, *The Refinement of America: Persons, Houses, Cities* (New York: Alfred A. Knopf, 1992), esp. 42-43. For a somewhat different perspective on the preoccupation with gentility and manners, consult C. Dallett Hemphill, "Middle Class Rising in America: The Evidence from Manners," *Journal of Social History* 30 (Winter 1996): 317-44. See also John F. Kasson, *Rudeness and Civility: Manners in Nineteenth-Century Urban America* (New York: Hill and Wang, 1990), 9-69.

religion." For Miller, true manners were not affectation but rather the out-working of Christian character. Yet his treatise showed preoccupations similar to the courtesy books, many of his admonitions counseling bodily restraint so as to avoid giving affront to delicate souls in polite society. He warned young ministers to guard against personal habits offensive in the company of others: unduly loud coughing, picking the teeth, laughing too heartily, yawning, combing the hair, or eating "with a rapidity or a greedi-ness which indicates a mind inordinately intent on the pleasures of eat-ing." He warned especially against an American proclivity to spit, noting that those who engaged in the habit "bespattered the clothes and persons of all who were sitting in their immediate vicinity."[15]

Along with many others in republican America, Miller dealt ambiva-lently with rank as a mark of gentility. One of the chief marks of clerical manners, he observed, was "condescension"; or, as he explained to young ministers:

> a large part of your social and professional intercourse will be with those who, according to popular language, are your inferi-ors. . . . It is, therefore, of peculiar importance that you acquire the art of treating such persons in a manner best adapted to soothe their feelings, inspire their confidence, and win their affections. This can only be done by habits of condescension; that is, laying aside every thing like an air of haughtiness or superiority.

Condescension, as described by Miller, avoided the appearance of haughtiness or superiority while implicitly recognizing that there were in fact "inferiors" in society. His admonitions concerning the minister's relationship with those of "wealth and high station" likewise exhibit a measure of unease. While the minister should never approach such peo-ple in a sycophantic manner, he did need to be aware that because of their position "any good impression made on them will be likely to ex-tend itself more widely," and he should always "let them see that Chris-tian duty is not inconsistent with the most perfect politeness."[16]

---

15. Miller, *Clerical Manners*, 17-18, 19, 20, 62, 71, 75, 76-79. If one is to judge from the not altogether unbiased account of Frances Trollope, an English visitor to America and mother of the future novelist Anthony Trollope, spitting was a common practice among American males; Frances Trollope, *Domestic Manners of the Americans* (London: Whit-taker, Treacher, and Co., 1832), 83, 171, 187.

16. Miller, *Clerical Manners*, 42, 132, 133.

Miller's vision of Christian gentility was not hierarchical after the fashion of Lord Chesterfield's *Letters to His Son.* It did not derive immediately from the world of aristocrats and royal courts. It had more in common with the culture of politeness fostered by the Scottish Enlightenment that influenced Princeton so profoundly. As Daniel Walker Howe has written of that culture, it encouraged a "politeness created for a world of coffeehouses, clubs, and debating societies — not of nobles or courtiers." In other words, it thrived in the sort of milieu in which Miller had participated in New York through the Friendly Club and other civic societies. Unlike aristocratic forms of gentility, this culture of politeness was not, at least in theory, closed to those of poor birth or low social station. By adopting its values, such persons were presumptive candidates for genteel status. In practice, Miller's ideal of Christian manners did exclude many, including the bumptious popular religious movements then flourishing in many parts of the country. Or, at minimum, it put them on probation until they manifested the fruits meet for refinement. Yet the notion of the Christian gentleman — with all its strengths and limitations — remained a goal of the seminary's implicit curriculum: not only would Princeton turn out learned, orthodox ministers; it would produce gentlemen.[17]

The Sabbath Conference

But there was, of course, more. The Plan of the seminary called for a union of "piety of the heart . . . with solid learning." Accordingly, Alexander and Miller took care to cultivate the religious life of those in their charge. When the seminary first opened, Alexander met his small classes in his own home, and he had them join with him in family worship. He also held at his home Sunday evening services where he preached. The popularity of these meetings spread from seminarians to townsfolk and undergraduates and prompted a move to a room in the college. When it likewise proved too small, the college offered the use of its refectory for the Sunday night worship. By January 1813, Alexander was reporting that approximately a hundred were attending.

Around 1816 Alexander abandoned the regular Sunday evening ser-

17. Daniel Walker Howe, *Making the American Self: Jonathan Edwards to Abraham Lincoln* (Cambridge: Harvard University Press, 1997), 54.

mons at the college and instituted Sunday afternoon conferences on "experimental religion." Many seminarians remembered these sessions fondly as one of the highpoints of their time at Princeton. Less formal than the classroom, these meetings permitted students and faculty to reflect upon religious devotion, the struggle against sin, and other practical matters encountered in a life of discipleship. After an opening hymn and prayer, one of the students introduced the topic for the day and then others in turn expressed their views. Once the students had their say, the professors spoke briefly, and the session was closed with additional prayer and singing. It is instructive to note some of the recurring themes treated in the conference: What is the difference between a true and a false sorrow for one's sin? What are the signs that one's heart has truly been changed? How does one grow in grace? What are the signs that a person has truly been called to the ministry? What is the relation of melancholy or depression to the religious life? When the professors held forth on these topics, they did so in very different ways. Alexander struck a more conversational and often more animated tone. "As he sat in his chair," said Alexander's son James, who was a student at the seminary in the 1820s, "he would begin with a low voice. . . . As he went on and drew more largely on his recollections and his consciousness, he seldom failed to kindle, and sometimes left all present in a state of emotion." Years later, when James Alexander served briefly as a faculty colleague of his father and when Archibald had grown distressingly frail, the son could still write that the old man "is nowhere so felicitous" as in the Sunday conference. By contrast, Miller was more methodical, precise, and reserved in manner. Yet students apparently appreciated both professors, and outside of the conference room both professors counseled the young men extensively about spiritual concerns.[18]

Since many of the themes expounded by Alexander echoed through his *Practical Sermons* and *Thoughts on Religious Experience,* an examination of those works suggests something of the tenor of the Sunday conference. A physician of the soul, Alexander charted the passage from spiritual death to life and the practical issues raised by this transformation. For example, what relationship did the catechizing and Christian nurture

---

18. Alexander, *Life of Archibald Alexander,* 421, 422; John Hall, ed., *Forty Years' Familiar Letters of James W. Alexander, D.D.,* 2 vols. (New York: Charles Scribner and Company, 1870), 2:104; Samuel Miller, *The Life of Samuel Miller, D.D., LL.D.,* 2 vols. (Philadelphia: Claxton, Remsen and Haffelfinger, 1869), 2:33, 34.

of children have to their ultimate rebirth in Christ? On the one hand, he implied that there was no guarantee that such training would avail at all. "Many children who have the opportunity of a good religious education," he warned, "learn scarcely anything of the most important truths of Christianity." Or again: "The education of children should proceed on the principle that they are in an unregenerate state, until the evidences of piety clearly appear." Alexander believed that God regenerated very few individuals in their early years. Yet nurture and Christian training were still of inestimable value, for God might use them to prepare the way for regeneration. The moment of conversion might be instantaneous — "there can be no medium between life and death," he insisted — yet the process by which God prepared a man or woman for that moment could be a gradual one "which may be going on from childhood to mature age." Alexander was also exceedingly cautious about claims that one could invariably date the moment of his or her regeneration or that a particular kind of deep sorrow for one's sin had to precede conversion. Alexander especially resisted the notion that the regenerated person possessed full confidence of his or her state. "Certainly, we should greatly prefer to stand in the place of some broken-hearted, contrite ones, who can scarcely be induced to entertain a hope respecting their acceptance, to that of many who boast that they never feel a doubt of their own safety. Men will not be judged in the last day by the opinion which they had of themselves." Among the other topics he took up was the necessity of distinguishing the true signs of conversion from "enthusiasm" — or the belief that God gave new revelations to the believer through audible voices or dreams. Alexander was also distressed by the fact that some associated religion with melancholy or depression — which he suggested might well be somatic conditions as much as spiritual. In dealing with these and many other issues, Alexander usually marshaled "case studies" to illustrate his points; and brooding over all his comments was the sense that at bottom the regenerated life was an unmerited gift of a gracious God.[19]

In these works, Alexander's love of piety sometimes seemed to trump learning and theology. "When faith is weak," he declared, "the true method of strengthening it, is not to be found in logical reasoning, but in

19. Archibald Alexander, *Thoughts on Religious Experience,* 3rd ed. (Philadelphia: Presbyterian Board of Publication, 1844), 13, 16, 26, 123; and *Practical Sermons: To Be Read in Families and Social Meetings* (Philadelphia: Presbyterian Board of Publication, 1850), 35. J. W. Alexander, *Life of Archibald Alexander,* 422, suggests that these two volumes convey the tenor of his father's presentations in the Sunday conference.

divine illumination. . . . All the most vigorous efforts of human reason, in the most gifted minds, can never produce one spiritual idea." Similarly, he suggested in the introduction to the *Practical Sermons* that nothing in the book "will be found offensive to the lovers of evangelical truth in other denominations," for "real Christians agree much more perfectly in experimental religion, than they do in speculative points." On the basis of this common experience, he dared to hope that the time will soon arrive "when all the disciples of Christ shall form one great brotherhood under the name of Christians!" But Alexander was not prepared to cede theological precision in order to promote piety. He began his reflections on religious experience with the warning that "a knowledge of the truth is essential to genuine piety; error never can, under any circumstances, produce the effects of truth." "Any defect in our knowledge of the truth," he continued, "must, just so far as the error extends, mar the symmetry of the impression produced." Piety might be the ultimate goal of learning and theology, but one could not produce sound religious commitment by sacrificing the intellect or theological exactitude. At the end of the day bad theology and poor learning created bad piety and ill-informed zeal.[20]

Students as the Makers of Their Own Education

The founders of the seminary, the directors, and the first professors had ideas of what they wished to accomplish, but students also shaped their own education at Princeton. One significant example of their contribution was support for the missionary movement. Perhaps as early as 1820, some students created a secret organization calling itself "the Brotherhood." Membership was based on "an expressed determination on the part of an applicant for admission of his purpose to devote himself, should his life be spared, to labor in the foreign field." The society was secret probably in imitation of a similar group of students that had begun at Williams College in Massachusetts. In 1806, a small number of devout Williams students who frequently met outdoors for prayer took shelter behind a haystack during a thunderstorm, and there they vowed to serve as foreign missionaries. The Haystack Prayer Meeting, an iconic moment in most histories of the American missionary movement, led the students to create a secret "Society of the Brethren" at Williams in support of the

20. Alexander, *Thoughts on Religious Experience*, 9; *Practical Sermons*, 6, 23.

cause. When some of them moved on to Andover Seminary, they organized a similar group there, and it was probably thence that Princeton students got the idea of the Brotherhood. Certainly the men associated with the Andover group played an initiatory role in the formation of the American Board of Commissioners for Foreign Missions (1810). But why the secrecy of these groups at Williams, Andover, and Princeton? Secrecy may have been partly inspired as a counter to the alleged conspiracy of the Illuminati, a movement of the radical Enlightenment that many Congregational and Presbyterian ministers feared was plotting to overthrow order and religion in the United States. (In point of fact, there had been such an organization, but in Bavaria; and even there it was largely defunct when the American clergy began sounding warnings about it.) Moreover, there was the example of Freemasonry — the secret society par excellence — which was growing dramatically at this time with its promise to promote benevolent ends for all. In any event, the secrecy of the Brotherhood was scarcely seen to be subversive by the faculty, who were sometimes party to it. As one student remarked, he was taken into the inner circle — "a wheel within a wheel" of the secret society — and on several occasions "Dr. Alexander . . . met with us in this inside organization, and we got from him a great deal of useful instruction and advice."[21]

But most of the activity of the students was done quite openly. In 1814, Princeton students organized the Society of Inquiry on Missions and the General State of Religion. The organization provided a means of acquiring knowledge, chiefly on religion and missions, from around the world. Its members carried on extensive correspondence with similar societies elsewhere in the United States and with missionaries in various parts of the world. It maintained a reading room with periodicals and journals open to the use of the seminary community. It created a "cabinet" to display artifacts acquired from missionaries. Eventually its activities led to visits from missionaries on furlough from their fields of labor. For example, in 1821 William Ward, an English Baptist missionary associated with the fabled William Carey, visited Princeton; and in 1854 Alexander Duff, Church of Scotland missionary to India, spoke in Princeton. In fact, a long procession of missionaries, some laboring in the United States and others

21. David Bays Calhoun, "The Last Command: Princeton Theological Seminary and Missions (1812-1862)" (Ph.D. Dissertation, Princeton Theological Seminary, 1983), 63, 64; Steven C. Bullock, *Revolutionary Brotherhood: Freemasonry and the Transformation of the American Social Order, 1730-1840* (Chapel Hill: University of North Carolina Press, 1996).

from abroad, came to campus. Through the Society of Inquiry students gave financial support to various missionary endeavors. The society also led students to engage in part-time work among those near Princeton — for example, in organizing Sunday schools and prayer meetings and in promoting revivals in local churches. In the seminary's early years, many students had a particular interest in ministry to the workingmen — many of them immigrants of Roman Catholic faith — who were building the Delaware and Raritan Canal, which went by the outskirts of Princeton and which, when completed in 1834, linked New York and Philadelphia. During the "long vacation," many students worked at greater distance as distributors of religious literature and Bibles or as temporary preachers in what, in the day's parlance, were considered "destitute places." The Society of Inquiry also appears to have functioned as an inspiration and prototype for other student societies devoted to special interests: the establishment of a scholarship fund, the study of Christian music, and the practice of conducting Christian worship.[22]

By these various activities, the students were doing multiple things. They acquired greater information and a larger perspective on the Christian mission. Although the word was not yet in vogue, seminarians were cultivating an ecumenical vision. The interest in mission also led students into various forms of temporary service that much later in the seminary's history would be called field work and brought under formal supervision by the school. The student interest in mission may also have hastened the directors' decision to hire John Breckenridge in 1836 as professor of pastoral theology and missions. Although he stayed only two years before leaving to work for the Presbyterian Board of Foreign Missions, his appointment gave him the distinction of being the first professor of mission in a North American seminary. Perhaps the most significant feature of this work was that it made students more active agents in their own educational and spiritual formation. The faculty served as advisors to many of these activities, but students had a much greater freedom to make their own decisions, especially when they were working in a Sunday school or a church, than when they were sitting in a classroom doing a recitation or listening to a lecture. One can find hints in the record that, at least from time to time, the faculty had reservations about the choices the students made.

One might take the example of a student named Flavel Mines, who

22. See Calhoun, "The Last Command," esp. 12-141.

attended the seminary in the late 1820s. Enthusiastic about the religious excitement generated by "new measures" in revivalism associated with Charles Finney, Mines took it upon himself, as Samuel Miller's son later recalled, to go "as a volunteer revivalist" to an area then called Jugtown or Queenstown, near the intersection of present-day Nassau and Harrison Streets in Princeton. "Having hastily caught up some of the ideas prevalent among Mr. Finney's admirers and followers, he here found a stage for exhibiting them, upon a small scale, with their usual issues in temporary excitement, and ultimate mischief and disrepute." Mines also labored for a short time at First Presbyterian among some who desired a more emotionally vibrant, evangelistic expression of the faith — a desire that, more than a decade later, led to the organization of the Second Presbyterian Church. The younger Miller in his account of Mines seemed to take some pleasure in noting that, having begun his ministerial career in the throes of evangelistic excitement, Mines "ended his ministry in the Episcopal Church, as an ultra high churchman."[23]

The story of Theodore Sedgwick Wright, the first African American student at Princeton Seminary, provides another example of students following their own lights. Born possibly in Rhode Island in 1797, he was reared in Schenectady, New York, and educated in New York City's African Free School. In 1825, he applied through his presbytery for admission to Princeton Seminary. On May 16, the board of directors noted under the heading "application for a colored student" that the Presbytery of Albany had "applied to the Board to have Theodore Wright, a free young man of color, admitted into this Seminary. Whereupon, resolved, that color shall form no obstacle in the way of his reception." While this policy is noteworthy given the practices of most schools at the time, the seminary may not have been entirely color-blind in its policy. By this time, the Theological Edifice — now known as Alexander Hall — was complete, and many students lived there; but Wright found lodging off campus, possibly with an African American widow. Unlike many students at the time, Wright stayed for the entire three-year course of study. At Princeton, Wright drummed up subscriptions for *Freedom's Journal,* founded in early 1827 by the Rev. Samuel Cornish, who served as pastor of the First Colored Pres-

23. Miller, *Life of Samuel Miller,* 2:238-39; also see John Frelinghuysen Hageman, *History of Princeton and Its Institutions,* 2 vols. (Philadelphia: J. B. Lippincott and Co., 1879), 2:125. Second Presbyterian Church later became St. Andrews Presbyterian and merged in the 1970s with the First Presbyterian Church to form today's Nassau Presbyterian Church. The sanctuary of St. Andrews is now the home of the Nassau Christian Center.

byterian Church in New York. The first newspaper published by an African American, *Freedom's Journal* quickly distinguished itself because of its opposition to the Colonization Society, a group that proposed to ameliorate the condition of African Americans and to promote their gradual emancipation by repatriating them to the land of their ancestors. Samuel Miller, presumably recruited by Wright, subscribed to the journal from its inception; but his subscription did not last long. This outcome was scarcely surprising, since the Princeton community, including the seminary faculty, had many ardent supporters of colonization — a commitment explored in greater detail in Chapter Six. According to Miller, he had subscribed to the journal in the "hope that it would be so conducted as to exert a favourable influence on the great cause of the improvement and final emancipation of the children of Africa throughout our country," but in this he was sorely disappointed. As he was planning to write a letter canceling his subscription, an acquaintance, "as cordial a friend to African rights . . . as any man in the land," asked Miller to send along a communication written under the pseudonym "Wilberforce." Finding himself in agreement with the piece, Miller included it with his letter of cancellation. To Miller's surprise, the junior editor, John Russwurm, not only printed the letter of "Wilberforce"; he also identified Miller as the person who had forwarded it and who had expressed approval of its sentiments. The gist of "Wilberforce" was that the journal, by publishing attacks on the Colonization Society — "this best friend of black men" — was actually severely damaging its own cause. The letter also expressed alarm over a recent article that, in the reading of "Wilberforce," called for social equality between the races and attempted to prove that blacks "deserve white wives, and are as good as the best, when they pay their money." Such talk, said "Wilberforce," would set back the cause of black liberation. In his editorial commenting on "Wilberforce," Russwurm remarked: "It is a fact, worthy of notice, that our bitterest enemies think not more contemptibly of us, than do Colonizationists generally — that nothing serves more, to keep us in our present degraded state, than the revolting pictures which are drawn by Colonization Orators." It was this attack, an attack directed at him by name, that prompted Miller to offer a public justification of his actions.[24]

24. *Freedom's Journal* 1 (September 7, 1827): 101-2, 103; (September 21, 1827), 110. I am greatly indebted to the independent research of Daniel Morrison while he was a Princeton Seminary student; Dan first led me to a number of these sources.

The impact of this imbroglio upon Theodore Wright is unclear. In an address in Utica, New York, in September 1837, Wright did allude to one effect of Miller's public pronouncement against *Freedom's Journal:* "I recollect at Princeton, where I was then studying, Dr. Miller came out with his letter, disapproving of the editor's views, and all the faculty and the students gave up the paper." But how did this affect Wright himself as the person at the seminary most closely associated with the journal? In his final year as a seminarian, how did he interact with his professors? Was he rebuked by Miller or one of the other professors for promoting the journal? Was there a coolness toward him? It is impossible to answer these questions, but several things are clear: Wright completed the full three years of the program, and he later as an alumnus spoke appreciatively of the students and faculty at Princeton; but he did *not* retreat an inch from anti-colonization sentiments. He was ordained and installed as Cornish's successor at the First Colored Presbyterian Church in New York in 1828, where he served until his death in 1847. During his nearly two decades as pastor, he also engaged in a dizzying round of social activism designed to protect and improve the lot of black Americans. He was one of the founders of the American Anti-Slavery Society in 1833, which called slaveholding a sin and called for immediate emancipation. When William Lloyd Garrison took that organization in a direction he deemed too heterodox and anti-church, Wright joined with others to create the American and Foreign Antislavery Society in 1840. He also participated in the organization of the small Liberty Party, organized by those who wished an unambiguous antislavery voice in the political process and despaired of achieving it through either of the major parties. Yet even as Wright moved to positions that his mentors abhorred, he went back to Princeton from time to time to renew acquaintances and participate in alumni activities. In 1836, when he attended a lecture on campus, he was subjected to a racial epithet and a brutal physical attack by a student from the college. Fortunately a seminarian intervened to stop the attacker. In a letter addressed to Archibald Alexander and published in William Lloyd Garrison's *Liberator,* Wright expressed a desire both to vindicate his own conduct during the ugly incident and to make clear his abiding love for the seminary.

> Permit me, sir, in the fullness of my soul to say, that I cherish feelings of profound respect and affection for my "Alma Mater," for the worthy professors and students. During the three years in which it

was my privilege to sustain an immediate connection with the Seminary, and the eight subsequent years, throughout the whole . . . I have enjoyed the immediate counsel and support of the beloved Professors, and a delightful intercourse with the students. . . . I always feel, when at Princeton, that I am in the midst of fathers and brethren, in the holy and responsible work to which we are devoted.

Wright's letter offered moving testimony to the esteem in which he held his professors and fellow students at Princeton. Yet there was also a not-too-subtle subtext. He had, after all, published his public appreciation of the seminary in a journal that symbolized a form of antislavery advocacy that his Princeton professors detested. Two years later Wright declared in a public address: "Colonization is the more dangerous as she comes to us in the garb of Piety. . . . Some have been led to look favorably upon this scheme because a great many good men have been engaged in it. But good men err; men are the same that they ever were, finite and fallible; and bad principles are very frequently found among good men." It would be surprising indeed if at least a fleeting thought of his Princeton mentors had not crossed his mind when he uttered those words.[25]

If students contributed to their own education in ways the faculty could not always anticipate or sometimes approve, what they did after they left Princeton was, of course, even more unpredictable. By soliciting subscriptions to *Freedom's Journal* during his student days, Theodore Wright had already given inklings of the trajectory his career would follow. More of an enigma was Elijah Parish Lovejoy, today honored as an early martyr to the cause of liberty for the slave and of freedom of the press. A plaque now hangs at the entrance to the Mackay Campus Center, commemorating his death in November 1837 in Alton, Illinois, at the hands of an armed mob outraged that his paper, the *Observer*, had taken a vigorously abolitionist stand and had called for the formation of a state auxiliary to the American Anti-Slavery Society. What makes Lovejoy a bit of a mystery is that one finds few signs of abolitionist zeal in his ear-

25. "Address of the Rev. Theodore S. Wright Before the Convention of the New York State Anti-Slavery Society, on the Acceptance of the Annual Report, Held at Utica, Sept. 20," *The Colored American*, October 14, 1837; "The Outrage at Princeton," *The Liberator*, November 6, 1836; *Friend of Man*, October 17, 1838. See also David E. Swift, "Black Presbyterian Attacks on Racism: Samuel Cornish, Theodore Wright and Their Contemporaries," *Journal of Presbyterian History* 51 (Winter 1973): 433-70.

lier life. To be sure, he came from an earnest religious upbringing in New England Congregationalism, his father having been a pastor in Maine. Nineteenth-century backgrounds of this sort often produced moral strenuousness as well as desire to do good for others and not infrequently spilled over into benevolent and reform causes, but not necessarily into full-blown abolitionism. When he graduated from Waterville (now Colby) College in 1826, he moved a year later to St. Louis, Missouri, where he ran a private school and edited a newspaper that became noted for its hostility to Andrew Jackson. Converted in a revival in 1832, he decided to pursue the ministry and spent approximately a year at Princeton Seminary. Little evidence of his reaction to the seminary exists, except an enthusiastic letter to his father in which Lovejoy wrote: "Come here, and I will introduce you to one of the best men in the world, — Dr. Alexander. He has few equals that I have ever seen." Most assuredly Lovejoy would not have received an abolitionist bias from Archibald Alexander, who regarded that position as fanatical madness. Alexander did, of course, believe that slavery was a social evil that would be gradually ended and that ex-slaves could be uplifted through colonization. Leaving Princeton after only a year, Lovejoy soon went back to St. Louis, where he organized a Presbyterian church and began the *Observer* as a religious paper. Slavery was initially but one of a series of issues that he examined. Although he thought steps needed to be taken at once to begin the end of slavery, he also insisted that "we do not believe that this change ought to be immediate and unconditional emancipation. We are entirely convinced that such a course would be cruel to the slave himself, and injurious to the community at large." But even this position was too radical for many in St. Louis, and Lovejoy chose to move the paper across the Mississippi River to Alton, Illinois. There resistance again emerged, and it appears that the ferocity of opposition actually caused Lovejoy to dig in his heels and move much closer to a flat-out abolitionism. Then came the violent denouement of November 1837.[26]

When one examines the experiences of students such as Flavel Mines, Theodore S. Wright, and Elijah Lovejoy, one is struck by the extent to which the choices and commitments of students themselves shaped the extracurricular part of their education and hence much of

26. Joseph C. and Owen Lovejoy, *Memoir of the Rev. Elijah P. Lovejoy* (New York: John S. Taylor, 1838), 54, 123. See also Merton L. Dillon, *Elijah P. Lovejoy, Abolitionist Editor* (Urbana: University of Illinois Press, 1961).

what they took away from Princeton. And this agency was not manifest simply as an aggregation of individual projects, each student making his own decisions in splendid isolation from others. As groups such as the Society of Inquiry demonstrated, student activities collectively shaped the educational experience. Moreover, the diversity of backgrounds added something to the learning experience. While a student, Archibald Alexander's son and future colleague on the faculty, James W. Alexander, wrote:

> In our societies one of my greatest pleasures is to observe the development of uncommon characters, a satisfaction which our institution affords in high degree, as it embraces specimens of every variety of American temper and manners which is not inconsistent with religion. We have the Yankee and the Kentuckian, ... the baccalaureate and the backwoodsman, the fastidious critic just emerged from a long confinement of the schools, and the rough unshapen child of nature fresh from the plough. ... Politeness is a thing known only nominally among students — I speak of the formulas of the *bon ton*. By mutual consent, we deal plainly with each other, and waive the observances of fashionable etiquette.[27]

Conclusion

James W. Alexander sounded exhilarated by the experience, but this diversity prompts a question: Was Princeton fulfilling the Plan? Was it turning out the pious, learned gentleman theologians — men of common views and shared theology — that Miller and Alexander wished? Undoubtedly it did in many cases, and one could compose a roster of distinguished alumni who fit the model. But one also gets hints that the professors, especially Miller, were not always satisfied with the quality or commitment of their students. In an opening lecture to the summer session in 1829, about the time that Mines was working his mischief, Miller lamented that seldom "have we been able to persuade as many as one-half of any class to continue their studies to the close of the prescribed period [that is, the full three years]. Many study but half the usual time; others not more than a third part; and some, after spending with us a

27. Hall, ed., *Forty Years' Familiar Letters*, 1:23.

single short summer session, have gone forth, and announced themselves to the churches as pupils of our Seminary." Miller was not exaggerating. Before 1840, only about a quarter of all of the seminary's students stayed for the entire three years. The basic problem was that presbyteries retained in their hands the power to ordain, and there was no requirement in the denomination's constitution that candidates for ordination had to complete a three-year seminary program. In other words, if a presbytery was prepared to ordain a student with one or two years of post-graduate theological education, it could do so. Moreover, by 1830 Princeton had several rivals. Even those Presbyterians who wanted a seminary education could make other choices: Western Seminary in Pittsburgh, Lane in Cincinnati, Auburn in the Finger Lakes region of New York, or Columbia Seminary in South Carolina.[28]

Several years later Miller authored a pamphlet setting out his concerns at greater length. He noted "the melancholy fact" that ministerial candidates often came to seminary and discovered "the miserable scantiness of their literary and scientific acquisitions" and had the sinking realization that they were not prepared "to enter with intelligence on several important departments of theological study." But discovering their deficiencies, they drew the wrong conclusion. Rather than seeking to engage in more and deeper study, they abandoned altogether their plans for seminary education and went "forth at once into the field of public labour." Miller was particularly incensed by the young men who, in the midst of the spiritual excitement of the Second Awakening, "have spurned the counsels of age and experience" out of a misplaced confidence that they were especially "skilled in originating and conducting revivals." Whenever he heard of such an individual, Miller sneered, "I take for granted, without further inquiry, that he is a man of small information . . . that he is a mass of inflated ignorance and spiritual pride." Although Miller's account was strongly one-sided, he was accurate in his discovery that professors could provide a very good course of study, but they could not dictate what students would do with it or even whether they would bother to take all of it.[29]

28. Miller, *Life of Samuel Miller,* 2:143. On the numbers completing the program, see the helpful study by Peter Wallace and Mark Noll, "The Students of Princeton Seminary, 1812-1929: A Research Note," *Journal of Presbyterian History* 72 (Fall 1994): 203-15.

29. Samuel Miller, *The Importance of a Thorough and Adequate Course of Preparatory Study for the Holy Ministry* (Philadelphia: Russell and Martien, 1832), 58-59, 82.

CHAPTER FOUR

The Professional Theologians

I N ITS EARLIEST years, Princeton Seminary provided a theological education only one or two steps above the apprentice system. Under that older scheme, a candidate for ordination studied with a single pastor, read whatever books the minister had in his library, accompanied him on pastoral duties, and usually boarded with him. In the first year of its existence, the seminary was very close indeed to this model. Despite the fact that the school had the offer of the college's facilities, much of the instruction and worship took place in Archibald Alexander's home. When Samuel Miller joined him as professor the following year, the connections between them and the students remained relatively intimate because of the small numbers. What James Alexander wrote of his father's relation with students at this time could be applied to both professors: the seminarians were "in a sense not merely learning of him but living with him. This continued to be the case for a number of years, for the seminary began with three and did not attain the number thirty until the fifth year of its existence." But even when the students were few or before classrooms and living quarters were built, the seminary was set on a trajectory away from the apprentice system. The Plan envisioned at least three professors, and this entailed not only a quantitative difference but a qualitative one from the old system. As Miller said at Alexander's inauguration, the creation of the seminary would "furnish a more extensive, accurate, and complete course of instruction." These professors would give *full* attention to their students and subject areas — an arrangement preferable to study under the tutelage of individual pastors with "neither the talents, learning, nor the leisure to do them justice." Students would also enjoy "one ample library" rather than the comparatively meager collections of most ministers. In short, the seminary would offer a theological education both broader and deeper than the previous method.[1]

In seeking to realize that vision, the church turned in its first faculty appointments to eminent ministers, men respected not only for their learning but also for their long service in the pastorate. At the time they came to Princeton Seminary, Archibald Alexander and Samuel Miller were 40 and 44 years old, respectively, each having spent approximately two decades in pastoral service before being called to the school. Subsequent appointments to the faculty in the next three decades indicated a new pattern. The two longest-serving individuals selected during that time — Charles Hodge and Joseph Addison Alexander — did not come to Princeton with significant pastoral service. Though both were deeply committed to the church, were ordained, and preached regularly, they embarked upon a ministry of scholarship early in their careers. Ensuing appointments at Princeton did not uniformly conform to this pattern, for persons with significant pastoral experience continued to be called to the faculty. However, Hodge and the younger Alexander did signify an important trend. The professional theological scholar was emerging as an important vocation. Clues to what that development meant may be gleaned from the lives, thought, and careers of these two extraordinary men.

Charles Hodge

Like Archibald Alexander's ancestors, Charles Hodge's grandfather, Andrew Hodge, and his two brothers were part of the tide of Scots-Irish immigration in the 1730s. Andrew Hodge became a successful merchant in Philadelphia, eventually buying a wharf on the Delaware River. Married to Jane McCullough, by whom he had fifteen children, Andrew and his family affiliated with the Presbyterian Church. When the denomination

---

1. James W. Alexander, *The Life of Archibald Alexander, D.D.* (New York: Charles Scribner, 1854), 273; [Samuel Miller, Archibald Alexander, and Philip Milledoler,] *The Sermon Delivered at the Inauguration of the Rev. Archibald Alexander, D.D. as Professor of Didactic and Polemic Theology in the Theological Seminary of the Presbyterian Church in the United States of America, to Which Are Added the Professor's Inaugural Address and the Charge to the Professor and Students* (New York: Whiting and Watson, 1812), 36, 37.

was split during the Great Awakening into New and Old Lights (or New and Old Sides), the Hodges went with the New Light party, favoring the revivals. Andrew helped to organize the New Side Second Presbyterian Church, which called the fiery Gilbert Tennent as pastor. (Ashbel Green, future president of the College of New Jersey and of the seminary board of directors, would be one of the subsequent pastors.) It was a mark of Andrew's prosperity that he was able to send his son Hugh, Charles's father, to college at Princeton, and then to help him secure a position as a trainee of Dr. Thomas Cadwalader, one of the city's most highly regarded physicians. After serving as a surgeon in the Continental army during the early part of the American Revolution, Hugh returned home, engaged in the family's mercantile business briefly, and then returned to the practice of medicine about the time his father died in 1790. When Hugh wed Mary Blanchard that same year, he was an up-and-coming physician, scion of a prosperous family, well connected through marriage and friendship to a number of other socially elite families. Hugh and Mary lost their first three children to the yellow fever and measles. In June 1796 was born Hugh Lenox Hodge, their first child who would survive to adulthood; shortly before midnight on December 27, 1797, Charles followed Hugh Lenox. Almost seven months later, Dr. Hugh Hodge died, himself a victim of yellow fever.[2]

To support herself and her two sons, Mary Hodge initially drew a very modest income from a share in the wharf and warehouse that Andrew Hodge had purchased years earlier. That money, however, depended upon trade coming through the port of Philadelphia — an inheritance ruined by the policies of the Jefferson and Madison administrations that restricted European commerce in the run-up to the War of 1812. Even before that loss, Mary had been forced to rent out part of her home to boarders. Eventually retreating to one room on the third floor, she let out the remainder to a relative. She found temporary relief from this confined space by visiting family in Virginia and Massachusetts and then returned to Philadelphia, where she managed to secure a somewhat larger dwelling; but she had to move several times and continued to support herself in part by taking in boarders. As Paul Gutjahr has summed up, "Only

---

2. In telling the story of Hodge's life, I am heavily indebted to Paul C. Gutjahr, who graciously shared portions of his study on Hodge while it was in process. Happily the work is now out as Paul C. Gutjahr, *Charles Hodge: Guardian of American Orthodoxy* (New York: Oxford University Press, 2011). A. A. Hodge, *Life of Charles Hodge* (New York: Charles Scribner's Sons, 1880), 1-9.

months after his birth, Charles Hodge's birthright consisted mainly of considerable social standing but precious little economic means."[3]

But Mary Blanchard Hodge was a determined woman. Despite her poverty, she helped to organize the Female Association for the Relief of Widows and Single Women of Reduced Circumstances. The group sometimes met in her home, collected money and supplies, and distributed them to women in need. Thus Mary Hodge participated in the founding of one of the many women's voluntary societies that profoundly shaped religious life in the nineteenth century. She was also determined that Hugh and Charles receive a good education. They were drilled in the catechism and periodically examined by their pastor, Ashbel Green. Since there was no free public education system for all young people in Philadelphia, she paid to enroll the boys in various schools, which often consisted of a single individual offering lessons in his home. In 1810 she sent her sons to a classical academy in Somerville, New Jersey, where they could receive a good education at a rate cheaper than in Philadelphia. Somerville also offered the attraction that Hugh and Charles had nearby a well-to-do first cousin, John Bayard, who could "exercise parental care" over the boys. Mary's commitment to her sons' advancement was evident in the advice with which she peppered her letters. She urged them, for example, to cultivate the gentility that would draw the attention of men of high station. In fact, the family background of the young Hodges and their good behavior was already allowing them to mingle in influential society. In Somerville, Charles gained *entrée* to the Frelinghuysens, a wealthy family of Dutch ancestry with a history of contributions to religious, political, and civic life. Hodge began what he later called "a revering friendship" with Theodore Frelinghuysen, future senator from New Jersey and the running mate of presidential candidate Henry Clay on the losing Whig ticket in 1844.[4]

After Somerville, the Hodge boys moved to Princeton. Hugh entered college early in 1812 as a member of the sophomore class. Charles, needing to study Greek first, went to the Princeton Grammar School before admission in the fall, likewise as a sophomore. In Princeton the family reunited again. Mary Hodge concluded that it would be cheaper to live in the village of Princeton than in urban Philadelphia. Renting a house on Witherspoon Street just across from the college, Mary boarded not only

3. Hodge, *Life of Charles Hodge,* 9; Gutjahr, *Charles Hodge,* 21.
4. Hodge, *Life of Charles Hodge,* 9-15.

Hugh and Charles but also cousins who were attending Princeton. To supplement her precarious income further, she took in wash from neighbors. By 1813, the cousins had either graduated or moved into the college dorm, and a new family joined the household — the widowed Catherine Bache and her three children. Bache's husband William, a grandson of Benjamin Franklin, had been a Philadelphia physician, and she herself was the sister of Dr. Caspar Wistar, professor of anatomy at the University of Pennsylvania and former president of the American Philosophical Society. When Hugh finished his Princeton education in the fall of 1814, Mary Hodge thus had a double claim to attention when she wrote to Dr. Wistar to ask him to take on Hugh as an intern in medical training: not only had Mary's husband been a fellow physician and good friend of Dr. Wistar; his sister now lived with Mary. Then, too, as she sought to help Hugh and Charles forward in the world, Mary could rely on the fact that Princeton's new president was the former pastor who had catechized her boys years earlier and who even now sometimes stopped by for tea on Witherspoon Street. Even though she and her boys had fallen into straitened circumstances, Mary was able at crucial moments to parlay her social connections into tangible benefits for them. And one of the benefits would not become apparent for some years. Catherine Bache's oldest child, Sarah, a girl then fourteen, would be remembered much later by Hugh Lenox Hodge as "well-grown, in blooming health, handsome, full of imagination; and exceedingly enthusiastic." In 1822 she and Charles Hodge would wed.[5]

On August 12, 1812, Charles Hodge attended the inauguration of Archibald Alexander, later describing himself as "a boy of fourteen, lying at length on the rail of the gallery listening to the doctor's inaugural address and watching the ceremony of investiture." Shortly before this, Alexander had come to the grammar school and had seen Hodge struggling over Greek. After that, said Hodge, "he never failed to notice me when I crossed his path." Indeed, the seminary professor sometimes took Hodge with him when he went out to preach on Sundays, and their relationship had become sufficiently close by 1816 that Hodge accompanied him on a six-week trip to Virginia. One need not be a devotee of psychohistory to discern that the boy who lost his biological father as an infant had found in Alexander an equivalent — a fact to which Hodge witnessed when he named his first son Archibald Alexander Hodge in

5. Hodge, *Life of Charles Hodge,* 18, 28, 29.

1823. This relationship — "a cord never broken," Hodge called it — endured throughout the lives of both men.[6]

When Hodge entered the college in the fall, Green was launching his revanche against the Samuel Stanhope Smith era. While most of the curriculum remained unchanged, the tougher discipline, the required study in the Bible, and the reintroduction of Witherspoon's *Lectures on Moral Philosophy* represented a departure from Green's immediate predecessor. So, too, did the decision to hire tutors primarily from among graduates or current students at the seminary. Green's desire to make the college a nursery of piety was apparent in virtually every phase of the school's life, and he achieved his goal, at least for a short moment, when religious revival broke out among the students in 1815. One of the first to signal a profession of faith was Charles Hodge, who joined the First (now Nassau) Presbyterian Church adjoining the campus. In addition to a deepened religious conviction, Hodge was absorbing through Witherspoon's *Lectures* and also in texts on other topics the principles of the Common Sense philosophy. For example, in Hugh Blair's *Lectures on Rhetoric and Belles Lettres* (1783), read as a text at Princeton, Hodge learned the nature of taste, or "the power of receiving pleasure from the beauties of nature and of art." He learned that taste is an intuitive sense possessed by all people, but one capable of improvement by use and by education. Moreover, taste is not a mere subjective preference; there is a correctness of taste by which the men of understanding will reject "counterfeit beauties." For a season particular circumstances may degrade taste in vulgar or superficial ways, but over time "the genuine taste of human nature never fails to disclose itself and to gain the ascendant over any fantastic and corrupted modes of taste." Blair allowed that these distortions "may have currency for a while," but they always vanish by the end of the day and "that alone remains which is founded on sound reason and the native feelings of men." Thus in the end even matters of taste were universal, precise, and governed by truths as self-evident as those in the moral and religious world of John Witherspoon and Ashbel Green. Hodge's education taught him to view knowledge — indeed, reality itself — as tidy and ultimately unambiguous.[7]

6. Hodge, *Life of Charles Hodge*, 19.

7. Hodge, *Life of Charles Hodge*, 23, 30-31; Hugh Blair, *Lectures on Rhetoric and Belles Lettres* (Philadelphia: T. Ellwood Zell and Co., 1866 [1783]), 16, 21, 25. For additional information on the study of belles lettres at Princeton, see Darrell L. Guder, "The History of Belles Lettres at Princeton: An Investigation of the Expansion and Secularization of Cur-

By the time he finished college in 1815, his health had become tenuous. His mother persuaded him to take a year off from study and to return with her to Philadelphia. After a year of general reading, visiting a well-to-do cousin near Wilkes-Barre in Pennsylvania, and taking the trip to Virginia with Alexander, Hodge's health was improved; and he entered Princeton Seminary in the fall of 1816. In seminary, Alexander further undergirded the philosophic tendencies already absorbed at the college. He heard little of the German "transcendental" philosophy, Hodge later noted. Alexander taught them to examine "mental phenomena on the inductive method," urged the seminarians to read Locke for method, and strongly commended such stalwarts of the Common Sense philosophy as Thomas Reid and Dugald Stewart. Although Alexander used Francis Turretin for theological instruction, he did so "to cultivate in his students the spirit and habits of original investigation." In his final year at the school, uncertain about the direction of his ministry, Hodge discussed his perplexity with Alexander and jokingly put himself at his teacher's disposal. "I may shock you when I come to tell you what to do," replied Alexander. Several months later in another conference, his mentor asked him without warning, "How would you like to be a professor in the Seminary?" He then indicated that, the General Assembly having the power of appointment, he could promise nothing, that Hodge should for the moment say nothing, but that he should spend the coming year learning Hebrew in Philadelphia "with some competent instructor."[8]

After finishing at the seminary late in 1819, Hodge went back to Philadelphia to live with his mother, to study Hebrew, and to preach in various churches. The Presbytery of Philadelphia licensed him on October 20, 1819, the same day that it also granted a license to Samuel Cornish — the future pastor of the First Colored Presbyterian Church in New York, editor of *Freedom's Journal,* and associate of Princeton Seminary graduate Theodore S. Wright. In 1820, upon recommendation of the seminary faculty and the board of directors, the General Assembly acted, authorizing the professors of the seminary "to employ an assistant teacher of the original languages of Scripture."[9]

Although teaching positions then did not conform to the standard

---

riculum at the College of New Jersey with Special Reference to the Curriculum of the English Language and Letters" (Dissertation, University of Hamburg, 1965).

8. Hodge, *Life of Charles Hodge,* 49-50, 51, 63, 65.

9. Hodge, *Life of Charles Hodge,* 69, 75.

ranks of academe in the twenty-first century, Hodge was something comparable to what today would be called an instructor or assistant professor on term appointment. Ordained on the basis of regular pulpit supply in a nearby church, Hodge threw himself with energy into that responsibility and into his teaching. Though the work was satisfying, he clearly wished for something more permanent — and at a higher salary — especially since he wished to marry Sarah Bache. By 1822, efforts to secure the long-planned third professor in oriental and biblical literature were afoot. Both Miller and Alexander wanted Hodge for the post, but since the final decision on the matter rested with the General Assembly, neither they nor the seminary directors could make the final decision. Miller told Hodge that the Assembly would "be acting in the dark" about his appointment unless the young man did something to make himself better known. Miller suggested, with Alexander's concurrence, that Hodge should publish an address he had given in December 1821 to the Society for Improvement in Biblical Literature. Hodge followed their advice, and the essay appeared early in the following year.[10]

The idea was excellent, for the address was admirably suited to assure the Assembly that Hodge was a competent, orthodox man to whom the third professorship could be safely entrusted. Although a very general treatment within a relatively brief fifty-one pages, the essay gave evidence that he understood the basic issues to address and the appropriate scholars upon whom to call in teaching biblical criticism and interpretation. But while Hodge could enumerate matters of textual variation within the Bible and could cite learned authorities, he also made clear that no one need fear anything unsettling in his version of biblical criticism. "God," he insisted, "is the real author of the sacred scriptures." The most important requisites of a good interpreter were thus "piety and a firm conviction of the divine origin of the Scriptures." If there were any doubts, the article alleviated them, for on May 24, 1822, the General Assembly elected Charles Hodge professor of oriental and biblical literature at Princeton Seminary. With his position secure and with a sizable increase in salary on the way, Charles married Sarah Bache several weeks later.[11]

As he settled into his long-term responsibilities of teaching biblical languages, exegesis, and interpretation, Hodge also founded in 1825 *The*

---

10. Hodge, *Life of Charles Hodge*, 87.

11. Hodge, *Life of Charles Hodge*, 92-95; Charles Hodge, *Dissertation on the Importance of Biblical Literature* (Trenton: George Sherman, 1822), 24, 26.

Biblical Repertory. Initially intended as a medium for the reprinting and translating of essays in biblical scholarship, the journal underwent a couple of title changes before assuming in 1837 the one by which it would be remembered: *Biblical Repertory and Princeton Review,* a title indicating the broader purview of theological and learned topics that the mature journal addressed. Except for a period when Hodge was abroad (1826-1828), he would be its editor for forty-three years. Of the initial reprints, slightly under half dealt in one way or another with issues raised by European, especially German scholarship. Robert Bridges Patton, professor of Greek at the college, cooperated with Hodge as interpreter. He had studied at Göttingen and received a Ph.D. there, only the second American to receive a European doctorate. Patton's example reinforced Hodge's growing conviction that European scholarship posed a danger and opportunity for orthodoxy. American Christians needed to know and benefit from that scholarship in order to refute its excesses.[12]

Hodge's *Dissertation on the Importance of Biblical Literature* had already signaled ambivalence about German scholarship. Germany, he declared, was "unquestionably . . . the country which had been the most distinguished for its progress in biblical literature." Through their arduous labors, German scholars had discovered many "materials which the friends of religion may employ for the illustration and defence of the word of God." Unfortunately, that same country "has also been the most remarkable for the prevalence of false doctrines and the most irreverent treatment of the sacred scriptures." Whether the riches of this scholarship were worth the risk of its possibly bad effect on piety was a matter that all people needed to resolve for themselves. The question came down to two things: whether one was able to read the German biblical scholarship with "sufficient skill . . . to separate the poison from the food" and whether one brought the right attitude to the study of the Bible. If we come to the Bible, Hodge noted, "as we would enter God's presence, and read its pages as we would hear his voice," then all learning about Scripture will be of benefit. "But if we come to the scriptures, as to the works of men, without reverence, and without prayer, trusting in ourselves, our rules, or our learning, the result will be disastrous." In a word, the question was whether the benefit of German learning could be attained without losing one's faith.[13]

---

12. Hodge, *Life of Charles Hodge,* 98-101.
13. Hodge, *Dissertation on the Importance of Biblical Literature,* 43, 44, 47, 50.

Hodge concluded that it could, or at least that he had to make the effort. Feeling himself unprepared for his theological professorship, he needed to grapple directly with the new theological scholarship emanating from Europe — neology as it was sometimes called — and made a formal request for a leave of absence from the seminary. With some misgivings that he might be corrupted by his exposure, Miller and Alexander gave their endorsement; and the board of directors approved. Hodge arranged for Sarah and their two young children to go live in Philadelphia with family; and John Williamson Nevin, a recent graduate of the seminary and a figure with whom Hodge would later conduct a major theological debate, was engaged to teach Hodge's courses during his absence. In October 1826, he left for France.[14]

One gets an idea of the sensibility impelling Hodge's journey by contrasting his initial reactions to Europe with those of another American traveler in the same year. Henry Wadsworth Longfellow, offered a job as professor of modern languages at Bowdoin College, went to the continent in May 1826 to prepare himself for his work. In subsequent sketches of his travels, Longfellow described his encounter with the great cathedral in Rouen shortly after his debarkation at Le Havre:

> If it had suddenly risen from the earth, the effect could not have been more powerful and instantaneous. It completely overwhelmed my imagination; and I stood for a long time motionless, and gazing entranced upon the stupendous edifice. I had before seen no specimen of Gothic architecture, save the remains of a little church at Havre, and the massive towers before me — the lofty windows of stained glass — the low portal, with its receding arches and rude statues — all produced upon my untraveled mind an impression of awful sublimity. When I entered the church, the impression was still more deep and solemn. It was the hour of vespers. The religious twilight of the place — the lamps that burned on the distant altar — the kneeling crowd — the tinkling bell — and the chant of the evening service that rolled along the vaulted roof in broken and repeated echoes — filled me with new and intense emotions.

14. See Hodge, *Dissertation on the Importance of Biblical Literature*, 100-201, for an account of the trip with copious quotations from Hodge's letters. I have benefited in this and following paragraphs from the astute analysis of the trip in Gutjahr, *Charles Hodge*, 101-19.

And the description went on to include "shadowy aisles," "the figures of armed knights upon tombs," and the presence of "the cowled and solitary monk" — the net effect of all this being that Longfellow felt as if he had been "transported back to the Dark Ages."[15]

Shortly after Charles Hodge landed at Le Havre, he, too, went to the great cathedral at Rouen. In a letter to Archibald Alexander, he described his impressions. After noting that on Sunday afternoon he had worshipped with a small group of Scottish and English expatriates in the city, he observed:

> I felt rejoiced to hear the praise of God in a foreign land in my own language, and could not help contrasting the beauty and simplicity of the service, both morning and evening, with the service I had witnessed in the early part of the day in the great cathedral. This is said to be the finest Gothic structure in France, and certainly to an eye accustomed to the church in Princeton it is sufficiently imposing. I saw it first late in the evening, and on entering its "long-drawn aisles," lighted only here and there by a dim lamp which scarcely revealed the lofty roof, I did not wonder that such places were trod with awe. In the morning I found at least fifty priests and other religious officers engaged in chanting the service, and about two hundred persons, principally poor, kneeling or sitting in different parts of the building. No one appeared attending to what was going on, or at least few. This building is said to have been built by William the Conqueror. One of the towers is two hundred thirty-six feet high, and another much higher was destroyed a few years ago by lightning.[16]

One must make due allowance for the genres and circumstances of the two writings: Longfellow had prepared a series of well-honed travel sketches designed to establish himself as a man of letters; Hodge was dashing off a hasty note to a mentor. Yet even with these allowances, the contrast remains striking. Longfellow allowed himself to be swept along by the aesthetic appeal of the Gothic cathedral. The distant light on the altar, "the shadowy aisles," and "the cowled monk" fired an imagination

---

15. Henry Wadsworth Longfellow, *Outre-Mer, or A Pilgrimage to the Old World*, 2 vols. (London: Richard Bentley, 1835), 1:26.

16. Hodge, *Life of Charles Hodge*, 107-8.

carrying him back to the Middle Ages. Hodge, while sensing the impressive size and beauty of the cathedral and acknowledging that he "did not wonder that such places were trod with awe," experienced no flights of imagination. His tone was reportorial and matter of fact — instead of being "transported back" to the eleventh century, he provided a factual account about the height of the tower and the identity of the builder. Moreover, the worship that filled Longfellow with a sense of mystery seemed to Hodge an instance of few people, if any, paying attention to what was going on; and the service compared poorly to the "beauty and simplicity" of the Protestant gathering among the English-speaking *emigrés*. Part of Hodge's reserve undoubtedly derived from traditional Protestant suspicions of Catholicism, but it also had to do with something equally basic to Hodge's orientation to the world. He appreciated emotion, beauty, and the power of the sublime — particularly as evoked by awe-inspiring scenes in nature, as, for example, when he first caught sight of the Alps — but he was not about to be swept along by unanalyzed imagination or feeling. He would observe patiently, gather his facts, and then make balanced judgments. That approach would mark not only his perception of an old cathedral. It would shape what he got out of his European trip and the kind of theologian he was becoming.[17]

After the short stop in Rouen, Hodge moved on to Paris, where he stayed several months. He enrolled in classes at the University of Paris in order to study with Sylvestre de Sacy, then recognized as a leading expert on Near Eastern languages. Cramming as many classes as he could into his days, Hodge took copious notes on Hebrew, Syriac, and Arabic grammar. In Paris, he met Edward Robinson, a former pupil of Moses Stuart and a future American biblical scholar of considerable eminence. Robinson dissuaded Hodge from his original plan to go to Göttingen by arguing that its faculty was too liberal and its professors past their prime; Halle, he contended, was the better place to pursue biblical studies. On this advice, Hodge moved to Halle, where he roomed next to Robinson. In Halle, Hodge attended the lectures of Heinrich F. W. Gesenius, arguably the leading Hebraist of his era, and theologian Julius Wegscheider, both of whom were regarded as rationalists hostile to traditional faith. There, too, he met August Tholuck, who represented a mediating theological position. Newly appointed to the faculty and about Hodge's age,

---

17. On the context of Longfellow's work, see Thomas H. Pauly, "*Outre-Mer* and Longfellow's Quest for a Career," *New England Quarterly* 50 (March 1977): 30-52.

Tholuck became a good friend of the American, and the two corresponded intermittently for the rest of their lives. After several months in Halle, Hodge went on to Berlin, where he spent most of the remainder of his European time. There he became acquainted with a wide variety of other important figures in the religious world: Johann Neander, a church historian and a Jewish convert to Christianity under the influence of Friedrich Schleiermacher; Ernst W. Hengstenberg, editor of the militantly conservative *Evangelische Kirchenzeitung* and an up-and-coming biblical scholar who defended precritical views; Otto and Ludwig von Gerlach, members of a family closely allied to political and confessional conservatism; and Guillaume ("Billy") Monod, son of a Protestant family involved in the promotion of the nineteenth-century evangelical awakening in France. In the spring of 1828, Hodge began the trip home, traveling through Switzerland, France, and Great Britain. Taking passage from Liverpool on August 1, he finally returned to Princeton in mid-September, after nearly two years away.

What had the trip meant for Hodge and his sense of vocation? Clearly he had begun to appreciate that German theology was not monolithic. Some, such as Gesenius and Wegscheider, though incredibly learned, were clearly opposed to significant parts of traditional faith, but others, such as Hengstenberg and the Gerlachs, stoutly defended the tradition. Others, such as Tholuck and Neander, adopted mediating stances. Perhaps equally significant, Hodge's personal encounter with some of the giants of European scholarship brought them down to ordinary size. When, for example, he first met Gesenius, Hodge was struck by the "frivolous . . . rather foppish appearance" of a 40-something man with "a silly laugh." Later he rendered a more positive estimate when he heard Gesenius lecture, but at one level the first impression remained: the man with the supposedly god-like knowledge had very mortal frailties. Perhaps even more significant, as Paul Gutjahr contends, Hodge had held his own in the company of his new friends and acquaintances and no longer seemed to have the nagging sense of unpreparedness or inferiority that had prompted him to go to Europe.[18]

Hodge did develop at least a marginal tolerance for ideas that once he might have scorned. Tholuck provides a case in point. Tholuck, whose friendship he always treasured and whose picture Hodge placed in his study near the end of his life, exhibited an intellectual eclecticism.

18. Hodge, *Life of Charles Hodge*, 115, 116; Gutjahr, *Charles Hodge*, 120.

"He was," his student Philip Schaff wrote, "original, fresh, brilliant, suggestive, eloquent, and full of poetry, wit and humor. He cannot be classed with any school. He was influenced by Pietism, Moravianism, Schleiermacher, Neander, and even Hegel." In Hodge's letters home one catches glimpses of this facet of Tholuck and of Hodge trying to make sense of it all. In one communication, he noted that Tholuck believed "that the pantheistic philosophy of the day was doing good inasmuch as it led men to entertain a 'deep religious feeling,' and showed them the insufficiency of neological systems." Tholuck also contended that while Schleiermacher and many other German theologians had pantheistic tendencies — they believed "that the material universe and the soul of man are of the divine essence" — they nevertheless affirmed the personality of God and the individuality of the human soul. He also argued that Schleiermacher was "an instrument of great usefulness, partly without designing it, or in a way which he did not contemplate. His authority stands so high that the respect he manifests for the Bible, and the reverence with which he speaks of Jesus Christ, has great influence. He has thus been the means of awakening the attention to religion of many young men." Hodge seemed much less appreciative of Schleiermacher. When Tholuck read "several passages" from the Berlin theologian, Hodge wrote, "they seemed to me to darken counsel by words without wisdom." Later, after hearing Schleiermacher preach, the reaction was similar: "The sermon was peculiar. The words were Biblical, but the whole tenor so general, the ideas so vague and indefinite, that it was impossible for me to understand exactly what he meant."[19]

In Germany Hodge encountered a type of thought he often found difficult to appreciate. If the theologian, like Tholuck, manifested a deep piety for Christ, Hodge could appreciate his learning and his faith. But clearly Hodge was not entirely comfortable with this sort of theology. After Tholuck had made the case that even pantheistic thought might, in the German context, be leading in a good direction, Hodge privately demurred, thinking it "a great misfortune that philosophy is mixed up with religion in this country, for it gives so abstruse and mystical a character to the explanation of important truths. . . . Thus, for example, they make

---

19. Hodge, *Life of Charles Hodge*, 120, 122, 123, 152; *New Schaff-Herzog Encyclopedia of Religious Knowledge*, ed. Samuel Macauley Jackson, 12 vols. (New York: Funk and Wagnalls, 1911), 11:420-21. Schaff's piece on Tholuck appears to have been edited by his son, D. S. Schaff.

faith to be the development of the life of God in the soul — that is — the divine essence everywhere diffused and the universal agent unfolding itself in the heart." On balance, German theology blurred too many distinctions Hodge thought important — it was too mystical, as he put it — to render a clear statement of the faith once delivered to the saints.[20]

Hodge's new theological self-confidence manifested itself in his reshaping of the journal he had founded. In the decades ahead, what would become known as the *Princeton Review* would no longer offer mere translations of previous biblical scholarship. With a much wider purview, the quarterly — now run by a self-styled "association of gentlemen" — would provide original essays on a wide variety of theological, cultural, ecclesiastical, and sometimes political issues. Although all of the "gentlemen" would serve as a board of editors, approving each essay published, Hodge would be the *Review*'s workhorse, editing most of the articles and writing many himself. With the *Review* as his special organ and with the self-assurance his two years of special training in Europe had conferred, Hodge was about to become, in E. Brooks Holifield's phrase, "the professional, the theologian who tackled just about every big aspect of the nineteenth century. . . . Hodge exemplified the nascent ideal of the professional theologian as an incisive and broad ranging thinker able to comment on any question of theology that might arise."[21]

Joseph Addison Alexander

If Hodge typified the wide range of the seminary theologian, Joseph Addison Alexander (1809-1860) illustrated this trait and another as well. Like Hodge, he had an extraordinary grasp of a wide variety of subjects and information, and particularly in the *Princeton Review* his essays covered a wide field. But his particular forte was his command of languages, ancient and modern, which allowed him to become Princeton Seminary's most significant biblical commentator prior to the Civil War. In a word, Joseph Addison Alexander offered an early hint of the way in which the seminary faculty would become the home of the highly spe-

---

20. Hodge, *Life of Charles Hodge,* 122.

21. E. Brooks Holifield, "Hodge, the Seminary, and the American Theological Context," in *Charles Hodge Revisited: A Critical Appraisal of His Life and Work,* ed. John W. Stewart and James H. Moorhead (Grand Rapids: Eerdmans, 2002), 128.

cialized scholar. There were countervailing trends to specialization in nineteenth-century Princeton, but Alexander's career set a trajectory in that direction.[22]

Born in 1809, the third son of Archibald and Janetta Alexander, Addison — as his family usually called him (or "Addy" when he was a boy) — was something of a prodigy. He was reading not long after the family moved to Princeton when he was 3; and as he recognized English words, his father often gave him slips of paper with Latin equivalents so that the boy was learning the two together. Eventually his extraordinary facility in languages allowed him to master more than twenty tongues. As a reader he was voracious. Even cast-off books tossed in the attic by the Alexanders became treasures to the young boy. Years later he recalled the excitement upon discovering in that garret Francis Lathom's Gothic potboiler *The Midnight Bell* with its ample supply of blood and horror. Yet he also found delight in Bunyan's *Pilgrim's Progress,* which, at about age 6, he read to the family's cook while providing his own commentary. Recognizing his precocity, Archibald and Janetta encouraged his self-culture and allowed him to postpone formal education until around age 8 or 9, when he began attending a classical school in town. Then came private tutorials in French (later Greek) with seminarian Robert Baird, and further lessons with him after Baird finished at the seminary and, for a time, ran his own school in Princeton.[23]

The freedom of the early portion of Addison's education allowed him to develop his interests to the fullest extent, but it also fostered a semi-monastic, solitary way of life whose effects permanently molded the young man's character. As an adult, he was ill-disposed to social amenities. With a few good friends and with children, he could and did unbend. Otherwise he usually shunned society. A bachelor until his death, he very nearly approximated the popular caricature of the total scholar, one whose highly structured life was disciplined toward the goal of maximum intellectual effort.

22. For general information about Joseph Alexander and his scholarship, see Henry C. Alexander, *The Life of Joseph Addison Alexander,* 2 vols. (New York: Charles Scribner, 1870); Marion Ann Taylor, *The Old Testament in the Old Princeton School, 1812-1929* (San Francisco: Mellen Research University Press, 1992), 89-166; and James H. Moorhead, "Joseph Addison Alexander: Common Sense, Romanticism and Biblical Criticism at Princeton," *Journal of Presbyterian History* 53 (Spring 1975): 51-66. Henry C. Alexander was the nephew of Joseph Addison Alexander.

23. Alexander, *Life of Joseph Addison Alexander,* 1:1-60.

Addison Alexander entered the junior class at the college in 1824, graduating two years later with highest honors. Where he would go professionally was unclear. Archibald hinted at his son's lack of clarity and at an emotional wall that even a father could not breach. Archibald wrote to his sister on the occasion of Addison's graduation, describing his son's academic achievements and the fact that he had delivered the valedictory address. "But to what use he will apply his learning and eloquence," Alexander remarked, "I know not. Probably he will be a lawyer and politician. His views on the subject of religion are known only to himself. He is so reserved that nobody attempts to draw him out." In fact, Addison made no immediate move toward a career or toward further defining his religious views. After his graduation, he lived at home for several years, continuing his wide-ranging studies and writing articles for papers and journals under pseudonyms. The breadth of his reading may be gauged by several entries in his journal during early 1829, when he was perusing works on church history, Arabic literature, Don Quixote in Spanish, Aristophanes, Chaucer, Dante, Spenser, and Shakespeare. His articles included brief discussions of contemporary events and politics, an essay on Persian poetry, exotic stories, and verses sometimes modeled on the themes of Byron's "Childe Harold." What his diverse writings said about his actual views and commitments is uncertain. "He loved," said his biographer, "to wear a literary mask, and to mystify his readers in every ingenious manner possible. It was also well known that he was fond of espousing sentiments which were at once novel and hard to defend." Perhaps he was also experimenting with these literary masks as a way of determining for himself a professional and personal identity.[24]

In 1829, Addison Alexander began to define that identity more clearly. He took a teaching position at the newly formed Edgehill School, and a year later he went back to the College of New Jersey as a tutor or adjunct in ancient languages and literature. With the assumption of a full-time job, and having moved out of his parents' home, Alexander confronted the issue of religious commitment. Although he had always attended church activities with regularity and had never given any indication of disbelief, he had not professed that quickening of the spirit so central to the piety in which he had been reared. In early 1830 he wrestled with a sense of deep religious inadequacy, much of which apparently involved his literary and intellectual interests. In January he recorded: "In-

---

24. Alexander, *Life of Joseph Addison Alexander,* 1:61-96; quotations from 93, 109.

tellectual enjoyment has been my idol heretofore. . . . I have indulged my imagination formerly too much. It must be mortified." Or again in March: "I have had something of a struggle today between my literary lusts, so to speak, and a sense of duty. I firmly believe, from experience as well as testimony, that an exclusive devotion to intellectual pursuits is one of the worst enemies with which the renewed soul has to grapple."[25]

As his spiritual state oscillated between hope and despair, Alexander, like his father before him, was eventually inclined to view his despondent moments as partly the result of melancholy. When Thomas Halyburton's *Memoirs* (1715) fell into his hands, Alexander felt that he had discovered a soul mate whose struggles paralleled his own. A Church of Scotland minister and the son of a minister, Halyburton had an experience similar to Alexander's, or so the latter thought: "Both minister's sons, and both ministers of the same communion — both guarded, in any unusual degree, by circumstances from exterior temptation — both outwardly exemplary, inwardly corrupt — both led to seek religion by distress." From Halyburton he learned the importance of *immediate* confession of sin. Failure to do so was to doubt the sufficiency of Christ's atonement and to fall into a subtle works righteousness, assuming that one's resistance to temptation, rather than the merits of Christ, constituted the grounds of spiritual security. Or as Alexander stated what he had discovered in Halyburton:

> To distrust the extent of . . . [God's] forgiving mercy through Jesus Christ, therefore, is an insult. It is in vain that the sinner talks about his unworthiness and the greatness of his sins. Poor wretch — if God thought of your unworthiness you might well despair; but it is to glorify Himself that He invites you! You may be sure, therefore, that He will receive you. This is an humbling but delightful doctrine.[26]

Addison Alexander had made his own a piety stressing the utter unworthiness of every person and emphasizing salvation as the free gift of God in Christ. Once he had resolved these issues, Alexander, like his father, was reticent to speak about his inner life. He, in company with other Princeton professors, stressed the importance of piety — what else were the Sunday afternoon conferences about? But unlike many forms of

25. Alexander, *Life of Joseph Addison Alexander*, 1:222.
26. Alexander, *Life of Joseph Addison Alexander*, 1:257, 258.

evangelicalism popular at the time, the Princeton version did not dwell on testimonies about one's own experience but chose instead to stress the objective grounds on which faith rested. Yet the formative power of his experience was apparent when, after his ordination some years later, Addison Alexander again and again wove the themes of this piety into the sermons that he preached.[27]

During his time of spiritual turmoil, Alexander concluded that his imagination and intellectual enjoyments needed to be mortified. In a sense they were, for most of his subsequent studies and literary productions had to do directly with biblical and other religious research. And yet the side of Alexander that as a boy had thrilled to Lathom's *The Midnight Bell* and as an adult loved Byron or took pleasure in literary elegance for its own sake was not so much abandoned as it was disciplined and restricted in its expression. Particularly among children of friends and family, he often reverted to playful fancy. For the young Caspar Wistar Hodge, the son of Charles and Sarah, he wrote assorted fables that he stitched by hand into volumes labeled *Wistar's Magazine*. An occasional Persian nature poem still found its way into his mature correspondence. After a trip to Europe, he spoke to his friends of the magnificent chorales, chants, and masses that he had heard in ornate Gothic cathedrals. To his family he admitted that the aesthetic appeal of a church choir in Rome had nearly overcome him. Yet his nephew added that, in print, Alexander "sedulously suppressed all outbursts of feeling" when he discussed his trips. Like Hodge encountering the cathedral in Rouen, Addison Alexander was not about to allow any feelings inspired by the exotic, the sublime, or the ancient to run riot. The imagination needed to be kept in bounds. His emotions may have resembled Longfellow's at the Rouen cathedral, but he would try to write about them more like Hodge.[28]

Alexander's trip to Europe, begun in 1833 after he had resigned his tutorship at the college, took him to England, France, Switzerland, Italy, and Germany. He met many of the same people whom Hodge had encountered several years earlier: Tholuck, Neander, and Hengstenberg. Very shortly before Schleiermacher's death, Alexander heard the famous German theologian preach. With regard to all these men, Alexander appears to have felt the greatest affinity for Hengstenberg. By contrast,

27. See, for example, Joseph Addison Alexander, *Sermons* (New York: Charles Scribner, 1860).

28. Alexander, *Life of Joseph Addison Alexander*, 26, 163-64.

Neander seemed to him too permissive. In an 1837 article in the *Princeton Review,* Alexander stated his comparison of the two succinctly:

> Neander and Hengstenberg are now acknowledged as the heads of parties, both evangelical in our sense of the term, but the latter [is] very strict, the former very lax, with respect to the diversity in sentiment and the proper course of conduct toward unbelievers. Neander looks upon all forms of error, involving any truth, as peculiar developments of mind and spirit, which are not to be coerced, but will, if properly controlled and guided, all come right at last. Hengstenberg maintains that religious truth is clearly revealed in a positive [i.e., a given, revealed] form, and must be definitely held on the authority of scripture.[29]

Alexander's assessment is illuminating as a clue to his own position. He felt that the "lax" view insufficiently protected the changeless verities of the Christian revelation; and although he honored the basic soundness of Neander's sympathies, his praise was lukewarm. On first hearing Neander, he wrote: "I take this opportunity to say that I have been agreeably disappointed." By contrast, of Alexander's view of Hengstenberg, his nephew wrote: "while he [Alexander] never yielded himself up to the slavish guidance of any teacher; he yet held this great scholar in the most exalted estimation." Alexander admired the tough-minded way in which Hengstenberg refuted naturalistic interpretations of biblical prophecies and miracles. But Hengstenberg was not ignorant of or naïve about the new learning. At one time a rationalist himself and trained by some of the Continent's best scholars, he used the philological tools of the new scholarship to defend traditional views. T. K. Cheyne, a late-nineteenth-century British biblical scholar, aptly described Hengstenberg's use of the new critical tools "as a brave attempt to save the citadel of orthodoxy at the cost of some of its outworks." That would be in general an accurate description of Alexander's program also, and it was appropriate that Cheyne called Addison Alexander an American disciple of Hengstenberg.[30]

Shortly after returning to America, Joseph Addison Alexander began

---

29. [Joseph Addison Alexander,] "Gleanings from the German Periodicals," *Biblical Repertory and Princeton Repertory and Princeton Review* 9 (1837): 199.

30. Alexander, *Life of Joseph Addison Alexander,* 1:327; T. K. Cheyne, *Founders of Old Testament Criticism* (London: Methuen and Company, 1893), 130, 131.

his career at Princeton Seminary in 1834, teaching biblical and oriental literature. First as an assistant to Charles Hodge (at the time still teaching biblical studies) and soon as a professor in his own right, the young Alexander quickly established a fearsome reputation among students, both for his prodigious learning and for his manner. He darted in the door at the last minute at the beginning of the class hour, lectured at a furious pace, and departed so quickly afterwards that students, still frantically writing to capture all his notes, looked up to see that he had gone. Even his nephew admitted that Alexander readily voiced "severe and unforbearing reproofs and sarcasms in class," especially to those he deemed lazy or pretentious. A student who called upon Alexander in his study discovered, when he overstayed a visit or strayed from its purpose, "that his absence would be very pleasant" to the professor. If staring at the floor, drumming his fingers on the chair, or whistling did not convey the message, Alexander simply turned to his desk and resumed work. That work, aside from an impressive number of essays for the *Princeton Review* (nearly eighty articles in twenty-six years), consisted chiefly of a series of biblical commentaries: on Isaiah (1846 and 1847), the Psalms (1850), Acts (1856), Mark (1858), and Matthew (1860).[31]

Alexander's scholarly life started about the time that German biblical scholarship gave the orthodox world a new shock in D. F. Strauss's *Life of Jesus* (1835), which dismissed most New Testament traditions about Jesus as mythic trappings. Addison Alexander penned a scathing review of the work. The "infidel theology," he said, "appears to have reached its consummation." Citing Tholuck, he saw that one work as having brought together "all the skepticism and unbelief of the age." Yet despite his fears concerning the direction of German critical scholarship, he was grateful for the vast erudition that it had amassed. When, for example, Gesenius's Hebrew lexicon was translated into English, Alexander welcomed the book as a significant contribution to biblical scholarship, despite the German's skeptical attitude toward orthodoxy. Alexander urged the necessity of learning from the labors of the European critics, even those with whom one disagreed profoundly. "The very fact," he explained,

> that neological propensities have led the scholars of that country
> to plow up the whole field for themselves and to examine every

---

31. For a list of J. A. Alexander's articles in the *Princeton Review* after 1843, see Alexander, *Life of Joseph Addison Alexander,* 2:865-67.

clod and pebble with a microscopic scrutiny, makes it certain that they must have turned up something. . . . The true course with respect to German labours and researches is not to look away from them or cover them with dust, but to seize upon their valuable products and convert them to our own use in the very face and teeth of those who after bringing them to light are often utterly unable to dispose of them.[32]

In his commentary on the prophecies of Isaiah, Alexander offered one of his most succinct evaluations of the radical critics. They erred, not because they were too critical or scholarly, but because they failed to adhere to those criteria. Their position was, he said, "to use a favourite expression of their own, *unkritisch* and *unwissenschaftlich,* i.e., neither critical nor scientific." To the critics' assumption that they brought an impartial spirit to the investigation of the Bible, Alexander retorted that they had smuggled an assumption into their work before they ever started. It was virtually a "foregone conclusion" that no event could be explained by way of divine inspiration or supernatural intervention; contrary evidence was discounted in advance. What paraded as scientific method possessed no settled principle except an amorphous "critical *Gefühl*," or feeling, that "the general presumption is against the truth and authenticity of everything traditional or ancient and in favor of whatever can by any means be substituted for it." A sane biblical criticism would not adhere slavishly to tradition, but it would give the benefit of the doubt to long-established views simply because their currency "shows how many minds" have been convinced of their truth. "Countervailing evidence" might indeed overturn the traditional, but only on compelling grounds. The essential difference between Alexander's view of a proper biblical criticism and that of the more radical German figures was the "same as that between the principle of English jurisprudence, that a person accused is to be reckoned innocent until he is proved guilty and the rule adopted by the criminal proceedings of some other nations that he ought to be held guilty till he proves his innocence."[33]

What, then, if anything did Alexander gain from the new scholar-

---

32. Alexander, "Gleanings," 198; Alexander, "Robinson's Gesenius," *Biblical Repertory and Princeton Review* 9 (January 1837): 88-101; Alexander, "Kitto's Cyclopædia of Biblical Literature," *Biblical Repertory and Princeton Review* 18 (October 1846): 561-62.

33. Joseph Addison Alexander, *The Prophecies of Isaiah,* 2 vols. (New York: Charles Scribner, 1870 [1846-1847]), 15, 24.

ship? He certainly acquired a matchless knowledge of the issues involved in the close textual study of the Bible — what is often called the lower criticism. He also sometimes handled creatively, even when he could not accept, the views of the higher criticism. His treatment of the prophecies in Isaiah offers a case in point. As one would expect, he rejected out of hand arguments that material from someone other than the prophet — someone presumed to be from a much later period — was incorporated into Isaiah's text. Alexander was referring especially to the later chapters (40 and afterwards) that dealt with predictions of the restoration of the Jewish people following the captivity in Babylon. On the other hand, he showed discomfort with the ways in which many orthodox interpreters had handled those "later prophecies." Treating them as having reference "throughout to the new dispensation and the Christian church," these exegetes opened the way to "an illimitable field of conjecture and invention . . . without any settled rule to guide or control" them. The result was to open the floodgates to all sorts of "extravagant conclusions" that could not be clearly demonstrated from the text. Alexander even expressed doubt about his mentor Hengstenberg's theory that these prophecies might have a double fulfillment: a "nearer and more remote realization of the same prophetic picture. . . . So that, for example, the deliverance [of the Jewish people] from Babylon by Cyrus insensibly merges into a greater deliverance from sin and ruin by Christ." Alexander feared that such theories might lead away from a careful study of the text and that a "general hypothesis or scheme" might lead to "a forced and artificial exegesis."[34]

In his New Testament research, Addison Alexander sometimes took issue with traditional interpretations as well as some of the newer critical theories. Stressing the literary integrity of each of the Gospels, he rejected German scholars' efforts to uncover a single primary source to which existing books might be reduced. He also developed serious reservations about a favorite project of orthodox commentators — the so-called gospel harmony, which purported to unify all the events of Jesus' life and all his sayings into one continuous chronological narrative. Noting the diversity among these harmonies, Alexander commented:

> The reason why this vast disparity and endless contradiction of harmonies need not shake the faith or trouble the composure of

34. Alexander, *The Prophecies of Isaiah*, 67-69.

the mere reader or spectator, is that he can often see from his position as such, what the harmonists are blind to, namely, that one grand result of all their labours is to make it highly probable, if not to prove, that these four books were never meant to be reduced to one, but to remain ever side by side, as four great pictures of the same great object, but with something peculiar to each, and no more admitting of amalgamation than so many literal paintings upon a canvass can be made perfect by being cut to pieces and then glued together.

Alexander was manifesting a deep respect for the literary integrity of each of the Gospels; and, while recognizing broad agreements and continuities among them, he believed that they should not be homogenized.[35]

Similarly, Alexander recognized the importance of understanding the Bible historically. "The Bible does not merely contain history, and that in large quantities," he wrote; "it is itself a history." To understand Scripture correctly, one must allow its historical narratives to illuminate the more discursive passages, "the historical scriptures . . . [being] more absolutely necessary to correct interpretation of the others, than the others are to it." Alexander's emphasis upon the historic portions of the Bible over its didactic parts and his respect for the diversities among the Gospels *could,* at least *in theory,* have led away from the assumption that theology was capable of being stated in a set of propositions or in a system of doctrine. In fact, Alexander made a potentially revolutionary claim: "Considered as a whole, . . . the word of God is not a prophecy, a prayer-book, or a system of doctrine, but a history in which all these elements are largely comprehended." Beyond such assertions lay, of course, the far more radical claim of many of the biblical critics that all human culture and artifacts — including the Bible and the Christian tradition — were the products of historical development. Neither Scripture nor any system of theology could thus provide truths uncontaminated by the flow of time. Genuine change and substantial historical development had, in this view, occurred both within the Bible itself and within subsequent Christian tradition. This assumption undergirded the work of those whom Alexander rejected as neologists, and he had no desire to enter their dangerous land. What is remarkable, however, is that at least

35. [Joseph A. Alexander,] "Harmonies of the Gospels," *Princeton Review* 28 (July 1856): 394.

on occasion his own biblical scholarship led him to skirt the border of the forbidden territory.[36]

Judged against what became the mainstream of American biblical scholarship by the end of the nineteenth century, Addison Alexander appears timid and conservative in his response to the critical method. By the standards of pre–Civil War America, however, he ranked among a handful of pioneering figures. He merits comparison to Moses Stuart, who in 1810 began a long career at Andover Seminary as professor of biblical studies. Stuart taught himself Hebrew, Arabic, and Syriac in order to be better prepared for his work. He also learned German through reading Johann Eichhorn's works. Despite the fear of the Andover trustees that German biblical criticism was inherently hostile to faith, Stuart pushed ahead in the confidence that this scholarship could be turned to the defense of orthodoxy. In fact, his views seldom strayed far from the traditional, his defense of the Mosaic authorship of the Pentateuch being a case in point. Edward Robinson, the former student of Stuart whom Hodge had met on his European trip, also provided a parallel to Alexander. Linked to the German academic community by marriage, Robinson translated many Continental works into English, but remained highly skeptical of the more radical claims of the neologists. He first pursued his career at Andover, subsequently as an independent scholar, and finally at Union Seminary in New York. His major scholarly achievement was a careful firsthand study of the topography of the Holy Land, which was published as *Biblical Researches in Palestine, Mount Sinai and Arabia Petraea* (1841) — a multivolume work that laid the foundation for later work in the region's historical geography. Of these three scholars, Robinson undoubtedly did the most original work and was one of the few nineteenth-century Americans to receive serious recognition on the Continent, Albrecht Alt later hailing his contributions. But at the end of the day, the similarities among Alexander, Stuart, and Robinson were greater than the differences. All three were profoundly conversant with the latest Continental biblical scholarship, sought to appropriate its benefits, and worked to refute what they deemed its excesses. They may be justly seen as founders of modern biblical scholarship in American theological education.[37]

36. [Joseph A. Alexander,] "The Historical Scriptures," *Princeton Review* 26 (July 1854): 484.

37. On these various figures, see Jerry Wayne Brown, *The Rise of Biblical Criticism in America, 1800-1870* (Middletown, CT: Wesleyan University Press, 1969).

In view of the strides that Addison Alexander had made in the field of biblical scholarship, the board of directors and General Assembly made an extraordinary request of him in 1851. For the previous two years, his brother James W. Alexander had served as professor of ecclesiastical history and church government — the position that Samuel Miller had held. But James was never fully happy in that capacity. Despite the strongly intellectual bent that he shared with his father and brother, he soon longed to return to the pastoral life. "I did not leave pastoral life willingly," he wrote shortly after beginning his professorship. "I foresaw the very evils I begin to feel; but they distress me more than I reckoned for. I miss my old women; and especially my weekly catechumens, my sick-rooms, my rapid walks, and my nights of . . . fatigue." When James did accept a pastoral call, Joseph Addison Alexander was asked to assume a redefined position as professor of biblical and ecclesiastical history. Despite profound misgivings, Addison Alexander felt that he could not resist a legitimate call, and he accepted. Though he threw himself into the new work with his customary energy, it ultimately proved frustrating to him, and he was delighted when in 1859 the seminary transferred him to the chair of Hellenistic and New Testament literature. Unfortunately, he had little time to develop this new chair. In 1860, Joseph A. Alexander died.[38]

The Nature of Professionalization in Early-Nineteenth-Century Princeton

The curious episode of Joseph Addison Alexander's changing chairs reveals something significant about the nature of the professionalization of theological education at Princeton. By today's standards, professors moved about the curriculum to an amazing degree. The changes resembled a cabinet reshuffle, with a president or a prime minister moving the same people around to different posts and sometimes reconfiguring the portfolios as well. Many examples abound. Archibald Alexander began in the field of didactic and polemical theology; in 1840 his responsibilities shifted to pastoral and polemical theology. At the same time, Charles Hodge, having been responsible for oriental and biblical literature, as-

---

38. John Hall, ed., *Forty Years' Familiar Letters of James W. Alexander,* 2 vols. (New York: Charles Scribner, 1860), 2:107; Alexander, *Life of Joseph Addison Alexander,* 2:698.

sumed the task of didactic theology for which he is most remembered. The young William Henry Green, who will recur later in these pages with a chapter devoted to his labors, began his seminary career teaching languages from 1846 to 1849, and then, after a brief pastorate, returned in 1851 to assume the post of oriental and biblical literature that Joseph Alexander was vacating to take on biblical and ecclesiastical history. When Joseph Alexander moved toward Hellenistic and New Testament studies in 1859, then Green was given unambiguous priority in the Old Testament field when his title was changed. Following the death of Joseph Addison Alexander in 1860, Caspar Wistar Hodge, who had been his friend and protégé since Hodge's childhood, returned to Princeton for a New Testament assignment. Called to the seminary in 1854, Alexander Taggart McGill first assumed responsibilities in pastoral theology, church government, and homiletics. By 1861, that position, while keeping history as part of the description, had been slightly altered to accommodate the appointment of James C. Moffatt, whose professorship was labeled simply church history.

One easily gets lost in these changes of job description, and several observations are in order to put this seeming game of academic musical chairs into perspective. Professionalization at Princeton Seminary did not mean that one picked a single part of theological learning and cultivated it extensively without much thought as to how it intersected the broader enterprise. Professionalization meant in the first instance, as Holifield would have it, the "ideal of the professional theologian as an incisive and broad ranging thinker able to comment on any question of theology that might arise." Yet it was also clear that shifts of portfolio worked better in some cases than others. For Hodge, the transfer from biblical studies to systematic theology placed him in what he — and others — perceived as his true calling. On the other hand, Joseph Addison Alexander transferred into ecclesiastical history out of a sense of duty more than joy. Although he threw himself into the task with his usual academic gusto, his reluctance sometimes could not be hidden. One former student later recalled thinking that Alexander "himself was never satisfied with this [i.e., the church history] department, and was even in our day anxious to get rid of it." Also, professionalization did not mean that positions were filled solely on the basis of impersonal, objective standards. To an extraordinary degree, the faculty was a network of family and kin. While this in-bred quality undoubtedly made for continuity of institutional self-understanding, it also had the potential to stultify. The relative lack of pastoral experience by both Charles Hodge and Joseph Addison Alexander also indicated another dimension of the professionalization of theological education. Both were ardent churchmen and filled pulpits, but the world of the study and the classroom seemed more their home than the day-to-day life of the pastorate. As Princeton took the first steps toward this kind of professionalization, it was setting in motion dynamics that would have long-term repercussions.[39]

39. Alexander, *Life of Joseph Addison Alexander,* 2:810.

CHAPTER FIVE

Princeton and the Presbyterian Schism of 1837

WHEN Princeton Seminary was founded, it was then the only seminary sponsored by the denomination as a whole. By 1835, there were five other Presbyterian seminaries — Auburn in upstate New York, Western (eventually Pittsburgh) Theological Seminary, Lane in Ohio, Columbia in South Carolina, and a school founded in Indiana that eventually would move to Chicago and become known as McCormick. In October of that year, a meeting was held that led to the formation of Union Theological Seminary in New York City. Although these schools were Presbyterian, they were created in different ways, some through synods or presbyteries and others through unofficial sponsorship by groups that were Presbyterian. Princeton still had claims to preeminence among Presbyterian seminaries but no monopoly.[1]

The growing number of seminaries had partly to do with convenience. The country was rapidly expanding westward, and many wished to have their theological training closer to home. The proliferation of seminaries also became entangled with theological differences emerging among Presbyterians. Two parties — commonly called New School and Old School — had emerged in the 1820s. By the 1830s, they were openly feuding for control of the Presbyterian Church. To a considerable extent, Lane Seminary in Ohio had New School sympathies; Auburn and Union in New York were decidedly New School. Theologically, there is no question Princeton's sympathies lay with the Old School. On the other

1. Robert T. Handy, *A History of Union Theological Seminary in New York* (New York: Columbia University Press, 1987), 1-23.

hand, as the school of the entire denomination, Princeton wished to exercise a moderating influence so as to prevent schism. As passions grew more heated, Princeton sometimes felt that it was in a no-man's-land between hostile parties. When push came to shove and division became inevitable, Princeton cast its lot wholeheartedly with the Old School. It was a fateful decision, shaping the identity of the school profoundly for decades to come.[2]

A History of Cooperation and Contention

The battle in which the seminary became embroiled had its most distant source in the complicated history of cooperation and disagreement that had marked the relationship between Congregationalists and Presbyterians. Congregationalists, largely from England, settled initially in New England after 1630. Presbyterians, some from England but even more from Ireland and Scotland, came in force in the eighteenth century and made their homes initially in the middle Atlantic from Pennsylvania to Virginia. The two groups disagreed over polity, Congregationalists distrusting the Presbyterian subjection of the local church to higher ecclesiastical authority. They also had memories of religious struggles in England, Scotland, and Ireland that had made them sometime foes as well as allies. Yet, differences notwithstanding, these groups often understood themselves as adherents of a common or at least similar tradition. The fate of the Westminster Confession of Faith provides a case in point. Drafted in the 1640s as the work of an English assembly with Scottish advisors, the confession eventually became the official creed of Scottish, Irish, and American Presbyterians. Although never adopted in England, Westminster did serve as a model in important respects for the Savoy Declaration (1658) of English Congregationalism, and its central tenets were reaffirmed by New England Congregationalists at the Reforming Synod of 1680 and the Saybrook Platform (1708). Congregationalism and Presbyterianism often appeared as variants of a common theological tradition. In fact, the precise boundary between the two was sometimes hard to determine. For example, the first American presbytery, orga-

2. In the paragraphs that follow, I draw upon my essay "'The Restless Spirit of Radicalism': Old School Fears and the Schism of 1837," *Journal of Presbyterian History* 78 (Spring 2000): 19-33.

nized in Philadelphia in 1706, had several members from Congregationalist New England; and the uncertain degree of authority the presbytery exercised over its ministers and congregations has led some to suggest that it was possibly more like a Congregationalist ministerial association than a presbytery as we know it today. On the other hand, Connecticut Congregationalists in the Saybrook Platform opted for connectional structures — consociations of churches — that looked to some suspiciously like presbyteries.[3]

Given the similarities between the groups and the sometimes murky boundaries dividing them, it is not surprising that Presbyterians and Congregationalists often maintained relaxed, cordial relationships in the eighteenth century. Thus, as noted earlier, the first three presidents of the unofficially Presbyterian college in Princeton — Jonathan Dickinson, Aaron Burr, and Jonathan Edwards — had roots in New England Congregationalism and had graduated from Yale. The ease with which ministers could shift between the denominations was paralleled by other forms of cooperation. For example, in 1766 Presbyterians and Connecticut Congregationalists approved mutual consultations that occurred annually until the eve of the Revolution. In the 1790s, both denominations agreed to grant representatives of the other body the privilege of vote as well as voice in its deliberations. The cooperative spirit found further embodiment in the Plan of Union (1801), which allowed the churches of the two denominations to collaborate in the formation of new congregations. In upstate New York, the two denominations eventually moved beyond cooperation toward amalgamation. In 1807, the Synod of Albany, in response to an overture from the Middle Association (Congregational), invited that group to become a "constituent part of our body." The synod offered the association's churches the right to continue conducting their internal affairs in accordance with Congregationalist usage while simultaneously enjoying the privilege of representation in the synod. In effect, the synod was proposing to make the association a presbytery under its jurisdiction. Approved by the General Assembly in 1808 and confirmed by the Middle Association, this Plan of Accommodation cleared the way for

3. Leonard J. Trinterud, *The Forming of an American Tradition: A Re-examination of Colonial Presbyterianism* (Philadelphia: Westminster Press, 1949), 14-37; Williston Walker, *Creeds and Platforms of Congregationalism* (Boston: Pilgrim Press, 1960 [1893]), 409-39, 463-523.

Congregationalist churches to enter en masse into Presbyterian affiliation while maintaining their own distinctive practices. The pattern set in 1808 was then followed subsequently in other parts of New York and in the Western Reserve of Ohio. How many churches were brought into Presbyterianism in this fashion has been a subject of dispute; but substantial numbers of originally non-Presbyterian congregations, probably in the hundreds, entered the denomination in the first several decades of the nineteenth century.[4]

Presbyterians also cooperated with Congregationalists through what today might be called parachurch organizations. In the first quarter of the nineteenth century, Protestants concerned about the promotion of specific causes — for example, foreign and home missionary work or the distribution of Christian literature — created voluntary benevolent societies. Nondenominational in character and outside formal ecclesiastical structure, these organizations were controlled by boards composed of individuals (often lay people) who represented only themselves, not their churches. The voluntary societies thus embodied a task-oriented ecumenism that brought Protestant Christians together in an *ad hoc* fashion. Although these organizations were formed both locally and nationally, it was at the national level that they gained great notoriety. A group of interlocking organizations known collectively as the evangelical united front or the benevolent empire took shape. To name only a few, these institutions included the American Board of Commissioners for Foreign Missions (1810), the American Education Society (1815), the American Bible Society (1816), and the American Home Missionary Society (1826). Although the benevolent empire had a broader constituency than the Presbyterians and Congregationalists, these two denominations provided the vast majority of the leaders and the workers for the voluntary societies. Through these organizations, then, the cooperation represented by the Plan of Union was increased

---

4. Nathan O. Hatch and Harry S. Stout, eds., *Jonathan Edwards and the American Experience* (New York: Oxford University Press, 1988); Bryan F. Le Beau, *Jonathan Dickinson and the Formative Years of American Presbyterianism* (Lexington: University Press of Kentucky, 1997); Patricia U. Bonomi, *Under the Cope of Heaven: Religion, Society, and Politics in Colonial America* (New York: Oxford University Press, 1986), 206; John Von Rohr, *The Shaping of American Congregationalism, 1620-1957* (Cleveland: Pilgrim Press, 1992), 263; Robert Hastings Nichols, *Presbyterianism in New York State: A History of the Synod and Its Predecessors*, ed. James Hastings Nichols (Philadelphia: Westminster Press, 1963), 70-86.

and so, too, was the blurring of boundaries between Presbyterianism and Congregationalism.[5]

Although these cooperative ventures with Congregationalists would later prove irritants among Presbyterians and eventually the source of bitter controversy, they were not so at the outset. No voices were raised in opposition when the Plan of Union was passed. The future leaders of Princeton Seminary concurred in the decision. Samuel Miller and Ashbel Green helped draft the plan, and Archibald Alexander carried the proposal to the Connecticut Congregationalists.[6]

Yet even as they cooperated with one another, Congregationalists and Presbyterians inched apart theologically. Despite their differences regarding polity, the two groups had originally shared a commitment to the federal theology that had its fullest creedal expression in the Westminster Confession. Called federal because of its stress on covenant (in Latin, *foedus*), this theology envisioned the human condition in terms of two covenants. In the first, God made a covenant of works with Adam, who stood as the representative for all humanity. By this covenant, Adam's transgression was imputed or assigned to his posterity, who, as a result, were born in a state of sin and were utterly incapable of doing God's will. Salvation came only through the covenant of grace made between God the Father and Christ. By his suffering on the cross, Christ vicariously paid the penalty for sin on behalf of the elect. His righteousness was counted as theirs, and only in this fashion could the elect be saved.[7]

By the end of the eighteenth century, some New England Congregationalists modified this theology. A group of ministers considered the disciples of Jonathan Edwards sought to improve and refine the doctrines of their master. Their leading figures included Samuel Hopkins, Joseph Bellamy, and Nathanael Emmons. Their movement, often called the

---

5. See, for example, Charles Foster, *An Errand of Mercy: The Evangelical United Front, 1790-1837* (Chapel Hill: University of North Carolina Press, 1960), 121-55; Clifford M. Drury, *Presbyterian Panorama: One Hundred and Fifty Years of National Missions History* (Philadelphia: Board of Christian Education, PCUSA, 1952), 52-76; Peter J. Wosh, *Spreading the Word: The Bible Business in Nineteenth-Century America* (Ithaca: Cornell University Press, 1994), 74.

6. James W. Alexander, *The Life of Archibald Alexander, D.D.* (New York: Charles Scribner, 1854), 233.

7. Earl A. Pope, *New England Calvinism and the Disruption of the Presbyterian Church* (New York: Garland, 1987), 5-30. This work is a published version of Pope's 1962 Ph.D. dissertation at Brown University.

Archibald Alexander (1772–1851), pastor at the Pine Street Presbyterian Church in Philadelphia from 1807 to 1812 and former president of Hampden-Sydney College in Virginia from 1796 to 1807, was chosen as the first professor of the new theological seminary of the Presbyterian Church in Princeton.

Ashbel Green (1762–1848) was pastor of the Second Presbyterian Church in Philadelphia from 1787 to 1812, chaplain to the United States Congress from 1792 to 1800, and the eighth president of the College of New Jersey (now Princeton University) from 1812 to 1822. He served as president of the Princeton Seminary Board of Directors from 1812 until his death in 1848.

The 1812 House was rented as the first home of Archibald Alexander in Princeton and the site of the first seminary classes, which were held in the study. Later moved to another location, it has now been purchased and restored by the seminary.

Samuel Miller (1769–1850), pastor at the First Presbyterian Church in New York City from 1793 to 1813, was called to be the second professor at Princeton Theological Seminary. He served as professor of ecclesiastical history and church government from 1813 to 1849.

Sarah Sergeant Miller (1778–1861) was the daughter of Jonathan Dickinson Sergeant, a Princeton attorney, member of the revolutionary Continental Congress, and later attorney general of Pennsylvania. She was a leader among Princeton women in devotional and benevolent work and took a special concern in providing education for poor children, both white and African American. *Portrait by John Wesley Jarvis*

Theodore Sedgwick Wright (1797–1847), class of 1828, was the first African American to attend and graduate from Princeton Theological Seminary. He became the pastor of the First Colored Presbyterian Church in New York City, where he was active in the antislavery cause and with his congregation aided runaway slaves escaping north to freedom in Canada.

Alexander Hall was designed by a New York City architect with Princeton roots, John McComb. The cornerstone was laid in 1815, and the building was ready for partial occupancy by 1817. It originally provided space for a classroom and oratory, a kitchen and dining hall, library rooms, and dormitory space. Today it serves largely as a dormitory, although the original oratory is still used for student prayer meetings and other functions.

Charles Hodge (1797–1878), class of 1819, returned to the seminary as a member of the faculty in 1820 and taught over 2,000 Princeton Seminary students before his death in 1878. He was the founding editor of what would become *The Princeton Review* and was a major voice in American Presbyterianism throughout the central years of the nineteenth century. Among his works are commentaries on Romans, Ephesians, and First and Second Corinthians, and a massive three-volume systematic theology.

Joseph Addison Alexander (1809–1860), son of Archibald Alexander, was a brilliant linguist, mastering not only the classical, biblical, and major and minor European languages, but also Arabic, Persian, Turkish, Ethiopic, Coptic, Sanskrit, Malay, and Chinese. He taught at Princeton Seminary from 1834 until his death in 1860, primarily in the field of biblical languages and literature.

Francis James Grimké (1850–1937), class of 1878, served for many years as pastor of the Fifteenth Street Presbyterian Church in Washington, D.C. Twice sold into slavery as a youth, he was freed following the Civil War and went on to become a leader in the African American community and one of the founding members of the National Association for the Advancement of Colored People in 1910.

Old Lenox Library was the first of a series of Princeton Seminary libraries that have stood on the corner of Mercer Street and Library Place. Constructed in 1843, it was built in the Gothic Revival style that was just beginning to come into vogue in Great Britain at the time, on land purchased for the purpose by New York philanthropist and Princeton Seminary board member James Lenox. Students could get the key and let themselves in whenever they needed to use a book in the earliest days.

New Lenox Library became necessary when Princeton Seminary's book collection outgrew the old Lenox Library. James Lenox again came to the seminary's aid and built a red brick High Victorian building behind the old library in 1879. It was designed by Richard Morris Hunt, the first American to study at the École des Beaux-Arts in Paris. It featured a large clerestory with many windows that allowed natural light to enter the library throughout the day. Around the balcony, overlooking the study area, were placed the portraits of Princeton Seminary faculty members from the earlier part of the nineteenth century.

Princeton Seminary faculty, 1871, left to right: James Clement Moffat, professor of church history from 1861 to 1888; Alexander Taggart McGill, professor of pastoral theology and homiletics from 1854 to 1883; Caspar Wistar Hodge, professor of New Testament literature and biblical Greek from 1860 to 1891; Charles Augustus Aiken, professor of Christian ethics and apologetics from 1871 to 1882, professor of Oriental and Old Testament literature and Christian ethics from 1882 to 1892; Charles Hodge, instructor in the original languages of Scripture from 1820 to 1822, professor of Oriental and biblical literature from 1822 to 1840, and professor of exegetical and didactic theology from 1840 to 1878; and William Henry Green, professor of biblical and Oriental literature from 1851 to 1900.

Archibald Alexander Hodge (1823–1886), class of 1847 and son of Charles Hodge, served as a missionary to India from 1847 to 1850 and a professor at Western Theological Seminary in Pittsburgh from 1864 until 1877, and returned to Princeton Seminary in 1877 to aid his aging father. He taught courses in exegetical, didactic and polemic theology at Princeton Seminary until his death in 1886.

Caspar Wistar Hodge Sr. (1830–1891), class of 1853 and son of Charles Hodge, taught New Testament literature and biblical Greek at Princeton Seminary from 1860 to 1891.

Francis Landey Patton (1843–1932), class of 1865, was a resident of Bermuda who pursued his higher education in Canada and the United States and went on to serve as professor of the relations of philosophy and science to the Christian religion at the seminary from 1881 to 1888. He then served as president of Princeton University from 1888 to 1902 before returning to Princeton Seminary as professor of the philosophy of religion and as the first president of Princeton Seminary, when that office was instituted, from 1902 to 1913.

William Henry Green (1827–1900), class of 1846, was a preeminent scholar of the Hebrew Scriptures whose textbooks for teaching Hebrew were widely used. He served as professor of biblical and Oriental literature from 1851 to 1900 and as senior administrative officer of the seminary from 1878 to 1900.

Benjamin Breckinridge Warfield (1851–1921), class of 1876, was professor of didactic and polemical theology at Princeton Seminary from 1887 until his death in 1921. He was the author of hundreds of scholarly articles and reviews and an ardent defender of traditional Calvinism as presented in the Westminster Confession.

George Tybout Purves (1852–1901), class of 1876, returned to Princeton Seminary from highly successful pastorates in Baltimore and Pittsburgh to serve as professor of New Testament literature and exegesis from 1892 to 1900.

John DeWitt (1842–1923), class of 1864, was a popular preacher and lecturer who had served churches in New York State, Boston, and Philadelphia, and taught at Lane Seminary in Cincinnati and McCormick Seminary in Chicago before becoming professor of church history at Princeton Seminary in 1892. He served in that post until his retirement in 1912. *Portrait by Howard Russell Butler*

Geerhardus Vos (1862–1949), class of 1885, was born in the Netherlands and immigrated to Grand Rapids, Michigan, when his father was called to serve a congregation there. He completed his basic theological studies at Calvin Theological Seminary in Grand Rapids and at Princeton Seminary and went on to earn his doctorate at the University of Strasbourg. After five years of teaching at Calvin Seminary, he was called in 1893 to teach in the field of biblical theology at Princeton, which he did until his retirement in 1932.

Princeton Seminary Faculty, 1904, from left to right: Geerhardus Vos, professor of biblical theology; Henry Wilson Smith, instructor in speech; Francis Landey Patton, president of the seminary and professor of the philosophy of religion; William Brenton Greene, professor of apologetics and Christian ethics; Joseph Heatly Dulles, librarian; Benjamin Breckinridge Warfield, professor of didactic and polemic theology; William Park Armstrong, professor of New Testament literature and exegesis; William Miller Paxton, professor of homiletics; James Oscar Boyd, instructor in Old Testament; John D. Davis, professor of Oriental and Old Testament literature; John DeWitt, professor of church history; and Robert Dick Wilson, professor of Semitic philology and Old Testament criticism.

New Divinity or sometimes Hopkinsianism, was an effort to render the Calvinist or Reformed position more consistent or coherent and thus more defensible in the age of Enlightenment.[8]

Their doctrinal "improvements" proceeded along several lines. The New Divinity theologians felt considerable unease at the notion that Adam's sin was imputed to subsequent generations or that people were condemned antecedent to any acts they committed. Human beings did not live under a double guilt, Adam's and their own. They were guilty only for sin that they themselves had done. Yet Hopkins and company did not reject the doctrine of original sin. Although a person was culpable only for his or her own crimes against God's law, every man and woman was, in consequence of Adam's fall, born with a corrupted disposition that made sin inevitable.

Just as the New Divinity theologians felt discomfort at the idea that Adam's sin was imputed to subsequent generations, they also were troubled by the notion that Jesus' righteousness paid the debt sinful humanity owed to God. From their perspective, traditional views of the vicarious or substitutionary atonement undercut the sovereignty of God and encouraged moral laxness. If Christ literally paid the penalty for the sinner's transgression, then the sinner's debts were canceled and he or she could legitimately demand salvation from God. Where was grace or the sovereign initiative of God in such a notion? To resolve this problem, the New Divinity theologians suggested a different model of the atonement. They replaced the debtor-creditor image with a governmental metaphor. Sin was not a debt owed God; it was a crime committed against the divine government. Punishment was necessary to uphold God's government, lest the law be flouted and sinners feel free to sin with impunity. The atonement, then, was not Christ's payment of the debt owed by the

8. In this and subsequent paragraphs on the New Divinity, I am heavily indebted to William Breitenbach, "The Consistent Calvinism of the New Divinity Movement," *William and Mary Quarterly* 41 (April 1984): 241-64; Joseph A. Conforti, *Samuel Hopkins and the New Divinity Movement: Calvinism, the Congregational Ministry, and Reform in New England between the Great Awakenings* (Grand Rapids: Christian University Press, 1981); David W. Kling, *A Field of Divine Wonders: The New Divinity and Village Revivals in Northwestern Connecticut, 1792-1822* (University Park: Pennsylvania State University Press, 1993); Mark Valeri, *Law and Providence in Joseph Bellamy's New England: The Origins of the New Divinity in Revolutionary America* (New York: Oxford University Press, 1994). These works present a more evenhanded assessment of the New Divinity than the often insightful (but also polemical) Joseph Haroutunian, *Piety Versus Moralism: The Passing of the New England Theology* (New York: Henry Holt, 1932).

sinner, for sin was a crime, not a debt. Instead, the atonement was Christ's bearing of the punishment due for the breaking of the law and an expression of God's aversion to sin.

The New Divinity also grappled with the perennial question of free will. In what sense, if any, did fallen humanity have the ability to do the will of God and in what sense did men and women sin of necessity? To answer these questions, Hopkins and others built on a distinction enunciated by their mentor Jonathan Edwards, who distinguished natural and moral necessity. Natural necessity derived from natural or mechanical laws: someone who falls off a cliff, for example, will of necessity plummet downward. That person has no freedom to reverse the law of gravity. But moral necessity was of a different order. Moral necessity referred to the fact that certain actions necessarily and certainly follow from the habits, dispositions, and motives of the heart. Since no external, mechanical law compelled an individual to sin, he or she possessed a natural freedom to avoid sin. However, since the dispositions and habits of the unregenerate were wicked, they would inevitably use that freedom to choose sin. In a word, men and women possessed a natural ability to refrain from sin, but not a moral ability since their souls were warped. Or, as William Breitenbach has summarized using another metaphor, "the distinction between natural ability and moral ability allowed the Hopkinsians to shunt divine sovereignty and human freedom past one another on parallel tracks."[9]

Although its adherents believed the New Divinity to be a preservation and restatement of orthodox Calvinism, opponents within both Congregationalism and Presbyterianism charged otherwise. For example, in 1798, the Presbyterian General Assembly reprimanded Hezekiah Balch, a Presbyterian minister in Tennessee, for espousing the views of Samuel Hopkins. In *A Contrast Between Calvinism and Hopkinsianism* (1811), Ezra Stiles Ely contended that the New Divinity undermined the Reformed understanding of the sinfulness of humanity and the nature of Christ's redeeming work. Encouraging sinners to think that they might contribute something toward their own redemption, it tended toward the ancient heresy of Pelagianism. In general, however, Presbyterians were not inclined to view the New Divinity in such dire terms. For example, after 1798 Balch appears to have continued to teach the offending views without any further censure from higher judicatories; and Ely's

9. Breitenbach, "Consistent Calvinism," 258.

blast against Hopkinsianism resulted in official ecclesiastical action to soothe rather than inflame the controversy. In 1817, a General Assembly committee chaired by Princeton Seminary's Samuel Miller reviewed a letter of the Synod of Pennsylvania written by Ely and charging error against the New Divinity. Although the committee commended "the zeal of the Synod" in attempting to promote "strict conformity" to the creedal standards of Presbyterianism, it regretted that ardor "on this subject should be manifested in such a manner as to be offensive to other denominations, and especially to introduce a spirit of jealousy and suspicion against ministers in good standing."[10]

By the late 1820s, however, this perception began to change with the emergence of the so-called New Haven theology and its leading proponent, Nathaniel William Taylor. Although scholars still debate the extent to which the theological pedigree of Taylor, professor of didactic theology at Yale, can be traced to Edwards and the New Divinity, he clearly took some of their assertions a step further than they had. For example, Taylor sometimes blurred the New Divinity's distinction between humanity's natural and moral ability and thus (in the opinion of critics) appeared to be suggesting that unregenerate humans had a power to effect their own salvation. Soon the theologians at Princeton Seminary, engaging in a sharp exchange in print with the New Haven theologians, pointed to the dangers of Taylorism. The Princetonians, however, while considering Taylorism to be beyond the pale of acceptability, continued to express a willingness to tolerate, somewhat grudgingly, the New Divinity. To Presbyterians further to the right than Princeton, the situation was more dire. Taylorism symbolized the direction of New England theology as a whole. The controversy compounded their fear that the New Divinity itself was unsound on such questions as total depravity, the imputation of Adam's sin, Christ's vicarious atonement, and the nature of regeneration.[11]

In this context, the Reverend Albert Barnes, a former student at Princeton Seminary, was brought to ecclesiastical trial for a sermon he

10. Miller's committee is quoted in Pope, *New England Calvinism*, 51; George M. Marsden, *The Evangelical Mind and the New School Presbyterian Experience: A Case Study of Thought and Theology in Nineteenth-Century America* (New Haven: Yale University Press, 1970), 39-45.

11. Pope, *New England Calvinism*, 62-106; Marsden, *Evangelical Mind*, 45-52; Bruce Kuklick, *Churchmen and Philosophers: From Jonathan Edwards to John Dewey* (New Haven: Yale University Press, 1985), 94-111.

had preached at his church in Morristown, New Jersey, in February 1829 during a revival. "The Way of Salvation" became an issue when Barnes answered a call to the pastorate of the First Presbyterian Church in Philadelphia in 1830. The city of brotherly love, perhaps poorly named from Barnes's point of view, was the center of conservative resistance to New England's theological innovations. Presbyterian leaders such as Ashbel Green, now firmly aligned with those wishing to purge the church of New England errors, argued that Barnes had compromised the integrity of the church's standards. He was accused of teaching views that put him at variance with the Westminster Confession on such matters as original sin, the atonement, and the ability of unregenerate humanity to respond to the call of God. Eventually Barnes's presbytery condemned the teaching of "The Way of Salvation" (though not Barnes personally), but in 1831, the General Assembly reversed that judgment against his sermon.[12]

Several years later, the pattern repeated itself. In 1835, after publishing a commentary on Romans, Barnes was tried anew, and this time he was suspended from his pulpit by the presbytery for allegedly teaching errors analogous to the ones of which he had been accused several years earlier. In 1836, the General Assembly again reversed the verdict.

Adding fuel to the desire to purge error from the church were violations of proper polity and behavior. The Old School objected that the New School was sending people (Congregationalist "committee men"), never properly ordained as ruling elders to represent their churches in presbytery, and presbyteries were sending them as commissioners to synod or General Assembly. They also believed that the various voluntary or benevolent societies had become a threat to Presbyterian agencies. Answerable to no church, the voluntary societies were in fact undermining Presbyterian ability to support and maintain their own enterprises. Even more shocking were the violations of decorum in worship and in congregational life that the New School was tolerating.

In short, the Old School complained that proper ecclesiastical order had dissolved, and nowhere were there more dramatic images of the religious world run amok than in upstate New York, the center of New School strength and the place where the Plans of Union and Accommodation had produced the heaviest Congregational influx into Presbyterianism. In the 1820s, Charles G. Finney, a lawyer (or possibly law clerk) turned evangelist, brought into the Presbyterian church a revivalism

---

12. Pope, *New England Calvinism*, 169-208; Marsden, *Evangelical Mind*, 52-55.

that many found suspect. Finney employed what were commonly called "new measures." Although the Methodists had actually pioneered in the use of these, Finney brought them into the "Presbygational" churches. The techniques included a pungent, colloquial style in the pulpit, protracted meetings, and the use of the anxious or mourner's bench where people concerned about the state of their souls were to be seated. When he conducted worship, Finney named sins with uncommon directness; and neither his sermons nor his prayers left much doubt as to the identity of the perpetrators. The evangelist tolerated — some would have said, encouraged — women to step outside their proper domain by speaking in "promiscuous assemblies." By the mid-1830s, Finney also condemned slave holding as sin and insisted that churches would not continue to enjoy revivals of religion unless they spoke forthrightly on the subject. While he claimed certain affinities to Edwards and the New England tradition, Finney was unabashedly and openly moving toward an Arminian view of the freedom of the will. Had Finney not been safely ensconced in overwhelmingly New School presbyteries at the beginning of his career, or had he not later switched his ministerial affiliation to the Congregational denomination shortly after he went off to teach at Oberlin College in Ohio, the Old School would almost assuredly have given him the same treatment it meted out to Barnes and others.[13]

Finney's ecclesiastical revolt paralleled larger changes unsettling the order of American society and culture. An economic transformation — a market revolution, gaining force in the several decades after the end of the war with Britain in 1815 — profoundly altered human relations. In the Northeast, the growing scarcity of land tore young men and women loose from the ties of blood, place, and prescribed social roles and hurled them westward or into the towns and cities. In the urban areas, artisans who had previously enjoyed some degree of status and independence were subjected to the more impersonal regime of wage earning. Among the growing middle classes, the nature of work tended to separate production from the home and produced a major rethinking of the proper roles of men and women. Among the new religious movements that had sprung out of the revivals, there were a number of

---

13. Charles G. Finney, *Lectures on Revivals of Religion*, ed. William G. McLoughlin (Cambridge: Harvard University Press, 1960 [1835]), 192. On Finney, see Charles E. Hambrick-Stowe, *Charles G. Finney and the Spirit of American Evangelicalism* (Grand Rapids: Eerdmans, 1996); and Keith J. Hardman, *Charles Grandison Finney, 1792-1875: Revivalist and Reformer* (Syracuse: Syracuse University Press, 1987).

women preachers. "By 1830," Catherine Brekus notes, "female preachers were more visible, more popular, and more aggressive than ever before." Even Presbyterians, who supposedly did not permit such things, were not untouched by the popular tide — witness the complaint against Finney's "promiscuous meetings" or the fact that the Presbytery of Philadelphia censured two churches in 1826 for allowing a female itinerant to occupy the pulpits. Beneath these specific changes was a transformation of consciousness that some historians have called a "democratization of mind" — a new outlook in which ordinary people vaunted their right to take charge of their own lives without the help of traditional authority and without deference to their "betters." Evidences of that determination appeared in the popular assault against professional elites in medicine and law and in the extension of suffrage to the vast majority of white males. With the electorate vastly widening, politics was increasingly converted into a form of popular mobilization and entertainment as the so-called second party system of the United States coalesced in the 1830s. As Robert Wiebe has written, it is little wonder that many observers professed to see in the young nation "only bursts of atomized behavior, a kinetic confusion that was undermining the last pillars of an old order."[14]

Another sign of the revolt against traditional authority was the rise of abolitionism. Exemplified by the formation of the American Anti-Slavery Society in 1833, abolitionism changed the tenor of antislavery thought. Prior to the 1830s, there existed in much of the North — and

14. Catherine A. Brekus, *Strangers and Pilgrims: Female Preaching in America, 1740-1845* (Chapel Hill: University of North Carolina Press, 1998), 276; Lois A. Boyd and R. Douglas Brackenridge, *Presbyterian Women in America: Two Centuries of a Quest for Status,* 2nd ed. (Westport, CT: Greenwood Press, 1996), 94; Gordon S. Wood, "The Democratization of Mind in the American Revolution," in *Leadership in the American Revolution,* Library of Congress Symposia on the American Revolution (Washington: Library of Congress, 1974), 63-89; Robert H. Wiebe, *The Opening of American Society: From the Adoption of the Constitution to the Eve of Disunion* (New York: Oxford University Press, 1984), 295. See also Richard D. Brown, *Modernization: The Transformation of American Life, 1600-1865* (New York: Hill and Wang, 1976), 74-158; David Hackett Fischer, *The Revolution of American Conservatism: The Federalist Party in the Era of Jeffersonian Democracy* (New York: Harper and Row, 1965), 188-99; Charles H. Sellers, *The Market Revolution: Jacksonian America, 1815-1846* (New York: Oxford University Press, 1991), 229-355; Chilton Williamson, *American Suffrage: From Property to Democracy, 1760-1860* (Princeton: Princeton University Press, 1960), esp. 117-259 and 545-67; Gordon S. Wood, *The Radicalism of the American Revolution* (New York: Alfred A. Knopf, 1992), 229-335.

also in some circles in the South — a conviction that slavery was an institution inconsistent with both Christianity and the spirit of the age. It was an anachronism that should and would disappear. The Presbyterian General Assembly expressed this view in 1818 when it branded slavery "a gross violation of the most precious and sacred rights of human nature" and asserted that it was "utterly inconsistent with the law of God." Yet this form of antislavery thought was exceedingly cautious. It recognized the difficulties of immediate emancipation, honored the property rights of slaveholders, never accused them of being sinners, and looked toward the eventual colonization of blacks in Africa once freedom was gradually and voluntarily attained. The abolitionists assaulted the peculiar institution much more directly. Asserting that slaveholding was a sin demanding repentance, they affirmed that slaves ought instantly to be set free and that, once freed, they should enjoy civil rights. Colonization, the abolitionists charged, was a morally bankrupt substitute for genuine antislavery conviction. With the aid of the penny press that now made possible a relatively cheap mass dissemination of printed material, abolitionists sent out reams of pamphlets and papers touting their message. Speakers fanned out to cities and towns where they preached the gospel of abolition. (The terminology is appropriate, for the meetings often had the air of a revival; and, in fact, support for abolitionism was frequently linked to the Finneyite style of evangelicalism.) When abolitionists ventured into countless northern communities, they were hounded from lecture halls by mobs often instigated and led by substantial citizens.[15]

It is against this backdrop of pervasive confusion and fear that the Presbyterian schism of 1837 must be set. Since abolitionism was arguably the most visible symptom of this ferment, historians have sometimes asked whether the controversy over slavery was the "real" issue dividing the Presbyterian Church in 1837. Framed in this fashion, the question has received a negative answer from most scholars who have studied the question closely. They have shown convincingly that the theological issues dividing the Old and New Schools antedated the explosive debate over slavery in the mid-1830s. Yet it is probably misleading to pose the question in a manner that draws a sharp distinction between concern for proper doctrine and concern with social issues such as slavery. These

15. Leonard L. Richards, *"Gentlemen of Property and Standing": Anti-Abolition Mobs in Jacksonian America* (New York: Oxford University Press, 1971), 81.

were not, in the experience of men and women in the 1830s, entirely separate matters but rather found linkage in a common fear. That fear was one rooted in the entire range of intellectual, religious, cultural, social, and political changes that America was experiencing in the 1830s. It was an anxiety that legitimate authority was under assault and collapsing.[16]

Whatever its relationship to that broader sense of legitimate authority at risk, the Old School certainly felt a mounting anxiety in the 1830s that Presbyterian order was in danger. The General Assembly that reversed Barnes's first conviction in 1831 marked a watershed. In addition to sanctioning apparent heresy, a majority in the Assembly also appeared to favor bringing the Presbyterian Boards of Education and Missions under the aegis of the interdenominational American Education Society and the American Home Missionary Societies. From the Old School perspective, here was double evidence of a dire threat to the denomination. How could the Presbyterian Church maintain its integrity if the General Assembly refused to defend theological purity and was prepared to turn over its educational and missionary enterprises to interdenominational organizations that it could not control?

By the end of 1834, a group of ardent Old School leaders spearheaded by Robert Breckenridge drew up and circulated the "Act and Testimony," a statement of errors they believed the New School was teaching or at least tolerating. Published in early 1835, the "Act and Testimony" garnered signatures of nearly 360 ministers and slightly over 1,700 ruling elders as well as the endorsement of a number of synods and presbyteries. The document consisted of a succinct enumeration of theological errors it associated with the New School, including the disbelief in the imputation of Adam's sin to the human race and a corresponding affirmation that sinners had the power to comply with God's commands, that regeneration is the human being's own act, and that Christ's suffering was not truly vicarious. In a word, the list of errors was aimed at the theological innovations coming from New England.

From the Old School's viewpoint, the General Assembly of 1836 brought the church to the edge of disaster. It reversed the second con-

---

16. For differing views, see C. Bruce Staiger, "Abolitionism and the Presbyterian Schism of 1837-1838," *Mississippi Valley Historical Review* 36 (December 1949): 391-414; Elwyn A. Smith, "The Role of the South in the Presbyterian Schism of 1837-38," *Church History* 29 (March 1960): 44-63; Marsden, *Evangelical Mind*, 250-51; Andrew E. Murray, *Presbyterians and the Negro: A History* (Philadelphia: Presbyterian Historical Society, 1966), 103-5.

viction against Barnes, and it reneged on the promise of the previous Assembly to assume oversight of the Western Foreign Missionary Society, founded by the Synod of Pittsburgh. The latter move signaled the Assembly's apparent refusal to sponsor any kind of denominationally controlled foreign missionary work. Together, the two actions reinforced the conservatives' perception that Presbyterianism was wandering yet further from its theology and polity. Just before the next General Assembly in May 1837, a convention of Old School Presbyterians met, plotted strategy, and sent a "Testimony and Memorial" to the Assembly. The document outlined in detail the now familiar grievances of the conservatives regarding irregularities of theology and practice within the New School, attributed the problems to the Plan of Union, and recommended its repeal on the grounds that the 1801 act had from the outset been unconstitutional. With a firm Old School majority, the General Assembly of 1837 did abrogate the Plan of Union. After efforts to negotiate a division with the New School failed, the Assembly dictated the terms of the split by expelling four synods that had been organized under the Plan of Union. When commissioners from the exscinded judicatories tried to take their places in the General Assembly of 1838, they were not recognized, and they proceeded to organize their own separate New School denomination.[17]

Princeton Seminary and the Old School

As passions within Presbyterianism heated up in the 1830s, Princeton Seminary moved cautiously. Theologically, the seminary's professors stood close to the Old School, but they feared that the vehemence with which its partisans pushed their crusade would divide the denomination. They abhorred this prospect, not only because it would rend the church they loved but also because schism might destroy the seminary. If division came, Princeton Seminary, as an institution established by the General Assembly, would be controlled by whichever party controlled the Assembly. Alexander, Miller, and Hodge feared that Old School extremists, failing in their effort to return Presbyterianism to simon-pure orthodoxy, might withdraw to form a new denomination, thus leaving

---

17. *Minutes of the General Assembly* (1837), 504. For further discussion of these events, see Marsden, *Evangelical Mind*, 59-87; Pope, *New England Calvinism*, 295-347.

current Presbyterian agencies — including Princeton Seminary — in the hands of the New School. That prospect was terrifying to them. Yet, as conflict within the church mounted, Princeton faced a threat from its right flank as well. Some Old School leaders, fearing that Princeton was not giving them sufficient backing, hinted at the possibility of creating a new seminary or throwing their support to one of the other schools. Princeton Seminary faced the danger that it might find itself without adequate financial support or without a constituency.

The caution of the Princeton faculty was illustrated by Samuel Miller's *Letters to Presbyterians*. Published first in the Philadelphia-based weekly the *Presbyterian* and then collected into a volume, the *Letters to Presbyterians* expressed Miller's horror of controversy. As one who had heard tales from his father of the "mournful effects" of the Old Side/New Side split of the previous century, Miller contemplated the prospect "of another rupture of our beloved church" with "anguish of spirit." He foresaw ugly fights dividing synods, presbyteries, and congregations — battles over church property, friend turned against friend, families in conflict with themselves. "Zion would lie dishonoured in the sight of an unbelieving world," Miller warned, "and all this for what?" But he also insisted that there was correct doctrine to be upheld and right practice to be observed. In accordance with their ordination vows, Presbyterian ministers must adhere unabashedly to the Westminster Confession. Although subscription to the creed did not demand "absolute uniformity in the mode of expounding every minute detail of truth," it did require an espousal of a full-bodied Calvinism, ruling out any form of Arminianism or Pelagianism. Miller scorned those unwilling to condemn doctrinal error unless it verged into blatant heresy such as "palpable Unitarianism." A church with such loose standards, he believed, would not be worth "keeping together." Similarly, he endorsed the importance of revivals, believing "that the church is warranted in looking and praying for revivals of religion far more glorious than the present generation, or indeed any other, has ever witnessed." Yet he also opposed the unscriptural system of revivals that led to protracted meetings, "bodily agitations," "unauthorized and unqualified persons" giving religious testimony or instruction, "females speaking and leading in prayer in promiscuous assemblies," and prayers for "particular individuals by name, as graceless or opposers of religion." Fearing that such practices discredited revivals and produced a bias against genuine awakenings, Miller nevertheless urged his readers: "Let no degree of abuse or disorder with which they have been attended, prejudice you against revivals themselves. Desire them, and pray for them with unwearied importunity."[18]

Miller also took what he deemed a middle position in the matter of voluntary societies. Many on the right of the Old School regarded the voluntary societies as usurpers of tasks properly performed by the judicatories of the church. Because they were not accountable to ecclesiastical courts, the voluntary societies might ultimately subvert church order and doctrine. By contrast, the New School viewed the societies as generally more effective instruments for action and favored them as more ecumenical, less sectarian ways in which Protestant Christians could work with one another. Miller argued that there was room enough for both denominational agencies and the voluntary societies. Building on the assumptions of his arguments against Hobart and the high church Episcopalians decades earlier, Miller allowed that cooperation with Christians outside one's own denomination was entirely appropriate, especially in the case of Bible or tract societies, where issues of differing denominational theologies were less likely to arise. He even affirmed that Presbyterians might simultaneously support both the non-denominational American Home Missionary Society and Presbyterian missionary agencies — a matter of hot contention between Old and New Schools in the 1830s. But cooperation with Christians of other communions, he insisted, should never entail the sacrifice of Presbyterian identity to a bland homogeneity or descend into an evangelical Protestantism of the lowest common denominator. "Can you as Presbyterians," he asked, ". . . abandon the appropriate institutions of your own church, and prefer those which, though devoted to the general interests of religion, have not in view the enlargement of that portion of Christ's family which you profess to believe is purer, more scriptural, and better adapted to promote the real prosperity of the Redeemer's kingdom than any other?"[19]

One of the national benevolent institutions — the American Education Society (AES) — had particular bearing upon Princeton Seminary. Organized in 1815 to raise and provide support to young men studying for the ministry, the society at its peak in 1838 gave aid to 1,141 students in a variety of schools from academies and colleges to seminaries. Because of

18. Samuel Miller, *Letters to Presbyterians on the Present Crisis in the Presbyterian Church in the United States* (Philadelphia: Anthony Finley, 1833), 11, 15, 89, 93, 152, 161-62, 189.

19. Miller, *Letters to Presbyterians*, 19, 20, 28.

the number of students it helped, the AES was positioned informally to help determine standards for theological education. In fact, one historian has called it "the nearest approach to anything resembling an external standard or an accrediting agency in the competitive anarchy of higher education in nineteenth century America." In many ways, the AES pushed theological education in a direction that Princeton very much wanted — toward a post-undergraduate three-year program. On the other hand, the power of the AES was troubling, for the institution advertised itself as non-denominational and non-sectarian. While those who would become New School Presbyterians created their own voluntary education society in 1818 — it merged eventually with the AES — those who would become known as Old School Presbyterians formed in the same year a board of education under the General Assembly. As early as 1829, the *Biblical Repertory* was expressing its concern about the AES approach. President James Carnahan of the College of New Jersey worried that the non-creedal AES, while currently orthodox, had nothing in its constitution preventing a new generation of leaders from using that powerful tool to subvert orthodoxy, just as Harvard College had in 1805 perverted the intentions of the donor of the Hollis professorship of divinity by appointing a Unitarian. "An open and confessed heretic," Carnahan warned, "seldom begins the work of corruption; but he succeeds to the confidence and power acquired by some zealous and faithful servant of the Lord Jesus, and then he employs the authority with which he is invested in spreading around him moral pestilence and death." His message was clear: the Presbyterian Church needed to keep separate its own board of education for the support of its seminaries. Miller echoed those concerns in his *Letters to Presbyterians*. While lauding the work of the AES and acknowledging that it had an important work worthy of support, he expressed suspicion of turning over Presbyterian theological education to it. Would that not be like a father giving over "the entire education of his children . . . into the hands of strangers"?[20]

---

20. Natalie A. Naylor, "'Holding High the Standard': The Influence of the American Education Society in Ante-Bellum Education," *History of Education Quarterly* 24 (Winter 1984): 479-94. The comparison of the AES to an accrediting agency is quoted in Naylor, 486, from George Schmidt, *The Liberal Arts College: A Chapter in Cultural History* (New Brunswick, NJ: Rutgers University Press, 1957). [James Carnahan,] "The General Assembly's Board of Education and the American Education Society," *Biblical Repertory, A Journal of Biblical Literature and Theological Science,* n.s. 1 (1829): 366; Miller, *Letters to Presbyterians,* 43.

Miller's adherence to Old School principles was unmistakable, but (aside from an occasional sarcastic comment) the *Letters to Presbyterians* set those principles forth with moderation. His goal was to express fundamental agreement with the basic convictions of the Old School while avoiding schism. Miller's way of dealing with the controversies surrounding Albert Barnes gave a practical illustration of his desire to keep the peace. A former student at Princeton Seminary, Barnes was a friend of the family and had served as a tutor to some of the Miller children. When Barnes sailed into difficulty after his transfer to the Philadelphia Presbytery, Miller tried to prevent the matter from exploding into a full-blown controversy. For example, when Ashbel Green indicated his intention to bring charges against Barnes in 1830, Miller tried to dissuade him. After the second charge was brought against Barnes in 1835 for allegedly erroneous opinions in his *Notes on Romans,* Miller wrote to his former student, urging him to examine himself. "Is all the blame attributable to your accusers? Have you done all in your power to guard against suspicious and offensive modes of expression?" But after Barnes had been convicted and the matter came on appeal to the General Assembly in 1836, Miller voted with the majority to overturn Barnes's conviction of heresy. Then, in an about-face, Miller introduced a resolution reprimanding Barnes for the views he had expressed in the *Notes on Romans.* Although the New School–dominated assembly would not accept even symbolic action against Barnes, Miller was maneuvering to make the point that Princeton was strongly Old School in sympathy but would not support rash action dividing the church.

In 1832, Archibald Alexander floated the idea of an alteration in the fundamental nature of the General Assembly. Noting that the annual meeting was degenerating into "a mere arena for fierce contention," Alexander proposed to end the fighting by removing the Assembly's function as a "high court of appeals." He envisioned this change as part of a larger restructuring of the denomination. Presbyteries would remain the basic ecclesiastical authority above the congregational level as they supervised churches, determined the ordination of clergy, and, where necessary, exercised discipline over their members. Appeal on such matters could be carried to the larger regional synod of which the presbytery was a part, and the synod would exercise the right of final decision now lodged in the General Assembly. Alexander then proposed boundaries for six synods — boundaries based chiefly on "geographical contiguity" but also on "similarity in views and habits." He also offered one additional suggestion to promote homogeneity within synods. If a presbytery in Pennsylvania, for example, concluded that it had greater affinity with the Synod of New York, it should be permitted by a two-thirds vote to switch to that synod. In short, Alexander's proposal devolved final judicial authority in the church upon synods, and these would be constructed to allow the like-minded to cluster together. With this decentralization of the denomination, what function would the General Assembly continue to have? It would serve as a bond of unity for the entire denomination, would collect information and publish it to give a comprehensive view of the denomination's ministry, and would maintain relations with other communions. It would also continue, Alexander added, to hold control over the assets legally committed to it — assets including Princeton Theological Seminary. There is no evidence that Old School partisans ever seriously entertained Alexander's proposal, but the fact that he offered it suggested his eagerness to avoid a split in Presbyterianism. It probably also hinted at his eagerness to keep the seminary out of the crossfire of conflict.[21]

Charles Hodge likewise tried to exercise a moderating influence. Robert Breckenridge wanted Hodge to sign the "Act and Testimony," but he refused to do so. He did help to hone the charges so that they would not be the imprecise or scattershot allegations that he thought had weakened the Old School case in the past. Yet, even having added his own improvements, he still would not sign because he thought the public letter an unwise tactic and some of its rhetoric offensive. As he later wrote in the *Biblical Repertory,* he disliked the "tone of confidence and superiority by which it is pervaded," as if the signers "alone were men of real courage." Although he did not use the word, Hodge apparently resented the nearly Manichean way in which some of the signers wished to use the document to force a crisis between the two sides. "It was designed," he complained, ". . . in order that the Assembly should be forced to retract [previous actions] or submit to have the church divided." Although he agreed with the basic theological complaints of the Old School, he wanted no part of what he perceived as their rule-or-ruin strategy.[22]

---

21. [Archibald Alexander,] "The Present Condition and Prospects of the Presbyterian Church," *Biblical Repertory and Theological Review* 4 (1832): 28-47.

22. [Charles Hodge,] "Act and Testimony," *Biblical Repertory and Theological Review* 7 (1835): 113, 127.

Archibald Alexander and Samuel Miller expressed a similar exasperation in 1835. Rehearsing their points of agreement with the Old School, they insisted that they had always been "the determined opponents of all those . . . leaning toward Arminian or Pelagian opinions in theology. . . . We have, again and again, warned our churches, that preferring irresponsible associations . . . to boards formed and superintended by our own ecclesiastical bodies" was dangerous. They had also sounded the alarm "against that system of novel and exciting 'measures' for promoting revivals of religion." But unlike their "ultra" Old School colleagues, they believed that the overwhelming majority within the church were theologically sound and that this majority was growing even greater. Miller and Alexander were convinced that if the Old School cause had been presented "with even tolerable discretion" — the clear implication was that they thought it had not been — the cause "would have invariably triumphed." Instead, the denomination was now a "bleeding church," and they noted wistfully that "moderate men have always fared badly between ultra partisans."[23]

By the latter part of 1836, it had become dangerous for the Princeton faculty to remain in what was becoming a no-man's-land between the "ultra partisans." That fall a delegation of some of the more ardent Old School leaders met with Archibald Alexander, J. W. Alexander, Miller, and Hodge in Hodge's study. Among these men were George Junkin, president of Lafayette College and one of the most fiery critics of the New School; Isaac V. Brown, a member of the seminary's board of trustees; and Cornelius C. Cuyler, a member of the board of directors. Although the tone of the meeting was apparently cordial, the professors were put on notice that their caution was not satisfactory to some in the Old School and that Robert Lenox, a wealthy backer of the seminary, was deeply concerned about the position of the seminary. As Isaac Brown later remembered, Lenox

> was, consequently, very solicitous that the Princeton delegation
> should ascertain whether the theological gentlemen there, who
> had seconded the revolt from the Act and Testimony, were deter-
> mined to persist in their course. Unless some favourable indica-
> tions should be given, he and others like-minded, had resolved to

23. [Archibald Alexander and Samuel Miller,] *Biblical Repertory and Princeton Review* 7 (1835): 57, 58, 59, 61, 65, 67.

abandon Princeton immediately to the control of the adversary, and take measures instantly to establish another seminary, on grounds entirely out of their reach. For this purpose, the money was ready in [the] bank; a beautiful site, with appropriate grounds and edifices, was selected; the principal officers for the institution were designated from among the most prominent in our church, and everything ready for action. But the delegates did not, on the whole, consider the condition of the seminary at Princeton, exposed as it was, sufficiently desperate to warrant so great a sacrifice and so decisive a change at that time. In this feeling our highly respected friends in New York cordially acquiesced.

For the moment, Lenox's plan had been stayed; but in Brown's recollection of the conference, much appeared to depend on the future ardor of Alexander, Miller, and Hodge in support of the Old School position. The fact that the unofficial delegation included a member of each of the seminary's governing boards no doubt underscored the gravity of the situation.[24]

In December, two days before Christmas, Miller wrote to a friend teaching at Western Theological Seminary in Pittsburgh that he was at last willing to separate "if we must go on as we have done for the last five or six years — in a state of perpetual strife and conflict." Yet he remained eager that the separation occur on terms favorable to the Old School and voiced again his fear that secession would leave the New School "in quiet possession of all our institutions, funds and boards, without exception." "Could you consent to give up your seminary, funds, buildings, books, etc., into their hands, and we, ours, and begin again from nothing? . . . If we should prove to be a minority in the next assembly, and should break away, in my opinion it would be, to give up all and go off beggars." But by April 1837, a few weeks before the General Assembly convened, Miller wrote a public letter acknowledging the inevitability of division and casting his lot with the Old School.[25]

Princeton now participated fully in the Old School maneuvers. When the "Act and Testimony" from Breckenridge was presented to the

---

24. Isaac V. Brown, *A Historical Vindication of the Abrogation of the Plan of Union by the Presbyterian Church in the United States of America* (Philadelphia: Wm. S. & Alfred Martien, 1855), 176; Samuel Miller, *The Life of Samuel Miller, D.D., LL.D.*, 2 vols. (Philadelphia: Claxton, Remsen and Haffelfinger, 1869), 316-17.

25. Miller, *Life of Samuel Miller*, 318.

Assembly in May, it was sent to a committee on which both Archibald Alexander and Ashbel Green served. The committee recommended the abrogation of the Plan of Union, and these two men who had helped bring it into existence thirty-six years earlier now argued that it was unconstitutional. When all of the work of division was done, the moderator placed Alexander on the committee to draw up a report and pastoral letter to the denomination at large. It was Alexander who presented that report to the Assembly. Then, in his annual report on the Assembly in the *Biblical Repertory and Princeton Review,* Charles Hodge vigorously defended the Old School position.[26]

In many ways the transformation of Princeton Seminary's role in Presbyterianism was epitomized by Hodge's major published foray into the field of church history, *The Constitutional History of the Presbyterian Church in the United States of America.* Published shortly after the schism, these two volumes represented an unabashed defense of the Old School position. At the beginning of his project, he noted that many New School advocates were claiming "that we owe our ecclesiastical existence to Congregationalists; that the condition of ministerial communion among us was assent to the essential doctrines of the Gospel [rather than assent to the essential doctrines of Calvinism]; and that the presbyterian form of government which our fathers adopted was of a very mitigated character." Through his reconstruction of the Presbyterian past, Hodge sought to demolish these contentions. In his account of the denomination's history, the Congregationalist input had been minimal, and Presbyterian ministers had always been expected to subscribe *rigorously* to the Westminster Confession of Faith. Despite his own family's origins in New Side Presbyterianism in the previous century, Hodge wrote as if the true lineage of Presbyterianism flowed through the Old Side. He also used his historical work to link Presbyterian polity to orthodoxy and looser structures to heterodoxy. When he looked at New England's Congregationalism and then surveyed "the obvious decline in the religious character of the people, and the extensive prevalence, at different periods, of fanaticism and Antinomianism, Arminianism, and Pelagianism," it was obvious to Hodge how essential Presbyterian polity was. Or, as he wrote:

26. [Charles Hodge,] "General Assembly of 1837," *Biblical Repertory and Princeton Review* 9 (1837): 407-85.

Where the preservation of the purity of the church is committed to the mass of the people, who, as a general rule, are incompetent to judge in doctrinal matters, and who, in many cases, are little under the influence of true religion, we need not wonder that corruption should from time to time prevail. As Christ has appointed presbyters to rule in the church according to his word, on them devolve the duty and responsibility of maintaining the truth. This charge is safest in the hands of those to whom Christ has assigned it.[27]

The *Constitutional History* was a sharp, polemical assessment of the Presbyterian past made more to justify the recent Old School actions than to offer a balanced assessment of the past. Its treatment of the New Side pained Archibald Alexander, who thought that Hodge had presented that group in too harsh a light and had been too lenient with the Old Side. Partly to redress the imbalance, Alexander produced his own *Biographical Sketches of the Founder and Principal Alumni of the Log College.* Hodge had not spoken his only word on theological diversity. This was a painful experience for both Hodge and Alexander, who sustained a relationship comparable to a father and son. The *Constitutional History* did not mean that Hodge and his Princeton colleagues would always defend everything that their denomination's General Assembly did in future years; but following the Presbyterian wars of the 1830s, a sharper defense of Old School ideas became even more central to Princeton Seminary's identity.[28]

27. Charles Hodge, *The Constitutional History of the Presbyterian Church in the United States of America,* 2 vols. (Philadelphia: William S. Martien, 1839-1840), 1:iv; 2:7, 72.

28. A. A. Hodge, *Life of Charles Hodge* (New York: Charles Scribner's Sons, 1880), 283; Archibald Alexander, *Biographical Sketches of the Founder and Principal Alumni of the Log College* (Philadelphia: Presbyterian Board of Education, 1851).

CHAPTER SIX

Princeton, Society, and Pre–Civil War America

W HEN Archibald Alexander presented to the General Assembly of 1837 the proposed pastoral letter explaining why the General Assembly had taken the drastic action of expelling several synods, his document dealt at length with errors of theology and polity. The pastoral letter also suggested that these errors were part of a deeper problem abroad in the land.

> One of the most formidable evils of the present crisis is the wide spread and ever restless spirit of *radicalism,* manifest both in the church and in the state. Its leading principle every where seems to be to level all order to the dust. Mighty only in the power to destroy, it has driven its deep agitations through the bosom of our beloved church. Amidst the multiplied and revolting forms in which it has appeared, it is always animated by one principle. It is ever the same leveling revolutionary spirit and tends to the same ruinous results. It has, in succession, driven to extreme fanaticism the great cause of revivals of religion, of temperance, and of the rights of man. It has aimed to transmute our pure faith into destructive heresy, our scriptural order into confusion and misrule.[1]

The descent into heresy and new measures revivalism was part and parcel of a fanaticism threatening to overthrow the social order itself.

---

1. *Minutes of the General Assembly of the Presbyterian Church in the United States of America from A.D. 1821 to A.D. 1831 Inclusive* (Philadelphia: Presbyterian Board of Publication, 1837), 657.

141

The fear ran so deep in some Old School quarters that it continued to smolder years after the division. As late as 1855, Isaac V. Brown, the seminary trustee who had met with the faculty in Hodge's study in 1836, still contended that "the palpable perversions of religious truth" in the New School would, if unchecked, have "prove[d] the programme to an age of infidelity, and introduce[d] upon the American stage the shocking theological panorama of universal derangement and confusion in the elements of the moral world; as a parallel to which we may point only to the reign of terror and triumph of ungodliness in the *French Revolution*." To understand how that overheated rhetoric might seem credible, we need first to understand what Princeton's ideal of the social order was.[2]

A Whiggish View of Society

The leaders of Princeton Seminary did not start from a single or unified view on all matters concerning politics or society — a fact apparent in the lives of the first three professors. From the beginning of his career, Archibald Alexander took little interest in matters of politics. In commenting on his father's attitude toward the War of 1812, J. W. Alexander wrote: "Privately, he lamented the policy which involved us in these troubles; but he never took any active part in politics, never preached a political sermon in his life, and indeed seldom voted at an election." By contrast, Samuel Miller early in his New York career ardently espoused Jeffersonian democracy, though his admiration for Jefferson had turned to contempt by the time he went to Princeton in 1813. Charles Hodge came from a family of strong federalist sympathies that were deepened when Jefferson's diplomatic policies toward Europe ruined the income his mother derived from the share in the Philadelphia wharf left by her late husband.[3]

Although they came from different perspectives, the other professors at the seminary seemed initially to be following Alexander's disengagement from politics. "On coming to Princeton in 1813," Samuel Miller recorded, "I resolved to begin a new course in regard to politics. I deter-

2. Isaac V. Brown, *A Historical Vindication of the Abrogation of the Plan of Union by the Presbyterian Church in the United States of America* (Philadelphia: William S. & Alfred Martien, 1855), iii.

3. James W. Alexander, *The Life of Archibald Alexander, D.D.* (New York: Charles Scribner, 1854), 379.

mined to do and say as little on the subject as could be deemed consistent with the character of a good citizen: to attend no political meetings; to write no political paragraphs; to avoid talking on the subject much either in public or private; to do little more than to go quietly and silently to the polls, deposit my vote, and withdraw." Charles Hodge maintained a deep, lifelong fascination with political and social matters, but that interest appears to have had little public manifestation before the 1830s. Concentration on religious nurture and theological formation reflected the redirection of Presbyterian educational efforts that had led to the creation of the seminary in 1812 and the replacement of Samuel Stanhope Smith with Ashbel Green at the college in the same year.[4]

But the seeming disengagement from politics did not indicate a lack of commitment to the public order or an absence of conviction about the centrality of Christianity to social welfare. At the heart of the Presbyterian understanding in the post-Revolutionary era was the belief that America's republican institutions were the products of Protestant Christianity and needed the maintenance of this religious heritage if those institutions were to endure. From this perspective the constitutional guarantee of religious freedom did not require the complete separation of church and state; it merely promised, in Fred Hood's words, governmental "neutrality toward the various Protestant denominations" and gave the churches an opportunity to create through voluntary persuasion "the true association between religion and patriotism" — that is, an unofficial establishment of religion in which Protestant values and morality would permeate and thereby protect the social order. It was this vision that American Presbyterians had in mind when in 1789 they struck out of the Westminster Confession the original passage about the civil magistrate's duty to see "that all blasphemies and heresies be suppressed, all corruptions and abuses in worship and discipline prevented," and replaced it with the assertion that "as nursing fathers, it is

4. Samuel Miller, *The Life of Samuel Miller, D.D., LL.D.,* 2 vols. (Philadelphia: Claxton, Remsen and Haffelfinger, 1869), 2:11. During the first decade of the seminary's life, political lines were less clear-cut as Federalism waned as a national political force. It ran its last presidential candidate in 1816. Virtually all political activity then took place within factions of the Democratic Republican party of Jefferson and Madison. While there were often abrasive contests at the local and national levels, there were no clear party battle lines until the 1830s and the emergence of the so-called second party system. See, for example, Michael F. Holt, *The Rise and Fall of the American Whig Party: Jacksonian Politics and the Onset of the American Civil War* (New York: Oxford University Press, 1999), 2-18.

the duty of civil magistrates to protect the church of our common Lord, without giving the preference to any denomination of Christians above the rest, in such a manner that all ecclesiastical persons whatever shall enjoy the full, free, and unquestioned liberty of discharging every part of their sacred functions, without violence or danger." Four years later, in his address to the Tammany Society in New York, Samuel Miller underscored the essential role that Christianity played in sustaining democratic republican institutions when he asserted that the gospel "tends to quench every extravagant thirst for power; to beat down every high thought, that exalteth itself against the general good; and to render men contented with those rights which the God of nature gave them." Or as Robert Baird, seminary graduate and sometime tutor of Addison Alexander, put the matter in the 1840s: "a people that believe in Christianity can never consent that the government they live under should be indifferent to its promotion since public as well as private virtue is connected indissolubly with a proper knowledge of its nature and its claims."[5]

These principles led Presbyterians into a controversy over the transport and delivery of the United States mail on Sundays. In 1810 Congress passed a law requiring postmasters to open their offices *any* day on which mail arrived. (In that era, mail was not delivered door to door but had to be picked up by recipients.) The law aroused a storm of opposition from a number of Protestant groups, with Presbyterians among the most active. By 1812 the General Assembly called not only for the repeal of the law requiring that the post offices be open on the Sabbath if mail had been delivered; it also demanded an end to the transporting of mail on Sundays. In cooperation with New England Congregationalists, they began a campaign to deluge Congress with petitions for a change in the postal policy. By 1815, approximately a hundred petitions from New England to Kentucky and from Maine to Delaware had arrived on Capitol Hill. Although sabbatarian protest was reduced to an ember by 1817, it was reignited by the General Assembly of 1826, which took the protest even further by urging a boycott of transportation companies that ran even a single stagecoach, canal boat, or steamship on Sunday. In Rochester, New York, Josiah

5. Fred J. Hood, *Reformed America: The Middle and Southern States, 1783-1837* (University, AL: University of Alabama Press, 1980); Samuel Miller, *A Sermon Preached in New York, July 4th 1793, Being the Anniversary of the Independence of the United States at the Request of the Tammany Society* (New York: Thomas Greenleaf, 1793), 22, 29, 30; Robert Baird, *Religion in America; or, An Account of the Origin, Progress, Relation to the State, and Present Condition of the Evangelical Churches in the United States* (New York: Harper and Bros., 1844), 116.

Bissell Jr., a Presbyterian elder and prosperous businessman, founded the Pioneer Line, a transportation company that ceased all Sunday travel but still managed to compete successfully with other businesses. Bissell helped organize yet another voluntary society — the General Union for the Promotion of the Christian Sabbath — that aimed to raise the consciousness of Americans on the matter. At this point Princeton joined the fray. In 1827, professors from the college along with Alexander and Miller from the seminary — Hodge was still in Europe — presented a petition calling for a community "ordinance prohibiting stages, wagons, etc., from passing through the town on the Sabbath."[6]

Several years later, Charles Hodge weighed in with an article in the *Biblical Repertory* on behalf of laws protecting Sunday observance. Hodge contended that the Sabbath promoted the welfare of society. His claims may sound extravagant or quaint by the standards of a later age, but they were widely shared in his own time. Asserting the day to be of "such incalculable importance" that "its proper observance is the only security for public morals," Hodge painted an idyllic picture of the Sabbath as the time when the social order was knit together and differences composed. When men and women assembled Sunday after Sunday for the public worship of God, Hodge explained:

The differences arising from wealth and other adventitious circumstances here disappear. The high are humbled without being depressed; the low are exalted without being elated. The cord, which vibrates in one breast, is felt in all the others, awakening the consciousness of community. . . . They learn that God has made of one flesh all dwellers upon earth . . . and has thus bound them together as one great brotherhood.

The laws that encouraged Sabbath observance and proscribed its desecration were not sectarian, for they voiced a common Christian — or at least Protestant — value. Here was an instance of the principle set forth in the revised American version of the Westminster Confession in 1789: the duty of "civil magistrates to protect the church of our common Lord,

6. Richard R. John, "Taking Sabbatarianism Seriously: The Postal System, the Sabbath, and the Transformation of American Political Culture," *Journal of the Early Republic* 10 (Winter 1990): 517-67; John Frelinghuysen Hageman, *History of Princeton and Its Institutions,* 2 vols. (Philadelphia: J. B. Lippincott and Co., 1879), 2:6.

without giving the preference to any denomination of Christians above the rest." In the 1831 article Hodge seemed to ground that duty in the fact that Christians enjoyed majority status in the United States. "As long as the great mass of the people profess the Christian religion, so long must government respect that religion." It was an argument strongly rejected by the then current administration of President Jackson and his allies in Congress.[7]

When he returned to the subject of Sunday laws nearly three decades later, Hodge's argument for the role of Christianity in public life had taken on a sharper edge. The faith's special status in America had to do with more than numbers. "This is a Protestant and Christian country," he thundered. "This does not mean merely that the great majority of the people are Protestant Christians. . . . As every tree or plant, every race of animals, so every nation has its own organic life. If you plant an acorn it developes into an oak; and as it grows it assimilates all that comes within the sphere of its activity." Since Protestants were the "progenitors of our country," they established the organic life to which others must conform. Hodge recognized that Roman Catholics, Jews, and some of atheist sentiments had immigrated to the United States. They were all permitted "to acquire property, to vote in all elections, made eligible to all offices, and invested with an equal influence in all public concerns. All are allowed to worship as they please, or not at all if they please." "Is this not liberty enough?" Hodge asked. From Hodge's perspective, it was enough indeed. One thing these people could not, in his view, claim was the right to set the moral tone or establish the ethos of America. Speaking to these more recent immigrants, Hodge concluded his article with a warning: "We [Protestant Christians] must obey God. We must carry our religion into our families, our workshops, our banking-houses, our municipal and other governments; and if you cannot live with Christians, you must go elsewhere."[8]

For Hodge, the Christian character of the nation was at stake in the battle over the Sabbath. So it was also in the question of honoring treaties with the Cherokee nation. After the American Revolution, the Cherokees signed a treaty relinquishing much of their traditional land in the

---

7. [Charles Hodge,] "The American Quarterly Review on Sunday Mails," *Biblical Repertory and Theological Review* 3 (1831): 103, 104, 105, 127.

8. [Charles Hodge,] "Sunday Laws," *Biblical Repertory and Princeton Review* 31 (1859): 757, 758, 767.

southeast United States. Yet within this restricted domain, chiefly in northwest Georgia with some overlap into adjoining states, they experienced what one of their most thorough students has called a renascence. Turning to their own purpose elements of white culture, they created prosperous farms, produced a written version of their language, launched newspapers, and established a republican form of government. White settlers were eager to expand into the lands of the native Americans and longed for their removal. In 1802, Georgia and the federal government signed a compact in which the state gave up land claims in territories further west in return for a commitment from the national government to the eventual removal of the Indian population. After 1802, the treaties with the Cherokees were renegotiated, further limiting their territory, until in 1819 they refused to cede any more land. Almost immediately Georgians started demanding the expulsion of the Cherokee, but Presidents James Monroe and John Quincy Adams resisted. With the election of Andrew Jackson in 1828, the supporters of removal gained a strong advocate in the White House; and the arguments over removal mounted dramatically. Protestant missionaries who labored among the Cherokee became ardent opponents of expulsion; and Protestant publications, voluntary societies, and especially women's organizations voiced outrage over the policy. Charles Hodge shared the anger over Jackson's Native American policy and wrote to his brother Hugh in October 1831 of his disgust "with the present miserable incumbent," adding: "Verily, I think I could in such a case join a rebellion, with a clear conscience, as I am sure I could with a full heart." A year and a half later, he wrote to Tholuck that America's "national character will be deeply stained" because "our present rulers" showed "disregard of solemn treaties" made with the Cherokee nation.[9]

Like many evangelical Protestants, Hodge and his Princeton colleagues held views that drove them into the anti-Jackson camp, which by 1834 called itself the Whig party. A term traditionally denoting opposition to executive despotism, "Whig" was an appropriate name for those who saw themselves fighting a man depicted by one of their cartoonists as

9. William G. McLoughlin, *Cherokee Renascence in the New Republic* (Princeton: Princeton University Press, 1986); McLoughlin, *Cherokees and Missionaries, 1789-1839* (New Haven: Yale University Press, 1984); Mary Hershberger, "Mobilizing Women, Anticipating Abolition: The Struggle Against Indian Removal in the 1830s," *Journal of American History* 86 (June 1999): 14-40; A. A. Hodge, *Life of Charles Hodge* (New York: Charles Scribner's Sons, 1880), 218, 230-31.

King Andrew I. Yet despite its origins in opposition to Jackson, there was more to the party than saying no to King Andrew. Making due allowances for the variations that exist in any broad-based political party, one can say that Whigs offered a positive program and vision: a strong national bank to provide the necessary capital to fuel economic growth, the use of tariffs to protect American industries, and federal support for "internal improvements" such as roads, canals, and railroads that would facilitate commerce and national unity. This was a program that prominent Whig Henry Clay put forth under the rubric "the American System." Although many evangelical Protestants were drawn to the Whig party, not all were. The way in which the evangelical ethos functioned within the two parties differed. "Under the second party system," Richard J. Carwardine observes, "both Whigs and Democrats annexed the support of evangelical Protestantism," but they did so in separate ways. "Whig evangelicals," he adds, "tended to look towards an active, benevolent government that would regulate social behavior and maintain moral standards. Democrats leant in the direction of a neutral state in which regenerate individuals regulated their own behavior voluntarily." In other words, within the Whig party the evangelical ethos was more public and activist — or, in the view of Democratic critics, more officious in meddling in the affairs of others. The Whig movement resonated with the themes of moral self-improvement, individual and collective, that also characterized the revivalism, reform movements, and voluntary societies of the evangelical united front. In fact, one might well argue, as Daniel Walker Howe has done, that this "evangelical organizing process was the religious precursor and counterpart of the so-called American System." There was irony in Princeton's affinity to the Whigs, for that was the same party to which people such as Albert Barnes, Charles Finney, and probably a great majority of New School Presbyterians adhered. This fact serves as a reminder that the Princetonians were not cranky reactionaries opposed flat out to the public and activist character of popular evangelical Protestantism with its moral crusades and voluntary societies. What they resisted was what they deemed to be the fanatical excess with which such activities were pursued by their New School opponents.[10]

10. Richard J. Carwardine, *Evangelicals and Politics in Antebellum America* (New Haven: Yale University Press, 1993), 35; Carwardine, "The Politics of Charles Hodge," in *Charles Hodge Revisited: A Critical Appraisal of His Life and Work,* ed. John W. Stewart and James H. Moorhead (Grand Rapids: Eerdmans, 2002), 247-97; Daniel Walker Howe, "The

At one time, the Whigs were commonly portrayed as the party of privileged elites and the Jacksonian Democrats as the advocates of the "common man." This stereotype contains an element of truth. Whigs did tend to have great strength among commercial and financial interests, often distrusted the newer immigrant groups, and sometimes feared that uninformed citizens might give way to class envy and oppose policies (usually pro-business) that made for progress. Charles Hodge manifested these Whig tendencies to a marked degree. He placed a premium on property rights, worried that widespread suffrage might ruin sane government, and favored a longer period of naturalization for immigrants prior to citizenship. The franchise, he believed, was not a universal right but rather a privilege that society bestowed upon those prepared to exercise it wisely. Hodge also exemplified the typical Whig emphasis upon moral discipline, which, to some degree, functioned as a way of controlling unruly immigrants and the lower orders of society. But in the first instance, the discipline for which Whigs called was *self*-discipline intended to improve the lot of everyone. By contrast, Jackson's Democrats did indeed claim to fight for the people against vested interests allegedly seeking unfair advantage, and they generally welcomed the newer immigrants, whom they often brought into their electoral coalition. On the other hand, "the people" by no stretch of the antebellum Democratic party's imagination included African Americans. While no political group had a monopoly on racism, it was particularly virulent within the party of Andrew Jackson. Moreover, the Democrats were far more likely than their Whig counterparts to seek opportunities for "the people" by acquiring new territories for settlement. Thus Andrew Jackson sanctioned the removal of the Cherokees, President Polk led the nation into war with Mexico in 1846 to secure more land, and some in the party longed to plant the American flag over Cuba. By contrast, the Whigs tended to see the promotion of opportunity for all less in terms of territorial expansion and more in terms of cultivating improvements within the space the nation already occupied. Moreover, the cause of public education and a whole range of humanitarian reforms usually found greater support among Whigs than Democrats.

Evangelical Movement and Political Culture in the North During the Second Party System," *Journal of American History* 77 (March 1991): 1223. There is some evidence that Old School Presbyterianism as a whole was more closely divided between the two major parties; Robert W. Doherty, "Social Bases for the Presbyterian Schism of 1837-1838: The Philadelphia Case," *Journal of Social History* 2 (Fall 1968): 69-79.

To observe, then, that nineteenth-century Princeton Seminary generally adhered to a Whig view of society is to say that it cannot be pigeonholed neatly by using terms such as "liberal" or "conservative" as they are commonly employed in the twenty-first century.[11]

Princeton and the Peculiar Institution

In 1818, the Presbyterian General Assembly had a serious moral issue thrown into its lap. It was asked to rule whether a church member, selling a slave who happened to be a fellow believer, should be brought to discipline if the slave did not wish to be sold. The General Assembly referred the issue to a committee chaired by Ashbel Green, president of the college and of the seminary's board of directors. The often-cited introduction to the report, passed unanimously by the Assembly, merits quotation at length.

> We consider the voluntary enslaving of one part of the human race by another, as a gross violation of the most precious and sacred rights of human nature; as utterly inconsistent with the law of God, which requires us to love our neighbour as ourselves, and as totally irreconcilable with the spirit and principles of the gospel of Christ, which enjoin that "all things whatsoever ye would that men should do to you, do ye even so to them." Slavery creates a paradox in the moral system; it exhibits rational, accountable, and immortal beings in such circumstances as scarcely to leave them the power of moral action. It exhibits them as dependent on the will of others, whether they shall receive religious instruction; whether they shall know and worship the true God; whether they shall enjoy the ordinances of the gospel; whether they shall perform the duties and cherish the endearments of husbands and wives, parents and children, neighbours and friends; whether they shall preserve their chastity and purity, or regard the dictates of justice and humanity.

11. Perhaps the classic example of the portrayal of Democrats as the party of the common people versus the Whigs as the party of the elites is Arthur M. Schlesinger Jr., *The Age of Jackson* (Boston: Little, Brown, and Co., 1945). For a now classic overview of the culture that informed the Whig party, see Daniel Walker Howe, *The Political Culture of the American Whigs* (Chicago: University of Chicago Press, 1969).

The report then asserted that it was the clear "duty of all Christians . . . to use their honest, earnest, and unwearied endeavours, to correct the errors of former times, and as speedily as possible to efface this blot on our holy religion, and to obtain the complete abolition of slavery throughout Christendom, and if possible throughout the world."[12]

The level of antislavery commitment behind these stirring words should not be overestimated, for the report made clear that "as speedily as possible" did not mean any time soon. "The number of slaves, their ignorance, and their vicious habits generally," said the assembly, "render an immediate and universal emancipation inconsistent alike with the safety and happiness of the master and the slave." Moreover, the report expressed sympathy with the plight of those "portions of the church and our country where the evil of slavery has been entailed upon them," and it warned "others to forbear harsh censures, and uncharitable reflections on their brethren, who unhappily live among slaves, whom they cannot immediately set free." In other words, the Assembly saw slaveholders as themselves slaves of a sort caught in a system they did not create, their predicament calling for compassion, not condemnation. The judicatory recommended several tangible steps to ameliorate the suffering of black Americans. Presbyterians might "patronize and encourage the society lately formed, for colonizing in Africa, the land of their ancestors, the free people of colour in our country." Masters were also encouraged to instruct their slaves in Christianity and to keep their families intact. With regard to the issue that occasioned the report, the Assembly advised that the case of any Presbyterian selling "a slave who is also in communion and good standing with our Church, contrary to his or her will" ought to be brought immediately to the attention of the proper judicatory for possible discipline. The same General Assembly issuing this statement had, a few days earlier, sustained the removal from the ministry of the Rev. George Bourne. Virginia's Lexington Presbytery had deposed Bourne for denouncing slaveholders as guilty of the worst form of theft — manstealing — and for attacking fellow clergy as complicit in the slave system.[13]

12. *Minutes of the General Assembly of the Presbyterian Church in the United States of America from Its Organization, A.D. 1789 to A.D. 1820* (Philadelphia: Presbyterian Board of Publication, 1847), 688, 692.

13. *Minutes, 1789 to 1820,* 692-94; John W. Christie and Dwight L. Dumond, *George Bourne and "The Book and Slavery Irreconcilable"* (Baltimore: Historical Society of Delaware and Presbyterian Historical Society, 1969), 47-65; Andrew E. Murray, *Presbyterians and the Negro: A History* (Philadelphia: Presbyterian Historical Society, 1966), 12-28.

The General Assembly's statement represented a transitional moment when antislavery sentiment was turning from optimism to caution. "Everywhere in the country," Gordon Wood has written of the 1780s, "most of the Revolutionary leaders assumed that slavery was on its last legs and headed for destruction." Between 1777 and 1804, northern states outlawed slavery or provided for the gradual emancipation of those in bondage. Even in the South, particularly the Upper South, many felt the institution to be waning. In some places the strict slave codes passed at the beginning of the eighteenth century were laxly enforced. Virginia, Delaware, and Maryland passed laws making it easier for masters to free slaves, and there was often talk in the South of the eventual demise of the institution. Then, in 1807, largely with southern acquiescence, Congress outlawed the foreign slave trade. But as early as the 1790s, there were also signs of growing wariness about antislavery rhetoric. The black rebellion in the French colony Saint-Domingue (Haiti), and later, in 1800, the revolt in Henrico County, Virginia, led by the artisan slave Gabriel, made many Southerners uneasy with loose talk about freedom or ameliorating the condition of slaves. Laws now obliged free blacks to carry papers or wear patches proving their freedom, and Virginia in 1806 passed a statute requiring that freed slaves depart the state. Also, with the invention of the cotton gin and the opening of new territories east of the Mississippi River, the use of slave labor spread rapidly and became more — not less — entrenched in southern economy and society.[14]

Within a year of the General Assembly's pronouncement, the tenacity of slavery's hold was manifest. A New York congressman in February 1819 proposed amendments to a bill allowing Missouri, still a territory, to draft a constitution and petition for statehood. He wanted Missouri's constitution to guarantee that no future slaves could be brought into the state and that the children born to those already in bondage in Missouri would henceforth be freed at age 25. His proposals met a nearly solid wall of resistance from southern leaders. Many of them insisted, however, that extension of the peculiar institution into Missouri would not perpetuate slavery but rather help to end it. By diffusing slaves more evenly throughout the country, extension would lower the ratio of blacks

---

14. Gordon S. Wood, *Empire of Liberty: A History of the Early Republic, 1789-1815* (New York: Oxford University Press, 2009), 508-42; quotation on 518; Douglas R. Egerton, *Gabriel's Rebellion: The Virginia Slave Conspiracies of 1800 and 1802* (Chapel Hill: University of North Carolina Press, 1993).

to whites in existing slave states and thus make it easier and safer for white governments to free them. One contemporary historian, allowing that this argument undoubtedly functioned in part to justify profits from slavery, also contends that it revealed an even deeper fear of southerners that they were trapped by their own system of bondage. Deliverance lay in "a vision of getting blacks safely out, of whitening a world, of removing the race to other plains." To that observation one might add that it was not only southern whites, but northern as well, who dreamt of "getting blacks safely out."[15]

One organization addressing this issue was the American Colonization Society (ACS), formally launched in January 1817. It was the ACS that the General Assembly endorsed a year later in its pronouncement on slavery because of the group's goal to colonize "in Africa, the land of their ancestors, the free people of colour in our country." One of those who played a role in the founding of the ACS was Robert Finley, a Presbyterian minister in Basking Ridge, New Jersey, a graduate of Princeton College, and a director of Princeton Seminary. Archibald Alexander later claimed that Finley called the "first public meeting which ever took place to consider the subject of African colonization in this country," that it occurred in the Presbyterian Church in Princeton, and that "most of the professors of the college and theological seminary" attended. Contemporary scholarship has played down the role of Finley and has seen the religious impulse as less central to the society's founding than the desire to rid the country of a potentially dangerous underclass of freed blacks. In fact, the widespread appeal of colonization in the early nineteenth century was its ability to blend together a variety of purposes and motives. The movement drew some who genuinely wished to improve the condition of blacks, others who were eager to purge the nation of its free black population, and many who no doubt wished to do both. Since the society did not challenge the property rights of slaveholders or brand them as sinners, it attracted less controversy than did the later abolitionist movement of the 1830s, which demanded the immediate, uncompensated emancipation of slaves. Many prominent figures, from Henry Clay to Millard Fillmore and Harriet Beecher Stowe, endorsed the colonization cause, and even in the midst of the Civil War President Lincoln initially toyed with the idea.[16]

15. William W. Freehling, *The Road to Disunion: Secessionists at Bay, 1776-1854* (New York: Oxford University Press, 1990), 144-61; quotation on 152.

16. Archibald Alexander, *A History of Colonization on the Western Coast of Africa* (Phil-

The depth of commitment within the seminary faculty to the colonization scheme was attested by the huge tome that Archibald Alexander wrote tracing the origins and progress of the movement. At more than six hundred pages, *A History of Colonization on the Western Coast of Africa* (1846) was by far his largest book. Various passages in the work hint at the appeal of colonization to Alexander. His bedrock conviction was the impossibility of blacks and whites living together on an egalitarian basis.

> Two races of men, nearly equal in numbers, but differing as much as the whites and blacks, cannot form one harmonious society in any other way than by amalgamation; but the whites and blacks, in this country, by no human efforts, could be amalgamated into one homogeneous mass in a thousand years; and during this long period, the state of society would be perpetually disturbed by many contending factions. Either the whites must remove and give up the country to the coloured people, or the coloured people must be removed; otherwise the latter must remain in subjection to the former.

Unable to envision an egalitarian biracial society in the United States, Alexander concluded that "we can confer a real benefit on the African race in no other way than by separating them from the whites, and removing them to the country of their fathers." Alexander did not ponder the (in)justice of racial prejudice, considered any struggle to overcome it futile, and in the end turned to a long view of history to construct a theodicy of slavery in which the sufferings borne by blacks were rationalized by God's ultimate purpose. "Why many of this unhappy race were ever permitted to be brought to America," he explains, "begins now to appear. They were sent here by a benignant Providence overruling the wicked passions of avaricious men, that they might be christianized and

---

adelphia: William S. Martien, 1846), 80. For a traditional view of the centrality of Finley and the evangelical motivation in colonization, see P. J. Staudenraus, *The African Colonization Movement, 1816-1865* (New York: Columbia University Press, 1961); for the alternate view, consult Douglas R. Egerton, "'Its Origin Is Not a Little Curious': A New Look at the American Colonization Society," *Journal of the Early Republic* 5 (Winter 1985): 463-80, and *Charles Fenton Mercer and the Trial of National Conservatism* (Jackson: University of Mississippi Press, 1989). Finley himself managed to appeal to multiple motives in his *Thoughts on the Colonization of Free Blacks*, as quoted in Isaac V. Brown, *Memoirs of the Rev. Robert Finley, D.D.* (New Brunswick, NJ: Terhune & Letson, 1819), 90-94.

civilized, and might carry back to their benighted countrymen, the principles of religion, freedom, and representative government."[17]

How strong the hold of colonization was in Princeton may be judged
from the fact that as late as 1877 — twelve years after the close of the Civil
War — Professor Alexander T. McGill of the seminary preached to the
Colonization Society, meeting in Washington, D.C., and lauded the fact
that it continued its work. In that year, when the remaining northern
troops were withdrawing from the South and the last of the Reconstruction governments fell to "Redeemers" determined to restore white supremacy, McGill asserted that politics, constitutional amendments, and
a federal army of occupation could do no more on behalf of the African
American. "No remedy here [within the United States] can advance him
another step," McGill suggested, "no mechanism of party can put on him
the true habiliment of manhood. We must send him home [to Africa],
when he is willing to go, and see that his home is attractive and safe, as it
was not when he was torn from it and sold from bondage to bondage."
Whatever one's assessment of the intentions of Archibald Alexander,
A. T. McGill, and others, colonization ultimately functioned as a way of
defusing or evading protest against slavery, racial prejudice, and discrimination.[18]

The seminary's approach to matters of slavery and race also derived
from its geographic location and its institutional connections. During
the school's first half-century, slavery in New Jersey was not yet dead. In
1804, a law decreed that all persons born to slaves after July 4 of that year
would be free people; however, they remained bound to serve their
mother's owner until adulthood — men until 25 years of age, women until 21. Those already in bondage in 1804 remained so until their deaths.
When the state decided in 1846 to abolish slavery in name, those still in
bondage remained permanent "apprentices." As late as 1860, the federal
census still recorded a handful of slaves in New Jersey. Moreover, both
the college and the seminary had significant numbers of students from
slaveholding states. The numbers fluctuated from year to year, but from
the 1820s through the 1840s the seminary usually drew between 20 and
30 percent of its student body from these areas. The bond with the South

17. Alexander, *History of Colonization*, 12, 17, 18.

18. Alexander T. McGill, *Patriotism, Philanthropy, and Religion: An Address before the
American Colonization Society, January 16, 1877* (Washington, DC: Colonization Society,
1877), 3-4.

was more, however, than a matter of having to accommodate the views of a student constituency from below the Mason-Dixon Line. It was also an issue of accountability, for as the seminary of the entire Presbyterian Church, Princeton was ultimately controlled by a General Assembly containing numerous representatives from the South.[19]

The seminary's involvement with slavery was also personal. Archibald Alexander had served a Virginia church that owned slaves, possibly during his pastorate; and when he and Janetta moved to Philadelphia, they brought a slave who later returned to Virginia. Samuel Miller grew up in a slaveholding family in Delaware. Although in New York City he spoke against slavery as an evil, he espoused the gradualist philosophy of emancipation and did not consider it a violation of his principles when he later used slave labor in Princeton. As his son wrote, "during the earlier part of his residence in New Jersey, [Miller] at several times held slaves under the laws providing for the gradual abolition of human bondage." In these instances, he had them "only for a term of years," except for one instance in which the seller lied about the status of a slave whose age made him liable to service for life. Without such labor, noted the son, "it was difficult otherwise to secure domestics." Because of the same difficulty, Charles Hodge also resorted to slave labor. In 1828, to provide assistance to his wife with household chores, he purchased a 16-year-old female who had five years to labor before being set free; and he may also have rented from the owner a slave named Cato, perhaps to help Hodge with the fields that he farmed near his house.[20]

Despite their personal and ecclesiastical entanglements, Alexander, Miller, and Hodge did, of course, endorse a *mildly* antislavery view. They looked toward the gradual and eventual demise of human bondage, regarded the repatriation of freed blacks to Africa as a valuable step in the right direction, and believed that in the meantime the holding of slaves was not a sinful act. While this outlook was in sync with what many Prot-

19. See, for example, Simeon F. Moss, "The Persistence of Slavery and Involuntary Servitude in a Free State (1685-1866)," *Journal of Negro History* 35 (July 1950): 289-314; Arthur Zilversmit, *The First Emancipation: The Abolition of Slavery in the North* (Chicago: University of Chicago Press, 1967); Graham Russell Hodges, *Root and Branch: African Americans in New York and East Jersey, 1613-1863* (Chapel Hill: University of North Carolina Press, 1999); Allen C. Guelzo, "Charles Hodge's Antislavery Moment," in Stewart and Moorhead, eds., *Charles Hodge Revisited*, 299-325.

20. Miller, *Life of Samuel Miller*, 2:300; Guelzo, "Charles Hodge's Antislavery Moment," 308.

estants then believed, a more strident kind of antislavery position came to the fore in the late 1820s and early 1830s. Among urban African Americans in the North, opposition to colonization mounted, typified by works such as Presbyterian minister Samuel Cornish's *Freedom's Journal* and David Walker's *Appeal.* In large measure because of stiffening resistance in the black community, a few white opponents of slavery began rethinking their own positions. The American Anti-Slavery Society (AAS), formed in 1833, unequivocally condemned slaveholding as a sin and rejected colonization as a bogus reform; it distracted from the true moral imperative: *immediate* emancipation of the enslaved. Although some in the AAS and its leader, William Lloyd Garrison, eventually turned to heterodox religious views and attacked the churches for their reticence to be forthrightly antislavery, much of the initial inspiration for abolitionism came from the spiritual energy generated by the revivals of the Second Great Awakening. Within the Presbyterian Church, this new outlook resulted in demands for a statement against human bondage more vigorous than the 1818 deliverance. For example, in 1835 the Presbytery of Chillicothe (Ohio) asked the General Assembly to declare that "buying, selling, or holding slaves, for the sake of gain, is a heinous sin and scandal," that trying to capture a runaway slave is "a scandalous sin," and that bequeathing slaves as property in one's will "is a great sin." With this sort of antislavery, the majority in the Assembly — as well as the faculty at Princeton Seminary — were distinctly ill at ease.[21]

In 1836 Charles Hodge took up his pen to write for the *Biblical Repertory* a lengthy essay detailing what he believed to be the proper attitude toward the question of slavery. On the basis of this piece and several others, one contemporary historian includes Hodge in a gallery of those whom he calls "early Northern proslavery ideologists." The classification is at once accurate and seriously misleading. The description is correct insofar as Hodge insisted that slavery was nowhere in the Bible condemned as sinful in itself. According to the Gospel accounts, Jesus never censured slaveholding, though he lived in a world where the institution abounded, and elsewhere New Testament authors enjoined slaves to

---

21. [Charles Hodge,] "The General Assembly of 1835," *Biblical Repertory and Theological Review* 7 (1835): 451. For an excellent account of the way in which the mood in the African American community affected the emergence of abolitionism in the white community, see Peter P. Hinks, *To Awaken My Afflicted Brethren: David Walker and the Problem of Antebellum Slave Resistance* (University Park, PA: Pennsylvania State University Press, 1997), esp. 91-115.

obey their masters. The Old Testament recognized and regulated the institution. "If God allowed slavery to exist," Hodge observed, "if he directed how slaves might be lawfully acquired, and how they were to be treated, it is in vain to contend that slaveholding is a sin, and yet profess reverence for the scriptures." Nor would the Princeton professor allow that slavery was wrong because it "interferes with the natural rights of a portion of the community." Every society "from the freest democracy to the most absolute despotism" curtailed natural rights to a greater or lesser degree.

> In England one man is born a peer, another a commoner; in Russia one is born a noble, another a serf; here one is born a free citizen, another a disenfranchised out-cast (the free coloured man), and a third a slave. These forms of society . . . are not necessarily just or unjust; but become the one or the other according to circumstances.

In short, natural rights — whether of slaves, women, children, or certain people deemed unfit to vote — could be legitimately curtailed based upon what a society felt was consistent with its interest at a given point of development. At bottom, Hodge suggested that the fundamental error of abolitionism was to confuse abuses of the slave system — for example, cruel treatment of those in bondage — with the institution itself. One should no more attack slavery as sinful in itself because some masters failed to practice the system in a humane way than one should reject parenthood as immoral because some men were bad fathers. Thus far Hodge had said nothing inconsistent with what the most ardent "proslavery ideologists" of the South themselves said.[22]

But the argument took an unexpected turn. Near the close of his article he declared that he trusted no one would take the essay to mean "that we regard slavery as a desirable institution or that we approve of the slave laws of the southern states." In fact, he professed to wish "the

22. Larry E. Tise, *Proslavery: A History of the Defense of Slavery in America, 1701-1840* (Athens: University of Georgia Press, 1987), 280. [Charles Hodge,] "Slavery," *Biblical Repertory and Theological Review* 8 (1836): 268-305; quotations on 287, 292, 295. For the fullest treatment of the proslavery argument in the context of the entire worldview of the Southern slaveholders, see Elizabeth Fox-Genovese and Eugene D. Genovese, *The Mind of the Master Class: History and Faith in the Southern Slaveholders' Worldview* (New York and Cambridge: Cambridge University Press, 2005).

extinction of slavery" as much as any abolitionist. His difference with the abolitionists concerned means. The "true method of Christians" in addressing the subject was "to enforce as moral duties the great principles of justice and mercy, and all the specific commands and precepts of the scriptures." "If it be asked," Hodge continued, "what would be the consequence of thus acting on the principles of the gospel, of following the example and obeying the precepts of Christ? We answer, the gradual elevation of the slaves in intelligence, virtue and wealth; the peaceful and speedy extinction of slavery." The South's choice lay "between emancipation by the silent and holy influence of the gospel, securing the elevation of the slaves to the stature and character of freemen, or to abide the issue of a long continued conflict against the laws of God." If the latter option were taken, Hodge had no doubt that the result would be "disastrous," possibly "a desolating servile insurrection." Here Hodge touched a nerve, for memories remained vivid of Saint-Domingue and more recently of the 1831 uprising led by slave preacher Nat Turner in southside Virginia. If someone objected that the elevation of slaves to the status of freemen might also entail their full citizenship, Hodge answered succinctly: "We admit that it is so." This conclusion to an essay, most of which was given to demolishing the case for abolitionism, would indeed seem to merit Allen Guelzo's assessment: "That Hodge could move almost at once from marshalling together Christ and the apostles to defend slavery, to a moment of apparently sober entertainment of emancipation and civil rights presents a double somersault of dizzying proportions."[23]

From Hodge's perspective, however, he was not doing somersaults. To change the metaphor, he was pointing to a sane, conservative middle road to social improvement. Unlike proslavery apologists who argued that the institution was a positive good for society and should be maintained indefinitely, Hodge believed that it was far from ideal and would someday end. But it would not terminate by denouncing slaveholders as moral criminals; abolitionists had actually impeded progress toward emancipation by producing "a state of alarming exasperation at the south, injurious to the slave and dangerous to the country." In their eagerness to end human bondage, they forgot that Christianity "was never designed to tear up the institutions of society by the roots." Christianity uplifted society by the gradual, almost imperceptible suffusion of its val-

23. Hodge, "Slavery," 302, 303, 304, 305; Guelzo, "Charles Hodge's Antislavery Moment," 314.

ues. With some alterations about specifics, Hodge continued to argue for what he deemed a commonsense middle path that would lead to the end of slavery without conflict. In 1844, he again expressed a belief that slavery could not last forever. "The only question is, how is it to end?" If slaves were deliberately kept "degraded," this policy would be "only to treasure up wrath for the day of wrath." But if Americans chose instead "to instruct, to civilize, to evangelize the slaves, to make them as good as we can, intelligent, moral, and religious," then the result "must be peace, a good conscience, and the blessing of God" — not to mention a gradual elevation of slaves to freedom in a way that did not rend the fabric of society. In 1849, he reasserted that "gradual improvement must lead to gradual emancipation," but by then he was no longer hinting at full citizenship for freed slaves. With warnings that the amalgamation of blacks and whites "must inevitably lead to the deterioration of both and fill the country with a feeble and degraded population," he reaffirmed the panacea of colonization in Africa.[24]

To those of a later era, the limits of the approach of Hodge and his colleagues to the question of slavery are all too painfully apparent. When they viewed the problem of slavery, they wanted a gradual, non-disruptive end to slavery — an end that would not tear apart the church, the seminary, or the nation. Looking for ways toward this increasingly elusive goal, they arguably exhibited a measure of genuine concern about the welfare of African Americans and desired a better future for them. But at the end of the day, their discussions and debates were within a *white* community of discourse; black Christians were not included as partners in the conversation. They were the objects of decisions that others — white others — would make about them. The voices of the increasingly vibrant black communities of the 1820s and 1830s were not heard. Hodge saw in his 1836 article a brief glimmer of blacks as full participants in civic life and decisions, but that status was one for which he thought the black community unready at present. For the moment, the voice of society at large — that is, white society — had to make all the choices. In his 1849 article touching on emancipation and colonization, Hodge went to the heart of what he understood to be the relationship between the white and black communities.

24. Hodge, "Slavery," 271, 292; Hodge, "Abolitionism," *Biblical Repertory and Princeton Review* 16 (1844): 579; Hodge, "Emancipation," *Biblical Repertory and Princeton Review* 21 (1849): 594, 603.

The slaves in this country are in a state of pupillage. They are minors. They stand in that relation of dependence and inferiority in which a state of minority essentially consists. They may therefore be rightfully treated as minors and disposed of without their consent in any way consistent with benevolence and justice. If a great good to them as well as to those they leave behind be designed in their removal, there is no principle of right violated in their expatriation.

At least at that moment and by his own description, Hodge's approach to African Americans rested on undiluted paternalism.[25]

Princeton on the Role of Women in Church and Society

Even as slavery and African Americans presented a challenge to Princeton's vision of an orderly America moving forward judiciously, so, too, did questions about the proper role of women. From the considerable research that has been done on women's history (and, more recently, on men's history), perhaps the one nearly universal conclusion is that gender is a historical construct. That is, except for basic physical differences, most of what people take to be the natures of men and women and their proper social functions are not determined by biology but are the product of particular cultures in specific times and places. In the eighteenth and nineteenth centuries, definitions of gender were in flux. The older notion of the male as patriarch of the family continued in virtually all quarters, but the idea was compromised and softened in significant ways, especially in middle- and upper-class communities. The romantic love and companionship uniting husband and wife — as well as woman's role as mother — assumed heightened importance. In the Revolutionary era, writers argued that republican motherhood required women to train their children in the virtues essential to the new political order. By the middle of the nineteenth century, this ideal had transmuted

25. Hodge, "Emancipation," 597. David Torbett, *Theology and Slavery: Charles Hodge and Horace Bushnell* (Macon, GA: Mercer University Press, 2006), makes an interesting argument that Hodge's biblicism not only led him, in the absence of specific scriptural condemnation of slavery, to oppose abolitionism but also forced him to take seriously passages asserting the unity of all humankind and served as a brake on his racism. How effective that brake against racism was, however, is open to question.

into a Victorian cult of domesticity in which the wife and mother re-
created in the home a little bit of Eden before the fall, a place of calm in
the midst of the hurly-burly of the competitive (male) world. Increasingly
regarded as naturally more attuned to religious matters than men,
women would find their calling in the spiritual nurture of their families
and in the promotion of benevolent causes. These changes in perceptions of the role of women contributed to important transformations in
the learning available to them. In the eighteenth century, women were
often schooled somewhat haphazardly, but in the early nineteenth century they had greater opportunity to acquire a liberal education comparable to what men might attain in academies or even colleges. If women
were to be genuine companions to their husbands, to fulfill the impera-
tives of republican motherhood, or to exercise spiritual influence upon
society, did they not also need an education of wider scope?[26]

Although these views have sometimes been interpreted to mean that
women were being excluded from a public role and confined to the private
realm, the reality was far more complex. For example, republican mothers
may have invested themselves chiefly in childrearing, but ultimately that
activity had public significance. Likewise the religious and benevolent
concerns believed to lie within the special province of women pointed outward into the world as well as into the home. Virtually everyone agreed
that women could form voluntary societies to help with the relief of the
poor, to support home or foreign mission, or to educate the young. But
some women carried religious influence into more controversial areas as
they formed organizations to combat prostitution, support abolitionism,
or promote temperance. Were they simply following the logic that women
were called to exert moral influence or were they transgressing into forbidden territory? It was not always easy to tell when the line had been
crossed, and debates over such questions frequently occurred.[27]

26. Out of the voluminous literature on this subject, I am particularly indebted to
Ruth H. Bloch, "American Feminine Ideals in Transition: The Rise of the Moral Mother,
1785-1815," *Feminist Studies* 4 (June 1978): 100-126; Bloch, "Changing Conceptions of Sexuality and Romance in Eighteenth-Century America," *William and Mary Quarterly* 60 (January 2003): 13-42; Mary Beth Norton, "The Evolution of White Women's Experience in Early
America," *American Historical Review* 89 (June 1984): 593-619; Leonard Sweet, "The Female
Seminary Movement and Woman's Mission," *Church History* 54 (March 1985): 41-55.

27. See, for example, Carroll Smith Rosenburg, *Disorderly Conduct: Visions of Gender
in Victorian America* (New York: Knopf, 1985); Lori D. Ginzberg, *Women and the Work of Benevolence: Morality, Politics, and Class in the Nineteenth-Century United States* (New Haven:

Conservative visions of domesticity seemed to fade the further one went from the center of cultural and religious prestige to the periphery. As Catherine Brekus has documented, upstart religious groups of the early 1800s — for example, the Christian Connection, the Freewill Baptists, the Methodists, the African Methodists, and the Millerite movement that looked for the return of Christ in the early 1840s — produced more than a hundred women preachers. Likewise, one could point to the women's rights activists, such as Elizabeth Cady Stanton, who gathered at Seneca Falls, New York, in 1848, and issued *The Declaration of Sentiments* in which they affirmed that "woman is man's equal," that man "has usurped the prerogative of Jehovah himself, claiming it as his right to assign to her a sphere of action, when that belongs to her conscience and her God." From a very different perspective, Joseph Smith and the Latter-day Saints (Mormons) rejected republican womanhood and the cult of domesticity. They did so out of no love for egalitarian views of the relation of men and women. Rather, they wished the restoration of a genuine patriarchy according to the model of the Old Testament and reinstituted polygamy ("celestial marriage"). Other alternative arrangements for the relationship between the sexes emerged in the Shakers, who rejected marriage in favor of celibacy, and in the community at Oneida, New York, where John Humphrey Noyes instituted a system of "complex marriage" by which *both* men and women shared multiple partners. That such diversities in relationships between women and men flourished in the early nineteenth century was a mark of the extent to which views of gender were contested terrain.[28]

Where did Princeton stand on these issues? Samuel Miller's *Brief Retrospect of the Eighteenth Century* (1801) provides the starting place for an answer. Noting that "it is much less than a hundred years since female education was lamentably, and upon principle, neglected," he rejoiced that in his own lifetime the problem had begun to find remedy. Now women's educational opportunities had improved dramatically, and "female talents [were] more justly appreciated" — a fact that "perhaps . . .

Yale University Press, 1990); Marilyn J. Westerkamp, *Women and Religion in Early America, 1600-1850* (London and New York: Routledge, 1999), 75-182.

28. Catherine A. Brekus, *Strangers and Pilgrims: Female Preaching in America, 1740-1845* (Chapel Hill: University of North Carolina Press, 1998); Lawrence Foster, *Religion and Sexuality: The Shakers, the Mormons, and the Oneida Community* (Urbana: University of Illinois Press, 1984). For a fascinating example of a "cultic" movement wanting to restore patriarchy, see Paul E. Johnson and Sean Wilentz, *The Kingdom of Matthias* (New York: Oxford University Press, 1994).

better [than any other] establishes the claim of the eighteenth century to much progress in knowledge and refinement." Miller's endorsement of the change was not, however, without fear that sometimes the transformation in attitude toward women had run into "certain extravagant and mischievous doctrines." As a case in point, he named Mary Wollstonecraft, whose *Vindication of the Rights of Woman* (1792) championed an end to hierarchical relationships between men and women and called for an age of genuine equality. In her, Miller saw arguments that would destroy all intellectual differences between men and women and open all "the duties and offices of life" to men and women alike. Miller was prepared to concede that women, "if it were practicable or proper to give them, in all respects, the same education as that bestowed on men, would probably discover nearly equal talents, and exhibit little difference in their intellectual structure and energies." He wanted, he insisted, "to see females receive the best education which their circumstances will afford," especially in view of their duty "of enlightening and informing the minds of the young." In some instances, it was even appropriate to have women study topics such as mathematics and metaphysics, often reserved to men. What Miller could not tolerate was any education of women premised on the breaking down of distinct gender roles. He offered a lurid description of where such confusion would lead.

> Let us suppose the various stations of civil trust to be filled indifferently by men and women; the places destined for the instruction of lawyers, physicians, and surgeons, to be occupied by a jumbled crowd of male and female students; the clerkships in counting-houses, and public offices, executed by a joint corps of male and female penmen; and the bands of labourers in manufactories formed without any distinction of sex. What would be the consequence of these arrangements? It would convert society into hordes of seducers and prostitutes. Instead of the regularity, the order, the pleasing charities, and the pure delights of wedded love, a system of universal concubinage would prevail. Seminaries of learning would be changed into nurseries of licentiousness and disease; the proceedings of deliberative assemblies would be perverted or arrested by the wiles of amorous intrigue; the places of commercial or mechanical business would become the haunts of noisy and restless lewdness; and all sober employment would yield to the dominion of brutal appetite.

Miller was turning to a ploy used not only by men but also by conservative women in the nineteenth century whenever they opposed women participating in a particular reform: to go beyond a certain point was to descend into gender confusion and immorality. What is easily forgotten in the midst of Miller's overheated and melodramatic rhetoric is that he *was* championing a broader education for women and a broader sphere of usefulness for them.[29]

One gets a sense of what that broader but still limited sphere might be by looking at the activities of his wife, Sarah Sergeant Miller, after the couple moved to Princeton. In 1816, she helped to form the Female Benevolent Society, which aimed to relieve the poor, provide care for the sick, and educate indigent children. As president of the society, she lobbied the First Presbyterian Church to provide the land on which to erect a school building. She was also involved in the creation of the Mount Lucas Orphan and Guardian Institute near Princeton and helped secure a financial endowment for it. When the Mount Lucas organization later closed, she arranged for the endowment to be transferred to the Ashmun Institute, founded in 1854 in Chester County, Pennsylvania, and subsequently renamed Lincoln University. Ashmun was created to provide higher education for African Americans. In addition to these activities, Sarah Miller supported — and often taught in — Sunday schools that educated Princeton's black and white children.[30]

From a brief account of the seminary published in 1822, one also learns of another acceptable outlet for women's benevolence: raising money to help the seminary. "The greater part . . . of the support which has been hitherto furnished to indigent students, in this institution," said the report, "has been derived from the contributions of female cent societies, in different parts of the church." In fact, "the liberality of pious females" had played an important role in supporting sixteen students; and the account went on to plead for the organization of still other societies of this sort. Thus, long before women were students or faculty at Princeton Seminary, they were helping to sustain it by their financial support.[31]

Speaking in late August 1825 to a Princeton women's organization supporting a female mission school in India, Ashbel Green emphasized

29. Samuel Miller, *A Brief Retrospect of the Eighteenth Century*, 3 vols. (London: Ellerton and Byworth, 1805), 3:126, 128, 132, 135, 136.

30. Miller, *Life of Samuel Miller*, 2:419; Hageman, *History of Princeton*, 122-23.

31. *A Brief Account of the Rise, Progress and Present State of the Theological Seminary of the Presbyterian Church in the United States at Princeton* (Philadelphia: A. Finley, 1822), 57.

both the imperative and the limits of women's engagement in benevolent activity. Green believed that women's participation in so many different kinds of societies augured "a better age approaching." He approved
women being engaged in Bible, tract, and charity societies as well as
helping support widow's and orphan's asylums. Especially they should
support missionary work among women of other lands, for only as
women "are raised from that state of ignorance and degradation in
which they have been sunk for ages past" can "the diffusion of Christianity . . . be general and lasting." Here in embryo was the rationale that
would later, under the rubric "woman's work for woman," be employed
on behalf of large-scale female involvement in missionary societies.
Green suggested that women could "take part in almost every plan and
effort for extending the Gospel, or for abating the sufferings, or meliorat-
ing the condition of mankind." Yet he did set limits on their activity. They
should always remember that, before they engaged in the support of
causes, they should "demonstrate that the influence of their religion has
rendered them better wives, better mothers, better daughters, better sisters, better neighbours, and better friends." Since the funds women contributed to worthy ends ultimately "must come from the purses of their
husbands, fathers, brothers," they needed to consult those men before
bestowing gifts. "Happy is that woman," said the president of the seminary's board of directors, "who always finds that she cannot do, what it is
improper for her to do as a woman." Chief of these improprieties was
that women "are in no case to be public preachers and teachers, in assemblies promiscuously composed of the two sexes."[32]

But what of women who turned to the medium of print to dissemi-
nate their theological views or to advocate various Christian causes? Old
Princeton offered an ambivalent response, as illustrated by Archibald Alexander's review of Catherine Beecher's *Letters on the Difficulties of Religion* in 1836. Beecher was the daughter of New School Presbyterian
Lyman Beecher, who, along with his friend Nathaniel William Taylor, was
driving the Old School crazy with theological innovations on issues of
human freedom and moral agency. Although Catherine Beecher differed
with her father on some issues, she dedicated the book to him, and the
flavor of the New England theology was apparent in many places in the

32. Ashbel Green, *The Christian Duty of Christian Women: A Discourse Delivered in the
Church of Princeton, New Jersey, August 23, 1825, before the Princeton Female Society* (Princeton: Princeton Press, 1825), esp. 8, 10, 11, 14, 16, 21, 22.

book, which sought to set forth an apologetic for the Christian faith. Praising her "for her strong good sense" and for the "general sobriety and correctness of her opinions," Alexander then took issue with her on a number of points: her tendency to weaken the doctrine of justification, to play down the role of the Holy Spirit, and to exalt the role of human agency in salvation. What is interesting in the context of the current question before us is the way in which Alexander related theological discussion to Beecher's gender. "We suspect," he said, "that she is inclined to meddle with too many things and with things out of her reach. We are glad that Paul has said so emphatically, 'I suffer not a woman to speak in the church.'" Although the apostle did not prohibit women from writing, Alexander believed that Paul would, if he were back in the flesh, warn women against "mixing themselves in theological and ecclesiastical controversies." He recommended that Beecher

> cease her efforts to untie the Gordian knots of theology and metaphysics. As she has studied the art of education and is said to excel in that department, let her be content to shine as an eminent instructor of the youth of her own sex. Or if that would be too great a restraint upon her prolific mind, we sincerely advise her to follow the example of Hannah More, and expatiate as widely as she will in the extensive field of Christian ethics, practical piety, and Christian manners.

It was highly suggestive that Alexander allowed that women might appropriately write on the subjects of manners, piety, and behavior, but not on theological and ecclesiastical matters. In the Princeton hierarchy of Christian education, theology and metaphysics were the normative fields to which piety and behavior had to conform. "Women authors," as Louise Stevenson has remarked, "thus assumed a sort of lady auxiliary status comparable to the status of Presbyterian women that joined in benevolent or charitable causes." The commendation of Hannah More as a worthy model was significant also, for she not only confined herself to "practical piety and Christian manners"; she also adhered to an essentially conservative view of society congenial to Alexander.[33]

33. [Archibald Alexander,] "Lectures on the Difficulties of Religion," *Biblical Repertory and Theological Review* 8 (1836): 515-45; quotations on 515, 544, 545; Louise L. Stevenson, "Charles Hodge, Womanly Women, and Manly Ministers," in Stewart and Moorhead, eds.,

As his citation of the Pauline injunction against women speaking in the church suggested, Alexander and his Princeton colleagues considered such texts decisive in determining the status of women. But why these texts and not others that spoke of women prophesying or speaking in tongues in front of what, in nineteenth-century parlance, were called promiscuous assemblies? Princeton certainly believed that the Lord had caused women to do these things, but they had done so in the days of revelation and miracles, when God sometimes suspended the usual rules of nature. The era of supernatural wonders, however, had ceased, and now on "ordinary occasions," said Ashbel Green, women "are absolutely required not to speak, but to keep silence in the churches." Also contributing to this interpretation was the belief that commonsense observations from nature and history supported the subordination of women. Charles Hodge, for example, said of the command that women should be subject to their husbands:

> The ground of the obligation, therefore, as it exists in nature, is the eminency of the husband; his superiority in those attributes which enable and entitle him to command. He is larger, stronger, bolder; has more of those mental and moral qualities which are required in a leader. This is just as plain from history as that iron is heavier than water. . . . This superiority of the man . . . cannot be denied or disregarded without destroying society and degrading both men and women; making the one effeminate and the other masculine.

Hodge also insisted that, even as the woman was subject to her husband, she was also exalted "to be the companion and ministering angel" to him. The way in which Hodge elided these nineteenth-century assumptions about gender with biblical passages about women and men — and thereby reified them as eternal verities — would seem to illustrate the dictum of Clifford Geertz: "Common sense is not what the mind cleared of cant spontaneously apprehends; it is what the mind filled with presuppositions . . . concludes."[34]

Charles Hodge Revisited, 167; Kathryn Kish Sklar, *Catharine Beecher: A Study in Domesticity* (New Haven: Yale University Press, 1973), 124-25.

34. Green, *Christian Duty of Christian Women*, 9-10; Charles Hodge, *A Commentary on the Epistle to the Ephesians* (New York: Robert Carter and Brothers, 1858), 312-13; Clifford Geertz, "Common Sense as a Cultural System," *Antioch Review* 33 (Spring 1975): 16-17.

What the Princeton professors believed about the role of women and what they believed about slavery were at the end of the day of a piece. In an 1844 article Charles Hodge identified the connection when he uttered one of his most savage condemnations of the abolitionist movement. "They seem to consider themselves above the scriptures, and when they put themselves above the law of God, it is not wonderful that they should disregard the laws of men." That rejection of the law of God manifested itself in "anarchical opinions about human governments, civil and ecclesiastical, and on the rights of women." "Let these principles be carried out," he thundered,

> and there is an end to all social subordination, to all security for life or property, to all guarantee for public or domestic virtue. If our women are to be emancipated from subjection to the law which God has imposed upon them, if they are to quit the retirement of domestic life, where they preside in stillness over the character and destiny of society, if they are to come forth in the liberty of men, to be our agents, our public lecturers, our committeemen, our rulers; if, in studied insult to the authority of God, we are to renounce the marriage contract, all claim to obedience, we shall soon have a country over which the genius of Mary Wolstoncraft [*sic*] would delight to preside, but from which all order and all virtue would speedily be banished.[35]

The thread running through this attack was Hodge's fear of "an end to all social subordination." A properly ordered society consisted of a series of such relationships — of humanity to God, woman to man, children to parents, slaves to masters, the morally unfit and uneducated to the best and brightest. He perceived abolitionism as the symptom of a disordered egalitarianism. By 1838, William Lloyd Garrison and his supporters had taken control of the American Anti-Slavery Society and were pushing a sweeping platform of reform: abolitionism, nonresistance (i.e., pacifism), women's rights, religious heterodoxy, attacks on all churches that failed to sever their involvement with slaveholders, and attacks upon the moral legitimacy of the federal constitution because the U.S. Constitution recognized slavery. There was in abolitionism a tendency

---

35. [Charles Hodge,] "West India Emancipation," *Biblical Repertory and Princeton Review* 10 (1838): 603-4.

toward anarchism, but Garrison and others like him did not interpret this stand as a repudiation of legitimate authority. Rather, they saw themselves tearing down all the intermediate and illegitimate forms of coercion standing between the individual and God. For the Princeton seminary leadership, it was, of course, quite otherwise. They believed in the possibility of genuine reform and progress, but it had to come step by step *through,* not around or over, the existing relationships of society.[36]

36. For an older but still insightful treatment of abolitionism, see Lewis Perry, *Radical Abolitionism: Anarchy and the Government of God in Antislavery Thought* (Ithaca, NY: Cornell University Press, 1973).

CHAPTER SEVEN

The Seminary, the Civil War, and Reconstruction

THE HOPE of achieving ordered progress through, not around or over, the existing relationships of society became exceedingly hard to sustain as social, political, and ecclesiastical structures fractured during the 1840s and 1850s. The settlement of America's disputed border claim against Great Britain in the Pacific Northwest, the annexation of Texas in 1845, and the subsequent war with Mexico dramatically increased the area of the nation, giving it virtually the same borders that the lower continental United States has today. In due course, these acquisitions would be organized by the federal government into territories and eventually be admitted as states. But which of the new states would permit slavery and which would prohibit the institution? How would the decisions be made? By continuing the principle of the Missouri Compromise of 1820, which set a geographic boundary north of which slavery could not exist, and south of which it could? Would the decision be left to the voters or legislatures in the respective states? Politics in the 1850s increasingly turned on these debates. The struggles disintegrated the Whig party after the 1852 presidential election. Out of the wreckage, the new Republican party emerged, winning the support of many former Whigs, some Democrats, and many from the small Liberty and Free Soil parties. In 1856, the Republican party fielded its first presidential candidate and made a respectable showing. The new party pledged to respect constitutional protection of slavery in the states where it already existed but to halt its spread into the newly acquired territories. Four years later, Republicans elected Abraham Lincoln on a similar platform against a Democratic party split into northern and southern wings that ran separate nominees and against a newly organized and short-lived Constitutional Union party. The election of Lincoln triggered the secession of various southern states during the winter of 1860-1861 and set the stage for the outbreak of the Civil War in April.[1]

Controversies in the Old School Church

The controversies in the nation had a counterpart in the churches. The major Methodist and Baptist denominations split along North-South lines in 1844 and 1845, respectively. In both instances, questions related to slavery were the direct cause of the schism. Yet the Old School Presbyterian Church, with which Princeton Seminary was affiliated, managed to hold together until 1861 and the beginning of the war. It did so largely because the General Assembly refused to take a stand against slavery. When overtures from some presbyteries requested a condemnation of slavery as sinful, the Assembly spelled out the position it believed to be biblical. A committee, including Professor A. T. McGill, then of Western Seminary and eventually of Princeton, prepared the report overwhelmingly adopted by the 1845 Assembly. "The church of Christ," said the General Assembly, "is a spiritual body, whose jurisdiction extends only to the religious faith, and moral conduct of her members. She cannot legislate where Christ has not legislated, nor make terms of membership which he has not made. The question, therefore, which this Assembly is called upon to decide, is this: Do the Scriptures teach that the holding of slaves, without regard to circumstances, is a sin, the renunciation of which should be made a condition of membership in the church of Christ?" The Assembly concluded that there were no scriptural grounds for an affirmative answer. Therefore, the church would exceed its authority if it condemned human bondage. But that was not to deny "that there is evil connected with slavery." To break up slave families and to treat servants in a cruel fashion, for example, were sinful practices. However, "neither the Scriptures nor our [church] constitution authorize this body to prescribe any particular course to be pursued by the churches under our care." The

---

1. The literature on these events is vast. Helpful introductions and overviews may be found in Daniel Walker Howe, *What God Hath Wrought: Transformation of America, 1815-1848* (New York: Oxford University Press, 2007), 658-855; and James M. McPherson, *Battle Cry of Freedom: The Civil War Era* (New York: Oxford University Press, 1988).

only proper path was to follow the example of the apostles: "to ameliorate the condition of slaves, not by denouncing and excommunicating their masters, but by teaching both masters and slaves the glorious doctrines of the gospel, and enjoining upon each the discharge of their relative duties." To demand a stronger statement about slavery, the Assembly concluded, would tend "to separate the northern from the southern portion of the Church; a result which every good citizen must deplore as tending to the dissolution of the union of our beloved country, and which every enlightened Christian will oppose as bringing about a ruinous and unnecessary schism between brethren who maintain a common faith." Charles Hodge, reviewing this deliverance and speaking on behalf of his colleagues at Princeton Seminary, rejoiced over the "harmonious decision." It confirmed his faith "that there is no serious difference of opinion on this subject, between the great majority of good men at the north and the south."[2]

But differences of opinion, partly over theology and partly over slavery, were growing. Under the intellectual leadership of men such as James Henley Thornwell, Southern Presbyterianism had begun to give distinctive twists to the Old School heritage. Southern theologians emphasized the spirituality of the church, which Thornwell once described as meaning that "the laws of the Church are the authoritative injunctions of Christ, and not the covenants, however benevolent in their origin and aim, which men have instituted of their own will." In other words, no matter how well-meaning certain moral reforms, such as the temperance cause or the colonization movement, might be, the *church as church* had no business supporting them. Individual Christians might, if they wished, exercise their liberty to support these causes, but the church itself dared not go beyond the moral and spiritual mission *explicitly* enjoined by the Bible. The idea of the spirituality of the church paralleled the espousal of what has been called *jure divino* Presbyterianism — the notion that the polity of the church was prescribed in detail from Scripture. In particular, Thornwell argued that the Bible did not sanction the creation of boards to administer missionary or other work; these activities belonged under the direct control of the divinely authorized

2. *Minutes of the General Assembly of the Presbyterian Church in the United States of America* [Old School], 11 (Philadelphia: William S. Martien, 1845), 11, 16, 17; [Charles Hodge,] "The General Assembly," *Biblical Repertory and Princeton Review* 17 (July 1845): 441.

church judicatories — presbyteries, synods, or General Assemblies — not with agencies that sometimes became semi-independent of the church courts that had authorized them. At the 1860 General Assembly, Hodge and Thornwell debated the issue. Although Hodge yielded to no one in his commitment that theology and practice had to derive from biblical warrant, he defended church boards on the grounds that Scripture did not prescribe every detail of polity. Or, as he put it, "The great principles of Presbyterianism are in the Bible; but it is preposterous to assert that our whole Book of Discipline is there. . . . The church must have freedom to adapt herself to the varying circumstances in which she is called to act." In addition to these differences of theology and polity, divergent views of slavery evolved. While the Princeton theologians and the leading Southern Presbyterian thinkers agreed that slavery was not in itself a sin and that the church had no right to condemn slaveholding per se, they did not agree on the desirability of human bondage. Southern thinkers increasingly portrayed slavery as a positive good that might continue indefinitely to the benefit of master and slave alike; the Princeton theologians tended to see slavery, while not sinful in itself, as a temporary form of social order destined to pass away as society advanced.[3]

Princeton and the Crisis of the Union

During the increasingly polarized late 1850s, Charles Hodge was moving along two different tracks simultaneously. With the crack-up of the Whigs, he found himself sympathetic to the Republican party and voted for its presidential candidates in 1856 and 1860. At the very time that he struggled to maintain the unity of the Presbyterian Church across sectional lines, his political convictions prompted him to vote for a party that, if victorious, would inflame the very southerners whom he was eager to keep within the Old School fold. His internal conflicts became public during the winter and spring of 1860-1861, when southern states

3. James H. Thornwell, *Collected Writings of James Henley Thornwell,* ed. John B. Adger and John L. Girardeau, 4 vols. (Richmond: Presbyterian Committee of Publication, 1871-1873), 4:469; [Charles Hodge,] "The General Assembly," *Biblical Repertory and Princeton Review* 32 (July 1860): 511-46; Hodge quotations on 518, 519; A. A. Hodge, *Life of Charles Hodge* (New York: Charles Scribner's Sons, 1880). For a thoughtful examination of Thornwell's life and theology, see James Oscar Farmer Jr., *The Metaphysical Confederacy: James Henley Thornwell and the Synthesis of Southern Values* (Macon, GA: Mercer University Press, 1986).

had begun seceding one by one and then formed the Confederate States of America. As crisis loomed, Hodge composed an article, "The State of the Country," for publication in the January 1861 issue of the *Princeton Review*. Without naming him specifically, Hodge began by rejecting Thornwell's sharp dichotomy between sacred and secular. "There are occasions," he asserted, "when political questions rise into the sphere of morals and religion; when the rule for political action is to be sought, not in considerations of state policy, but in the law of God." Such, he believed, was the case of possible secession. Although the South had legitimate grievances against abolitionists, there were appropriate remedies under the Constitution. No moral justification existed for the rending of a Union that, by the original agreement, was perpetual. Hodge also used language that anticipated Lincoln's appeal for loyalty to the Union in his March 4 inaugural address, when the president predicted that "the mystic chords of memory, stretching from every battle-field, and patriot grave, to every living heart and hearth-stone, all over this broad land, will yet swell the chorus of the Union." In his January article, Hodge evoked remembrance that "the blood of Northern and Southern patriots flowed in a common stream, and their ashes lie mingled in the same graves." Until recently, such was "the common sentiment of the country," North and South; and anyone suggesting disunion "would have been associated, in the estimation of his countrymen, with Benedict Arnold." Hodge predicted that, should disunion actually occur, its authors would be judged in precisely this fashion by future generations.[4]

By the time the Presbyterian General Assembly convened in Philadelphia on May 16, 1861, civil war had already begun. A month earlier, Confederate batteries had fired on Fort Sumter, still under Federal control in the harbor of Charleston, South Carolina, and thereby ignited a storm of patriotic fervor within the North. The Rev. Gardiner Spring of New York introduced resolutions in the General Assembly that would avow "our obligations to promote and perpetuate, so far as in us lies, the integrity of these United States, and to strengthen, uphold, and encourage, the Federal Government." After considerable parliamentary maneuvering, and under great public pressure from outsiders who wanted tangible evidence that Presbyterians were loyal to the Union, the resolutions passed.

---

4. [Charles Hodge,] "The State of the Country," *Biblical Repertory and Princeton Review* 33 (January 1861): 1-36; quotations from 1, 2; Roy P. Basler, ed., *Abraham Lincoln: His Speeches and Writings* (Cleveland: World Publishing Co, 1946), 588.

Hodge, who served as a commissioner to the Assembly, opposed the action and wrote a protest signed by nearly sixty others. The gist of the protest was that the General Assembly, which still represented both North and South (though the southern presbyteries sent few commissioners), was attempting to decide a point of constitutional law disputed between the two regions: Was the citizen's ultimate loyalty to the state or to the Federal Union? The Assembly's action "pronounces or assumes a particular interpretation of the [U.S.] Constitution. This is a matter clearly beyond the jurisdiction of the Assembly." Or, as Hodge said in a later explanatory passage about the reason for the protest: "Our church was as much divided as the country. It was the case of a mother who was called upon to take part for one child against another." Hodge also insisted that those who signed the protest were "loyal to the Constitution and the Federal Government. They regarded the war which had been declared against the Union, as one of the most unjustifiable and wicked upon record. . . . Why then did they refuse to avow them [their sentiments of loyalty to the Union] in and through the General Assembly? For the same reason that they would refuse, at the command of an excited multitude, to sing the 'Star-Spangled Banner' at the Lord's table. They refused because in their judgment it was wrong and out of place." The Assembly responded to the Hodge protest by quoting "an able article in the January number of the *Princeton Review*," which included the comments: "There are occasions when political questions rise into the sphere of morals and religion; when the rule of political action is to be sought, not in consideration of state policy, but in the law of God." The Assembly said it concurred with what Hodge had written a few months earlier: the present moment and the Assembly's own action were illustrations of his principle. Despite the at least temporary break-up of the Union, Hodge had hoped to maintain the unity of the Old School Presbyterian denomination across the lines of political division and armed conflict. At best that outcome was a long shot, and the passage of the Spring resolutions made schism all but certain. In December 1861, representatives of the Southern Old School formally organized the Presbyterian Church in the Confederate States of America.[5]

---

5. *Minutes of the General Assembly of the Presbyterian Church in the United States of America* [Old School], 16 (Philadelphia: Presbyterian Board of Publication, 1861), 330; [Charles Hodge,] "The General Assembly," *Biblical Repertory and Princeton Review* 33 (July 1861): 542, 543-44. Despite being eighty years old, the fullest treatment of the Old School and the war is found in Lewis G. Vander Velde, *The Presbyterian Churches and the Federal Union, 1861-1869* (Cambridge: Harvard University Press, 1932), esp. 21-131.

Like the denomination as a whole, Hodge and his Princeton colleagues were slow to embrace the end of slavery as a war aim. But then, so
was President Lincoln and much of the North with him. Although abolitionists clamored almost from the beginning of the conflict to make the
struggle a crusade against slavery, the president proceeded cautiously. For
a time after Sumter, he had considerable bipartisan support for suppressing the rebellion; but the president knew that much of the support would
evaporate if he announced a campaign to free slaves. Moreover, border
states that had not sided with the Confederacy might well have done so
had Lincoln acted precipitously against the peculiar institution, and their
defection could have lost the war. Ironically, had the struggle ended with a
swift Union victory in 1861, slavery would probably have survived for the
foreseeable future. But the war dragged on month after month, and by 1862
the conflict became particularly bloody. In the western theatre, chiefly in
Tennessee, Union armies under General Ulysses S. Grant achieved significant if costly success, but in the east Federal armies failed to capture Richmond and suffered other disastrous reverses before managing to turn
back a Confederate invasion of Maryland at the battle of Antietam on September 17, 1862, the single bloodiest day in American history. By this time, a
larger sector of public opinion was prepared for more radical war aims.
Many called for the freeing of slaves in the areas in rebellion as a way of
crippling the Confederacy, and large numbers of Protestant clergy argued
that Union reverses indicated divine punishment for slavery and signaled
God's desire that the oppressed be set free. Lincoln's own strategic sense
and his ruminations on the mysteries of God's purposes in the midst of
war led him in the same direction. After Antietam, he announced his intention to free slaves in those areas still in rebellion on January 1, 1863. On
January 1, he fulfilled his pledge, issuing the Emancipation Proclamation.
His constitutional justification was that, as commander in chief in time of
war, he was confiscating enemy property. Slavery was not constitutionally
ended until the Thirteenth Amendment, passed by Congress in January
1865 and ratified by December of that year.[6]

In 1864, the Old School General Assembly endorsed the expansion of
war aims. Choosing to ignore its more equivocal statement of 1845, the As-

6. I have treated in greater detail the changing attitude of the churches and of the Lincoln administration toward antislavery as a war aim in James H. Moorhead, *American Apocalypse: Yankee Protestants and the Civil War, 1860-1869* (New Haven: Yale University Press,
1978), 82-128. On the importance of Antietam and the events leading up to it, see James M.
McPherson, *Crossroads of Freedom: Antietam* (New York: Oxford University Press, 2002).

sembly quoted the 1818 deliverance that stigmatized "the voluntary en-slaving of one portion of the human race by another as a gross violation of the most precious and sacred rights of human nature, as utterly inconsis-tent with the law of God, . . . and as totally irreconcilable with the spirit and principles of the gospel of Christ." The 1864 statement further declared:

> Whether a strict and careful application of this advice would have rescued the country from the evil of its condition, and the dangers which have since threatened it, is known to the Omniscient alone. Whilst we do not believe that the present judgments of our Heav-enly Father, and Almighty and Righteous Governor, have been in-flicted solely in punishment for our continuance in this sin; yet it is our judgment that the recent events of our history, and the present condition of our Church and country, furnish manifest to-kens that *the time has at length come, in the providence of God, when it is His will that every vestige of human slavery among us should be effaced, and that every Christian man should address himself with industry and earnestness to his appropriate part in the performance of this great duty.*

The Assembly also observed that the president had indicated that he would not "consent to the reorganization of civil government within the seceded States upon any other basis than that of emancipation." In the loyal states where slavery still existed, the statement noted that "mea-sures of emancipation, in different stages of progress, have been set on foot," and plans "for an amendment to the Federal Constitution, prohib-iting slavery" had begun. The Assembly expressed its conviction that "the interests of peace and of social order" were thus "identified with the success of the cause of emancipation."[7]

Hodge gave a cautious endorsement to the actions of the 1864 Gen-eral Assembly. But he was deeply concerned lest observers draw the wrong implication from either the deliverance or his backing of it. "We wish, however to have it distinctly understood," he insisted,

> that we have not changed our ground on the subject of slavery. We hold now precisely what we held in 1836, when the subject was

---

7. *Minutes of the General Assembly of the Presbyterian Church in the United States of America* [Old School], 17 (Philadelphia: Presbyterian Board of Publication, 1864), 297, 298, 299; italics are in the original.

first argued in these pages. What is more important, it should be known that the Old-school Presbyterian church has not changed her doctrinal teaching by the recent action of the General Assembly. God and truth are immutable; and a church vacillates in doctrine only when deserted by God. The General Assembly has not declared all slaveholding to be sinful; it has not contradicted, retracted, or modified its formal and explicit teachings of 1845; it simply declares that slavery, as it exists in this country, (that is, the slave-laws of the Southern states,) is an unjust and anti-christian institution.

Hodge felt compelled to insist that the Old School had not gone over to abolitionism — that is, the belief that slavery was in itself a sin. For Hodge, change was difficult to accept, not only in others, but especially in himself. He felt compelled to maintain that he had held uniform views over the years. That compulsion was no doubt a heavy psychological burden to bear in a revolutionary age.[8]

Princeton and Reconstruction

The Civil War was a deeply painful experience for Hodge partly because he worried about family members in the service. His son John fell ill with typhoid while in the army, and his brother-in-law General David Hunter suffered a wound in battle; but fortunately both survived. Hodge was dismayed by reports of horrific casualties and of initial Union defeats putting an end to the hope of a brief war. He appears as well to have suffered a challenge to some of his most fundamental assumptions about the nature of the world. Part of the problem was his need for consistency and stability, rooted perhaps in part in the psychology of a man left fatherless at a young age. Yet, whatever its sources in Hodge's biography, the need for consistency was also grounded in his epistemology. Like Alexander and his mentors at the College of New Jersey, he adhered to the universality of self-evident principles that people of common sense must everywhere perceive. One catches a glimpse of that confidence in his grateful

8. [Charles Hodge,] "The General Assembly," *Biblical Repertory and Princeton Review* 36 (July 1864): 548-49. Hodge's most sustained effort to prove his consistency on matters of slavery and civil war came in [Charles Hodge,] "The Princeton Review on the State of the Country and of the Church," *Biblical Repertory and Princeton Review* 37 (October 1875): 627-57.

observation that the General Assembly's 1845 deliverance on slavery cor-
roborated his belief "that there is no serious difference of opinion on this
subject, between the great majority of good men at the north and the
south." Once the war broke, he could, of course, no longer hold to this
rosy view of good people rising above the passions of their time and
place to reach moral consensus. In the summer of 1865, as he reflected
on the previous years of war, he sounded a more somber note that deserves to be cited at some length.

> Popular bodies, whether ecclesiastical or secular, are in a great
> measure organs of public spirit. They give utterance to the opin-
> ions, temper, and feelings of the communities to which they be-
> long.... We see even staid Episcopalians among the foremost and
> most violent in asserting Southern dogmas, the ministers often
> going beyond the politicians in their zeal and extravagance.
> Southern Presbyterian Synods and General Assemblies, to the
> great sorrow and chagrin of their Northern brethren, have been
> among the foremost in the assertion of extreme Southern doc-
> trines and in the manifestation of sectional animosity.... It would
> betray great self-ignorance and self-conceit, to assume that we
> here at the North, and our Northern Synods and Assemblies, are
> free from the operation of this law; that we are so elevated, so en-
> lightened, so self-possessed, that we can rise above these disturb-
> ing elements, and think, speak, and act simply under the guidance
> of right principles and of correct opinion.... It is easy to say that
> we are right and they are wrong. This in the present case is, no
> doubt, in a great measure, true. But it is not because we are right,
> that we go with those around us, any more than it is because the
> South is wrong, that Southern ecclesiastical bodies go with the
> people of whom they form a part. It is largely in both cases, be-
> cause every man, and every body of men, are more or less subject
> to the controlling influence of public opinion, and of the life of the
> community to which they belong.[9]

For Hodge, this passage was an unusual one. It reflected an appreciation of the influence of context in shaping values and ideas — an aware-

9. [Charles Hodge,] "The General Assembly," *Biblical Repertory and Princeton Review*
37 (July 1865): 458-514; quotations on 505-6.

ness fitting somewhat awkwardly with his more accustomed confidence in the power of all sane minds to perceive self-evident truths. One wonders what the result might have been if Hodge had incorporated this insight more fully into the *Systematic Theology* with which he capped his career. Perhaps his three-volume opus would have exhibited a bit more reticence to make so many unqualified assertions or manifested a greater willingness to make allowance for the way in which time and place have shaped theological discourse.

Hodge's effort to dampen self-righteousness among northerners and to promote a magnanimous view of southern errors occurred at a time when Old School policies toward the South distressed him. In fact, he wrote the passage cited above in a commentary on the action of the 1865 General Assembly of the northern Old School. The General Assembly had laid down rules for presbyteries examining southern or border state ministers who wished to be received into membership. They had to give evidence that they had not willingly supported the rebellion. If they had done so, they needed to renounce those errors. Moreover, any minister who held "that the system of negro slavery in the South is a Divine institution" or espoused the doctrine in the founding of the Southern Church that it had "the peculiar mission . . . to conserve the institution of slavery" could not be received by a presbytery unless he repented of those views. On the floor of the Assembly, William Henry Green, professor at Princeton Seminary, opposed the regulations as unnecessary; and in his report on the General Assembly Hodge opposed them as creating tests of fellowship that went beyond scriptural warrant and the denomination's constitution. In the same article, Hodge also made passing comment on the growing enthusiasm within the Old School denomination for reunion with the New School. In a revealing aside, Hodge noted that those most prominent in pressing for reunion with the New School "were the most zealous in pressing through these extreme measures with regard to the Southern ministers." He accused them of being inconsistent. The Old School advocates of reunion "do not require that they [the New School] should repent of their sin in breaking up the union of the church, in supporting or tolerating false doctrine."[10]

These comments signaled what was soon even more apparent. If

10. *Minutes of the Presbyterian Church in the United States of America* [Old School], 17 (Philadelphia: Presbyterian Board of Publication, 1865), 562-64; Hodge, "General Assembly" (1865), 512.

there were to be any ecclesiastical reunions, Hodge preferred to bring together the two Old Schools, North and South, rather than to have a combination with the New School. Hodge respected the theological movement that had occurred within the New School. He especially appreciated the theology of Union Seminary's Henry Boynton Smith, who had helped allay many previous objections to the New School. But despite this fact, Hodge still felt doctrinally more comfortable with the Southern Old School. Of his reluctance to reunite with the New School, Paul Gutjahr has commented perceptively:

> Hodge's resistance to the reunion provides some interesting insights into his lifelong aversion to change, and his views on sharing fellowship with those who differed from him theologically. Thirty years earlier, Hodge had been one of the strongest advocates for exploring ways to keep the Presbyterian Church from dividing institutionally into New and Old School sides. Few had worked harder to try to limit the influence of Ashbel Green's inflexible Ultra faction in an attempt to keep the denomination together. Three decades later, Smith had taken Hodge's former role as the moderating voice of reconciliation, while Hodge came to resemble Green or one of his Ultras from the 1830s. He could not support a return to a common Presbyterian body because like so many changes in his life he saw this one as utterly unnecessary. Each body had established itself as a respected and ably functioning entity. There was no need to disturb this equilibrium, particularly when he saw that it would mean compromising one another's theological views.

For Hodge, maintaining theological equilibrium appeared easier with his recent Old School allies below the Mason-Dixon Line than it did with the New School. However, the Southern Presbyterian animosities spawned by the Spring resolutions, the bitterness of the Confederacy's defeat, and post-war anger over the northern Assembly's actions in 1865 (then reiterated in 1866) ended any possibility of early reunion; but the merger with the New School was consummated in 1870. Despite his previous opposition, Hodge greeted reunion with grace.[11]

---

11. Paul C. Gutjahr, *Charles Hodge: Guardian of Orthodoxy* (New York: Oxford University Press, 2011), 341. On reunion with the New School, see George M. Marsden, *The Evan-*

His preference for the theologically more conservative southern church paralleled his attitude toward the politics of Reconstruction. Once the guns were stacked at Appomattox, the victorious North had to decide what it would do with its victory. Hodge had rather definite opinions on the matter and shared them with the readers of the *Princeton Review* in July 1865 as part of a eulogy to Abraham Lincoln, whose death by assassin's bullet he deeply mourned. Hodge urged that the nation "be as magnanimous and generous in victory as we were brave and constant in conflict." He warned that harsh policies "exasperate instead of subduing; they exalt criminals into martyrs"; and he feared that they might result in making the South into a permanently disaffected minority analogous to "what Ireland is to England." Hodge wished generous amnesties to the rebels and a quick restoration of the states of the Confederacy to their former place in the Union once they had ratified the Thirteenth Amendment. On the matter of extending the vote to ex-slaves, Hodge asserted that, while "the colour of the skin" should not be a basis for denying the vote, "it is a dictate of common sense that no man, whether white or black, has a right to exercise any privilege for which he is not qualified." Hodge found himself sympathetic to the Reconstruction policies of President Andrew Johnson, who had taken office after the death of Lincoln. "How wonderfully," he wrote to his brother Hugh on Christmas Day 1865, "God has controlled and guided President Johnson. He has acted with consummate wisdom." When Johnson vetoed a bill extending the powers of the Freedmen's Bureau in February 1866, Hodge praised the "veto message [as] conclusive" and said the Congress should sustain the president. The bureau, created in March 1865, was designed as a temporary agency to provide aid to the newly freed slaves. But as several southern states by the fall of 1865 passed codes designed to restrict the ability of African Americans to testify in court and tried to limit their mobility by forcing them into labor contracts that constituted a state of virtual peonage, some in the bureau — and their friends in Congress — wished to expand the power of the bureau to serve as a protector of the freed people. For example, in places where blacks' legal rights were restricted, courts operated by the bureau or the military would be allowed to take

gelical Mind and the New School Presbyterian Experience: A Case Study of Thought and Theology in Nineteenth-Century America* (New Haven: Yale University Press, 1970), 199-229; for illuminating documents from the era, consult *Presbyterian Reunion: A Memorial Volume, 1837-1870* (New York: De W. C. Lent, 1871).

jurisdiction to secure justice. Johnson opposed — and Charles Hodge agreed with him — this expansion of federal power at the expense of the states and objected to creating what he regarded as a specially protected class of citizens. By contrast, the so-called Radical Republicans — led, perhaps most notably, by Representative Thaddeus Stevens — wished to treat the southern states as conquered territories subject to military rule and to use the opportunity to confiscate the land of Confederate plant-ers, redistribute it as homesteads to the ex-slaves, guarantee black suf-frage, and thereby create an independent African American yeomanry. Although many recent historians have portrayed Stevens and other Rad-ical Republicans as laudable reformers aspiring to a more egalitarian so-ciety, Stevens and company were considered by conservatives in their own time as dangerous, vindictive men. Certainly Charles Hodge held that view. To Hugh, he wrote in his Christmas letter of 1865: "Pennsylva-nia ought to be ashamed of such a representative as Thaddeus Stevens." Or the following summer: "Any body led by Thaddeus Stevens must be led to evil." And in the fall of 1866, he accused the Radicals of being "out-rageously wicked men," the evidence offered in his letter being their de-sire for "universal suffrage and the disfranchisement of the white popu-lation in the South — giving the whole power to the negroes and a few hundred renegade white men in every State." Hodge overstated his case. The disenfranchisement to which he alluded was the proposal of the Radicals that ex-rebels be denied the vote for a time as punishment for rebellion and until they showed their willingness to accept the new or-der. Only a small portion of the Radical agenda was attempted, and even that flamed out quickly. By 1877, the last of the Reconstruction govern-ments had fallen, and the way was soon clear over the next several de-cades for the states of the old Confederacy to create the legal apparatus of Jim Crow.[12]

A man of conservative temperament, Hodge had confronted and ac-cepted, often with difficulty, dramatic changes wrought on the bloody fields of battle in places such as Shiloh, Gettysburg, and the Wilderness. When the struggle ended, his basic caution reasserted itself. Glad that slavery had ended, he could not imagine further systemic changes such

12. [Charles Hodge,] "President Lincoln," *Biblical Repertory and Princeton Review* 37 (July 1865): 435-58; quotations from 455, 457. Hodge, *Life of Charles Hodge*, 486, 487, 488. On Reconstruction policies, see Eric Foner, *Reconstruction: America's Unfinished Revolution, 1863-1877* (New York: Harper and Row, 1988); Hans L. Trefousse, *Thaddeus Stevens: Nineteenth-Century Egalitarian* (Chapel Hill: University of North Carolina Press, 1997).

as land reform, universal suffrage, or the prolonged Federal presence in the South that would have been necessary to create a more egalitarian America. He could only conceive of *gradual* improvement coming through existing institutions and relationships. Given the realities of prejudice and power in both the South and the North, that meant very little change at all. One should not, of course, single out Charles Hodge or his Princeton colleagues as if they alone favored this approach or bore some unique responsibility for it. They were part of a great multitude.

Black Students at Princeton Seminary in the 1870s

A new seminarian in 1874 offered a local example of Princeton's essential conservatism on the mores of racial interaction. Matthew Anderson was born in 1848 in Greencastle, Pennsylvania, to a free black family of farmers whose Presbyterianism stretched back to the eighteenth century. Set in the prosperous Cumberland Valley in a state where slavery had been outlawed, Greencastle was regarded by some in the black community as a "glory land" because of the opportunities it offered, and this designation would have appeared quite apt, for only a few miles to the south lay the border of Maryland, where slaveholding remained legal. Greencastle was scarcely free of racial prejudices or *de facto* segregation, but the prospects for African Americans were, compared to many places, favorable. Matthew Anderson's grandfather had owned several sawmills, and his father was a respected member of the community. In fact, the Andersons were remembered by at least "one longtime resident," as C. James Trotman remarks, "as the aristocrats within Greencastle's black community." Trotman suggests that Anderson had acquired a sense of security within the black community and also had enjoyed a unique opportunity to witness "the complexity of moving back and forth between two cultures [black and white], which must have taken place frequently if not daily in view of the business activities involving his father and grandfather." From his background, Anderson remembered much later, he derived a "craving desire . . . for an education." His purpose was "that we might be permitted under God to do a work that would establish the equal manhood of the Negro, and stamp to the earth the thought of his inferiority, as well as the slangs and imputations which were being hurled at him by an unreasonable and thoughtless nation, whose boasted land, the land of liberty, was theirs as a legacy from the Pilgrim fathers." He went to Oberlin College but interrupted his collegiate career by two years of teaching in a school under the sponsorship of the Presbyterian Board of Freedmen in Salisbury, North Carolina. After college, he headed off to theological studies, first at Western Seminary for only a few days and then, in response to a more favorable offer, on to Princeton Seminary in the fall of 1874.[13]

He had corresponded with Professor Alexander T. McGill about the possibilities at Princeton and was promised "flattering inducements, much better than they gave in the Western Seminary." Upon arriving in Princeton, he called upon McGill, who mistook him for a workman come to do a job. In response, Anderson handed McGill the letter the professor had written inviting him to Princeton. Speaking of himself in the first-person plural, Anderson continued his recollection: "A study of the old Doctor's face as he glanced over his own letter was as good as a play. For a moment he looked intensely at the letter, then raised his eyes and glanced at us, then scrutinized the letter again, after which he reached out his hand and said, 'Mr. Anderson, I'm glad to see you. I didn't know, Mr. Anderson, that it was you I was writing to. Take a seat.'" Struggling to contain his amusement at McGill's discomfiture, Anderson kept his replies to polite yeses and nos. When McGill said that he would give him "a note of introduction to a most estimable colored lady" in town who would give him lodging and board, Anderson politely resisted, reminding McGill of the "inducements" he had been offered. A flustered McGill replied that he thought Anderson "would feel more at home among your own people," especially since there were no other black students enrolled at that time and since "none [had] ever roomed in the dormitories." Anderson then firmly drew a line: "Dr. McGill," he replied, "it was because of the dormitories and their furnishings we came . . . ; as to our being more at home among the colored people, we feel we have been with both

---

13. Matthew Anderson, *Presbyterianism: Its Relation to the Negro* (Philadelphia: John McGill White, 1897), 135-36, 155; C. James Trotman, "Matthew Anderson, Black Pastor, Churchman, and Social Reformer," *American Presbyterians: Journal of Presbyterian History* 66 (Spring 1988): 11-21; Trotman, "Race, Reform, and Religion in the Life of Matthew Anderson," *Princeton Seminary Bulletin* 9 (1988): 143-55; William P. Conrad, *Glory Land: A History of Greencastle's Negro Community* (Shippensburg, PA: Beidal Printing House, 1983). See also Edward L. Ayers, *In the Presence of Mine Enemies: War in the Heart of America, 1859-1863* (New York: Norton, 2003), which compares Franklin County, Pennsylvania, where Greencastle is located, to Augusta County, Virginia, and in the process offers numerous insights about the nature of the world in which Matthew Anderson grew up.

classes all our lives, besides we have not come to Princeton to be entertained, but to study." McGill then provided him with a note to carry to Dr.
Moffatt, asking the latter to secure Anderson a room in what is today Alexander Hall. Moffatt expressed uncertainty about the availability of a
room, but after consulting with a custodian, took Anderson to "a room
which evidently had been used as a storage room, from the quantity of
old broken chairs, bedsteads and shutters that were in it." Anderson
chose to accept the quarters on the assumption that once he was in the
dorm, he could bargain for better. After a couple of weeks, one of his
more well-to-do classmates came to call upon Anderson and, appalled
by the room's condition, told Anderson that there was a vacancy across
the hall that he should request to occupy. At this point, Anderson made
his move. He went to Moffatt and said that he would like to be assigned
to the vacant room rather than the "lumber room" where he was currently quartered. Frustrated, Moffatt blurted out the real reason for the
original assignment: "'We never had any to room in the seminary before,'
he retorted, referring to Negro students." With the issue of discrimination now clearly named, Anderson took his unequivocal stand:

> It makes no difference to us whether you ever did or not, Doctor,
> . . . we are going to room there, and have a suitable room, too, be-
> cause we were assured by the corresponding secretary, Dr. McGill,
> that a good room, well furnished, would be given us in the sem-
> inary building should we come, and if we can't get this we will
> leave.

Moffatt said nothing "but nervously assigned us the desired room." Anderson concluded his narrative of the episode with triumphant satisfaction: "This ended our battles at old Princeton on the race question. From
this time until we graduated we could not have been better treated in
any school, than we were at Princeton, both by faculty and students."[14]

Writing about this incident from the perspective of more than twenty
years, Anderson struck a remarkably generous note. Despite what he
called Princeton's "little weakness on the subject of the Negro," he gave
the school credit for the fact that "there never was the day in the history of
the seminary when her doors were closed against the Negro student,
which is not true of some seminaries of other denominations, even now

14. Anderson, *Presbyterianism,* 164-68.

in the North." Undoubtedly he felt anger at his treatment, but an inner self-confidence coupled with a sense of humor allowed him to assert his rights firmly while maintaining calm dignity. These traits served him well during a distinguished career as the founding pastor of the Berean Presbyterian Church in Philadelphia. In addition to his pastoral labors — or, as he probably would have said, as an extension of them — he established the Berean Building and Loan Association, a bank that never closed even during the Great Depression, and also the Berean Manual and Training School. His wife, Caroline Still Anderson, became one of the first African Americans to graduate from the Women's Medical College of Philadelphia; and the Berean ministries drew on Dr. Anderson's expertise in the establishment of prenatal classes, nurseries, and vocational instruction for women. In addition, in 1893 Matthew Anderson helped organize the Afro-American Presbyterian Council, a forerunner in some respects of the black caucuses organized in mainstream Protestant churches during the 1960s. He and his wife embodied a vision of ministry to the whole person, to economic and social concerns as well as the spiritual. As Anderson fulfilled his ministry, he did so proudly as a Presbyterian, but with a warning to his fellow coreligionists and to his alma mater:

> We are a Presbyterian of the Presbyterians; the very fibre of our mental make-up being Presbyterian; before this nation came into existence our grand sires were in the Presbyterian Church, and we are firm in the belief that the Presbyterian Church is the church for the Negro, but we are forced to say that before the Presbyterian or any other church can have any great success in getting hold of the Negro, the fountain head of that church, the schools of the prophets must be right towards him. For if the Theological Schools are wrong in their attitude towards the Negro, the young men they send out as ministers will be wrong in their attitude towards him, and if the ministry is wrong, the people whom they teach will be wrong also, for like priest like people. Let Princeton Seminary, the fountain head of the Presbyterian Church turn about and make herself perfectly right in regard to the Negro.[15]

15. Anderson, *Presbyterianism,* 168, 169; Trotman, "Race, Reform, and Religion." For his own description of a portion of his ministry, see Matthew Anderson, "The Berean School of Philadelphia and the Industrial Efficiency of the Negro," *Annals of the American Academy of Political and Social Science* 33 (January 1909): 111-18.

During Anderson's time at Princeton, three additional black students joined the student body: Hugh M. Browne and Francis J. Grimké in Anderson's middle year and Daniel W. Culp in his senior year. All four availed themselves of the reciprocal relation the seminary had with the college and took classes there, especially with President James McCosh. According to Anderson's account, their attendance caused no difficulty until Culp, the most dark-skinned among them, came to class. As Anderson recalled it, "when Culp walked in the class room with his book under his arm, it was too much, for the young bourbons of the South. They had been able to stand black, and blacker, but when the blackest came into their classic halls, they bolted." They demanded that McCosh force Culp to withdraw, the president refused, and the southerners then boycotted his classes. Lest Culp be scared off, Anderson said that he and the other black students met with him, "strengthened his nerve, and he continued to attend the lectures."[16]

Despite these painful difficulties, Anderson's friends persisted through the seminary program and subsequently pursued very different careers. Hugh M. Browne served as a licensed stated supply preacher at the Witherspoon Street Church in Princeton while a student but does not appear to have proceeded to ordination. A few years after completing that assignment, he taught in the College of Liberia. Back in the United States, he headed the Department of Physics in the M Street High School in Washington, D.C., from 1886 to 1897 and then for several years held a comparable post at Hampton Institute. After a brief tenure as principal of the Colored High School in Baltimore, he became head of the Institute for Colored Youth in Cheyney, Pennsylvania, where he subsequently started the Training School for Teachers. After retiring in 1913, he spent a year in Germany studying vocational education and devoted his retirement to "the devising and construction of mechanical appliances." Although he did not pursue an ordained ministry, he gave an address before the American Academy of Political and Social Sciences in 1906 and discussed the African American past and future in terms of analogy to Israel's exodus from Egypt to the promised land. In the process he offered a historical theodicy endowing slavery with meaning.

> I have no excuse to offer for slavery; nevertheless it has brought us
> into contact with a more advanced race, and whatever of civiliza-

16. Anderson, *Presbyterianism*, 175, 176.

tion and development we now possess came to us by means of it. The blessings to Israel in Egypt were mightier than the hardships endured, and I am persuaded that we shall, by and by, acknowledge the same concerning our bondage in this country.

For the moment, what his people most needed to appropriate from that civilization, what they needed to begin an exodus to their promised land, was training in practical, vocational skills. At Cheyney, he explained, the instruction had to do with "helpful precept and practice along all the lines of every-day activity." He insisted that his students — and their parents — would benefit not so much from "nicely prepared essays and speeches" as they would from "the teacher's ability to actually perform, after the most approved and economic methods, the every-day activities of the housewife and the husbandman." This philosophy stamped him as a disciple of Booker T. Washington, head of the Tuskegee Institute and advocate of black advancement chiefly through vocational training and a willingness to eschew (at least publicly) questions of social and political equality. Browne left no doubt of his feelings about Washington: "let me testify that if ever there was a man sent of God to a needy people at the psychological moment, Booker T. Washington is one. And I would further testify that the support which the white people have given him is to-day the rainbow of promise that the door of hope will not be closed to the brother in black." Although there was some ambiguity in his expressions of hope for his people, Browne seemed to look beyond "citizenship *de jure* and *de facto* in these United States" in favor of "a developed African race in Africa" with the "United States . . . [as] the greatest of the schools from which the founders and builders of this African nation are to be graduated." In any event, Browne was eager to make clear to his audience at the American Academy that the improvement of his people in the United States would not lead "to the bugbear of Negro domination or the scarecrow of amalgamation." Returning to the biblical analogy, he declared: "In Egypt Israel was a family and a tribe: in the wilderness she became a nation. God made the black race for a nation."[17]

17. Hugh M. Browne, "The Training of the Negro Laborer in the North," *Annals of the American Academy of Political and Social Science* 27 (May 1906): 117-27; quotations from 117, 118, 121, 123, 125, 127. The biographical details about Browne are derived from *Princeton Theological Seminary Biographical Catalogue: 1909*, comp. Joseph H. Dulles (Trenton, NJ: MacCrellish and Quigley, 1909), 364; and from an obituary in the NAACP magazine *The Crisis* 27 (February 1924): 180-81.

After leaving Princeton, Daniel W. Culp served a small Presbyterian Church in Laurens, South Carolina, under the sponsorship of the Freedman's Board of the northern Presbyterian Church. He held that post for a year, then moved to Jacksonville, Florida, as pastor of the Laura Street Presbyterian Church. When asked to head the Stanton Institute, the largest black college in Florida, he added that responsibility to his pastoral duties until overwork prompted him to give up the latter entirely for the work of the Institute. Subsequently he served as a pastor and educator as a Congregationalist under the auspices of the American Missionary Association and held posts in Florida, Alabama, and Tennessee. While in Tennessee, he felt increasingly called to medical work, left his pastorate to pursue the study of medicine in schools in Michigan and Ohio, and eventually worked as a doctor in Georgia and Florida. He also developed an interest in the creation of an African American literature. As he made clear in the preface to his anthology, *Twentieth-Century Negro Literature* (1902), he wished to meet several needs: to combat the "considerable ignorance, on the part of the white people of this country, of the intellectual ability of the Negro"; to provide role models and "character sketches" for "the aspiring Negro youth of the land"; to give a "correct idea of the progress made by the Negro since his Emancipation"; and to provide a synopsis of the thought of "educated Negroes on . . . political, religious, civil, moral and sociological problems." Culp, in short, was making a rudimentary attempt to create a canon of African American thought that would achieve respect outside the community and inspire emulation from within.[18]

Of Anderson's three seminary classmates, Francis J. Grimké (1850-1937) arguably attained the greatest acclaim. The son of a South Carolina planter and one of his female slaves, Grimké was sold by his white half-brother to a Confederate officer during the Civil War. At the close of the war, a patron from the Freedman's Aid Society facilitated Grimké's education at Lincoln University, not far from Philadelphia. He excelled in his classes; and a newspaper story brought him and his brother Archibald, also born to the same parents and also studying at Lincoln, to the attention of their father's sisters. The aunts, Sarah Grimké and Angelina Grimké Weld, had become disillusioned with slavery as young women, left South Carolina for residence in the North, and established them-

18. D. W. Culp, *Twentieth-Century Negro Literature* (Naperville, IL: J. L. Nichols and Company, 1902), 5, 6.

selves as advocates of abolitionism. They had not known of their nephews prior to reading the newspaper article, made contact with them, and helped subsidize their educations. Archibald went on to study law at Harvard and joined a prominent firm. Francis studied law for a time at Lincoln and then Howard University before deciding to enter Princeton Seminary in 1875. After leaving Princeton in 1878, he assumed the pastorate of the Fifteenth Street Presbyterian Church in Washington, D.C., where he remained until his retirement in 1928, except for four years spent in Jacksonville, Florida, for reasons of health. From 1885 to 1889, he served the Laura Street Church when his seminary friend Daniel W. Culp left that pastorate.[19]

In Washington, Francis Grimké acquired a reputation as a powerful preacher whose sermons exhibited the solid biblical exposition and conservative theology that he had learned from Charles Hodge and others at Princeton. (Hodge had once confided to James McCosh that he found Grimké "equal to the ablest of his students.") It was a mark of the esteem in which Grimké was held among the Presbyterians of the District of Columbia, black and white, that he was elected moderator of the Washington Presbytery in 1880. He did not achieve popularity, however, by ducking the hard social questions of the day. At the time, many white Americans suggested that the source of what they called "the race problem" was the lack of education and of self-discipline among black people — some even suggesting that the problem derived from a supposed moral decline among blacks once the restraints of slavery had been removed. Grimké had nothing against the virtues of education, self-discipline, and temperance; in fact, he preached them vigorously as a means to social uplift. But he scoffed at those who would blame African Americans themselves for the problems they faced, and he forthrightly condemned the systematic discrimination and denial of rights to black citizens. After about 1895, he drew back from Booker T. Washington and Washington's unwillingness to confront the evil of the Jim Crow system. In 1913, in commemoration of the fiftieth anniversary of Lincoln's Emancipation Proclamation, he warned: "At the end of these fifty years, we find nearly all the rights guaranteed to us under the constitution, especially under the Four-

19. On Grimké's life and work, see Henry Justin Ferry, "Francis James Grimké: Portrait of a Black Puritan" (Ph.D. Dissertation, Yale University, 1970); and Louis Weeks, "Racism, World War I and the Christian Life: Francis Grimké in the Nation's Capital," in *Black Apostles: Afro-American Clergy Confront the Twentieth Century,* ed. Randall K. Burkett and Richard Newman (Boston: G. K. Hall, 1978), 57-75.

teenth and Fifteenth Amendments, practically nullified in a large section of the country. In the South we have been disfranchised. We have no rights, civil or political, which the white man is bound to respect." But what astounded him even more was that those "whose fathers fought and died to save the Union, and through whom freedom and the great amendments to the constitution came, can stand silently by and see the same rebel spirit that sought to destroy the Union set upon the colored man and rob him of his rights." Grimké argued that the recrudescence of the rebel spirit "is an affront to every loyal white man who fell during the war or who fought for the Union and the cause of freedom." When the biracial National Association for the Advancement of Colored People (NAACP) came into being in 1910 to press a more aggressive agenda in protection of the civil rights of African Americans, the historian will rightly think of persons such as W. E. B. DuBois, Ida B. Barnett-Wells, or Oswald Villard as founding figures. But Francis Grimké; his wife, Charlotte Forten Grimké, who was an important black leader in her own right; and his brother Archibald were also supporters. Francis and Charlotte Grimké were likewise at the center of an important intellectual group in Washington through their Saturday Circle, where, as Wilson J. Moses observes, "prominent blacks from all over the United States found the opportunity to share ideas with receptive audiences."[20]

Within the Presbyterian Church, Francis Grimké fought with equal vigor against efforts to draw a color line. When the northern Presbyterian Church considered reunion with the southern church in the late 1880s after wartime passions had cooled a bit, it was clear that the price of reunion with the South would be separate presbyteries and synods for African Americans. "Organic union," Grimké observed, "is a good thing, but it is by no means the most important thing. It is better to do the right thing than be organically united." On that occasion, the southern church's rejection of the proposal ended, for the moment, the idea of segregated judicatories. But the scheme returned again when the Presbyte-

20. Francis J. Grimké, *Fifty Years of Freedom* (n.p.: n.p., 1913); Wilson J. Moses, "The Lost World of the Negro, 1895-1919: Black Literary and Intellectual Life before the 'Renaissance,'" *Black American Literature Forum* 21 (Spring-Summer 1987): 68. For those interested in pursuing Grimké's thought at length in his own words, see *The Works of Francis J. Grimké*, 4 vols., ed. Carter G. Woodson (Washington, DC: Associated Publishers, 1942). For an excellent analysis of the way in which the issues of equal justice were frequently ignored or suppressed in this era, see David W. Blight, *Race and Reunion: The Civil War in American Memory* (Cambridge: Harvard University Press, 2001).

rian Church in the U.S.A. (PCUSA) negotiated for reunion with the Cumberland Church and offered that denomination the option of segregated judicatories. Despite much PCUSA opposition to the union on the grounds that the Cumberland Church would bring Arminianism into the Calvinist fold, and despite the opposition of Grimké, his friend Matthew Anderson, and others, the PCUSA approved the union as did the Cumberland Presbyterians in 1906. When the issue had come before Grimké's own Washington Presbytery in April 1905, he spoke vigorously against it because the proposal introduced segregation into the laws of the church:

> It may not be popular, but we must stand up for principle. The Presbyterian General Assembly worked itself up into a frenzy against exhibiting the Liberty Bell on the Sabbath, but it was willing to set up the color line. Verily, this is tithing mint and anise and cumin and omitting the weightier matters of the law. . . . I sometimes wonder how God can sit still and see such things going on in the Presbyterian Church.

Despite the applause that Grimké's impassioned appeal triggered, and despite the supporting argument of Presbyterian elder and Supreme Court Associate Justice John Harlan, the Washington Presbytery voted 41 to 23 in favor of the merger, including the segregation clause.[21]

THE VOTE THAT DISHEARTENED Grimké in April 1905 may stand as a valedictory to much that the Presbyterian Church and Princeton Seminary had done as well as to much they had left undone throughout the preceding century. Princeton Seminary was born near the beginning of the decade when the Presbyterian Church offered its most forthright statement against slavery. Drafted chiefly by Ashbel Green, who headed the seminary's board of directors, the statement branded slavery "as utterly inconsistent with the law of God" and urged all Christians "to use their honest, earnest, and unwearied endeavours . . . to obtain the complete abolition of slavery throughout Christendom." Yet, as we have already seen, that seemingly unequivocal stand was quickly followed by the assertion that the "number of slaves, their ignorance, and their vicious habits generally render an immediate and universal emancipation in-

21. Henry Justin Ferry, "Racism and Reunion: A Black Protest by Francis James Grimké," *Journal of Presbyterian History* 50 (Summer 1972): 80, 87, 88.

consistent alike with the safety and happiness of the master and the slave." In short, prudential considerations trumped the urgency of ending slavery. By the 1830s, when Charles Hodge drafted his famous article "Slavery," he held out the hope that "acting on the principles of the gospel, of following the example and obeying the precepts of Christ," would yield "the gradual elevation of the slaves in intelligence, virtue and wealth," as well as "the peaceful and speedy extinction of slavery." But, of course, in the meantime the radicalism of abolition had to be foresworn, and the date for "the speedy extinction of slavery" was pushed somewhere into the indefinite mists of the future. In 1845, the Old School Assembly took the position, approved strongly in the pages of the *Princeton Review,* that it could ameliorate the condition of the slave only by teaching "the glorious doctrines of the gospel, and enjoining upon each [master and slave] the discharge of their relative duties." Any effort to be more specific about programs or policies might split the denomination and contribute to the dismemberment of the Federal Union. Then, during the war, the *Princeton Review* finally endorsed the ending of slavery as a goal signaled by God's providence; but it did so because emancipation served the larger aim of preserving the Federal Union. One can understand how, from the perspective of the leaders of Princeton Seminary, these priorities made sense. But from the vantage point of those, whether black or white, who believed the primary moral imperative of the hour was to eliminate slavery and its legacy, it must have seemed that Princeton and the Presbyterian Church always seemed to manifest genuine concern about slavery and its legacies, only to find other matters that almost invariably took precedence. It is this history that has prompted Gayraud S. Wilmore, a senior statesman among contemporary African American Presbyterians, to declare: "No church was more high-sounding and profound in its theological analysis of slavery and did less about it."[22]

To its credit, Princeton Seminary did, as Matthew Anderson acknowledged, accept black students at a time when many other schools did not. But these students were not able to room on campus until Anderson himself forced the issue with McGill and Moffatt. After Anderson had done so, the coming to campus over the next two years of Francis Grimké, Hugh M. Browne, and Daniel W. Culp appeared not to have cre-

22. Gayraud S. Wilmore, *Black and Presbyterian: The Heritage and the Hope* (Philadelphia: Geneva Press, 1983), 62.

ated a similar stir about housing. However, in his 1897 memoir Anderson claimed to have it "from good and reliable authority" that, once his cohort of black students had graduated,

> not a single Negro student, has roomed in one of the buildings, though a number have graduated from the seminary since then. The only exception, if it can be called an exception, being in the case of a Negro student, who was taken in for a short time by one of the other students while making a fight for a room, at the beginning of his junior year, who afterwards drew a room, but gave it up and took a room in one of the colored families of the town, through pressure which had been brought to bear upon him by the Seminary.

This account gains credibility from the fact that Professor Benjamin Warfield announced in 1911, as if it were a new policy, that black students could room on campus. Two years later, when the opportunity arose to put the policy into action, Warfield's determination created a private donnybrook between him and Assistant Professor J. Gresham Machen, who was usually on his senior colleague's side in most matters.[23]

23. Anderson, *Presbyterianism*, 169.

Chapter Eight

Charles Hodge and the Tradition Codified

B Y THE 1840s, Princeton Seminary had weathered a crisis. The school was no longer suspended between the two contending parties within the Presbyterian Church, too conservative for the New School and too moderate for the ultra–Old School faction. Princeton was now unambiguously an Old School institution in an exclusively Old School denomination. Any lingering fear about the seminary falling into hostile hands vanished once the Supreme Court of Pennsylvania, the state in which the General Assembly had incorporated, ruled in 1839 against a New School claim to the assets of the denomination. Before that decision, the seminary experienced some exceedingly anxious moments, for a lower Pennsylvania court had found in favor of the New School, and Princeton's fate had hung in the balance. Within a few years of the Pennsylvania decision, Princeton's enrollments had recovered from a drop during the time of crisis, finances rebounded, and a new library building arose in 1843. That library was donated by James Lenox, son of Robert Lenox, who in 1836 had threatened to take his money elsewhere if Princeton did not hew rigorously to an Old School line. The elder Lenox had died in 1839, and now the son was signaling satisfaction with the course Princeton had followed. He did hedge his bets, however, by putting into the legal document bestowing the library to the seminary a clause specifying that if the school ever passed from the control of the Presbyterian Church or veered from the distinctive doctrines of the Westminster Confession, the grant would become "null and void."

The clarity brought by the division of the Presbyterian Church and

Princeton's unequivocal identification with the Old School was liberating in that it allowed the seminary to voice theological convictions freely within a relatively united denomination. But this did not mean the absence of theological controversy. Especially through the pages of the *Princeton Review,* the seminary defined its distinctive position in conversation with — and often in opposition to — various other schools and thinkers. Then, during the Civil War and its immediate aftermath, the relationship between Old School and New School Presbyterians changed dramatically. Both of the churches lost their southern components — the relatively tiny number of Southerners in the New School withdrew in 1857, and the much more substantial number of Old School Southerners left at the start of the Civil War to form a separate denomination. With these secessions, the northern Old and New Schools were drawn together by a common, fervid loyalty to the Union. That experience, coupled with the fact that the New School had repudiated many of the excesses the Old School feared in the 1830s, made what would have seemed unthinkable at that time a reality in 1870: the two branches of Presbyterianism reunited in a single denomination. Spokesmen at Princeton Seminary had opposed reunion, but accepted it with grace once the issue was decided. Nevertheless, Princeton continued to think of itself as perpetuating a decidedly Old School point of view; and this self-perception would prove to be a source of conflict some decades down the road.

At the center of Princeton's life for these years of transition, from the schism of 1837 to the reunion of 1870 and slightly beyond, was Charles Hodge. In 1841, Hodge moved to the chair of didactic and polemic theology when Archibald Alexander reconfigured his teaching responsibilities. Given the importance the seminary attached to sound doctrine and systematic theology, this move placed Hodge in what was arguably the premier spot at the school, and his editorship of the *Princeton Review* already made him its public face or voice. Then, with the death of Samuel Miller in 1850 and of Archibald Alexander the following year, Charles Hodge became the senior member of the faculty. Thus, over the years from the divisions of the 1830s through the 1870s, Charles Hodge was the single most important figure in defining and codifying the Princeton Theology of the nineteenth century.

Charles Hodge and the Faith Once Delivered to the Saints

Many interpreters have taken a single often-quoted remark as a summary of Old Princeton. Hodge himself provided the comment on April 24, 1872, when Princeton Seminary hosted a celebration of his fifty years as a professor. Schools across the country and around the world sent greetings, or their representatives appeared in person. At the same time, the three volumes of Hodge's *Systematic Theology* had begun to roll off the presses. Although Hodge would live another six years and author an additional book — his assessment of Darwinism — the semi-centennial was a time of summing up; and the honoree offered his own summary, including the comment: "I am not afraid to say that a new idea never originated in this Seminary." In many classes on American religion, this one sentence has become the humorous tagline in lectures caricaturing the Princeton Theology as utterly reactionary, ossified, and out of touch with contemporary thought.[1]

Conservative the theology surely was, but a more nuanced assessment of Hodge and Old Princeton is needed. Henry A. Boardman, speaking on behalf of the board of directors at the semi-centennial, provided a start toward that appraisal when he lauded Hodge for publishing "the only comprehensive work on systematic theology in our own or any other language, which comprises the latest results of sound scriptural exegesis, discusses the great themes of the Augustinian system from an evangelical standpoint, and deals satisfactorily with the sceptical speculations of modern philosophy and science." A professor from the Theological Institute of Connecticut (today the Hartford Seminary Foundation) likewise gave a clue to Hodge's appeal when, to laughter from the audience, he said of Hodge's views, "I doubt whether you have the right to put your imprimatur especially on it, as the 'Princeton Theology.' It is the theology of the Reformation. It is the theology which the fathers of New England . . . taught, and which we can teach on the basis of their teaching." Hodge, in short, was being praised that day, not because he had rejected the new out of hand, but for an achievement more subtle. With a knowledge of "the latest results of sound scriptural exegesis" and thoroughly familiar with modern philosophy and science, Hodge used

---

1. *Proceedings Connected with the Semi-Centennial Commemoration of the Professorship of Rev. Charles Hodge, D.D., LL.D. in the Theological Seminary at Princeton, N.J., April 24, 1872* (New York: Anson D. F. Randolph and Company, 1872), 52.

that expertise to restate and reaffirm a theological heritage that stretched from a solid rock of biblical authority, to Augustine, to the Reformation, and thence to the present. "The Princeton Theology," as E. Brooks Holifield has observed,

> was therefore much more than a set of beliefs about biblical infallibility. It was also more than simply a return to the seventeenth century. It was an effort to defend Westminster Calvinism against innovators and critics by showing that seventeenth-century doctrines met the standards of nineteenth-century philosophy, properly understood.[2]

A prime example of Hodge's commitment to meeting contemporary standards appeared in what is perhaps the second most famous passage from his work, this one lengthier than the first. In his discussion of proper theological method set forth near the beginning of his *Systematic Theology,* he declared: "The Bible is to the theologian what nature is to the man of science. It is his store-house of facts; and his method of ascertaining what the Bible teaches, is the same as that which the natural philosopher adopts to ascertain what nature teaches." That method was empirical in nature. "It is the fundamental principle of all sciences," Hodge explained, "and of theology among the rest, that theory is to be determined by facts, and not facts by theory. As natural science was a chaos until the principle of induction was admitted and faithfully carried out, so theology is a jumble of human speculations, not worth a straw, when men refuse to apply the same principle to the study of the Word of God." Yet this induction was not empirical in a narrow sense, for it made room for the facts of human consciousness as well as the facts of God's spirit working in the soul of the believer. Hodge insisted that his empiricism was "perfectly consistent, on the one hand, with the admission of intuitive truths, both intellectual and moral, due to our constitution as rational and moral beings; and, on the other hand, with the controlling power over our beliefs exercised by the inward teachings of the Spirit, or, in other words, by our religious experience." What Hodge was seeking to accomplish was the assembling of all the relevant "facts" — from the Bible and from human consciousness in

2. *Proceedings Connected with the Semi-Centennial Commemoration,* 47-48, 81; E. Brooks Holifield, *Theology in America: Christian Thought from the Age of the Puritans to the Civil War* (New Haven: Yale University Press, 2003), 389.

general as well as from the souls of the regenerate in particular — into a single system of theology that would have the same objective grounding as what today one might popularly call the "hard" sciences. Without such facts — precise and irrefutable — the foundation of Christian truth would lose its firmness and sink into a morass of subjectivism. The anxiety that theology would wander into such a swamp was one of the perennial fears of the Princeton theologians.[3]

In the tradition of Witherspoon and Alexander, Hodge sought to wed Reformed orthodoxy with the epistemological assumptions of the Common Sense philosophy and the Baconian ideal, both of which became almost ubiquitous in American colleges and seminaries of the pre–Civil War era. Some scholars have questioned whether at the end of the day this was an appropriate marriage. Strongly God-centered, classic Reformed theology sensed acutely the limits of sinful humanity's capacity to know God or to capture in human discourse the mystery of the divine. To the extent that men and women could know God, it was through God's gracious self-revelation and because of the divine accommodation to human frailty. Yet, in choosing the Common Sense philosophy, Hodge and his colleagues seized upon a tradition born among Scottish Moderates of the eighteenth century who were generally eager to construct an anthropocentric system diminishing mystery and vaunting the natural capacity of humans to grasp, analyze, and define ultimate reality. More than fifty years ago, in a ground-breaking article on the influence of the Scottish philosophy in America, Sydney Ahlstrom put the matter this way:

> As this philosophy was adopted, the fervent theocentricity of Calvin . . . was sacrificed and a new principle of doctrinal interpretation was increasingly emphasized. Self-consciousness became the oracle of religious truth. Man's need rather than God's Word became the guide in doctrinal formulation. . . . The adoption of the benign and optimistic anthropology of the Scottish Moderates by American Calvinists veiled the very insights into human nature which were a chief strength of Calvin's theology. . . . There resulted a neo-rationalism which rendered the central Christian paradoxes into stark, logical contradictions that had either to be disguised or

---

3. Charles Hodge, *Systematic Theology*, 3 vols. (New York: Charles Scribner, 1872-1873), 1:10, 14-15.

explained away. Reformed theology was thus emptied of its most dynamic element. A kind of rationalistic *rigor mortis* set in.[4]

Subsequent authors, while accepting the thrust of Ahlstrom's argument, have put a finer point on the analysis. Mark Noll, for example, contends that the Common Sense philosophy did not determine the specific doctrines that Hodge held — large swaths of the *Systematic Theology* repeated views that Reformed theologians such as Turretin had already stated. However, that philosophy did profoundly affect the *way* in which Hodge construed theological method. Correct procedure entailed treating the Bible as a storehouse of reliable, discrete facts to be sorted and assembled inductively into a system analogous to the work of Sir Isaac Newton. Or, as Noll writes, "The example of Newton encouraged" belief "that the end product of theology was a system of certain truths, grounded on careful induction from simple facts, eschewing hypothetical flights of fancy, and providing a universal and unvarying picture of God and his ways." Thus Hodge and many other evangelicals "assumed that when they applied scientific Common Sense to Scripture and God-given experience more generally, they could derive a fixed, universally valid theology."[5]

The Core of a "Fixed, Universally Valid Theology"

For Hodge, a crucial aspect of that "universally valid theology" was the principle of representation, or the notion that Adam and Christ had acted on behalf of others, the transgression of the former being counted against all subsequent human beings and the righteousness of the latter being reckoned to the saved. Without this representative principle, he believed that the biblical account of sin and redemption was unintelligible. From his 1830 essay "Inquiries Respecting the Doctrine of Imputation," through

4. Sydney E. Ahlstrom, "The Scottish Philosophy and American Theology," *Church History* 24, no. 3 (1955): 268-69. For a contrary view of the role of the Common Sense philosophy in the Old Princeton Theology, see Paul Kjoss Helseth, *"Right Reason" and the Princeton Mind: An Unorthodox Proposal* (Phillipsburg, NJ: P & R Publishing Co., 2010).

5. Mark A. Noll, "The Irony of Enlightenment for Presbyterians in the Early Republic," *Journal of the Early Republic* 5 (Summer 1985): 149-75; Noll, "Common Sense Traditions and American Evangelical Thought," *American Quarterly* 37 (Summer 1985): 216-38. Noll's focus in these articles is much broader than Hodge, but the latter provides a key illustrative figure. The quotation is from "Common Sense Traditions," 224-25. See also Holifield, *Theology in America*, 173-96, 370-89.

his commentary on Romans (1835), and down to the publication of his *Systematic Theology* (1872-1873), Hodge maintained the importance of the parallel offices performed by Christ and Adam. Just as Adam's transgression was imputed to his descendants and brought them to ruin, so, too, Christ's righteousness was imputed to the redeemed and opened the path of salvation. Hodge flatly rejected theologies that evaded or mitigated the stark claim that, on account of the sin of Adam, every subsequent human being entered the world as a condemned sinner, and this prior to any particular sin he or she committed. Although he did not use the precise language, Hodge's theology affirmed the famous line from a New England Puritan primer: "In Adam's fall, we sinnèd all." Just as emphatically, Hodge insisted that the righteousness of Christ was credited to the redeemed, even though they had in themselves no such virtue. Hodge regarded imputation as more than one instance of a range of possible theories about the nature of sin and redemption; it was the reality itself. It "is neither a theory nor a philosophical speculation," he insisted, "but the statement of a scriptural fact in scriptural language."[6]

His defense of representation and imputation testified to Hodge's adherence to the covenant theology of the Westminster Confession, but it also signaled a willingness to sail against prevailing theological winds. Many nineteenth-century theologians felt uneasy claiming that the actions or character of one person could determine the moral status of another — the idea seemed unfair and manifestly out of keeping with the individualistic, democratic sentiments of the era. These theologians tended to see sin and redemption in terms of the sum total of particular choices made by free men and women, often found older notions of original sin overblown if not repugnant, and in general viewed salvation from an anthropocentric perspective. Although Hodge was not entirely immune to those sentiments, he generally adopted a more God-centered approach. Moreover, he understood the corporate dimension of the drama of sin and redemption, sensing that it consisted of more than the aggregation of all the religious decisions made by men and women. Or, as he put the matter, he opposed the prevalent view "which teaches that happiness is the great end of creation; that all sin and virtue consist in

6. Charles Hodge, *A Commentary on the Epistle to the Romans* (Philadelphia: Grigg and Elliot, 1835), 226; Hodge, *Systematic Theology,* 2:121-22; Hodge, "Inquiries Respecting the Doctrine of Imputation," *Biblical Repertory and Theological Review* 2 (1830): 425-72; Hodge, *Essays and Reviews* (New York: Robert Carter and Brothers, 1857), 323.

voluntary acts; that moral character is not transmissible, but must be determined by the agent himself; that every man has power to determine and to change at will his own character, or to make himself a new heart." This outlook represents "every man as standing by himself, and of course denies any such union with Adam as involves the derivation of a corrupt nature from him." It plays down "union with Christ, as the source of righteousness and life," and makes his sacrifice "scarcely more than a device to render the pardon of sin expedient, and to open the way to deal with men according to their conduct. Attention is turned from him as the ground of acceptance and source of strength, and everything made to depend on ourselves." As Hodge's remarks indicate, he regarded imputation and the principle of representation as more than isolated doctrines whose demise would have little impact on other aspects of Christian teaching. Rather, they were part of the theological keystone, and their removal would cause the entire arch of Christian teaching about sin and redemption to collapse. Hodge hinted that imputation satisfied an important psychic need within humanity as well, a need to know that forgiveness was not cheaply or easily given. "The enlightened conscience," he claimed, "is never satisfied until it sees that God can be just in justifying the ungodly; that sin has been punished. . . . It is when he thus sees justice and mercy embracing each other, that the believer has that peace which passes all understanding." Such peace required the believer to know that his or her security came entirely from without, from the gracious action of God in Christ, and not from the strength of one's faith or moral achievement. In short, the defense of imputation was not only a matter of upholding doctrinal truth; it was essential to offering authentic pastoral comfort to troubled souls. Although much of his defense of representation and imputation turned on appropriate biblical passages, Hodge also enlisted the supposed common sense of humanity. The principle on which imputation rests, he asserted, "finds a response in the very constitution of our nature. All men are led as it were instinctively to recognize the validity of this principle of representation. Rulers represent their people; parents their children; guardians their wards."

Hodge's defense of the covenant theology of Westminster would lead one to suppose that he desired strict adherence to that confession of faith, and the assumption is correct. Upon his installation as professor, Hodge along with his colleagues had, of course, taken the exceedingly strict creedal vow, including the statement: "I do solemnly promise and engage, not to inculcate, teach, or insinuate any thing which shall appear to me to contradict or contravene, either directly or impliedly, any thing taught in the . . . Confession of Faith or Catechisms." Yet, when Hodge wrote of creedal subscription, it was not the seminary vow that he discussed but rather the Presbyterian ordination requirements, which suggested somewhat less restrictive endorsement of Westminster. In the ordination vows, every minister declared that he "receives and adopts the Confession of Faith of this church, as containing the system of doctrine taught in the Holy Scriptures." This avowal did not, Hodge made clear in 1858, permit ministers to pick and choose among the confession's doctrines as if they constituted a smorgasbord, but neither did the declaration mean that clergy had to endorse every statement in the confession. "There are hundreds of ministers in our church," he declared — and at this time he was speaking of an entirely *Old School* denomination, ". . . who do not receive all the propositions contained in the Confession of Faith and Catechisms." To start requiring them to do so would be "simply absurd and intolerable." Although, by today's standards, Hodge's concept of subscription would generally be deemed quite limiting, it was, in the context of mid-nineteenth-century Old School Presbyterianism, firm but charitable, middle-of-the road more than reactionary. In a very different theological climate nearly eighty years later, some still found a spirit of breadth in Hodge's essay. In 1937, President John A. Mackay, seeking to woo Emil Brunner to the faculty, wished to convince the European theologian that his intellectual liberty would not be unduly infringed by the creedal subscription required of Princeton professors. In his effort to convince Brunner that coming to Princeton would not entail donning a theological straitjacket, Mackay sent him a copy of Hodge's 1858 article.[7]

But even when allowance is made for Hodge's willingness to permit a *modest* theological diversity, his writings still leave the impression of a man eager to mark off truth from error. He felt that the church, to adapt a metaphor of historian James Turner, was sailing through treacherous waters; and the "hand on the tiller" needed to be "rock steady." Hodge sought to provide that sure hand. Through his essays in the *Princeton Review,* he identified the shoals on which faith might run aground and attempted to guide the church safely around them. Among the dangers he identified were, of course, the innovations of the New England theologians and their

---

7. *A Brief History of the Theological Seminary of the Presbyterian Church, at Princeton, New Jersey* (Princeton: John Bogart, 1838), 15; [Charles Hodge,] "Adoption of the Confession of Faith," *Biblical Repertory and Princeton Review* 30 (1858): 685, 688.

New School fellow travelers. In his exchanges with those of this persuasion, he argued against weakening the connection between the sin of Adam and his posterity, altering the doctrine of atonement, and exalting the sinner's role in his or her salvation — the errors Princeton identified with the New Divinity of Samuel Hopkins, Nathanael Emmons, and Joseph Bellamy, but especially with the New Haven theology of Nathaniel William Taylor. Hodge directed some of his sharpest barbs against Charles G. Finney, the upstate New York evangelist whose use of new measures in the promotion of revivals — the reliance on protracted meetings, the anxious bench, and other such devices — deeply offended Old Schoolers. Hodge shared that distaste and located the problem in Finney's defective theology. As Hodge suggested in an 1832 article, Finney illustrated the logical end point of New England modifications of Calvinism. Hodge objected that Finney's zeal to win converts caused him to magnify human agency in regeneration unduly. "When sinners are thus represented as depending on themselves," Hodge observed, "God having done all he can, how they can be made to feel that they are in his hands, depending on his sovereign grace, we cannot conceive." He argued that the theological effect of the evangelist's preaching was to render the cross of Christ and the agency of the Holy Spirit superfluous. After Finney had gone to teach at Oberlin College in Ohio and transferred from Presbyterianism to Congregationalism, he published *Lectures on Systematic Theology* (1846), which only confirmed Hodge's belief that the evangelist had taken New England theology beyond the pale. The book was, Hodge acknowledged, "in a high degree logical," but he was not complimenting Finney, for the evangelist had employed an entirely *a priori* method of argument, not the inductive method favored by Princeton. Starting from what Hodge called the "first truths of reason," ignoring the "common consciousness of men," and without adducing any arguments from the Bible, Finney proceeded to overturn traditional Christian teaching about the nature of moral duty, sin, virtue, and human free agency.[8]

8. James Turner, "Charles Hodge in the Intellectual Weather of the Nineteenth Century," in *Charles Hodge Revisited: A Critical Appraisal of His Life and Work*, ed. John W. Stewart and James H. Moorhead (Grand Rapids: Eerdmans, 2002), 41; [Charles Hodge,] "The New Divinity Tried," *Biblical Repertory and Theological Review* 4 (1832): 300, 301; Hodge, *Essay and Reviews*, 245, 257. For contemporary assessments placing Finney within the context of the New England tradition, see Charles E. Hambrick-Stowe, *Charles G. Finney and the Spirit of American Evangelicalism* (Grand Rapids: Eerdmans, 1996), and Allen C. Guelzo, "An Heir or a Rebel? Charles Grandison Finney and the New England Theology," *Journal of the Early Republic* 17 (Spring 1997): 61-94.

Hodge's complaint about revivals was larger than his objection to one man's theology. The Princeton professor questioned the heavy reliance placed upon them in the United States and on occasion dismissed them as an American "idiosyncracy" *(sic)*. He acknowledged the debt owed by the churches to the revivals promoted by Jonathan Edwards, George Whitefield, the Tennents, and others in the previous century; but he felt that many of his contemporaries had fallen into the "error of regarding these extraordinary seasons as the only means of promoting religion," when in fact continued reliance on them might actually do harm. The "paroxysms" of revivals on occasion "may be highly useful, or even necessary, just as violent remedies are often the only means of saving life. But such remedies are not the ordinary and proper means of sustaining and promoting health." Hodge believed that American Christians should place far more emphasis on week in, week out Sunday worship, and especially upon the nurture that took place — or should take place — within Christian families. Theologically, he rooted this conviction in the Reformed notion that "the children of believers are introduced into the covenant into which their parents enter with God, and that the promises of that covenant are made no less to the children than to the parents. He promises to be their God, to give them his Spirit, to renew their hearts, and to cause them to live." That did not mean that, in every case, the children of believers would be regenerate, but in the main, God "has established a connexion between faithful parental training and the salvation of children, as he has between seed-time and harvest." Many American Christians failed to remember this truth because they ignored the fact that "men are not isolated individuals, each forming his own character by the energy of his will." People are shaped by relationships, communities, and circumstances into which they were born or otherwise found themselves through no decision of their own. Here again Hodge took occasion to ring the doctrinal chimes in favor of imputation and representation.[9]

Hodge had allies in the struggle against undue reliance on revivals. One of these was John Williamson Nevin, a former student who had stayed on after completing his studies to teach Hodge's classes while the latter was in Europe from 1826 to 1828. After leaving Princeton, Nevin accepted a call as a professor of biblical literature at Western Seminary (one of the predecessor institutions of today's Pittsburgh Theological Seminary), and in 1840 he assumed a professorship at the German Re-

9. Hodge, *Essays and Reviews,* 305-6, 307, 320, 324.

formed Seminary (now Lancaster Theological Seminary) in Mercersburg, Pennsylvania. In 1843, his small book *The Anxious Bench* offered a biting attack against the system of new measures revivalism that he believed to be nothing less than a "heresy," a "Babel of extravagance," undermining the ordinary means of grace offered in regular preaching, worship, the sacraments, and catechesis. When *The Anxious Bench* appeared, the *Princeton Review,* in a brief notice, signaled its approval. The "main argument," said the reviewer, was "unanswerable"; the system of new measures revivalism, while promoted by "pious but misguided brethren," was creating "wide-spread spiritual mischief."[10]

The Problem of History and Development

Soon, however, Hodge found himself at loggerheads with his erstwhile student. During his years in Pittsburgh, Nevin had learned the German language and began reading J. A. W. Neander's church history as well as other current German works in theology and philosophy. Nevin's studies contributed to a profound shift in his thinking that came to fruition when he moved into the German cultural orbit at Mercersburg, and particularly after he was joined on the faculty in 1844 by Philip Schaff, a Swiss-born scholar educated in Germany by some of the leading theological figures: among others, F. C. Baur, I. A. Dorner, F. A. G. Tholuck, E. W. Hengstenberg, and Neander. These teachers ran the gamut from the more radical Baur to the reactionary Hengstenberg, with the others occupying more mediating positions. Schaff himself stood on moderate to conservative ground. However, he brought with him a set of commitments and ideas that, along with those of Nevin, would shape what became known as the Mercersburg Theology — a theology that set Charles Hodge's teeth on edge.[11]

10. Charles Yrigoyen Jr. and George H. Bricker, eds., *Catholic and Reformed: Selected Theological Writings of John Williamson Nevin* (Pittsburgh: Pickwick Press, 1978), 19, 21; review of Nevin, *The Anxious Bench,* in *Biblical Repertory and Princeton Review* 16 (January 1844): 137.

11. For a now classic analysis of the Mercersburg Theology, see James Hastings Nichols, *Romanticism in American Theology* (Chicago: University of Chicago Press, 1961); the same author offers a much briefer sketch of Nevin in *Sons of the Prophets: Leaders in Protestantism from Princeton Seminary,* ed. Hugh T. Kerr (Princeton: Princeton University Press, 1963), 69-81.

Hodge's discomfort surfaced as Nevin and Schaff began elaborating their views. In his *Mystical Presence* (1846), for example, Nevin contended that American Protestants had lost the richness of the classic Reformed understanding of the Eucharist. Aside from Zwingli, who tended to reduce it to a memorial ordinance, Calvin and others of the sixteenth century regarded the Supper as conveying the real spiritual presence of Christ. The triumph of what Nevin called "modern Puritan theory" had reduced the Eucharist to a pale shadow of this earlier vision. Repudiating transubstantiation, he nevertheless insisted that Protestants needed to recover a more robust doctrine — one in which "the sacrament is made to carry with it an *objective* force. . . . It is not a sign, a picture, deriving its significance from the mind of the beholder. The virtue which it possesses is not put into it by the faith of the worshipper." For Nevin, the Eucharist stood at the center of worship. Here Christ shared his life with believers — his human as well as his divine life — and they became part of Christ's body, the church, and thus in some sense an extension of the incarnation.[12]

Another statement of the Mercersburg Theology appeared in the publication of an expanded version of Schaff's inaugural lecture, *The Principle of Protestantism* (1845), offering an overview of Christian history. Central to the entire presentation was an understanding of church history as organic development. The Reformation, for example, did not simply negate medieval Christianity but grew out of it, redressing its one-sided stress on objectivity and external authority. Unfortunately, Protestantism in reaction had careened to another extreme. Schaff explained:

> As Catholicism towards the close of the Middle Ages settled into a character of hard, stiff objectivity, incompatible with the proper freedom of the individual subject, now ripening into spiritual manhood; so Protestantism has been carried aside, in later times, into the opposite error of a loose subjectivity, which threatens to subvert all regard for Church authority.

As a result of the Protestant revolt against church authority, a "sect system," nowhere more apparent than in the United States, shivered the body of Christ into fragments, and that crumbling "must be a source of deep distress" to anyone who has a sense of the church "as the commu-

---

12. John W. Nevin, *The Mystical Presence: A Vindication of the Reformed or Calvinistic Doctrine of the Holy Eucharist* (Philadelphia: King and Baird, 1846), 61, 173-76.

nion of saints." Schaff ended on a note of hope, for he believed that the organic development of Christianity was carrying it toward a day "when walls of partition as they now divide sect from sect should be broken down, and the whole Christian world brought not only to acknowledge and feel, but also to show itself evidently one."[13]

These two early works of Nevin and Schaff established the themes that reverberated through their collaboration over the next decade: a respect for the entirety of the Christian tradition, a sense of its organic development over the centuries, the centrality of sacramental life, a commitment to an ecumenical vision of the church, and the hope of the denominations one day becoming empirically what they already are in essence: the one holy catholic or universal church. Beneath these motifs lay the conviction that God's relationship to humanity was not to be understood mechanically or abstractly but rather in terms of the divine-human life of Christ flowing into the church.

Charles Hodge ignored Nevin's *Mystical Presence* for two years before taking up his pen to refute it. With voluminous quotations from sixteenth-century figures, he attempted to show that his former student had misrepresented the sources and distorted the Reformed doctrine of the Supper. The scholarly consensus is that Hodge came off second best in the ensuing exchange. As James H. Nichols demonstrated fifty years ago, Hodge drew largely on the sources already assembled by Nevin and often cited them "out of context in accordance with his own ideas of theological propriety." He could do so, Nichols argues, because he saw the past as "an armory of theological tenets, and a man had a right to pick and choose as he would." Nichols's point is astute, for Hodge had difficulty understanding history as development, at least in the sense suggested by Nevin and Schaff. Hodge, of course, was no fool; he understood that customs, institutions, and ideas altered over time. He could even allow that, within limits, what was morally and politically appropriate — for example, the amount of liberty to be given to a people or the form of government they should have — depended upon context. But when it came to the faith once delivered to the saints, he balked at notions of development. In a review in 1854 of Schaff's *History of the Ap-*

13. Philip Schaff, *The Principle of Protestantism as Related to the Present State of the Church*, with an introduction by John W. Nevin (Chambersburg, PA: Publication Office of the German Reformed Church, 1845), 117, 131, 205. At this point, Schaff was spelling his name as "Schaf" but would shortly add the extra "f."

ostolic Church, Hodge registered a strong dissent against the notion that there could be a genuine evolution of Christianity or that each age could receive its understanding of the gospel only as filtered through the church and its tradition.

> Christianity is a system of doctrines supernaturally revealed and now recorded in the Bible. Of that system there can be no development. . . . No doctrine can ever be unfolded or expanded beyond what is there revealed. The whole revelation is there, and is there as distinctly, as fully, and as clearly as it ever can be made, without a new supernatural revelation. . . . Instead of the Church of one age being dependent for its life upon those which precede it, and obliged to gain access to Christ and the truth through them, we all have direct access to Christ and his word.[14]

Part of Hodge's queasiness had to do with whence the Mercersburg Theology came and whither it tended. Its source made him suspicious. Shaped by German views in which the divine and human sometimes merged into one evolving reality — Hodge evoked the specter of Hegel here — Mercersburg might open the gates to pantheism. It also endangered the unambiguous clarity of God's revelation. The logical outcome of the developmental principle espoused by Nevin and Schaff was that "Christian doctrine is not a definite form of truth revealed in the Scriptures, but the variable form in which the Christian consciousness or life expresses its cognitions," and hence the ghost of Schleiermacher as well as the shade of Hegel lurked in the background. But at the end of the day, Hodge feared that all the talk of development and organic life would give the ecclesiastical game away to Roman Catholicism. The emphasis upon the church as the extension of the incarnation and as the essential community through which the individual believer receives the life of Christ might prove a "road leading Rome-ward." Hodge's concern was not without merit. By the 1840s and 1850s, the so-called "church question" occupied many minds. From the United Kingdom in the previous decade had come the Oxford or Tractarian movement, advocating that Anglicanism rediscover its Catholic roots; and some, most notably John Henry (later

---

14. Nichols, *Romanticism in American Theology,* 90; [Charles Hodge,] "Dr. Schaff's *Apostolic Church*," *Biblical Repertory and Princeton Review* 26 (1854): 157, 163. Hodge's 1848 review of *Mystical Presence* is reprinted in Hodge, *Essays and Reviews,* 341-92.

Cardinal) Newman, eventually found their way to Rome. By the 1840s, Tractarianism was influencing an already existing high church party within American Episcopalianism, some fifty of whose priests or seminary graduates took the same path as Newman. Nevin himself, during what he called a period of "dizziness," came close to conversion to Roman Catholicism before turning back.[15]

Theology and Language

During the years of debate with Nevin and Schaff, Hodge also entered into another controversy — one involving the nature, or possibly even the *existence,* of theology as a subject of systematic study. Horace Bushnell, American Congregationalism's most creative thinker, triggered the dispute. In 1848, this pastor from Hartford, Connecticut, lectured in the three major theological schools of New England: Harvard, Yale, and Andover. The following year, he published those addresses as *God in Christ,* to which he added a "Preliminary Dissertation on Language." The book advanced controversial views about the divinity of Christ and the atonement, but its deepest challenge came from Bushnell's view of the place of theology in the life of the Christian community. To the shock of many, he argued that carefully wrought creeds or doctrines might impede "the true reviving of religion" and could produce unnecessary conflict. Theology was not bad in itself, but Christians had mistaken the nature of this discourse. Following notions he gleaned from his teacher Josiah W. Gibbs at Yale and from Samuel Taylor Coleridge's *Aids to Reflection,* Bushnell contended that language originated at the level of physical reality to denote things that can be seen, touched, or heard. As language moved to the realm of the non-sensible, to the things of the spirit, it used the words and ideas developed in the realm of the senses as metaphors or symbols. To expect any single theological system or creed to give precise definition to the Christian faith was thus an "effort to make language answer a purpose that is against its nature." Because words "are inexact representations of thought, mere types or analogies," Bushnell argued, ". . . it follows that language will ever be trying to mend its own deficiencies, by multiplying its forms of representation." In other words, *more*

15. Hodge, "Dr. Schaff's *Apostolic Church,*" 171, 180, 192; Nichols, *Romanticism in American Theology,* 192-217.

theologies, not fewer, might be needed; but they had to be received as so many *partial* approximations of truth. Moreover, he insisted that "any sufficient or tolerably comprehensive theology" cannot be achieved "save through the medium of an esthetic elevation in the sensibilities of our souls." As Robert Bruce Mullin has observed, Bushnell was asking his readers "to accept a new model for the vocation of the theologian." While theologians and ministers had "seen themselves as analogous to practitioners of other learned professions," Bushnell was suggesting "that a theologian was not like a doctor or lawyer but more like a poet plumbing his soul."[16]

Edwards Amasa Park, professor at Andover Seminary, picked up the challenge that Bushnell had issued. As his first name implied, Park came from a family committed to the theological heritage of Jonathan Edwards, his father having studied with New Divinity minister Nathanael Emmons. Park continued the line by spending his career trying to systematize and defend the Edwardsean or Consistent Calvinist heritage. In May 1850, he addressed a convention of Congregational ministers in Boston on the subject "the theology of the intellect and of the feelings." He conceded Bushnell's point that much in the Bible did indeed appeal to the feelings, emotions, and imagination rather than the intellect. Using his own rather lush image, he asserted: "In the Bible there are pleasing hints of many things which were never designed to be doctrines. . . . I would say that these ideas . . . are like oriental kings and nobles, moving about in their free, flowing robes; but in many a scholastic system they are like the embalmed bodies of those ancient lords." (As a defender of the New Divinity, Park suggested, for example, that biblical images depicting the imputation of Adam's sin to subsequent men and women were to be treated as a theology addressed to the feelings, not as a literal truth to be commended to the intellect.) Park strongly resisted, however, the notion that religious language could be dissolved entirely into metaphor or doctrine into poetry. Above the feelings stood a theology of the intellect that "comprehends the truth just as it is." The latter theology consisted of rational propositions exhibiting "preciseness both of thought and style" and contained "no ambiguous, mystical or incoher-

---

16. Horace Bushnell, *God in Christ* (New York: Charles Scribner's Sons, 1876 [1849]), 55, 72, 280, 308; Robert Bruce Mullin, *The Puritan as Yankee: A Life of Horace Bushnell* (Grand Rapids: Eerdmans, 2002), 149; see also Conrad Cherry, *Nature and Religious Imagination: From Edwards to Bushnell* (Philadelphia: Fortress Press, 1980), 158-230.

ent sentence." Without this sturdy theology, the feelings might lead Christianity into "wild or weak sentimentalism"; but on occasion the theology of the feelings might serve as a warning system for the theology of the intellect. If a particular doctrinal formulation consistently failed to strike a responsive chord in the hearts of the people in the pews or invariably seemed to them repugnant, then "we may infer that we have left out of our theology some element which we should have inserted, or have brought into it some element which we should have discarded. *Somewhere it must be wrong.*" Park, of course, insisted that in the end it was the intellect that adjudicated matters of doctrine; but he hoped that recognition of the role of the feelings in religion would reduce the areas of theological contention. Or, as D. G. Hart has summarized: "By distinguishing between intellectual and emotional language, theologians could avoid embittered quarrels over doctrines that were primarily products of the feelings."[17]

Hodge reacted swiftly and negatively to both Bushnell and Park. Previously he had offered qualified praise of Bushnell for his *Discourses on Christian Nurture.* Hodge appreciated the Hartford pastor's groundbreaking work, for it echoed Hodge's concern that the American churches were paying too much attention to revivals and not enough to the role of families in shaping the piety of their children. However, Hodge thought Bushnell failed to ground his argument theologically: *Christian Nurture* rested upon naturalistic premises rather than upon God's promise that the children of believers were included within the covenant of grace. With the appearance of *God in Christ,* Hodge found almost nothing to commend and virtually everything to condemn. He disagreed not only with Bushnell's reinterpretations of particular doctrines but also with the way in which his view of language undermined the theological enterprise itself. While Bushnell's general theory of language contained "nothing either new or objectionable," Hodge argued that the "whole absurdity and evil lie in the extravagant length to which he carries his principles." Bushnell, convinced of the limitations of language, had concluded that "there can be no such thing as a scientific theology; no

---

17. Edwards A. Park, *The Theology of the Intellect and of the Feelings* (Andover: Warren F. Draper, 1850; reprint from *Bibliotheca Sacra*), 4, 15, 18, 35; Anthony C. Cecil Jr., *The Theological Development of Edwards Amasa Park: Last of the "Consistent Calvinists"* (Missoula, MT: Scholar's Press, 1974); D. G. Hart, "Poems, Propositions, and Dogma: The Controversy over Religious Language and the Demise of Theology in American Learning," *Church History* 57 (September 1988): 310-21. Hart's quotation is on 316.

definite doctrinal propositions; creeds and catechisms are not to be trusted." As his final assessment of the author of *God in Christ*, Hodge uttered a sad dismissal: "He is a poet, and neither a philosopher nor theologian; a bright star, which has wandered from its orbit, and which must continue to wander, unless it return and obey the attraction of the great central orb — God's everlasting word."[18]

In several articles, Hodge also took issue with Park's notion that the feelings advanced a theology different from the theology of the intellect. He rejected the distinction and suggested that it was merely "a convenient way of getting rid of certain doctrines, which stand out far too prominently in Scripture" to be ignored. Thus, on Park's hypothesis, anyone opposed to a particular doctrine could reject it by asserting that biblical passages in its support were merely "passionate expressions designed not to be intelligible" but to evoke the feelings. "What doctrine of the Scriptures," he asked, have modern skeptics ". . . by that simple process, failed to explain away?" Hodge believed that it would prove fatal to theology to allow "the principle that right feeling may express itself in wrong intellectual forms." Hodge flatly rejected the idea, for he saw it unraveling the authority of Scripture, allowing the dismissal of venerable doctrines, and melting solid theological discourse into vapor.[19]

Bushnell's notion of language — and to a lesser extent Park's — struck at the core of Hodge's understanding. He could never consent to the romantic notion that language was symbolic, that its vocabulary always had a certain incompleteness and ambiguity, and that therefore it needed to use multiple, sometimes apparently contradictory statements — metaphor stacked against metaphor, as it were — in order to gain a better approximation of the truth. Hodge recognized the presence of metaphor in language, realized that it had to be interpreted differently than more prosaic language, and understood that failure to treat it according to its character would produce absurdities. Nevertheless, he insisted, "figurative language is just as definite in its meaning and just as intelligible as the most literal. . . . Such language, when interpreted according to established usage, and made to mean what it was intended to express, is not only definite in its import, but it never expresses what is false to the intellect. The feelings demand truth in their object; and no utterance is natural or effective as the language of emotion, which does

18. Hodge, *Essays and Reviews*, 439, 471.
19. Hodge, *Essays and Reviews*, 543, 545, 554, 606.

not satisfy the understanding." Contemporary scholar John W. Stewart notes how Hodge made his point with an apt metaphor of his own.

> Bushnell's view of language, Hodge charged, resembled "the fine rolling frenzy" of a kaleidoscope. Such a whirling of patterns "may be well enough for him to amuse himself with that pretty toy; but it is a great mistake to publish what he sees as discoveries, as though a kaleidoscope were a telescope." Hodge's point was clear: Romantics saw mere images; common sense Princetonians saw what was real.[20]

Hugh Blair's *Lectures on Rhetoric and Belles Lettres* (1783), widely used in American colleges in the nineteenth century and read by undergraduates at Princeton, was one likely source of Hodge's ideas of language. Both he and Park alluded to Blair's *Lectures* in their exchange. A product of the Scottish Enlightenment, the book depicted language as a precision instrument. Language "is become a vehicle by which the most delicate and refined emotions of one mind can be transmitted, or, if we may so speak, transfused into another." Although recognizing the widespread use of dramatic images in primitive language, Blair contended that "the understanding has gained ground on the fancy and imagination." Indeed, the use of figures of speech did not obscure meaning or put a cloud of ambiguity about it. Quite the contrary, such forms of expression permitted the communication of meaning with nuance and precision. "By their means," said Blair, "words and phrases are multiplied for expressing all sorts of ideas; for describing even the minutest differences; the nicest shades and colours of thought; which no language could possibly do by proper words alone, without assistance from tropes." This was a theory of language consonant with the other aspects of Scottish realism. Just as the common sense of humanity could perceive the world as it really is, so also language could communicate with precision that reality from one mind to another. Nor did the metaphors and figures of the imagination undermine rational discourse; rather, they served as ornaments or dress, rendering words in speech or in print with greater clarity and exactness. At the end of the day, there was one

---

20. Hodge, *Essays and Reviews*, 548; John W. Stewart, *Mediating the Center: Charles Hodge on American Science, Language, Literature, and Politics* (Princeton: Princeton Theological Seminary, 1995), 57.

language, not two, according to Blair; and for Hodge, in matters of religious discourse, there were not two theologies — one for the intellect and another for the feelings — but a single theology. Or, as Hodge put it: "Neither the cognition without the feeling, nor the feeling without the cognition completes the idea of religion. It is the complex state of mind in which those elements are inseparably blended, so as to form one glowing, intelligent apprehension of divine things, which constitutes spiritual life. *But in this complex state the cognition is the first and the governing element.*"[21]

Hodge's view of language meshed with his notion of biblical authority. Language was capable of conveying solid, objective knowledge; and biblical infallibility assured that theology possessed such knowledge to communicate. Hodge maintained that the Bible, inspired by God, was utterly truthful and reliable. Or, in his words, "the Scriptures of the Old and New Testaments are the Word of God, written under the inspiration of the Holy Spirit, and are therefore infallible." This inspiration "is not confined to moral and religious truths, but extends to the statements of facts, whether scientific, historical, or geographical." As noted earlier, Hodge was seeking to ground theology in hard "facts," which, through patient use of the Baconian method of induction, would produce a system of theology having the same objective standing as the other sciences. In short, an infallible Bible provided the necessary storehouse of facts assuring the objectivity of theology. But Hodge was also doing more than affirming theology's claim to be a science. By asserting that biblical infallibility extended beyond "moral and religious truths" to include "scientific, historical, or geographical" facts, Hodge was making claims that impinged upon geology, biology, history, and other fields of study. He was also implicitly inviting those camels to stick their noses into theology's tent. But how could he do otherwise, since he believed that all truth, whether learned from the test tube or from Scripture, had come from God and must therefore cohere?[22]

---

21. Hugh Blair, *Lectures on Rhetoric and Belles Lettres,* 3 vols. (London: Strahan and Caddell, 1787 [1783]), 1:124, 157, 360; Hodge, *Essays and Reviews,* 607-8; emphasis added to Hodge's quotation. See also Jack Kligerman, "'Dress,' or 'Incarnation' of Thought: Nineteenth-Century American Attitudes toward Language and Style," *Proceedings of the American Philosophical Society* 117 (February 16, 1973): 51-58; Conrad Cherry, *Nature and Religious Imagination: From Edwards to Bushnell* (Philadelphia: Fortress Press, 1980), 158-230.

22. Hodge, *Systematic Theology,* 1:152, 163.

Theology and Science

Historians often remember Hodge's last years for his book *What Is Darwinism?* (1874), which soundly criticized Charles Darwin's evolutionary theory. Hodge's critique needs to be set within the context of a lifetime of interest in scientific study. His father had been a leading physician in Philadelphia, his older brother Hugh won acclaim as a pioneer in gynecology and obstetrics at the University of Pennsylvania, and Hodge himself had intended to pursue medicine as a career until he felt a call to the ministry. During his year of independent study after graduating from the College of New Jersey, Hodge attended lectures on physiology and anatomy at the University of Pennsylvania. Interest in science remained an abiding passion after he became a professor at the seminary. By John W. Stewart's calculation, about 20 percent of the articles Hodge commissioned or accepted for publication for the *Princeton Review* dealt with scientific topics. Notable scientific figures from the college such as mathematician Albert Dod, chemist John Maclean, and physicist Joseph Henry (later head of the Smithsonian Institute) frequently joined him for soirées in his study. Exceptionally well informed about scientific matters, Hodge had strong opinions as to what proper science should be. A true scientist adhered to the Baconian method of induction. Eschewing premature conclusions or rash speculation, a true scientist patiently accumulated facts until the data supported appropriate generalization. Along with many other nineteenth-century Protestants, Hodge believed that research pursued in this fashion would yield, in historian T. D. Bozeman's suggestive phrase, a "doxological science," demonstrating the order and intelligent design of God's universe.[23]

Whenever he discerned science moving away from that method, Charles Hodge did not hesitate to point out its errors. For example, he took on theories suggesting multiple human origins or polygenesis. In 1850 the Swiss naturalist Louis Agassiz, who had won appointment at Harvard several years earlier amid both widespread public and professional acclaim, published articles asserting that the various peoples of the earth had separate origins rather than descent from a common pair of ancestors. Although he did not press the theory of multiple origins to mean that hu-

23. Stewart, *Mediating the Center,* 28; Theodore Dwight Bozeman, *Protestants in an Age of Science: The Baconian Ideal and Antebellum American Religious Thought* (Chapel Hill: University of North Carolina Press, 1977).

mans constituted separate species and he indicated a respect for the biblical creation account, others were not so restrained. Josiah Nott and George R. Gliddon in *Types of Mankind* (1854), to which Agassiz contributed an introductory essay, argued vigorously for the polygenetic theory. They suggested that blacks and whites were separate species, and they drew upon the work of the recently deceased Samuel Morton, who had studied craniology, using over a thousand skulls from different periods of history. Measuring the skulls to determine brain capacity, Morton concluded that the various "races" could be clearly differentiated and that blacks were clearly inferior to whites and had been so since the beginning of recorded time. Morton, Gliddon, and Nott constituted the leaders of an American school of ethnology or physical anthropology much in vogue for a couple of decades in the mid-nineteenth century.[24]

Charles Hodge wrote forcefully against the school. In an 1859 article in the *Princeton Review,* he demonstrated considerable familiarity with their arguments and devoted the bulk of his essay to a careful survey — and refutation — of the evidence for multiple origins. He spent so much energy on the subject because he deemed something essential to the biblical message to be at stake: "the unity of mankind." That unity was, he insisted, "intimately connected with the whole system of revealed truth." The Bible declares that all men and women everywhere are in thrall to sin because of Adam, and in Christ redemption for all is proclaimed. For that reason, Christians preach the gospel to the ends of the earth. "We go," he said, "and nowhere, from Greenland to Caffraria [in southern Africa], do we find any class of men to whom the gospel is not the grace of life; none who do not need it, or who are not capable of being partakers of the salvation which it offers." Polygenesis called into question the veracity of the biblical witness and the universal validity of the Christian message. Hodge also sensed something ethically troubling in the ethnology of Nott, Gliddon, and Morton. He realized that, in part, it drew its motivation from a desire to provide an intellectual rationale "for the perpetuity of African slaveholding" and from a wish "to excommunicate a portion of our race from the church universal of humanity." Recently, historian Nell Irvin Painter has written of the "dour legacy" left by the American school of anthropology: "the fetishization of tall, pale, blond, beautiful Anglo-Saxons; a fascination with skulls and head measurements;

24. Jon H. Roberts, *Darwinism and the Divine in America: Protestant Intellectuals and Organic Evolution, 1859-1860* (Madison: University of Wisconsin Press, 1988), 26-29.

the drawing of racial lines and the fixing of racial types; [and] the ranking of races along a single 'evolutionary' line of development." Hodge was not immune to racial biases, but in this instance he resisted.[25]

Hodge did not, however, believe that the theologian should invariably adopt a posture of confrontation with the scientist. Ideally, the two should act as partners, not opponents. Their fields "in many points overlap each other." Their methods differed in that science worked by "induction and analogy" on the empirical facts of nature and theology on the facts of revelation. "Let each," he advised, "pursue its course independently yet harmoniously. Neither should ignore the other." Several years later, Hodge had occasion to elaborate those themes. In January 1863, the *Princeton Review* published an article on religion and science by Joseph Clark, a Pennsylvania minister and businessman. Clark professed complete faith in the reliability of Scripture but also called for granting full freedom to scientific inquiry. He noted how on previous occasions the church had had to adjust its understanding of the Bible in light of scientific discovery and suggested that reinterpretation might again need to occur. The conservative *New York Observer* charged that the author had conceded far too much to science. He — and by implication the editor of the *Princeton Review* — were allowing "that in scientific matters, faith in Moses and Paul" must give way to modern theories. How could the opinions of fallible mortals be allowed to impeach the Word of God? Two weeks later, Hodge replied, asserting that the *Observer* misstated the case. True "science," he explained, "is not the opinions of man, but knowledge." Science, he went on to say, consists of "the ascertained truths concerning the facts and laws of nature. To say, therefore, that the Bible contradicts science is to say that it contradicts facts, is to say that it teaches error; and to say that it teaches error is to say it is not the Word of God." Hodge gave the example of the long exploded theory "that the earth stood still in space." Just because the church had for centuries maintained that the Bible taught this view, "shall we go on to interpret the Bible so as to make it teach the falsehood that the sun moves round the earth, or shall we interpret it by science and make the two harmonize?" At the same time, Hodge insisted that true science cannot "contradict the Bible" and warned against believers too quickly adopting the

25. [Charles Hodge,] "The Unity of Mankind," *Biblical Repertory and Princeton Review* 31 (January 1859): 108, 112, 144, 149; Nell Irvin Painter, *The History of White People* (New York: Norton, 2010), 200.

latest fads of the scientific community. The proper Christian course was to "calmly wait until facts are indubitably established, so established that they command universal consent among competent men, and then they will find that the Bible accords with those facts." Harmony, independence, and mutual respect — these qualities were to characterize the interaction between theology and science. Whenever science seemed to contradict Scripture, Christians should not panic, knowing that, when all the facts had come in, biblical revelation would be vindicated.[26]

As the allusion to Copernican cosmology suggested, vindication did not always entail confirmation of previous interpretations of Scripture. It might require instead serious reassessment. Hodge understood that geology was forcing his generation to reconsider its understanding of the creation account in Genesis. For example, James Hutton's *Theory of the Earth* (1785) accounted for the formation of the earth solely by natural processes that had "no vestige of a beginning — no prospect of an end." Charles Lyell's *Principles of Geology* (1830-1832) proposed that the earth was formed over an immensely long period by uniform natural laws that were everywhere active. Could the biblical story of divine creation within six days be reconciled with the new theories? In his *Systematic Theology,* Hodge noted that some had treated the creation story as "an allegory without any historical basis, any more than the parables of our Lord," but he regarded this solution as dangerous. The first chapters of Genesis included the narrative of "the creation and probation of man" and constituted "the foundation of the whole plan of redemption." For Hodge, the impasse with geology was broken, not by surrendering the historicity of the first and second chapters of Genesis, but by reading the account in a new way. He found help from scientist James Dwight Dana of Yale, who had compiled a chart in which the long eras of geologic time were equated with the "days" of creation in Genesis. Hodge was sufficiently impressed to reproduce Dana's compilation in the *Systematic Theology.* Since the word "day" was sometimes used in Scripture for an indefinitely long period, and since Dana's proposal brought Genesis into a "most marvelous coincidence" with the facts of science, Hodge concluded that the presumption must lie in favor of this reading. The fact that Dana was

---

26. Hodge, "Unity of Mankind," 104; the *Observer*'s critique of the *Princeton Review* and Hodge's reply are contained in Charles Hodge, *What Is Darwinism? and Other Writings on Science and Religion,* ed. Mark A. Noll and David N. Livingstone (Grand Rapids: Baker, 1994), 51-56; quotations on 52, 54.

a devout Congregationalist layman and that other scientists favoring a similar rapprochement, such as his good friend Arnold Guyot from the college, were also practicing Christians no doubt made Hodge more willing to approve this resolution of the problem.[27]

Hodge could never see his way clear to a comparable intellectual reconciliation with Charles Darwin's theory of evolution. Darwin had advanced the hypothesis in his master work *On the Origin of Species* (1859), but this book was only the latest of a number of proposals that plants and animals had gradually developed into their current forms. Although others had advanced some form of the developmental hypothesis, the power of Darwin's work lay in the fact that he offered what appeared (at least to many) a compelling explanation of the manner in which evolution occurred. Nevertheless, his work was initially rejected in large segments of the American scientific community, and this fact allowed religious leaders to regard it as a passing fancy that they need not take seriously. But by the mid-1870s, the religious intelligentsia had begun to realize that the transmutation hypothesis was winning over scientists. It was also getting some favorable notices from theological leaders, even in Charles Hodge's Princeton. President James McCosh of the college, for example, indicated that he thought Darwin's insights should not be rejected out of hand. "It is useless," he warned in an address at the 1873 meeting of the Evangelical Alliance in New York, "to tell the younger naturalists that there is no truth in the doctrine of development, for they know that there is truth, which is not to be set aside by denunciation." McCosh suggested that it might be a better strategy to emphasize "the religious aspects of the doctrine of development" while also pointing to the limitations of the theory and warning that it could not serve as an explanation of everything.[28]

At the same conference, Hodge rose to make a pointed observation

27. Hodge, *Systematic Theology,* 1:568-74; quotations on 568-69, 571. See also Herbert Hovenkamp, *Science and Religion in America, 1800-1860* (Philadelphia: University of Pennsylvania Press, 1978).

28. James McCosh, *Christianity and Positivism: A Series of Lectures to the Times* (New York: Wilbur B. Ketcham, 1871), 67-96; Philip Schaff and S. Irenaeus Prime, eds., *History, Essays, Orations, and Other Documents of the Sixth General Conference of the Evangelical Alliance* (New York: Harper and Brothers, 1874), 270. See also for this and the next several paragraphs Roberts, *Darwinism and the Divine;* and J. R. Moore, *The Post-Darwinian Controversies: A Study of the Protestant Struggle to Come to Terms with Darwin in Great Britain and America, 1870-1900* (Cambridge: Cambridge University Press, 1979).

about evolutionary theory: "The great question which divides theists from atheists — Christians from unbelievers — is this: Is development an intellectual process guided by God, or is it a blind process of unintelligible, unconscious force, which knows no end and adopts no means?" While McCosh saw theistic possibilities in the evolutionary hypothesis, Hodge was less sanguine, at least in regard to the Darwinian version of the theory. Shortly after the meeting of the Evangelical Alliance, Hodge's final book, *What Is Darwinism?* (1874), expressed his intellectual difficulties. The basic hurdle he could not overcome — "the grand and fatal objection to Darwinism" — was "the exclusion of design in the origin of species." Hodge acknowledged that some Christians did indeed endorse biological evolution, but they always emphasized that God's superintending providence directed the process. He himself saw no way that Darwin's version of the theory could be made consistent with design. It was based, as he had implied in his brief remarks at the Evangelical Alliance, on a "blind process of unintelligible, unconscious force." Although he exempted Darwin as a person from the charge, Hodge believed that Darwinism as an idea led to an exclusion of God from the universe and hence a *de facto* atheism. Moreover, he thought that the very notion that a species could be evolved from a single cell was a "*prima facie* incredibility" and that the immense amounts of time needed to produce such change "must be counted by millions or milliards of years." "Here," he asserted, "is another demand on our credulity."[29]

Darwinism also signaled a troubling mentality that was growing more common. Hodge was concerned that many restricted the term "science" to "the facts of nature or of the external world" and believed that "the senses are the only sources of knowledge." Against that bias, Hodge insisted that God "has given to the human mind intuitions which are infallible, laws of belief which men cannot disregard any more than the laws of nature." If these intuitions no longer counted as knowledge, moral philosophy and theology were put out of business or at the very least were demoted to matters of mere opinion and unsubstantiated faith. This arrogance in the name of science was all the more infuriating to Hodge when its practitioners hypothesized well beyond hard evidence and then claimed that their expertise exempted them from criticism by nonprofessionals. Those outside the circle of experts, he insisted, "have

---

29. *Sixth General Conference of the Evangelical Alliance*, 318; Hodge, *What Is Darwinism?* 138, 139, 152.

the right to judge of the consistency of the assertions of men of science and of the logic of their reasoning" and "the right to reject all specula- tions, hypotheses, and theories which come in conflict with well- established truths." Although he gave credit to Darwin for allowing that he had only shown the plausibility of evolution, not proved it, the style of reasoning in *On the Origin of Species* annoyed Hodge. "His mode of argu- ing," the Princeton professor grumbled, "is that if we suppose this and that, then it may have happened thus and so." Hodge counted himself among those in whom such reasoning "rouses indignation." Nor would he admit a possible reconciliation between science and religion secured by placing them in different dimensions of reality. He took a verbal swipe at John S. Henslow, a botanist and Church of England clergyman, who "says Science and Religion are in different spheres of thought." "This," Hodge warned, "is often said by men who do not admit that there is any thought at all in religion, [who maintain] that it is merely a matter of feel- ing. The fact, however, is that religion is a system of knowledge as well as a state of feeling." In some respects, Hodge would have made his life as a theologian easier had he drawn a line between science and religion more sharply, giving each a separate domain. He might, as some theologians were already doing after the manner of Henslow, have suggested that re- ligion dealt with issues of ultimate meaning or value, the why of exis- tence, whereas science dealt with the empirical mechanics of the uni- verse. But if Hodge had done so, he would have been conceding defeat in the intellectual battles he had fought for decades — for example, his re- sistance to Schleiermacher's reduction of religion to sensibility and his struggle against Bushnell's transformation of theology into poetry. Hodge was not about to give away the game in his twilight years.[30]

The Legacy of Charles Hodge

When Charles Hodge died in Princeton on June 19, 1878, two of his sons constituted his most immediate and obvious legacy to the seminary. Caspar Wistar Hodge and Archibald A. Hodge both continued on the fac- ulty where they had taught with their father. Wistar Hodge had begun as a professor at the seminary in 1860 in New Testament, following the death of Addison Alexander, and A. A. Hodge came as an assistant to his

30. Hodge, *What Is Darwinism?* 130, 131, 137, 138, 140.

father in 1877 with the understanding that he would eventually assume the senior Hodge's chair. Professor "Arch" had a relatively brief career at the seminary, his service being terminated by death in 1886. Wistar continued until his death in 1891. Then in 1901 his son and namesake, Caspar Wistar Hodge Jr., joined the faculty in didactic and polemical theology and served until his demise in 1937. On balance, the Hodges compiled a remarkable record. Except for a single decade, a Hodge was on the faculty from 1822 until 1937. Combined, their years of service to the seminary totaled approximately one hundred thirty.

Caspar Wistar Hodge was the second of Charles's sons. Tutored by Addison Alexander, who was both friend and mentor as well perhaps as a kind of older brother to him, Wistar then studied at the College of New Jersey and the seminary, served brief pastorates in the Williamsburg section of Brooklyn as well as in rural Oxford, Pennsylvania, and then returned to teach at the seminary from 1860 until his death. At his memorial service, Francis L. Patton suggested that the greatest influence upon Wistar had been Addison Alexander, to whom "he was indebted for those scholarly ideals that made him so painstaking in his work and . . . so dissatisfied with it." Perhaps, too, his father's commanding reputation may have set the bar of achievement so high that Wistar was reluctant to put his thoughts in print. In any event, he published very little save the privately printed lecture syllabi that were designed for his students, an occasional sermon, and some reviews. When he reviewed a book, he often did not obtrude his own opinions. His comments, Patton observed, "would tell you more about the book itself" than his estimation of the subject. Of course, when he did declare theological convictions, they represented the rock-ribbed orthodoxy for which his father had contended. The younger Hodge, however, did not see himself as a controversialist and was content to devote his labors chiefly to close attention to New Testament analysis.[31]

Archibald A. Hodge, the firstborn of Charles and Sarah Hodge, had a broader experience and more expansive personality than his younger brother. Theorists of family dynamics might speculate that he exhibited the confidence typical of the oldest child. After his education at the Col-

---

31. Francis L. Patton, *Caspar Wistar Hodge: A Memorial Address* (New York: Anson D. F. Randolph and Co., 1891), 15, 28. For outlines of his courses, see C. W. Hodge, *Syllabus of Lectures on Apostolic History and Literature* (Princeton: Princeton Press, 1887); idem, *Synopsis of Lectures on New Testament Criticism* (Princeton: Princeton Press, 1878). These works by Hodge are available through the Internet Archive.

lege of New Jersey and the seminary, he wed Elizabeth Halliday and was ordained, and the two left for India in 1847 to serve as missionaries in Allahabad, India. Elizabeth's serious illness and Hodge's own health problems forced their return to the United States in 1850. For nearly fifteen years, Archibald Hodge then held several successive pastorates: in northeastern Maryland near the Pennsylvania and Delaware borders; in Fredericksburg, Virginia; and in Wilkes-Barre, Pennsylvania. In 1864, he accepted a call to serve as professor of theology at Western Theological Seminary, and the following year he also assumed the pastorate of the North Presbyterian Church in Allegheny City (now part of Pittsburgh). He continued to hold both positions until returning to Princeton to serve as his father's associate in 1877. He thus came to Princeton with a range of experiences as a missionary in India, a pastor in the United States, and a theological professor.

His first major work was *Outlines of Theology*, which he delivered initially as a series of Sunday evening lectures to his congregation in Fredericksburg and then issued in an expanded edition in 1878. Especially in its original form, the *Outlines* drew heavily upon notes he had taken from his father's lectures at the seminary — a fact he openly and gladly acknowledged. Throughout his career, he made few substantive changes from his father's views, though the younger Hodge did hold out the possibility of rapprochement between theology and the theory of biological evolution. He contributed an introduction to Joseph S. Van Dyke's *Theism and Evolution* (1886). A former tutor at the college and graduate of the seminary, Van Dyke offered, in James R. Moore's words, "a timid book" concerned "more with defending the faith from evolution than with scrutinizing the faith in its light." Hodge's introduction was equally cautious, putting severe limitations on the sort of evolution that could be consistent with Christianity. Without conceding that evolution had been conclusively demonstrated, he affirmed that

> Evolution considered as the plan of an infinitely wise Person and executed under the control of His everywhere present energies can never be irreligious; can never exclude design, providence, grace, or miracles. Hence we repeat that what Christians have cause to consider with apprehension is not evolution as a working hypothesis of science dealing with facts, but evolution as a philosophical speculation professing to account for the origin, causes, and ends of all things.

If evolution were eventually established as more than a theory, Archibald Hodge felt sure that it could never account for the origin of life, nor the origin of consciousness, nor the moral sense of humanity. These "could have been introduced into the flow of natural evolution only by an immediate act of God." While somewhat more open to the idea of evolution than his father, A. A. Hodge had not moved very far from him.[32]

Archibald Hodge also held to views of society consonant with his father's. Just as Charles Hodge had argued that the United States was a Christian nation, the son not only held that this was so but wished to have the principle formally enshrined in the Constitution. In 1864, during the Civil War, some Protestants formed a group to lobby for the amendment of the Preamble to the United States Constitution to recognize "Almighty God as the source of all authority and power in civil government, the Lord Jesus Christ as the Ruler among the nations, [and] his revealed will as the supreme law of the land." Although most of the organizers of the movement, which became known as the National Reform Association, were drawn from some of the smaller American Presbyterian churches whose lineage traced to the Covenanter tradition in Scotland, the proposal received the endorsement of several denominations, including the Old School Presbyterian General Assembly. Archibald Hodge supported the amendment and addressed a meeting of the National Reform Association when it met in 1874 in Pittsburgh, just across the river from where he taught at Western Theological Seminary. In his telling, amending the Preamble would not be a novelty but a recognition of "the hitherto universally admitted fact, that Christianity is an element in the common law of the land." But now "an historical crisis" called for making legally explicit that which had been previously implicit. That crisis derived from "disappointed political and social theorists [who] have recently immigrated to our land, who are disseminating theories of human rights and of man's relation to God which are as inconsistent with the facts and traditions of our government as with the Christian religion." He did not specify who these "disappointed" immigrants were; but they threatened to take away what in one breath he described as the "immemorial faith of our Saxon race," and in the next moment identified more

32. A. A. Hodge, *Outlines of Theology*, rewritten and enlarged (Chicago: Bible Institute Colportage Association, 1878); Joseph R. Van Dyke, *Theism and Evolution: An Examination of Modern Speculative Theories as Related to Theistic Conceptions of the Universe*, with an introduction by Archibald A. Hodge (London: Hodder and Stoughton, 1886), xviii, xx.

broadly to include all the Christian immigrants, including Catholics, who had come to America.[33]

In one of a series of popular lectures he gave in Philadelphia in 1885, the year before his death, he returned again to a similar theme. On that occasion he decried the effort to strip religion from the public schools, warned of "unholy laws and customs of divorce" growing like a "cancer," and sounded the alarm against the "desecration of our ancestral Sabbath." Alluding to recent labor unrest, he expressed dire fears for the nation:

> Whence come these portentous upheavals of the ancient primitive rock upon which society has always rested? Whence comes this socialistic earthquake, arraying capital and labor in irreconcilable conflict like oxygen and fire? Whence come these mad nihilistic, anarchical ravings, the wild presages of a universal deluge, which will blot out at once the family, the school, the church, the home, all civilization and religion, in one sea of ruin?

For A. A. Hodge, the solution to the social problems of the late nineteenth century lay in maintaining "the crown-rights of Jesus" over all of life — in the family and in the state as well as in the church.[34]

Archibald Hodge had a flair for dramatic expression that prompted some to think him a better teacher than his father. His hearers appreciated his ability to condense difficult theological arguments and to provide vivid illustrations. One of his first students at Princeton, the Scot C. A. Salmond, who took classes with both Charles and Archibald, admired the elder but found the younger a more dynamic teacher. (Of course, due allowance must be made for the fact that Charles was then in declining health and nearing death.) Salmond penciled into his notebook "a few of the sparks struck out in the class-room" by A. A. Hodge. For example, when he wished to emphasize the importance of having and defending definite theological views, Archibald remarked: "It is a miserable thing when men get so broad and charitable as never to have

---

33. "Address of Dr. Hodge," *Proceedings of the National Reform Convention* (Philadelphia: Christian Statesman Association, 1874), 81-85; quotations on 82, 84. Gaines M. Foster, *Moral Reconstruction: Christian Lobbyists and the Federal Legislation of Morality, 1865-1920* (Chapel Hill: University of North Carolina Press, 1992), 27-30.

34. Archibald Alexander Hodge, *Popular Lectures on Theological Themes* (Philadelphia: Presbyterian Board of Publication, 1887), 286, 287.

any fighting. Rather let us have the Inquisition and a little blood-letting, than a dead apathy about religious doctrine." With his penchant for wit and colorful illustration, it is sometimes difficult to know how seriously to take his verbal flourishes. His colleague Francis Patton thought that "he had somewhat against any man who could not appreciate a joke . . . and was never happier than when he met his match in an encounter of wit." Thus when Salmond alluded to Hodge's experience as a missionary in India, he remarked that one abiding result of those years was "an intense admiration for British rule, which often showed itself in a half-earnest, half-jocular disparagement of the institutions of the Model Republic" (i.e., the United States). Patton made a similar point: "Aristocratic sympathies were very strong in him, and they found expression sometimes in an extravagant avowal of Toryism that was partly jest, and partly based upon a real conservatism of sentiment respecting the philosophy of social life." Given Hodge's penchant for hyperbole and sarcasm, how much, then, does one make of vigorous affirmations of Toryism or melodramatic warnings about socialistic earthquakes and everything in civilization adrift in a sea of ruin? At the very least, one may observe that A. A. Hodge often exhibited pugnacity and sharpness of tongue to a degree greater than his father.[35]

Of course, it was not only Charles Hodge's bloodline that continued his legacy at Princeton. His former students who joined the faculty did likewise. Among these was Francis Landey Patton. A native of Bermuda born in 1843, Patton received an education in an academy there and then went on to Knox College and the University of Toronto in Canada. After studying at Princeton Theological Seminary from 1863 to 1865, he was ordained to the Presbyterian ministry and served several pastorates in the greater New York City area — in Manhattan, in Nyack, and finally in Brooklyn. During this time, he published his first book, *The Inspiration of the Scriptures* (1869), which gave him higher visibility within the church. In 1872, the Presbyterian Theological Seminary of the Northwest in Chicago called him to a professorship in didactic and polemic theology. Cyrus McCormick, a wealthy philanthropist for whom the seminary was ultimately named, was the major funder of the school and the central

---

35. C. A. Salmond, *Princetoniana: Charles and A. A. Hodge, with Class and Table Talk of Hodge the Younger* (New York: Scribner and Welford, 1888), 68, 69, 100, 165; Francis L. Patton, *A Discourse in Memory of Archibald Alexander Hodge, D.D., LL.D.* (Philadelphia: Times Printing House, 1887), 55, 57.

player in the appointment of Patton. As one decidedly committed to the Old School before the reunion, he was eager that the professor of theology in the Seminary of the Northwest be an influence for Old School views. In Patton, he seemed to have found the ideal person — a rising scholar with impeccable Old School training but, at 29, much too young to have taken part in the battles between the now reunited parties and thus less likely to offend former New School partisans. But within two years he did indeed offend them. In 1874, Patton took on one of Chicago's most popular Presbyterian ministers. In charges filed with the presbytery, he accused David Swing of preaching sermons out of accord with the Westminster Confession. He provided numerous specifications indicating that Swing had used "vague and ambiguous statements," leading to the conclusion that he "does not sincerely receive and adopt the Confession of Faith." Responding to the charges, Swing declared that he adhered to Westminster "as rendered by the former New School Theologians" and avowed his firm belief "in the evangelical sense" in the "inspiration of the Holy Scriptures, the Trinity, the divinity of Christ, the office of Christ as a mediator when grasped by an obedient faith, conversion by God's Spirit, man's natural sinfulness, and the final separation of the righteous and wicked." After lengthy proceedings, Patton summarized his case. It was not, he insisted, a matter of whether former New School views could be tolerated; it was rather a case of whether "Swing holds a theology which is consistent with the integrity of the Calvinistic system." If Swing's views were deemed to be in harmony with Calvinism, said Patton, using a kind of slippery slope argument, "we might raise the question whether a man might be an atheist and be in good and regular standing in a Christian church." The subsequent overwhelming 48 to 13 vote against sustaining the charges indicated how far out of sympathy with Patton the Presbyterians of Chicago were. One also gets hints in the press coverage of the trial that the community at large was likewise not favorable to Patton. One description of him, as he prepared to make his case, declared: "Professor Patton, calm and bloodless as the spirit of Hamlet's father, arose and began."[36]

36. William L. McEwan, "Dr. Francis L. Patton," *Princeton Seminary Bulletin* 27 (1933): 4-9; Francis L. Patton, *The Inspiration of the Scriptures* (Philadelphia: Presbyterian Board of Education, 1869); William T. Hutchinson, *Cyrus Hall McCormick: Harvest, 1856-1884* (New York: D. Appleton-Century Co., 1935), 250-66; *The Trial of the Rev. David Swing before the Presbytery of Chicago* (Chicago: Jansen, McClurg and Co., 1874), 8, 13, 20, 186; *The World's Edition of the Great Presbyterian Conflict: Patton vs. Swing* (Chicago: Geo. McDonald and

Patton may have lost Chicago, but he was playing to another audience. He was trying to sway the Presbyterian denomination and was prepared to appeal the case to a higher judicatory. Swing, however, withdrew from the Presbyterian ministry, and he and his supporters organized an independent congregation. The episode did not hamper Patton's career; in some quarters it made him more attractive as a defender of orthodoxy. Elected moderator of the General Assembly in 1878, he preached later in the year at the meeting of the Pan-Presbyterian Council in Edinburgh and was offered a theological post at the Presbyterian Theological College in London. As a life-long subject of the British crown, he was tempted but declined, at least partly because of Cyrus McCormick's entreaties. However, McCormick's pleas were not enough to hold Patton in Chicago in 1881 when Princeton Seminary offered him the Stuart Professorship of the Relations of Philosophy and Science to Christian Religion. As Patton construed the position, it dealt with the fundamental question of what he called "the argumentative status of Christianity." Was it possible to give evidence — evidence available to both believer and unbeliever alike — that "Christianity is a divinely revealed religion"? The claim "that it cannot be proved true, but that it accredits itself to the religious consciousness" he found utterly inadequate. Or, as he summed up the matter in a memorable aphorism: "I have no confidence in the philosophy that first throws the intellect into bankruptcy and then pensions us on an allowance of faith." To demonstrate that Christianity derived from genuine knowledge was a task to which he set himself in the remainder of his time at Princeton. In one capacity or another, he stayed in the community more than thirty years. He continued in his post at the seminary until 1888, when he was named president of the college to succeed James McCosh. During his presidency at the College of New Jersey — it officially became Princeton University during his tenure — he continued to teach a course on theism at the seminary. Resigning from the college in 1902, he then became the first president of Princeton Theological Seminary the following year, and he would serve in that capacity until 1913, when he retired back to his home in Bermuda.[37]

And, of course, others who will appear in pages that follow would

---

Co., 1874), 107. See also William R. Hutchison, "Disapproval of Chicago: The Symbolic Trial of David Swing," *Journal of American History* 59 (June 1972): 30-47.

37. Francis L. Patton, "The Place of Philosophy in the Theological Curriculum," *Princeton Review* 7 (January 1882): 103-24; quotations from 106, 107, and 108.

also be considered the intellectual inheritors of Hodge's legacy. One thinks preeminently of William Henry Green in biblical studies, Benjamin B. Warfield in systematic theology, and J. Gresham Machen in biblical studies.

Conclusion

But simply to enumerate subsequent professors who taught at Princeton and adhered to the central features of his theological system only begins to capture Hodge's legacy. A fuller accounting, much too large for one volume and probably big enough to occupy multiple scholars through most if not all of their careers, would be to trace lines of influence through the lives and work of the several thousand students who studied with Hodge during his long tenure. And then one would also have to go forward into the present to take into account the various theological schools in the United States and around the globe that continue to study Hodge, not simply out of historical interest, but because they consider his work to be a viable theological option for the twenty-first century. Or one would have to trace Hodge's influence to contemporary conservative thinkers such as Robert C. Sproul, or Hodge's mode of apologetic to current popularizers such as Josh McDowell. The list could go on indefinitely.[38]

A complete list might also move along unaccustomed paths. Because an individual is seldom monolithic and unchanging in thought — even a person as concerned with consistency as Charles Hodge — his or her intellectual legacy seldom moves in one direction only. Thus it matters greatly if one claims to stand in the tradition of the Hodge of the early to mid-1830s, who strove mightily for Presbyterian unity against those whom he perceived as extremists of both the Old and New Schools; or whether one makes the Hodge of the late 1860s, the one who opposed reunion with the New School, the definitive embodiment of the man. Or one might look at Hodge's breadth of interests, from politics, to the latest developments in science, and to the commentaries on contemporary culture that filled the pages of the *Princeton Review.* Some of Hodge's successors (both avowed friends and foes of his theology) have reduced him

---

38. Paul C. Gutjahr, *Charles Hodge: Guardian of American Orthodoxy* (New York: Oxford University Press, 2011), 377-85.

to conservative Presbyterian theology, opposition to Darwinism, or the debate over biblical infallibility. All of these were indeed a part of his legacy; but understood in the context of his own time and not simply as a precursor to the Presbyterian conflicts of the 1920s, he was also much more and deserves to be remembered as such.[39]

39. For further development of the theme of Hodge's legacy, see my afterword in Stewart and Moorhead, eds., *Charles Hodge Revisited*, 328-34.

CHAPTER NINE

William Henry Green and Biblical Studies

THREE YEARS after the death of Charles Hodge, Archibald A. Hodge, now successor to his father in the chair of didactic and polemical theology, and Benjamin B. Warfield of Western Theological Seminary published an essay on the topic "Inspiration." The article appeared in *The Presbyterian Review,* a relatively short-lived experiment — nine years — in joint publishing among the Presbyterian seminaries, with Princeton and Union Seminary in New York supplying the two editors. Until his death, A. A. Hodge represented Princeton, and Charles A. Briggs, Union. Designed to provide a unified voice for the reunited Old and New Schools, the *Review* ultimately collapsed in part because of serious theological differences between the two seminaries. The series of which "Inspiration" was a part helped to reveal those differences.[1]

"Inspiration," which set forth with new precision the notion of biblical inerrancy, is sometimes seen as Old Princeton's chief contribution to the fundamentalist movement that arose in the early twentieth century. There is considerable merit in this portrayal, for inerrancy did indeed figure prominently in that later movement. But analyzed in the context of the 1880s, the article suggested a somewhat more complicated agenda. To be sure, one need only read the famous definition of inerrancy by Hodge and Warfield to see the deeply conservative — some might say reactionary — trajectory on which they were launched: "all the affirmations of Scripture of all kinds, whether of spiritual doctrine or duty, or of physical or historical fact, or of psychological or philosophical principle, are with-

---

1. A. A. Hodge and B. B. Warfield, "Inspiration," *Presbyterian Review* 2 (April 1881): 225-60.

out error, when the *ipsissima verba* of the original autographs are ascertained and interpreted in their natural and intended sense." In short, the exact words of the original manuscripts of the Bible, interpreted naturally, were without error, not only in matters of faith and practice, but also in their incidental affirmations regarding historical fact, geography, philosophy, or psychology. This strong assertion of biblical inerrancy was an effort to defend the faith from what Hodge and Warfield perceived as destructive forms of biblical scholarship that were on the rise.[2]

What is often missed in the article is the authors' desire to confer legitimacy, within appropriate boundaries, on a thoroughgoing critical examination of the biblical texts and the human circumstances through which they came to be written. Hodge and Warfield, while believing the Scriptures divine in their inspiration, also saw them as human in origin. For example, each of the biblical writers

> drew from the stores of his own original information, from the contributions of other men, and from all other natural sources. Each sought knowledge, like all other authors, from the use of his own natural faculties of thought and feeling, of intuition and of logical inference, of memory and imagination, and of religious experience. Each gave evidence of his own special limitations of knowledge and mental power and of his personal defects, as well as his powers.

"The Scriptures," they added, "were generated through this divinely regulated concurrence of God and man, of the natural and the supernatural, of reason and revelation, of providence and grace." The word "concurrence" was crucial. Because God had providentially superintended the human element in Scripture, no Christian need fear the results of unbiased scholarly inquiry into the Bible. Thus at the same time that Hodge and Warfield were exalting the error-free quality of the Scriptures, they were also encouraging a searching examination of every aspect of the Bible's context and origins. In this they continued and deepened the commitment to a developmental view of the Bible as the record of God's progressive self-disclosure that Joseph Addison Alexander had already to some degree suggested.[3]

2. Hodge and Warfield, "Inspiration," 238.
3. Hodge and Warfield, "Inspiration," 229, 230.

What they proposed in their 1881 article was symptomatic of the potentially conflicting tendencies in the seminary's life as the nineteenth century closed and the twentieth dawned. The school was defining its position ever more sharply, sometimes defiantly, against the tide of current opinion in the religious and intellectual world. Yet, at the same time, Princeton was trying to embrace new knowledge and views. At the end of the day, this tension proved difficult to sustain, but both plotlines are part of the story of Princeton, and both need to be told. Although many people contributed to that story, in the field of biblical studies, the career of William Henry Green illustrates it with particular force.

"The Hebrew Teacher of His Generation"

One of those exemplifying Princeton's oscillation between rejection and embrace of modern scholarship was William Henry Green, who succeeded Joseph A. Alexander in the chair of biblical and oriental literature in 1851. Born in Groveville, New Jersey, not far from Princeton, in January 1825, Green was the son of a prosperous lumber merchant and a descendant of Jonathan Dickinson, first president of the college of New Jersey. He received his early education in Groveville and Lawrenceville as well as at a classical academy in Easton, Pennsylvania. In 1837 he matriculated at Lafayette College (also in Easton), finished the full course of studies in 1840, and thus received his baccalaureate degree at the age of 15. He stayed on at the college as mathematics instructor for two years, then entered Princeton Seminary and completed the program in 1846, having taken off a year during his divinity studies to teach at Lafayette again. As a student at the seminary, Green was a prize pupil and protégé of Joseph Alexander, and he was asked to stay on as an instructor in Hebrew, a position he held from 1846 to 1849. From 1849 to 1851, he served as pastor of the Central Presbyterian Church in Philadelphia. When Alexander moved into biblical and ecclesiastical history in 1851, Green was called to his mentor's chair, which, with a slight change of title, he held until his death in 1900.[4]

In 1896, at the fifty-year celebration of Green's first appointment, his

---

4. John D. Davis, "William Henry Green," *Presbyterian and Reformed Review* 11 (July 1900): 377-96; Marion Ann Taylor, *The Old Testament in the Old Princeton School (1812-1929)* (San Francisco: Edward Mellen Press, 1992), 167-252.

classmate, the Rev. Theodore L. Cuyler, remarked that Green seemed cut out for the academic life from the moment he appeared among his fellow students. "He leaped at once to the front," Cuyler recalled, "the foremost scholar of the class, the foremost scholar in the Seminary. He took to Greek as if he had been born at Athens; he took to Hebrew as if he had been the son of a rabbi in Jerusalem. He seemed to us not so much as a student, but as an incipient professor." Yet, despite his obvious gifts, Green was cut from different cloth than Joseph Alexander. Another former student at the semi-centennial suggested that their differences may have made Green a better teacher than Alexander for the majority of seminarians. James F. McCurdy, who had gone on to become an assistant to Green and then a major light of ancient Near Eastern studies at the University of Toronto, observed that Alexander seemed to absorb languages and literatures as "undivided wholes by a species of intuition" and thus had little "consciousness of a process in his appropriation of a language or its literature." In the classroom he "came upon his students with an almost overpowering rush of information. . . . Fortunate were those who could swim with such a current." In contrast, Green knew how to establish a step-by-step process by which students could master language and put it to use. "What Green stood for in the teaching of oriental languages," McCurdy observed, ". . . was method and system." This he did first in the classroom and then through several books: *Hebrew Grammar* (1861); *Hebrew Chrestomathy* (1864), which contained selections from the Old Testament and included grammatical notes; and *Elementary Hebrew Grammar with Reading Lessons* (1866). "Thus, with rare sureness and clear-sightedness," said his former pupil, "he became the Hebrew teacher of his generation in Princeton — not in Princeton merely, but in America; in fact, the most influential Hebrew teacher of his time among English-speaking men." McCurdy's warm tribute was all the more significant because he had moved by the time of his remarks much farther toward accommodation with the higher criticism than had his mentor.[5]

According to historian and biblical scholar Marion Ann Taylor, McCurdy's praise of Green as a teacher of Hebrew was fully deserved. "Green's work in Hebrew grammar in the early sixties," she observes, "represented a major contribution to the field of Hebrew studies in

5. *Celebration of the Fiftieth Anniversary of the Appointment of Professor William Henry Green as an Instructor in Princeton Theological Seminary* (New York: Charles Scribner's Sons, 1896), 32, 33, 69.

America." Although he drew upon the previous work of Continental scholars such as Heinrich Ewald, Wilhelm Gesenius, and Isaac Nordheimer, he added his own touches that made his work particularly useful to students, and his grammar went through a number of editions. But, as Taylor goes on to observe, his demanding yet ultimately encouraging manner with students in and out of the classroom at Princeton probably did even more to advance the study of Hebrew in North America. Students "who came to him to discuss the option of dropping Hebrew," Taylor notes, "left his study with new resolve to take it up again, having been convinced that their ministry would be severely hampered without a working knowledge of Hebrew."[6]

It was a mark of Green's standing within the fellowship of American biblical scholars that he was asked to head the American Old Testament committee of translators preparing the Revised Version of the Bible. The revision movement had begun in the Church of England, which appointed in 1870 a translation committee composed chiefly of Anglicans but also including some scholars from the major dissenting denominations. The British committee subsequently asked Americans to join in the project; and Philip Schaff, by this time at Union Seminary in New York, chaired the American group. As the most recent student of American movements for biblical revision has noted, "Schaff assembled an ecumenical committee whose membership roster, like its British counterpart, read like a *Who's Who* of scholars and divines." Nine Protestant denominations were represented on the committee. At the time of the final constitution of the committee in November 1872, members included, among others, former President Theodore Dwight Woolsey of Yale; Daniel D. Whedon, editor of the *Methodist Quarterly Review;* Professor Henry Boynton Smith of Union Seminary; Ezra Abbott of Harvard; Lutheran theologian Charles Porterfield Krauth, who also served as vice provost of the University of Pennsylvania; and Calvin E. Stowe, husband of novelist Harriet Beecher Stowe and a professor of biblical studies at Hartford Seminary. Princeton Seminary had three professors on the revision team: Green and Charles Aiken on the Old Testament committee, and Charles Hodge on the New Testament.[7]

6. Taylor, *Old Testament in the Old Princeton School,* 177, 178.

7. Peter J. Thuesen, *In Discordance with the Scriptures: American Protestant Battles over Translating the Bible* (New York: Oxford University Press, 1999), 44; *Documentary History of the American Committee on Revision* (New York, 1885), 75-76. No publisher is listed

Revision was fueled in part by the discovery of new, more ancient manuscripts of the Bible by Constantin von Tischendorf between 1844 and 1860 — most notably the Codex Sinaiticus at the St. Catharine Monastery on Mount Sinai — and by the opening of the Vatican archives to scholars. With these manuscripts, older than the scholarly community had possessed before, it appeared possible to achieve a more accurate rendition of the biblical text — and hence a more accurate English translation. The fact that many of the words in the King James Bible had become archaic or had acquired somewhat different meanings in contemporary usage also argued for revision. Although the committee occasionally wavered between seeing its task as deciding the historicity of particular passages or viewing its mandate as determining the best original text, its predominant approach was textual. The lower, not the higher, criticism was generally deemed the province of the committee. This conservative approach suited the prevailing temper of American biblical scholarship at the time, and it certainly fit the disposition of William Henry Green.[8]

Green and Biblical Criticism "Born of Unbelief"

From his earliest publications, Green demonstrated that he had been shaped by Joseph Alexander's appreciation for — *and* his desire to place limits upon — the historically conditioned character of the Old Testament. For example, in an 1851 review Green pondered the question of prediction or foreshadowing of Christ in the Old Testament. On the one hand, he expressed a lack of patience with those who ransacked the Old Testament in order to find "all that bears a real or seeming analogy to the history of Christ" and then "erect out of these random and violently sundered fragments a figure of him that was to come." Green found this approach deficient on multiple counts. It led to a "capricious" exegesis of the Hebrew Scriptures, and it tended to ignore "the signifancy [*sic*] of the Old Testament for Old Testament times." What meaning would such a document have had for its own contemporaries, "for whom it was pri-

---

for the latter; the volume bears above the title the phrase "private and confidential," and below includes the comment, "prepared by order of the committee for the use of the members"; copy in the Princeton Theological Seminary library.

8. Thuesen, *In Discordance with the Scriptures,* 43-61.

marily and especially designed"? Or, as we might state the objection, such interpretation yanked the writings out of their historical context. Green's desire to set the Old Testament documents within their own times included a willingness to allow that some customs and beliefs of the Israelites might have originated with other Near Eastern peoples. "Wherever it can be shown, therefore, that a particular rite had its parallel among the heathen, or wherever it can be made probable that it had its origin in Egypt, we feel no difficulty in the admission, and think that in so doing we do not derogate in the least from its divine enactment and authority." And yet there was something in the Old Testament that made it unique and lifted it above its context. "There is no copying of pagan institutions, and introducing them with their pagan errors attached, into the worship of God; but symbols, which were used in those institutions and profaned to idolatrous ends, are set in new combinations, purged of their profane ideas, and made to point to God and holiness." But the supreme illustration that the Old Testament stood above its times lay in the fact that, despite the propensity of some interpreters to find Christ in the Hebrew Scriptures in unwarranted places or ways, nevertheless, by God's revelation, Christ *was* there. "The unquestionable authority of the New Testament," Green averred, "requires us to believe that Moses and the prophets wrote of Christ."[9]

In the latter half of his career, Green restated the same critical perspectives even more clearly and bluntly. In the introduction to *Moses and the Prophets* (1883), a book expanding reviews that he had already published as articles, Green declared in a passage that merits extended quotation:

> No objection can be made to the demand that the sacred writings should be subjected to the same critical tests as other literary productions of antiquity. When were they written, and by whom? For whom were they intended, and with what end in view? . . . Every production of any age bears the stamp of that age. It takes its shape from the influences then at work. It is part of the life of the period, and can only be properly estimated and understood from being viewed in its original connections. Its language will be the language of the time when it was produced. The subject, the style

9. [William Henry Green,] "Kurtz on the Old Covenant," *Biblical Repertory and Princeton Review* 23 (July 1851): 451, 454, 457, 471, 473.

of thought, the local and personal allusions, will have relation to the circumstances of the period. . . . Inspiration has no tendency to obliterate these distinctive qualities and characteristics which link men to their own age. It is as true of Paul and Isaiah as it is of Plato and Virgil. . . . If now inspired writings, like others, are in all their literary aspects the outgrowth of their own age, then the most thorough scrutiny can but confirm our faith in their real origin; and if in any instance the view commonly entertained of their origin or authorship is incorrect in any particular, the critical study which detects the error, and assigns each writing to its proper time and place, can only conduce to its being better understood and more accurately appreciated.

But having made that significant concession to the critical method, he noted that the unique character of the Scriptures "as a revelation from God" must always be remembered. Any "criticism which denies this at the outset . . . is under a bias which must necessarily lead to false conclusions. There is a Biblical criticism which is born of unbelief, and there is a Biblical criticism which has sprung from a reverent faith in the Divine Word." In short, believing criticism had to make room for revelation and the supernatural.[10]

Green's most often remembered works were those in which he took scholars to task for conceding too much to a criticism "born of unbelief." His first major publication as a controversialist was a response to John William Colenso, Anglican bishop in Natal, South Africa, who had published in 1862 the first volume of *The Pentateuch and the Book of Joshua Critically Considered*. Colenso's work represented the labors of a dedicated amateur who had with impressive diligence devoured within a few months all the German biblical scholarship he could find. Colenso's work sought to demonstrate the factual unreliability of the Pentateuch and thereby to call into question the precepts based on those accounts. "The bishop proposes," Green remarked with some justice, "by arithmetic to overthrow the Mosaic record." Colenso took, for example, biblical verses such as "And Moses called all Israel and said unto them . . ." and then proceeded to demonstrate how it would have been impossible for the entire nation to stand within earshot; or he took the mention in Exodus of the Is-

10. William Henry Green, *Moses and the Prophets* (New York: Robert Carter and Brothers, 1883), 17-18.

raelites dwelling in tents in the wilderness and computed that they would have needed 200,000 tents and between 200,000 and 500,000 oxen to carry the tents! From whence, the bishop wanted to know, could these supplies be found? With heavy sarcasm and point-by-point refutation, Green sought to demonstrate that Colenso's objections were puerile.[11]

In passing, Green also commented on the genealogies of the Old Testament. Although Colenso had not directed much of his fire at the reliability of these particular records, Green addressed the issue in some detail. For example, in comparing the priestly lineages in 1 Chronicles 6:3-14 and in Ezra 7:1-5, Green observed that the latter had six fewer names. He explained this discrepancy as a result of the biblical authors' "disposition to abbreviate genealogies by the omission of whatever is unessential to the immediate purpose." Then, a couple of pages later in a footnote, he added that if it were ever shown by science — he did not concede that this had yet happened — "that the race of man has existed upon the earth for a longer period than the ordinary Hebrew Chronology will allow, we would be disposed to seek the solution in this frequent, if not pervading, characteristic of the Scriptural genealogies." Green was addressing a potential impasse between biblical interpretation and science regarding the antiquity of humanity. In 1650 Archbishop James Ussher of Ireland had published his computations, based in large measure on the Old Testament genealogies, and concluded that the week of creation began on October 22, 4004 B.C. These calculations found their way into the marginal notes of many Bibles and were widely accepted by the nineteenth century. For at least several decades prior to Green's comments, scientific research had raised questions about the age of the earth, but it was only by the 1860s that geologists and paleontologists were coming to an agreement that human beings had also existed much longer than previously thought. Faced with a choice between biblical and scientific chronologies, Green was offering a way beyond the dilemma. His conclusions provided conservative Christians a way of reconciling the antiquity of humanity with the biblical record. As historian Ronald L. Numbers has demonstrated, Green's conclusions, adopted by Charles Hodge and Benjamin Warfield, aided those theologians in coming to terms with contemporary science. Today Green still figures as an authority in some conservative evangelical dis-

---

11. William Henry Green, *The Pentateuch Vindicated from the Aspersions of Bishop Colenso* (New York: John Wiley, 1863), 15, 52-54, 69-73.

cussions of the relation of science and religion. Ironically, in a work aimed at defending traditional Old Testament interpretation, Green also pointed to a way of accepting scientific conclusions that some conservative Christians found subversive of the Bible.[12]

Although most Americans joined Green in pooh-poohing Colenso, more formidable foes seemed to lurk by the end of the 1870s. Of special importance in revealing to Americans the advance of higher critical views was the case of William Robertson Smith, elected in 1870 professor of Hebrew and Old Testament exegesis at the Aberdeen Free Church College (subsequently Christ's College), Scotland. In 1875, he was selected to be part of the Old Testament section working on what became the Revised Version of the Bible. He also wrote commissioned articles on biblical studies for the ninth edition of the *Encyclopedia Britannica,* the first two of these pieces appearing in 1875. Accused of heresy and the violation of his ordination vows as a minister in the Free Church, Smith was involved in a series of complicated ecclesiastical trials lasting for several years. During this time he set forth his views in popular lectures later published as *The Old Testament in the Jewish Church* (1881) and *The Prophets of Israel* (1882). At the end of the process, a vote of no confidence in the Free Church General Assembly brought his ouster from the college in Aberdeen, and Smith eventually won appointment at Cambridge.[13]

What was it that Smith had said that was so offensive and why did it matter so much across the water in the United States? He made a favorable presentation of the views of scholars such as Abraham Kuenen of the Netherlands and the Germans Karl Graf and Julius Wellhausen. All three — though Graf and Wellhausen were most identified with the hypothesis — suggested that the Pentateuch was not the product of a single author, certainly not Moses, and that it was composed of multiple traditions reflecting various stages of Israel's religious development. Not only did the theory impeach Mosaic authorship; it also suggested that the Pentateuch in its final version distorted the historical development of Israel. For example, the Deuteronomic law actually made a late appearance during the reign of Josiah, and the Levitical law after the time

12. Green, *The Pentateuch Vindicated,* 124, 125, 128; Ronald L. Numbers, "'The Most Important Biblical Discovery of Our Time': William Henry Green and the Demise of Ussher's Chronology," *Church History* 69 (June 2000): 257-76.

13. See William Johnstone, ed., *William Robertson Smith: Essays in Re-assessment* (Sheffield: Sheffield University Press, 1995).

of the Jewish exile. In a word, the history of Israel was not what it seemed to be on first reading. In his popular lectures, Smith argued that the new views did not threaten faith but continued traditional Protestant commitment to careful study of the Bible. "Accordingly," he declared, "the first business of the Reformation theologian is not to crystallize Bible truths into doctrines, but to follow, in all its phases, the manifold inner history of the religious life which the Bible unfolds." Since the Bible was composed of a number of pieces written at various times by different authors, "it is our business to separate these elements from one another, to examine them one by one, and to comprehend each piece in the sense which it had for the first writer." In short, the higher criticism — Smith helped to popularize the term — was an extension of classic Protestant principles. In America, his case drew attention not only from weighty theological journals but also from the popular religious paper the *Independent* and even the *New York Times*. It was of particular interest in Presbyterian Princeton, which had important ties not only to Scotland but also to the Free Church, with which both the college and seminary felt an especial bond, President James McCosh himself having been one of the founding ministers of the denomination in 1843.[14]

Despite the winsome way in which Smith made his case, Green was not buying. In reviewing *The Old Testament in the Jewish Church,* Green did acknowledge his "high respect for the learning and ability of the author" and commended him for "a remarkable faculty for presenting subjects that are commonly regarded as dry and technical, in a lucid and attractive manner." But these good qualities notwithstanding, Green judged the Aberdeen professor "deficient in well-balanced judgment." He thought the professor's mode of argument "about as rational as though some critic were to deal with the Constitution of the United States in a similar manner, erecting its several articles into distinct codes, assigning them to different periods of the national history." As he analyzed the case, Green seemed almost shocked that the higher criticism should appear in such a quarter. It was as if the Trojan horse had been wheeled into the citadel of orthodoxy. The imbroglio over Smith revealed that "barriers of distance and of language, in which we found our safety from

14. W. Robertson Smith, *The Old Testament in the Jewish Church: Twelve Lectures on Biblical Criticism* (Edinburgh: Adam and Charles Black, 1881); and Smith, *The Prophets of Israel and Their Place in History* (Edinburgh: Adam and Charles Black, 1882); quotations from *Old Testament in the Jewish Church,* 16, 20. See Warner Bailey, "William Robertson Smith and American Bible Studies," *Journal of Presbyterian History* 51 (Fall 1973): 285-308.

the critical battles that have raged in Germany, are suddenly thrown down and the conflict is at once transported to our own shores."[15]

Much of the remainder of Green's academic career was given to the defense of traditional views of the Old Testament. In 1888, William Rainey Harper, then a professor at Yale University and editor of *Hebraica,* invited Green to participate in an examination of the question of the Pentateuch. Through a series of polite, learned exchanges, Harper summarized the case for composite origins and Green the case for Mosaic authorship. Drawing upon the work he had done for these essays, Green produced his two major final works, both published in 1895: *The Unity of the Book of Genesis* and *The Higher Criticism of the Pentateuch.* Green claimed that he had carried only one presupposition into his discussion with Harper: "that the Pentateuch as inspired of God was a true and trustworthy record; everything else was to be determined by the evidence which it should supply." But not surprisingly, he concluded that the notion of multiple sources had no reasonable foundation. It was a will-o'-the-wisp "which has misled critics ever since into a long and weary and fruitless search through fog and mire, that might better be abandoned for a forward march on *terra firma.*" The firm ground was the traditional belief that Moses authored the Pentateuch, that it was thus not the product of a later era in Israel's history, and that it accurately portrayed the events it reported. With painstaking attention to detail, Green assaulted the arguments used to support multiple origins. For example, the different Hebrew names used for God did not indicate divergent traditions, but the fact "that there is an appropriateness in employing one rather than the other in certain connections." Or again: he claimed that Genesis presented itself as "a continuous and connected whole, written with a definite design." In short, any seeming diversities "of diction, style, and conception" were "either altogether factitious" or the result of "the differences in subject matter and not of a diversity of writers." Undergirding his objections to composite origins was his conviction that the theory originated in flawed presuppositions. "It is noteworthy," he observed in the conclusion to *The Higher Criticism of the Pentateuch,*

> that the partition hypotheses in all their forms have been elaborated from the beginning in the interest of unbelief. . . . All the acknowledged leaders of the movement have, without exception,

15. Green, *Moses and the Prophets,* 27, 33, 34, 43, 72.

scouted the reality of miracles and prophecy and immediate divine revelation in all their genuine and evangelical sense. Their theories are all inwrought with naturalistic presuppositions, which cannot be disentangled from them without their falling to pieces.[16]

Green and the Briggs Case

By the time Green wrote those words, a growing number of American biblical scholars disagreed with him about the authorship of the Pentateuch and about other matters concerning the higher criticism. But they would not have acknowledged that their views either came from or led to "naturalistic presuppositions" or that critical theories served "the interest of unbelief." In fact, some of the most eager partisans of the new scholarship in America were persons who saw in it a gospel — good news — that would revive genuine religion. William Rainey Harper, the friend with whom Green had the polite exchange over the Pentateuch, was a case in point. A product of a Presbyterian home and later a convert to the Baptist faith, Harper knew Hebrew by the time he graduated college at age 14, had a Ph.D. from Yale at 19, and after a string of brief academic appointments was back at Yale at 30, teaching in Semitic studies and the divinity school. In 1892, he became the first president of the newly founded University of Chicago, where he created a biblical studies program virtually synonymous with higher criticism. Behind this dynamo of academic and administrative energy lay the conviction that the new biblical scholarship would place the Christian faith upon a surer foundation. In addresses to students at Chicago he asserted his firm belief that anyone who studies the Christian message "honestly and fearlessly, regardless of the mass of rubbish which tradition has gathered about it" will ultimately come to a surer faith. Charles A. Briggs, who had co-edited the *Presbyterian Review,* likewise advocated a strong dose of historical criticism as the thing most needed to reawaken the church's spirit. A convert during the Prayer Meeting Revival of 1857-1858, Charles Briggs had a sense of religious calling that his exposure to German learning under Isaac Dorner only deepened, and

16. William Henry Green, *The Unity of the Book of Genesis* (New York: Charles Scribner's Sons, 1895), viii, ix, 541, 554, 596; Green, *The Higher Criticism of the Pentateuch* (New York: Charles Scribner's Sons, 1895), 157.

he carried a missionary zeal about critical studies with him to his teaching at Union Seminary. When transferred to a new chair at Union in 1891, he used his inaugural address to compare the higher criticism to the work of the clearing of brush in early spring.

> The farmers are at work with axe, and saw, and knives, the instruments of destruction, cutting off the limbs of trees, and pruning vines and bushes, and rooting out weeds; fires are running over the fields and meadows, the air is filled with smoke, and it seems as if everything were going to destruction. But they are destroying the dead wood, dry and brittle stubble, and noxious weeds. They are removing them out of the way of the life that is beating beneath the surface of the ground, and throbbing in tree and bush. In a few days the fields will be mantled in living green, the trees and bushes will wave their leaves joyously, and deck themselves with blossoms of every variety of beauteous form and color, and the world will rejoice in a new spring-time.

In the eyes of William Henry Green, the higher criticism served unbelief, but for Harper, Briggs, and others of their ilk it promised a reinvigoration of faith. Or, to use Briggs's metaphor, it was the springtime of faith, not winter.[17]

Briggs's inaugural address created a furor in which William Henry Green eventually became embroiled, but Princeton's negative relation to Briggs did not begin with that address. For more than a decade Green and his colleagues had found Briggs an irritant. In the series of articles in the *Presbyterian Review* of which the Hodge-Warfield article on "Inspiration" was the first, Briggs wrote an essay entitled "The Right, Duty, and Limits of Biblical Criticism." There he offered partial endorsement of the Hodge-Warfield position but demurred on the matter of verbal inspiration, which he called a "scholastic theory" not found in the Reformation creeds. He also rejected their notion of inerrancy — "a matter to be decided by biblical research" and not to be "determined by *a priori* defini-

---

17. William Rainey Harper, *Religion and the Higher Life: Talks to Students* (Chicago: University of Chicago Press, 1904), 108; Charles Augustus Briggs, *The Authority of Holy Scripture: An Inaugural Address* (New York: Charles Scribner's Sons, 1891), 66-67. See also James P. Wind, *The Bible and the University: The Messianic Vision of William Rainey Harper* (Atlanta: Scholar's Press, 1897); Mark S. Massa, *Charles Augustus Briggs and the Crisis of Historical Criticism* (Minneapolis: Fortress Press, 1990).

tions and statements." Then, too, Briggs denied the Princeton view that a book's canonical status rested upon authorship and insisted that it was the witness of the Holy Spirit that authenticated the writing's status. Subsequently, Briggs gathered together earlier research about the Westminster Assembly (a small part of which had already appeared in the *Presbyterian Review* article) and published it in 1889 as *Whither? A Theological Question for the Times*. Although focused upon the Westminster Confession and its authors, the book was clearly a polemic in favor of the revision of that creed — a cause that was gathering steam in many quarters of American Presbyterianism at the time. The work honored the Westminster Standards as a "most precious doctrinal achievement" of the Puritan era, but then insisted that they "are not true disciples of the Westminster faith who would confine" Presbyterians to the Westminster documents and "make them the barriers to progress." Briggs left no doubt that the Princeton theologians were prime offenders in this regard; and, setting Princeton's teeth further on edge, he cited specific instances in which he alleged that these stout defenders of Westminster had sometimes themselves altered the confession's teachings — and often not for the better. On behalf of Princeton, it was the college's McCosh who issued a somewhat sarcastic rejection of Briggs's argument in *Whither? O Whither? Tell Me Where* (1889). In this context, Briggs, already a faculty member at Union, was transferred to a new chair at Union Seminary and delivered his inaugural address, "The Authority of Holy Scripture," in January 1891. For a scholar usually as meticulous as Briggs, the address was rather shocking in its boldness and lack of nuance. He argued, for example, that there were three sources of divine authority — church, reason, and Bible — and seemed to suggest that the three were coequal, or at least left their exact relationship unclear. Moreover, he enumerated six barriers to a proper understanding of the Bible. Among these were verbal inspiration, tying "the authenticity of the Scriptures" to the question of authorship, and the theory of inerrancy — he dismissed this as "a ghost of modern evangelicalism to frighten children." He also rejected the notion of biblical prophecy as "minute prediction," saying that "many of these predictions have been reversed by history." Likewise, he thought that the tendency to view biblical miracles as supernatural abrogation of natural law prevented many from understanding the Bible aright. Given the inflammatory nature of his language, Briggs seemed to be baiting those who disagreed or perhaps was trying to rally what he perceived as a silent majority of moderately liberal Presbyterians awaiting a champion. If so, he badly misjudged the temper of the denomination. By the time the General Assembly convened in May, more than sixty presbyteries had requested the Assembly to take action against Briggs. The election of William Henry Green as the moderator along with the appointment of President Francis Landey Patton of the College of New Jersey as chair of the standing committee on theological seminaries testified to the conservatism of the commissioners.[18]

The events of the next several years seemingly vindicated the dominance of Princeton's views within the denomination. Patton's committee recommended to the 1891 Assembly that it veto Briggs's election to his new chair, and it did so. Prior to the reunion of 1870, Union, although a *de facto* New School institution, had remained independent of formal ecclesiastical control. At the time of the reunion, the board of directors as a gesture of good faith agreed to submit future faculty appointments to the General Assembly for approval or rejection. When the General Assembly invoked the veto in 1891, Union claimed that, as a transfer to a new position within the faculty, Briggs's latest appointment did not require Assembly approval. The Assembly refused to accept this interpretation, and Union Seminary voided its agreement with the Presbyterian Church in the USA, thereby returning to its independent status. Faced with the choice, Union decided to keep Briggs and forfeit its formal affiliation with the Presbyterians. This action did not, however, end Briggs's travail. After lengthy ecclesiastical proceedings, the 1893 General Assembly found him guilty of violating his ordination vows and deposed him from the ministry. Five years later he took orders as an Episcopal priest. Princeton also appeared victorious in 1892 when the General Assembly in the so-called Portland Deliverance (the body was meeting in Portland, Oregon) declared of the Bible: "Our Church holds that the inspired Word, as it came

---

18. Charles A. Briggs, "The Right, Duty, and Limits of Biblical Criticism," *Presbyterian Review* 2 (1881): 550-79; quotations from 551, 552; Briggs, *Whither? A Theological Question for the Times,* 3rd ed. (New York: Charles Scribner's Sons, 1890 [1889]), 274; Briggs, *Authority of Holy Scripture,* 35, 38; James McCosh, *Whither? O Whither? Tell Me Where* (New York: Charles Scribner's Sons, 1889). Briggs also published a major work, *American Presbyterianism: Its Origin and Early History* (New York: Charles Scribner's Sons, 1885), which sought, *contra* Hodge's *Constitutional History,* to demonstrate that a greater measure of theological diversity had existed in colonial Presbyterianism. For a succinct overview of these events, see Lefferts A. Loetscher, *The Broadening Church: A Study of Theological Issues in the Presbyterian Church since 1869* (Philadelphia: University of Pennsylvania Press, 1954), 48-62.

from God, is without error." Despite some ambiguity in the deliverance's wording, the Assembly's intent appears to have been to throw the full weight of the denomination behind the Princeton view of Scripture.[19]

Yet these were arguably costly victories. With the Briggs case splashed across the front pages of newspapers, his opponents may have done more to spread knowledge of and support for the higher criticism among the general public than to retard it. S. D. F. Salmond, professor at the Free Church College at Aberdeen and co-editor with Briggs of the International Theological Library, wrote to his friend shortly after the latter was removed from the Presbyterian ministry. He expressed shock that a "great church like yours . . . should commit itself to a definition of the inerrancy of Scripture which must make it the gazing stock and object of wonder to intelligent Christians everywhere." In fairness, one must add that the extreme self-confidence, if not abrasiveness and arrogance, with which Briggs made his case also contributed to his ouster from the Presbyterian ministry. The irony was that Briggs, in the total spectrum of scholarly opinions about the higher criticism throughout the Euro-American world, clearly placed somewhere in a conservative to mediating position. His conservatism became apparent a few years later when he contemplated (but was dissuaded from) seeking the dismissal of a younger Union colleague who had cast doubt on the virgin birth! If Briggs was presently to be upset by the direction of the higher criticism in America, how much more would Princeton soon find itself at odds with major trends in the scholarly world in the early twentieth century.[20]

In 1900, after several years of poor health, William Henry Green died. His more than half-century of service to the seminary marked notable accomplishments. He had trained several generations of young men in Hebrew and promoted that study throughout North America by his grammars. His standing as a learned textual scholar was confirmed by his selection to head the Old Testament section preparing the Revised Version of the Bible. The fact that William Rainey Harper invited him to present the counterargument to Graf and Wellhausen in the pages of *Hebraica* attested to his academic stature. Yet it was also clear that the prevailing scholarly consensus had by the 1880s begun to move away from Green.

19. For a discussion of the Briggs case and its impact on Union Seminary, see Robert T. Handy, *A History of Union Theological Seminary in New York* (New York: Columbia University Press, 1987), 69-94.

20. Salmond to Briggs, quoted in Loetscher, *Broadening Church*, 62.

CHAPTER TEN

Princeton in the Age of Warfield

BENJAMIN Breckinridge Warfield was a couple of months shy of his thirty-sixth birthday when he assumed the seminary's professorship of didactic and polemical theology in 1887. At his formal inauguration the following May, he praised his predecessors in the post — Archibald Alexander, Charles Hodge, and A. A. Hodge. He assured the community that "the theology of Charles Hodge is within me and that this is the theology which, according to my ability, I have it in my heart to teach." This was not merely a *pro forma* bow, but an accurate description of the course Warfield would follow. During his nearly thirty-four years at Princeton, he never wrote a systematic theology; rather, he assigned Hodge's three volumes to his students. It is not that his pen lay idle over the decades. After Warfield's death, his brother Ethelbert culled through his essays to assemble ten substantial volumes; and enough articles were left over for John F. Meeter years later to compile two more books. These volumes stretched across an extraordinary range of topics, and among the major areas Warfield touched were biblical and textual criticism, Christology, revelation and inspiration, Augustine, Tertullian, Calvin, the Westminster Assembly, and perfectionism. The essays displayed the learning of a polymath as he commented on biblical studies, church history, practical issues of church life, and numerous "secular" studies. These forays, despite their diversity, did not scatter into dilettantism. They remained focused by a powerful intellect and theological vision that represented the apogee of Old Princeton.[1]

1. *Inauguration of the Rev. Benjamin B. Warfield, D.D., as Professor of Didactic and Po-*

Warfield's Background and Early Career

Warfield came from a landed family with money, slaves, and influential connections. His father, William, who was descended from a Puritan who had settled in Virginia, owned the estate Grasmere near Lexington in the "Bluegrass" area of Kentucky, where Benjamin was born on November 5, 1851. The elder Warfield was an authority on cattle production, and that interest continued in the son, who, in addition to his many theological works, authored essays on the breeding of cattle. His father was part of a prominent Whig family, and his paternal grandfather had been a good friend of Senator Henry Clay. Through his mother, Mary Cabell Breckinridge, Warfield was connected with a number of well-known figures in church and state: John Breckenridge, who served as professor at Princeton Seminary in the 1830s and married Samuel Miller's daughter Margaret; Robert J. Breckenridge, the ardent Old School partisan who sometimes gave headaches to Hodge and Alexander in the years before the 1837 split; and John Cabell Breckinridge, vice president of the United States under President James Buchanan (1857-1861) and one of the two Democrats running for president in 1860 when the party split. During the Civil War, the Warfields and Breckinridges illustrated the division that split many border state families: Benjamin's grandfather, Robert J. Breckinridge, a strong Unionist who had lobbied as late as 1849 for a new Kentucky constitution providing for gradual emancipation, was temporary chair of the political convention that renominated Abraham Lincoln for the presidency in 1864. John Cabell Breckenridge, the cousin of Warfield's mother, became a Confederate general. Benjamin Warfield's father served as a Union officer during the war, supported emancipation, and remained ardently Republican in his political sympathies. The divisions engendered by politics, slavery, and war left enduring rifts within the extended Warfield/Breckinridge clan.[2]

---

lemic Theology (New York: Anson D. F. Randolph and Co., 1888), 5. The ten volumes comprising the *Works of Benjamin B. Warfield,* published by Oxford University Press, are as follows: vol. 1: *Revelation and Inspiration* (1927); vol. 2: *Biblical Doctrines* (1929); vol. 3: *Christology and Criticism* (1929); vol. 4: *Studies in Tertullian and Augustine* (1930); vol. 5: *Calvin and Calvinism* (1931); vol. 6: *The Westminster Assembly and Its Work* (1931); vol. 7: *Perfectionism, Part 1* (1931); vol. 8: *Perfectionism, Part 2* (1932); vol. 9: *Studies in Theology* (1932); vol. 10: *Critical Reviews* (1932). See also Benjamin B. Warfield, *Selected Shorter Writings,* 2 vols., ed. John E. Meeter (Phillipsburg, NJ: Presbyterian and Reformed Publishing Company, 1970, 1973).

2. See Bradley J. Gundlach, "'B' Is for Breckinridge: Benjamin B. Warfield, His Mater-

Benjamin Warfield, then, came from a prominent family that owned slaves yet disliked the institution of slavery and welcomed its end. One may get a sense of how that complicated legacy worked itself out in his life and thought in two essays that he published in the late 1880s, the first in January 1887, while he was teaching at Western Seminary at Pittsburgh and preparing to move to Princeton. The time the essays were written is significant. The last of the Reconstruction governments in the South had fallen a decade earlier, and "Redeemers," as they styled themselves, had taken political control of the states in the old Confederacy with the goal of reestablishing white supremacy. Through lynching and other acts of violence, blacks were prevented from exercising the freedoms they had ostensibly won as a result of the war; and legislatures enacted Jim Crow segregation laws. After the last of the Federal troops were withdrawn from the South in 1877, there was little political will at the national level to try to guarantee the rights of the freed people.[3]

In this setting, Warfield penned "A Calm View of the Freedman's Case," a plea for support of the Presbyterian Board of Missions to Freedmen, whose purpose was to promote both education and evangelization for southern blacks. His appeal was a curious mixture of paternalism, rationalization, and condescension on the one hand and, on the other, a realization of the evil of slavery's systemic legacy and a fervent hope for a more egalitarian future. As the son of a family that had possessed more than two dozen slaves, Warfield was eager to acquit slaveholders of undue responsibility for the current plight of the freed people. The "slaveholders did what they could to teach a true Christianity to their slaves," he said, and he added: "Let anyone simply compare the average self-respecting Negro in America with the naked savage of the African forests, and thank God for the miraculous change." Like most other whites, Warfield assumed that African Americans had experienced a moral declension since emancipation. However, unlike many others, he did not attribute this fact to some moral defect in African Americans themselves. Warfield maintained that "by its very nature, slavery cannot allow its victim a will of his own; that it leaves him master of none of his deeds;

---

nal Kin, and Princeton Seminary," in *B. B. Warfield: Essays on His Life and Thought*, ed. Gary L. W. Johnson (Phillipsburg, NJ: Presbyterian and Reformed Publishing, 2007), 13-53; James C. Klotter, *The Breckinridges of Kentucky, 1760-1981* (Lexington: University Press of Kentucky, 1986).

3. See, for example, Eric Foner, *Reconstruction: American's Unfinished Revolution* (New York: Harper and Collins, 1988).

that it permits him ownership in nothing. Who need ask of the moral effect of such a state of things?" The solution proposed by Warfield was that the spirit of caste — both North and South, in church and in state — be utterly rooted out. He condemned those who invariably tried "to make the Negro know 'his place' — as if, forsooth, his place as a man was not side by side with men, and his place as a Christian was not in the midst of God's children. Are we today to reverse the inspired declaration that in Christ Jesus there cannot be Greek and Jew, circumcision and uncircumcision, barbarian, Scythian, bondman, freeman?" Today we would rightly wish to have heard from Warfield a less benign assessment of the master's role in slavery, a more forthright condemnation of the violence and terrorism wreaked on blacks, or a clear recognition that they themselves were active agents in their own liberation and improvement, not merely the passive recipients of what benefactors might choose to offer. Yet, given the range of white opinion on issues of racial justice in the late nineteenth century, Warfield's views would place him toward the more progressive end of the spectrum.[4]

Warfield's position on this matter sometimes put him in conflict with his ecclesiastical interests. In the late 1880s, the Northern and Southern Presbyterian denominations had begun very tentative conversations about the terms on which they could reunite. Nothing came of this for several generations, for reunion did not occur until 1983. Given the strength of traditional Old School Presbyterianism in the South and its closeness to the Princeton tradition, it was Warfield's inclination to pursue reunion. But he gagged on one of the chief requirements of the southern church — one that he feared his northern counterparts were prepared to allow. That is, he feared that the northern church would accede to racially segregated congregations, presbyteries, and synods. This, he concluded, would be for Christians "under the pressure of their race antipathy, [to] desert the fundamental law of the Living God, that in Christ Jesus there cannot be Greek and Jew, circumcision and uncircumcision. . . ." The issue of racial segregation in the house of God returned when the Presbyterian Church in the U.S.A. considered reunion with the Cumberland Presbyterians in 1906, and again the price of union included

4. Benjamin Warfield, "A Calm View of the Freedmen's Case," *The Church at Home and Abroad*, January 1887, 62-65, in *Selected Shorter Writings*, 2:735-42; quotations on 736-37, 741. For an excellent discussion of these issues, see Bradley J. Gundlach, "'Wicked Caste': B. B. Warfield, Biblical Authority, and Jim Crow," *Journal of Presbyterian History* 85 (Spring/Summer 2007): 28-47.

the willingness of the PCUSA to accept racially divided judicatories. Although Warfield opposed the reunion, he gave doctrinal reasons and appears to have said nothing about the question of drawing the color line in the church. At Princeton itself, Warfield sought integration against the wishes of some of his seminary colleagues. In 1911, he told the faculty that if a black student came to Princeton "there was no objection to having him room in the dormitory." When such a case arose in 1913, Warfield advised the registrar to give the student a room on campus; and he was housed in Brown Hall. This action reduced assistant professor J. Gresham Machen, who believed in the practice of segregation, to a smoldering fury against his former teacher, now senior colleague and ally on most theological questions.[5]

But to tell this account is to get ahead of the story. Warfield's home conditioned him in other important ways as well. It nurtured a love of both the Calvinistic tradition and scientific interests. According to the memories of his brother Ethelbert (a member and for a time president of the seminary board of directors), each Warfield had to memorize the Westminster Shorter Catechism by age 6 and subsequently had to master the biblical texts annexed as support for each answer. Then the children moved on to the Larger Catechism! At age 16, Benjamin Warfield made a formal profession of faith in the Second Presbyterian Church of Lexington. As a youth, he dabbled as a collector of birds' eggs, butterflies, and geological specimens. He read James Audubon's works on ornithology and perused Darwin's volumes. He was already, according to his recollection, "a Darwinian of the purest water." After secondary education in private schools in Lexington, he went off to the College of New Jersey in 1868, entering the sophomore class the same year that James McCosh became president. At college, he participated in the literary societies, helped edit the *Nassau Literary Magazine,* won prizes in debate and essay, and excelled especially in mathematics and physics. At his graduation in 1871, his perfect marks in those last subjects no doubt accounted for his winning a fellowship in science for further study in Europe. Upon his father's advice, Warfield turned down the fellowship on the grounds that he did not need the money for travel abroad and that

5. [Benjamin B. Warfield,] "Drawing the Color Line," subtitled "A Fragment of History," *Independent,* July 5, 1888, in *Selected Shorter Writings,* 2:743-50; quotation from 748. This article Warfield published under the pseudonym "Disinterested Spectator." See also Gundlach, "'Wicked Caste,'" 42.

the terms would limit his options for study. Sailing to Europe in 1872, Warfield spent a short time in Edinburgh before moving on to the Continent. From Heidelberg he wrote in the summer of his intention to study for the ministry. Upon returning to Kentucky, he served as the livestock editor of a farmers' journal until he entered Princeton Seminary in the fall of 1873. The episode of the declined fellowship and the subsequent European tour is suggestive of both family affluence and family dynamics. Clearly his was a privileged family; and while he received many opportunities, he was not indulged. Given opportunities, he was expected to use them to good effect, and he did.[6]

After completing his studies at Princeton in 1876, Warfield preached at a church in Dayton, Ohio, for several months and in August married Annie Pearce Kinkead, daughter of a Lexington attorney. The Dayton church called Warfield as its regular pastor, but he declined, wishing to go back to Germany for study at Leipzig. Upon arriving, Warfield and his new bride discovered that the professor with whom he had planned to study had died several months earlier, and he chose instead to attend the lectures of Christoph Ernst Luthardt and Franz Delitzsch. Both stood to the right of center on the spectrum of German theological scholarship. Luthardt was a theologian noted for his *Apologetic Lectures on the Fundamental Truths of Christianity,* which had been translated into multiple English printings. Delitzsch, a distinguished Hebraist, gave some ground to the new biblical scholarship, but nevertheless stoutly rejected any "historical criticism . . . [that] denies miracle, denies prophecy, denies revelation." The true criticism "starts from an idea of God, from which the possibility of miracle follows." Delitzsch, immensely learned, was a favorite of many American commentators. While the Warfields were in Germany, they also had an experience that shaped the remainder of their lives. Caught in a violent afternoon thunderstorm while the couple was walking, Mrs. Warfield was traumatized and never fully recovered. For much of the remainder of her days she lived as a partial recluse, and the last couple of years before her death in 1915 she was confined to bed. In the absence of adequate medical information about her condition, the reason that the storm proved so life-changing remains uncertain. Her

6. Ethelbert D. Warfield, "Biographical Sketch of Benjamin Breckenridge Warfield," in Benjamin B. Warfield, *Revelation and Inspiration,* v-ix; Benjamin Warfield, "Personal Reflections of Princeton Undergraduate Life: IV — The Coming of Dr. McCosh," *Princeton Alumni Weekly* 16 (1916): 650-53; David B. Calhoun, *Princeton Seminary,* vol. 2: *The Majestic Testimony, 1869-1929* (Carlisle, PA: Banner of Truth Trust, 1996), 117.

husband, according to surviving accounts, manifested a tender care for his invalid wife. When they moved to Princeton, their residence would be on campus at a short distance from the classrooms, and Warfield was seldom far away. As Hugh Thomson Kerr has observed,

> "Devoted" hardly contains the weight of Benjamin's loyal commitment to his life-long companion. He guarded, protected, and stood by her while pursuing his full teaching and writing assignments. He himself, by his own choice, became house-confined and scarcely ever ventured more than an hour or two from her side.

Thus B. B. Warfield rarely traveled outside Princeton and sat on relatively few church committees.[7]

After brief service as assistant pastor in the First Presbyterian Church in Baltimore, Warfield accepted a position in New Testament exegesis and literature at Western Theological Seminary in greater Pittsburgh in 1878. Irony attended the appointment, for in his student days Warfield, then expressing an interest in pursuing math and science, protested that he had no need to study Greek. His antipathy had been long overcome by 1878. In his inaugural address at Western he decried "a certain looseness of belief" in the contemporary church and defended what he took to be a major tenet of the Westminster Confession of Faith: "the church doctrine of the plenary inspiration [equated by Warfield with 'verbal inspiration'] of the New Testament." Here we see a dress rehearsal of themes that he and A. A. Hodge shortly elaborated further. His argument proceeded point by point through a series of what Warfield deemed unassailable assertions: the New Testament writers claimed to be inspired by God, a claim that he believed entailed error-free teaching; none of the contemporaries of the writers refuted that claim; no one has been able to undermine the authenticity of the writings — that is, no one has demonstrated any of these works to have been written by anyone other than the purported author; and critics had not proved a single error in any of the sacred writings. Ergo, "the Scriptures stand before us au-

---

7. See, for example, Christoph Ernst Luthardt, *Apologetic Lectures Given on the Fundamental Truths of Christianity,* trans. from the 7th German ed. (Edinburgh: T&T Clark, 1873); Franz Delitzsch, "The New Criticism: A Series of Lectures Given by Dr. Franz Delitzsch to His English Exegetical Society," *The Hebrew Student* 1 (May 1882): 6. Hugh Thomson Kerr, "Warfield: The Person Behind the Theology," *Princeton Seminary Bulletin* 25 (2004): 80-93; quotation from 85.

thenticated as from God. They are, then, just what they profess to be; and criticism only secures to them the more firmly the position they claim."[8]

Historians and theologians continue to disagree about the assertions that Warfield made in the inaugural address and then in greater detail in his joint article with A. A. Hodge, "Inspiration." Was what he described as "church doctrine" in fact such? Was it so even for the Westminster Confession, let alone the rest of the Christian tradition? And, even if one granted that the idea was present earlier, was the notion of verbal inspiration and infallibility only *one* of the ways in which the truthfulness of the biblical witness could be construed? Had the idea held the central place in theology that Warfield and Hodge appeared to give it? Were there more appropriate alternate ways of conceiving the authority of Scripture and interpreting it? To put it mildly, there has been no consensus on these issues. Hodge and Warfield themselves sometimes seemed to diminish the importance of the doctrine. One should never, they observed in the 1881 essay, "allow it to be believed that the truth of Christianity depends upon any doctrine of Inspiration whatever. Revelation came in large part before the record of it, and the Christian Church before the New Testament Scriptures." In fact, in his inaugural address at Western Seminary, Warfield had allowed: "Without any inspiration we could have had Christianity; yea, and men could still have heard the truth, and through it been awakened, and justified, and sanctified and glorified." Why then was something immensely significant at stake in the doctrine of verbal inspiration and infallible Scripture? Warfield went on to answer that question: "But to what uncertainties and doubts would we be the prey! — to what errors, constantly begetting worse errors, exposed! . . . Revelation is but half revelation unless it be infallibly communicated; it is but half communicated unless it be infallibly recorded." A firm authority, precise and error-free, was essential if Christians were to avoid wandering off into fantasies and dreams.[9]

8. *Discourses Occasioned by the Inauguration of Benj. B. Warfield to the Chair of New Testament Exegesis and Literature in Western Theological Seminary* (Pittsburgh: Nevin Brothers, 1880); quotations on 17, 18, 45.

9. *Discourses Occasioned by the Inauguration*, 46; A. A. Hodge and B. B. Warfield, "Inspiration," *Presbyterian Review* 2 (April 1881): 225-60; quotation from 227. Ernest L. Sandeen, *The Roots of Fundamentalism: British and American Millenarianism, 1800-1930* (Chicago: University of Chicago, 1970), 103-31; and Jack B. Rogers and Donald McKim, *The Authority and Interpretation of the Bible: An Historical Approach* (San Francisco: Harper and Row, 1979), have argued that the Hodge-Warfield understanding of inspiration repre-

Warfield's conviction of the error-free character of the original Scripture put limits on his use of criticism, but it also energized his biblical studies. Since the Bible was the very word of God and since God had chosen to use humans — without suppressing their individual feelings, intuition, imagination, or even many of their defects and limitations — it was vital to understand the way in which the Bible came to be, who wrote its various books, and the circumstances and times for which they wrote. It was especially crucial to establish the closest possible approximation to the original text. While at Western, he prepared *An Introduction to the Textual Criticism of the New Testament*. The book was vintage Warfield, by turns accessible and highly technical. For example, he made the student understand that textual criticism was simply a continuation of a practice in which he had already engaged. "Whenever, for instance, we make a correction in the margin of a book we chance to be reading, because we observe a misplaced letter or a misspelled word, or any other obvious typographical error, we are engaging in processes of textual criticism." But soon the student was moving through the intricacies of different kinds of writing in the Greek text — uncial and miniscule — and learning how to plot the lines of the great manuscript families with all their subgroups and then decide which textual variant is most likely. Some of the pages of *An Introduction* look almost more like scientific tables than prose. Warfield's pedagogy might start where the learner was, but it presumed that he would quickly move at breakneck speed into the realms of the highly technical.[10]

Warfield's evaluation of his own teacher — Charles Hodge — says a great deal about the former's own ideal of a biblical scholar. Asked to assess Hodge as an exegete, Warfield replied with candor:

> He made no claim, again, to critical acumen; and in questions of textual criticism he constantly went astray. Hence it was that of-

---

sented a historical innovation. By contrast, John D. Woodbridge, *Biblical Authority: A Critique of the Rogers/McKim Proposal* (Grand Rapids: Zondervan, 1982), emphasizes that positions similar to the Princeton view of inspiration were common and antedated the Princeton Theology's formulation. For alternate ways — what he calls "failed alternatives" — to the type of hermeneutic represented by Old Princeton and most other Protestants of the era, see Mark A. Noll, *America's God: From Jonathan Edwards to Abraham Lincoln* (New York: Oxford University Press, 2002), 402-21.

10. Benjamin B. Warfield, *An Introduction to the Textual Criticism of the New Testament* (Toronto: S. R. Briggs, 1887), 5.

ten texts were quoted to support doctrines of which they did not treat; and a meaning was sometimes extracted from a passage which it was far from bearing. But this affected details only, the general flow of thought in a passage he never failed to grasp, and few men could equal him in stating it. . . . [But] Theology was his first love.

Warfield did excel in the minutiae of textual work that Charles Hodge had passed by perhaps too hastily. Yet for Warfield, too, theology was ultimately his first love. When the untimely death of Archibald A. Hodge left Princeton's chair of didactic and polemical theology vacant, the seminary directors called Warfield to the post, and he accepted, remembering that Charles Hodge had also begun his seminary teaching as a professor of biblical studies.[11]

Warfield's Vision of the Theological Enterprise

At his Princeton inauguration in the spring of 1888, Warfield offered a comprehensive vision of his new task — indeed, of the entire range of studies within the theological seminary. "The Idea of Systematic Theology Considered as a Science" stood as a fitting prolegomenon to what Warfield would undertake at Princeton.

In that lecture, Warfield sought to draw out the implications of the assertion that theology is a science, a "science which treats of God and of the relations between God and the universe." With this simple definition, he ruled out common misconceptions. Theology was not a historical discipline, for it "seeks to discover not what has been or is held to be true, but *what is ideally true;* in other words, it is to declare that it *deals with absolute truth* and aims at organizing into a concatenated system all the truth in its sphere" (emphases added). The study of past religious thought and its development constituted a valuable science in its own right — and one upon which theology should draw — but it was not itself theology. Or again: theology, strictly speaking, could not exist in multiple forms, for "this all-embracing system will brook no rival in its sphere, and there can be two theologies only at the cost of one or both of them being imperfect, incomplete, false." To be sure, from the perspective of

---

11. A. A. Hodge, *Life of Charles Hodge* (New York: Charles Scribner's Sons, 1880), 590.

historical study, one could speak of Pelagian or Augustinian theologies, or of Calvinist and Arminian theologies. But *as theology,* only one of the systems could be correct, for theology dealt with "absolute truth." Nor was theology the "science of faith," as some suggested who would base the discipline on the religious affections or moral consciousness of humanity. The history of Christian thought and experience was indeed a valuable contributor to theology, but it was not itself theology proper. Theology had its ground in God's revelation; and while God had indeed disclosed himself in part through the human mind and its moral-religious experience, in the structure of the world, and in his providence, these were inadequate guides unto salvation. Preeminently God disclosed himself through "the revelation . . . in His written Word — in which are included the only authentic records of the revelation of Him through the incarnate Word." With this understanding of the nature and sources of theology, Warfield explained how other disciplines served it. First, apologetics "prepares the way for all theology by establishing its necessary presuppositions without which no theology is possible — the existence and essential nature of God, the religious nature of man which enables him to receive a revelation from God, the possibility of a revelation." Apologetics "thus places the Scriptures in our hands for investigation and study." Then "exegetical theology receives these inspired writings from the hands of apologetics, and investigates their meaning." Once exegesis has done its work, it hands off the results to biblical theology, which assembles "scattered results of continuous exegesis" into patterns and themes. These larger motifs of biblical theology, more than the individual bits of data produced by exegesis, then provided grist for the mill of systematic theology.[12]

On first glance, Warfield's inaugural address appears to confirm the frequent portrayal of Old Princeton as advancing a theology of static propositions. Thus Warfield ardently contended for the notion that theology is about the "ideally true" or "absolute truth," and notions suggesting that truth itself somehow developed were as deeply troubling to Warfield as they had been to Charles Hodge. Yet Warfield also realized that Christian understanding of the truth had grown in significant ways. In a decade in which the phrase had acquired currency, Warfield indicated that there was a sense in which orthodoxy was progressive. In a fascinating passage, he talked about the development of doctrine:

12. *Inauguration of the Rev. Benjamin B. Warfield,* 12-13, 18, 23.

Justin Martyr, champion of the orthodoxy of his day, held a theory of the intertrinitarian relationship which became heterodoxy after the Council of Nice; the ever-struggling Christologies of the earlier ages were forever set aside by the Chalcedon fathers; Augustine determined for all time the doctrine of grace, Anselm the doctrine of the atonement, Luther the doctrine of forensic justification.

To attempt to go back to a much earlier theology and take it as adequate for the present made no more sense than going back to ancient theories of medicine or astronomy. "The physician," he asserted, "who would bring back to-day the medicine of Galen would be no more mad than the theologian who would revive the theology of Clement of Alexandria. Both were men of light and learning in their time; but their time is past, and it is the privilege of the child of to-day to know a sounder physic and a sounder theology than the giants of that far past yesterday could attain." Such development was not, however, an invitation to open-ended revision or to rejection of previously gained truths. Unlike medicine or astronomy, theology basically had all its facts laid before it once the biblical canon was closed, but over the centuries Christian thinkers encountered different issues and were forced to think through the implications of its facts and doctrines. As theology developed, the scope for legitimate change narrowed. In fact, said Warfield, "we are ever more and more hedged around with ascertained facts, the discovery and establishment of which constitute the very essence of progress." The conclusion: "Progress brings progressive limitation."[13]

One of the areas that Warfield marked as offering distinctive advance was the field of biblical theology. In an essay written at the dawn of the twentieth century, Warfield acknowledged that the "new discipline . . . came to us indeed wrapped in the swaddling-clothes of rationalism" and "rocked in the cradle of the Hegelian recasting of Christianity." In other words, its first advocates touted it as a way of overturning the corruptions of traditional theology, and they often believed that truth was a historically relative entity, changing with time and place. For Warfield, this sort of development in theology was not progress, but regress, usu-

---

13. *Inauguration of the Rev. Benjamin B. Warfield,* 35-36. For an examination of the idea of the possibility — and limits — of development in Warfield's theology, see James Samuel McClanahan Jr., "Benjamin B. Warfield: Historian of Doctrine in Defense of Orthodoxy, 1881-1921" (Ph.D. Dissertation, Union Theological Seminary, Richmond, VA, 1988).

ally a relapse into some long-exploded heresy. Nevertheless, he believed "a more mature form" of biblical theology was emerging and augured a deeper understanding of God's revelation.

> If men have hitherto been content to contemplate the counsel of the Most High only in its final state — laid out before them, as it were, in a map — hereafter it seems that they are to consider it by preference in its stages, in its vital processes of growth and maturing. Obviously a much higher form of knowledge is thus laid open to us; and were this discipline the sole gift of the nineteenth century to the Christian student, she would by it alone have made good a claim on his permanent gratitude.

By the time Warfield penned these words, Princeton had added its own biblical theologian in the person of Geerhardus Vos (on whom see the next chapter).[14]

For Warfield, none of these matters was of purely speculative or theoretical interest, for all theology was at bottom *practical* theology. In the inaugural address, he insisted that systematic theology "is an eminently practical science," and "the systematic theologian is pre-eminently a preacher of the Gospel." Designed to "save and sanctify the soul," theology needed to be properly mastered so that the minister might "make the most efficient use of it for its holy purpose." In fact, to "misconceive it in its parts or in its relations" was to promote a piety "dwarfed or contorted." In an article for the *Homiletic Review,* he complained of those who championed spiritual ardor over learning as the thing most needed for "the practical work of the ministry." "Give us not scholars, it is said, but plain practical men in our pulpits — men whose simple hearts are on fire with love to Christ and whose whole energy is exhausted in the rescue of souls." Stated in these terms, Warfield allowed, the choice was clear. He, too, would prefer "a warmly evangelistic ministry" to a "chilly intellectualistic" one; but the dichotomy was false, for a preacher could be both theologically learned and "on fire with love to Christ." Indeed, the effective minister was ultimately the one who understood the truth of the gospel thoroughly — that is, the one who understood it *theologically.* "Systematic theology is, in other words," Warfield said,

14. Benjamin B. Warfield, "A Century's Progress in Biblical Knowledge," *Homiletic Review,* March 1900, in *Selected Shorter Writings,* 2:12.

the preacher's true text-book. Its study may be undertaken, no doubt, in a cold and unloving spirit, with the mind intent on merely scholastic or controversial ends. In that case it may be for the preacher an unfruitful occupation. But so undertaken it has also lost its true character. It exists not for these ends, but to "make wise unto salvation." And when undertaken as the means of acquiring a thorough and precise knowledge of those truths which are fitted to "make wise unto salvation," it will assuredly bear its fruit in the preacher's own heart . . . and in the lives of the hearers.

For Warfield, solid training in systematic theology and in the other classical disciplines was the foundation of all practical theology, which consisted primarily in applying and rightly dividing the truths that systematic theology had discovered.[15]

Whatever reservations people then or now might harbor about Warfield's position, he offered a cogent view of the theological enterprise and its place in the world of learning. Apologetics established the reasonableness of faith and revelation; then exegetical theology went to work on the Scriptures, interpreting their meaning verse by verse and book by book; biblical theology constructed those pieces into larger entities; and finally systematic theology assembled everything into an overall portrait of God's nature and his relationship with humanity. Or, as Warfield might put it, theology "concatenated" the truths about God into their proper proportion to one another. Theology was also the fulfillment of every other systematic study undertaken by humanity: "All science without God is mutilated science, and no account of a single branch of knowledge can ever be complete until it is pushed back to find its completion and ground in Him." Whatever subject Warfield touched — whether it was the knowledge of God in Calvin's theology, the latest textual studies of biblical books, the history of the Westminster Assembly, or passing observations drawn from contemporary writers such as Arthur Conan Doyle or H. Rider Haggard — Warfield approached the topic with immense erudition. One has the sense that he read and absorbed virtually everything, and he almost always exuded the serene

---

15. *Inauguration of the Rev. Benjamin B. Warfield,* 37, 38, 39; Benjamin B. Warfield, "The Indispensableness of Systematic Theology to the Preacher," *Homiletic Review,* February 1897, in *Selected Shorter Writings* 2:281, 288.

confidence that he could bring the subject or the author he was citing into subjection to the theological *imperium.*[16]

The depth of Warfield's commitment to rational argument, particularly as an apologetic tool for persuading people of the reasonableness of Christianity, became apparent in his response to the major Dutch Calvinist theologians, Abraham Kuyper and Herman Bavinck. Warfield considered the two to be among the foremost contemporary defenders of Reformed orthodoxy, and both were invited to the seminary to deliver the Stone Lectures, Kuyper in 1898 and Bavinck in 1908. Warfield admired not only the cogency of their statements of Calvinist orthodoxy but also their comprehensive vision of the Christian duty to shape *all* of life — its cultural, intellectual, and social aspects as well as its religious ones — in accord with an appropriate Christian worldview. He was puzzled, however, that the two did not set nearly as much store by apologetics as he did. Assuming that the effects of the fall had corrupted the intellect, they believed that Christians and non-believers would reason from different assumptions and thus come to different conclusions; apologetics thus played a limited role in the theological enterprise. As George Marsden has expressed the matter, Warfield assumed "that intellectually the believer and the non-believer stood on common ground." To be sure, he never suggested that intellectual argument could bring a person to saving knowledge; only the Holy Spirit could do that. However, argument from universally recognized facts and self-evident truths — here one hears the echoes of the Common Sense philosophy — were essential tools that the theologian must use. In a review of one of Bavinck's books, Warfield declared:

> We are not, we repeat, absurdly arguing that Apologetics will of itself make a man a Christian. But neither can it be said that the proclaimed gospel itself can do that. Only the Spirit of life can communicate life to a dead soul. But we are arguing that Apologetics has its part to play in the Christianizing of the world: and that this part is not a small part. . . . Christianity must think through and organize its, not defense merely, but assault. It has been placed in the world to *reason* its way to the dominion of the world. And it is by reasoning its way that it has come to its king-

16. *Inauguration of the Rev. Benjamin B. Warfield,* 30.

ship. By reasoning it will gather to itself all its own. And by reasoning it will put its enemies under its feet.[17]

Dangers in Contemporary Theology

Those enemies, Warfield recognized, would not always yield easily. He often acknowledged that he was up against powerful foes. Less than a decade into his Princeton professorship, he discussed the dilemma theologians of his era faced. Sympathetic allies in Scotland found the essay so compelling and timely that they reprinted it with an introduction by Professor James Orr of Edinburgh. "We are accustomed," Warfield began, "to regard theology as the queen of the sciences, and Systematic Theology as queen among the theological disciplines. But these are not days in which lofty claims are readily allowed." As Warfield saw it, the problem came largely from supposed friends of Christianity who tried to save religion by destroying theology. He found a chief offender in Albrecht Ritschl, a German theologian whose ideas exercised an important influence in liberalizing sectors of American Protestantism at the close of the nineteenth century. Ritschl wanted to free the faith from metaphysical theory, slough off the dogmatic accretions of the centuries, and ground it in the experience of justification and reconciliation mediated through the Christian community by the historical Jesus. But who was that Jesus? Warfield feared that disciples of Ritschl were willing to "let historical criticism do its worst, let it evaporate into the mist of myth every fact on which men have been accustomed to found Christianity[;] Christianity will remain untouched: it is constituted by this one fact only — Jesus Christ." Unfortunately this "Christ of critical history" is one "of whom we can say but this — that He lived and died and left behind Him the aroma of a life of faith." The Christ of the tradition, the divine-human savior, was thus reduced to a faint whiff of what Christian theology had claimed him to be. Or alternately, Warfield noted, critics of theology — and here he offered French Protestant Auguste Sabatier as a case in point — argued that Christianity should be understood primarily as life, a growing pul-

17. George M. Marsden, *Fundamentalism and American Culture: The Shaping of Twentieth Century Evangelicalism, 1870-1925* (New York: Oxford University Press, 1980), 115; Benjamin B. Warfield, "A Review of *De Zekerheid des Geloofs*," *Princeton Theological Review*, January 1903, in *Selected Shorter Writings*, 2:120-21.

Charles Rosenbury Erdman (1866–1960), class of 1891, served as professor of practical theology at Princeton Seminary from 1905 until 1936. The seminary's Erdman Hall, on the site of their former home, is dedicated to Charles Erdman and his wife, Estelle Pardee Erdman, "in grateful remembrance of the gracious hospitality of their home so freely extended, even until their last days, to generations of students." *Portrait by Peter G. Cook*

Joseph Ross Stevenson (1866–1939) served as president of Princeton Theological Seminary from 1914 until 1936. Prior to coming to Princeton Seminary he taught church history at McCormick Theological Seminary in Chicago and served as a pastor in New York City and Baltimore.

J. Gresham Machen (1881–1937), class of 1905, served as professor of New Testament at Princeton Seminary from 1906 until 1929 and at Westminster Theological Seminary from 1929 to 1937. He was a leading figure of conservative Presbyterianism and helped found the Presbyterian Church of America in 1936, which was renamed the Orthodox Presbyterian Church in 1939.

Miller Chapel, dating to 1833, was the second building constructed on the Princeton Seminary campus, and is here shown in its original location facing Mercer Street to the east of Alexander Hall. At the center of Princeton Seminary's worship life from that day until the present, it was built by Princeton carpenter and builder Charles Steadman in the Greek Revival style that was popular in his day. It is named for the Seminary's second professor, Samuel Miller, who taught at Princeton Seminary from 1813 until his retirement in 1848 at the age of 79. It has been renovated several times. In 1933 it was moved further back from the street and turned 90 degrees to face the inner campus of the Seminary, next to Stuart Hall (seen to the left rear of Miller Chapel in the photo).

John Alexander Mackay (1889–1983), class of 1915, served as president of the seminary and professor of ecumenics from 1936 until 1959. He had been a missionary in Latin America from 1916 to 1932, was a leading figure in the ecumenical movement, and helped to establish the World Council of Churches. *Portrait by Alfred Jonniaux*

Stuart Hall is probably the most visible sign of the Stuart family's generosity to the seminary; it serves to this day as the main classroom building of the seminary. It is difficult to summarize all that the Stuart family — Robert Leighton Stuart, his brother Alexander Stuart, and his wife, Mary Macrae Stuart — meant to Princeton Seminary in the nineteenth century. In addition to Stuart Hall, they gave substantial

monetary gifts to increase the seminary's general endowment and to meet its ongoing operational expenses, established a Stuart professorship of philosophy, provided for faculty housing, and contributed books to the library. Hodge Hall was also funded from a bequest left to the seminary by Mary Macrae Stuart.

Springdale has housed every president of the seminary since 1899. The land on which Princeton Seminary now stands was originally part of a larger farm known as Springdale, owned by the Stockton family; the seminary acquired several acres of the farm from the son of Richard Stockton, a signer of the Declaration of Independence, when it began. In the middle of the nineteenth century, Commodore Robert F. Stockton engaged the Scottish-born American architect John Notman to design a home on the remaining farm property as a wedding gift for his eldest son, Richard Stockton. It was eventually purchased by Princeton Seminary from Richard Stockton's grandson, Bayard Stockton Jr.

Muriel Van Orden Jennings (1905–2000), class of 1932, was the first female graduate of Princeton Seminary. Her ministry focused especially on children and youth, and for over fifty years she was associated with the Montrose (PA) Children's Camp. Among other projects, the Montrose Children's Camp brought inner-city children from Harlem of diverse ethnic backgrounds to the countryside for an interracial Christian camp experience with local children from Pennsylvania.

Emil Brunner, a noted Swiss theologian, was a guest professor of systematic theology at Princeton Seminary for the school year 1938–1939.

Elmer George Homrighausen, shown here with fellow Princetonian Albert Einstein, was the Thomas Synnott Professor of Christian Education at Princeton Seminary from 1938 to 1954 and held the Charles R. Erdman Chair of Pastoral Theology from 1954 until 1970. He served as dean of the seminary from 1955 to 1965.

Bruce Metzger (1914–2007), class of 1938, taught New Testament at the seminary for forty-four years, from 1940 until 1984. He became the first incumbent of the George L. Collard Chair of New Testament Language and Literature in 1964. During his tenure he also served as the chair of the committee of translators that produced The New Revised Standard Version of the Bible.

Otto Piper (1891–1982) taught at the Universities of Göttingen and Münster, but he was dismissed from his teaching post in Germany when the Nazis came to power for his outspoken views on the proper relation between church and state. After an interim period of several years as a refugee in Great Britain, he came to Princeton Seminary as a visiting professor, teaching systematic theology in the academic year 1937–1938. Eventually he became the first holder of the Helen H. P. Manson Chair in New Testament Literature and Exegesis until his retirement in 1962.

Emile Cailliet (1894–1981), best known for his work as a Pascal scholar, was the Stuart Professor of Christian Philosophy at Princeton Seminary from 1948 until 1959.

George Stuart Hendry (1904–1993) was born in Aberdeenshire in Scotland and served a parish in Scotland from 1930 until 1949. He occupied the Charles Hodge Chair of Systematic Theology at Princeton Seminary from 1949 until his retirement in 1973. He is pictured here on the right with President James McCord (left) and Swiss theologian Karl Barth (center).

Lefferts Augustine Loetscher (1904–1981), class of 1928, spent most of his life in Princeton, where his father, Frederick William Loetscher (1875–1966), class of 1900, served as professor of homiletics and then of church history at Princeton Seminary until 1945. Lefferts Loetscher was called to the seminary in 1941, where he taught with a special focus on American church history until his retirement in 1974.

Edward Atkinson Dowey Jr. (1918–2003), class of 1943, served as a naval chaplain during the Second World War, completed his doctoral work on John Calvin under Emil Brunner at the University of Zurich, and joined the Princeton Seminary faculty in 1957 after teaching church history at McCormick Theological Seminary from 1953 to 1957. He became the Archibald Alexander Professor of the History of Christian Doctrine in 1982 and retired from the faculty in 1988. He was especially known for his work in chairing the committee that prepared the Book of Confessions and the Confession of 1967 of the United Presbyterian Church in the USA.

Edward Jabra Jurji (1907–1990), class of 1942, was born in Latakia, Syria, and studied at the American University of Beirut. He taught at Mosul and Baghdad and came to the United States in 1933 to complete his graduate work at Princeton University. An authority on the Middle East and a leading Arab-American scholar, he began his teaching at Princeton Seminary in 1939, teaching in the fields of Islamic studies and comparative religion, and at the time of his retirement in 1977 was professor of the history of religions.

James Iley McCord (1919–1990) served as president and professor of systematic theology at Princeton Seminary from 1959 until 1983. During his tenure the seminary significantly increased its endowment, and McCord oversaw the construction of major new housing projects for both faculty and students. He founded the Center of Theological Inquiry in Princeton in 1982 and served as its chancellor from 1983 to 1989. He was also a recipient of the Templeton Prize for Progress in Religion in 1986. *Portrait by Herbert E. Abrams*

Thomas William Gillespie (1928–2011), class of 1954, served as president and professor of New Testament at Princeton Seminary from 1983 to 2004, bringing twenty-nine years of pastoral experience to the position. He preached regularly in Miller Chapel and placed a strong emphasis on theological education in service to the larger church. He oversaw an increasing diversification of the seminary faculty and student body; was instrumental in establishing the Institute for Youth Ministry, the Center for Barth Studies, the Abraham Kuyper Center for Public Theology, and the Joe R. Engle Institute of Preaching at Princeton Seminary; and was responsible for bringing the offices of the Hispanic Theological Initiative to the Princeton Seminary campus.

sating reality "of which . . . [theology] is only a reflection." Thus "it follows," Warfield concluded wryly, "that changeableness in doctrine is not an evil, but a sign of abounding life. The more unstable a doctrine is, the more living it is." Warfield discounted any effort to reduce Christianity to an imprecisely defined "life" and suspected any thinker who claimed to believe in the fundamental facts of God's redemptive activity while at the same refusing to endorse the doctrines usually associated with those facts. "What Christianity consists in," he insisted, "is facts that are doctrines, and doctrines that are facts." The two could not be separated.[18]

Warfield found American theologians and religious scholars succumbing to similar looseness of teaching, or outright heresy, and he did not hesitate to take them on. When Charles Briggs, for example, tried to show in *Whither? A Theological Question for the Times* that the Westminster Confession did not affirm biblical inerrancy in the way that Princeton taught, Warfield challenged Briggs's interpretation of the historical evidence. He also worked behind the scenes, apparently at the request of his colleague William Henry Green, to draw up a paper specifying the ways in which Briggs's 1891 address, *The Authority of Holy Scripture,* taught doctrines incompatible with the Presbyterian Church's doctrinal standards. When Henry Preserved Smith of Lane Seminary, a Presbyterian school in Cincinnati, spoke out in defense of Briggs and criticized the notion of plenary inspiration, Warfield pounced with a negative review in 1895. Warfield expressed equal displeasure with Arthur C. McGiffert, a young colleague of Smith at Lane who moved to Union Seminary in New York in 1893 to assume a post in church history. McGiffert had studied with Adolf von Harnack in Germany, and his inaugural address demonstrated how deeply Harnack had influenced him. Harnack's massive studies of the history of Christian dogmatic development reflected a conviction, gleaned initially from Albrecht Ritschl, that the history of Christian doctrine entailed the intrusion of alien modes of thought upon the simple message of primitive Christianity. McGiffert echoed these concerns in his inaugural, *Primitive and Catholic Christianity.* Averring that the historian's duty was to observe "if Christianity has assimilated any elements from without" and then "to trace those elements or accretions to their sources," he proceeded to trace what he regarded as the major transformation of Chris-

18. Benjamin B. Warfield, *The Right of Systematic Theology* (Edinburgh: T&T Clark, 1897), 15, 34, 48-49, 56, 79. On Ritschl, see Claude Welch, *Protestant Thought in the Nineteenth Century,* vol. 2: *1870-1914* (New Haven: Yale University Press, 1985), 1-30.

tian history, the church's transition from its primitive state to Catholicism. The early Christian community, he asserted, was characterized by "the spirit of religious individualism," the belief "that every Christian believer enjoys the immediate presence of the Holy Spirit, through whom he communes with God, and receives illumination, inspiration and strength sufficient for his daily needs." But then, under the impact of Stoic, neo-Platonic, and ultimately Gnostic influences, the Christian community changed from a fellowship of the Spirit into an institution regulated by a fixed canon (the Bible), governed by bishops, and defined by creeds. McGiffert suggested that the Protestant Reformation had only partly recovered the ethos of the primitive church and needed to go further. "The true statement of the Protestant position," he declared, "is not that the Word of God, contained in the Scriptures of the Old and New Testaments," is the final authority but rather "that the Spirit of God is the sole and ultimate authority for Christian truth — the Spirit of God who spoke through the Apostles and who still speaks to his people." Warfield was mortified. All external authority, whether of canon or polity, had been relegated to post-apostolic Christianity — a historical reading that would, in his judgment, "surrender the whole body of Christian doctrine as being no part of essential Christianity, but the undivine growth of ages of human development." From Warfield's perspective, McGiffert and others in the Ritschlian camp had obliterated the objective basis for Christian theology and guaranteed the triumph of unbelief. Warfield again registered his conviction that the only way Christian preachers and theologians could attain "a lasting hold upon men" was through "the bold proclamation of positive, dogmatic truth, based on external, divine authority." As in the case of Briggs, Warfield had a majority in the Presbyterian Church at his back. After losing an appeal to the General Assembly, Smith was suspended from the Presbyterian ministry in 1894; and McGiffert, in a similar plight and sensing the odds against him, asked the New York Presbytery to remove his name from the rolls in 1900.[19]

19. Henry Preserved Smith, *Inspiration and Inerrancy: A History and a Defense* (Cincinnati: Robert Clarke and Co., 1893); Arthur Cushman McGiffert, *Primitive and Catholic Christianity: An Address* (New York: John C. Rankin, 1893), 18, 19, 43; Benjamin B. Warfield, "Professor Henry Preserved Smith on Inspiration," *Presbyterian and Reformed Review* 5 (1894): 600-653; Warfield, "The Latest Phase of Historical Rationalism," *Presbyterian Quarterly* 9 (January and April 1895): 36-67, 185-210; quotations on 37, 49. See also Barry Waugh, "A Manuscript of B. B. Warfield concerning the Trial of Charles A. Briggs," *Westminster Theological Journal* 66 (2004): 401-11.

Efforts to Revise the Westminster Confession

Warfield regarded the Westminster Confession as one of the best statements of "positive, dogmatic truth." Accordingly, he did not view favorably efforts within the Presbyterian Church to revise it. Dissatisfaction with aspects of Westminster — at least, unhappiness with Old School interpretations of the standards — had surfaced among New School Presbyterians decades earlier. Shortly after the reunion of the two branches of the denomination in 1870, there were rumblings about possible creedal change, even as others within the larger Reformed family were openly discussing the nature of creedal subscription and the possibility of revision. The question had agitated the various Presbyterian churches of Scotland for some years. The Alliance of Reformed Churches Throughout the World Holding the Presbyterian System (formed in 1875) had investigated the possibility of drafting a consensus creed; and American Congregationalists, who for years had served alternately as allies or as sparring partners for their Presbyterian counterparts, adopted the so-called "Commission" Creed in 1883. Desire for change in the Presbyterian Church in the U.S.A. took concrete form when more than a dozen presbyteries sent overtures to the 1889 General Assembly, asking for creedal revision. The General Assembly sent the matter back to the presbyteries by asking them whether they desired any revisions and, if so, to what extent. After several years of debate and the submission by the Assembly of recommended changes, the attempt failed, in part because the trials of Charles A. Briggs, a prominent advocate of revision, discredited the movement in some quarters and otherwise distracted the denomination.[20]

In the debate, Warfield spoke out strongly against any alterations. His basic contention was that they were unnecessary. The "moderation, fullness, lucidity, and catholicity of its [Westminster's] statement of the Augustinian system of truth" have made it "the best, safest and most acceptable statement . . . that has ever been formulated." Moreover, since Presbyterian ministers and elders had to accept the confession only for "system of doctrine," they had a measure of liberty in subscription and need not worry about disagreements over quibbles. The supposed is-

20. A. Taylor Innes, "The Creed Question in Scotland," *Andover Review* 12 (July 1889): 1-15; Williston Walker, *The Creeds and Platforms of Congregationalism,* with an introduction by Douglas Horton (Philadelphia and Boston: Pilgrim Press, 1960 [1893]), 577-84.

sues that needed to be addressed by addition or amendment, Warfield insisted, were based on a misreading of the confession. Some critics objected that the phrase "elect infants dying in infancy" implied that some infants would in fact be damned — a reading the Princeton professor dismissed "as one of the most astonishing pieces of misinterpretation in literary history." Others complained that God's predestinating decrees needed to be balanced by a firmer affirmation of God's love for all, but Warfield insisted that the confession already made abundantly clear that "God's electing grace is the expression of His infinite love for men." When the Assembly in 1892 did endorse and send to the presbyteries a series of changes for their approval or disapproval, Warfield's anxiety mounted. Unlike his earlier comments suggesting that the issues of revision were mere quibbles, his words now suggested that the very integrity of Presbyterian theology and the credibility of its witness to the world were at stake. If the proposals were adopted, Presbyterians would be compelled to ask, he noted ominously, do "we still have a Confession which is Calvinistic and can be accepted"? He concluded his reflections with a challenge:

> It is not a time in which to whisper the truth in doubtful phrases, but to shout it from the housetops in the clearest and sharpest language in which it can be framed. Distinctive Calvinism must be upheld. . . . Let him that is fearful and trembling, indeed, return and depart. But though there be but a Gideon's hundred left, if they will take but their lights in their hands . . . and blow with their trumpets . . . the sword of the Lord will get them victory.

Warfield did not have to decide where this heated rhetoric might lead, for the proposed revisions failed to win approval. A decade later, when the denomination did make minor changes in the confession and issued a Declaratory Statement clarifying the sense in which it understood the confession, Warfield, though initially opposed to the changes, concluded that the Calvinistic system had not been compromised.[21]

---

21. John DeWitt et al., *Ought the Confession of Faith to Be Revised?* (New York: Anson F. D. Randolph, 1890), 40, 54, 121; Benjamin B. Warfield, "The Final Report of the Committee on Revision of the Confession," *Presbyterian and Reformed Review* 3 (1892): 329, 330.

Warfield and Popular Religion

In his zeal for Reformed orthodoxy, Warfield directed much of his fire at liberal views that would in the 1920s be targets of the fundamentalist movement. But he also criticized movements that would later be associated with fundamentalism. He had little sympathy, for example, with the premillennial theories then gaining currency in many Protestant quarters. Premillennialism taught that Christ's Second Advent would occur *before* the church's golden age on earth, or the millennium of Revelation chapter 20 — hence the term "premillennial." The more common view of American Protestant leaders had been postmillennialism, the notion that Christ would return *after* the millennial age. By the mid-nineteenth century, postmillennialism often served as an incentive for Christians to promote revivals, religious benevolence, and reform as a way of nudging history toward the millennium. Sometimes it became a religious equivalent to notions of cultural and social progress and underwrote the idea that the United States had a special mission in world history. By contrast, the premillennial faith — especially a new variant called dispensationalism, often traced to the Englishman John Nelson Darby — offered a very different vision of the future. Pronouncing the current age corrupt, dispensationalists scoffed at the postmillennial dream of the church helping to inaugurate the millennium. They looked for the Rapture, Jesus' removal of true believers from the earth prior to the tribulations near the end of the age. Wars, increasing decadence, and the restoration of the Jewish people to Palestine were also expected signs of the end. They also assumed that the gospel needed to be preached to all nations before the end came, though they did not interpret this injunction to mean that in fact the majority of the world would be converted to Christianity. Through annual Bible study conferences, meeting for a quarter-century after 1875, through Bible institutes created to provide basic theological education to Christian workers, and through the Scofield Reference Bible (1909), dispensationalism created a subculture that influenced the rise of twentieth-century fundamentalism. A significant part of dispensationalism's appeal was that it purported to uphold the inerrancy of Scripture and the supernatural character of Christianity at a time when biblical criticism and liberal theology had called these assumptions into question.[22]

22. James H. Moorhead, *World without End: Mainstream American Protestant Visions of the Last Things, 1880-1925* (Bloomington: Indiana University Press, 1999). See also

Although Warfield did not write at length on eschatology, he found premillennialism highly suspect. His views were closer to postmillennialism, even though he did not quite fit into that category either. One gets a sense of how greatly his approach to the apocalyptic literature differed from that of the premillennialists in an article he published in 1904. For someone who believed in the verbal inerrancy of Scripture, his preliminary remarks about the interpretation of the book of Revelation are striking: the task of interpreting the work is not so much a matter of "minute philology" as it is of "broad literary appreciation." Determination of "the meaning of the Apocalypse," he continued,

> is a task . . . not directly of verbal criticism but of sympathetic imagination: the teaching of the book lies not immediately in its words, but in the wide vistas its visions open to the fancy. It is the seeing eye here, therefore, rather than the nice scales of linguistic science, that is needful more obviously than in most sections of Scripture.

In the apocalyptic genre, infallible teaching had less to do with the assertions of individual verses than with the broad picture that the book limned; thus the book cried out for a different hermeneutic than the discursive portions of the Bible. Warfield's comment is a reminder that his notion of biblical inerrancy sometimes functioned as a more subtle and discriminating tool than is commonly supposed. At precisely this point he broke decisively with dispensationalists, who treated apocalyptic and prophetic writings as if they were encrypted texts that, once decoded, would yield predictive precision verse by verse. Warfield also believed that the broad picture outlined in Revelation as well as in other portions of Scripture would not sustain the notion that Christ had to come on the clouds of heaven, like a warrior chieftain, in order to win the world. He granted the dispensationalist assumption that "the Gospel assuredly must be preached to the whole world as a witness before the Lord comes." But unlike the premillennialists, he assumed that this preaching accomplished more than simply converting a few individuals in each

---

Sandeen, *Roots of Fundamentalism;* Marsden, *Fundamentalism and American Culture,* esp. 43-71; and Timothy Weber, *Living in the Shadow of the Second Coming: American Premillennialism, 1875-1982,* enlarged ed. (Chicago: University of Chicago Press, 1987), esp. 3-104.

place. "These visions seem to go farther," he insisted, "and to teach that the earth — the whole world — must be won to Christ before he comes." This vision of the church's destiny — a view he shared with Charles Hodge — sounded distinctly postmillennial, yet technically it was not. Warfield did not use Revelation 20 as the basis of his view of the triumph of the church prior to the Second Coming, for he believed that the so-called millennium of that chapter described the saints in heaven. Nor, for the most part, did Warfield follow those postmillennialists who sometimes made the earthly triumph of Christianity appear merely a religious gloss on secular progress; and he seldom, if ever, used eschatological imagery as a way of trumpeting the United States' special mission. But he did believe that Christianity had a mission to transform and redeem all aspects of life and culture, not simply to pluck persons from eternal damnation. "For it is only as we realize," he said in a somewhat different context, "that God is saving the world and not merely one individual here and there out of the world, that the profound significance of the earthly life to the Christian can be properly apprehended." This was a view fundamentally separating Warfield from the millenarians.[23]

If Warfield's criticisms of premillennialism were relatively few, he had much more to say against another tendency among evangelical Protestants. Throughout the nineteenth century, various movements held out the possibility of believers' attaining in this life a more exalted holiness, a greater triumph over sin, than most had previously thought possible. American Methodism, growing dramatically in the nineteenth century, disseminated John Wesley's ideal of a second blessing that could bring perfect love and freedom from all known sin. But the message did not cease at the borders of one denomination. For example, at Oberlin College after the mid-1830s, Charles Finney, one of Old Princeton's great nemeses, advanced similar sentiments; and in 1858 the New School Presbyterian minister William E. Boardman espoused what he called in a book of the same name, *The Higher Christian Life*. After the Civil War, one stream of the holiness movement spoke in a Wesleyan idiom and derived the vast majority of its adherents from that tradition. Another current of holiness flowed from the Keswick movement, which grew out of a series of meetings organized in England in 1873 by Americans William Boardman and Hannah Whittall Smith along with her husband, Robert Pearsall Smith.

23. Benjamin B. Warfield, "The Millennium and the Apocalypse," *Princeton Theological Review* 2 (1904): 599-617; quotations on 602, 616.

Designed to promote holiness, the meetings drew an enthusiastic response, prompting the holding after 1875 of a regular conference at Keswick in England's Lake District. Under the influence of Anglican clergyman H. W. Webb-Peploe, Keswick teaching evolved into a distinctly non-Wesleyan form of perfectionism. Webb-Peploe stressed that Christians might triumph over all known sins, but he rejected what he believed to be the teaching of many Methodist interpreters: namely, that the innate sinfulness of human nature could be eradicated in this life. Men and women, said the Keswick teachers, remained liable to sin all their days; but if they yielded themselves to Christ, his grace would counteract their sinful nature, give them victory over sin, and empower them for greater Christian service — as long as they maintained the posture of surrender. The emphasis upon power for service was in particular a hallmark of the movement. Keswick ideas spread to the United States in part through speakers at summer conferences at Northfield, Massachusetts, organized by the premier evangelist of the era, Dwight L. Moody. Charles G. Trumbull, who edited *The Sunday School Times,* advanced both dispensationalism and the victorious life through that popular magazine. Trumbull, in fact, was typical of many late-nineteenth-century conservative Protestants who simultaneously endorsed the higher or victorious life even as they adhered to some form of premillennialism.[24]

In a series of careful essays, Warfield evaluated the permutations of the holiness movement and found little to approve. Behind the late-nineteenth- and early-twentieth-century figures such as the Smiths or Charles Trumbull, he saw the shadows of Charles Finney and John Wesley — and, still further back, Jacobus Arminius and Pelagius. In Warfield's assessment, the higher or victorious life movement suffered, whatever its precise form, from a fatal flaw: holding an inadequate view of the depth of sin, it assumed that there was something that the human being could contribute to redemption and was unwilling to rest on God in Christ alone for salvation. "God stands always helplessly by," Warfield mocked in an article three years before his death, "until man calls Him into action by opening a channel into which His energies may flow. It sounds dreadfully like turning on the steam or electricity.... Everywhere and always the initiative belongs to man; everywhere and always God's

24. Marsden, *Fundamentalism and American Culture,* 72-101. James H. Moorhead, "The Quest for Holiness in American Protestantism," *Interpretation* 53 (October 1999): 365-79, views the holiness movement within the broad sweep of American religious history.

action is suspended on man's will." Alluding to the fact that dispensational premillennialism and the various notions of the higher life had become theological fellow travelers, he remarked acidly:

> For the world they look every day for the cataclysm in which alone they can recognize God's salvation; and when it ever delays its coming they push it reluctantly forward but a little bit at a time. For themselves they cut the knot and boldly declare complete salvation to be within their reach at their option, or already grasped and enjoyed.[25]

In October 1917, in a series of lectures at Columbia Theological Seminary in South Carolina, Warfield took on another feature of popular religion that he believed represented a departure from orthodoxy: the notion that the miracles and other charismatic gifts manifest in the ministries of Jesus and his apostles had continued beyond the biblical era and indeed might occur today. The Princeton professor had no doubt that Christianity could not exist without the supernatural. He had told the Princeton community at an opening convocation more than twenty years earlier that "the supernatural is the very breath of Christianity's nostrils." His Columbia addresses did not indicate any change of mind. "When our Lord came down to earth," he declared at the beginning of his first lecture, "He drew heaven with Him. The signs which accompanied His ministry were but the trailing clouds of glory which He brought from heaven, which is His home." But Warfield believed that the signs accompanied revelation in order to attest its validity. Revelation being complete, miracles also ceased. This position was a classic Protestant one, originally developed as a Reformation polemic against superstitions and corruptions supposedly introduced by Roman Catholicism during the medieval period. In his early lectures, Warfield repeated the traditional allegation but updated the critique to include contemporary interest in healings at Lourdes in France; those more recent phenomena, like their medieval counterparts, represented "an infusion of heathen modes of thought into the church."[26]

25. Benjamin B. Warfield, "The Victorious Life," *Princeton Theological Review* 16 (1918), in *Studies in Perfectionism,* ed. Samuel G. Craig (Phillipsburg, NJ: Presbyterian and Reformed Publishing, 1958), 349, 397, 398.
26. Benjamin B. Warfield, "Christian Supernaturalism," *Presbyterian and Reformed*

Judging from the space he devoted to the subject in his lectures, Warfield harbored at least as much concern that some contemporary Protestants were seeking to replicate the signs and wonders of the biblical era. One group insisted, for example, that the healings in the Bible were wrought in accord with psychological laws everywhere operative; in other words, biblical signs and wonders were not miracles in the traditional sense. They exemplified natural laws of the mind that, if properly understood, allowed people today to produce similar healing. In this category Warfield included various forms of so-called mind cure, the most extreme being Christian Science, which he deemed to be little more than pantheistic nonsense. In this class he also placed less offensive groups such as the Emmanuel Movement. That movement, inaugurated in 1905 by Elwood Worcester and Samuel McComb, attempted to unite medical doctors and ministers in a program of joint therapy stressing upbeat religious counseling. McComb explained that the goal of Emmanuel's therapy was "to substitute for false or inadequate ideas of God and of His relations to men a conception of His real character as Christ reveals it, until the sufferer feels as if God were a new being, the very embodiment and guarantee of all his better aspirations and ideal longings." This, McComb argued, would bring healing. Although Warfield allowed that the approach probably did offer some healing benefit, he was troubled by the apparent reduction of religion to a form of medical treatment. "We confess to being chilled," he said, "when we hear of such things as 'religious faith and prayer' being looked upon as therapeutical agents for the cure of disease, and administered to patients as such. . . . We are too accustomed to thinking of faith and prayer as terminating on God, and finding their response in His gracious activities, to feel comfortable when they are turned back on themselves and — while still, no doubt, addressed to God — used as instruments for moving man."[27]

Warfield was also troubled by a group of Protestants, often holding

Review 8 (1897): 61; Warfield, *Counterfeit Miracles* (New York: Charles Scribner's Sons, 1918), 3, 61. For a perceptive treatment of the argument over the miraculous and Warfield's role in it, see Robert Bruce Mullin, *Miracles and the Modern Religious Imagination* (New Haven: Yale University Press, 1996), esp. 210-13; also useful is Raymond J. Cunningham, "From Holiness to Healing: The Faith Cure in America, 1872-1892," *Church History* 43 (December 1974): 499-513.

27. Warfield, *Counterfeit Miracles,* 203-4; Elwood Worcester and Samuel McComb, *The Christian Religion as a Healing Power: A Defense and Exposition of the Emmanuel Movement* (New York: Moffatt, Yard and Company, 1909), 63, 203.

premillennial or perfectionist views, who argued that the biblical promises of miraculous healings had not ceased but could be expected to continue, especially as the last days drew nigh. He dismissed some of these people out of hand — for example, John Alexander Dowie, who had organized a utopian community north of Chicago and who contributed to the early Pentecostal movement. But he took more seriously other late-nineteenth-century figures such as Baptist pastor A. J. Gordon, founder of what later became Gordon-Conwell; William Boardman, who had written *The Higher Christian Life* and also published *The Great Physician;* and Charles E. Cullis, an Episcopal layman and homeopathic physician, who founded the Home for Indigent and Incurable Consumptives in Boston. Warfield also took note of similar individual and healing facilities in Europe. How seriously he regarded these phenomena may be judged by the fact that he not only analyzed their exegesis of the Bible and the soundness of their theology; he also cited articles from the *American Journal of Psychology* as well as the opinions of famous physicians such as William Osler, a founding member of the Johns Hopkins School of Medicine, and Jean-Martin Charcot, a distinguished pioneer in the fields of neurology and psychology. Here one sees Warfield's conviction that ultimately the truth of science must be congruent with the truth of Scripture. (Perhaps here one also sees — though this is speculation — a husband who had recently lost his invalid wife and who had possibly pored through medical literature, hoping in vain to find a cure for her.) In various ways, the advocates of divine healing tried to connect Christ's redemption of humanity from sin to the notion of redemption from disease. As with other forms of mind cure, Warfield had no doubt that some of the practices they advocated might have a therapeutic value, but he insisted that it would be a mistake to think of such healing as miraculous. He particularly feared that those who looked for a miracle would ignore the means to health that God had provided in the natural order. Or, as he observed:

> He who prays for a harvest, and does not plough, and sow, and reap, is a fanatic. He who prays for salvation and does not work out his own salvation is certainly a Quietist, and may become an Antinomian. He who prays for healing and does not employ all the means of healing within his reach — hygiene, nursing, medicine, surgery, — unless God has promised to heal him in the specific mode of precise miracle, is certainly a fanatic and may become also a suicide.

Even though the would-be healers were correct that ultimately redemption was for the body as well as the soul and would bring release from disease as well as from sin, they misunderstood the process by which God brought about this end — an end that would not be fully achieved until the Last Judgment and the next life. For an inveterate Calvinist like Warfield, to claim for this life too much in the way of perfection, whether of the spirit or of the flesh, was to misunderstand how God worked.[28]

Warfield could on occasion participate in common ventures with people who held views on holiness, millenarianism, or healing that he did not share. The most notable instance was his contribution to the series of twelve paperback volumes, *The Fundamentals,* published between 1910 and 1915. Warfield wrote on the absolute centrality of the deity of Christ for Christianity. Funded by wealthy California oilmen Lyman and Milton Stewart, the larger project was organized by persons who adhered to premillennialism and to some form of higher life theology. But the harder forms of dispensational theology were largely ignored in the essays because the promoters of the volumes wished to assemble a broad coalition to combat perceived modernist deviations from classic Christianity. They also wanted a common front against historic enemies such as Roman Catholicism as well as new sectarian movements — for example, the Russellites or Watchtower Society (today known as the Jehovah's Witnesses) and Mary Baker Eddy's Christian Science. More than three million individual volumes were sent *gratis* to seminarians, theological professors, clergy, Sunday school superintendents, missionaries, and YMCA and YWCA secretaries.[29]

About the same time that he wrote for *The Fundamentals,* Warfield also published an article on Calvin's doctrine of creation, which asserted that the Genevan reformer, though he obviously knew nothing of modern science and its notions of evolution, had presented a doctrine of creation fully consistent with those theories. It had long been Warfield's view that the hypothesis of biological evolution, if it were not construed to exclude God's ultimate superintendence of the process nor to deny the special creation of the human soul, might be consistent with a Christian worldview. He resisted strenuously, of course, any interpretation

28. Warfield, *Counterfeit Miracles,* 165, 176-77; Grant Wacker, "Marching to Zion: Religion in a Modern Utopian Community," *Church History* 54 (December 1985): 496-511; Scott M. Gibson, *A. J. Gordon: American Premillennialist* (Lanham, MD: University Press of America, 2001).

29. Marsden, *Fundamentalism and American Culture,* 118-23.

that barred divine teleology from the world. He was also deeply suspicious of those thinkers who turned evolution into a grand theory of everything — the key to the explanation of society, history, and theology itself. Down that interpretive path lay the road to the subjectivism and relativism that he — like Charles Hodge before him — believed would destroy Christian faith itself. These caveats notwithstanding, it is remarkable that in 1915, only a few years before some who shared Warfield's distrust of modernism launched an anti-evolution crusade, he was still asserting the possible compatibility of Christianity with the theory.[30]

Conclusion

Benjamin Warfield does not fit easily into the stereotypes forged after the religious conflicts of the 1920s and '30s. He founded his beliefs on an inerrant Bible that he also thought to be thoroughly human. Theology, rock solid as the faith once delivered to the saints, was a progressive science as well. God created the heavens and the earth, but evolution might well prove an accurate scientific hypothesis.

In the latter years of his life, Warfield's position on the theological landscape of higher education was becoming a lonelier one, as illustrated by a 1910 symposium in the pages of the *American Journal of Theology*. Warfield, William Adams Brown of Union Seminary, New York, and Gerald Birney Smith of the University of Chicago assessed "the task and method of systematic theology." Reasserting ideas that he had espoused for decades, Warfield insisted that theology was "an attempt to reflect in the mirror of the human consciousness the God who reveals himself in his works and word, and as he has revealed himself"; it was emphatically *not* the study of the religious experience and ideas of those who have called themselves Christians, as important as these might be. By contrast, William Adams Brown, who had studied with Harnack and taught church history before taking up theology, insisted that the study of history was quite central to the task of the theologian. "Modern theology is

---

30. Benjamin Warfield, "Calvin's Doctrine of the Creation," *Princeton Theological Review* 13 (1915), in *Calvin and Calvinism*, 304, 305. On the complexities and changes of Warfield's thought on evolution, see David N. Livingstone and Mark A. Noll, "B. B. Warfield (1851-1921): A Biblical Inerrantist as Evolutionist," *Isis* 91 (June 2000): 283-304; and Bradley John Gundlach, "The Evolution Question at Princeton, 1845-1929" (Ph.D. Dissertation, University of Rochester, 1995), 105-49.

primarily concerned with finding out what Christianity is as an actual fact of human experience," and the only way to do that was to follow Christianity through all of its historic manifestations. Gerald Birney Smith, though a former student of Brown and himself indebted to the Ritschl-Harnack tradition, thought theology had to move beyond it. He suggested that theology had to give up the dream of an absolute standard of truth in favor of a functional, down-to-earth approach. Smith asked, "If, by analyzing the historical conditions underlying the formulation of religious belief in the past, we understand its significance, would not an equally thorough analysis of the conditions of modern life suggest the form of religious belief which would contribute most powerfully to life's victory in our day?" In other words, the ultimate test for theology was to produce religious and moral ideals that would help men and women meet the pressing issues of the twentieth century. Smith and others like him represented a pragmatic view well described by Louis Menand. That notion assumed "that ideas are not 'out there' waiting to be discovered, but are tools — like forks and knives and microchips — that people devise to cope with the world in which they find themselves." Because ideas "are provisional responses" to specific circumstances, "their survival depends not on their immutability but on their adaptability." That was a view obviously quite alien to Benjamin Warfield and his Princeton colleagues.[31]

At the same time, Warfield also adhered to positions that put him at odds with popular movements gaining strength in conservative sectors of Protestantism. Students with premillennial and holiness ideals certainly came to Princeton to study, and Warfield did not manifest the animus toward their ideas that he did against liberalism. In fact, on matters of biblical authority and certain areas of traditional doctrine such as the deity of Christ, he shared much with them. Yet he clearly was ill at ease with the growing fascination with holiness and millenarian ideas among conservative Protestants.

31. Benjamin B. Warfield, Williams Adams Brown, and Gerald B. Smith, "The Task and Method of Systematic Theology," *American Journal of Theology* 14 (April 1910): 192-233; quotations from 204, 206, 223; Louis Menand, *The Metaphysical Club* (New York: Farrar, Straus and Giroux, 2001), xi-xii. On Brown and Smith, see Gary Dorrien, *The Making of American Liberal Theology: Idealism, Realism, and Modernity, 1900-1950* (Louisville: Westminster John Knox Press, 2003), 21-62, 256-62. For a classic overview of the rise of liberalism in America, see William R. Hutchison, *The Modernist Impulse in American Protestantism* (Cambridge: Harvard University Press, 1976).

Princeton was becoming isolated on both its right and left flanks, but to some degree this situation was scarcely new. At its founding, the seminary's leaders perceived themselves as standing between the extremes of radical Enlightenment and unlettered piety. One thinks of the young Archibald Alexander, piecing his way between the world of the skeptical, Deist writers admired by educated Virginians and the raucous evangelical faith of the Separate Baptists. Or one recalls the efforts of the seminary in the 1830s, while Old School in sympathy, trying to keep the two factions from splitting the Presbyterian Church. Or again, the efforts of Hodge in 1860 come to mind as he attempted to hold both southern and northern wings of the Old School together even as the nation dissolved into Civil War. In each of these cases, Princeton was forced to make choices and adapt to changing realities. Except for some minor changes in curriculum to which we will come in due course, it was not clear during the lifetime of Warfield what changes, if any, Princeton would have to make. In fact, signs of isolation were not the only omens for Princeton. There was also evidence that Princeton was succeeding quite nicely just as it was, at least within its primary community of reference — the Presbyterian Church. Briggs was forced out of the Presbyterian ministry for his views on biblical authority, as were Henry Preserved Smith and Arthur Cushman McGiffert; the General Assembly in 1892 affirmed something very close to the Warfield-Hodge view of inerrancy; and creedal revision of Westminster, when it finally came in 1903, did not seem to Warfield so very damaging after all.

And yet there was something new in the spirit of the age. Writing of the late nineteenth century, the liberal Congregationalist Washington Gladden observed that there was "considerable relaxation of the rigidity of theological dogmatism, and . . . [an opening of] the way for the examination of many traditional beliefs. There was 'the sound of a going in the tops of the trees,' — the spirit of inquiry was abroad." That sound in the trees was being heard even in Princeton, and what it meant was not yet entirely clear.[32]

---

32. Washington Gladden, *Recollections* (Boston and New York: Houghton Mifflin Company, 1909), 262.

CHAPTER ELEVEN

Hints of Change and Missionary Visions

T HEIR ACADEMIC celebrity notwithstanding, William Henry Green
and Benjamin B. Warfield did not, of course, constitute the entirety of the seminary faculty at the end of the nineteenth century. Others added their own distinctive contributions to the institution. In fact,
a major turnover of professors occurred in the late 1880s and early
1890s. In 1893, at his formal induction as the Stuart Professor of the Relations of Philosophy and Science to the Christian Religion, William
Brenton Greene observed: "This . . . is no ordinary occasion in the history of the Seminary. We are passing through a crisis unexampled,
probably, in the career of any similar institution. Of the seven professors who first welcomed me here as a student sixteen years ago, but
one remains; so terrible have been the ravages of death in that unequalled Faculty." Aside from William Henry Green, none of the professors of 1877 left: the Hodges (Charles, A. A., and Caspar Wistar),
Charles Aiken, A. T. McGill, and James C. Moffatt were all gone. To that
list might be added Francis L. Patton, who, appointed the year after
Greene graduated from the seminary, moved to the presidency of the
College of New Jersey in 1888, though he continued to teach a course on
theism at the seminary. These vacancies led to a series of appointments between 1887 and 1893: Warfield as professor of didactic and polemical theology in 1887; John D. Davis as professor of Hebrew in 1888
(he had already served as instructor for two years); three faculty members in 1892 — George T. Purves in New Testament, John DeWitt in

church history, and Greene as the Stuart professor — and finally, in 1893, Geerhardus Vos as professor of biblical theology.[1]

The demographic effect was dramatic. In 1886, shortly before A. A. Hodge died, the youngest two professors had been in their late 50s, the remainder being over 60 and one over 70. By 1893, except for William Henry Green and William Paxton who were in their late 60s, Princeton had a much younger faculty. The oldest of the new appointees was DeWitt at 50. Vos, a youthful 31, was the youngest of the lot; the others were in their late 30s or early 40s. But the generational shift did not indicate a fundamental change in the theological orientation of the seminary. If anything, a younger faculty — Warfield himself offering the prime example — defended, honed, and reinvigorated the tradition they had inherited from Alexander, Miller, and the elder Hodge. Of these new professors, George Purves was the only one who had a relatively short tenure. After eight years, he returned to the pastorate at Fifth Avenue Presbyterian Church, where his deeply lamented death cut short his service only eighteen months after his departure from Princeton. The others — William Brenton Greene, Geerhardus Vos, John Davis, and John DeWitt — served between twenty and thirty-nine years. These four men also exhibited interesting variations, standing as a reminder that, despite continuity and shared commitments, they were not simply copies of one another or their predecessors. They provide a window into inklings of change, albeit subtle, in Princeton Seminary. And at the same time Princeton Seminary was redoubling its commitment to the foreign missionary enterprise in ways that could likewise be regarded as a harbinger of transformation.

William Brenton Greene

Perhaps most like Warfield was William Brenton Greene. A native of Rhode Island, he attended college at Princeton, graduated as valedictorian in 1876, taught school for a year, and then returned to Princeton for the three-year program at the seminary. After ordination in 1880, he served churches in Boston and Philadelphia before his appointment to

---

1. *Inauguration of William Brenton Greene, Jr., D.D., as Stuart Professor of the Relations of Philosophy and Science to the Christian Religion* (New York: Anson D. F. Randolph and Co., 1893), 9, 32.

the seminary in 1892. The title of Greene's chair stressed the relation of science to Christian faith, but the school envisioned his academic assignment more broadly. Delivering the charge to the new professor on behalf of the directors, Ebenezer Erskine reminded him that, despite the designation of his official title, his chair actually "covers the whole department of Apologetics." Greene's inaugural address signaled that wider conception of his task, with science constituting but one of the issues with which his teaching would deal. His address — "The Function of Reason in Christianity" — offered a spirited defense of the role of the rational in Christian faith. While recognizing that some thinkers had gone astray by making too much of reason, Greene felt that the primary temptation of the age lay in "the folly and sin of acting as if God, who is the supreme reason, could be irrational." He saw such foolishness in the widespread notion that while "we feel and realize spiritual truth, . . . we cannot express it" in propositions. For too many, religion consisted in "sensibility" rather than in "cognitive powers." They had gotten matters backwards. Quoting Harvard philosopher Francis Bowen, Greene insisted that feeling "is a state of mind consequent on the reception of some idea." Since sensibility and feeling came from the impact of ideas, Christians could not rely on vaguely articulated feelings. They needed to marshal facts and arguments on behalf of the faith. Reason could, for example, present "evidence that Scriptures are the Word of God, and so to be received on His [God's] authority." In subsequent writings, Greene limned a fuller portrait of the apologetic task. Through careful observation of the universe about us and of the self-evident moral and religious perceptions within us — the spirit of John Witherspoon, Thomas Reid, and Dugald Stewart lived on in Greene — apologists could demonstrate the reality of a world outside themselves: moral obligation, immortality, and the existence of a supernatural, personal God. By establishing these facts, apologetics cleared away obstacles to Christian belief. Apologetics could not, of course, bring spiritual rebirth to anyone — only the Holy Spirit could do that. Moreover, Greene allowed that "sin has darkened the intellect as well as corrupted the heart." But properly employed, the intellect could be the instrument by which, as Warfield would say, Christianity might "*reason* its way to the dominion of the world."[2]

---

2. *Inauguration of Greene*, 38, 50, 54. On Greene's apologetics, see Tim McConnel, "The Old Princeton Apologetics: Common Sense or Reformed?" *Journal of the Evangelical Theological Society* 46 (December 2003): 647-72.

For Greene, the importance of careful reasoning extended beyond apologetics and played an important role in theology proper. It was the instrument by which the Christian made precise judgments about doctrine, and Greene decried efforts to blur differences among theological traditions. In an article in 1906, he deplored "broad churchism," which he defined as "the tendency to regard Church union as more important than Church distinctions." He saw it as "one of the great foes of Christian living," for it weakened acuity of doctrinal judgment and ultimately tended toward "mental suicide." It dishonored God by making his truth of less account than Christians' "intention and conduct. Hence, ethics soon supplants dogmatics. What is the duty that God requires of man? becomes the question. The inquiry, What are we to believe concerning God? loses all but a merely academic interest." Convinced that "broad churchism" had seduced far too many, he believed that "simple and practical preaching of 'the whole counsel of God' is the supreme need of the hour."[3]

Greene's concern for theological precision did not mean indifference to Christian practice. Near the close of his inaugural address, he suggested that apologetics might make the case for Christianity from the ethics it promoted and from its impact upon society.

> The examination of her [Christianity's] ethics should prove to us that to behold the "fulfilment of all righteousness" we must turn to the words and works of her Author. The investigation of her sociological applications and achievements should demonstrate to us that the regeneration of society requires no new and artificial scheme of life, but simply the practical recognition in all spheres of the Gospel of Christ.

Greene's references to ethics and to sociology were more than nods to those concerns, for at the time of his appointment it was understood that his academic responsibilities would include these areas. The board of directors made the assignment more explicit in 1903 by altering the title of his chair to the Stuart Professorship of Apologetics and Christian Ethics. In substance, this was the same job description that Charles Aiken had assumed in 1871, though under him the social dimension of ethics received relatively little attention. But Greene's years at Princeton coincided

---

3. William Brenton Greene Jr., "Broad Churchism and the Christian Life," *Princeton Theological Review* 4 (1906): 306-16; quotations on 306, 309, 310, 316.

with a growing Protestant engagement with what many at the time called the "social question." The influx of immigrants from eastern and southern Europe, the sprawling growth and disorder of many cities, and the labor unrest manifest in numerous strikes and punctuated by occasional violence prompted many to ponder what the churches might do to promote peace and equity within society. For example, in the same year that the seminary board of directors changed the name of Greene's chair, the Presbyterian Church in the U.S.A. created a Department of Church and Labor, which sought to engage the working classes and their concerns more effectively. The first such agency in any of the major Protestant denominations, the department represented an institutional expression of a rising Social Gospel movement aimed at making the redemption of society a subject of theological reflection and a goal of ministry.[4]

Greene shared many of the concerns of Social Gospel proponents but dissented from the theology and practices they recommended. He agreed that the social order had come to a crisis, he concurred that the church had a major responsibility for the welfare of society, and on occasion he used language about "bringing in the kingdom" that echoed Social Gospel rhetoric. However, he found the usual Social Gospel prescriptions to be wrongheaded. When the Baptist church historian Walter Rauschenbusch called for the clergy to make the "pressing questions of public morality" a focus of "the teaching function of the pulpit" and when fellow Presbyterian Charles Macfarland declared that the minister should be "the guide, the director" of movements to eradicate tuberculosis or to improve the lot of the laboring classes or to espouse one of any number of reform movements, Greene demurred. The church's mission, he insisted, is not

> fundamentally or even chiefly social. It is primarily and characteristically individual, and it is above all religious. It contemplates

4. *Inauguration of Greene*, 68. On the Social Gospel, see Christopher H. Evans, *The Kingdom Is Always but Coming: A Life of Walter Rauschenbusch* (Grand Rapids: Eerdmans, 2004); Paul T. Phillips, *A Kingdom on Earth: Anglo-American Social Christianity, 1880-1940* (University Park: Pennsylvania State University Press, 1997); Donald K. Gorrell, *The Age of Social Responsibility: The Social Gospel in the Progressive Era, 1900-1920* (Macon, GA: Mercer University Press, 1990); C. Howard Hopkins, *The Rise of the Social Gospel in American Protestantism, 1865-1915* (New Haven: Yale University Press, 1940); and Ronald C. White Jr., *Liberty and Justice for All: Racial Reform and the Social Gospel, 1875-1925* (San Francisco: Harper and Row, 1990).

saving men from sin rather than society from poverty, making them "new creatures in Christ Jesus" rather than surrounding them with opportunities for education and culture. It holds that it is thus, and only thus, that the church can do her work in the world. . . . It is thus that she will best meet the crisis and redeem society and bring in the kingdom.[5]

Greene believed that God had established three great "institutes" for society: the church, the family, and the nation. Each had a distinct function to perform: the church to offer true worship to God, the family to nurture the human affections, the state to guarantee justice. When the church made social reform a direct object, it abandoned its true calling. Its primary function was to preach the gospel of redemption from sin, without which no genuine social reform would likely occur or endure. Moreover, if the clergy offered guidance on specific policies or programs for the reconstruction of society, they claimed for themselves an expertise they did not possess. Ministers should indeed preach, for example, the biblical injunction that "the laborer is worthy of his hire"; but that does "not tell us," Greene added, ". . . how much in a given case is the hire of which the laborer is worthy, how far he is justified in disregarding public interests when he strikes, to what degree his unions may interfere with individual liberty." Similarly, whether public utilities should be owned by the state or whether the government should regulate corporations were issues of great moment, but Scripture offered no clear answers. Thus the clergy should not use the pulpit to declaim on such matters, and the church as church had no warrant to advocate one position over another. He thought the "Social Creed of the Churches" adopted by the Federal Council of Churches in 1908 to be a prime instance of ecclesiastical overreaching. Christians, as individuals inspired by biblical teaching, should indeed support appropriate reforms and benevolent causes. However, too deep an entanglement in these concerns by the church as an institution would detract from its central mission.[6]

Greene failed to draw out the full implications of his social ethics and sometimes manifested contrary impulses. As Earl W. Kennedy has

---

5. William Brenton Greene Jr., "The Church and the Social Question," *Princeton Theological Review* 10 (July 1912): 380, 381. For a brief sketch of Macfarland, see Susan Curtis, *A Consuming Faith: The Social Gospel and Modern American Culture* (Baltimore: Johns Hopkins University Press, 1991), 114-27.

6. Greene, "The Church and the Social Question," 389, 390.

noted, his views were often "ambivalent and ambiguous." While recognizing that government might sometimes need to redress social injustices, he seemed even more afraid of the "totalitarian state, socialism, and the repression of individual initiative." On matters relating to the relationship of labor and capital, he recognized that concentrations of economic power in large conglomerates posed problems, but he often seemed equally worried about government efforts to limit hours of work or to guarantee a minimum wage. In alluding to the vast disparities of wealth in American society, he exhibited no sympathy for policies to promote the redistribution of income. "Instead of trying to cripple . . . the multi-millionaire, we should pray all the more earnestly that God would enable him to recognize and to discharge his stewardship." In many passages, Greene seemed to be sounding an argument for what has been called "rugged individualism." "The trend of our age," he warned,

> is toward the depreciation of the individual. Machinery has ruled out handicraft. The lecture has taken the place of private instruction. The shepherd of souls who knows his own sheep by name is giving way to the evangelist who converts sinners in the mass and who has no sheep of his own to know by name or even by sight. Sociology is a more popular study than theology and the reason is that it puts stress not on individual regeneration but social reformation. . . . In affirming the individuality of each man's relation to God . . . [Christianity] affirms both what is most essential in the foundation of any true sociology, and also that which in our day most demands recognition.[7]

But despite Greene's use of individualistic rhetoric in these instances, he was not celebrating an atomized society and economic order whose principles were utterly libertarian and devoid of regulation. Behind his notion of the three "institutes" were hints of an older, more organic conception of society. Although the Whig party was long since dead as a political organization, Greene exhibited the spirit of the Whig ideology that had shaped antebellum Princeton so profoundly. Like the Whigs, he saw

7. Earl William Kennedy, "William Greene's Treatment of Social Issues," *Journal of Presbyterian History* 40 (June 1962): 92-112; quotations on 101, 107; William Brenton Greene Jr., "The Bible as the Text-Book in Sociology," *Princeton Theological Review* 12 (January 1914): 6-7.

society sustained by mediating structures such as church and family and protected by a modestly active state. He envisioned a unity of interest among social classes and anticipated gradual improvement of society through piety, self-discipline, and material progress. Even if his advocacy fell far short of what many Social Gospel supporters desired or what Franklin Roosevelt's New Deal enacted several decades later, Greene clearly wished society to exhibit something more than a laissez-faire ideology. His rhetoric was conflicted, but so, too, was that of many other conservatives of his era — and beyond — who struggled with the relationship of free market ideology to traditionalist views of society.[8]

Geerhardus Vos

Geerhardus Vos, the youngest member of the faculty at the time of his appointment in 1893, came from a background quite different from that of previous Princeton professors. In 1881, at the age of 19, he emigrated from the Netherlands with his parents to Grand Rapids, Michigan, where his father assumed the pastorate of a congregation of the Christian Reformed Church (CRC). The Vos family began its American residence at the start of the largest wave of Dutch immigration to the United States (1880-1920) and just as the previously tiny CRC began to grow dramatically. It did so in large measure due to its appeal to many of those newly arrived from the Netherlands and also because the denomination won over some disaffected Midwestern congregations from the larger Reformed Church in America. Along with the Reformed churches in the Netherlands, the CRC was profoundly affected by the Neo-Calvinist movement, of which Abraham Kuyper (1837-1920) was the leading light. At various times a pastor, an editor, founder of and professor at the Free

---

8. Gillis J. Harp, "Traditionalist Dissent: The Reorientation of American Conservatism, 1865-1900," *Modern Intellectual History* 5 (2008): 487-518, offers a helpful discussion of the struggle within American conservatism in the late nineteenth century. Harp sees Greene as an example of "traditionalist dissent." See also Gaines Foster, "Conservative Social Christianity, the Law, and Personal Morality: Wilbur F. Crafts in Washington," *Church History* 71 (December 2002): 799-819. Crafts delivered lectures at Princeton Seminary in February 1895 that were published as *Practical Christian Sociology: A Series of Lectures at Princeton Theological Seminary and Marietta College on Moral Reforms and Social Problems,* rev. 4th edition (New York: Funk and Wagnalls, 1907 [1898]); the volume opened with letters of approbation from William Henry Green and George Purves.

University in Amsterdam, member of parliament, and eventually prime minister of the Netherlands, Kuyper was arguably one of the most significant theorists of Calvinism and its place in modern society. Kuyper's writings are far too numerous and complex to summarize in a single chapter, much less a few lines, but several points merit brief comment. Kuyper wished as strongly as the Hodges or Warfield to reaffirm the central emphases of the Reformed heritage, but his mode of making the case differed from that of his Princeton counterparts. They believed, as this study has noted repeatedly, in a particular kind of apologetics. Arguments inductively made from the observed facts of the external world as well as from the self-evident truths of human consciousness could make a convincing case for the reasonableness of Christianity and clear the way for its intellectual reception. Kuyper, assuming that the regenerate and unregenerate minds operated on different principles, had much less confidence in this enterprise. For him the more useful activity was to identify the ideas that shaped every movement in history or lay behind each nation and group. Influenced partly by philosophic idealism, Kuyper believed that ideas were the drive shaft of history; and if one tracked them to their sources, they invariably had religious implications. He advocated what he called "principial thinking" that exposed these ideas and traced their organic development through history. At its worst, Kuyper's approach led to facile historical generalizations; but at its best, as James Bratt has remarked, it prompted "fresh, serious thinking about a wide range of concerns" and forced people to identify the presuppositions on which they operated. These notions provided an important backdrop to the intellectual and religious development of Geerhardus Vos.[9]

Despite the fact that Vos's father was affiliated with the Dutch seceder church, which normally remained aloof from the larger culture, the family sent Geerhardus to a public school in Amsterdam. When the elder Vos accepted the call that took him to the United States, his son abandoned plans to study at the seceder seminary at Kampen and instead enrolled at the Christian Reformed Church's theological school (now Calvin Theological Seminary) in Grand Rapids. He went on to Princeton Seminary, received advanced standing, and finished in 1885.

9. For an excellent discussion of the neo-Calvinist movement in the Netherlands and its impact in America, see James D. Bratt, *Dutch Calvinism in Modern America: A History of a Conservative Subculture* (Grand Rapids: Eerdmans, 1984), esp. 14-54; quotation on 18.

He scored an academic coup at Princeton by winning the Hebrew Fellowship for his thesis, published in 1886 as *The Mosaic Origin of the Pentateuchal Codes,* with an introduction by William Henry Green. As Green's introduction acknowledged, the book provided neither an exhaustive treatment of current scholarship nor an original contribution to the topic, but it did offer "an admirable introduction" for "intelligent readers" to issues at stake in contemporary Old Testament research — no mean achievement for a 24-year-old writing in his second language. With the money he received from the fellowship, Vos spent three years in Europe, studying first in Berlin and then at the University of Strasbourg. From the latter institution he received a doctorate in 1888 for a textual analysis of a medieval Arabic manuscript. While in Europe, he met Kuyper, who offered him a professorship at the newly founded Free University in Amsterdam; but Vos had already committed himself to returning to Grand Rapids to teach at the Christian Reformed seminary. There he was one of only three professors and carried a burdensome teaching load. He also found himself embroiled in theological controversy. Vos held to supralapsarianism — that is, to the version of Calvinism teaching that God decreed the election of the saved *before* the Fall of Adam — and his views created a brouhaha within the CRC. Most likely weary of both his heavy class load and being the occasion of strife, Vos finally accepted, after having initially turned down, an offer to join the faculty at Princeton in the newly established chair of biblical theology.[10]

In creating the position, Princeton was following the example of other schools, but the development was quite recent on the American scene. As late as 1880, no major American seminary or divinity school had a professorship devoted solely to biblical theology, even though the subject had been widely taught on the Continent for some time. The classic charter for the field had come from Johann Philip Gabler, who declared in his inaugural address at the University of Altdorf in 1787 ("A Discourse on the Proper Distinction between Biblical and Dogmatic Theology and the Boundaries to Be Drawn for Each"): "Biblical theology is historical in nature and transmits what the sacred writers thought about the things of God." This work was preparatory, according to Gabler, to the systematician's task, which "is didactic in nature and transmits the

10. Geerhardus Vos, *The Mosaic Origin of the Pentateuchal Codes* (New York: A. C. Armstrong and Son, 1886), vii; Ransom Lewis Webster, "Geerhardus Vos (1862-1949): A Biographical Sketch," *Westminster Theological Journal* 40 (Spring 1978): 304-17.

philosophizing of a particular theologian concerning Godly things in terms of his own mode of thinking, historical situation, denomination and school." In other words, biblical theology was descriptive, setting forth the teachings and worldviews of the various biblical writers; systematic theology was normative, using biblical theology for its reflection and judgment. As biblical theology gained currency in American schools in the 1880s and 1890s, its proponents often saw it as a means to reform traditional dogmatics. In 1895, Professor George Gilbert of the Chicago Theological Seminary announced: "Now it is the mission of biblical theology to furnish the weapons of truth with which errors in existing dogmatics, where there are such, may be destroyed, and to co-work, in the most friendly way, with systematic theology in the construction of a system of doctrine which shall speak when the Bible speaks, and be silent when the Bible is silent." So, too, when Charles Briggs delivered his famous description of contemporary scholars "at work with axe, and saw, and knives" to destroy "the dead wood" of outdated theological views, he was speaking as Union's new professor of biblical theology. It is little wonder, then, that Geerhardus Vos at his installation at Princeton observed that the birth of his discipline "took place under an evil star."[11]

Vos and his colleagues were not prepared to concede the field of biblical theology to critics of orthodoxy. Used properly, biblical theology adhered to the actual mode of God's activity disclosed in Scripture. While systematic theology treated revelation "as the material for a human work of classifying and systematizing according to logical principles," the biblical theologian "applies no other method of grouping and arranging these contents than is given in the divine economy of revelation itself." God's work of revelation "is a work covering ages, proceeding in a sequence of revealing words and acts. . . . The truth comes in the form of growing truth, not truth at rest." In part, God gave his truth in this fashion as an accommodation to the frailty of men and women. God's truth "so far transcends our human capacities, [it] is such a flood of light, that it had, as it were, gradually to be let in upon us, ray after ray, and not the full radiancy at once." Revelation also involved temporal movement be-

11. For the Gabler quotation, I am indebted to Karlfried Froehlich's translation as cited in Bernhard W. Anderson, "Tradition and Scripture in the Community of Faith," *Journal of Biblical Literature* 100 (1981): 5-6. George H. Gilbert, "Biblical Theology: Its History and Its Mission, II," *Biblical World* 6 (November 1895): 359, 364; *Inauguration of the Rev. Geerhardus Vos, Ph.D., D.D, as Professor of Biblical Theology* (New York: Anson D. F. Randolph and Company, 1894), 24.

cause of its very character. Revelation was more than the disclosure of timeless truths. "It constitutes," he explained,

> a part of that great process of the new creation through which the present universe as an organic whole shall be redeemed from the consequences of sin and restored to its ideal state, which it had originally in the intention of God. Now, this new creation, in the objective, universal sense, is not something completed by a single act all at once, but is a history with its own law of organic development.

Vos spoke in language redolent of the idealism and romanticism that had influenced him. Throughout the inaugural address, words such as "organic," "development," and "growth" recurred, pointing to the conviction that revelation is process and activity, life unfolding according to its own inner nature. Vos also contended that biblical theology's way of presenting revelation as "growing truth, not truth at rest" also cleared Christianity of the common charge that its doctrines rested "on an arbitrary exposition of some isolated proof-texts." Instead, biblical theology showed how those doctrines "grow out organically . . . from the stem of revelation." Vos, of course, was not the first biblical scholar at Princeton to have a sense of the importance of history, context, and development in Scripture. Both Joseph Addison Alexander and William Henry Green had emphasized the same points to varying degrees, but Vos did so with much greater force.[12]

Vos did add important qualifications to his understanding of the historical nature of revelation and warned against distortions of biblical theology. Too often the field was made to conform to contemporary theories of evolution. Vos thought biblical theology especially vulnerable to this misuse, for "its principle of historic progress in revelation seems to present certain analogies with the evolutionary scheme." Whatever the merits of evolution as an hypothesis in biology — Vos appeared to leave that question open — he vigorously dissented from the manner in which it was frequently applied as a theory explaining everything. "Evolution is bent upon showing that the process of development," Vos charged,

---

12. *Inauguration of Vos,* 9-10, 11; John Halsey Wood Jr., "Dutch Neo-Calvinism at Old Princeton: Geerhardus Vos and the Rise of Biblical Theology at Princeton Seminary," *Zeitschrift für Neuere Theologiegeschichte* 13 (2006): 1-22, 40.

is everywhere from the lower and imperfect to the higher and relatively more perfect forms, from impure beginnings through a
gradual purification to some ideal end. So in regard to the knowledge of God, whose growth we observe in the Biblical writings,
evolution cannot rest until it shall have traced its gradual advance
from sensual, physical conceptions to ethical and spiritual ideas,
from Animism and Polytheism to . . . Monotheism.

From that perspective, biblical theology recounted a developing religious consciousness, gradually sloughing off primitive and erroneous
notions of faith and ethics for higher and better ones that reached their
culmination in the New Testament. For Vos, studies based on this prem-
ise were emphatically not biblical theology. The discipline required that
"we . . . fix our gaze on the objective self-revelation of God, and only in the
second place . . . observe the subjective reflex of this divine activity in the
religious consciousness of the people." Biblical theology, in short, was a
history of *God's* acts and of *God's* revelation. It was not a phenomenology
of the Christian religious experience; nor did it imply that revelation was
"associated with anything imperfect or impure or below the standard of
absolute truth." Vos denied that the historical character of revelation in
any way relativized truth or limited it because of its appearance at particular times and places; rather, "the historic setting has been employed
by God for the very purpose of revealing the truth, the whole truth, and
nothing but the truth."[13]

Vos is not an easy thinker to categorize. He envisioned revelation as a
dynamic process — "growing truth, not truth at rest" — and he conceived
history, redemption, society, and the church as organic realities. Speaking
this language, he manifested the influence of Dutch Neo-Calvinism and
also indicated a receptivity to idealistic and romantic modes of thought
that had generally discomfited the Old Princeton theologians more accustomed to the Scottish Common Sense tradition. Yet on central theological affirmations he found himself at one with his Princeton colleagues. Like them, he would not allow that the historical character of
revelation implied imperfection in its earlier stages or that temporal context in any way dimmed the truth that God was disclosing. Unlike
Charles A. Briggs, he certainly did not see biblical theology as a pruning
tool for hacking away the "dead wood" of systematic theology. Nor would

13. *Inauguration of Vos*, 25, 26, 31-32.

he entertain the suggestion that progressive revelation was but a form of natural historical development. Revelation indeed occurred within history, but history did not limit it. The supernatural ultimately trumped history. Vos was attempting to reassert what he understood to be orthodox Calvinism, but to do so in an intellectually reinvigorated fashion with new tools and perspectives appropriate to his age.

In his scholarly work, Vos paid particular attention to incorporating traditional Reformed covenant ideas with his conception of progressive revelation. The eschatology of Paul was also a major interest of his research, as was the notion of the Kingdom of God in the teaching of Jesus. Beyond his contributions to biblical studies, he played a role in introducing to Princeton the Dutch Neo-Calvinism typified by Abraham Kuyper and Herman Bavinck, the latter a lifelong friend of Vos. Yet in general his immediate impact was limited. Although some students found him extraordinarily stimulating — the very model of the complete scholar — others saw his instruction as ponderous and, when not required, avoided his classes. Moreover, his scholarly productivity declined significantly around World War I, when he largely ceased to write the incisive reviews that had characterized his first quarter-century at Princeton. When he published *The Pauline Eschatology* in 1930, this was done privately, not through a major press, though the work was reprinted in 1953 by Eerdmans. During the controversies at the seminary and in the Presbyterian Church in the 1920s, Vos said or wrote little publicly about the conflicts, though his sympathies lay with the more conservative party. This intensely private man chose instead to give public expression to a lifelong interest by publishing volumes of his poetry. His relative silence on the controversies, his contemplative poetry, the decline in scholarly productivity, a certain dryness in the classroom — all of these no doubt contributed to the waning of his influence. But perhaps Vos's studies fell victim to the larger problem that Mark Noll has diagnosed in Princeton's biblical scholarship during the early twentieth century. It "never succeeded in setting the tone for either the academic or the popular worlds. It was too conservative for the first, too learned (and Calvinistic) for the second."[14]

14. Marion Ann Taylor, *The Old Testament in the Old Princeton School, 1812-1929* (San Francisco: Mellen, 1992), 261-67; George Harinck, "The Poetry of Theologian Geerhardus Vos," in *Dutch-American Arts and Letters in Historical Perspective*, ed. Robert P. Swierenga, Jacob E. Nyenhuis, and Nella Kennedy (Holland, MI: Van Raalte Press, 2008), 69-80; Peter J. Wallace, "The Foundations of Reformed Biblical Theology: The Development of Old Testament Theology at Old Princeton, 1812-1932," *Westminster Theological Journal* 59 (1997):

John D. Davis

Another young faculty member appointed as professor in the great turn-over of the late 1880s and early 1890s was John D. Davis, whose background was more typical of the usual seminary appointee than Vos's. A native of Pittsburgh born in 1854, he entered Princeton University as an undergraduate in 1875, a bit older than most students, his matriculation having been delayed by his family's financial reverses, which forced him to work for several years as a bank teller. Excelling as a student, he appears to have had a choice between two fellowships — one in classics, the other in philosophy. Years later, Davis's colleague Frederick Loetscher claimed that President McCosh had wanted Davis to choose the philosophy fellowship, but that the young man, Loetscher surmised, already had a "fondness for concrete knowledge" and a "rather pronounced aversion . . . to the abstractions of metaphysical thought." After a year of study in classics at Bonn and then further travel in Europe, Davis returned to Princeton in 1881 as a seminarian. As Vos would do a few years later, Davis finished the program in two years, and also won the Hebrew Fellowship, allowing him to study subsequently at the University of Leipzig in the field of Old Testament. He concentrated particularly on the nascent field of Assyriology, and that interest appeared in his first scholarly publication, *Genesis and Semitic Tradition* (1894), which compared the biblical account of creation through the stories of the flood and the tower of Babel with similar narratives in the Babylonian tradition. Back in the United States in 1886, he returned to an instructorship in Hebrew at the seminary that he had held briefly before going to Leipzig. The same year Princeton University awarded him a Ph.D., chiefly on the basis of the work he had done in Germany. By 1888, the seminary named him to a chair in Hebrew and cognate languages, changed the name of the chair in 1892 to Semitic philology and Old Testament history, and then in 1900 transferred Davis to the chair previously held by William Henry Green. Davis remained in that position until his death in June 1926.[15]

41-69; George Harinck, "Herman Bavinck and Geerhardus Vos," *Calvin Theological Journal* 45 (2001): 18-31; James T. Dennison Jr., "Geerhardus Vos: Life Between Two Worlds," *Kerux* 14 (Summer 1999): 18-31; Mark A. Noll, *Between Faith and Criticism: Evangelicals, Scholarship, and the Bible in America* (San Francisco: Harper and Row, 1986), 56.

15. Frederick W. Loetscher, "John D. Davis," *Princeton Theological Review* 24 (October 1926): 529-67; John D. Davis, *Genesis and Semitic Tradition* (New York: Charles Scribner's Sons, 1894).

After his study of Genesis, his major scholarly work was *A Dictionary of the Bible,* first published in 1898 and then expanded and ultimately going into four editions. In his preface to the book, Davis stated that his goal was "to furnish a thorough acquaintance with things biblical." To achieve that goal the *Dictionary* "has been made a compendium of the facts stated in the Scriptures, and of explanatory and supplementary material drawn from the records of the ancient peoples contemporary with Israel." The book amply illustrated Frederick Loetscher's point that Davis had "a fondness for concrete knowledge." Despite his own very conservative leanings, Davis was generally fair in recording the arguments of critics. For example, in the 1911 edition he cited Julius Wellhausen's opinion on various matters at least eighteen times, though usually to disagree. According to Loetscher, who had had Davis as a teacher as well as a colleague, the same attention to detail and thoroughness in covering all viewpoints marked his classroom. In his instruction of senior students, Davis was less interested in working through the themes of an Old Testament book as a whole or relating its contents to systematic theology than he was in taking a few disputed passages, having students research them in the commentaries, and then arguing the merits of the various interpretations. While some seminarians thrived on this approach, others apparently found it maddening to have as many unresolved questions as assured answers at the end of the day. On occasion, when his students pressed him for definitive answers, they received a "Perhaps" or "Possibly so." "His occasional Hamlet-like irresolution," Loetscher felt, was rooted in an intellectual honesty that refused to oversimplify "the difficulties which historical scholarship . . . dare not evade." Yet underneath the candor, the questions, and the willingness to wait for more light was Davis's "serene confidence in the truthfulness and trustworthiness of the sacred history."[16]

Davis had little inclination to push himself into the limelight and no desire to engage in controversy. Even when he had become the senior professor at the seminary, he sometimes sat through a faculty meeting without making a comment. He seldom preached outside of Princeton or took on ecclesiastical responsibilities other than attendance at his own presbytery. Despite his conservatism, he took no public part in the arguments over revision of the Westminster Confession. "He had no zeal for

16. John D. Davis, *A Dictionary of the Bible,* 3rd ed. revised (Philadelphia: Westminster Press, 1911), iii; Loetscher, "John D. Davis," 548.

controversy," Loetscher wrote, "but thought that training the children of the kingdom in sound biblical learning was better for them and for the kingdom than was the promotion of strife among brethren." No doubt contributing to these qualities was a somewhat introverted character that preferred the solitude of the study, and who found sufficient outlet for his sociability in the company of his family — his wife and their six children.[17]

John DeWitt

Following the retirement of James Moffatt two years earlier, the board of directors selected John DeWitt as professor of church history in 1892. He came to Princeton after having spent ten years as a seminary professor, first at Lane Seminary in Cincinnati and then at McCormick Seminary in Chicago. The first seventeen years of his ministry he had served as pastor of churches in upstate New York, Boston, and Philadelphia. He thus arrived in Princeton with substantial experience both in the pastorate and as a professor.

Perhaps as notable as the range of his professional experience was the scope of his theological training and sympathies. He was born on October 10, 1842, the son of the pastor of the Market Square Presbyterian Church in Harrisburg, Pennsylvania. William Radcliffe DeWitt's pastorate in Harrisburg — his only charge in a ministry extending nearly a half-century, from 1818 to his death in 1867 — had illustrated a measure of ecclesiastical independence. Although an Old School man, the elder DeWitt believed that the acts expelling the New School synods in 1837 were unconstitutional, and he repudiated the jurisdiction of both of the rival denominations in 1838. In 1840 he chose to affiliate with a New School presbytery and carried his congregation with him. John DeWitt's education mirrored his father's breadth. After studying in Old School Princeton, both at the college and the seminary, he took an additional year of study at the New School's Union Seminary in New York, where he was deeply influenced by Henry Boynton Smith and by William G. T. Shedd. Smith played a major role in reorienting New School theology. During a year of study in Germany, Smith had fallen under the spell of Tholuck and developed the central emphasis of his thought: a belief that

17. Loetscher, "John D. Davis," 564.

theology must find its center in the incarnation. That conviction prompted in Smith a deeper appreciation for the Reformed tradition as well as an ecumenical commitment, and he was a major architect of the New School's reunion with the Old. On the other hand, Shedd before the reunion adhered to the Old School and thus stood out as something of an oddity at Union; but he was a very unusual Old Schooler. As a college student, Shedd was exposed to the influence of Samuel T. Coleridge and his *Aids to Reflection* by Professor James Marsh at the University of Vermont. Despite his own theological conservatism, Shedd exhibited, especially in the earlier part of his career, an appreciation for romanticism and idealism unusual among Americans of orthodox persuasion. Shedd inspired DeWitt's own aesthetic sense, particularly an appreciation of literature and a love of the English "lake poets" — a love that DeWitt expressed in an article commending Wordsworth as a valuable help to preachers. From both of his Union Seminary mentors DeWitt acquired a sense of church history as more than a collections of dates and events; it was primarily an account, as he quoted Henry Boynton Smith, of "the course of one shaping, overmastering and progressive power, before which all others have bowed, and that is the spiritual kingdom of God, having for its object the redemption of man."[18]

DeWitt remained essentially conservative throughout his career. When revision of the Westminster Confession was first attempted a year after he had gone to McCormick, DeWitt opposed the enterprise. In the second go-round, when revision was accomplished, he served on the committee that drafted changes in the confession and proposed a brief statement adopted by the General Assembly in 1902. Although he dissented from some of the group's recommendations, DeWitt won the plaudits of his fellow committee member and more liberal Princeton neighbor, Henry van Dyke, who recalled after his colleague's death: "Dr.

18. *The Centennial Memorial of the Presbytery of Carlisle,* 2 vols. (Harrisburg, PA: Meyers Printing and Publishing, 1889), 2:131-42; Frederick W. Loetscher, "John DeWitt," *Princeton Theological Review* 22 (1924): 177-234. DeWitt attested his own indebtedness to Shedd in a tribute written on the occasion of the latter's death; John DeWitt, "William Greenough Thayer Shedd," *Presbyterian and Reformed Review* 6 (1895): 295-322. DeWitt, *Church History as a Science, as a Theological Discipline, and as a Mode of the Gospel: An Inaugural Discourse* (Cincinnati: Elm St. Printing, 1883), quotation on 29-30; DeWitt, "The Homiletical Value of Wordsworth's Poetry," *Presbyterian Review* 3 (1882): 241-63. On Shedd, see Cushing Strout, "Faith and History: The Mind of W. G. T. Shedd," *Journal of the History of Ideas* 15 (January 1954): 153-62.

DeWitt's contribution was of special value because of his knowledge of church history, his broad scholarship, and his irenic spirit." Van Dyke also singled out DeWitt's "practical experience as pastor and preacher" as a major source of his helpfulness on the committee.[19]

In DeWitt's own mind there was a clear connection between the work of the pastor and that of the historian. In the pastorate, he had on occasion preached Sunday afternoon sermons about historical topics and urged the senior classes at Princeton to do so. "In God's Revelation," he explained, "truth is embodied; it is given in the concrete; it is made known in the career of a people, or is incarnated and exemplified in the life of an individual." Church history offered the tangible, the readily apprehended, examples of truth that might move and inspire. Moreover, DeWitt said that historical sermons presented truth in a way that was "catholic and irenic" and thus likely to be winsome rather than controversial. In part this assertion grew out of his conviction that the vocation and method of the church historian differed from that of the systematic theologian. In his inaugural address at Lane Seminary, he offered as a case in point the Calvinist response to Arminianism. For the theologian, the evaluation is clear cut. "Arminianism is truth, or it is error." But for the historian, even one of "Calvinist prepossessions," the standard of judgment is different. The historian evaluates the phenomenon "as a system in action. . . . He meets it in the lives of the Wesleys; in the rise of that great evangelical communion which . . . has so abundantly blessed both England and our own country." In a word, church history allows the pastor to see that, while the theology of Methodism may represent serious error, we may invite the local Methodist pastor "as a brother beloved, to our pulpits and to our meetings for prayer" and "gladly unite with him as one of the host of the elect in labor for the redemption of the world." Church history, DeWitt believed, promoted "a catholic and irenic" spirit.[20]

Princeton and the Evangelization of the World in This Generation

That "catholic and irenic" spirit was also encouraged by the fact that Princeton Seminary at the end of the nineteenth century shared Ameri-

---

19. Loetscher, "John D. DeWitt," 223.

20. John DeWitt, "Relations of Church History to Preaching," *Princeton Theological Review* 5 (1907): 105, 106; DeWitt, *Church History as a Science,* 34, 35, 49.

can Protestantism's growing interest in world mission. To unpack the implications of this statement, one must first emphasize the word "growing," for commitment to the cause of mission existed from the school's outset. The Plan of the Seminary gave as one of the purposes of the institution "to found a nursery for missionaries to the heathen, and to such as are destitute of the stated preaching of the gospel." Students organized the secret Brotherhood in support of the missionary cause and also created the more public Society of Inquiry on Missions and the General State of Religion. The directors called John Breckenridge in 1836 as the first professor to have the study of mission as an explicit part of his job description. Charles Hodge sat on the Presbyterian board of foreign missions and the board of domestic missions for many years, and his son "Archie" (A. A. Hodge) went, along with his wife, as a missionary to India until her ill health forced their return. Frank F. Ellinwood (class of 1853) served as corresponding secretary of the board of foreign missions from 1871 to 1907. Then, too, one could add the long list of Princeton seminarians who went on to foreign missionary service. In an address at the centennial of the seminary in 1912, Robert E. Speer, himself a onetime student at the seminary and then a corresponding secretary of the Presbyterian board of foreign missions, estimated that from its founding to 1875, the seminary "sent one out of every eighteen of its students abroad."[21]

But by the 1880s, something dramatic occurred across the landscape of American Protestantism. It had begun with women's organizations after the Civil War. The organization of a Woman's Board of Missions (Congregational) in 1868 soon found eager imitators among women in other denominations. By 1915, more than three million women held membership in forty denominational women's missionary societies. In 1888, the Student Volunteer Movement (SVM) came into existence. Through its traveling agents, the movement preached the imperative of foreign missions on campuses around the country. In the next half-century, the SVM persuaded thousands of young men and women to pledge themselves to work abroad, heightened support for the cause within the American

---

21. *Plan of the Theological Seminary of the Presbyterian Church in the United States of America* (Elizabethtown, NJ: Isaac A. Kollock, 1816), 6; A. A. Hodge, *Life of Charles Hodge* (New York: Charles Scribner's Sons, 1880), 384-85; *Princeton Theological Seminary Biographical Catalogue,* comp. Joseph H. Dulles (Trenton, NJ: MacCrellish and Quigley, 1909), 215; *The Centennial Celebration of the Theological Seminary of the Presbyterian Church in the United States of America* (Princeton: Trustees of the Seminary, 1912), 420.

churches, and raised to prominence dynamic young leaders, such as Speer and John R. Mott, who exercised decisive influence on the shape of American Protestantism for decades to come. The watchword of the SVM — "the evangelization of the world in this generation" — stirred many American campuses as profoundly as civil rights or the anti-war movement touched a later cohort of students. Between 1880 and the early 1920s, major Protestant denominations dramatically increased the size of their missionary staff abroad and had a corresponding increase of program and personnel at home to support these far-flung enterprises.[22]

Princeton was one of the centers of this activity. In 1875, Royal and Eliza Wilder, who had worked as missionaries in India under the aegis of various agencies at different times, including the Presbyterian board of foreign missions from 1870 to 1875, settled in Princeton. Three years later Royal Wilder began publishing the *Missionary Review* (later renamed the *Missionary Review of the World*). Robert Wilder, the son of Royal and Eliza, entered college at Princeton in 1881 filled with zeal for mission, attending conferences on the subject and making important contacts, including the acquaintance of A. T. Pierson, who had become a prominent Presbyterian pastor. Right after his graduation from Princeton — delayed a year because of a period of ill health — he went to the first conference for college students organized at Mt. Hermon, Massachusetts, by the famous evangelist Dwight L. Moody. There Robert Wilder introduced the theme of foreign missions, and he and Pierson persuaded Moody to allow them to conduct special meetings on the subject. These meetings resulted in one hundred students — honored in missions lore as the "Mt. Hermon Hundred" — who pledged themselves to service in the foreign field. Two years later the Student Volunteer Movement was formally created. Even before the official organization of the SVM, Wilder threw himself into a whirlwind of travel to more than 160 campuses during 1886 and early 1887. His itinerary took him in March 1887 to his alma mater, Princeton, where Robert E. Speer, nearing the end of his sophomore year, heard him speak and was moved to take the SVM pledge. After graduation in 1889, Speer spent a year as a traveling agent for the SVM and then

22. Patricia R. Hill, *The World Their Household: The American Woman's Foreign Mission Movement and Cultural Transformation, 1870-1920* (Ann Arbor: University of Michigan Press, 1984); Dana L. Robert, *American Women in Mission: A Social History of Their Thought and Practice* (Macon, GA: Mercer University Press, 1996), esp. 125-88; William R. Hutchison, *Errand to the World: American Protestant Thought and Foreign Missions* (Chicago: University of Chicago Press, 1987).

in 1890 entered Princeton Seminary to prepare for a vocation as a foreign missionary. In his middle year, Frank Ellinwood visited Speer and offered him a post as one of the executives at the board of foreign missions. Speer accepted the offer without completing the three years at the seminary and was never ordained to the ministry, but spent his entire career as an executive of the board of foreign missions.[23]

The interest in mission at Princeton was more than a peripheral phenomenon affecting a student here or there. According to Speer's 1912 calculation, the percentage of students serving in foreign missions — one in eighteen between 1812 and 1875 — doubled after 1875 to one in nine. He particularly gloried in the class of 1902, "with the largest percentage of its matriculated students going out to the foreign field, thirteen out of fifty-nine, — one out of four and a half." By their more recent calculations broken down somewhat differently, Mark Noll and Peter Wallace come up with a rise in the number of Princeton seminarians going abroad as missionaries from a low of 3.9 percent from 1815 to 1829, to 7.2 percent for the period from 1880 to 1929, and peaking at 8.2 percent in the 1910s and 1920s. Despite some disparities in the number crunching, the overall conclusion is the same. Princeton Seminary experienced a significant surge in the number of foreign missionaries it sent out after 1880. The deepening concern for mission also resulted in a new series of annual lectures, initiated by students and to a significant degree funded by them, called (appropriately) the Student Lectures in Missions.[24]

What did these developments mean for the way in which Princeton understood its task or viewed the world? A single or simple answer is not easily given. At one level, the growing commitment to mission fulfilled on a grand scale the hope expressed in the Plan: "to found a nursery for missionaries to the heathen." But more students going to the foreign field, greater numbers of missionaries abroad, and bigger boards with larger budgets brought qualitative as well as quantitative change. For one thing, by the end of the century Protestant missions had been established in a number of places for at least a generation, and now visiting lecturers on the seminary campus or missionary literature available to

23. James F. Findlay Jr., *Dwight L. Moody: American Evangelist, 1837-1890* (Chicago: University of Chicago Press, 1969), 345-55.

24. *Centennial Celebration,* 420; Peter Wallace and Mark Noll, "The Students of Princeton Seminary, 1812-1929: A Research Note," *Journal of Presbyterian History* 72 (Fall 1994): 210, 212. On Speer, see John F. Piper Jr., *Robert E. Speer: Prophet of the American Church* (Louisville: Geneva Press, 2000).

students offered better information about those places, their indigenous religions, and the unique problems young churches faced in each of the different contexts. Many of the Student Lecturers in Missions dealt in detail with the missionary movement in some part of the contemporary world. For example, in the 1893-94 lectures, William Imbrie (PTS, 1870), just back from Meiji Gakuin school in Tokyo, discussed the Presbyterian and Reformed churches in Japan; and Benjamin Henry (PTS, 1873) four years later spoke of the situation in China based on more than twenty years of labor. Henry's published work had a tendency to fall into stock images that were derogatory, such as the "absurd and monstrous contradictions" of Chinese ancestor worship, but he nevertheless stressed the importance of the missionary's need "to study their [the Chinese] manners and customs, habits of life, and folk-lore" if one were to communicate effectively with the Chinese; and his book *The Cross and the Dragon* did precisely that. Imbrie seemed more appreciative, even lyrical at times, about Japanese culture and history, and noted its complexity. "The longer one lives in Japan the less the disposition to generalize with confidence and without qualification." He showed considerable sensitivity to the need to translate the gospel message into terms that would be understood in the Japanese context, and he quoted with approval comments he had heard from a Japanese Christian: "Spurgeon would have failed in addressing . . . assemblies in Japan; and so would Moody, if he had made the addresses which he made in Scotland and America." Imbrie even suggested that this translation might extend to creeds as well. "The church of Christ in every land and every age," he observed, "should have a Confession suited to its own peculiar needs." In light of such comments, the assessment of a more recent scholar seems apt: "Imbrie displayed a warmth and understanding toward the views of his Japanese colleagues that was exceptional." Even among officials of the Presbyterian board of foreign missions, scarcely a hothouse of theological liberalism, there was an insistence that the finality of Christ needed to be asserted in a way showing respect for non-Christian peoples. Thus Frank F. Ellinwood, writing in 1896 for the *Presbyterian and Reformed Review* edited by Warfield, condemned "the prevalence of a sentimental plea for the brotherhood of men and Fatherhood of God" that ignored the need for redemption in and through Christ alone. He particularly directed his fire at the 1893 World's Parliament of Religions in Chicago, at which many advocates suggested that the various religions needed to recognize that each offered a path to God. Yet, having reasserted the uniqueness of the Christian gospel, Ellinwood also acknowledged that missionaries did need to proceed with greater discretion than they had sometimes shown in the past.

> Missionary addresses will not hereafter be illustrated by the exhibition of idols and other evidences of depravity (intelligent Hindus and Buddhists have indignantly pointed to the images and pictures of the church); on the contrary there will be more of the tact of Paul when he referred to the altar of the unknown God.

It was also time, Ellinwood made clear, to be done with the idea that it was unnecessary "to know anything about what the non-Christian peoples believe or disbelieve since the one aim is to tell the 'Old, Old Story.'"[25]

Princeton also heard lecturers who dealt cautiously, if at all, with a major Protestant disagreement over the rationale for the missionary enterprise. The watchword of the Student Volunteer Movement, often attributed to A. T. Pierson, had its origin in a premillennial interpretation of Matthew 24:14, "The gospel of the kingdom shall be preached in all the world for a witness unto all nations; and then shall the end come." By this reading, the task of the movement was not to win the majority of men and women in the mission fields to Christian belief, still less to transform or Christianize whole societies. Some, probably many, would be saved, but the primary task was to fulfill the mandate that the gospel be preached to all the world within a generation so that the end might come. By contrast, moderate to liberal Protestants aimed at a more expansive goal to occur within the current age. As a Baptist theologian argued, "We seek the conversion of individuals to Christ, . . . we build up the institutions of Christianity, and we seek to leaven the entire life of the

---

25. B. C. Henry, *The Cross and the Dragon, Or Light in the Broad East* (New York: Anson D. F. Randolph and Company, 1885), 133, 234; William M. Imbrie, *The Church of Christ in Japan: A Course of Lectures* (Philadelphia: Westminster Press, 1906), 22, 75, 105; *Biographical Catalogue* (1909), 24, 325, 329. I have been unable to locate the specific lectures that Henry and Imbrie gave at Princeton and am using published writings on topics that appear similar to the topics of their lectures at the seminary. The assessment of Imbrie is from Augusta Moore Stoehr, "Mission Cooperation in Japan: The Meiji Gakuin Textbook Controversy," *Journal of Presbyterian History* 54 (Fall 1976): 338. F. F. Ellinwood, "Present Hindrances to Missions and Their Remedies," *Presbyterian and Reformed Review* 7 (April 1896): 193-210; quotations from 198, 202, 203. On the Parliament of Religions, consult Richard Hughes Seager, *The World's Parliament of Religions: The East/West Encounter, Chicago, 1893* (Bloomington: University of Indiana Press, 1995).

community with Christian influence and quality. In a word, we labor with the purpose that the people and their life shall become and remain thoroughly Christian, and the human race at length be Christianized." Yet in practice, at least until the second decade of the twentieth century, the debate was not so sharply joined. In fact, there existed what William R. Hutchison has called a tacit "collaboration in which cultural enthusiasms and promotional needs outweighed theological differences. This alliance depended in part upon both sides to accept — in fact to utilize — the ambiguities in the watchword's key term: 'evangelization.'"[26]

In the Student Missions Lectures given by James S. Dennis, one sees an example of the ways in which "evangelization" could be made to cover a great deal. A Princeton Seminary graduate of 1867 and a missionary to Syria for over twenty years, he had the distinction of being invited to give the student lectureship twice. The title of his first series of lectures in 1892-1893 was "Foreign Missions after a Century," and the second series, three years later, "Christian Missions and Social Progress." In the first series, he left no doubt that "the object of missions . . . is to give the Gospel to those who need it." And everyone needed it, for God appointed the gospel of Christ as "the one supremely blessed instrumentality for illumining the mind, arousing the conscience, leading to repentance, subduing, melting, and humbling the heart, and giving a gracious energy to the will." But the centrality of personal regeneration and witnessing to the gospel of redemption meant more than the spoken word. It "includes," said Dennis, "Christian education, Christian literature, Christian philanthropy, and Christian evangelization. It implies organized churches, native agencies, and Christian institutions planted in heathen soil upon a self-supporting and self-propagating basis." After their delivery, he developed his second set of lectures into a three-volume behemoth that offered an apparently exhaustive — and exhausting — catalogue of the beneficial social results of the missionary movement in nonwestern lands. Wherever Christianity had taken hold, it promoted industrious habits, restrained gambling, elevated the status of women and children, abolished cannibalism, introduced modern medicine, brought relief from famine, established orphan asylums, promoted sanitation,

26. William Newton Clarke, *A Study of Christian Missions* (New York: Charles Scribner's Sons, 1900), 52; Hutchison, *Errand to the World*, 118. See Dana L. Robert, "'The Crisis of Missions': Premillennial Mission Theory and the Origins of Independent Evangelical Missions," in *Earthen Vessels: American Evangelicals and Foreign Missions, 1880-1980*, ed. Joel A. Carpenter and Wilbert R. Shenk (Grand Rapids: Eerdmans, 1990), 29-46.

developed industrial training, produced better government, wrought technological advance, and produced a more prosperous standard of living. In this way, Dennis gave a sociological apologetic testifying to the divine origin of the missionary enterprise.[27]

The Student Lectures in Missions frequently put a premium upon cooperation among the various denominations. As Dennis stated the issue in his first series of lectures at the seminary:

> A conviction is growing that there is danger of waste in the multiplication of agencies in many fields, and that practical cooperation is the true method for reducing expenses, especially where churches of the same polity are working side by side, whose differences in creed are rather matters of shading in doctrine than of divergence in essentials.

These calls for comity agreements or possibly even ecclesiastical mergers made sense according to the pragmatic test of efficiency. They could also potentially be subversive of the rigorous theological precision that Princeton Seminary had always wished to preserve. They might even smack of the "broad churchism" that William Brenton Greene and others at the seminary condemned.[28]

Conclusion: Princeton at the Dawn of the Twentieth Century

Future accounts of Princeton Seminary will undoubtedly continue to feature Benjamin Warfield and William Henry Green as commanding figures, and rightly so. But other things were going on at the seminary in addition to the work and influence of these two men. William Brenton Greene, for example, serves as a reminder that social Christianity did flourish at Princeton. It was certainly not the Social Gospel as commonly understood. It was not the message of Walter Rauschenbusch or Charles

27. *Biographical Catalogue*, 24, 306; James S. Dennis, *Foreign Missions after a Century* (New York: Fleming H. Revell, 1893), 201, 213, 215; Dennis, *Christian Missions and Social Progress: A Sociological Study of Foreign Missions*, 3 vols. (New York: Fleming H. Revell, 1897-1906). For an examination of Dennis's thought, see William H. Berger, "James Shepard Dennis: Syrian Missionary and Apologist," *American Presbyterians: Journal of Presbyterian History* 64 (Summer 1986): 97-112.

28. Dennis, *Foreign Missions after a Century*, 222.

Macfarland, summoning the church to campaign for structural changes in society; nor was it a call for the church to make the redemption of society its immediate object. It was instead a call for the church to contribute to reform by indirection. As the instrument through which God regenerated sinful human beings, the church did its part for social transformation by preaching the renovation of men and women, one by one, through the grace of God. Despite the apparent individualism of such rhetoric, Greene did not hold an atomized view of the social order. He was promoting a vision of a properly ordered society in which the church, along with the other divinely appointed institutions of family and state, contributed to the creation of a better world. Many would have disputed the adequacy of his program to address the problems of the day, but it did indicate a social consciousness, albeit an essentially conservative one. That conservatism looked back toward a Whig notion — with its emphasis upon mediating structures, piety, self-discipline, and the unity of interests of all groups — more than it did toward an unbridled laissez-faire and libertarian vision.

Some of the lesser-known Princeton professors of this era also demonstrate that unexpected intellectual and theological impulses were at work (at least around the edges) in the bastion of Old School theology and Common Sense Realism. Who would have expected, for example, to find in John DeWitt a church historian trained at the unofficially New School Union Seminary — and by a professor (W. G. T. Shedd) who admired Coleridge? Who would have anticipated DeWitt himself recommending to his Princeton students that they cultivate a love of Wordsworth's poetry as an aid to preaching? In an institution widely perceived as teaching Christian truth as timeless propositions, one would perhaps not expect to find DeWitt insisting that church history aimed at analyzing theology "as a system in action" and that the result might be a more flexible and charitable judgment than the systematic theologian would render. Then there was Vos, influenced by philosophic idealism and Kuyperian Calvinism, who insisted that biblical theology presented "growing truth, not truth at rest" — a phrase that could be taken to suggest that truth was in process and not fully captured in static propositions.

The various professors also approached their tasks with differing temperaments and styles. Glenn T. Miller has written of "a theological bravado" in the rhetoric of nineteenth-century Princeton. "The Princeton theologians," he observes, "exhibited an almost Kierkegaardian willingness to suspend themselves over forty thousand fathoms and dare

the sea to engulf them. They acted almost as if strong belief itself was evidence of theological masculinity, and any sign of weakness would cost
them their theological manhood." One can indeed discern that attitude
within much that came from the pens of Old Princeton, but other attitudes were communicated as well. Vos, for instance, had distaste for
public disputation and often managed to express views obliquely. When
the Presbyterian Church was considering creedal revision a second time
and hearing calls for the church to make an unqualified affirmation of
the love of God for all humanity, Vos did not directly oppose revision. Instead, he delivered the 1901 opening convocation address at the seminary, "The Scriptural Doctrine of the Love of God" — an address in
which he painstakingly catalogued the many places in the Bible in which
the love of God was, if not absent, at least carefully balanced with other
divine attributes. Against the richness and complexity of the biblical witness, Vos contrasted the contemporary "demand that God's love, and
nothing but His love shall be made the keynote of every message Christianity has to bring to the world." John DeWitt, as will be remembered,
opposed the first revision attempt and, while serving on the committee
that eventually proposed change, nevertheless dissented from some of
the recommendations. But he did so in a spirit so constructive that even
wholehearted supporters of revision would later praise the positive
spirit he brought to the endeavor. Or one might recall the work of John
Davis, who took no part in the revision controversy or other public theological squabbles of the day. Instead, he buried himself in the minutiae of
textual and historical research, and even in those areas sometimes
hedged his bets with a "Perhaps" or "Possibly so" when faced with disputed questions.[29]

One must quickly add, of course, that none of these individuals
ever hinted, privately or publicly, at significant disagreements with the
historic theological stance of the seminary or with one another. To a
man, they were conservative. Yet they did exhibit shades of difference,
shaped in part by various backgrounds, fields of study, and personal
dispositions. It is doubtful that even a close observer would have seen
any portent of rift in these distinctions; yet Princeton Seminary was no
monolith.

29. Glenn T. Miller, *Piety and Profession: American Protestant Theological Education,
1870-1970* (Grand Rapids: Eerdmans, 2007), 9-10; Geerhardus Vos, "The Scriptural Doctrine
of the Love of God," *Presbyterian and Reformed Review* (January 2002): 1-37; quotation on 1.

In its commitment to the growing foreign missions movement, Princeton Seminary was firm in its adherence to the finality of Jesus Christ, but it was also opening itself to a diversity of voices. These were voices calling the school to wrestle with the specific beliefs of other religions and not, as Frank Ellinwood would have it, simply to point to idols or to paint pictures of unrelieved depravity. The voices sometimes called, with Imbrie, for a recognition that "the church of Christ in every land and every age should have a Confession suited to its own peculiar needs"; or, with Dennis, they proclaimed a message asserting that sometimes efficacy in mission might trump precision in theology.

CHAPTER TWELVE

Curriculum, Conflict, and the Seminary's Mission

O N NOVEMBER 13, 1906, Charles Rosenbury Erdman was formally installed as professor of practical theology at Princeton Seminary. His
chair had been newly expanded to include English Bible as well as a
number of other areas. In his inaugural address, the new professor explained that the times demanded an expanded place in the curriculum
for practical theology and an enlarged understanding of its scope. He
noted that the modern church exhibited many "novel features"; among
them were "increased intricacy of church organization," greater emphasis upon "social service," "the scientific development" of Sunday school
instruction, and the "enlarging sphere of benevolent and missionary
boards." Merely to enumerate these new realities was, he thought, to
"suggest the necessity of reconstructing and developing" practical theology. With candor and tact, he recognized that the board of directors, in
establishing his new chair, had also created a "delicate and difficult problem. It is to so adjust this enlarged department to the Seminary curriculum as to do no injustice to the other departments while meeting the imperious demand of the times in establishing this new chair." Erdman's
comment was an understatement. The decision to establish his position
had already proved more than "delicate and difficult." It had sparked disagreement within the faculty and portended even more serious division
in the future.[1]

The argument over Erdman's appointment in English Bible and

---

1. Charles R. Erdman, "Modern Practical Theology," *Princeton Theological Review* 5
(1907): 82, 83, 88.

practical theology was a sign of something much larger than a parochial turf war among academics. The struggle involved the theological vision of the seminary, and it signaled an effort to come to terms with changes in theological education, in higher education more generally, and in the churches that the seminary served. Behind those transformations lay equally profound changes within American society and culture. As Princeton Seminary entered this new world and attempted to meet what Erdman called "the imperious demands of the times," it was unknowingly creating within the institution a crack that would eventually expand into a chasm.

A New World for Theological Education

American higher education in the post–Civil War era benefited from an immense infusion of money from public and private sources. The Morrill Act, passed by Congress and signed into law by President Lincoln in 1862, authorized money from the sale of public lands to be given to the states for colleges offering agricultural and technical training, though more traditional subjects were not forbidden. Wealthy philanthropists such as Ezra Cornell and Johns Hopkins brought into being universities bearing their names. John D. Rockefeller, by a huge infusion of cash and the inspired choice of William Rainey Harper as president of the school, turned a small Baptist college into the University of Chicago, which quickly became a pacesetter in American higher education. Already well-established schools such as the College of New Jersey, Yale, and Harvard benefited from the financial largesse of wealthy donors and thus were able to add new buildings, enlarge faculties, and create better libraries.[2]

More money, buildings, books, and professors did not mean that schools simply purveyed a grander version of the same education they had offered in the antebellum era. Greater resources facilitated qualitative changes. Although colleges and universities did not hew to a single line, higher education in the decades after the Civil War exhibited fre-

---

2. For a classic analysis of the developments in higher education in the post–Civil War era, see Laurence R. Veysey, *The Emergence of the American University* (Chicago: University of Chicago Press, 1965). For anyone interested in the implication of these changes for the role of religion in higher education, George M. Marsden provides essential reading in *The Soul of the American University: From Protestant Establishment to Established Nonbelief* (New York: Oxford University Press, 1994).

quently recurring patterns. Knowledge became increasingly specialized and areas of study proliferated as faculties began to segment into the departmental divisions taken for granted in academe today. Specialization manifested itself also in the founding of various learned societies in history, economics, science, and the social sciences. Within the field of theological studies, for example, the Society of Biblical Literature and Exegesis was organized in 1880 and the American Society of Church History in 1888. Under the influence of ideals gleaned partly from the German universities, schools in the vanguard of educational change emphasized research as essential to the professor's task. His (very occasionally, her) responsibility was not merely to transmit received knowledge to students, but to advance the frontiers of knowledge in his specialty. The Ph.D. degree came to symbolize this aspiration. But due to differences in institutional and cultural contexts, this degree did not necessarily mean the same thing in America as it did, say, in the German setting. While the German universities tended to view specialized knowledge as a means toward the achievement of broader cultivation *(Bildung)* of the individual and as contributing to the formation of a worldview *(Weltanschauung),* the American university often lacked this counterbalance to specialization. This was particularly true in the land grant college with its emphasis on the acquisition of particular scientific or technical skills. At the undergraduate level, the multiplication of courses and areas of study made it impossible for students to take every offering or even to approximate that goal. Schools created an elective system that presented varying degrees of choice. That system — soon followed by the expectation that study would entail majoring in specific disciplines — freed students from the lockstep of a totally prescribed curriculum, but some critics also feared that it would weaken the common knowledge that all college graduates should share and that it might undercut the moral and religious element they believed vital in true education.[3]

An exchange in 1885 between Harvard president Charles William Eliot and Princeton's James McCosh at the Century Club in New York City offered a notable instance of the differing views. "Under an elective system," Eliot boasted of Harvard's program, "the great majority of students use their liberty to pursue some subject or subjects with a reason-

---

3. Alexandra Oleson and John Voss, eds., *The Organization of Knowledge in Modern America, 1860-1920* (Baltimore: Johns Hopkins University Press, 1979); see esp. the essays by John Higham, 3-18, and Fritz K. Ringer, 409-29.

able degree of thoroughness. This concentration upon single lines develops advanced teaching, and results in a general raising of the level of instruction." In other words, the elective system allowed students to flourish in a field of their own choosing and to become more than superficial dabblers in a variety of areas. At the same time, faculty could offer a higher level of instruction and more profound intellectual culture. Thus the elective system, specialization, and the research ideal all cohered. Eliot wished to extend student freedom to include behavior outside the classroom. Rather than policing their conduct as the *in loco parentis* model attempted — a task Eliot thought difficult in any event — the university should treat them as responsible adults. To treat them as children was to invite childish behavior.[4]

Although McCosh allowed the desirability of permitting some elective freedom and worked hard to secure for Princeton scholars of the first rank, he saw danger written all over Eliot's policy. "Education," McCosh maintained, "is essentially the training of the mind — as the word *educare* denotes — the drawing forth of the faculties which God has given us." Those faculties could best be trained via "a Trinity of studies: in Language and Literature, in Science, and in Philosophy. Every educated man should know so much of each of these. Without this, man's varied faculties are not trained, his nature is not fully developed and may become malformed." He feared that an undisciplined elective system would lead to precisely such deformity, and he was particularly distressed that a student might never study moral philosophy — previously the foundation of education in American colleges. Without the undergirding of that instruction and in the absence of parietal rules, the college or university might ultimately turn out irreligious and immoral graduates. He drew a picture of young men living amid the urban centers where Eliot wanted to locate universities. There, "in the midst of saloons, and gambling-houses, and temples of Venus," the young men were to be left to their own devices without supervision and without the wholesome influence of moral and religious instruction.[5]

McCosh feared what the new model of higher education might mean

4. "Liberty in Education," in Charles William Eliot, *Educational Reform: Essays and Addresses* (New York: Century Company, 1901), 123-48.

5. James McCosh, *The New Departure in College Education* (New York: Charles Scribner's Sons, 1885), 8, 10-11, 21. On McCosh, see J. David Hoeveler Jr., *James McCosh and the Scottish Intellectual Tradition: From Glasgow to Princeton* (Princeton: Princeton University Press, 1981).

for the seminaries and the churches. If, for example, the requirement in classic languages were abolished, what would become of students who, late in their college careers, felt a call to ministry but had never studied Greek? They might be deterred from going to seminary, and the supply of candidates for the ministry would diminish. In this prospect, McCosh read a portent of a future "division of colleges into Christian and infidel." While his fears may have been too lurid, he had legitimate reason for concern about the impact of the elective model for undergraduates upon the training of clergy. Seminary education had presumed that students would come with at least some knowledge of classic languages. If Greek disappeared as a required undergraduate course, perhaps some might, as McCosh feared, be deterred from going to seminary. Or perhaps, if a prior knowledge of Greek became increasingly rare, the seminaries would themselves have to find a way of adding the subject to their own already overcrowded programs. As Glenn T. Miller has observed:

> The decline of classical studies was a crisis for seminary curricula. The traditional seminary program was an extension of the collegiate study of classical literature and was, in effect, advanced study of the Bible in Greek and Hebrew as well as some theology and church history. Undergraduate study more or less merged into seminary study. . . . Most students arrived at the seminary well drilled in language skills, often able to read Greek with little difficulty, and primed to learn Hebrew. By 1900 that type of student was a rare bird.[6]

Despite overheated rhetoric about young men being left morally adrift "in the midst of saloons, and gambling-houses, and temples of Venus," McCosh had accurately identified another potential problem for seminaries: the new system for undergraduate education failed to require the study of moral philosophy, at least as previously understood. McCosh himself wrote *Our Moral Nature* (1892), one of the last textbooks in this genre. As taught in the American college, that discipline had established what purported to be self-evident truths about the moral nature of the universe and of the existence of God. This course served not only to integrate the undergraduate curriculum on a moral and theistic

---

6. McCosh, *New Departure*, 18; Glenn T. Miller, *Piety and Profession: American Protestant Theological Education, 1870-1970* (Grand Rapids: Eerdmans, 2007), 123-24.

basis but also to provide an apologetic paving of the way for Christianity. It laid a foundation upon which subsequent theological education could build. One remembers how Archibald Alexander began his work with first-year seminarians by offering lectures "in mental and moral science" to provide "a transition from college work." But where was the transition if collegiate work did not require moral philosophy? What was the connection between undergraduate training and seminary education?[7]

In addition to the issue of what they taught (or failed to teach) and apart from the question of their educational philosophies, the research universities by their mere existence altered the place the theological seminary had occupied during the first half of the nineteenth century. As Natalie Naylor has demonstrated, antebellum seminaries, as the first successful graduate professional schools to be established in America, not only educated a considerable number of parish clergy but also trained many of those who served as the founders of colleges, the presidents of those schools, and much of the professoriate. "The theological seminary," Naylor remarks, "was both the mother of colleges and a functional equivalent of the university in ante-bellum America." But once the post–Civil War research university arrived and began granting the Ph.D., the seminary's role within the scheme of higher education became less central.[8]

Some wished to recast theological education after the pattern of the new university; and, not surprisingly, leaders of universities with divinity schools spearheaded the endeavor. Charles W. Eliot, for example, called in 1883 for the elective principle in the education of ministers as well as of undergraduates; and he argued that the university, preferably in an urban and cosmopolitan environment, was the best place for such education. Sixteen years later, William Rainey Harper echoed the call, proposing that the first year of seminary education consist of a general introduction to the basic theological disciplines and that the remainder of the program should concentrate in one of the fields of study. He, too, assumed that a university in a city was the logical place to educate clergy.

7. D. H. Meyer, *The Instructed Conscience: The Shaping of the American National Ethic* (Philadelphia: University of Pennsylvania Press, 1972), 20-22, 130; Douglas Sloan, "The Teaching of Ethics in the American Undergraduate Curriculum, 1876-1976," *Hastings Center Report* 9 (December 1979): 21-41.

8. Natalie A. Naylor, "The Theological Seminary in the Configuration of American Higher Education: The Antebellum Years," *History of Education Quarterly* 17 (Spring 1977): 17-30; quotation from 27.

Harper urged that theological students be given the opportunity to become familiar with scientific subjects, modern psychology, and English Bible and literature. Perhaps most surprisingly for one whose academic passion was Hebrew, he concluded that the language should no longer be required in seminaries. At bottom, Harper was issuing what he styled "a plea for a curriculum which encourages specialism in the ministry, as opposed to the current curriculum, which requires the same work of every man." It was also a plea for greater integration of the practice of ministry into the program of study, for Harper assumed that appropriate field work or internships should be part of theological education. Finally, Harper and other advocates of the divinity school model wanted a theological curriculum transcending denominational particularities and embodying an ecumenical — or at least a pan-Protestant — perspective.[9]

Transformations in American society and in the churches also fed the desire for new patterns of theological education. From the 1880s onward, the "new immigration" (mainly from southern and eastern Europe) threatened Protestant hegemony. Well-publicized labor strikes, disorder in the nation's burgeoning cities, and muckraking journalism calling attention to hideous poverty among the underclass stoked fears of social upheaval. At the same time, the power of giant corporations and the wealth flaunted by the very rich — this was the era when Thorstein Veblen coined the phrase "conspicuous consumption" — prompted other fears. Anxious that they might be crushed between the upper and nether millstones, many in the broad, if somewhat ill-defined, middle class turned to reform — a desire that peaked in the politics of the Progressive era during the first two decades of the twentieth century. Many church leaders, proponents of what came to be known as the Social Gospel, also sought to address these problems. After 1880, a number of urban congregations moved beyond traditional forms of outreach to provide community services such as libraries, gymnasiums, non-alcoholic "saloons," medical clinics, employment bureaus, kindergartens, and workingmen's clubs. Styled institutional churches, these bod-

9. Charles W. Eliot, "On the Education of Ministers," *Princeton Review* 12 (April 1883): 340-56; W. R. Harper, "Shall the Theological Curriculum Be Modified and How?" *American Journal of Theology* 3 (January 1899): 45-66; quotation on 56. See W. Clark Gilpin, *A Preface to Theology* (Chicago: University of Chicago Press, 1996), 81-112; Conrad Cherry, *Hurrying toward Zion: Universities, Divinity Schools, and American Protestantism* (Bloomington: Indiana University Press, 1995), esp. 1-25; James P. Wind, *The Bible and the University: The Messianic Vision of William Rainey Harper* (Atlanta: Scholars Press, 1987).

ies aimed at what Charles L. Thompson, pastor of one such Presbyterian congregation in New York City and an 1861 alumnus of Princeton Seminary, called "salvation for the whole man for the regeneration of society." Closely allied to these ventures were settlement houses where volunteers lived for a time, seeking to rebuild society through face-to-face encounters among individuals of different classes. Out of these labors came a push for new specializations in ministry and new areas of study such as social work and sociology. In short, the Social Gospel generated new forms of ministry and gave impetus to the trend for the inclusion of innovative courses and specialties in theological education.[10]

Another potential challenge to the theological seminary came from the various Bible schools and training institutes founded after 1880. Although not the first, the institution founded by famed evangelist Dwight L. Moody in Chicago became the best known and often a prototype for subsequent schools. Moody believed that urban ministry required talented lay people who, with modest training, could be equipped for evangelistic work in the cities. In 1886 he challenged the people of Chicago to raise a quarter of a million dollars to support such an endeavor. He exhorted: "I believe we have got to have gap-men — men who are trained to do city work. . . . They have got to know the people and what we want is men who . . . go right into the shop and talk to men. Never mind the Greek and Hebrew, give them plain English and good Scripture." In theory, most of the Bible schools did not compete against the seminaries because they were training lay people, not clergy, for Christian work. Their closest counterpart in late-nineteenth-century American education was the normal school, which offered rudimentary training so that one could teach, usually at the elementary level. Most normal schools provided education pitched at the high school level or slightly above. In fact, the proliferation of Bible schools paralleled the growth in high school education. In 1890, approximately 200,000 young people in the United States attended high school; by 1920, that figure had soared to nearly two million. By the latter year at least forty Bible schools had been established in various parts of the United States. Through this network of schools were disseminated premillennialism, biblical iner-

10. Charles L. Thompson, quoted in Aaron I. Abell, *The Urban Impact on American Protestantism, 1865-1900* (Cambridge: Harvard University Press, 1943), 156; Arthur J. Vidich and Stanford M. Lyman, *American Sociology: Worldly Rejections of Religion and Their Directions* (New Haven: Yale University Press, 1985), demonstrate the way in which American sociology had Protestant origins in the late nineteenth and early twentieth centuries.

rancy, holiness, and in some instances divine healing and the manifestation of the primitive charismata.[11]

Despite the fact that the Bible schools aimed at training lay people, they offered a new vision of theological education potentially at odds with the seminaries. Moody's remark about putting aside Hebrew and Greek for "plain English" could be taken as a veiled critique of the seminary, and other leaders were sometimes sharper. A. J. Gordon, founder of the training school that eventually evolved into Gordon-Conwell, was particularly critical of the seminaries. He warned that the ministry was in danger of being "impoverished by an excess of learning, and that it shall attach the first importance to German learning and to Greek philosophy"; he hoped "that no more chairs might be endowed in the theological institutions for teaching the relations of Christianity to science" and that "courses in polemics, which stuff men's heads full of the history of all the heresies which have afflicted the church from the beginning might be shortened more and more, and that the time thus saved might be given to studying the Bible and practicing with the 'sword of the spirit.'" Moreover, as the decades passed, there were more and more Christian workers — often pastors as well as lay leaders — trained by these schools. Of course, the pull of academic respectability eventually made Bible institutes into colleges or seminaries. Witness the transformation of the Bible Institute of Los Angeles into Biola University and of A. J. Gordon's training school into Gordon-Conwell Seminary.[12]

Clearly, important differences divided the divinity schools from the Bible institutes. They offered education at different levels of sophistication, and the theologies animating them diverged widely. In the divinity schools some form of Protestant liberalism held sway, while the Bible institutes advanced millenarian, holiness, and biblicist views. In time those differences made the two enemies. Indeed, in the first stages of the fundamentalist controversy during and immediately after World War I, the struggle sometimes appeared to be a cross-town battle between the University of Chicago and the Moody Bible Institute. Yet one should not

11. Virginia Lieson Brereton, *Training God's Army: The American Bible School, 1880-1940* (Bloomington: Indiana University Press, 1990); Moody quoted on 53. See also James F. Findlay Jr., *Dwight L. Moody: American Evangelist, 1837-1899* (Chicago: University of Chicago Press, 1969), 321-38. Figures on high school attendance are from the federal census as cited in Edward J. Larson, *Summer for the Gods: The Scopes Trial and America's Continuing Debate over Science and Religion* (Cambridge: Harvard University Press, 1997), 24.

12. Brereton, *Training God's Army,* 67.

miss a common point that advocates of both types of institution were making: theological education needed to be engaged more effectively with the actual practice of ministry and to be more in tune with the life of the church in a rapidly changing America.[13]

Princeton and the Call for a New Education

When Charles W. Eliot issued his call for an elective system of theological education in the April 1883 issue of the *Princeton Review,* Francis L. Patton replied for Princeton swiftly and negatively. Patton allowed that there might be a place in seminaries for electives, but only within severe limits. He was certain that any system allowing "a young man to be graduated from a theological seminary without having studied Old or New Testament exegesis, ecclesiastical history, or systematic theology is radically wrong." In 1896, Benjamin Warfield added his voice to the debate. It was vital, he insisted, to achieve clarity about the function of a theological seminary.

> Our theological seminaries are not the theological departments of
> universities, but training schools for the Christian ministry.... They
> do not exist primarily in order to advance theological learning, but
> in order to impart theological instruction; their first object is not
> investigation, but communication.... Our theological seminaries
> are not training schools for the Christian ministry in general, but,
> specifically, training schools for the Presbyterian ministry.

In short, Warfield along with Patton rejected the elective principle, specialization, and the pan-Protestant ideal that inspired the divinity schools at Harvard and the University of Chicago.[14]

Warfield had not given up the ideal of students doing rigorous research or studying at the advanced level. But these goals should be achieved through "a rich body" of extracurricular courses, through

---

13. See Grant Wacker, "The Holy Spirit and the Spirit of the Age in American Protestantism, 1880-1910," *Journal of American History* 72 (June 1985): 45-62, for a broader discussion of some of the common emphases of liberalism and the higher life movement.

14. Francis L. Patton, "On the Education of Ministers: A Reply to President Eliot," *Princeton Review* 12 (July 1883): 66; Benjamin B. Warfield, "The Constitution of the Seminary Curriculum," *Presbyterian Quarterly* 10 (October 1896): 413, 414.

prizes and fellowships for postgraduate study, or through a fourth year of education after the required work was completed. He did admit that electives could, in theory, be permitted in the curriculum itself *if* rigorous distribution requirements were enforced to ensure adequate preparation in the several areas of study. However, a system of this sort would require, he believed, more faculty than most seminaries had or could afford to hire, and thus the issue of an elective curriculum was moot. He rejected the addition of "clinics" — that is, field work — as part of the course load, and he dismissed as "sheer folly" talk about the "over-educated ministry" or calls to make theological education more practical. In this regard, professors needed to do a better job of getting "the bridge built which would practicalize in their own minds the intellectual training that we give our students." In other words, seminaries did not need to make significant adjustments in their curricula; they needed to do a better job of showing students that their studies in Hebrew, in Greek exegesis, or in systematic theology were in fact the best preparation for the practice of ministry. Regarding the demand for more study in English Bible, Warfield allowed that some students did need more work in this area. Yet he remained adamant that "our theological seminaries can never make 'the English Bible' the basis of their instruction." Quoting a speaker at a recent meeting of the Presbyterian Alliance, Warfield hinted that perhaps each student should "at the close of his theological course . . . be prepared to pass an examination on the contents of the Bible from Genesis to Revelation." Warfield was prepared to supplement the seminary's heavily prescribed curriculum with extra courses, to make provision for an additional year of specialized study beyond the three-year program, and possibly to add an examination in English Bible. But he was opposed to altering the curriculum itself, which he deemed sound.[15]

As the new century dawned, Princeton Seminary gave little sign of veering from its course, and the appointment of Francis Landey Patton in 1902 as the school's first president confirmed the impression. Earlier that year, Patton had resigned as president of the university when faced with a palace coup that would have left him with the title but not the power of the office. Frustration had gradually built among some of the faculty, trustees, and alumni, who felt that Patton was not up to the job of making Princeton into a first-rate modern university. One of the ongoing problems of his tenure was the proliferation of courses. The difficulty

15. Warfield, "Constitution of the Seminary Curriculum," 435, 439.

was an unexpected result of policies begun by James McCosh, Patton's predecessor from 1868 to 1888. Although McCosh had no desire to give the elective system free rein and insisted on maintaining the distinctively Christian (as well as unofficially Presbyterian) character of the college, he was also determined to keep Princeton abreast of Yale and Harvard professionally. The search for excellence brought talented young professors who wished to be able to teach courses in their specialties, and hence the number of electives multiplied. The process continued under Patton and reached what P. C. Kemeny styles "curricular chaos." Although Patton was not responsible for setting these developments in motion, he did not seem to have a plan or vision for dealing with them. He also angered some when he was unwilling to appoint the promising young historian Frederick Jackson Turner because the latter was a Unitarian. Moreover, Patton showed little interest in creating a first-rate graduate school, and he had a style of management that many found indolent. In early 1902, several professors, including Woodrow Wilson, meeting with two trustees, hatched the plan that resulted in Patton's resignation and Wilson's election to the presidency of the university. Meanwhile, the boards of the seminary and then the General Assembly took the needed steps to create the office of the president of the seminary, and Frances L. Patton was selected. His administrative style, regarded as overly laid-back at the university, suited practice at the seminary quite well. Professors at the seminary were accustomed to running the day-to-day affairs of the school with a senior member presiding. Patton's notion of himself as first among equals rather than chief executive matched these expectations. His inaugural address also indicated that, just as he had taken on David Swing in Chicago more than a quarter-century earlier, he was still ready to do battle for the faith.

> Sooner or later I am sure the eyes of men will be opened and they will see — would to God they might see it now! — that the great battle of the twentieth century is in its final issue a struggle between a Dogmatic Christianity on the one hand and an out-and-out naturalistic philosophy on the other.[16]

16. Francis L. Patton, "Theological Encyclopædia," *Princeton Theological Review* 2 (1904): 136. For an excellent overview of Patton's presidency of the university, see P. C. Kemeny, *Princeton in the Nation's Service: Religious Ideals and Educational Practice, 1868-1928* (New York: Oxford University Press, 1868-1928), 87-125; quotation on 90.

Many of the appointments to the faculty in the first decade of the twentieth century likewise gave little evidence of innovation or willingness to change. Robert Dick Wilson came from Western Seminary in 1900 to serve as professor of Semitic philology and Old Testament criticism. In 1901, Caspar Wistar Hodge Jr., the last of the Hodges to teach at Princeton, began his career as an instructor in New Testament, moved to didactic and polemical theology in 1907, and eventually succeeded to Benjamin Warfield's chair after the latter's death in 1921. William Park Armstrong assumed the professorship of New Testament literature and exegesis in 1903 after having served as instructor in the field for four years. Also, in 1906, J. Gresham Machen started his career as a New Testament instructor at Princeton. Although these men sometimes differed on tactics, they would seek to perpetuate largely unchanged the legacy of Old Princeton.

The Appointment of Charles Erdman and Rumbles of Controversy

But Princeton Seminary was beginning to feel pressure for change in the first decade of the twentieth century. That pressure no longer came only from outside the seminary, but also from within. In 1903, students petitioned the board of directors for the inclusion of English Bible in the curriculum. Since the seminary's biblical courses entailed close textual readings of books in the original languages, the student request was in part a plea for a broader overview of the Bible — a study emphasizing the use of Scripture in preaching and in pastoral work. The appeal may also have reflected the fact that many students no longer had a strong background in the classical languages. The board responded with assurances that it appreciated student concerns and promised that "plans now in progress of formulation" would meet the needs expressed by the student body. In the meantime, the matter was referred to the board's committee on curriculum for study and recommendation. The faculty had already moved to discount the petition. In two statements written by Warfield and adopted by his colleagues, the faculty defended the current curriculum and emphatically resisted as "a fatal mistake" the substitution of English Bible for exegesis in the original languages. The faculty suggested that the problem did not lie with Princeton's curriculum but rather in many students' inadequate preparation, whether in the lack of sufficient Bible reading in their childhood homes or in their subsequent formal schooling. It was simply not the business of the seminary to remedy prior defects in student training. If seminarians felt they needed more knowledge in English Bible, they should turn to personal study of Scripture or to supplemental extracurricular courses that were already available to them.[17]

The report of the board of directors' curriculum committee in April 1904 took a more sympathetic stance toward student concerns. The committee recommended, among other things, that a department of English Bible should be created with the purpose "to secure as far as possible, on the part of every student, a general knowledge of the contents of the Old and New testaments; and to provide for a study of the several books with special reference to their use in the pastoral and missionary service of the Church."[18]

In 1905, Charles Rosenbury Erdman was called to the post of professor of practical theology and took up his seminary duties a year later. His previous history in some respects fit what one would expect of a professor in Old Princeton. He graduated from the College of New Jersey in 1886 and then, after a year of teaching in a private school in Germantown, Pennsylvania, returned to the seminary. In 1891, he completed his studies and assumed pastorates first in Philadelphia and then in Germantown. He married Mary Estelle Pardee, daughter of a wealthy coal merchant, in 1892. Thus, with a well-connected marriage and two Princeton educations, Erdman exhibited the ties to families of wealth or prominence and the Princeton pedigree typical of many of the seminary's professors in the first century of its life.

In other respects, Erdman was decidedly not from the usual mold. His father, William Jacob Erdman, had been a New School Presbyterian minister educated at Union Seminary, New York. The elder Erdman also served as the secretary of the Niagara Bible Conference, which convened annually between 1875 and 1900 and provided a major forum for the growing premillennial movement. Through his participation in the summer conferences sponsored by Dwight L. Moody at Northfield, Massachusetts, W. J. Erdman also became familiar with the Keswick move-

17. "Report of the Faculty of Princeton Theological Seminary to the Board of Directors on the Study of the Bible," Princeton, May 1, 1903. My discussion of the curriculum question has been greatly informed here and in following paragraphs by Ronald T. Clutter, "The Reorientation of Princeton Theological Seminary, 1900-1929" (Th.D. Dissertation, Dallas Theological Seminary, 1982).

18. "Report of the Committee on Curriculum," Princeton, April 25, 1904.

ment. Both premillennial and holiness themes appeared throughout his ministry; but they did not, as was often the case, foster a spirit of contention. William Erdman was, as his son later recalled, "a harmonizer" — a fact demonstrated in his pastorate in the late 1870s at the Chicago Avenue Church in Chicago, where congregants from diverse denominational backgrounds, drawn together by Dwight Moody's revivals, worshiped side by side. Similar commitments appeared in Charles Erdman's ministry. For example, he wrote an essay for the *Fundamentals* on the importance of the doctrine of the Second Coming. He later wrote a book, *The Spirit of Christ: Devotional Studies in the Doctrine of the Holy Spirit* (1928), in which the influence of the holiness movement was apparent. Charles Erdman set forth these potentially controversial themes in an irenic way. For example, in discussing the Second Advent, he recognized that the subject often generated disagreement and warned against "unkindly criticism of fellow Christians." The doctrine was of value "not for idle dreaming, but for the immediate task of evangelizing a lost world." It was a characteristic note that Erdman struck throughout his career. As historian Bradley Longfield has summed up the matter, "the overwhelming sense of Erdman's writings was that Christian living took precedence over matters of precise doctrine." For example, when he wrote a manual for instructing those preparing for the Lord's Supper, he suggested as possible texts both *Christian Doctrine* by Princeton's impeccably orthodox William Brenton Greene and *Being a Christian* by the liberal Social Gospel pastor Washington Gladden. Yet it was never doubted, even by those who came to oppose him, that Erdman was personally conservative in his own theological views.[19]

Very much like Dwight L. Moody, whom he had known and about whom he wrote an admiring biography, Charles Erdman esteemed Christian piety and a willingness to submerge many theological differences in Christian service to the world as vital. Those commitments were manifest in the range of Erdman's activities: a member of the Presbyterian board of foreign missions and its president from 1928 to 1940;

19. Charles Erdman, "The Coming of Christ," in *The Fundamentals: A Testimony to Truth*, 12 vols. (Chicago: Testimony Publishing Company, 1910-1915), 11:98; Erdman, *The Return of Christ* (New York: George H. Doran Company, 1922); Erdman, *Coming to the Communion: A Manual of Instruction for Preparatory Classes and Private Study* (Philadelphia: Presbyterian Board of Education and Sabbath-School Work, 1912), 11; Bradley J. Longfield, *The Presbyterian Controversy: Fundamentalists, Modernists, and Moderates* (New York: Oxford University Press, 1991), 141.

one of the founders of the Princeton chapter of the YMCA; pastor of the First Presbyterian Church in Princeton from 1924 to 1934 while still working full time as a professor; and numerous civic engagements. Somehow he also managed to write thirty-five books, including numerous biblical commentaries that analyzed the English text in a lucid fashion useful for devotions or for preparing sermons. He carried these responsibilities with humor, kindness, and sociability. Upon his death in 1960, faculty colleagues remembered "his prodigal generosity in making personal calls, presenting gifts, and assisting with financial aid those who were in need." They also recalled his facility with "the witty retort" and his ability at alumni gatherings to lead in song. "From the raucous 'McNamara's Band,' through 'Carry Me Back to Ol' Virginny,' he led us to the deeply moving spiritual 'Steal Away, I Ain't Got Long to Stay Here.'" That same tribute, however, also sought to correct any misapprehension that his popular touch or his writings on practical matters made him an intellectual lightweight. The memorial mentioned his faithful attendance at faculty symposia where heavy theological works were discussed and noted how in one instance he reported extemporaneously on "a most difficult book in continental theology in such a manner as to be unequalled."[20]

Despite these testimonials at his death, Erdman's professorship was not uniformly welcomed at its beginning. Benjamin Warfield acted as if the courses of the new professor affronted the integrity of the seminary program. Having already gone on record that the introduction of English Bible into the curriculum would be disastrous, Warfield, in the later words of registrar Paul Martin,

> served notice upon the Registrar that Dr. Erdman's elective courses would not receive his necessary approval as minors in the registration by candidates of B.D. courses in the Department of Systematic Theology, and maintained this ruling through the successive years. It can be said without fear of contradiction that disparagement of Dr. Erdman's courses has been a state of mind of the "majority" of the Faculty through his whole term as a professor.[21]

20. Charles R. Erdman, *D. L. Moody: His Message for Today* (New York: Revell, 1928); Elmer G. Homrighausen, Charles T. Fritsch, and Bruce M. Metzger, "In Memoriam: Charles Rosenbury Erdman," *Princeton Seminary Bulletin* 54 (November 1960): 36-39; quotations on 37, 39.

21. Quoted in Clutter, "Reorientation of Princeton Theological Seminary," 75.

The belittling of Erdman's work derived in part from the conviction that biblical study for curricular credit should involve close examination of the text in the original languages. Anything less represented a lowering of standards. One might also speculate that Erdman's background in Keswick and premillenarian circles might have rendered him somewhat suspect in Warfield's eyes. A deeper issue, not fully voiced until later in Erdman's tenure, may have been his willingness to tolerate or ignore theological differences in the name of shared devotion to Christ and common mission. This smacked too much of the "Broad Churchism" that Warfield and many of his Princeton colleagues profoundly distrusted. But underlying all was the belief of these professors that ultimately nothing was more necessary — nothing more practical — than firm grounding in the Bible in its original languages, a firm grasp of the tradition, and a thorough understanding of Christian doctrines in their interrelatedness.

Student grievances over the curriculum did not cease with Erdman's appointment. In 1909, some students petitioned the board of directors to complain about the manner in which certain professors taught their classes. They singled out Francis Patton, William P. Armstrong, and John Davis as particularly culpable of poor teaching. Another part of the petition called for more practical courses such as sociology. The *New York Times* reported the protest and noted that the students' petition objected "to the slovenly, dull, and uninspiring way in which Dr. Patton delivers his lectures in Theism and Dr. William Park Armstrong conducts his work in New Testament history." According to an interview with one student, "You could hardly hear them, and it was all we could do to keep awake." The student claimed that some of his peers had earlier raised these concerns with Patton, who dismissed them sarcastically. Once the petitioners sent their grievances to the board of directors, Patton was incensed that they had gone over his head and used a class period to excoriate the protesters. A formal faculty letter expressed to the board its concern that the protesters were attempting to usurp a role in the governance of the institution.[22]

The board decided to investigate the matter further. Already concerned about a dip in enrollment and the fact that prospective students might in some instances be turning to other Presbyterian seminaries where part-time church employment was more readily available, the di-

22. *New York Times*, April 6, 1909.

rectors could hardly have been pleased to have stories of student dissatisfaction splashed across newspapers. (The numbers of students who had come to Princeton in the first decade of the twentieth century had declined about 15 percent over the numbers in the 1890s.) Shortly after receiving the student petition and the faculty letter, the directors created a committee to investigate the possibility of curricular changes. Its report in October 1909 recognized that the church faced a world that the founders of the seminary could not have imagined and observed that a number of contemporary issues might be profitably addressed in the curriculum: among others, "the relation of the church to the poor in the community, . . . the church and wage earners, the church and non English speaking peoples in this country, the church and civic and social reforms, the church and administrative agencies and finances." The committee also observed that it had heard complaints from alumni who remained "intensely loyal to everything in Princeton" and yet who questioned parts of the curriculum. According to those complaints,

> sometimes weeks at a stretch have been consumed in lectures in certain of the departments upon subjects of remotest interest to the pastors . . . while other matters in the same department, which are very important to the pastor, have been practically overlooked. It is intimated by way of explanation that this is so because professors who had themselves never been pastors have no true conception of the relative importance of different subjects to the actual work of the ministry.

Among the changes recommended was more opportunity in the curriculum to study "the practical duties of the Christian minister in their relation to the concrete conditions of the present time."[23]

In the end, the curricular change was cosmetic. Warfield again wrote a vigorous defense of the traditional curriculum, and the board of directors backed off, adopting rather modest recommendations. These included postgraduate work in every department and the listing of the appropriate courses in the catalogue, more emphasis upon the possibility of a fourth year of study, the establishment of graduate fellowships for

23. "Report of the Supervising Committee," October 1909. I base the 15 percent decline on figures accumulated by Peter Wallace and Mark Noll, "The Students of Princeton Seminary, 1812-1929: A Research Note," *Journal of Presbyterian History* 72 (Fall 1994): 204.

seminarians elsewhere who might wish to pursue advanced study at Princeton, a request that the seminary president annually offer "a short series of popular lectures" for the students, and the insertion of one credit hour into the curriculum to address "the church's relation to practical problems." That hour was to be gained by removing from the fixed course of study one hour of English Bible and turning it into an extracurricular elective or a course that could be taken in a fourth year. In short, the basic three-year program remained almost unaltered.[24]

The Centennial of the Seminary and Mixed Messages

In 1910, about the time of the curriculum decision, Princeton Seminary sought to address the obvious problem of image that bad publicity had created. It issued what, by the standards of the era, was a glossy publication filled with numerous pictures of the campus. The title — *A Modern School of the Prophets* — gave evidence that the seminary was feeling pressure to demonstrate that it provided an up-to-date education for ministry. The booklet noted that the seminary was bound by its original Plan to a course of study that had for nearly a century sent out "men of missionary zeal, evangelistic fervor, pastoral loyalty, and scholarly ability." Yet, recently "a great agitation . . . in the secular as well as the religious press" had called for "a widening of the scope of theological training." A student for the ministry, noted the pamphlet, had even asked his presbytery to permit him to substitute an examination in sociology for one in Hebrew — a petition the presbytery denied. While Princeton applauded the presbytery's decision, it also avowed its own determination "to provide the broadest possible training consistent with thoroughness." The pamphlet observed that the 1909 General Assembly had appointed a committee designed to consider "the matter of training our young men for an efficient ministry" in light of "urgent social needs" and of the needs of home and foreign missions. The resolution also assumed training in "the business methods of practical church administration." Professing itself "in hearty accord with this action," the seminary took pride in noting that Princeton graduates had played prominent roles in bringing the initiative to the General Assembly. The seminary also, in the pamphlet's words, took "additional pleasure" in pointing to the fact that,

24. Clutter, "Reorientation of Princeton Theological Seminary," 86.

even before the Assembly's action, Princeton had addressed the issue. The seminary had selected Charles Erdman to expand the curriculum in the area of practical instruction, and the board of directors had appointed a committee to work with the faculty "in arranging a curriculum that will embrace so far as possible everything essential to the equipment of an efficient ministry." These facts "show that the Seminary is in touch with the world of to-day."[25]

The remainder of the pamphlet touted the school's favorable location, roughly midway between Philadelphia and New York. That site allowed students to investigate urban ministry with only an hour's train trip, and one of the trustees had arranged "for a systematic visitation of the churches and missions of Philadelphia by students to study and engage in evangelistic work." Similarly, the seminary, the pamphlet noted, "is nearer a larger number of Presbyterian churches than any other seminary, and encouragement to practice in preaching is given so far as it does not interfere with the more important work of preparation for preaching." The booklet also stressed the proximity to the university and the opportunities to hear lectures there and to take some elective courses. In the closing section introducing the faculty, the booklet highlighted those who had had experience as pastors before introducing on another page those who did not.[26]

Two years later, in early May 1912, the seminary celebrated its centennial anniversary. As one would expect on such an occasion, the tone was largely celebratory. Messages of congratulation poured in from church bodies and theological schools throughout the world. Addresses lauded the distinguished alumni who had served as pastors, missionaries, and college or seminary educators. Speakers hallowed the memory of storied professors — the Alexanders, the Hodges, William Henry Green, and others. But the addresses also hinted at anxieties and tensions within the community. No doubt with fresh memories of the student protest of 1909, President Patton acknowledged the importance of the seminary having "a number of men who when they speak to students in regard to the work upon which they are about to enter can speak out of an affluent ministerial experience"; but he observed that Charles Hodge had never held a pastorate and that in the contemporary world of

---

25. *A Modern School of the Prophets: The Theological Seminary of the Presbyterian Church in the United States of America, Princeton, New Jersey* (n.p., n.d.), 4, 5, 6.

26. *A Modern School of the Prophets,* 8, 9, 11-14.

scholarship certain fields had become so "highly specialized" that it was undesirable to insist that those teaching them should have significant pastoral experience. Aware, too, of the student demand for courses in sociology, he warned that graduates who went forth from Princeton thinking their "great work is to engage in the development of social morality" would misunderstand the real nature of their call. In the spirit of Hodge's 1872 comments at his semi-centennial celebration, Patton emphasized that Princeton proudly stood where it had a hundred years earlier. Without question, he conceded, science had given a better understanding of "days" in the creation account, and textual criticism had produced "a better text of the New Testament"; but none of "these improvements made necessary any modification of our belief as to the authority of Scripture or as to the dogmatic content of the Scripture."[27]

William Hallock Johnson, a professor of Greek and New Testament at Lincoln University (Pennsylvania) as well as a Princeton Seminary alumnus of the class of 1896, commended his alma mater for maintaining its rigorous adherence to Reformed theology and for holding fast to its traditional curricular standards, especially in Greek and Hebrew. "In these days of specialized Biblical criticism," he remarked, "it would be certainly a misfortune if the decision of Biblical questions should be taken out of the hands of the ministry, and relegated to a learned and cloistered caste." Yet at the same time Johnson thought that Princeton needed to do more — far more — in other areas: "Our hope and dream for Princeton is that with expanding resources, she should offer, in some way, as extra-curriculum or elective, or fourth year or graduate courses, all the subjects which might be taught by the theological university." Johnson imagined Princeton offering specialized courses "in all the philosophies, in all the Biblical books, in all the doctrines, in all the periods of church history, in the philosophy and psychology of religion, in ethics and economics and sociology." He envisioned Princeton sending forth a stream of "sociological experts, men with the modern outlook upon social problems, and able to apply the most exact and scientific methods to their study and to their solution."[28]

John Grier Hibben, the newly installed president of Princeton University, brought warm greetings from the seminary's sister institution

---

27. *Centennial Celebration of the Theological Seminary of the Presbyterian Church in the United States of America at Princeton, New Jersey* (Princeton, 1912), 343, 352, 368.

28. *Centennial Celebration*, 447, 448-49.

and rejoiced in the common heritage of the two schools. Calling that heritage one of the "most cherished possessions" of the university, he pledged "to remain true to the gospel" that the founders of both institutions professed. But he qualified the vow carefully, saying that the university was Christian "in a broad spirit of tolerance" that welcomes "all the sects of Christendom." Nor did Hibben sound much like Patton or Warfield when he said that the university joined the seminary in adhering to "a spiritualistic philosophy in an age of materialistic and utilitarian creeds." Warfield and Patton would have agreed heartily, but they would also have insisted on fleshing out the assertion with a number of distinctively evangelical tenets. Hibben's attitude reflected what had taken place at the university under Woodrow Wilson. The number of university trustees associated with the seminary had fallen virtually in half; and faculty appointments, while still heavily Protestant, were less Presbyterian and even included Catholic and Jewish scholars. Wilson had for a time ditched the Bible courses that Francis Patton had assigned to his son George; and when Wilson revived the Bible courses a few years later, he brought in the theologically liberal Lucius Miller, a graduate of Union Theological Seminary, to teach them. Wilson also publicly distanced the university from any overt ties to the Presbyterian Church because he wished Princeton to qualify for money from the Carnegie Foundation to help establish a faculty pension fund. (The foundation refused to provide funding to denominationally related colleges.) None of this meant that there was overt hostility between the seminary and the university or that privileges of reciprocity had ceased. It was more a case of the university and seminary going somewhat different ways and having much less in common.[29]

The most poignant address at the centennial came from Charles Beatty Alexander, a grandson of Archibald Alexander and also a New York lawyer as well as a trustee of Princeton University. After fond reminiscences about the seminary, Alexander concluded:

One does not have to be a professional theologian to be aware that the kind of thought for which Princeton Seminary has always stood most firmly is now attacked persistently from many quarters. Voices come to us from across the sea and are raised here at home telling us that the sun is fast setting upon the old faith, and

29. *Centennial Celebration,* 559, 560; Kemeny, *Princeton in the Nation's Service,* 148-64.

that the doctrines taught here will pass away like those of the Athenian and Roman schools. It may be said that in our own country the Seminary stands in a somewhat isolated position.[30]

Beneath the overwhelming chorus of celebration and affirmation at the centennial were other notes: Patton's defiance of the spirit of the age; Johnson's satisfaction with Princeton, coupled with a conviction that the institution could do much more; Hibben's slightly distant embrace of the seminary; and Alexander's elegiac wistfulness for an era that might be passing. None of the speakers called for a change in the seminary's basic theological stance. These were responses to the nagging undertone that perhaps Princeton needed to make some adaptation to a rapidly changing world. The centennial year was, after all, also a year when modernism had triumphed in major divinity schools and when the Social Gospel was at the peak of its intensity in the Protestant churches. It was also a year in which Woodrow Wilson, now the governor of New Jersey, would be elected to the American presidency on a platform calling for significant reforms in American life.

J. Ross Stevenson and Other New Appointments

In 1913, Francis Patton retired, having reached the age of 70. Benjamin Warfield served as acting president until the board of directors selected J. Ross Stevenson, one of its own number, as the seminary's new leader a year later. The selection was contested, for a minority of the search committee had wished to offer the position to Warfield. Unlike Patton or Warfield, who had spent the greater portion of their careers in the seminary or university world, Stevenson had served chiefly as a pastor. A native of Westmoreland County in southwestern Pennsylvania and a graduate of Washington and Jefferson College, he had gone to McCormick Theological Seminary and subsequently spent a year in Berlin studying church history and New Testament. Upon his return from Europe in 1890, he was ordained to serve a church in Sedalia, Missouri. In 1894, he moved to Chicago to teach church history at McCormick Seminary. Eight years later he returned to pastoral ministry, first at the Fifth Avenue Presbyterian Church, New York City, and then from 1909 to 1914 at

30. *Centennial Celebration,* 466.

the Brown Memorial Church in Baltimore. In 1902, he joined the board of directors at Princeton Seminary and also became a member of the board of foreign missions, a post he held until his death. In fact, Stevenson served ultimately on fifteen to twenty committees of the denomination. In 1915, as he neared the end of his first year of service as president of the seminary, the General Assembly elected him moderator. In choosing Stevenson for the presidency of Princeton, the directors chose a highly respected pastor and denominational statesman, yet one with advanced academic training and experience as a professor. He appeared admirably equipped to bridge the gap that some feared had opened between the seminary and the church at large.[31]

The appointment prompted mixed reactions. J. Gresham Machen, for example, when he got wind of the possibility, wrote to his mother: "Stevenson's notions about theological education are ruinous . . . and then of course you know what an extremely weak man Stevenson is." But others saw him as a man attuned to the problems of the days as well as to theology and as one who could help the institution recoup its loss of influence throughout the church. It was not that Stevenson was thought by anyone to be a modernist or liberal. His prepossessions were conservative, but he had little inclination to pick fights over doctrine. His conservatism was irenic, and he preferred to stress issues of evangelism, service, and ministry.[32]

When the seminary community assembled in the First Presbyterian Church for his formal installation in October 1915, President Stevenson set a tone very different from that of his predecessor. In 1903, Patton had offered a learned overview of the entire range of the theological curriculum, noting its various components and the way theological educators since the Reformation had assembled those pieces. Patton put the pieces together in much the same fashion that Benjamin Warfield had in his inaugural address in 1888: systematic theology was the culminating synthesis of every other subject, and its contemporary task was to make war against an alien worldview threatening the very existence of Christianity. When Patton offered the charge to his successor in 1915, the military metaphor recurred. "This Theological Seminary is a training camp for

---

31. See the biographical sketch by Robert E. Speer, "Dr. Stevenson as a Presbyterian Churchman," *Princeton Seminary Bulletin* 33 (1940): 4-11.

32. Ned B. Stonehouse, *J. Gresham Machen: A Biographical Memoir* (Grand Rapids: Eerdmans, 1954), 216.

soldiers of the cross. It is also a fortress." He closed with the wish that under Stevenson "the friends and foes alike of historic Christianity . . . may feel constrained to say — 'There, there, in Princeton Theological Seminary, is to be seen the Gibraltar of the Christian faith.'"[33]

In his inaugural, Stevenson deftly balanced old concerns with a new vision. He affirmed points with which Patton would heartily concur: that it was, for example, "the glory of this institution that she has been thorough and fearless in her scholarship" and yet nevertheless always "sought to place and to hold men on the one and only foundation — the living Christ — God manifest in the flesh, the power of God unto salvation from sin and endless death by His atoning, expiatory sacrifice." Patton would also have nodded assent to the statement that "traditional theology had . . . a clear positive and soul satisfying faith and a definite, consistent and compelling message," unlike what many accommodations to "present-day thought" offered. Yet Stevenson also saw something valuable in the demand that the gospel be restated in contemporary idiom, for "it requires the minister to make the unchanging message apprehensible to the modern mind." He also found a constructive side in the clamor for a Social Gospel. While granting that the Christian message centered on a message of regeneration wrought supernaturally by the Spirit, he also insisted that "individual evangelization, sooner or later, compels social amelioration" and that "to establish a city of God in which there will be no slums is the task of the Church of the living God." At the same time, Stevenson called for a deeper "spiritual culture" in the seminaries. He feared that "over-occupation with class-room work and premature ministerial functions" worked against this end. "Each department of instruction, groaning under the burden of its indispensability," he remarked, "clamors for the maximum of available time, while the American utilitarian spirit is holding out all sorts of allurements for the pursuit of practical efficiency. Consequently there is little time, or leisure, or interest left for the lost art of reflection." The seminarian must also graduate with "a national and international outlook and a humanity embracing passion" and a corresponding zeal for an ecumenical worldwide mission. While Patton's charge had ended with the image of Princeton as an immovable Gibraltar, Stevenson's address closed with a more dynamic image: Princeton Seminary, by the grace of God, training "the leaders of the coming day,

33. Patton, "Theological Encyclopædia"; Patton, "Charge to Dr. Stevenson," *Princeton Seminary Bulletin* 9 (1915): 15, 18.

so that through them the knowledge of God shall cover the earth and the kingdom of His truth and love be established."[34]

There were also new or reassigned faculty inaugurated to chairs shortly before and after Stevenson's installation, and these changes likewise hinted at a partial shift of mood at Princeton. Frederick W. Loetscher offers a case in point. Born in 1875 in Dubuque, Iowa, to parents who emigrated from Switzerland, he graduated from Princeton University in 1896 and later received an M.A. and Ph.D. from the university. He also completed studies at Princeton Seminary in 1900 and then continued with additional work at Berlin and Strasbourg. He was an instructor in church history at Princeton Seminary from 1903 to 1907, then left to serve as a pastor in Philadelphia for several years. In 1910, he returned to teach homiletics at Princeton, but in 1913 the board transferred him to a professorship in church history, which he held until his retirement in 1945. Loetscher's inaugural address, "Church History as a Science and Theological Discipline," was undoubtedly one of the longer examples of that genre, running to forty-eight pages in the *Princeton Theological Review*. Although Loetscher was theologically conservative, he believed generosity of spirit and tolerance to be among the gifts that the study of history conferred upon theological reflection. "Church History is of inestimable benefit to the systematic theologian," Loetscher claimed, "because it inculcates in him the right temper for his scientific labors. It delivers him from the temptation which . . . too often has become his besetting sin, the harsh and repellent dogmatism that so readily degenerates into rancor and makes it next to impossible for him to grasp the truth in its ripeness." It is history that "gives theological opinion its proper life-context, and thus enables even the polemic writer to differ in generous and genial fashion from his foe."[35]

After Loetscher moved from homiletics to church history, J. Ritchie Smith was called from the pastorate of the Market Square Presbyterian Church, Harrisburg, Pennsylvania, to teach preaching. Born in Baltimore in 1852, he received his education at both the College of New Jersey and Princeton Seminary. During two successful pastorates, he established a reputation as a solid preacher and also authored a substantive essay, "Au-

---

34. J. Ross Stevenson, "Theological Education in the Light of Present Day Demands," *Princeton Theological Review* 14 (1916): 83-95; quotations on 85, 87, 88, 89, 91, 95.

35. Frederick W. Loetscher, "Church History as a Science and as a Theological Discipline," *Princeton Theological Review* 13 (January 1915): 1-48; quotations on 38.

gustine as an Exegete" (1904) as well as the book *The Teaching of the Gospel of John* (1903). The book drew upon conservative biblical scholarship but did so without descending into polemic and without being unduly technical. Its conservatism was attested by support from the author's seminary friend, Benjamin B. Warfield, and its irenic practical character was confirmed by encouragement from another Princeton classmate — Henry van Dyke, professor of English at the university and an evangelical liberal of broad church sympathies. In his inaugural address at the seminary, Smith reminded his hearers that both the Bible and preaching were but means to an end: "It is not the word printed or preached, but the Divine Word, incarnate for the sake of men, that is the power of God unto salvation."[36]

One must remember that not all faculty appointments after 1910 reflected the temperamentally mild conservatism of Stevenson, Ritchie, Erdman, or Loetscher. Having served as an instructor in New Testament since 1906, J. Gresham Machen was given the post of assistant professor of New Testament literature and exegesis in 1914. In his inaugural address in May 1915, Machen issued a dire warning that the gospel was at risk in contemporary theology. He focused his argument upon the scholarly quest for the historical Jesus, which had proceeded on the assumption that the Jesus of history could be disentangled from the Christ of faith with which the tradition had enshrouded him. The enterprise attempted to remove every element of the supernatural from Jesus' life and undercut the integrity of the biblical narratives. Machen closed with a call to battle:

> Let us not deceive ourselves. The Bible is at the foundation of the Church. Undermine that foundation, and the Church will fall. It will fall, and great will be the fall of it. . . . The Church is in perplexity. She is trying to compromise. She is saying, Peace, peace, when there is no peace. And rapidly she is losing her power. The time has come when she must choose. God grant she may choose aright!

This attitude would have significant consequences for the seminary in the decade ahead.[37]

---

36. J. Ritchie Smith, "Augustine as an Exegete," *Bibliotheca Sacra* (1904); Smith, *The Teaching of the Gospel of John* (New York: Fleming H. Revell Company, 1903), esp. 20; Smith, "The Place of Homiletics in the Training of the Minister," *Princeton Seminary Bulletin* 9 (1915): 9-14; quotation on 14.

37. J. Gresham Machen, "History and Faith," *Princeton Theological Review* 13 (July 1915): 337-51.

Curriculum Reform Again

Early in the Stevenson era, the issue of curriculum again returned. In the fall of 1914 the board of directors asked the faculty to form a special committee on curriculum to meet with a corresponding committee from the board. Growing out of President Stevenson's concern that an overloaded course of study denied students sufficient choice or time for reflection, a proposal for reducing required hours was placed before the faculty committee. Again rising to the defense of the existing curriculum, Warfield argued that he could not give adequate coverage to the various theological topics if his hours were reduced, that cutting the hours in Hebrew would make it impossible to teach the language adequately, and that introducing greater elective freedom would cause students to choose easier courses and thus, in the phrase of today, lead to a "dumbing down" of the educational program. In December 1914, a meeting between the curriculum committee of the faculty and the comparable body of the board produced two proposals for consideration by the entire faculty: a reduction of the number of hours in the required curriculum and the creation of greater elective freedom for students.[38]

After a series of faculty votes and maneuvers, a reduced required curriculum with the addition of electives was approved. Throughout the voting, Benjamin Warfield, William Brenton Greene, Geerhardus Vos, and Caspar Wistar Hodge remained stalwart defenders of the existing curriculum. Although Robert Dick Wilson, J. Gresham Machen, and William Park Armstrong were in basic sympathy with the position of Warfield's bloc and generally voted with them in the early rounds of the process, they appear to have made the pragmatic decision that some reform needed to be made in order to forestall more drastic changes. So they joined in the final vote with the colleagues who had most strenuously supported reform: Ross Stevenson, John Davis, Frederick Loetscher, and J. Ritchie Smith.[39]

Overall, the changes were quite modest indeed. More than 85 percent of the courses were still prescribed, and fewer than 15 percent could be taken as electives. The major difference from the older system was that one now had to take a few electives to receive a degree; previously such courses were entirely at the discretion of the student. Moreover, all

---

38. Clutter, "Reorientation of Princeton Theological Seminary," 95-106.
39. Clutter, "Reorientation of Princeton Theological Seminary," 95-106.

of the courses listed as electives (the "extracurriculum," according to the language of the time) were in the areas of Semitic philology, Old Testament, New Testament, church history, apologetics, and systematic theology. There was virtually no opportunity for the student to use the electives to skimp on the so-called classical disciplines in favor of "practical" courses. Given the relatively minor nature of the changes, one suspects that opponents had anxieties much deeper than a variation in a course here or there, or an hour subtracted from one requirement and added to another area. Beneath the battle over curriculum were deeper fears that would come into focus ever more sharply in the following decade.[40]

40. *Catalogue of Princeton Theological Seminary* 9, no. 4 (1916): 37-48.

Chapter Thirteen

The Fundamentalist Controversy and Reorganization

T HE YEARS during and after World War I — then called the Great War — produced an extraordinary outpouring of both extravagant hope and fear within the United States. When the nation entered the conflict in 1917, it did so with dreams of a grand outcome. President Woodrow Wilson, son of a Presbyterian manse and less than a decade earlier the president of Princeton University, depicted the conflict as a war to end all wars and as a struggle to make the world safe for democracy. At the close of the conflict and after a peace agreement had been concluded at Versailles in 1919, Wilson submitted the treaty to the Senate with a provision for a League of Nations. In his accompanying message, he portrayed the League as the beginning of "a new order which would rest upon the free choice of peoples." He saw the United States leading the way in this endeavor. "The stage is set," he declared, "the destiny disclosed.... America shall in truth show the way. The light streams upon the path ahead, and nowhere else."[1]

Yet, bright hopes notwithstanding, many exhibited considerable fear of those whom they considered alien or un-American. At the outset of the war, fear of the "Hun" (the German) verged on paranoia and created serious problems for Americans of German origin. After the armistice and in the wake of the Bolshevik Revolution in Russia, fear was displaced

---

1. *New York Times,* July 11, 1919. On the larger context, see Thomas J. Knock, *Woodrow Wilson and the Quest for a New World Order* (New York: Oxford University Press, 1992); Alan Dawley, *Changing the World: American Progressives in War and Revolution* (Princeton: Princeton University Press, 2003).

onto supposed subversives of foreign birth. Nativist anxieties found voice in a resurgent Ku Klux Klan, re-founded in 1915 and transformed from a purely southern into a national organization. By the mid-1920s, the Klan had hundreds of thousands of members and sympathizers from the Deep South, to the Pacific Northwest, Indiana, and New Jersey. The Klan's platform no longer emphasized anti-black appeals alone — although these remained very much a part of the message — but now included anti-immigrant, anti-Catholic, and anti-Semitic sentiments. Such prejudices fueled the immigration restriction legislation of 1921 and 1924 and the establishment of a quota system that was severely discriminatory against peoples coming from anywhere other than western and northern Europe. Stimulated partly by the migration of larger numbers of African Americans from the rural south to northern cities, brutal anti-black riots occurred shortly after World War I. Given these manifestations of racism and ethnic bias, it is little wonder that historian John Higham once characterized the period as "the tribal twenties."[2]

Some feared a breakdown of morals, and their anxieties were often tinged with considerable worry about changing gender roles. They pointed to divorces mounting in number, birth rates falling among Anglo-Saxon Americans, and women continuing to enter the workforce in greater numbers. The so-called new woman, recently enfranchised by the Nineteenth Amendment and perhaps most graphically symbolized by the flapper of the 1920s, asserted her independence of both home and traditional mores. Many also feared that the flouting of the Eighteenth Amendment, which banned the sale and manufacture of alcoholic beverages, likewise threatened the moral fiber of the nation. Although some of these trends had been the object of concern for several decades, they appeared especially dangerous in the surcharged atmosphere after the war. On the outcome of these matters, many felt, hinged the fate of Christian civilization in America.[3]

In the midst of these hopes and anxieties, American Protestants turned the tribalism of which Higham wrote in upon themselves. It

2. David M. Chalmers, *Hooded Americanism: The History of the Ku Klux Klan*, 3rd ed. (Durham, NC: Duke University Press, 1987), esp. 28-38; John Higham, *Strangers in the Land: Patterns of American Nativism, 1860-1925*, 2nd ed. (New York: Atheneum, 1971), 158-330.

3. Higham, *Strangers in the Land*; Joshua Zeitz, *Flapper: A Madcap Story of Sex, Style, Celebrity, and the Women Who Made Modern America* (New York: Crown, 2006); Margaret Lamberts Bendroth, *Fundamentalism and Gender, 1875 to the Present* (New Haven: Yale University Press, 1993), esp. 2-72.

would be simplistic to suggest that the social and cultural fears of the day caused this outcome, for the theological differences at the heart of the fundamentalist-modernist controversy had existed for several decades. The premillennial ideas, the holiness views, and the distrust of theological liberalism had roots deep in the nineteenth century, as George Marsden has demonstrated. But, as he has also observed, "there is nonetheless no doubt that the sense of cultural crisis following World War I shaped and modified the movement in important ways. Certainly the post-war crisis helped to intensify feelings, increase militancy and harden resistance to change." Even during the war itself, one might note illustrations of this hardening — and it was not only conservatives who became more militant. For example, University of Chicago professor Shirley Jackson Case spoke of "The Premillennial Menace" that threatened the American war effort. "Under ordinary circumstances," he commented, "one might excusably pass over premillennialism as a wild and relatively harmless fancy." But his article made clear that the times were not ordinary, and millenarianism was no longer harmless. It was a threat to the democratic way of life, lent itself to use by socialist radicals (the International Workers of the World or "Wobblies") who desired the overthrow of American institutions, and threatened to paralyze the nation in time of war. Incensed by attacks on their patriotism, premillennialists protested that it was their enemies — men like Case — who promoted Germanic ideals fatal to Christianity and America alike. At the 1918 Prophetic Conference in Philadelphia, one premillenarian identified the "ripe, rank, rotten, new theology made in Germany" as the "abomination of abominations in the modern religious world." "Permeating and poisoning our theological seminaries" (including especially the University of Chicago Divinity School), this modernism prepared the way for both apostasy and the war. "If the churches of Great Britain, America, and France, fifty years ago," he remarked, "had fought this iniquity, this infamous thing, there never would have been any war in the world now."[4]

The fundamentalist-modernist controversy was fought on two major fronts: within the larger American culture as a battle over evolution;

4. George M. Marsden, *Fundamentalism and American Culture: The Shaping of Twentieth-Century Evangelicalism, 1875-1925* (New York: Oxford University Press, 1980), 201; Shirley Jackson Case, "The Premillennial Menace," *Biblical World* 52 (July 1918): 16-23; Cortland Myers, "War on German Theology," in *Light on Prophecy: A Coordinated, Constructive Teaching,* ed. William L. Pettingill et al. (New York: Christian Herald, 1918), 176, 181.

and within certain churches, chiefly the Northern Baptist denomination and the Presbyterian Church in the U.S.A. In the years after the end of World War I, conservative Christian groups lobbied for and won in a number of state legislatures the passage of statutes outlawing the teaching of biological evolution in public schools — a movement that most contemporary Americans know, if at all, from the dramatically powerful but historically flawed 1960 movie *Inherit the Wind*. The struggle in the Baptist and Presbyterian churches involved efforts to enforce stricter theological conformity to traditional views. The conservatives' ultimate goal was to force modernists to withdraw from the denominations or to be ousted. In the Presbyterian controversy, the denominational battle was intimately tied to a struggle within Princeton Seminary itself. The result of those intertwined struggles was the permitting of a greater degree of theological latitude within the Presbyterian Church and the reorganization of the seminary in 1929.[5]

The Beginnings of the Presbyterian Conflict and Princeton Seminary

As noted earlier, Presbyterian conservatives had previously won notable victories against modernism or liberalism. In the Portland Deliverance of 1892, for example, the General Assembly had aligned itself with the Princeton position when it declared: "Our Church holds that the inspired Word, as it came from God, is without error." The ouster or forced withdrawal of Charles Briggs, Henry Preserved Smith, and Arthur C. McGiffert had likewise attested the conservatism of Presbyterianism. Even the creedal revision that Princeton had opposed seemed relatively innocuous when it came to pass in 1903. Then in 1910 the General Assembly defined five doctrines as "essential and necessary." (Here the Assembly echoed the language of the act by which the Westminster Standards were made the official creed of the Synod of Philadelphia in 1729. The Adopting Act, as it was soon called, required all ministers to subscribe to the Westminster Confession of Faith but did not mandate that they af-

5. For a thoughtful account of the trial and of the way subsequent mythology about the event altered its significance, see Edward J. Larson, *Summer for the Gods: The Scopes Trial and America's Continuing Debate over Science and Religion* (Cambridge: Harvard University Press, 1997), esp. 225-46.

firm every jot of Westminster, only its "essential and necessary articles," which were not explicitly identified.) The five articles singled out by the Assembly were (1) the inerrancy of Scripture, (2) the virgin birth of Christ, (3) his death on the cross as vicarious sacrifice "to satisfy divine justice," (4) his bodily resurrection, and (5) the reality of the miracles by which Christ "showed his power and love." Although these items were singled out as essential, the General Assembly did not wish to be understood as limiting the essential articles to these points alone, for it added: "Others are equally so." The Assembly further instructed that no one was to be received into the ministry unless he was willing to accept these and other essential and necessary articles. Subsequently, in 1916 and again in 1923, the Assembly reaffirmed this deliverance.[6]

Officially the Presbyterian Church was committed to these items, but the fact that it felt compelled to assert them, and then reaffirm them two more times, indicated that they were apparently at risk in some quarters. Concern focused particularly upon the Presbytery of New York, which sometimes ordained those who expressed doubts about one or more of the articles; often these ordinands had graduated from Union Seminary, which had broken its affiliation with the Presbyterian Church after the denomination had rejected Briggs. Complaints about the presbytery's actions in ordaining supposedly dubious candidates had actually been the occasion for the passage of the 1910 General Assembly deliverance and continued to be an irritant for many conservatives.

The greatest long-term challenge to the five points, however, came not from those who overtly rejected them but from a transformed attitude toward theology itself. One may illustrate this more subtle challenge in the person of Henry van Dyke of Princeton Seminary's class of 1877. Also a graduate of the College of New Jersey and one of the many American students who took a period of study in Germany after seminary — in his case for two years in Berlin, part of that time with Isaak Dorner — van Dyke went on to a varied career as pastor of the Brick Presbyterian Church in New York City, professor of English literature at Princeton University, service as moderator of the General Assembly in 1902-1903, and chair of the committee that proposed the creedal revision and declaratory statement adopted in 1903. Van Dyke also served as the

6. Lefferts A. Loetscher, *The Broadening Church: A Study of Theological Issues in the Presbyterian Church since 1869* (Philadelphia: University of Pennsylvania Press, 1954), 90-98.

chair of the committee that produced *The Book of Common Worship for the Presbyterian Church* in 1906; and when his Princeton friend Woodrow Wilson became president of the United States, he tapped van Dyke for diplomatic service in the Netherlands and Luxembourg. He was famous also for his poetry, now little esteemed, and his book *The Story of the Other Wise Man,* a fictional account of a fourth wise man, which sold hundreds of thousands of copies. Assessment of van Dyke as a religious and theological leader has produced a wide range of characterizations: one author lists him among "moderate conservatives," and another counts him with the modernists. Sydney Ahlstrom, one of the leading historians of American religion in the last half-century, characterized van Dyke as an exponent of "a mediating theology remarkably attuned to the mood of the age, yet warmly evangelical." Depending on which passage one cites from van Dyke, each of these designations might be apt; but judged as a whole, his thought was that of a warmly evangelical preacher not overly concerned with minute doctrinal precision. This trait was not so much intellectual sloppiness as it was a conviction about the mystery of God and of faith. For example, in *The Gospel for a World of Sin* (1899), he made clear at the outset: "This book is not meant to present a theory of the Atonement. On the contrary, it is meant to teach that there is no theory broad or deep enough to embrace or explain the fact." He explained further:

> . . . the Atonement is the work of God's love in its bearing upon man's sin. Therefore it must include more than we can explain. What Christ did to take away the sin of the world was precisely all that was needed, neither more nor less. What we know of this need is what we know about the Atonement. One man sees one segment of the circle more clearly. Another man sees another segment. No man sees the whole circle. But if each one sees his little arc of experience in right relation to the centre, he sees it as part of the truth. The false theories of the Atonement are those which claim to be final and exclusive.[7]

7. Kathryn Lofton, "The Methodology of the Modernists: Process in American Protestantism," *Church History* 75 (June 2006): 397; John Abernathy Smith, "Ecclesiastical Politics and the Founding of the Federal Council of Churches," *Church History* 43 (September 1974): 363; Sydney E. Ahlstrom, *A Religious History of the American People* (New Haven: Yale University Press, 1972), 815; Henry van Dyke, *The Gospel for a World of Sin* (New York: Macmillan, 1899), vii-viii.

Charles Lemuel Thompson, who finished the course of study at the seminary in 1861, affords another instance of a changing outlook toward the theology he had learned at Princeton. After a series of pastorates from Cincinnati to Chicago, Pittsburgh, and New York, in 1898 he took on, at nearly the age of 60, the position of general secretary of the Presbyterian Church's board of home missions and held the post until he was 75. Shortly after Thompson's death, one appreciative colleague observed that when the general secretary came to the board "his office had but one clerk. He left it in 1914 an elaborate organization for national service, with departments adapted to express the sympathy of Christians for Indians, Mexicans, wage earners, farmers, immigrants, Alaskans." Far from pursuing an easy course in the last part of his career, he presided over a proliferation of departments and ministries. He also pioneered, said another former colleague, in the creation of an ecumenical "Home Missions Council" through which he pursued "his two great passions — an America won for Christ, won in every phase and aspect of its life, and a Protestantism united in His service." From the vantage point of his old age and retirement, Thompson evaluated the theological training he had received at Princeton. He remained profoundly grateful "for the anchorage given me there in a very conservative theology." But he also indicated how his ministry moved him in other directions:

> I am not conscious of feeling any reaction against it for a decade or more. But, as gradual as the approach of daylight, there came across my mind the feeling that I could not fully preach that theology. As, however, I was never a doctrinal preacher it troubled me but little. I simply put Hodge and Shedd further back on my shelves, and gave myself to practical sermonizing where their presence was not felt. . . . If any one should care to ask me today, "What is your theology now?" I am afraid I should be obliged to answer, It is not a well articulated system at all. If I think of it as a chain, there are missing links. Further, I do not know as much about the mysteries of divine revelation as once I knew. . . . But faith abides. I am surer every day of the Fatherhood of God, of the sufficient and efficient sacrifice of Christ, of the value of Christian character, the power of the Gospel to save men, the final award [*sic*] and the blessedness eternal of all who believe. For much that is beyond and between — I wait.

As one given to "practical sermonizing" and committed to creating and effectively administering new ministries first in his various churches and then at the board of home missions, there was an evangelical pragmatism about Thompson.[8]

As one looks at the cases of van Dyke and Thompson, one senses at least two dimensions to the subtle shift in the church's attitude toward its theology. Van Dyke, while affirming the major evangelical points of Calvinism, also implied in a fashion reminiscent of Horace Bushnell that any great truth of the gospel, such as the atonement, defied reduction to a single theory, for "there is no theory broad or deep enough to embrace or explain the fact." In the case of Thompson, one likewise sees a minister who firmly adhered to a Christ-centered message — the "sufficient and efficient sacrifice of Christ . . . [and] the power of the Gospel to save men." But Thompson, too, by his own confession, was no longer deeply concerned to have "a well articulated system" with all the "missing links" supplied. Thompson's willingness to live with these unanswered questions seemed to have much to do with the fact that he was preoccupied with creating new forms of ministry and the administrative structures to support them. His career represented a major transformation taking place within the Presbyterian Church as well as in other denominations between the late nineteenth century and the 1920s. In their eagerness to carry out the foreign missionary enterprise, to engage in home missions to new immigrants, and to reach the laboring classes that often seemed to be alienated from the churches, Presbyterians sent out more workers into specialized ministries and had more agencies to support these workers. As the number and size of programs and personnel grew, Presbyterians experienced the frustrations common to other denominations: lack of coordinated planning, the difficulty of raising money for so many different enterprises, and rivalries among agencies. The result was an increasing pressure toward administrative centralization in order to fund and coordinate the various enterprises of the church. Theological disputation seemed to distract from this goal and therefore should be curtailed. Thus, as early as 1893, over two hundred Presbyterians, upset by the strife created by the Briggs affair, signed "A Plea for Peace and Work," written by Henry van Dyke. The document declared:

8. *Charles Lemuel Thompson: An Autobiography,* ed. Elizabeth Osborn Thompson (New York: Fleming H. Revell, 1924), 30, 120-22, 276, 280.

As Ministers of Jesus Christ, and working Pastors in the Presbyterian Church, we are filled with the gravest fears lest the usefulness of the Church should be hindered, her peace disturbed and her honor diminished by the prevalence of theological controversy and strife over doctrines which are not essential. . . . It is in this spirit that we join our voices in a plain, straight-forward, fraternal expression of the desire for harmony and united devotion to practical work.[9]

During and shortly after World War I, Princeton Seminary faculty found themselves on different sides of issues relating to these institutional dynamics. In 1918, the General Assembly recorded its "profound conviction that the time has come for Organic Church Union of the Evangelical Churches of America" and authorized overtures to other denominations for the purpose of formulating a specific plan. The committee to which the task was assigned included both J. Ross Stevenson and Charles R. Erdman as well as William Henry Roberts, the Assembly's stated clerk and former Princeton Seminary librarian (1877-1886). At the same time the denomination also explored the possibility of reunion with the "southern" Presbyterian Church. Various cooperative ecumenical ventures had, of course, preceded this overture — for example, the organization of the Federal Council of Churches in 1908, in which Roberts and the Presbyterian Church had played important roles. The Great War, however, added fresh impetus to the search for new avenues of joint work and service. As one Presbyterian put the matter in 1922, the war "revealed to American Protestantism its essential unity. . . . But while the war disclosed to the churches their essential unity, it showed them at the same time that they lacked the agencies through which that unity could express itself effectively in action." The proposal for organic union was

---

9. [Henry van Dyke,] "A Plea for Peace and Work," three-page leaflet (n.p., 1893), p. 1. On the proliferation of structure in Presbyterianism during these years, see James H. Moorhead, "Presbyterians and the Mystique of Organizational Efficiency, 1870-1936," in *Reimagining Denominationalism,* ed. Robert Bruce Mullin and Russell E. Richey (New York: Oxford University Press, 1994), 264-87; Richard W. Reifsnyder, "The Reorganizational Impulse in American Protestantism: The Presbyterian Church (U.S.A.) as a Case Study, 1788-1983" (Ph.D. Dissertation, Princeton Theological Seminary, 1984); and Louis Weeks, "The Incorporation of American Religion: The Case of the Presbyterians," *Religion and American Culture* 1 (Winter 1991): 100-118. See also Ben Primer, *Protestants and American Business Methods* (Ann Arbor, MI: UMI Research Press, 1979).

one effort to remedy the problem and find a path to effective expression of unity. Interdenominational meetings in response to the Presbyterian overture produced the Philadelphia Plan — so named because of the place it was drafted. Even though the original goal had been organic union, the plan fell far short of that end. It guaranteed that "each constituent Church reserves the right to retain its creedal statements, its form of government in the conduct of its own affairs." There would, however, be a council of the united churches whose purpose was "to prevent overlapping, friction, competition or waste in the work of the existing denominational boards or administrative agencies." The council "shall direct such consolidation of their missionary activities as well as of particular Churches in over-churched areas as is consonant with the law of the land or of the particular denomination affected." While these formulae seemed to leave each denomination with its own internal polity and creed intact and possibly gave it a veto over any proposed consolidations, the council was nevertheless to be given power to "direct," not recommend, consolidation. This vagueness did not help efforts to win support for the proposal. Moreover, the murky boundaries between this proposed council and the already existing Federal Council, not to mention the council's undefined relationship with another new ecumenical venture just launched — the Interchurch World Movement — probably guaranteed rejection. When the General Assembly of 1920 asked the presbyteries to make a preliminary decision about creating an American Council of United Churches, they said no by a decisive margin. Similarly negative opinions arose from Princeton Seminary. Notwithstanding the support of the proposal by Stevenson and Erdman, most of the faculty disliked it.[10]

J. Gresham Machen voiced their sentiments in sharp terms. The proposal for an American Council of United Churches, he said in a letter to his mother, was a "great disaster and disgrace." If adopted, it would mean "that the Presbyterian Church . . . will have given up its testimony to truth." He wrote to Stevenson in protest and suggested that at the 1920 General Assembly "there was launched the most dangerous attack not

10. *Minutes of the General Assembly of the Presbyterian Church in the United States of America,* n.s. vol. 18 (Philadelphia: Office of the General Assembly, 1918), 154; William Adams Brown, *The Church in America: A Study of the Present Conditions and Future Prospects of American Protestantism* (New York: Macmillan, 1922), 101; for a brief analysis in the Assembly's minutes of the committee's views about the rejection of the Philadelphia Plan, see *Minutes,* n.s. vol. 21 (1921), 84.

only upon the Reformed Faith but upon the Christian religion in general which had appeared in America in recent years." Since Stevenson had presented to the Assembly the report recommending that the Philadelphia Plan be sent to the presbyteries for their concurrence, Machen's note could hardly be read as anything other than a stinging rebuke to the president.[11]

J. Gresham Machen and the Travail of Princeton Seminary

In the early 1920s, Machen became a powerful conservative voice both within the seminary and within the Presbyterian Church. He attained greater scholarly recognition in 1921 with the publication of *The Origin of Paul's Religion*. Delivered the same year as the Sprunt Lectures at Union Seminary in Richmond, the volume provided a learned argument against the common view that Jesus had preached a message about the fatherhood of God and God's kingdom and that Paul, instead of teaching the religion *of* Jesus, had turned Christianity into a message *about* Jesus. Even some scholars who did not agree with Machen thought his argument and learning merited review and comment. Then, in 1923, Machen published *Christianity and Liberalism,* a work addressed to a larger popular audience. In it, he made the arresting claim that "despite the liberal use of traditional phraseology modern liberalism not only is a different religion from Christianity but belongs in a totally different class of religions."[12]

Given the important role that he played in the troubles of Princeton in the 1920s, it is useful to trace the path that brought Machen to his convictions. Born to an affluent Baltimore family in 1881 as the second of three sons, Machen was reared in a home where Southern traditions were venerated. His father, Arthur, had spent his childhood on a farm in Fairfax County, Virginia, and eventually took up the practice of law in Baltimore in the 1850s. Arthur Machen's sympathy for the Confederacy during the Civil War prompted him to turn down an appointment as a district attorney because he feared that the position would have forced him to prose-

11. Ned B. Stonehouse, *J. Gresham Machen: A Biographical Memoir* (Grand Rapids: Eerdmans, 1954), 305. Machen to Stevenson quoted in Ronald T. Clutter, "The Reorientation of Princeton Theological Seminary, 1900-1929" (Th.D. Dissertation, Dallas Theological Seminary, 1982), 111-12.

12. J. Gresham Machen, *The Origin of Paul's Religion* (New York: Macmillan, 1921); Machen, *Christianity and Liberalism* (New York: Macmillan, 1923), 7.

cute active southern sympathizers. In the years after the war, his law practice flourished, and in 1873 he married a young Georgia woman twenty-two years his junior. Mary ("Minnie") Gresham, daughter of a successful entrepreneur and former mayor of Macon, was a southern belle boasting the adornments of a college education and travel abroad. She loved Victorian poetry, and in 1903 she published *The Bible in Browning*. While her father lived, she regularly took the children to visit the family home. Machen's later memories of these trips suggested a "courtlier, richer, life, and a broader culture" than that of modern northern society, and his recollections of his mother's ancestral home were suffused with a nostalgic glow: "On College Street, in Macon, Georgia, stands a typical Southern mansion, almost hidden by luxuriant shrubs and tall magnolias. In front of the house, supporting the roof, stand four tall fluted pillars. These pillars are hollow, and were used during the war to hide the family silver from the Yankees." These lines conjure up the image of the romanticized but now lost Old South that Margaret Mitchell turned into her bestselling 1936 novel *Gone with the Wind*. But while that side of Minnie Gresham Machen indeed existed — she belonged, for example, to the United Daughters of the Confederacy — she gave her sons a view of the world containing more than moonlight and magnolias. Mrs. Machen nurtured them in a sturdy Presbyterian piety that required memorization of the Westminster Confession and the reading of *The Pilgrim's Progress*. In Baltimore, the Machens joined a Presbyterian congregation that had withdrawn from the northern Old School in 1867 in order to affiliate with the southern Presbyterian denomination, in which the ideals of James Henley Thornwell and his notion of the spirituality of the church lived on. Arthur Machen communicated to his boys a love of classical learning. Although he enjoyed contemporary literature, he took particular pleasure in reading the New Testament or Thucydides in Greek as well as Caesar and Horace in Latin. Classical learning, long valued in western culture, had held a particular place among the educated in the American South. Thus Basil Gildersleeve, a native of the South and the nation's foremost classicist in the late nineteenth century, described the classics, as Eugene Genovese and Elizabeth Fox-Genovese have commented, "as 'the offspring of a healthy humanity' — by which he meant that they taught historical continuity, critical perspective, and 'eternal norms.'"[13]

13. D. G. Hart, *Defending the Faith: J. Gresham Machen and the Crisis of Conservative Protestantism in Modern America* (Baltimore: Johns Hopkins University Press, 1994), 10-18;

In 1898, J. Gresham Machen began studies in classics at Baltimore's Johns Hopkins University, where Gildersleeve had been teaching for a quarter-century. Gildersleeve did more than perpetuate a traditional southern love of the classics; he also brought to the subject an exacting philological approach that he had learned during study in Germany. Impressed by his mentor's intellectual rigor, Machen stayed a year beyond graduation to participate in Gildersleeve's doctoral seminar. In addition to exemplifying meticulous scholarship, the Hopkins classicist no doubt appealed to the pro-southern cultural and political biases of Machen. In probably his most widely known essay, Gildersleeve, a part-time staff officer for two Confederate generals during the Civil War, insisted that "the cause we fought for and our brothers died for was the cause of civil liberty, and not the cause of human slavery." The South had upheld ideals of states' rights and localism that had enduring value. Even if "the complete centralization of the government shall prove to be the wisdom of the future, the poetry of life will still find its home in the old order, and those who loved their State best will live longest in song and legend." It was a vision of America that Machen himself continued to cherish. After leaving Johns Hopkins, Machen went on to Princeton Seminary. At this time he was far from convinced that he had a ministerial vocation. His experience at seminary apparently did not provide encouragement in this direction, for the classroom work often bored him and he resented required attendance — a policy more appropriate to "a boarding school," he complained. He derived enjoyment from the courses he took at the university but did not allow his studies there or at the seminary to interfere with the pleasures of watching football, taking day trips to New York City, or playing games of tennis. His insouciance, one suspects, was at least partly a pose, because he did well enough academically to win the New Testament fellowship and to have his work published in the *Princeton Theological Review.* He held the confidence of Francis L. Patton, already a friend of the Machen family; and William Park Armstrong also saw great promise in him. Machen decided to continue his studies in Europe, but chose not to use the New Testament Fellowship to fund the trip

---

Bradley J. Longfield, *The Presbyterian Controversy: Fundamentalists, Modernists, and Moderates* (New York: Oxford University Press, 1991), 28-38. On the role of the classics in southern thinking, see Elizabeth Fox-Genovese and Eugene D. Genovese, *The Mind of the Master Class: History and Faith in the Southern Slaveholders' Worldview* (Cambridge: Cambridge University Press, 2005), 249-304; quotation on 250.

so that he would feel no obligation to return to Princeton or to pursue the ministry.[14]

From 1905 to 1906, Machen studied at Marburg and Göttingen, where he heard the lectures of major biblical scholars Wilhelm Bousset, Adolf Jülicher, and Johannes Weiss; but it was Wilhelm Herrmann of Marburg who most fascinated and challenged him. Arguably the leading contemporary liberal theologian of the Euro-American world, Herrmann stood in the tradition of Albrecht Ritschl and had little use for metaphysics. Nor did he think that the thing of central importance for Christianity was the precise historical record of Jesus' life, for scholarship constantly readjusted its assessment of those facts. But he did believe that the Bible presented a compelling portrait of Jesus that could — and did — transform subsequent generations of men and women who took it seriously. "True faith," as Bradley Longfield remarks of Machen's interpretation of Herrmann, "was grounded in an encounter with the inner life of Jesus — an experience unassailable by history or science." It is little wonder that Machen hardly knew what to make of him. With his rejection of metaphysics and his deriding of efforts to prove Christianity from the demonstrable historicity of everything in the Bible, Herrmann departed dramatically from the apologetic method Machen had learned from the Common Sense tradition of Princeton. "Herrmann," he wrote his brother, "affirms very little of that which I have been accustomed to regard as essential to Christianity." And yet Machen could not deny the evangelical zeal of the Marburg professor. "There is no doubt in my mind but that he is a Christian, and a Christian of a particularly earnest type." Machen confessed in a letter to his father a few weeks earlier that he found Herrmann's "devotion to Christ" to be deeper "than anything I have known in myself during the past few years." Yet even as Herrmann threw him into intellectual and spiritual turmoil, Machen was discovering a renewed appreciation for his seminary education, for he realized that his professors there, especially Armstrong, had already acquainted

14. Longfield, *Presbyterian Controversy*, 28-53; Hart, *Defending the Faith;* Basil Gildersleeve, *The Creed of the Old South, 1865-1915* (Baltimore: Johns Hopkins Press, 1915), 51-52; the essay that lent its name to the title of Gildersleeve's book originally appeared in *The Atlantic* in 1892. The articles based on the work for which Machen won the New Testament prize appeared as J. Gresham Machen, "The New Testament Account of the Birth of Jesus, First Article," *Princeton Theological Review* 3 (1905): 641-70; Machen, "The New Testament Account of the Birth of Jesus, Second Article," *Princeton Theological Review* 4 (1906): 36-81.

him with the state of German biblical scholarship and had supplied the intellectual tools with which it might be evaluated and often refuted.[15]

Upon his return from Germany, Machen still had qualms and career uncertainties, but Armstrong enticed him into accepting a one-year appointment at Princeton beginning in the fall of 1906. An appointment at this level required no creedal subscription and no commitment to seek ordination. Yet, as year succeeded year and reappointments followed, Machen settled his misgivings. By 1914, he was prepared to receive ordination as a minister in the Presbyterian Church in the U.S.A. — thus formally severing any official connections to the southern Presbyterian denomination — and to become assistant professor of New Testament literature and exegesis in the same year. His inaugural address left no doubt that he had identified with the tradition of Warfield, Patton, and Armstrong. Calling the liberal quest for the historical Jesus a failure, he asserted that the church must robustly assert the supernatural origins of Christ and of Scripture. Underlying his summons was the argument he had set forth at the opening of the 1912-1913 academic year in an address entitled "Christianity and Culture." As he made clear from his first sentence, his concern was with the same issue that had preoccupied the founders of the seminary: "the relation between knowledge and piety." But the old problem had taken on new dimensions reflecting the changing nature of higher education. "Our whole system of school and college education," he observed,

> is so constituted as to keep religion and culture as far apart as possible and ignore the question of the relationship between them. . . . From this activity the study of religion was banished. We studied natural science without considering its bearing or lack of bearing upon natural theology. We studied Greek without opening the New Testament. We studied history with careful avoidance of the greatest of historical movements which was ushered in by the preaching of Jesus. In philosophy, the vital importance of the study for religion could not be entirely concealed, but it was kept as far back as possible in the background.

Machen was speaking from firsthand experience. Although he had been reared in a home with old-fashioned religious ideals, his undergraduate

---

15. Longfield, *Presbyterian Controversy,* 41; Hart, *Defending the Faith,* 21-28.

education at Johns Hopkins took place in one of the new research-oriented universities, where, as George Marsden has put it, Christian hopes were to be achieved by "methodological secularization."[16]

In this situation, the temptation for Christians was either to adapt Christianity to standards of knowledge hostile to the gospel or to withdraw from contact with the world of contemporary ideas in order to get on with the practical business of preaching the gospel. Both alternatives, Machen believed, were disastrous. The proper response to contemporary learning was not to succumb to its blandishments or to isolate oneself from it in "a sort of modernized intellectual monasticism." Rather, "let us go forth joyfully, enthusiastically to make the world subject to God." Machen understood that some might shrink from the task because engagement with modern learning entailed risks of falling into doubt — risks of the sort he had taken in going to Johns Hopkins or in studying at Marburg and Göttingen. "Is it not far easier to be an earnest Christian if you confine your attention to the Bible," he asked rhetorically, "and do not risk being led astray by the thought of the world? We answer, of course it is *easier* . . . just as it is easier to be a good soldier in comfortable winter quarters than it is on the field of battle." But the Christian calling in the contemporary age was to fight unbelief on the battleground of ideas. "The chief obstacle to the Christian religion to-day lies in the sphere of the intellect," he declared. "What is to-day matter of academic speculation begins to-morrow to move armies and pull down empires." It was because he saw such dire consequences arising from the neglect of correct thinking that he was appalled at what he perceived as the doctrinal sloppiness and indifference underlying the American Council of United Churches supported by Stevenson and Erdman.[17]

But the threats did not end there. In 1918 the First Presbyterian Church in New York City had called as its preaching minister Harry Emerson Fosdick, a Baptist liberal who had already made a name for himself as the author of a number of popular religious books. On May 21, 1922, Fosdick preached the sermon "Shall the Fundamentalists Win?" which confronted those demanding conformity to what they called essential doctrines of Christianity. Fosdick took up such matters as the virgin

16. J. Gresham Machen, "History and Faith," *Princeton Theological Review* 13 (July 1915): 337-51; Machen, "Christianity and Culture," *Princeton Theological Review* 11 (1913): 1; George M. Marsden, *The Soul of the American University: From Protestant Establishment to Established Nonbelief* (New York: Oxford University Press, 1994), 156.

17. Machen, "Christianity and Culture," 5, 7, 8, 10.

birth, the inerrancy of Scripture, and belief "in a special theory of the atonement — that the blood of our Lord, shed in a substitutionary death, placates an alienated Deity." He denied that these theories were essential to Christianity, urged mutual tolerance among those holding different views, and declared that disputes about such matters diverted believers from the real mission of Christianity. Here was an instance in which people "tithe mint and anise and cumin, and quarrel over them, when the world is perishing for the lack of the weightier matters of the law, justice, and mercy, and faith." Why, he asked, should churches be made into "a cockpit of controversy when there is not a single thing at stake in the controversy on which depends the salvation of human souls. . . . And there is one thing that does matter — more than anything else in all the world — that men in their personal lives and in their social relationships should know Jesus Christ." If Fosdick's sermon had stayed within the walls of First Church, perhaps subsequent controversy would not have occurred or at least would have been muted; but John D. Rockefeller Jr. funded the printing and distribution of the sermon to clergy across the country. Numerous conservative Presbyterians were outraged, among them Clarence Macartney, Princeton Seminary class of 1905 and newly elected member of the school's board of directors. Macartney preached a refutation of Fosdick — "Shall Unbelief Win?" — and persuaded the Presbytery of Philadelphia in October 1922 to send an overture to the General Assembly requesting that it instruct the Presbytery of New York "to take such action as will require the preaching and teaching in the First Presbyterian Church . . . to conform to the system of doctrine taught in the Confession of Faith."[18]

Although the Fosdick affair did not by itself prompt Machen to assemble his thoughts into a book against the dangers of modernism, it did render the project timely. The result was *Christianity and Liberalism,* published early in 1923. From beginning to end, the book exhibited the rhetoric of sharp dichotomy. The Christian churches faced a major challenge from "the modern lust of scientific conquest" — that is, the desire to subject all spheres of life to the presumptions of a naturalistic scientific method. It did no good, said Machen, for Christians to attempt to

---

18. Harry Emerson Fosdick, "Shall the Fundamentalists Win?" *Christian Work* 102 (June 10, 1922): 716-22; Clarence E. Macartney, "Shall Unbelief Win? An Answer to Dr. Fosdick," *Presbyterian,* July 13, 1922, and July 20, 1922. For an account of this event from Fosdick's perspective, see Robert Moats Miller, *Harry Emerson Fosdick: Preacher, Pastor, Prophet* (New York: Oxford University Press, 1985), 93-149.

appease this enemy by surrendering a few outposts, the supposedly non-essential doctrines "that the liberal preacher has abandoned in the interests of peace." The enemy only pressed further demands. "In the intellectual battle of the present day," he warned, "there can be no 'peace without victory'; one side or the other must win." But the burden of Machen's polemic was not against the modern temper per se; it was against the liberals who thought they could strike a compromise with it. Not only would they find themselves scorned by the advocates of a full-throated modernity; they would, if honest, have to recognize that in trying to reconcile the gospel to the age they had "really relinquished everything distinctive of Christianity." He took them to task for treating doctrine as a provisional statement of Christian experience when, in fact, "a creed is not a mere expression of Christian experience, but on the contrary it is a setting forth of those facts upon which experience is based." Further, he charged liberalism with toppling the Bible from the position of authority and replacing it with a dependence on "the shifting emotions of sinful men." Liberalism treated Christ "as an Example and Guide," a mere "example for faith," whereas true Christianity regarded him as savior and as "object of faith." It ignored the transcendence of God and the utter sinfulness of humanity, forgetting that humanity needed supernatural redemption and regeneration from beyond itself. And so the list of discrepancies between Christianity and liberalism went on. Machen allowed that individual liberals might not espouse the full implications of their position, and some might even be Christians. "But one thing is perfectly plain — whether or no liberals are Christians, it is at any rate perfectly clear that liberalism is not Christianity." Whatever the status of individual liberals, the logic of liberalism would triumph, for "logic is the great dynamic, and the logical implications of any way of thinking are sooner or later certain to be worked out. And taken as a whole, even as it actually exists to-day, naturalistic liberalism is a fairly unitary phenomenon; it is tending more and more to eliminate from itself illogical remnants of Christian belief." Liberalism represented a slippery slope down which one inevitably slid toward unbelief, and therefore no compromise with liberalism was possible. Since that was the case, "separation between the two parties in the Church is the crying need of the hour."[19]

Allied to Machen's willingness to separate was a conception of the church as a voluntary society. "An evangelical church," he explained, "is

19. Machen, *Christianity and Liberalism*, 3, 6, 7, 19, 79, 96, 160, 173.

composed of a number of persons who have come to agreement in a certain message about Christ and who desire to unite in the propagation of that message, as it is set forth in their creed on the basis of the Bible." Therefore, if individuals found that they had come to disagree with the standards of a church, they should in honesty withdraw; and if they failed to do so, those who adhered to the original standards could justly remove them. In a worst-case scenario, if a majority of a church departed from the original standards, then those still adhering to those purposes might in good conscience withdraw and form a new church. Of Machen's conception of the church, historian Lefferts Loetscher observed: "For him the Church was, in essence, a voluntary society, created *de novo* by contract by people who find themselves in theological agreement. . . . This was good Anabaptist doctrine and might even pass for Congregationalism, but it certainly was not Presbyterianism." There is considerable justice in Loetscher's assessment; but Machen was scarcely the originator of that view of the church, even among Presbyterians. In fact, if one examines debates about creedal subscription in Ulster Presbyterianism as far back as the 1720s, there were already hints of the contractual notion in some of the polemics.[20]

A more immediate origin of Machen's ecclesiology was his devotion to southern traditions. He held a libertarian view of government. As a devotee of the Confederate Lost Cause, he believed that liberty in the first instance meant states' rights and minimal federal government. Unlike many Southerners, however, who overcame their suspicion of extending federal power at least in the matter of the Eighteenth Amendment and its ban on the manufacture and sale of alcoholic beverages, Machen insisted that Prohibition was not only unbiblical but an unwarranted intrusion into personal liberty. His opposition to governmental intrusion extended to the state and local level. He viewed with alarm increasing intrusions into education by states and localities and even grumbled that jaywalking ordinances unduly infringed liberty. One of the great threats to American liberty — and its culture — was the spirit of collectivism. He used part of the introduction to *Christianity and Liberalism* to expound the point. He

20. Machen, *Christianity and Liberalism*, 168; Loetscher, *Broadening Church*, 117. See, for example, Peter Brooke, *Ulster Presbyterianism: The Historical Perspective, 1610-1970* (New York: St. Martin's Press, 1987), esp. 89-91, on the creedal debates; also A. W. Godfrey Brown, "A Theological Interpretation of the First Subscription Controversy (1719-1728)," in *Challenge and Conflict: Essays in Irish Presbyterian History and Doctrine,* ed. J. L. M. Haire (Antrim: W & G Baird Ltd., 1981), 28-45.

wrote mournfully of the decline of music, literature, poetry, and the other arts. He attributed this degeneracy to the "narrowing of the range of personality which has been going on in the modern world. The whole development of modern society has tended mightily toward the limitation of the realm of freedom for the individual man." In an allusion to novelist Sinclair Lewis's portrayal of the bland hypocrisy and conformity of the American small town, Machen voiced anxiety that the loss of freedom would make the nation "one huge 'Main Street,' where spiritual adventure will be discouraged and democracy will be regarded as consisting in the reduction of all mankind to the proportions of the narrowest and least gifted of the citizens." "Are we forever condemned," he asked, "to live the sordid life of utilitarianism? Or is there some lost secret which if rediscovered will restore to mankind something of the glories of the past?" Machen believed that the answer lay in the recovery of the Christian religion, by which he meant "certainly not the religion of the modern liberal Church, but a message of divine grace, almost forgotten now, as it was in the middle ages, but destined to burst forth once more in God's good time, in a new Reformation, and bring light and freedom to mankind." For Machen, the restoration of proper doctrine was the main concern, but he had no doubt that the preservation of the libertarian ideals he prized for society also hung in the balance. "God grant," he prayed, "that there may come a reaction, and that the great principles of Anglo-Saxon liberty may be rediscovered before it is too late!" The phrase "Anglo-Saxon liberty" conveyed perhaps more than Machen realized, for his libertarian vision did *not* include opposition to laws enforcing racial segregation or otherwise discriminating against African Americans.[21]

Machen's roots in southern Presbyterianism also influenced his views of the nature of the church. James Henley Thornwell, the major theologian of nineteenth-century Presbyterianism in the South, had argued that Scripture offered no warrant for the church to create boards or agencies to supervise missionary or other activities. All such endeavors needed to be under the direct control of church judicatories, and Thornwell feared that boards would become partially independent of church courts. Because of Thornwell's enduring influence, southern Presbyterians were slower than their northern counterparts to develop an ecclesiastical bureaucracy. Also, Thornwell not only justified secession of the southern states from the Union in 1860-1861; he believed that

---

21. Machen, *Christianity and Liberalism,* 10, 15-16.

when the Old School General Assembly pledged its loyalty to the Federal government in 1861, this was a violation of the spirituality of the church and justified the withdrawal of southern Presbyterians to form their own denomination. Moreover, Machen's home congregation had withdrawn from the northern church to affiliate with the southern after the war. As Bradley Longfield sums up: "Secession, in Machen's heritage, provided not only an acceptable, but, in many respects, an honorable solution to irreconcilable disagreements of principle."[22]

This was the attitude that Machen brought to a conflict that rapidly escalated over the next several years. In 1923, the General Assembly took up the overture from the Philadelphia Presbytery regarding Fosdick and did instruct New York Presbytery to take action to bring the teaching and preaching of First Church into accord with "the system of doctrines taught in the Confession of Faith." The Assembly also reaffirmed the five essential doctrines it had specified in 1910. Protest was not long in coming, and it originated in the study of Robert Hastings Nichols, professor of church history at Auburn Theological Seminary. Nichols had drafted a document prior to the 1923 Assembly, but in light of its action Nichols and others revised the original statement and published it in January 1924 with the signatures of 150 Presbyterian clergy. By May it was reissued bearing the names of 1,274 ministers. Popularly known as the Auburn Affirmation, the document challenged the constitutional right of the General Assembly to define unilaterally essential doctrines of the Westminster Confession, "since the constitution of our church provides that its doctrine shall be declared only by concurrent action of the General Assembly and the presbyteries." Moreover, the Auburn Affirmation asserted that it was a theological error "to commit our church to certain theories concerning the inspiration of the Bible, and the Incarnation, the Atonement, the Resurrection, and the Continuing Life and Supernatural Power of our Lord Jesus Christ." The signers indicated that they all espoused "these great facts and doctrines," and some regarded "the particular theories contained in the deliverance of the General Assembly of 1923 as satisfactory explanations of these facts and doctrines. But," the signers continued, "we are united in believing that these are not the only theories allowed by the Scriptures and our standards as explanations of these facts and doctrines of our religion." In short, the Auburn Affirmation charged that the Assembly had exercised a power it did not possess and

22. Longfield, *Presbyterian Controversy*, 52.

that it had, in any event, placed more restrictions on legitimate theological expression than either the Westminster Confession or the Bible required. The authors closed with a fervent plea: "Finally, we deplore the evidences of division in our beloved church, in the face of a world so desperately in need of a united testimony to the gospel of Christ. We earnestly desire fellowship with all who like us are disciples of Jesus Christ."[23]

The Auburn Affirmation and Machen's *Christianity and Liberalism* represented the extreme poles of the controversy within the Presbyterian Church. Nichols and the co-signers of the Auburn Affirmation believed that the great "facts and doctrines" of the confession admitted of various permissible explanations and theories. The standards were a big tent, as it were, under which various acceptable opinions could coexist, and on this broad evangelical basis Presbyterians could preserve both "the unity and freedom of our church." Machen, by contrast, spoke for exclusivists who saw little room for reinterpretation of the confession without beginning the descent into apostasy. The Auburn Affirmation not only called for toleration but also questioned the power of the General Assembly (without the concurrence of the presbyteries) to issue a definitive interpretation of the standards. Machen, for all of his usual suspicion of centralized power, was quite eager to have the General Assembly place severe limits on theological interpretation. Many conservatives stood somewhere between Auburn and Machen. J. Ross Stevenson offered a case in point. Shortly after the Auburn Affirmation appeared, Stevenson published a response. Through a historical analysis of the Adopting Act of 1729, Stevenson concluded that it was indeed constitutional for the General Assembly to make definitive and binding statements regarding ministerial subscription to the Westminster Confession of Faith. Stevenson feared that "the loose terms of subscription" advocated by the Auburn Affirmation would allow "that a minister may be in good and regular standing in the Presbyterian Church even though he does not accept the clear teaching of the Confession of Faith." Yet, in contrast to Machen's book, Stevenson's article did not exhibit a fear of widespread apostasy or manifest any eagerness to ferret out supposed theological offenders. Stevenson represented a conservative position, uncomfortable with the degree of latitude that the Auburn Affirmation

23. The various revisions that resulted in the Auburn Affirmation are examined in Charles E. Quirk, "Origins of the Auburn Affirmation," *Journal of Presbyterian History* 53 (Summer 1975): 120-42.

espoused, but also irenic in spirit. These two types of conservatism at Princeton Seminary had clashed before. The disagreement between them was about to become even more fierce and public.[24]

The pulpit of First Presbyterian Church in Princeton fell vacant in 1923, and J. Gresham Machen was invited to serve as stated supply. He used his sermons to promote an exclusivist theological vision and warn of the dangers of modernism. In protest, Professor Henry van Dyke made a prominent display of his dissatisfaction by ceasing to attend worship at the church. In a letter to the session, also sent to the press, van Dyke temporarily surrendered his pew. He wrote that he would not fritter away his time "in listening to such a dismal, bilious travesty of the Gospel. Until he is done, count me out, and give up my pew in the church." When Machen resigned the temporary post, the session asked Charles Erdman to fill the pulpit, and by late 1924 the latter was called as the regular pastor of the First Church — a post he held until 1934, two years before his retirement from the seminary. When Erdman began preaching at First Church, van Dyke returned to his accustomed pew. In January 1925, this action prompted the editor of *The Presbyterian,* a theologically conservative periodical published out of Philadelphia, to wonder what van Dyke's action signified with regard to the seminary: "Does the return of such a pronounced modernist as Dr. van Dyke to the old church, under the new pastor, mean that he is anticipating more liberal preaching under the new regime? . . . Does this action of Dr. van Dyke signify that two parties are developing in the faculty of Princeton Seminary, or does it simply show a confusion outside?" An incensed Erdman wrote, insisting that the disagreements at Princeton had nothing to do with differences of theology but instead entailed questions of "spirit, methods, or policies." Erdman also added a barb: "This division would be of no consequence were it not for the unkindness, suspicion, bitterness and intolerance of those members of the faculty, who are also editors of *The Presbyterian.*" Erdman subsequently indicated that he was not referring to Machen when he wrote those words, but the denial seemed a bit disingenuous since Machen was the only faculty member at the seminary who sat on the periodical's board of editors.[25]

24. J. Ross Stevenson, "The Adopting Act of 1729 and the Powers of the General Assembly," *Princeton Theological Review* 22 (1924): 96-106; quotation on 96.

25. On the incident at First Presbyterian Church, see Arthur S. Link, ed., *The First Presbyterian Church of Princeton: Two Centuries of History* (Princeton: First Presbyterian Church, 1967), 93-96; Longfield, *Presbyterian Controversy,* 131.

Erdman's irritation was understandable. In nearly two decades on the faculty, he had endured, mostly with forbearance, the condescension of colleagues who behaved as if his English Bible and other courses had debased the curriculum. Then, after the Great War, the majority of the faculty had publicly opposed the plan for organic union of Protestant churches that he and Stevenson both prominently endorsed. In the months before Erdman's outburst to the *Presbyterian,* difficulties with colleagues had intensified. In early 1924, Erdman was nominated for moderator of the General Assembly, ran against Clarence Macartney, and narrowly lost. The majority of the seminary faculty opposed Erdman's election. Then, in October 1924, a group of Princeton seminarians voted to withdraw from the Theological Seminary Conference of the Middle Atlantic Union and to organize a more conservative League of Evangelical Students. While not opposed in principle to the creation of the new organization, Erdman questioned its wisdom. For many years Erdman had been the faculty representative to the student group, but his lukewarm response to the new association prompted a movement among some students for a new advisor. The faculty then passed over Erdman and chose Professor Robert Dick Wilson for the post. Most campus battles remain arcane affairs unnoticed by the larger public, but this story was picked up by major newspapers and thus broadcast to all that Princeton was divided against itself. A few months later, in early 1925, when his presbytery again nominated Erdman to be General Assembly moderator, the majority of his seminary colleagues — Professors William Park Armstrong, William Brenton Greene, J. Gresham Machen, and Geerhardus Vos — signed a pamphlet setting forth reasons why Erdman should *not* be elected moderator. In May, shortly before the Assembly convened, Machen publicly condemned Erdman's candidacy. While he acknowledged Erdman's personal orthodoxy, he claimed that he was functioning as a stalking horse for the "modernist and indifferentist party in the church." Erdman replied: "I have always been a Fundamentalist in my beliefs. I refuse to be labeled as a Modernist or liberal, but if any men of liberal theological views desire to vote for me this year it is, of course, their privilege to do so." On this second try for office, Erdman was elected, and he quickly made clear that healing the controversy in the church would be the top priority of his year as moderator.[26]

26. Longfield, *Presbyterian Controversy,* 149.

The Presbyterian Controversy Resolved
and the Reorganization of the Seminary

At the General Assembly of 1924, Macartney's narrow victory over Erdman had signaled a triumph of the most conservative forces in the denomination; but the Assembly nevertheless moved cautiously, unwilling to take the church to the brink of schism. For example, it chose to make no response to the Auburn Affirmation, and it postponed a final decision on the Fosdick case by switching the immediate question from theology to polity. The Assembly concluded that Fosdick, as a non-Presbyterian occupying a Presbyterian pulpit for a prolonged period, was an anomaly to proper order. Therefore, the Presbytery of New York was instructed "to take up with Dr. Fosdick this question to the end that he may determine whether it is his pleasure to enter the Presbyterian Church and thus be in a regular relationship with the First Presbyterian Church of New York as one of its pastors." The Assembly also avoided an immediate decision on the cases of two young men — Henry Pitney Van Dusen and Cedric Lehman — whom the Presbytery of New York had licensed to preach despite their refusals to affirm the virgin birth; instead, it sent the matter down to the synod (an intermediate judicatory between the General Assembly and the presbytery) for action. In effect, these moves rescinded nothing that the General Assembly had done previously but avoided pushing the liberal faction into a corner. By the time the next Assembly gathered in 1925, Fosdick had taken the Presbyterians off the hook by deciding that he did not wish to enter their ministry and by severing his relationship to the First Church.[27]

But the matter of Van Dusen and Lehman returned. The Judicial Commission of the General Assembly, in response to a request from New York to clarify the relative powers of presbyteries vis-à-vis the General Assembly in the licensing and ordaining of candidates, ruled that the General Assembly had the power to review decisions by presbyteries and that, since several General Assemblies had affirmed the virgin birth to be an essential doctrine of the confession, the Presbytery of New York should not have proceeded to license Van Dusen and Lehman. The matter was remanded to the presbytery for appropriate action. In advance of the commission's report, Henry Sloane Coffin, then pastor of the Madison Avenue Presbyterian Church in Manhattan, had already caucused with the other

27. Loetscher, *Broadening Church,* 124.

commissioners of the New York Presbytery and prepared a statement of protest in the event of such a ruling. He had also secured a promise from Moderator Erdman that the protest could be presented to the Assembly. In essence, Coffin informed the Assembly that the New York Presbytery would stand upon the constitutional principle that the General Assembly could not "change or add to" the requirements for ordination "without submitting such amendment to the Presbyteries for concurrent action." In a word, New York would stand by the view of the constitution set forth in the Auburn Affirmation, and there was more than a little hint of willingness to defy the Assembly and possibly to withdraw from the denomination. In this charged atmosphere, Erdman relinquished the chair to the vice moderator so that he himself could introduce a resolution calling for the creation of a special commission of fifteen members "to study the present causes making for unrest" in the church and to report back to the next Assembly with the goal that "purity, peace, unity and progress of the Church" be promoted. Seconded by both conservative and liberal leaders, the motion passed unanimously. Erdman appointed a commission composed chiefly of moderate conservatives.[28]

During the intervening year, the special commission of fifteen met four times to draft a report that it presented in 1926, with an additional follow-up in 1927. Overwhelmingly approved by the Assembly in both years, the report, without naming Machen or any other ultraconservative specifically, rejected the charge that the denomination faced widespread departure from the faith within its own ranks. The commission also found that original jurisdiction in matters of the examination and ordination of candidates resided with presbyteries. While the General Assembly clearly had power on an appellate basis to review these decisions on a case-by-case basis, it should be wary of issuing categorical statements with regard to "essential and necessary" articles of faith, for the Assembly could not unilaterally alter the church's constitution. "The Constitution of the Presbyterian Church," the commission said in echo of the Auburn Affirmation, "can be amended only by the General Assembly and the Presbyteries acting concurrently." In effect, the report, without explicitly saying so, was asserting that the Assembly had exceeded its power when it tried to erect the five points into "essential and necessary" articles. The commission's report also provided a valuable historical section, demonstrating, in the words of Lefferts Loetscher more than a

28. Loetscher, *Broadening Church*, 125-36.

quarter-century after the report, that "the American Presbyterian Church has been from the beginning a combination of diverging tendencies, maintained in fairly equal balance." Thus, from a historical perspective, it was far too simplistic for the "extreme conservatives" to assume that "their theological perspective and theirs alone was simon-pure American Presbyterianism, and that their liberal opponents represented a sinister deviation from this straight line." Particularly suggestive was the assertion of the commission that

> The principle of toleration when rightly conceived and frankly and fairly applied is as truly a part of our constitution as are any of the doctrines stated in that instrument. . . . Toleration as a principle applicable within the Presbyterian Church refers to an attitude and a practice according to which the status of a minister or other ordained officer is acknowledged and fellowship is extended to him, even though he may hold some views that are individual on points not regarded as essential to the system of faith which the Church professes. Presbyterianism is a great body of belief, but it is more than a belief; it is also a tradition, a controlling sentiment. The ties which bind us to it are not of the mind only; they are ties of the heart as well. There are people who, despite variant opinions, can never be at home in any other communion. They were born into the Presbyterian Church. They love its name, its order and its great distinctive teachings. In its fellowship they have a precious inheritance from their forebears. Their hearts bow at its altars and cherish a just pride in its noble history. Attitudes and sentiments like these are treasures which should not be undervalued hastily nor cast aside lightly.

The adoption of the special commission's report was not intended to devalue theology, but it did imply that the ties binding the denomination were more than theological in a purely intellectual sense. Loyalty to Presbyterianism meant loyalty to a community — to its congregations, its schools, its boards, its mission programs, its ethos or way of life. That loyalty, at least *to some degree* (a degree never fully specified), transcended questions of agreement or disagreement on points of doctrine.[29]

29. *Minutes of the General Assembly of the Presbyterian Church in the U.S.A.*, 3rd ser., vol. 5, 1926 (Philadelphia: Office of the General Assembly, 1926), 62-87; quotation on 78-

By 1926, it was clear that the seminary was deeply divided; and to the detriment of the institution, its internal divisions were being displayed to the public. At the level of the faculty, there existed a majority party composed of J. Gresham Machen, William Park Armstrong, Geerhardus Vos, Oswald Allis (an assistant professor of Semitic philology since 1922 and an instructor twelve years prior to that time), Caspar Wistar Hodge Jr., Robert Dick Wilson, and William Brenton Greene. The minority consisted of Ross Stevenson, John Davis (who died in late June 1926), Frederick Loetscher, and J. Ritchie Smith. But the divisions were not simply within the faculty. The original Plan of the Seminary provided for governance by the board of directors with ultimate authority lodged in the General Assembly. For reasons of civil law, it became necessary in the 1820s to incorporate the seminary under a board of trustees who would take fiduciary responsibility for the assets of the school. Unfortunately, by the 1920s the two boards found themselves often divided, with the majority of the board of directors in sympathy with the faculty majority and the majority of the trustees sympathetic to the faculty minority. Hence, Princeton found itself with a faculty deeply divided, the two boards of governance often out of sync with each other, and a president who did not enjoy the confidence of the majority of either the faculty or the board of directors. The seminary appeared to be a study in institutional dysfunction.

The struggle intensified in 1926. A proposal to move Machen to another chair at the seminary made him a further point of contention. With the impending retirement of William Brenton Greene from the chair of apologetics and ethics, the board of directors proposed to move Machen to Greene's chair. With the denomination as a whole opting for greater inclusiveness with the adoption of the report of the special commission of 1925, Machen and his allies viewed the maintenance of a rigorously Old School Princeton as possibly the last redoubt within the Presbyterian Church against an encroaching tide of liberalism.

A number of individual trustees and directors requested the Assembly to appoint a committee to investigate the condition at the seminary with the goal of harmonizing differences and promoting its welfare. In

---

79. The people who turned the tide toward a greater toleration of divergent views have sometimes been styled "moderate conservatives" or denominational loyalists. See William J. Weston, *Presbyterian Pluralism: Competition in a Protestant House* (Knoxville: University of Tennessee Press, 1997).

his capacity as president of the school, Stevenson strongly supported the proposal. In his remarks to the Assembly, he emphasized that Princeton was "an agency of the combined old school and new school"; its purpose was to "represent the whole Presbyterian Church and not any particular faction of it." Thinking of the sorts of students who were likely to be attracted if the position of Machen and his allies won the day, Stevenson asked, "Shall Princeton Seminary . . . be permitted to swing off the extreme right wing as to become an interdenominational Seminary for Bible School–premillennial–secession fundamentalism?" Machen, of course, was not a premillennialist but was prepared to make common cause with them in the interest of the greater good of defeating liberalism. From the perspective of Machen's opponents, the issue was not conservatism versus liberalism — all the Princeton professors were conservative by any reasonable definition of the term. "The real point at issue," Lefferts Loetscher wrote, ". . . was whether orthodoxy and tolerance were compatible."[30]

The Assembly chose to appoint the special committee and to postpone a confirmation vote on Machen until the results of the report were received. After making several trips to Princeton to interview the various constituencies of the school, the committee made recommendations enacted by the 1929 General Assembly. The Assembly merged the boards of trustees and directors into a single body of trustees; the two preexisting boards each made up one-third of the members of the new board of trustees, with the final third being new appointees. Given the nature of the persons chosen for the new board, it had a somewhat more centrist composition. Also, the office of the president of the seminary was strengthened. Although all members of the existing faculty were invited to remain, there was a major secession. J. Gresham Machen, Robert Dick Wilson, and Oswald Allis saw the change as the first step toward the destruction of Old Princeton and resigned to form the nucleus of Westminster Theological Seminary, which opened its doors in the fall of 1929 in the greater Philadelphia area. They were also joined by Cornelius Van Til, who had just been offered a position at Princeton but turned it down to go to Westminster.

---

30. Loetscher, *Broadening Church*, 154; his discussion on 136-48 still remains the best succinct description of the events.

Aftermath

For those who remained, the trauma of losing approximately half their colleagues must have been painful indeed; and the sting must have been made worse for Loetscher and Stevenson because Ritchie retired that fall, and they could scarcely share any feelings of loss, of anger, or of relief with those who remained, for both Vos and Armstrong had strong sympathies for the seceders. Years later Ned Stonehouse, the first serious biographer of Machen, claimed that "the wife of one of those concerned [i.e., either Mrs. Vos, Mrs. Armstrong, or Mrs. Hodge] once told me, following the establishment of Westminster, that it was very difficult to work for one institution and pray for another." One must wonder what institutional and interpersonal dynamics were shaped in that environment and were perhaps unconsciously perpetuated in later generations of Princeton faculty.[31]

But the work of the school needed to go forward. Among others, Samuel Zwemer, a missionary of many years through the Reformed Church in America, was appointed professor of the history of religion and mission in 1929; and the following year Henry Snyder Gehman began a long tenure as biblical scholar. Of course, the fall of 1929 also brought the beginnings of the Great Depression, and the rebuilding of the seminary faced economic as well as psychological barriers.

---

31. Stonehouse, *J. Gresham Machen*, 450.

CHAPTER FOURTEEN

John A. Mackay: Continuity and New Direction

O N FEBRUARY 2, 1937, John Alexander Mackay was formally inaugurated as the third president of Princeton Seminary. The seminary
community and visiting dignitaries gathered in the recently completed
neo-Gothic chapel of Princeton University for the ceremonies. On behalf
of the board of trustees, Robert E. Speer gave the charge to the new president. No doubt with the troubles of 1929 in mind, he struck a careful balance, affirming both continuity and change. Asserting that "we glory in
our heritage," he encouraged Mackay to "saturate your mind and spirit
with the early history of the Seminary, and especially with the biographies of the great triumvirate of Dr. Alexander, Dr. Samuel Miller, and Dr.
Hodge." These "were men of clear and unflinching conviction"; but, Speer
added, "they were also men of fair and generous temper." No doubt
thinking of the role they had played in trying to keep the Presbyterian
Church together in the years before the 1837 schism, Speer remarked that
those "of more contentious spirit spoke of them with a touch of derision,
as 'the Gentlemen at Princeton.'" Their heritage of solid theology and
sound reasoning needed to be preserved. But so, too, did their spirit of
warmth and devotion. "The words of [poet John Greenleaf] Whittier,"
Speer insisted, "have been illustrated to generation after generation of
students in the lives of the men who have taught here: 'Warm, sweet, tender even yet,' — those are the very words that describe what we have
seen here — as far removed as anything could be from a cold intellectu-
alism of theoretical theology." From his own time as a student at the university and seminary, Speer added personal reminiscences of attending
an evangelistic meeting at which "the little round red-headed speaker

[A. A. Hodge made] . . . the most moving appeal with the tears coursing down his cheeks." And he recalled William Henry Green, affectionately remembered as "Rabbi Green," and "the tenderness and beauty of his personal devotion to God." The implicit message was clear: Princeton continued to value its heritage and did not concede it to those who had withdrawn in 1929. Speer implied that those who had seceded from the seminary had at best a partial appreciation for Princeton's heritage. Speer was equally straightforward in asserting that the tradition was dynamic, not a relic or museum piece. As he said to Mackay, "we are laying on you not only this duty preserving the heritage but also the duty of enlarging and enriching it."[1]

In his inaugural address, entitled "The Restoration of Theology," Mackay did not deal directly with the Princeton tradition nor even allude to the school's recent troubles until very near the end of his remarks. He focused on a much larger issue: the "sense of uprootedness and spiritual homelessness" afflicting America and Europe. The "greatest cultural need at the present time," he averred, "is a consistent world view, a *Weltanschauung,* as the Germans call it"; and only theology could address this want — "great theology, theology that brings to a focus the rays of light that streamed from above in Jesus Christ." Contemporary philosophy and metaphysics could not meet the demand of the hour, for they had nothing to say about "the stark reality of sin" and humanity's need for redemption. He insisted further that the "most potent cultural forces of our time are theologies rather than philosophies." In Mackay's view, both communism and fascism were *de facto* religions. The communist "feels himself to be invincible because the stars in their courses fight against the Sisera of the Bourgeoisie. Thus while he fights against religion he does so in the name and in the strength of a religious faith which is rooted in the nature of things." Similarly, German fascism, said Mackay, quoting Nazi theorist Alfred Rosenberg, held "that the Nordic Blood presents that mystery by which the ancient sacraments are superseded and transcended." Against these essentially idolatrous views of human community, one founded upon class and the other upon "blood or soil or national tradition," Christians had to exemplify "that universal community which came into being at Pentecost and which recognizes no barriers of soil or blood or class." To realize that goal, the church uni-

---

1. Robert E. Speer, "Charge to the President," *Princeton Seminary Bulletin* 31 (April 1937): 2, 3, 5.

versal "needs a theology that will give it resistance-strength, communal cohesion, and expansive power. It needs the theology that is inherent in the Biblical records and the tradition of historic Catholic Christianity, a Theology of the Word."[2]

Mackay acknowledged that even in certain conservative circles in America there was a "dislike, or at least wariness, of theology and theological discussion." That caution "derives from unforgettable experiences of divisions caused by theological differences" — a remark undoubtedly triggering painful memories within his audience, who had recently witnessed schism in their own midst. Yet the church should not shrink from "first class theological discussion," for only thus could there be a chance of getting beyond the "weak, undogmatic and invertebrate faith" too common in the churches. Warfield, Patton, or Machen would have warmed to that language. But it was none of these whom Mackay cited in his summons to restore theology. He turned largely to Europeans who a few years earlier would have been unknown to his hearers: contemporaries Karl Barth and Emil Brunner, as well as the only recently rediscovered nineteenth-century Danish thinker Søren Kierkegaard. From Brunner, he drew a caution about theology even as he was urging its recovery:

> The fact that God's Word is not a static theory, that it is not a Word which man can manipulate as he chooses, but that it is a living personal challenge has been forgotten. When dogma has ceased to be witness, that is, to point to something behind and above itself, then it is fossilized into a concrete "Word," a fetish.[3]

Mackay closed his inaugural address with a confident expression that "the Reformed tradition to which Princeton Seminary belongs has a role of unprecedented importance to play in the world of today and of tomorrow. If we of today are faithful, the great days of this Seminary are not all in the golden past." He was even bolder in the letter to alumni that he appended to his inaugural address when it was sent out in the *Princeton Seminary Bulletin*. He suggested that "strong tides of thought are running in the direction of Princeton's historic position. . . . The future is

---

2. John A. Mackay, "The Restoration of Theology," *Princeton Seminary Bulletin* 31 (April 1937): 7-18; quotations on 7, 8, 9, 11, 12, 13.

3. Mackay, "The Restoration of Theology," 15, 16. The quote was from Emil Brunner, *The Mediator.*

ours if we have faith to grasp it." The seminary, he seemed to say, stood at a providentially significant moment — to use the New Testament term, a *kairos*. Both he and Speer had made plain at the inaugural ceremony that they were laying claim to the legacy of Old Princeton. They also made it clear, to use their terms, that the tradition was not going to be fossilized but rather enlarged and enriched. New voices would be heard and new ideas advanced in service to an old vision.[4]

Years of Preparation

John Alexander Mackay was born in Inverness in the Highlands of Scotland in 1889, the eldest of the five children of Duncan Mackay, a tailor and clothier, and Isabella Macdonald Mackay. His parents reared their children in the Free Presbyterian Church after it seceded from the Free Church in 1893. The secession occurred in response to the Free Church's passage of a declaratory act interpreting the Westminster Confession so as to emphasize the love of God and to downplay human depravity and God's predestination of the elect. It was an act bearing similarity to the declaration adopted by the Presbyterian Church in the U.S.A. in 1903. The Free Presbyterians, holding to a rigorous interpretation of the confession, rejected this leniency, generally avoided contact with other groups, did not permit musical instruments in worship, and sang only from the Psalms. Years later, Mackay recalled in an address to the Princeton Seminary community that he needed no one to tell him "about sectarian Protestantism," for the church in which he was brought up held "that our ideas and practices were so much purer than the ideas and practices of others that we were not on any account to mingle with them in religious fellowship." And yet Mackay also testified that he owed "more than tongue can tell" to the Free Presbyterians, for it was in their fellowship "that Christ first spoke to me."[5]

The occasion was a communion season in 1903 at the village of

4. "Dr. Mackay's Message to the Alumni," *Princeton Seminary Bulletin* 31 (April 1937): 20.

5. John Mackay Metzger, *The Hand and the Road: The Life and Times of John A. Mackay* (Louisville: Westminster John Knox Press, 2010), 1-18; James Lachlan MacLeod, *The Second Disruption: The Free Church in Victorian Scotland and the Origins of the Free Presbyterian Church* (East Linton, Scotland: Tuckwell Press Ltd., 2000); John A. Mackay, "The Glory and Peril of the Local," *Princeton Seminary Bulletin* 48 (1955): 11.

Rogart north of Inverness. Despite the desire of the sixteenth-century Scottish reformers for a monthly or quarterly celebration of the sacrament, the actual observance of the supper became much less frequent, especially in the Highlands. Shortages of ministers, poverty among the people, and religious disruptions were among the reasons for the infrequency. When celebrated, the communions were solemn events stretching over a number of days, with periods of fasting, preparatory services, and examination by ministers or elders to determine whether one should be admitted to the supper. On the day of the communion itself, the tables were fenced — that is, barred to all but those who had received a token at the time of the examination. Often a service of thanksgiving was held the day following the communion. Because of the numbers of people attending these seasons, they were often held outdoors in the summer. These large gatherings attracted gawkers and peddlers, thus sometimes creating around the edges a bit of the atmosphere of a carnival — hence the term "holy fairs" that Robert Burns gave them in 1785 — but at their core was a particularly intense form of spirituality.[6]

At Rogart in 1903, John Mackay entered that world of religious experience. Years later, in a book exploring the meaning of the letter to the Ephesians, Mackay gave his fullest account of the experience:

> I was a lad of only fourteen years of age when, in the pages of the Ephesian Letter, I saw a new world. I found a world there which had features similar to a world that had been formed within me. After a period of anguished yearning, during which I prayed to God each night the simple words "Lord, help me," something happened. After passionately desiring that I might cross the frontier into a new order of life which I had read about, which I had seen in others whom I admired, I was admitted in an inexplicable way, but to my unutterable joy, into a new dimension of existence.... My life began to be set to the music of that passage which begins, "And you hath he quickened, who were dead in trespasses and sin" (2:1).
>
> I had been "quickened"; I was really alive. The quickening came in this wise. It was a Saturday, towards noon, in the month

6. Leigh Eric Schmidt, *Holy Fairs: Scottish Communions and American Revivals in the Early Modern Period* (Princeton: Princeton University Press, 1989), 49, 68, 109, and *passim*. See also Paul K. Conkin, *Cane Ridge: America's Pentecost* (Madison: University of Wisconsin Press, 1990).

of July of 1903. The "preparation" service of an old-time Scottish Communion season was being held in the open air among the hills, in the Highland parish of Rogart, in Sutherlandshire. A minister was preaching from a wooden pulpit. . . . But something, someone, said within me that I, too, must preach, that I must stand where that man stood.

Mackay recounted how "the rest of the summer I literally lived in the pages of a little New Testament which I had bought for a British penny." He was particularly moved by the letter to the Ephesians and its portrayal of a cosmic Christ. "It was," he recounted, "the cosmic Christ that fascinated me, the living Lord Jesus Christ who was the center of a great drama of unity, in which everything in Heaven and on earth was to become one in him." Mackay's description of his "quickening" displays some similarity to Jonathan Edwards's account of his own transformed sense of reality in the wake of conversion, and that fact is not surprising, for soon Mackay was avidly reading Edwards.[7]

Awarded a scholarship, he began his secondary education in the fall of 1903 at the Inverness Royal Academy, where he formed friendships with John and Donald Baillie, both of whom subsequently became distinguished theologians. After graduating in 1907, Mackay briefly attended Glasgow University, but a fellowship made possible his transfer to Aberdeen. Since no Free Presbyterian congregation existed there, Mackay first attended a Free Church and then joined a Baptist chapel. His time at Aberdeen was punctuated by two different periods of absence during which he undertook theological studies with a tutor of the Free Presbyterian Church, first in Inverness and then subsequently in Wick. Much later, in 1958, in the address opening the final academic year of his presidency at Princeton, Mackay painted a memorable picture of those theological studies: "there were three of us who studied together under the direction of a scholarly pastor away in the Scottish North Country. We occupied a room together within the sound of the North Sea breakers in the fishing port of Wick. We studied and slept together in the same room, two in one bed, and one in another." Although nostalgically rendered, the description of three young students cramped into a single room in an out-of-the-way fishing port at the north of Scotland also con-

7. John A. Mackay, *God's Order: The Ephesian Letter and This Time* (New York: Macmillan, 1953), 6-8.

veyed the sense of limitation that Mackay ultimately felt with his Free Presbyterian affiliation. At Aberdeen he studied widely, taking honors in philosophy, and engaged in a number of student activities that broadened his perspectives. In 1910 he heard Robert E. Speer, of the Presbyterian board of foreign missions, present an eloquent case for mission and for young men and women to consider whether they were called to the foreign field. Mackay's extensive reading, his experience of worship in churches other than the Free Presbyterian, a growing sense of the body of Christ as an ecumenical fellowship transcending the denominations, increasing contacts with people in the Free Church, and then the information that the Free Church was eager to sponsor a missionary to Latin America and would be pleased if that person were Mackay himself — all of these events led to the moment in 1913 when he resigned as a candidate for the ministry in the Free Presbyterian Church. The fact that he had, at roughly the same time, spoken before a Free Church near his home congregation in Inverness infuriated the Mackay family's pastor, and they in turn joined their son in leaving the Free Presbyterians to join the Free Church.[8]

Mackay had won a fellowship in philosophy that allowed him to pursue further education. He decided to go to Princeton Seminary and arrived at the school in September 1913. The choice was a logical one, for Mackay already had positive associations with Princeton. He knew, for example, that Robert Speer, whom he greatly admired, had studied at the seminary; and the pastor of the Free Church where the Mackay family transferred its membership recommended Princeton heartily. Since the Disruption of 1843 when the Free Church came into existence, there had been a special bond with Princeton. William Cunningham, Free Church theologian and church historian, came to visit Charles Hodge the year of the disruption; and the two found an immediate rapport. Then in 1868 the Free Church gave the College of New Jersey its new president in the person of James McCosh. Because Mackay had already done previous theological work, he finished the program at Princeton in 1915 after only two years. His reactions to the faculty were mixed. He believed that Erdman and Machen were excellent preachers, but other professors chiefly scholars. In fact, he found the general tone of spiritual life to be somewhat chilling, though with the coming of J. Ross Stevenson in

8. John A. Mackay, "Theological Triennium: For What?" *Princeton Seminary Bulletin* 52 (1959): 5.

Mackay's second year, the young Scot sensed "a more serious tone" among the students. He praised Stevenson as "a man of spiritual power who is in intense sympathy with the life, difficulties, and aspirations of the students," but that sympathy apparently did not translate into much direct involvement with students. In fact, the faculty generally remained aloof outside the classroom. The most notable exception was Charles Erdman, who regularly invited students to his home. Nearly six decades later, well into his retirement, Mackay used the introduction to his baccalaureate sermon to the class of 1971 to praise Erdman. He declared that "the personality, teaching, and friendship of Professor Charles Erdman proved to be one of the most creative experiences in my life! For this man became for a young Scottish student the finest pattern he had known of what it means to be a Christian."[9]

Mackay used his time at Princeton to prepare for the missionary vocation he envisioned. He read appropriate books — such as Samuel Zwemer's *Life of Raymond Lull,* the late medieval lay missionary who sought the conversion of Jews and Muslims — and examined the biographies of John L. Nevius and Walter M. Lowrie, nineteenth-century Princeton Seminary graduates who had served as missionaries to China. He attended the Student Volunteer Movement's convention in Kansas City over the Christmas break, 1913-1914. He also wrote a thesis, "The Idea of Revelation," in his second year, which won him the theology prize in 1915. With it came funds that he could use to travel for further study. Where to travel was not immediately self-evident. By 1915, Great Britain, France, and Russia were at war with Germany and its allies. Thus one usual course of study for fellowship recipients — a trip to visit universities on the Continent — was not feasible, especially for a citizen of the United Kingdom. Knowing that Mackay planned to work as a missionary in Latin America, Benjamin Warfield recommended that the young man spend time in Spain in order to understand better the language and culture of the people to whom he would be ministering. In the meantime, the Free Church had authorized Mackay to make a fact-finding tour of South America. After completing his studies at Princeton, Mackay embarked on May 14, 1915, on a voyage that would take him through the Panama Canal — it had been open slightly less than a year — and on to Peru, Bolivia, Chile, Uruguay, and Argentina. By the end of September he had returned to the United Kingdom and delivered his report to the Free

9. John A. Mackay, "The Great Adventure," *Princeton Seminary Bulletin* 64 (1971): 31.

Church, including a recommendation that an educational mission be established in Lima, Peru. Then, after several weeks at home in Scotland, he headed off for his year of study in Spain.[10]

From the fall of 1915 until the summer of 1916, Mackay studied in Madrid except for brief periods of travel to other places in Spain. Madrid was then a relatively open place intellectually, and he lived in the Residencia de Estudiantes — a community inspired and organized by Francisco Giner de los Ríos, the great Spanish champion of academic freedom and research, who had died only a few months before Mackay's arrival. Some years later, Mackay said that Giner resembled Christ teaching "his disciples on the hill slopes beside the placid sea." Through the Residencia at various times came such figures as Salvador Dali, Luis Buñuel, José Ortega y Gasset, and Miguel de Unamuno. During Mackay's stay in Madrid, Unamuno was already 51 years old and an established scholar at the University of Salamanca, but he visited Madrid from time to time, staying at the Residencia during his sojourns. On one of these, Mackay met him and was quite taken by Don Miguel. Over the Christmas break, the young man visited Unamuno in his home in Salamanca and was cordially received. More than anyone else he encountered in Spain, Unamuno left a profound impact upon John Mackay — a fact attested not only by the numerous references in Mackay's subsequent writings but also by a portrait of Unamuno that hung in his study when he returned to Princeton.[11]

While Giner symbolized to Mackay Christ teaching by the Sea of Galilee, he saw in Unamuno the Christ "who drove the merchants from the temple." A Basque of passionate intensity, Unamuno attacked every form of religious hypocrisy. He believed that the realities of the Christian message were not found in "bloodless logic," and the true religious life did not bring certainty and peace but an "agonizing struggle." For Unamuno, "truth breaks and life is fulfilled only upon the road when one is pressing onwards, loyal to the heavenly vision." From Don Miguel, Mackay learned to appreciate the great mystics of the Spanish tradition, especially John of the Cross and Teresa of Avila. If he had a saint, Mackay would say thereafter, it was Teresa. The ascetic and moral character of Unamuno

---

10. Metzger, *Hand and the Road*, 45-60.

11. H. McKennie Goodpasture, "The Latin American Soul of John A. Mackay," *Journal of Presbyterian History* 48 (Winter 1970): 265-92; "John A. Mackay: Influences on My Life," interviewer Gerald W. Gillette, *Journal of Presbyterian History* 56 (Spring 1978): 20-34.

also impressed his Scottish admirer. He dressed simply, he did not smoke, and in a time and place where prevailing mores tolerated the taking of mistresses, Unamuno maintained strict fidelity to his wife. Don Miguel's learning also awed Mackay. If he found a foreign author whom he wished to read, he sought to master the appropriate language in order to study the original. Thus he learned Danish in order to read Kierkegaard. His mentor's emphasis that truth was found in the midst of struggle and journey — "only upon the road when one is pressing forward" — resonated with strands of piety in which Mackay himself had been reared. One of the first books given John as a boy was an illustrated edition of John Bunyan's *Pilgrim's Progress,* the classic expression of a Puritan piety depicting the Christian's path to salvation as an arduous journey through sin, doubt, and temptation. Perhaps Unamuno's greatest contribution to Mackay was to deepen his awareness that within the Spanish-speaking world a religious tradition already existed upon which the Protestant missionary might draw. That tradition — the "other Spanish Christ," Mackay would later call it — though overlaid by contradictory elements, was something indigenous within Hispanic Christianity to which the Protestant could appeal.[12]

After his fruitful year in Spain, John Mackay returned to Scotland to be commissioned by the Free Church as missionary to Peru. On August 16, 1916, he married Jane Logan Wells, and in mid-October the couple sailed for their new home and work in South America.

The Missionary Years

Arriving in Lima near the close of 1916, John Mackay put into effect his goal of establishing an educational mission. He arranged to take over an existing school that was failing financially and transferred it to a new location under the auspices of the Free Church, with himself as the principal. Both he and Jane Mackay also took on a part of the instructional responsibilities as well as much of the labor to get the new building ready for students. In March 1917, the school opened for instruction under the

12. John A. Mackay, *The Other Spanish Christ: A Study in the Spiritual History of Spain and South America* (Eugene, OR: Wipf and Stock, 2001 [1933]), 147; Solomon Lipp, "Francisco Giner de los Ríos — Modern Educator of Spain," *History of Education Quarterly* 2 (September 1962): 168-81.

name Escuela Anglo-Peruana. It began with approximately forty students and within two months had eighty-five. Despite some personnel problems and the difficulties of communicating with the Free Church's foreign missionary committee back in Scotland, the school prospered; and by the 1918-1919 school year, Mackay expanded it to include instruction at the secondary level, secured yet another site, and renamed the institution the Colegio Anglo-Peruana to signify the higher, more advanced learning the school would be offering. The certification of the school was made possible, in part, by the fact that Mackay had in the meantime received educational credentials from the University of San Marcos in Lima. During his first year in the city, he presented a thesis on Unamuno that was accepted at San Marcos and opened the way for him subsequently to give lectures and offer courses there. Mackay had quickly begun to establish his credibility among Peruvians.[13]

The Mackays had started their labors in Peru at a propitious moment. In February 1916, less than a year before they arrived, the Congress on Christian Work in Latin America was held in Panama. Because of qualms among "high church" Anglicans about designating a Roman Catholic region as a mission field, Latin America had been excluded from formal discussion at the World Missionary Conference at Edinburgh in 1910. Behind the scenes, Robert E. Speer lobbied for a meeting to address the topic and continued to do so until his efforts bore fruit in the 1916 gathering of delegates from Latin America, primarily missionaries, and from churches and other agencies elsewhere around the globe. Native Latin Americans constituted fewer than 10 percent of the delegates, and many missionary interests, such as faith missions and the nascent Pentecostal presence, were not represented. Nevertheless, the gathering represented the beginnings of an ecumenical awareness among Protestants working in the region and created a continuing committee of cooperation to sustain and deepen that awareness. The moment was also particularly auspicious in Peru itself. After the congress, regional meetings took place, including one in Lima in March 1916. The public character of the meeting represented, according to one account, "a radical innovation — a Protestant meeting held openly, without apology, in a theatre and with police protection!" A meeting of this character was possible because of constitutional change. The previous November the words "and permits no other form of public worship" were stricken from

13. Metzger, *Hand and the Road*, 92-120.

the constitutional clause recognizing Roman Catholicism as the national church. The Catholic Church still enjoyed great privileges and could bring pressure to bear upon Protestants, but public activity by non-Catholics was now legally permitted. The same account also suggested a political undertone to the meeting. While most of the audience "consisted of humble and devout members of the evangelical missions," others seemed to be jeering Catholicism more than cheering the evangelical message. To these people, the observer opined, Protestants owed the recent change in the constitution. They constituted a "liberal party" standing "for democracy, free speech, freedom of conscience, and social progress through education." That group perceived Roman Catholicism as a threat to their vision for society. Thus "missionaries feel that in many ways these liberals are their allies, and the liberals in turn see possibilities of great good for their country implicit in the evangelical movement." The comment was prescient of trends that would shape the Latin American ministry of John Mackay.[14]

Through his connection with San Marcos University, Mackay became part of a network of young Peruvian intellectuals who hoped for a regeneration of their nation and its culture. Prominent among them was Víctor Andrés Belaúnde, a professor of philosophy at San Marcos who both before and after his time in academe served as a diplomat for his country, including work at the United Nations following World War II. (His family's continuing influence in national affairs was attested when his nephew Fernando Belaúnde Terry served as president of Peru for two terms, one in the 1960s and the other in the 1980s.) Víctor Belaúnde had founded a literary review *(El Mercurio Peruano)* in 1918 through which cultural, religious, political, and social issues were discussed. Among the influential contributors to the review was Francisco García Calderón, who spent much of his life in Europe and had played a role in the Paris Peace Conference in 1919. John Mackay himself was invited to contribute articles to *El Mercurio.*[15]

In 1921 Mackay wrote an essay, "Religious Currents in the Intellectual

14. Harlan P. Beach, *Renaissant Latin America: An Outline and Interpretation of the Congress on Christian Work in Latin America, Held at Panama, February 10-19, 1916* (New York: Missionary Education Movement, 1916), esp. 14-15, 231; [Committee on Cooperation in Latin America,] *Regional Conferences in Latin America* (New York: Missionary Education Movement, 1917), 7, 8, 9, 10. Harlan Beach was professor of the theory and practice of missions at Yale University.

15. Metzger, *Hand and the Road,* 110-16.

Life of Peru," for the New York–based *Biblical World*. He noted, as had the observer at the Lima meeting in March 1916, that many nonreligious thinkers recognized "the social value of evangelical effort" and respected it for "devotion to philanthropic enterprises." "At the present moment," Mackay remarked wryly, "the warmest defender of Protestant missions in the national Congress is . . . a professed atheist." But Mackay believed that something more than a non-believing appreciation of the social utility of religion was stirring in Peru. He cited the writings of his fellow contributors to *El Mercurio* — Belaúnde and García Calderón — as cases in point. The former had an eclectic admiration for thinkers as diverse as Pascal, Spinoza, Kant, and Renan; and he had formed "a love of Christ," a virile "Christ who will whip the low mercantile spirit out of the hearts of the people, who will expose the hollowness of the traditional religious cult, who will not appear simply as the 'crucified in weakness,' but rather as the 'risen one that was dead and is alive for evermore.'" For his part, García Calderón, under the influence of Catholic modernism, "hails a regenerated Catholicism as the morning star of the new era." Despite Mackay's respect for the religious yearning and desire for reform manifested in such thinkers, he remained firm in his conviction that "only Protestant Christianity can save Peru for God." Clearly he believed that the trends among Peruvian intellectuals had created a providential opening for the message to be heard. He closed, however, with an important caveat to the North American readers of the *Biblical World:* "Let the term pan-Americanism be blotted out of missionary literature." It was tainted with an association — undoubtedly he meant a thinly disguised U.S. claim to primacy in the Americas — "that is not congenial politically or sentimentally to many of the most serious minds on the southern continent."[16]

In 1925 another major congress on Christian work met in Montevideo, Uruguay. Immediately prior to that event, a smaller gathering on education convened as well. John Mackay took a prominent role in both meetings. At the congress, he delivered one of the two opening addresses, his being in Spanish. The address elicited effusive praise from a Spanish delegate: "I never knew that a foreigner could speak with such eloquence in Spanish." The work of the congress was assigned to six commissions, each assigned a different task. Mackay chaired the group that presented a report on special religious problems in South America.

16. John A. Mackay, "Religious Currents in the Intellectual Life of Peru," *Biblical World* 6 (April 1921): 192-211; quotations on 203, 207, 209, 210, 211.

The report expressed concern about attitudes sometimes manifested by missionary agencies themselves. It warned against boards that, in the words of one correspondent, "do not know, nor appear to have any special desire to know" the countries to which they are sending workers. It advised that "South Americans are becoming increasingly sensitive about what they regard as the inveterate incomprehension of missionaries." The report also highlighted the religious obstacles to the Protestant cause — for example, hostility from the Roman Catholic Church, particularly the tendency of the ecclesiastical hierarchy to ally with reactionary governments and to resist liberal efforts on behalf of religious freedom. But in the midst of difficulties, there was an encouraging sign among many students — a new seriousness and engagement with intellectual issues. "The champions of this new mental attitude," said the report, "proclaim that intellectuals should not be simple spectators of life's drama, but actors in it. . . . They should be prophets of glories to come and not priests of glories spent." To capture and direct that mood, the Protestant churches needed to embody a "new prophetic spirit" in which "Scripture and literature, art and science must be made vocal, to broadcast through South American lands the eternal connection between sin and suffering." The goal was to "touch life at as many points as possible." As "comprehensive a program as possible of missionary activity" was required so that all the "different aspects of life may lead the thoughts of men to the Christ." To achieve this comprehensive program, the evangelical movement should hesitate to import European or North American ecclesiastical forms that might have little use in the South American context. In fact, the missionaries *"should make provision for the delivery of a religious message without the ordinary trappings of a religious service.* It is our conviction that the greatest opportunity of the present hour in South America is theirs who will deliver God's message as it was once delivered by the sea of Galilee and on the Athenian Areopagus without any of the elements of worship." Mackay's was a vision of a missionary enterprise centered on the person of Christ, innovative in its methods, and cognizant of the fact that redemption entailed not only salvation of individual souls (though that was absolutely essential) but also of "literature, art and science" — in short, the totality of human life.[17]

---

17. *Christian Work in South America: Official Report of the Congress on Christian Work in South America at Montevideo, Uruguay, April 1925,* 2 vols. (New York: Fleming H. Revell, 1925), 2:299-377; quotations on 300, 309, 365, 366, 367.

Mackay had no illusion that this task would always be easy. Formidable obstacles remained, and the report highlighted an incident from Peru.

> The government and the [Roman Catholic] Church recently attempted to consecrate the Peruvian Republic to a bronze effigy of the "Sacred Heart." Everything was ready for the imposing ceremony, which was to take place in the principal plaza of Lima. A few days, however, before the event, a united movement of students and workmen, backed by the city press and public opinion, so alarmed the authorities that the projected consecration was suspended, and has not been heard of since. Five months later, the leader of this movement, who was a teacher in an Evangelical school in Lima, was deported, and an attempt was made at the same time to deport the head of the school.

The teacher was Víctor Raúl Haya de la Torre, one of the instructors at the Colegio Anglo-Peruano; and the head of the school was, of course, Mackay himself.[18]

John Mackay met Haya, the son of a wealthy family from the north of Peru, sometime after the latter came to Lima in 1917. Mackay not only offered him a position at the college; he also became a friend and mentor to him. From 1919 to 1923, Haya served as president of the Peruvian Association of Students; and under his leadership the group sought to realize a dream talked about in Latin American educational circles since the turn of the century: "the creation of university extensions," in the words of Jeffrey Klaiber, "to spread the cultural wealth of the old and very elitist universities to the new working classes emerging in many parts of Latin America." Haya led what was called the Popular University. Its "faculty" were drawn from among students and a few professors at San Marcos whom Haya persuaded to donate their time, and those who attended the classes came chiefly from among laborers or field hands. Mackay admired the work that the students' organization carried out among these people. "Not only were the rudiments of education imparted, but instruction was given in hygiene and civics by a volunteer band of enthusiastic young undergraduates"; and "Indians in the valleys and high Pumas of the Andes saw a hope for the future." Mackay also respected the way in

---

18. *Christian Work in South America*, 2:335-36.

which Haya, after being cut off financially by his parents "on account of his radicalism," lived close to starvation and, instead of renouncing his views, "resolved to dedicate himself to the cause of the proletariat." Yet above all Mackay found in Haya someone who understood "that the human problem is spiritual before it is economic." When Peruvian President Leguía in 1923 sanctioned a plan to have Archbishop Emilio Lissón rededicate Peru to the Sacred Heart of Jesus, Haya mobilized protest against the action. He assembled a diverse group that included anarchists, Catholics, Protestants, and both students and faculty from the Popular University. Calling itself the "Popular Front of Manual and Intellectual Workers," the group marched through Lima on the scheduled day of dedication in condemnation of the proposed action. Government forces attacked the protesters, and in the mêlée several people died, but Haya still managed to speak. In the midst of the confusion, the ceremony of reconsecration could not proceed. Students at San Marcos barricaded themselves on the campus and prepared to defend against government invasion. Once the archbishop announced that the rededication would be abandoned, the protest faded.[19]

Haya's own situation remained precarious. His health was broken by bronchial pneumonia, and, fearing the government might arrest him, he found refuge with the Mackays. At risk to themselves, they hid him in their school's boarding department, located outside the center of Lima. There Jane Mackay nursed him until he recovered from his illness. To lessen the chance of discovery, the Mackays told neither the students at the boarding department nor their own children of Haya's presence. By mid-summer, with health recovered and governmental pressure seemingly eased, he went back to his teaching at the college. Mackay himself had delayed a planned lecture trip out of the country and now felt the situation permitted him to leave. But in early October, the police seized Haya and deported him. In 1924, during his exile, Haya founded the Alianza Popular Revolucionaria Americana (Apra), of which he was

---

19. Metzger, *Hand and the Road*, 121-28; Jeffrey L. Klaiber, "The Popular Universities and the Origins of Aprismo, 1921-1924," *Hispanic American Historical Review* 55 (November 1975): 693-715; quotation on 694; Mackay, *Other Spanish Christ*, 194, 197. Although the focus is upon Methodist education, Rosa del Carmen Bruno-Jofré, *Methodist Education in Peru: Social Gospel, Politics, and American Ideological and Economic Penetration, 1888-1930* (Waterloo, Ontario: Wilfrid Laurier University Press, 1988), observes a broader linkage of Protestant schools and the YMCA to Haya de la Torre and other leaders of APRA and thus emphasizes Protestantism as one of the contributors to the Aprista ideology.

leader until his death in 1979. He returned to Peru in 1930, and the next year he ran for the presidency as the candidate of the Apristas and narrowly failed of election. Following defeat, he endured a brief imprisonment and other times abroad, and the Aprista party was prevented from participating in elections. In 1962, when the ban had been lifted, he won an apparent plurality in another run for the presidency, but a military coup prevented him from taking office. Shortly before his death, Haya was elected head of the constituent assembly of Peru — the only elective office in government that he ever held. Of course, during the time he was associated with John Mackay's school in Lima, Haya was not yet the leader of a political party. He was simply a charismatic young man, an organizer of students and workers, who longed for a more just social order and believed that Christian faith was an important component of that vision. Religion was one of the most persistent themes in the life of Haya and of the party he founded. As Klaiber has observed, "in the case of Peru no other movement compared to the Aprista party for its frequent appropriation of Christian symbolism." The influences that shaped Haya were many, but John Mackay undoubtedly contributed much to the religious aspects of his thought.[20]

John and Jane Mackay's willingness to protect a wanted man was not only a personally courageous decision; it potentially put their school at risk. When Mackay returned to Peru in 1923 after his speaking tour, he had difficulty getting past Peruvian immigration officials. For a time thereafter, Roman Catholic leaders waged a verbal campaign against him, his teachers, and their school in hopes of having them expelled and the school eliminated. Mackay also had to reassure his Free Church sponsors that he had not turned the college into a hotbed of politics. This was not a ploy, for John Mackay was always first and foremost a Christian minister and educator promoting a vision of spiritual renewal. Yet Mackay also believed that the gospel, as he would say in Montevideo in 1925, had to "touch life at as many points as possible"; and as "comprehensive a program as possible of missionary activity" was needed in order that the "different aspects of life may lead the thoughts of men to the Christ." In fulfill-

20. Metzger, *Hand and the Road,* 122-28; Jeffrey L. Klaiber, "Religion and Revolution in Peru," *The Americas* 31 (January 1975): 289-312; quotation on 307. For other accounts of Haya providing useful but sometimes critical assessments, see Frederick B. Pike, "Visions of Rebirth: The Spiritualist Facet of Peru's Haya de la Torre," *Hispanic American Historical Review* 63 (August 1983): 479-516; and Richard Lee Clinton, "Apra: An Appraisal," *Journal of Interamerican Studies and World Affairs* 12 (April 1970): 280-97.

ing that mandate, the boundary between spiritual renewal and political protest could sometimes become a rather porous one.

Despite that temporary opposition, the Anglo-Peruvian College survived and prospered. Its success and stability allowed John Mackay to dream of a wider horizon of ministry. John R. Mott, the great missionary and ecumenical statesman who among his many responsibilities represented the YMCA, had broached with the Free Church as early as 1921 the possibility that Mackay might be "loaned" to the Y for a period of international service throughout Latin America. In 1926, John Mackay went much further than a temporary job switch. He resigned from the college and gave up his lectureship at San Marcos. His new job description was special lecturer and writer on religion under the South American Federation of YMCA's. Under this arrangement, Mackay was, as an early biographer of Mott put it, set free from a sphere of action limited primarily to Peru "in order that he might do his remarkable work of spiritual and intellectual interpretation of Christianity to the literati of the Spanish-speaking republics of Latin America." Despite his new field of labor, the Free Church hoped to keep its connection with Mackay by persuading him to maintain membership in one of its presbyteries. He deeply valued his friendships in the church, but he wrote to the head of the Free Church's foreign missionary committee to explain why he could not maintain the affiliation:

> My loyalty henceforth must be loyalty to a cause rather than to an institution. In the present chaotic condition of the religious world, in which the orthodoxies and the heterodoxies are scattered piecemeal throughout the denominations, and at a time when it is evident that there must be new alignments, I am unwilling to accept any denominational label. I have given my life afresh to the living God for His cause and His glory and to belong officially to the ministry of any given denomination would only tend to embarrassment and misinterpretation.[21]

The YMCA gave Mackay a venue for the kind of ministry he had praised at the Montevideo Congress. Like Jesus by the Sea of Galilee or Paul at the Areopagus, he had found a place where he could deliver "a re-

---

21. Basil Mathews, *John R. Mott: World Citizen* (New York: Harper and Brothers, 1934), 349; Metzger, *Hand and the Road*, 152.

ligious message without the ordinary trappings of a religious service." Many young men who probably would not set foot within the door of a church sanctuary would come to the YMCA. Moreover, work through the Y had the advantage of allowing Mackay to avoid being dragged into ecclesiastical controversies that were tangential or even detrimental to confronting people with the person and claims of Christ. Mackay worried that requiring members of the Y to be affiliated with an evangelical church was too restrictive. He was happier with the revised 1931 formula adopted by an international YMCA that made loyalty to Jesus Christ, rather than membership in a church, the requirement for Y membership. This is not to say that Mackay's goal, as he said in a letter to a friend, was to create a vague or diffuse "influence" of Christianity throughout Latin America, though that indeed was valuable; rather, he aimed to generate "passionate hearts which in virtue of a personal experience of divine power become themselves generators of a new 'movement' in thought and life." The forms and institutions, Mackay seemed to be saying, would adjust themselves accordingly if the spiritual center of the Y's message were put front and center.[22]

Reminiscing nearly fifty years after he had gone into work with the Y, Mackay recalled:

> While Jesus Christ became increasingly real and meaningful to me, I had lost faith in the church, I mean the church as an organization, a structure. I continued to attend church services, but I no longer belonged to any denomination.
>
> As I reflect on this mood it would appear that two phenomena produced my antichurchism. The first was my disillusionment with the two denominations to which I had ecclesiastically belonged. The second was the tragic phenomenon of the Hispanic Catholic Church to which I had devoted a great deal of study. This church throughout the centuries had become Christ's patron, relegating Him to a very secondary position. The result: I lost faith in the church.[23]

In assessing how he might best fulfill his new ministry, Mackay concluded that lightning trips through as many cities as possible would pro-

22. Metzger, *Hand and the Road,* 156-57.
23. John A. Mackay, "Let Us Remember," *Princeton Seminary Bulletin* 65 (1972): 28.

duce superficial results. The better approach was to spend an intensive period of work in a few cities each year and then dedicate the remainder of the time to writing. By concentrating on selected localities, Mackay believed that he would get a more thorough knowledge of particular individuals as well as their communities and thus be able to address them more effectively. Then, when he sat down at his desk at home to write, his words would reflect a deeper knowledge of the situation on the ground. During his years of service for the Y, he produced numerous articles and two books in Spanish. From 1926 to 1929, the family made their home in Montevideo, though his travels took Mackay away from his wife and the children for long stretches of time. After a furlough in 1929-1930, they secured a residence in Mexico City for the remainder of Mackay's work with the YMCA.[24]

His travels took him throughout Latin America and, among many other places, to Jerusalem in 1928 for the meeting of the International Missionary Council. That conference signaled a change in mood from the gathering at Edinburgh eighteen years earlier. Few representatives from the younger churches had come to Edinburgh, and the sessions often used quasi-military images to describe parts of the world awaiting "occupation" by Christian forces — imagery reinforced by John R. Mott, the presiding officer at most of the Edinburgh sessions, when he began the closing address with the declaration: "The closing of the Conference is the beginning of the conquest." At Jerusalem, attendance included an increased number of people from the younger churches, and a broader range of issues were addressed. On the agenda were matters such as religion and industrialization as well as Christianity and race. Various papers probed the relationship of the Christian message "to non-Christian systems of thought." Major essays addressed Hinduism, Buddhism, and Islam. In the presentations lurked profound questions: How should Christians assess these faiths? Did Christianity represent their repudiation, their fulfillment, or something in between? The conference also treated what some considered a much greater threat to the missionary enterprise than any of the alternative religions of the world. "No student of the deeper problems of life," said Professor Rufus M. Jones of Haverford College in Pennsylvania, "can very well fail to see that the greatest rival of Christianity in the world to-day is not Mohammedanism, or Buddhism, or Hinduism, or Confucianism, but a world-wide sec-

24. Metzger, *Hand and the Road*, 153-82.

ular way of life and interpretation of the nature of things." By "secular" Jones meant any "way of life" that regarded God or "a realm of spiritual reality" as unessential. His paper prompted much discussion, especially his assertion that "secular civilization" was on the rise in the United States and Europe. This perception *potentially* undercut the assumption that the world divided neatly into Christian countries that sent out missionaries and non-Christian ones that received them.[25]

During the discussion of Rufus Jones's paper, John Mackay observed that many of the laments about "secular civilization" failed to make an important distinction. Individuals, groups, and nations sometimes pursued altruistic as well as egoistical aims. "In the altruistic aspects of our civilization," he observed, "we find ends which are identical with Christian ends. The passion for truth wherever it may be found, the willingness to sacrifice for that truth, even though any reference to God is left out of account, provide certain values which Christianity must not fight." From Mackay's perspective, the great problem was not the altruistic aspirations in secular civilization, but the difficulty of fulfilling them. At this point, the gospel offered the solution: "Christianity is the birth of the eternal Christ in the human soul, which then does good, becomes good and creates goodness. In this combination is the solution of our problem." He further developed his assessment of the missionary situation in a paper, "The Evangelistic Duty of Christianity," presented to the Jerusalem conference. Mackay believed that more and more the person of Christ attracted those who were not, in any conventional sense, believers. Thus some contemporary Hindus admired the Christ-likeness of Mahatma Gandhi, a communist like the French Henri Barbusse respected the ethics of Jesus while seeing Christians as his betrayers, and the Argentine writer Ricardo Rojas considered himself an "œcumenical Christian . . . belonging neither to the Roman Catholic nor to the Protestant communion." To take advantage of this unprecedented opportunity to proclaim the gospel, the missionary needed to "win a right to be heard." Unless he offered "some human value that the group he proposes to evangelize can appreciate, . . . he will not be seriously listened to." What that meant was that one had to "present that aspect of Christ or of

25. On Edinburgh, see Brian Stanley, *The World Missionary Conference, Edinburgh 1910* (Grand Rapids: Eerdmans, 2009); on Jerusalem, *The Christian Life and Message in Relation to Non-Christian Systems,* vol. 1 of *Report of the Jerusalem Meeting of the International Missionary Council* (London: Oxford University Press, 1928), 284.

truth which the situation requires." For much of Latin America, he believed that the situation required a knowledge of the Christ who satisfied a hunger for social justice. He told of "an apostle of social reform" whom he knew — almost assuredly Haya de la Torre — who had said that "the name of God nauseated in his mouth every time he tried to utter it, because from his boyhood up God had been associated with social crimes and injustices he abhorred." The appropriate response to someone like Haya "was to draw attention to the denunciations launched against the injustices of their time by the prophets of the Old Testament, and to the prophetic masculinity of Jesus when He cleared the temple courts of godless traffickers, and indicted the official religion of his time as an unholy alliance with Mammon." In short, Mackay insisted that missionaries tailor their message in some degree to the context of those whom they addressed, that they earn the right to be heard, and that they respect the hunger for truth and justice even when it appeared without reference to the name of God. Yet to engage in mission in this fashion, Mackay insisted, the Christian churches also needed to re-center themselves upon the fundamental fact of the gospel: Christ as "the incarnate revelation of God" — the cross and resurrection "as the supreme redemptive act in which the initiative belonged to God." Only as the church "attained a sense of the cosmic significance of Jesus and a fresh experience of a Divine Lord" could it march forth "as an army with banners." The sense of the Christ in whom all things cohered, the vision that had enthralled a lad of 14 at a summer communion season in Rogart, remained at the center of Mackay's view of mission.[26]

From late 1929 into 1930, Mackay went on a furlough that took him back to Europe. He had the opportunity to visit once again with Unamuno and Haya de la Torre, both of whom were in exile from their respective countries — the former in France just across the border from Spain, and the latter in a suburb of Berlin. Mackay also arranged to meet a thinker whose views had shaken the theological world. For several months, he and his family lived in Bonn, Germany, where Karl Barth was just beginning his time on the theological faculty. Mackay attended Barth's lectures and the weekly evening meetings for students in Barth's home. He got to converse with Barth privately as he tutored him in En-

26. *Christian Life and Message*, 411, 443, 444, 452, 454, 456-57. Although Mackay did not specify in his Jerusalem address who had said that the name of God once nauseated him, he attributed the comment to Haya in *The Other Spanish Christ*, 194.

glish. On a side trip to Switzerland, he also met Emil Brunner and Eduard Thurneysen, other significant participants in the reorientation of Protestant thought. Without becoming a slavish devotee of the new movement, Mackay was profoundly impressed by what he encountered in Bonn and Switzerland. In a letter to a Latin American friend who was a fellow worker for the YMCA, Mackay offered his assessment. "Karl Barth and his friends," he suggested, "are rehabilitating in contemporary thought the concept of God held by the great Hebrew prophets as well as that of Jesus Christ." In recent times, "the immanence of God has been emphasized at the expense of his transcendence." All of this Mackay admired as he did also the way in which "the Barthians transcend modernism and orthodoxy." "From my point of view," Mackay added,

> one can escape a sterile and weak relativism on the one hand and on the other the absolutism of an authoritarian hierarchy built on a particular revelation whose absolute form we have in Jesus Christ. If God has spoken, he also speaks. In this way particular situations in life are not resolved by simple general rules even if they are taken from the Bible but by a specific word that is relevant since God is not only our ancestor but also our contemporary. Thus, there is a plan from him for all the different moments of life and history.

In short, to espouse God's truth was not simply to adhere to timeless "general rules if they are taken from the Bible," but to hear the word that the living God was speaking in Christ through Scripture in the present situation.[27]

Mackay also resonated with "the new emphasis that is placed on faith as the means of initiation and progress in the spiritual life, the realistic analysis of sin and its implications in human life, and the recognition that the Christian, in his time, must live at the highest level for his time placing on all his actions the stamp of eternity and not to be under the illusion that what he and his contemporaries call progress is not necessarily identified with the kingdom of God." Yet Mackay also had reservations about the new theology. He found Barth's seeming lack of interest in the historical Jesus distressing, and "equally disturbing" was Barth's unwillingness to allow "that spiritual life can be considered as

27. Metzger, *Hand and the Road*, 193.

something in itself or as a possession of the Christian." For one nurtured on Bunyan and other Puritan writers about the pilgrimage of faith, for a man who had come to love John of the Cross and Teresa of Avila, this deficiency was a serious one.[28]

Mackay as Secretary for the
Presbyterian Board of Foreign Missions

After returning from furlough in Europe, the Mackays and their four children established residence in Mexico City. But while the work was rewarding, it would prove to be brief. Since 1928, Robert E. Speer had periodically sought to secure the services of Mackay for the board of foreign missions of the Presbyterian Church in the U.S.A. In 1932, Mackay accepted the offer, and in June he became a secretary of the board with special responsibility for Latin America. Since the late 1920s, during his period of disillusionment with churches, Mackay had begun to rethink his position. The contacts he had made with Barth, Brunner, and others during his time on the Continent played an important role in his reappraisal of the church. "Long reflection on the Latin American situation convinces me," he wrote to a friend, "that creative and lasting work must be done through the Church." Yet Mackay never narrowly focused his concern upon the church as an institution. For him, the church was always first and foremost a *community* gathered in loyalty to Jesus Christ and seeking to carrying out Christ's mission to the world.[29]

Mackay came to the board at a moment when major conflict broke around it. In 1932, the so-called Layman's Report on the missionary movement appeared. The study had grown out of an initiative by John D. Rockefeller Jr. and eventually won tentative approval from seven denominational boards. Under the leadership of Harvard professor William E. Hocking, a fifteen-person commission of appraisal visited mission areas and, along with professional staff, issued seven volumes of findings. In addition, the commission issued a summary volume, *Re-Thinking Missions,* written chiefly by Hocking, which ignited the controversy. In addition to irritating many by suggestions that missionary personnel abroad were often not up to their jobs, the report seemed to traditionalists to of-

28. Metzger, *Hand and the Road,* 194, 195.
29. Metzger, *Hand and the Road,* 209-12; quotation on 211.

fer a rather anemic purpose for missions: missionary work should be a kind of "foreign service or ambassadorship" that would "seek with people of other lands a true knowledge and love of God, expressing in life and word what we have learned through Jesus Christ, and endeavoring to give effect to his spirit in the life of the world." Sharing one's own convictions, embodying them in lives of service, and seeking common ground with those of other faiths appeared to be the ultimate aim of missions. More traditional goals of the enterprise — Christian "conquest" of the world through conversions, the supplanting of other religions, and the assertion of the finality of Jesus Christ — seemed to be abandoned or played down. In responding to the report for the Presbyterian board, Robert E. Speer, ever the gentleman, praised the good motives of the commission of appraisal and even allowed that some of their specific recommendations deserved consideration. However, he flatly rejected the basic theological premises of the report. "For us, Christ is still *the* Way," he insisted, "not *a* way, and there is no goal beyond Him or apart from Him, nor any search for truth that is to be found outside of Him."[30]

Mackay issued his own critique of the Hocking report in the April 1933 issue of the *International Review of Mission*. Gracious like Speer, Mackay indicated that specific recommendations should be evaluated on their own merits; and he commended Hocking "for having offered a corrective to what has been the root weakness of popular American Christianity — ... its virtual disdain of theology, its supreme and exclusive preoccupation with so-called practical issues." It was unfortunate, said Mackay, that many had responded to the theological section of the report either with "unequivocal rebuttal" or "unqualified approval," neither of which shed much light on the subject. The real tragedy of the report was that it put forward an inadequate assessment of the current situation in the world, oversimplified the nature of Christianity, and showed superficial understanding of the missionary objective. The Hocking report assumed that there was "an emerging world culture" in which all religions faced a common enemy in the secularism that was emptying "the vessels of life of all spiritual content." In fact, claimed Mackay, since the Jerusalem conference of 1928, perceptive thinkers were

---

30. William Ernest Hocking, chairman of the commission of appraisal, *Re-Thinking Missions: A Laymen's Inquiry after One Hundred Years* (New York: Harper and Brothers, 1932), 27, 59. On the Hocking report and controversies generated by it, see William R. Hutchison, *Errand to the World: American Protestant Thought and Foreign Missions* (Chicago: University of Chicago Press, 1987), 158-75.

beginning to understand that the problem of secularism was not quite what they thought at that time. The "empty vessels are filling up with strong fresh wine" — communism, fascism, various nationalisms, and militant new religions such as Theosophy. Amid these "crusading forces . . . , no missionary expression of Christianity which has not sufficient conviction and passion at the heart of it to turn it into a crusading movement stands the slightest hope of success." Given these realities, the Hocking report sounded more like "the requiem of a thought day that is dying rather than the trumpet of dawn of a day that is coming." To generate the requisite conviction and passion, Christians needed to rediscover the central meaning of Christianity and to give affirmative answer to the most pressing theological questions of the hour:

> Is Jesus Christ the expression of special activity from God's side and not merely an achievement from man's side, a redemptive gift as well as a normative ideal? In a word, did God give Jesus, was God in Him in such a way that He became the centre of history, inaugurating by His death and resurrection a new epoch in cosmic history?

To answer these questions positively was also to say what was the true aim of missions: "To make Jesus Christ inescapable for men everywhere. Not acceptable but inescapable, the only possible solution, the only saviour of men who have become deadly in earnest about the problem of living."[31]

The position taken by the board of foreign missions did not satisfy J. Gresham Machen, who by this time had been at Westminster Seminary for several years. In the past he had groused about the board, but now he mounted a frontal assault. Pearl Buck, author of the best-selling *The Good Earth* (1931) and still nominally a Presbyterian missionary, gave him another target. She praised the Hocking report "as a masterpiece of constructive religious thought" and dismissed traditional views of the purpose of missions. For Machen and his allies, the fact that she was not instantly repudiated confirmed fears that Speer and the board tolerated doctrinal looseness. (Buck, who had not been drawing a salary from the board for some time, eventually resigned to spare the church further em-

---

31. John A. Mackay, "The Theology of the Laymen's Foreign Missions Inquiry," *International Review of Mission* 22 (April 1933): 174-88; quotations on 175, 178, 181, 184, 187.

barrassment.) Although his dissatisfaction lay chiefly with matters of theology, a personal element undoubtedly colored Machen's thinking. Charles R. Erdman, his old faculty nemesis at Princeton, chaired the board of foreign missions, and Speer, its executive secretary, had served on the special committee of 1925 that refuted Machen's charges of creeping apostasy in the denomination. Speer had also favored the 1929 reorganization of the seminary. In early 1933, Machen requested the New Brunswick Presbytery to send an overture to the General Assembly that, in effect, would rebuke Speer's policies. After presentations by both Machen and Speer before presbytery, the former's motion was defeated handily. By reason of its adoption in another presbytery, however, the overture did make its way to the Assembly, where it lost again, this time by a margin so overwhelming that negative votes were not even counted. The stage was set for the denouement of the Presbyterian controversy in which Princeton had figured prominently. Machen and his allies organized an Independent Board of Foreign Missions, and in 1934 the General Assembly declared the new board unconstitutional, ruling that Presbyterians should sever connections to it. The Presbytery of New Brunswick in 1935 suspended Machen from the ministry for failing to abide by the Assembly directive, and the following year the General Assembly upheld the suspension. Machen quickly took steps to organize a separate church, which, after a subsequent change of name, called itself the Orthodox Presbyterian Church. It succeeded in carrying fewer than 1 percent of Presbyterians into secession. Less than a year later, Machen was dead; his new denomination was already riven with disputes, and he himself had been ousted from the leadership of the Independent Board of Missions.[32]

Mackay was deeply angered by the attacks on Speer and the board, but he took no part in the controversy at the Assembly of 1933 because he was in Latin America at the time. Mackay wrote to a friend about the failed attack on the board and on Speer:

> Dear old Robert E., how my heart has been sore for him! . . . I am
> not a controversialist by nature, but one of these days my Celtic

---

32. Lefferts A. Loetscher, *The Broadening Church: A Study of Theological Issues in the Presbyterian Church since 1869* (Philadelphia: University of Pennsylvania Press, 1954), 148-55; D. G. Hart, *Defending the Faith: J. Gresham Machen and the Crisis of Conservative Protestantism in Modern America* (Baltimore: Johns Hopkins University Press, 1994), 147-59; Grant Wacker, "Pearl S. Buck and the Waning of the Missionary Impulse," *Church History* 72 (December 2003): 852-74.

blood is going to boil and Dr. Machen is going to know it. He will find that he can't take out a patent on Christianity and then indict for daring to be a Christian a man whom I adore, without a violent clash with me. When the next barrage comes I hope to be on the spot.

What Mackay most wanted was to make a positive witness for the gospel, not to engage in what he regarded as unnecessary and sterile controversy.[33]

He was far more at home presenting his case positively, as he did in his first book in English. During his time in Mexico City, Mackay had begun writing the book — he had already authored three in Spanish. It appeared shortly after he had taken his position with the board of foreign missions of the Presbyterian Church in the U.S.A. Mackay called his work *The Other Spanish Christ: A Study in the Spiritual History of Spain and South America.* In it, he sought to acquaint English-speakers with an aspect of the Hispanic religious tradition with which they were not familiar. In addition to the Catholicism of the conquistadors, of the Inquisition, of the authoritarian Roman Catholic Church, and of the piety that seemed to know only the Christ hanging upon the cross, not the resurrected one, there was an alternate tradition: the tradition of Teresa of Avila and of Bartholomé de Las Casas, who opposed the conquest of the native peoples of Latin America. It was a tradition that had been recovered by Giner and Unamuno and was thus stirring in the Spanish world again. He saw signs of hope of its spread in the establishment of the Spanish Republic in 1931 and in the near election of Haya de la Torre to the Peruvian presidency.[34]

From the perspective of the close of the twentieth century, Luis N. Rivera-Pagán, who himself taught at Princeton Seminary in two different posts, has observed both the limitations and the extraordinary durability of Mackay's book. It may be criticized for too easily conflating the diversities of multiple Latin American traditions with those of Spain; it seemed "unable to decipher the hidden strength of popular Catholicism"; and it exhibited "a rather naive understanding of the Spanish and Latin American political situations." But on balance and viewed in the context of the time, the book holds up remarkably well. Rivera-Pagán remarked that the work showed a knowledge of and respect for Latin

---

33. Quote from Metzger, *Hand and the Road*, 218.
34. Mackay, *Other Spanish Christ.*

American intellectual currents and writers scarcely "to be expected in the thirties, particularly from a Scots Calvinist missionary." Thus Mackay remains in many Latin American quarters today a beloved and revered figure.[35]

Mackay introduced the book with an image from the Old Testament. In an early prophecy, Jeremiah saw "an almond spray in bloom" — one of the first plants to flower in the spring — but nearby was "a seething cauldron" (Jer. 1:11-13). These pictures suggested both renewal and destruction. "A new Springtime is clearly coming," wrote Mackay, "but who will venture to predict what God's spring breezes will first blow over pampa and sierra, whether the aroma of almond blossom or the froth of the storm-brewing pot?" This prophetic vision would recur frequently to John Mackay in subsequent addresses and writings. It was, he thought, an apt figure for the time in which he was living.[36]

John Mackay and "God's Terrible Springtime"

In addition to Speer's ultimately successful effort to bring Mackay to the board of foreign missions, there had been attempts since the late 1920s to lure him to American seminaries. In 1926, Western Theological Seminary in Pittsburgh wanted Mackay for a chair in systematic theology. After the death of William Brenton Greene in 1928, J. Ross Stevenson and Charles Erdman both pressed Mackay to consider taking the position in apologetics and Christian ethics. Mackay turned down these posts. When the presidency of Princeton Seminary was due to become vacant with the imminent retirement of J. Ross Stevenson, the search committee offered the position to Mackay, who politely said no. Mackay declined these positions because he understood his call to be that of a missionary. But Princeton wanted Mackay for the presidency and persisted. As he mulled over the offer again, Mackay recalled years later, the decisive moment in his decision to accept was the advice of a "Methodist friend of

35. Luis N. Rivera-Pagán, "Myth, Utopia, and Faith: Theology and Culture in Latin America," *Princeton Seminary Bulletin* 21 (2000): 142-60; quotations on 143, 144, 147; C. René Padilla, "Evangelical Theology in Latin American Contexts," in *The Cambridge Companion to Evangelical Theology,* ed. Timothy Larsen and Daniel J. Treier (Cambridge: Cambridge University Press, 2007), 259-73; Samuel Escobar, "The Missionary Legacy of John A. Mackay," *International Bulletin of Missionary Research* 16, no. 3 (July 1992): 116-22.

36. Mackay, *Other Spanish Christ*, x.

mine" who "said to me that a theological seminary can be a mission field." How seriously Mackay took that dimension of the call was apparent when he was named by the board of trustees not only president of Princeton Theological Seminary but also professor of ecumenics — ecumenics meaning, according to Mackay's definition in a book produced early in his retirement, "everything that concerns the nature, functions, relations and strategy of the Church Universal, when the latter is conceived as a missionary community."[37]

John Mackay came to Princeton at a moment when many Protestant thinkers were engaged in a major theological reassessment. The origins of that rethinking may be traced, among others, to persons whom Mackay met on his furlough in Europe during 1929-1930: Karl Barth, Emil Brunner, and Eduard Thurneysen. These thinkers and others like them did not agree on all issues, but they shared common concerns. The slaughter of the Great War, economic dislocation and depression, and subsequently the rise of fascist dictators made former confidence in western superiority as well as faith in progress appear to have been naive. Since Protestant liberalism had often underwritten optimism by stressing an indwelling God manifest in the spirit of the age, many found liberalism woefully inadequate to the current crisis. With renewed appreciation of Christian themes neglected by their recent predecessors, they returned to older sources of wisdom — preeminently to the Bible and to the Protestant reformers of the sixteenth century — in order to frame a sturdier theology. As they turned to the Bible, these theologians approached it differently than their liberal predecessors, who tended to find there a record of humanity's evolving religious consciousness. The newer theologians viewed the Bible primarily as the medium through which *God* spoke, often in accents strange to the human ear. Yet for all their respect for the biblical witness as divine revelation, they did not reject critical scholarship out of hand, nor did they espouse notions of biblical inerrancy. They neither fought battles over the Mosaic authorship of the Pentateuch nor engaged in disputes about the number of writers who composed the book of Isaiah. They did, however, take with utmost seriousness what they saw as the central themes of the Bible: the fallen nature of humanity and the unmerited, redeeming love of God in Christ, which alone bridged the chasm opened by sin. Faith in divine redemp-

37. Gillette, interviewer, "John A. Mackay: Influences on My Life," 33; John A. Mackay, *Ecumenics* (Englewood Cliffs, NJ: Prentice-Hall, 1964), viii.

tion was not achieved simply by holding correct theological views, as if God and salvation were objects one could possess. Faith was primarily a response of trust to the encounter with the living God in Jesus Christ, not the espousal of timelessly true propositions about God.

This theological temper took hold in America more slowly than in Europe; but by the late 1920s, signs of change had begun to appear in the United States as well. For example, in 1926 Henry Pitney Van Dusen of Union Seminary wrote *In Quest of Life's Meaning,* suggesting that, contrary to usual renditions of liberalism, Jesus was a source of empowerment and new life, not simply a moral example for humanity. The same year, Francis Pickens Miller, a layman active in the World Christian Student Federation and the YMCA, edited *The Church and the World,* which summoned the church to rise above its uncritical adaptation to modern culture. Two years later, Douglas Horton, then a Congregationalist pastor in the greater Boston area, published an English translation *(The Word of God and the Word of Man)* of Karl Barth's *Das Wort Gottes und Die Theologie;* and Reinhold Niebuhr, already a critic of liberalism, became professor of ethics at Union Seminary in New York. In 1932, Niebuhr published *Moral Man and Immoral Society,* which argued trenchantly that injustice was far more intractable than an older religious liberalism, preaching good will and brotherhood, could allow. Shortly afterward, Walter Marshall Horton of Oberlin College declared in *Realistic Theology* (1934): "With Reinhold Niebuhr, I find that the attempt to face the exigencies of our times is driving me 'politically to the left, theologically to the right' — thus bringing me into simultaneous relations of sympathy with Christian orthodoxy on the one hand and with social radicalism on the other." After 1931, Reinhold's younger brother, H. Richard Niebuhr, from his post at the Yale Divinity School, developed his own critique of the liberal tradition in a number of essays and books. One of the most powerful of these was a volume that he co-edited with Francis Miller and Wilhelm Pauck. *The Church Against the World* (1934) contended that American Protestantism had essentially allied itself with nationalism, capitalism, and human-centered visions of reform; in the process, it had lost its identity. "If the church," wrote H. Richard Niebuhr in one of his contributions to the volume, "has no other plan of salvation to offer to men than one of deliverance by force, education, idealism, or planned economy, it really has no existence as a church and needs to resolve itself into a political party or a school." Instead, the church needed to recover its transcendent point of reference in the eternal purpose of God. As such views gained currency in the intellectual centers of Protestantism, they were described by different names: "Neo-orthodoxy," "Barthianism," the "theology of crisis," "dialectical theology," "Christian realism," and "neo-Reformation theology" were among the most frequent descriptors. Some continued to identify with the liberal tradition, but did so as "chastened" liberals or neo-liberals. A complete account of Protestant thought in the 1930s would require the addition of many other important figures and the drawing of careful intellectual distinctions among them. But for the purpose of understanding the world of theological education into which John Mackay entered when he became president of Princeton Seminary in 1936, this brief overview underscores why he could boast that "strong tides of thought are running in the direction of Princeton's historic position."[38]

Perhaps Mackay exaggerated just a bit, for those currents were not moving toward Benjamin Warfield's doctrine of inerrancy or toward William Henry Green's defense of the Mosaic authorship of the Pentateuch. But a new generation of theologians did have far greater sympathy for the central insights of the orthodoxy Princeton had represented. Moreover, Princeton itself was moving. John Mackay had not repudiated the older Princeton tradition — nor would he ever do so — but his election to the presidency did represent a course correction in its trajectory. Because both Princeton and other schools were reorienting their thinking, convergence was now a possibility. Princeton Seminary's third president could much more readily find common ground with people from places like Yale Divinity School or Union Seminary than was conceivable in the days of Francis Patton. In fact, John Mackay quickly became a major leader among "ecumenical Protestants" — that is, among those denominations and theological schools that provided the bulk of the support and direction to groups like the Federal Council of Churches (the National Council after 1950), to organizations such as the YMCA, the Student Volunteer Movement, and the World Student Christian Federation, and to the various conferences and movements leading up to the formation of the World Council of Churches in 1948.[39]

---

38. See William R. Miller, ed., *Contemporary American Protestant Thought: 1900-1970* (Indianapolis: Bobbs-Merrill, 1973); Sydney E. Ahlstrom, "Continental Influence on American Christian Thought Since World War II," *Church History* 27 (September 1958): 256-72; Walter Marshall Horton, *Realistic Theology* (New York: Harper and Brothers, 1934), ix; H. Richard Niebuhr et al., *The Church Against the World* (Chicago: Willett, Clark, and Company, 1935).

39. I derive this usage of "ecumenical Protestantism" from David A. Hollinger, "The

A brief overview of only *some* of Mackay's outside activities during his years as president of Princeton Seminary underscores the important role he played, not only within the Presbyterian Church, but also within broader intellectual and religious circles. Even while working for the board of foreign missions, he had already become part of the Theological Discussion Group, a twice-a-year gathering of younger theologians initially organized by Henry Pitney Van Dusen. Among the other members of the group were Wilhelm Pauck; Walter M. Horton; John C. Bennett of Union; the Niebuhr brothers; Samuel McCrea Cavert, the general secretary of the Federal Council of Churches; and Paul Tillich, who had recently fled to America from Hitler's Germany. The lone black member of the group was Benjamin E. Mays, then dean of the School of Religion at Howard University; and Georgia Harkness, initially of Elmira College in New York State and by 1939 a professor at Garrett Biblical Institute (now the Garrett-Evangelical Theological Seminary) in Evanston, Illinois, broke the gender barrier as the only woman invited to join. From today's perspective, the presence of the latter two people in the Theological Discussion Group may have epitomized tokenism; but given the social and cultural attitudes in many ecclesiastical circles at the time, their inclusion also pointed to a growing awareness that the church, if it were to be truly the church, had to transcend barriers of race, nation, and gender.[40]

Members of the Theological Discussion Group played important roles in preparing for the 1937 Oxford Conference on Church, Community, and State. Mackay wrote the initial draft of a statement for the conference section on the universal church and the world of nations. He coined the phrase that became the motto of the conference: "Let the church be the church." Five years later, at the Delaware Conference sponsored by the Federal Council in March 1942 — it was so named because the delegates met on the Methodist Seminary campus in Delaware, Ohio — Mackay was again a major figure. This first large gathering of ecumen-

---

Realist-Pacifist Summit Meeting of March 1942 and the Political Reorientation of Ecumenical Protestantism in the United States," *Church History* (September 2010). See also William R. Hutchison, ed., *Between the Times: The Travail of the Protestant Establishment in America, 1900-1960* (Cambridge: Cambridge University Press, 1989).

40. Heather A. Warren, "The Theological Discussion Group and Its Impact on American and Ecumenical Theology, 1920-1945," *Church History* 62 (December 1993): 528-43. For more on Harkness and Mays, see Gary Dorrien, *The Marking of American Liberal Theology: Idealism, Realism, and Modernity, 1900-1950* (Louisville: Westminster John Knox Press, 2003), 390-430.

ical Protestants following the United States' entry into World War II drew together not only leading clergy from the denominations but also notable Protestant lay people such as Alfred M. Landon, the Republican candidate for president in 1936, and John Foster Dulles, a future secretary of state under the Eisenhower administration. The then current secretary of state, Cordell Hull, sent a special representative to the meeting. The nature of the attendees attested to the cultural clout and prestige that this ecumenical gathering carried. The resolutions of the conference, issued as *The Churches and a Just and Durable Peace*, helped to set the discourse within which plans for a post-war world were drawn up. At the Amsterdam assembly that launched the World Council of Churches in 1948, Mackay was again present as a member of the provisional committee, then later of the WCC's central committee. He served as moderator of the General Assembly of his own Presbyterian Church in the U.S.A. from 1953 to 1954. In 1954, he was also elected to a five-year term as president of the World Alliance of Reformed Churches. This brief list touches only a few of the many significant responsibilities that Mackay undertook in addition to his duties as president of Princeton Seminary.[41]

But more important than the list of committees chaired and meetings attended was the vision of Christianity that these activities expressed and that Mackay sought to have the seminary embody. The reinvigorated belief in the church that marked his thought from the 1930s onward gives an important clue to that vision. When he coined the phrase "Let the church be the church," he meant it as something more than a tautology. In *A Preface to Christian Theology* (1941), he offered the draft he had prepared for the Oxford Conference:

> *Let the Church be the Church.* Let the Church *know herself,* whose she is and what she is. Discerning clearly her own status as the community of Grace, the organ of God's redemptive purpose for mankind, she must by a process of the most merciless self-scrutiny, become what God intended her to be.... This involves a revivified sense of God as the real living God, the "god of the whole earth," over against a God who is no more than a dialectical process or a member of a polytheistic pluralism. This means con-

---

41. On the Delaware Conference and its aftermath, see Hollinger, "Realist-Pacifist Summit Meeting"; Dennis L. Tarr, "The Presbyterian Church and the Founding of the United Nations," *Journal of Presbyterian History* 53 (Spring 1975): 3-32.

cretely that the Church recognize herself to be the Church of Christ, the organ of God's purpose in Him. It must be her ceaseless concern to rid herself from all subjugation to a prevailing culture, an economic system, a social type, or a political order. Let the Church live; over against all these let the Church stand.

In sum, Mackay wanted the church to know itself as the community witnessing to the redemptive activity of God; and since God was not defined by a particular culture, economic system, or form of political government, neither should the church be limited by these.[42]

Mackay believed that his era especially required the church to be the church. *A Preface to Christian Theology* appeared only months before the United States' entry into a war already engulfing much of Europe and Asia. The totalitarian regimes were claiming that the state and the nation could justly demand absolute loyalty from their peoples. In so doing, they had overstepped their legitimate bounds and became demonic. Totalitarianism, however, was only a symptom of a deeper problem. Arising out of the vacuum left by the "disintegration which inevitably follows the absence of meaning," totalitarianism reflected, according to Mackay, the lack of an overarching or transcendent worldview. "However great was the diversity existing among the nations of the west," he suggested of the past, "and despite their recurring conflicts, they all professed loyalty to a common Christian tradition which had been the basis of their culture and the inspiration of their institutions. This particular unity was called Christendom, a unity which has now, alas, been totally disrupted." Mackay's elegiac tone notwithstanding, he did not suppose that previous patterns of relations between church and state should be restored. Too close a connection between church and state had proven, he believed, disastrous for both. In his beloved Latin America, the frequent alliance of Roman Catholicism with repressive regimes appalled him. The collapse of the Spanish Republic and the triumph of General Francisco Franco, in alliance with powerful elements of the Roman Catholic Church, he regarded as unalloyed disaster. For Mackay, the *Caudillo's* Spain provided a grim example, as he said in 1951, of "a State controlled by a Church, or rather transformed into a Church, which exceeds in fanaticism and ruthlessness anything that the Christian ages or the history of religion can show. When the State becomes a Church, the Church-

42. John A. Mackay, *A Preface to Christian Theology* (New York: Macmillan, 1941), 171.

State which results assumes the attributes of Deity and becomes the Devil." Mackay did not wish the church to ally with the state or to seek power for itself. Rather, as a community defined by the transcendent, it served to remind the secular power of its own limits and that it stood, too, under an obligation to something higher than itself. "While not aligning herself with any political party or faction, or unfurling the banner of any social theory or group," Mackay insisted, "the Church sets forth in the boldest relief her diagnosis of unhappy situations in which the welfare of men is being compromised and the principles of righteousness violated." Yet the church had something to offer still more powerful than moral critique. "The Gospel entrusted to the Church," he declared, "is not a great imperative, but a great indicative. It does not consist primarily in a call to realize certain human ideals, but to accept certain divine realities. It does not invite men to achieve something; it invites them to receive something. It makes available for them new life which God Himself offers them, upon the basis of which a new world may be built." By embodying that new life in new men and women and in a new kind of community, the church introduced into human history the power by which a new social order could come into being.[43]

Any reading of Mackay will err if it fails to recognize his profound sense of the grace of God, his passionate commitment to the person of Jesus Christ, *and* his equally strong conviction that the grace of God must be made manifest in the life of the church as well as in the quest for social justice in the world. So, too, that grace was accompanied by judgment. Mackay's opening address to the seminary community on September 26, 1950, offers an illustration of the way in which he wove those themes together. His fondness for arresting images and flowery language showed in the title, "Splendor in the Abyss." He spoke scarcely three months after the United States had, in concert with United Nations allies, again committed armies to battle, this time to defend South Korea against an invasion from the North. As Mackay made clear, the pain of that struggle was personal for Princetonians. Missionaries had gone from the seminary to serve in Korea, and Koreans themselves had studied there. South Korea's President Syngman Rhee, Mackay noted, had

---

43. Mackay, *A Preface to Christian Theology,* 143, 173, 175; Mackay, "Church, State, and Freedom," *Theology Today* 8 (July 1951): 228. See also Mackay's "Religion and Government: Their Separate Spheres and Reciprocal Responsibilities," *Theology Today* 9 (July 1952): 204-22.

lived in Hodge Hall while studying at the university, and he singled out for special note the Rev. Kyung Chik Han of the class of 1929, who had gone on to pastor "the leading church in Korea." What was transpiring in Korea was part of ominous trends that reminded Mackay of Milton's *Paradise Lost,* wherein the poet saw "a universe of death" and "a dark, unbounded, infinite abyss." Yet even in this darkness there were signs of divine hope and redemption. Changing to a different trope, Mackay employed an image to which he recurred frequently over the years. Twentieth-century Christians were living through one of God's "terrible Springtimes." He looked, he said, "in this Springtime, for the destruction and the passing of many things which we have revered with idolatrous devotion. For Spring in nature, let us not forget, is a time of devastating floods, as well as of fragrance and flowers." God's blessing and judgment were apparent in what would commonly be called both the secular and the religious realms. The willingness of the United Nations to resist North Korean aggression, to stand for "principles of international order," and to come to the aid of "a beloved and afflicted people . . . is a positive manifestation of God's Springtime." But Mackay also asserted that the larger communist movement in various parts of the globe represented God's judgment on social injustice. "Unless we take seriously," he thundered, "what the Bible says in the Old Testament and in New about responsibility for the poor and the oppressed, God's judgments shall be in the earth." Likewise, he saw mixed signals in contemporary religious movements. Ecumenism, particularly as it had begun to blend questions of faith and order with the question of mission, gave hope that "ecclesiastical harmony and theological understanding" would "become the occasion for an aggressive missionary policy." Yet against positive omens stood negative trends resistant to ecumenism: Roman Catholicism, which tended to "deify" itself as the sole expression of the church; and, among Protestants, the dispensationalists, who called on Christians to abandon "traditional Christian churches" and in effect made their motto "Schism be thou my good" — a view that Mackay regarded as little different than the cry of Milton's fallen archangel: "Evil be thou my good." One would expect these opinions from an ecumenical Protestant in 1950, but more surprising were other movements Mackay identified as positive signs of God's springtime. The young Billy Graham, who only a year earlier had burst into national fame with revivals in Los Angeles, had yet to achieve the widespread acceptance in mainstream circles that he would later attain, but already Mackay welcomed his ministry. At a time when most mainstream Protestant leaders either ignored Pentecostal churches or dismissed them out of hand, Mackay put in a good word for them, too. "These groups," he acknowledged, "are oftentimes dismissed as Christianity's 'lunatic fringe' because of certain objectional features which they manifest. Yet, according to the clear evidence of spiritual results, they are doing a great work in which Christ is present."[44]

Mackay's interest in Pentecostalism had been initially sparked by his years in Latin America, and he continued to monitor the religious situation there. In September 1953, in an address assessing the current situation south of the Rio Grande, he told the Princeton Seminary community that he greatly admired the fact that Pentecostals had brought to those "living literally on the brink of misery" the realization "that they were sons and daughters of the living God." And the impact was not limited to the spiritual realm, for "the Pentecostals have succeeded in raising the masses out of their degradation" and had given them not only a faith but also "an interest in life and education." Mackay was noting what subsequent students of religion have sometimes argued: namely, that the Pentecostal movement in Latin America promoted social uplift by encouraging education, self-discipline, and communal ties. At about the same time, Mackay formed a friendship with a South African Pentecostal who had moved to America in 1948, believing he had a call to bring the Pentecostal witness to traditional Christian denominations. Learning of Mackay's openness, David DuPlessis phoned him in Princeton in early 1952, had a good conversation, and received an invitation to visit. The visit went well, and DuPlessis took delight in John Mackay's remark: "I would rather put up with the uncouth life of the Pentecostal, than be bound by the ascetic death of the formal churches." Mackay eased DuPlessis's way into ecumenical circles and introduced him at the International Missionary Council meeting in Willingen in July 1952 as his "great Pentecostal friend." In 1956, Mackay had him back to Princeton for an extended stay, and he returned again in April 1959 when Mackay introduced him to visiting theologians Markus Barth and Thomas Torrance. DuPlessis also received an invitation to give the Student Missions Lectureship that fall, which he did shortly after James I. McCord became the new president of the seminary. During Mackay's retirement, after a charismatic movement had arisen within the Presbyterian

---

44. John A. Mackay, "Splendor in the Abyss," *Princeton Seminary Bulletin* 44 (1950): 5-15; quotations on 5, 8, 9, 12, 13.

Church and produced controversy in some congregations and presbyteries, leaders of the movement consulted Mackay, who helped bridge the gap between them and the denominational leadership. He was also influential behind the scenes in getting the General Assembly to commission a study of the charismatic movement.[45]

<h2 style="text-align:center">"A Letter to Presbyterians"</h2>

During 1953-1954, when Mackay served as moderator of the General Assembly of the Presbyterian Church in the U.S.A., fear of communism stood at high tide. In the years since the close of World War II, America had witnessed much of eastern Europe fall under the domination of the Soviet Union, had seen Russia develop the atomic bomb within several years of the United States, and had watched as Mao led a successful communist takeover of China. The following year his regime entered the war against the United States in Korea; and the conflict dragged into a protracted, bloody stalemate, ending with an armistice in July 1953, just a couple of months after Presbyterians elected John Mackay moderator. Faced with the frustrations of the Cold War, some Americans looked for enemies within. Had China been "lost" because, in the parlance of the day, communists, fellow travelers, or dupes within the government encouraged this result? Had the Soviet Union developed the atomic bomb due to American spies covertly passing along information? The congressional investigation of Alger Hiss, former official in the State Department, resulted in charges, hotly denied by Hiss, that he had disclosed classified documents. The statute of limitations had run out on the charge of spying, but he was eventually convicted of perjury after an initial trial resulted in a hung jury. Julius and Ethel Rosenberg, arrested in 1950 and charged with providing information on the bomb to the Soviet

---

45. John A. Mackay, "Portent and Promise in the Other America," *Princeton Seminary Bulletin* 47 (1954): 13; Joshua R. Ziefle, "The Place of Pentecost: David Johannes du Plessis, the Assemblies of God, and the Development of Ecumenical Pentecostalism" (Ph.D. Dissertation, Princeton Theological Seminary, 2010); Robert R. Curlee and Mary Ruth Isaac-Curlee, "Bridging the Gap: John A. Mackay, Presbyterians, and the Charismatic Movement," *American Presbyterians: Journal of Presbyterian History* 72 (Fall 1994): 157-72. For an example of a sociologist's reflections on the Pentecostal movement in Latin America, see David Martin, *Tongues of Fire: The Explosion of Protestantism in Latin America* (Oxford: Blackwell, 1990).

Union, were convicted and ultimately executed. After 1950, Senator Joseph McCarthy came to embody fears of communist subversion. Often crude and savage in manner, he claimed to possess evidence that the government was riddled with communists and their sympathizers. He seldom named individuals or offered specific evidence to substantiate his charges; but before his fellow senators censured him in 1954, he had managed to cast aspersions of disloyalty upon the State Department, elements of the United States army, and the American clergy. Others raised the issue of "red" clergy before McCarthy did. In March 1953, for example, Donald Jackson, congressman from California, rose on the floor of the House to charge that John Mackay's friend, the Methodist Bishop G. Bromley Oxnam, had for a long time "served God on Sunday and the Communist front for the balance of the week." Then in June, McCarthy appointed a new staffer, J. B. Mathews, who shortly published in a conservative magazine an article entitled "Reds and Our Churches." Mathews, who had once served as a Methodist clergyman and in the 1930s was sufficiently left-wing to attack the New Deal as pro-business and insufficiently radical, made a dramatic charge in the essay's first sentence: "The largest single group supporting the Communist apparatus in the United States today is composed of Protestant clergymen." Among those presented as an example was John Alexander Mackay.[46]

Upon his election as moderator in May, Mackay had already issued a sharp statement expressing fear that anti-communism was becoming for many "a substitute religion" and "the new idolatry." While he had no doubt of the evil of communism, he found equally dangerous the fanatical spirit willing to violate the rights of individual conscience or to hold people guilty by reason of "casual association" with others who may have espoused questionable views. Behind this fanaticism lurked a "Fascist demon" ready "to assert itself in our own and other countries." During the summer and fall, Mackay pondered the need for an official letter to the Presbyterian Church to set forth clearly and positively the theological is-

46. Robert Moats Miller, *Bishop G. Bromley Oxnam: Paladin of Liberal Protestantism* (Nashville: Abingdon Press, 1990), 569; Rick Nutt, "For Truth and Liberty: Presbyterians and McCarthyism," *Journal of Presbyterian History* 78 (Spring 2000): 51-68; Mathews's quotation on 58. For an excellent overview of anti-communism in the period, see James T. Patterson, *Grand Expectations: The United States, 1945-1974* (New York: Oxford University Press, 1996), 165-205. On the life, career, and tactics of McCarthy, consult David M. Oshinsky, *A Conspiracy So Immense: The World of Joe McCarthy* (New York: Oxford University Press, 2005).

sues posed by McCarthyism. As moderator, he proposed to the General Council — which functioned as a kind of executive committee of the denomination between the then annual meetings of the General Assembly — that it send such an epistle. With little if any precedent for this action, some hesitated initially; but in the end a letter drafted chiefly by Mackay and adopted unanimously by the council with modest changes went out on November 2, 1953, to all presbyteries and sessions. At the same time, the letter was given to the press and sent to the president of the United States, the secretary of state, and Presbyterian members of Congress.[47]

"A Letter to Presbyterians," which has been compared to the Barmen Declaration of the Confessing Church in Germany in 1934, readily granted that "the menace of Communism" and its "undoubted aim . . . to subvert the thought and the life of the United States" required "appropriate precautions." But the gist of the letter was that fear of communism had bred dangerous excess: "a subtle but potent assault on basic human rights" that one could see in the tendency of some congressional investigations to "become inquisitions" and in attacks upon "citizens of integrity and social passion." "Treason and dissent," warned the letter, "are being confused." Noting that the church "has a prophetic function to fulfill," the letter reminded Presbyterians that the "Church does not derive its authority from the nation but from Jesus Christ" and that it therefore owed "its supreme and ultimate allegiance" to him. That loyalty did *not* mean that the church had a mandate "to present blueprints for the organization of society and the conduct of government," but it did have a prophetic duty "to proclaim those principles, and to instill that spirit, which are essential for social health." One of these was the preservation of "the majesty of truth . . . at all times and all costs." Mackay believed that principle to be at grave risk in the Cold War, when "falsehood is frequently preferred to fact if it can be shown to have greater propaganda value." He warned that the "demagogue . . . is coming into his own on a national scale." According to the demagogue's "philosophy, if what is true 'gives aid and comfort' to our enemies, it must be suppressed." The statement saw "a painful illustration" of this tendency in the fact that men and women were being "condemned upon the uncorroborated word of former Communists," who may simply have transferred "their allegiance

47. John A. Mackay, "The New Idolatry," *Theology Today* 10 (October 1953): 382-83. For more on the General Council's letter, see James H. Smylie, "Mackay and McCarthyism, 1953-1954," *Journal of Church and State* 6 (Autumn 1964): 352-65.

Bernhard Word Anderson (1916–2007) served as professor of Old Testament theology at Princeton Seminary from 1968 until 1982. Among many honors and awards, he held the office of President of the Society of Biblical Literature in 1979–1980 and the office of Dean of Drew University School of Theology from 1958 to 1963.

Johan Christiaan Beker (1924–1999) was born in Gorrsel, the Netherlands, and left for the United States following World War II. A specialist in Pauline studies, he began teaching at Princeton Seminary in 1966 and retired in 1994 as the Richard J. Dearborn Professor of New Testament Theology.

Seward Hiltner (1909–1984) served as professor of pastoral theology at the Divinity School of the University of Chicago from 1950 to 1961, and as professor of theology and personality at Princeton Seminary from 1961 until 1980. He was a leading pioneer in the field of clinical pastoral education.

James Edwin Loder (1931–2001), class of 1957, joined the Princeton Seminary faculty teaching in the field of Christian education in 1962, and was serving as the Mary D. Synnott Professor of the Philosophy of Christian Education at the time of his death. He had a deep interest in the relationship between psychology and theology and in the processes of human creativity and transformation.

James Hastings Nichols (1915–1991) came to Princeton Seminary in 1962 as the Mary McIntosh Bridge Professor of Modern Church History and served in that capacity until his retirement in 1983, also serving as academic dean of the seminary from 1970 to 1979. Previously he had taught on the faculty of the Divinity School of the University of Chicago. He attended the Second Vatican Council in Rome in 1962 as an official Protestant observer. *Portrait by Béla Schmidt*

Karlfried Froehlich was born and grew up in Germany, where his father was a Lutheran pastor in Meissen. He completed his doctoral degree at the University of Basel, where he also served as secretary and assistant to the New Testament scholar Oscar Cullmann. He came to Princeton Seminary in 1968 and at the time of his retirement in 1992 was the Benjamin B. Warfield Professor of Ecclesiastical History.

Kathleen McVey serves as the Joseph Ross Stevenson Professor of Church History. She came to Princeton Seminary in 1979 and is a specialist in early and Eastern church history, with a particular focus on Syriac Christianity.

M. Richard Shaull (1919–2002), class of 1941, was for twenty years a missionary, seminary professor, and university administrator in South America before coming to teach at Princeton Seminary in 1962. At the time of his retirement in 1980 he was the Henry Winters Luce Professor of Ecumenics. In his retirement years he served with the Volunteers in Mission in Costa Rica, Guatemala, and Mexico, and served with a delegation of religious leaders who observed the elections in Nicaragua in 1990.

Samuel Hugh Moffett, class of 1942, and Eileen Flower Moffett, class of 1955, served as missionaries in Korea from 1955 until Sam's appointment as the Henry Winters Luce Professor of Ecumenics and Mission at Princeton Seminary in 1981. Sam received emeritus status at Princeton Seminary in 1986 and published a major history of Christianity in Asia during his retirement years. Eileen Moffett, whose field is Christian education, served as director of the Korea Bible Club movement. *Portrait by Ewan McClure*

Samuel Wilson Blizzard Jr. (1914–1976), class of 1939, joined the Princeton Seminary faculty in 1957. He served as director of student studies from 1965 to 1967, as dean of instruction in 1967–1968, and as chair of the history department in 1963–1964 and again from 1969 to 1971. At the time of his retirement in 1975 he held the Maxwell M. Upson Professorship in Christianity and Society.

Daniel Leo Migliore, class of 1959, began his teaching career of forty-seven years at Princeton Seminary in 1962 in the field of New Testament. After a few years he moved to the field of systematic theology and served as the Arthur M. Adams Professor of Systematic Theology and as the Charles Hodge Professor of Systematic Theology before his retirement in 2009.

Charles Converse West began teaching Christian ethics at Princeton Seminary in 1961 and retired from the seminary in 1991 as the Stephen Colwell Professor of Christian Ethics. He was academic dean of the seminary from 1978 to 1984. He served as a missionary in China from 1947 to 1950, as an ecumenical worker in Germany from 1950 to 1953, and on the staff of the Ecumenical Institute of the World Council of Churches in Bossey, Switzerland, from 1956 to 1961. Among his special concerns were the witness of Christianity in Communist-dominated countries and the ecumenical mission of the church.

Edler Garnet Hawkins (1908–1977) began his ministry at Saint Augustine Presbyterian Church in New York City in 1938, which under his leadership grew to be a multiracial, multilingual congregation of over 1,000 members. He became the first African American Moderator of the General Assembly of the United Presbyterian Church in 1964 and, after serving as a visiting professor and consultant in field education, was called to Princeton Seminary in 1971 as professor of practical theology and coordinator of black studies. He also served on the General Board of the National Council of Churches and on the Central Committee of the World Council of Churches. *Portrait by Dorothy Whitehead*

Sang Hyun Lee was born in Korea and educated in North America. He taught for ten years at Hope College in Holland, Michigan, before joining the Princeton Seminary faculty in 1980 as assistant professor of theology. In 1984 he became the first director of the seminary's program for Asian American theology and ministry, and in 1987 he was named the first holder of the seminary's Kyung-Chik Han Chair in Systematic Theology. In addition to Asian American theology, Professor Lee specializes in the writings of Jonathan Edwards. He retired after teaching at Princeton Seminary for thirty years in 2011; a lecture series, the Sang Hyung Lee Lecture in Asian American Theology, has been established in his honor.

Freda Ann Gardner, a graduate of the Presbyterian School of Christian Education in Richmond, Virginia, was the first tenured woman faculty member at Princeton Seminary. She taught Christian education at the seminary beginning in 1961 and served as the director of the School of Christian Education at Princeton Seminary from 1979 through 1992, retiring as the Thomas W. Synnott Professor of Christian Education in 1992. She was chosen as Moderator of the Presbyterian Church (USA) in 1999.

Katherine Doob Sakenfeld came to Princeton Seminary as an instructor in the department of biblical studies in 1970 and holds the William Albright Eisenberger Chair of Old Testament Literature and Exegesis. She was director of the seminary's Ph.D. studies program from 1993 to 2009. She served as general editor of the New Interpreter's Dictionary of the Bible, as a coeditor of the Oxford Study Bible, and as a member of the New Revised Standard Version translation committee, and has published several biblical commentaries and many articles, particularly exploring premonarchical biblical narratives, feminist biblical hermeneutics, and the relation of the biblical message to the concerns of marginalized groups and in diverse cultural contexts.

Luis Rivera-Pagán, a native of Puerto Rico, was the visiting Mackay Professor of World Christianity in the 1999–2000 academic year and returned in 2002 to take up the Henry Winters Luce Chair of Ecumenics and Mission, in which he served until his retirement in 2007. He previously taught at the Evangelical Seminary of Puerto Rico and at the University of Puerto Rico. Among his interests are the relationship of theology and literature, the role of Christianity in the conquest of Latin America, and issues of war, peace, and nonviolence.

Geddes Whitney Hanson came to study for a doctorate at Princeton Seminary after ten years in congregational ministry in New York City, Philadelphia, and Indianapolis. He has held both academic and administrative positions at Princeton Seminary. He was assistant and associate director of professional studies from 1969 until 1977, taught courses in the department of practical theology with a special focus on pastoral administration beginning in 1969, and served for a period of time as director of the seminary's continuing education program. He was named the Charlotte Newcombe Professor of Congregational Ministry in 1996 and retired in 2009. In 1992 the Association of Black Seminarians established a lecture series in his name to honor "his outstanding academic and spiritual guidance to the students of Princeton Theological Seminary."

Yolanda Pierce joined the Princeton Seminary faculty in 2007 as the Elmer G. Homrighausen Associate Professor of African American Religion and Literature. She also serves as liaison to the Princeton University Center for African American Studies. She teaches courses in African American religious history, womanist theology, and literature and religion.

Jane Dempsey Douglass served as the Hazel Thompson McCord Professor of Historical Theology at Princeton Seminary from 1985 to 1998. She was the first woman president of the World Alliance of Reformed Churches, the first woman president of the American Society of Church History, and the first woman holder of a named chair at Princeton Theological Seminary. She had a strong ecumenical interest and was an active leader in Lutheran-Reformed dialogue for many years.

Iain Richard Torrance is the sixth president of Princeton Theological Seminary and professor of patristics. A native of Scotland, he taught at Queen's College, Birmingham (England), the University of Birmingham, and the University of Aberdeen in Scotland, where he also served as dean of the Faculty of Arts and Letters prior to coming to Princeton in 2004. In 2003 he was elected Moderator of the General Assembly of the Church of Scotland. He has also served as chaplain to Britain's armed forces and chaplain to Her Majesty the Queen in Scotland. His scholarly focus has been especially in the areas of early Christian thought, the ethics of war, and bioethics, and he has been an active participant in the dialogue between the World Alliance of Reformed Churches and the Orthodox church. *Photo courtesy of Robyn Torrance*

from one authoritarian system to another." Perhaps the most dangerous attitude the Cold War engendered was the tendency to make a fetish of security, and the statement developed that point at some length.

> That we have the obligation to make our nation as secure as possible, no one can dispute. But there is no absolute security in human affairs, nor is security the ultimate human obligation. A still greater obligation, as well as a more strategic procedure, is to make sure that what we mean by security, and the methods we employ to achieve it, are in accordance with the will of God. Otherwise, any human attempt to establish a form of world order which does no more than exalt the interest of a class, a culture, a race, or a nation, above God and the interests of the whole human family, is foredoomed to disaster.[48]

The letter went on to observe that powerful "revolutionary forces" were at work in the world — forces that constituted "in great part the judgment of God upon human selfishness and complacency." None of this implied that communism represented, as its adherents believed, the wave of the future. It would ultimately fail. "No political order can prevail which deliberately leaves God out of account. . . . For that reason Communism has an approaching rendezvous with God and the moral order." In fact, because that system would ultimately fail, Americans should "ever be on the lookout for the evidence of change in the Communist world, for the effects of disillusionment, and for the presence of a God-implanted hunger." Therefore, the letter advocated a willingness by American leaders to "take the risk, even the initiative, of seeking face-to-face encounter with our enemies." Although the statement did not mention China, Mackay himself had argued since Mao's rise to power in 1949 that the People's Republic should — contrary to United States policy — be officially recognized and diplomatic contacts established. The statement closed with a call for "spiritual calm" and a reminder: "Loyalty to great principles of truth and justice has made our nation great; such loyalty alone can keep it great and ensure its destiny."[49]

48. "A Letter to Presbyterians Concerning the Present Situation in Our Country and in the World," *Theology Today* 11 (April 1954): 15-21; quotations on 16, 17, 18, 19; Daniel L. Migliore, "'The Majesty of Truth': Meditations on 'A Letter to Presbyterians,' 1954," *Princeton Seminary Bulletin* 6 (1985): 78-80.

49. "Letter to Presbyterians," 20, 21.

As "A Letter to Presbyterians" indicated, John Mackay could assume the mantle of prophetic social protest, and that side of him still appeared even into his ninth decade. His baccalaureate address to the class of 1971 sounded a warning about U.S. policies in much of the world. He decried American involvement in the Vietnam War as "the disastrous and meaningless struggle that continues to go on in Southeast Asia." With regard to Latin America, he referred to the "involvement of our government in facilitating the emergence of the present Brazilian regime which is one of the most tyrannical regimes in Latin American history," and he sadly noted the "tragic fact that our country's attitude toward Brazil has not been inspired by concern for the many millions of impoverished people in that country who live a dehumanized life." He noted "the revolutionary expectation" that was rising in the region and that had acquired powerful symbols in the deaths of the Colombian priest Camilo Torres and of the Cuban revolutionary Che Guevara, who had gone to fight in Bolivia. Unlike many American students who romanticized these figures — then and later it was common to see college-age youth wearing T-shirts with the image of Che — Mackay did not idealize them. But he did see them as God's warning. "More and more," he said,

> I reach the conviction that, unless governments in the Western hemisphere take seriously the tragic condition of the Latin American masses, the living God of the Hebrew prophets will bring into the contemporary scene the counterpart of that pagan monarch whom Jeremiah, speaking in the name of the Lord God of Israel, called "Nebuchadnezzar, my servant."

Yet even as Mackay appeared ready to go to the barricades with students more than sixty years his junior, his message also sounded another note. His hope for justice lay ultimately in the reinvigoration of a commitment to the Christ who loved all people and empowered those who would trust him. Mackay expressed gratitude for signs of renewal in Catholicism and cited "the Christian witness of that great Brazilian, the Roman Catholic bishop, Helder Camara," who, despite a military coup in 1964 and despite being considered a dangerous man by many supporters of the junta, continued to advocate the cause of the poor. He also praised Chilean Pentecostals as another instance of the proper "incarnational approach" to ministry among the deprived. "By what they were and did they opened up the way for an enthusiastic response to the Christian gospel."[50]

Mackay defied facile labels. He illustrated this fact perhaps most graphically when, five years before his baccalaureate sermon to the 1971 graduates, he went back to the seminary to speak at the dedication of a plaque in honor of James Reeb, class of 1953 — a plaque still hanging on the wall beside the front entrance to the campus center. In 1965, Reeb, then a social worker and a Unitarian Universalist minister in Boston, went to Selma, Alabama, in support of demonstrations for voting rights led by Martin Luther King Jr. Brutally beaten by a gang of thugs on March 9, he died two days later in a Birmingham hospital. Unlike the shooting death of a black activist several weeks earlier, the murder of the white Reeb captured the attention of the nation and contributed to President Lyndon Johnson's decision to go before Congress on March 15 to press for the enactment of a voting rights bill. Mackay's address in 1966 expressed both great admiration and a sad reservation about Reeb. On the one hand, "Reeb represented America at its best, and Princeton Seminary at its best, on the crucial racial issue." With regard to "James Reeb's human concern and the cause for which he died, I find myself at one with him." Perhaps feeling the need in an activist age to establish his own credentials, Mackay observed how often he had been called a communist because of stands he had taken, and he noted his association with the National Advisory Committee on Farm Labor, which worked on behalf "of the indigent migrant workers, whose woes have been so shamefully exploited in our country." It was a cause, he said, that gave him the "exciting experience" of working in company with several extraordinary men: Frank Porter Graham, a former president of the University of North Carolina who had defended the academic freedom of his school by inviting Bertrand Russell and Langston Hughes to give public lectures; A. Philip Randolph, founder of the Brotherhood of Sleeping Car Porters and pioneer civil rights leader who proposed the 1963 March on Washington; and Norman Thomas, a champion of social justice and perennial leader of America's Socialist party. What troubled Mackay about Reeb was that a

> beloved, sincere and courageous man came to ignore and brush aside the commandment to love God, which is both the Christian pivot of human obligation and the inspiration of creative concern

50. Mackay, "Great Adventure," 31, 36, 37.

for others. The love of one's neighbor ... became for him a substitute for the First Commandment which is "to love God with all one's heart, soul, strength and mind." ... James Reeb made concern for others the one ultimate source, norm and objective of human behavior. These two commandments, however, belong together. When they are separated in such a way that either one becomes the sole absolute, or a substitute for the other, tragedy ensues.

For Mackay the only adequate hope for the social justice for which he longed, for which he and his wife Jane had hidden the young Haya de la Torre, for which he had risked controversy by writing "A Letter to Presbyterians," was what he liked to call a "luminous" encounter with Jesus Christ. Over the years, Mackay saw ever-expanding meaning in what he had experienced at Rogart in 1903, but that encounter remained at the center of his life, work, and thought.[51]

Mackay's Vision for Princeton Seminary

In 1936, Mackay came to the leadership of Princeton with definite views about what a theological seminary should be, and the central features of that vision remained constant throughout his twenty-three years of leadership. If one puts together remarks that he made near the beginning of his tenure with addresses in the waning years of his service, one sees the continuity of purpose during his presidency.

In a statement to alumni and friends of the seminary in January 1939, Mackay offered a metaphor to explain the nature of theological education. A countryside, he said, might be observed from "the turret of the old castle atop its rocky eminence" or it might be viewed from "the road along which a wayfarer travels." A modern theological seminary must have a "double vision from the turret and the road. It must scan the unchanging landmarks seen from the ancient fortress and blend them with the ever changing prospect that greets the traveler's eye. These two, the changeless and the changing, must be focussed into a single vision in the outlook of the theological seminary that would fulfill its mission today in the service of Christ and His Church." Both perspectives were essential;

51. John A. Mackay, "A Representative American of the Sixties: James Joseph Reeb," *Princeton Seminary Bulletin* 60 (1966): 33-39; quotations on 35, 37.

to abandon either would entail betrayal of Princeton's task. The seminary would, he admitted, "be disloyal to the Christian faith were it to cease to set forth the everlasting truths of the Gospel, with a constantly renewed sense of their grandeur." However, it would also be faithless "to the needs of men should it fail to be interested in the highways and byways of contemporary life in order to understand the human situation and meet its need." "The Princeton dream," he concluded, pressing the image even further, "is to blend the stability and strength of the fortress with the mobility and concern of the moving cavalcade."[52]

Two years later, in his *Preface to Christian Theology,* Mackay made the same point by contrasting the differing views one gets by observing life from the balcony and from the road, and he also used a slightly different way of stating the polarities of theological education.

> In recent generations in America seminaries have been of two main types. One type of seminary has been exclusively interested in breaking up the white light of revelation into its constituent facets. It has had little or no interest in the problems of contemporary people, nor has it shown the relevance of divine truth to the situation in which men and women live and move. The other type has been interested more or less exclusively in the problem of the horizontal, that is to say, the problems of man's life in society. In its classrooms theological thinking has not been based upon divine revelation. Theology has been little more than a department of sociology. What we need today is a union of these two types. The vertical and the horizontal emphases must intersect in a prophetic approach to the world of our time; the eternal must challenge the temporal.

As Mackay's comments indicated and as he had stressed in his inaugural address, he had no sympathy with any school that made the study of theology simply one option among many or that turned seminary education into a study of human problems. Nor did theological education consist chiefly in the acquisition of certain vocational skills. But neither was theology to be examined apart from its intersection with the "world of our time." It needed to be taught and learned in a new fashion. It could not — or should not — be considered simply as a system of eternal truths, refracted into their logical components. The age needed a theology of the

---

52. John A. Mackay, "The Outlook," *Princeton Seminary Bulletin* 32 (January 1939): 1.

road — a theology in motion, so to speak, as the word of God encountered human need in particular times and places.[53]

"Christian theology today," Mackay said, "has a missionary role to fulfill, of a kind that has not been required since the early Christian thinkers outthought the pagan world." He said this, not simply because he had served as a missionary in Latin America, but because he believed that twentieth-century churches and their theological schools existed amid a new cultural and intellectual reality. "Time was," he observed,

> when both thought and action in secular society were basically determined by Christian conceptions. When that was so, theology could follow, without loss to life, a purely technical, scholastic, sectarian course. But when things, taken for granted for centuries, are called in question, and total disintegration threatens, and secular theologies [i.e., fascism and communism] emerge, Christian theology is invested with a new missionary role.

In this new world, theology and seminaries had to grapple more immediately with intellectual, cultural, and social challenges. The age was one that, in Mackay's view, was witnessing the disruption of Christendom. Describing the United States in the era when Mackay began his presidency, historian Robert Handy has called the years between 1920 and 1940 the time of the "second disestablishment" — a period when Protestant churches in particular, having been legally disestablished in the late eighteenth or early nineteenth centuries, were manifestly losing the ability to shape the values and assumptions of the culture. Of course, this loss was far from complete. One need only recall the 1942 Delaware Conference sponsored by the Federal Council of Churches, where John Mackay rubbed shoulders with Alfred Landon, John Foster Dulles, and a special representative from Cordell Hull's State Department to disabuse oneself of the notion that he and other ecumenical Protestants had been shoved into marginality. Yet Mackay rightly discerned that the place of Christianity within the culture was changing and that theological education needed to take cognizance of the fact.[54]

---

53. Mackay, *A Preface to Christian Theology,* 25.

54. Mackay, *A Preface to Christian Theology,* 24; Robert T. Handy, *A Christian America: Protestant Hopes and Historical Realities,* 2nd ed. (New York: Oxford University Press, 1984), 159-84.

After more than two decades at the helm of Princeton Seminary, Mackay used his last opening convocation on September 30, 1958, to offer a valedictory reflection on the question: "What is the ideal which a theological education should fulfill?" First, after three years of hard study "every seminary student, not to speak of every teacher," should "have a massive, luminous, theological structure, as the guide of his life." Reminiscing about his own formation, Mackay singled out four thinkers who had helped him to achieve that goal. He remembered how "in my mid-teens I wrestled with that masterpiece of American metaphysics, Jonathan Edwards's *Freedom of the Will.*" The other three were teachers he encountered in person and recalled fondly. At Aberdeen he admired J. B. Baillie, "who was no mere teacher of the history of ideas" but "an unashamed Hegelian." Mackay did not agree with Baillie's "main ideas," nor did Baillie demand that his students do so. What he did require was "that we should possess accurate knowledge, that we should think clearly, that our thoughts should be governed by a rigorous logic." Of his years as a seminarian at Princeton, he recalled his debt "to that supremely great teacher, Benjamin B. Warfield, a true master by the vastness of his theological knowledge, and the penetration of his dialectical acumen. 'Bennie' Warfield opened up to us the Reformed System." And then there was "that great Spaniard, Miguel de Unamuno ... [who] felt that Spanish intellectuals lacked a world-view and that they needed it." The thinkers whom Mackay cited were diverse, but they shared a common quest: through rigorous learning and clarity of thought they offered a comprehensive view of the world. Mackay desired that every graduate of Princeton leave possessing such a vision. "Not that your theology will then be complete," he added, "no, but it will be something vertebrate, which you will proceed to clothe with flesh and sinews." In other words, one needed the structure, the organizing principle, but the process of filling it out would be a continuing post-graduate process as one traveled the road of faith and ministry.[55]

But an intellectual "structure of truth," important as it was, required something more. One needed to recall, he said, quoting Kierkegaard: "Subjectivity is truth." At one level, Mackay was simply enunciating in different language the principle that Princeton had espoused from the beginning: piety and learning needed to accompany one another. As if implicitly acknowledging that he was saying nothing new, he cited a figure much admired by Old Princeton, Thomas Chalmers, and discussed the way in

55. Mackay, "Theological Triennium," 5, 6, 7, 8.

which this guiding spirit in the formation of the Scottish Free Church in 1843 had preached and prayed eloquently before he was, through illness, brought to apprehend what Chalmers himself called "the magnitude of eternity." Mackay did not quibble over whether one described this transforming experience as conversion or, with more modern thinkers, styled it the discovery of "the dimension of depth." Nor did he insist that the experience be sudden and datable; it might equally well be a gradual process. But however it happened and whatever nomenclature described it, that personal encounter with the divine was essential to complete theological formation. Mackay's emphasis upon spiritual experience stood in the great Princeton tradition, but his use of the language of Kierkegaard — "subjectivity is truth" — suggested a provisionality to theological systems and propositions that would have troubled the Hodges or Warfield. Mackay put the matter thus in 1955: "Christian truth is *personal* truth, it is commitment to a Person, loyalty to a Person who is the Sovereign Lord. And that Person, the Living Christ, is ever moving beyond the frontiers of today. His truth cannot be contained within rigid dogmatisms, nor His Kingdom within narrow ecclesiastical boundaries."[56]

The "theological triennium" at Princeton also entailed two other goals. It was not enough for students to sequester themselves in the library or in dorm rooms in order to crack the books. Nor was it sufficient that in chapel or upon their knees in private prayer they experienced the grace of God. The seminary was to be a Christian community, not a mere aggregation of devout and theologically literate individuals. *"We must incarnate the Faith in corporate living,"* Mackay insisted, adding: "We can speak of the Church on the Princeton Seminary campus, as we can of the Church at Corinth, and the Church at Rome." In his travels around the world on behalf of the seminary, said Mackay, nothing gave him greater satisfaction than to encounter alumni who, "whatever their race or nationality, or denominational background, felt that they were welcome on this campus and they belonged to a single community of faith." In his earlier 1955 address, he had contended that Princeton Seminary, while under the auspices of the Presbyterian Church in the U.S.A., was "never intrusive" in its denominationalism. With its student body composed of representatives of many churches and from various parts of the globe, Princeton had a unique opportunity "to live ecumenically at the local

56. Mackay, "Theological Triennium," 8, 10; Mackay, "The Glory and Peril of the Local," *Princeton Seminary Bulletin* 48 (1955): 11.

level" and thus demonstrate the reality of ecumenicity to the church universal as it sent out graduates to serve around the nation and world. Finally, said Mackay, *"we must discern the world relevance of the faith."* Solid theological learning, an existential encounter with God in Christ, a community incarnating the faith — all of these found their end in mission to the world. "You must while in seminary," he exhorted, "strive to fix your gaze on the world and to move out into the world" in order to develop *"a prophetic outlook upon contemporary history."* Before he closed his reflections, he gave some examples of what that outlook might mean for his era. In the late 1950s, with much popular religion involving the quest for peace of mind or using faith as a way of distinguishing America from Soviet Russia — "We are not atheists like the communists" — Mackay thundered that God was not to be patronized. Instead "of seeming to chum up with Deity, of becoming Christ's 'cronies,'" Christians need to be "His true friends and loyal servants." Aside from noting that their future work required prospective clergy to learn homiletics and church polity and to engage in field work, he did not specify further curricular implications of his vision of the "theological triennium." But one obvious inference should be underscored: if men and women were to keep their gaze fixed on the world and develop "a prophetic outlook" on the contemporary scene, they needed sometime during their three years to reflect on those matters. Theological education could not simply be about theology, biblical studies, practical theology, or church history considered in isolation from the larger cultural, intellectual, and historical realities of which they were a part.[57]

MACKAY'S VISION for the seminary stood in continuity with that of the older Princeton. His stress upon the training of a learned ministry echoed the founders. His emphasis upon theology as the central task of the seminary as well as his conviction that theology treats "something that is objective and which must be studied with all the resources of learning" and that we are "not dealing with sentiment" were themes that Mackay's admired teacher "Bennie" Warfield would have endorsed. Mackay's belief that theology derived from God's revelation, that its focus should be christocentric, and that the Bible is the witness to that revelation adhered to the Princeton tradition. Also, Mackay spoke in accents that Old

57. Mackay, "Theological Triennium," 10-12; Mackay, "Glory and Peril of the Local," 9. The italics are in the original.

Princeton would have approved when he declared in 1941 that theology "does not consist primarily in a call to realize certain human ideals, but to accept certain divine realities. It does not invite men to achieve something; it invites them to receive something. It makes available for them new life which God Himself offers them." Mackay's stress on piety, even many of the authors he had learned to love as a child and often quoted as guides to the pilgrimage of faith, came from the same Puritan Reformed lineage that had informed the Plan of the Seminary. Certainly Mackay's sense of mission to the world — though somewhat broader than the nineteenth-century notion of sending out missionaries — likewise exemplified a commitment manifest early in Princeton's life. One might even say that Mackay's willingness to comment on contemporary events — whether the rise of fascism and communism, political events in Latin America, or McCarthyism — bears more than a passing resemblance to the political and social interests manifested in the pages of the *Princeton Review* under the editorship of Charles Hodge.[58]

It would, of course, be as inaccurate to suggest that nothing had changed with Mackay as it would be to imply that he represented a complete rupture with Old Princeton. In important ways, he did take the school in new directions. He was uninterested in refighting the battles of the 1920s, for he saw them as fruitless and irrelevant to the contemporary situation. He adhered to a notion of God's revelation as a dynamic process. Along with Barth, Unamuno, Kierkegaard, Brunner, and others, he was less confident than previous generations of Princetonians that static propositions could contain God's truth. As he wrote in a *Theology Today* article that appeared several months after his retirement: "We shall have to move fast and far, if we would keep abreast of truth. This is particularly so where Christian truth is concerned. For Christian truth is not so much something that we have as something that has us. . . . To grasp that for which Jesus Christ the Truth has grasped us will be our task of a life-time." Or, as he had said five years earlier in an address to the World Presbyterian Alliance meeting in Princeton: "Theology must be constantly reformed to bring it closer to the everlasting Word of God, and to make it more relevant to the problems and concerns of living men. . . . Light has not ceased to break forth from Holy Scripture."[59]

58. Mackay, "Theological Triennium," 6.

59. John A. Mackay, "Keep Moving Beyond," *Theology Today* 16 (October 1959): 317; Mackay, "The Witness of the Reformed Churches," *Theology Today* 11 (October 1954): 383.

From the perspective of the history of Princeton Seminary, the crucial question posed by the institution's third president is this: How did Mackay's vision shape seminary life, its programs, curriculum, faculty appointments, and even the physical structure of the campus itself? To these questions, our account now turns.

CHAPTER FIFTEEN

Reshaping the Seminary, 1936-1959

D URING HIS twenty-three-year presidency, John A. Mackay had an extraordinary opportunity to reshape the school. Several of the most
conservative members of the faculty's majority had, of course, left with
J. Gresham Machen in 1929. Others prominently identified with Machen's
point of view were passing from the scene during the early years of
Mackay's tenure. In early 1937, Caspar Wistar Hodge Jr. died. Due to failing health, William Park Armstrong took a reduced load in 1940, and he
died four years later. Although Frederick W. Loetscher continued his professorship until 1945, he had been quietly a part of the faculty minority in
the 1920s and now strongly favored the new direction that Mackay
brought to the school. Also, in 1936, Charles R. Erdman retired at the
same time as President Stevenson, and thus the two bêtes noires of the
ultraconservatives were no longer on the scene. In other words, the principal belligerents on both sides of the conflict of the 1920s were gone
from the seminary, presenting the institution with the chance of a new
beginning.

Of course, some of those who started teaching at the seminary in the
post-reorganization period of Stevenson's presidency — from the fall of
1929 or later — did carry on into the Mackay years. Donald Mackenzie,
named professor of biblical theology in 1933, continued until 1941. But
only a few of the holdovers from the previous administration stayed
more than a decade into Mackay's presidency. Among those who did
were the following: John Kuizenga, appointed in 1930 to systematic theology and continuing until 1947; Andrew Blackwood, called to a post in
homiletics in 1929 and teaching until 1950; and Edward Howell Roberts,

who started as an instructor in systematic theology in 1930, moved into homiletics, and served as registrar and later as dean before his death in 1954. The longest serving was Henry Snyder Gehman, who started his career at the seminary as an instructor in New Testament Greek in 1930 and then moved into Old Testament, retiring only two years before Mackay himself. Given the fact that a system of faculty search committees did not yet exist to fill vacancies, John Mackay, in informal consultation with his faculty colleagues, had a relatively free hand in recommending new faculty to the board of trustees and thus in reshaping the direction of the school. Under Mackay, the expansion of presidential power conferred in the 1929 reorganization began to make a significant difference in the life of the institution.

Mackay signaled a new direction very early in his presidency when, in the 1938-1939 academic year, he brought Emil Brunner to campus as a guest professor. For recent generations of theological students, Brunner, if remembered at all, is seen as the junior partner in the dispute with Karl Barth over natural theology. Yet, as Douglas John Hall has observed, Brunner's voice "was the one that first made the 'new theology' being spawned in Europe *personally* known to the English-speaking world." His year at Princeton was one of the means by which he did so. As that year drew to a close, Mackay reported to alumni that Brunner's presence "stirred the campus in a creative way by his efforts to refocus and restate the everlasting verities." Through a series of other, long-term faculty appointments, Mackay also promoted a course correction for the seminary. Moreover, the Tennent College of Christian Education, previously in Philadelphia, was brought to campus and housed in newly purchased facilities vacated by the Hun School. With the Tennent School of Christian Education, the first significant number of women students came to Princeton. Perhaps because of the fact that they were studying for a degree in religious education and not seeking ordination, there was little recorded discussion of the gender question. Departments were consolidated in a way comparable to their current form, and curriculum was revamped. The seminary added a doctoral program that saw its first graduate in 1944, created *Theology Today* the same year as a new voice for itself, started a summer Institute of Theology, and expanded its facilities with the new Speer Library and a campus center. The campus center did away with the former eating clubs and provided a common place for all students to eat, and thereby in Mackay's view promoted more of a sense of community among seminarians. But

Mackay's aspiration for the seminary was most fully demonstrated in the faculty appointments he approved.[1]

Overtures to Behavioral Science: Homrighausen, Bonnell, and Blizzard

One of the first long-term faculty appointments under Mackay nearly misfired. In 1937, he and Elmer G. Homrighausen both attended the World Conference on Church, State, and Society in Oxford. At the meeting, Mackay offered Homrighausen a position as professor of Christian education, and the latter accepted. The board of trustees duly endorsed the president's choice and sent the matter to the 1938 General Assembly for approval. Homrighausen took up his post as professor-elect during the second semester of the 1937-1938 academic year while awaiting confirmation by the Assembly. Usually *pro forma,* ratification proved difficult to secure in this instance. Several allies of J. Gresham Machen in his struggle against reorganization in the 1920s, two of them former directors (Clarence Macartney and Samuel Craig) and one a former assistant professor at the seminary (Oswald Allis), led the charge against Homrighausen, who was deemed highly suspect because he had what conservative critics charged was a weak view of the inspiration and authority of Scripture and because he had translated some of Karl Barth's writings into English. The fact that the appointment coincided with the guest professorship of Brunner also raised fears that the seminary was about to be overrun with the new theology from Europe. From the perspective of many conservatives, Barth and Brunner were not critics of modernism but rather Trojan horses for its entry into the church. Sensing that the appointment might fail, Mackay did not press for a vote in 1938, did some ecclesiastical politicking in succeeding months, and secured approval of Homrighausen at the 1939 General Assembly.[2]

1. Douglas John Hall, *Remembered Voices: Reclaiming the Legacy of "Neo-Orthodoxy"* (Louisville: Westminster John Knox Press, 1998), 75; John A. Mackay, "The One Hundred and Twenty-seventh Commencement," *Princeton Seminary Bulletin* 33 (July 1939): 2. For an overview of the institutional issues, see George L. Haines, "The Princeton Theological Seminary" (Ph.D. Dissertation, New York University, 1966). I base the comments on the Tennent school on examination of the relevant records by a research assistant.

2. For a conservative perspective on these issues, see Edwin H. Rian, *The Presbyterian Conflict* (Grand Rapids: Eerdmans, 1940), ch. 14. Later, Rian concluded that he had erred in

Born in 1900 in Iowa to a German Reformed family, Elmer G. Homrighausen later recalled his religious upbringing as one that instilled fear in him. "My boyhood religion was a matter of dread at the thought of God's judgment. Religion was related to things solemn — to death, to heaven and hell. The moral law hung like a sword of Damocles over my defenseless head." And from this perspective, he saw "God as an all-seeing judge, his church the place to which I *had* to come, and his minister the spy and vicar of God." Yet the Elmer Homrighausen described by his Princeton colleagues and students was anything but fearful or conscience-driven. They remembered an exuberant man whom they often fondly called "Homy" (or "Homey") — a man whose zest for life inspired them and whose kindness allowed him to share their joys and to empathize with their sorrows. They depicted a teacher able to hear and fairly restate a hostile question without belittling the student who raised it. Homrighausen attributed his joy and enthusiasm to the fact, learned by him much later, that at the age of 2 he was not expected to live. Thereafter, he said, "I determined to thank God every day the sun rose, and to live that day to the fullest."[3]

Homrighausen studied at Mission House College (now Lakeland College) in Wisconsin and then at the Mission House Theological School, where the Mercersburg theology of John Williamson Nevin and Philip Schaff had profoundly shaped the educational philosophy. Finishing at Mission House in 1923, he went on that fall for a year of study at Princeton Seminary, where he took courses from faculty on both sides of the then deeply divided school. He was particularly influenced by an adjunct professor, George Johnson, who had graduated from the seminary in 1896 and was a professor of theology at Lincoln University. Johnson's course "The Psychology of Religion" introduced Homrighausen, in at least a rudimentary fashion, to the social scientific study of religion as well as to the ideas of Karl Barth, still largely unknown in America in 1924. After his year at Princeton, Homrighausen was ordained in the Reformed Church in

leaving the Presbyterian Church in the U.S.A., returned to the denomination, and served as Assistant to the President for Promotion under James I. McCord.

3. For information on Homrighausen, I am indebted to "Elmer George Homrighausen, 1900-1982," *Princeton Seminary Bulletin* 4 (1983): 45-49; Dana R. Wright, "Elmer G. Homrighausen," http://www2.talbot.edu/ce20/educators/view.cfm?n=elmer_homrighausenxxxx (accessed on June 11, 2011). As a student, I took a class with Homrighausen in 1970, the year before he retired. My own experience of his teaching and personality accords with the testimony of others.

America and served pastorates in Freeport, Illinois (1924-1929), and in Indianapolis, Indiana (1929-1938). During his pastorates he continued advanced studies at the University of Chicago, the University of Dubuque Theological Seminary, and Butler University. From his encounter with Shirley Jackson Case and Shailer Mathews at Chicago, he gained deepened appreciation of liberal theology and the historical-functional approach to religion dominant among the Chicago thinkers. It was an approach perhaps most succinctly stated by Case in *The Christian Philosophy of History* (1943), where he wrote that anyone who would understand how the world "has taken on its present character — physical, social and cultural — . . . must acquaint himself with the processes of historic evolution." Only in this way "can he discover the genesis and function of social institutions, of prevailing customs and ideas." The appeal of liberal theology and of a historical-functional approach to Christianity was apparent in theses that Homrighausen submitted for advanced degrees: for example, a reflection on the new views of history and their relation to the role of church history in theological education that he submitted to Dubuque for the S.T.M. in 1928, and a dissertation on Justin Martyr that won him a Th.D. from the same school two years later.[4]

Yet Homrighausen's curiosity about Barth, begun at Princeton, had deepened by the mid-1930s, and he translated two volumes of sermons by the Swiss theologian into English. In 1935 he also published his first book, *Christianity in America: A Crisis,* which signaled a movement toward a position akin to Barth's. In the book, Homrighausen blamed the theological liberalism he had found attractive a few years earlier for much that was wrong in the American churches: their superficial activism, a facile optimism that could not adequately address the human condition, and a preoccupation with human experience rather than the God-centered proclamation of the gospel of redemption through Christ. Yet this was no summons to return to traditional Protestant conservatism. He called for an existential approach similar to that of the early Karl Barth, whose insights Homrighausen was trying to render in an idiom appropriate to the American scene. Existential assessment meant "that the whole person enters, is drawn into, the event it seeks to under-

---

4. Shirley Jackson Case, *The Christian Philosophy of History* (Chicago: University of Chicago Press, 1943), 77, 78. In framing my assessment of Homrighausen, I am indebted to Gordon S. Mikoski and Richard R. Osmer, *With Piety and Learning: The History of Practical Theology at Princeton Theological Seminary, 1812-2012* (Zurich: Lit Verlag, 2011), 103-6, 117-31.

stand." It does not confuse "the mere human idea of a thing" nor "dogma about it . . . with the thing itself, its reality and its sovereign life. Never does existential thinking seek exhaustively and rationally to control the object of its study. On the contrary, it allows the thing studied to study the observer." For a man like Samuel Craig, who adhered to the views of Old Princeton, *Christianity in America* insufficiently protected the authority of the Bible. For Edwin Aubrey, a professor at the University of Chicago, Homrighausen's critique had some merits, but also serious flaws. "The questions are too many to be pushed aside with *obiter dicta*," Aubrey said. "The insistence on the pure objectivity of revelation overlooks two hundred years of serious reflection on the nature of knowledge." The responses of Craig and Aubrey typified the reception that the "Neo-orthodoxy" of Homrighausen and others like him often received from ultraconservatives and those still strongly committed to the liberal tradition. Too like modernism for the one, it seemed too reactionary and obscurantist to the other.[5]

After Homrighausen had finally run the gauntlet of General Assembly approval, he gave his inaugural address as the Synott Professor of Christian Education on October 10, 1939. He recognized that some traditionalists dismissed the field as "a newcomer which has emerged on the rising tide of psychological, historical and sociological studies." He allowed that the Religious Education Association, formed in 1903 by figures such as William Rainey Harper and Shailer Mathews, was indeed of recent origin; and he also saw more than a grain of truth in the assertion that in its current form religious education was often "a child of liberalism," that it had imbibed much from the philosophy of John Dewey and others that was destructive of Christianity, and that it had "capitulated to a naturalistic and positivistic idea of religion." The fundamental problem was that "too many Christian educators in the professional field . . . lack balance and depth. They lack church-relatedness." Yet he insisted that, rightly understood, Christian education was as old as the biblical tradition itself. He viewed his task, as a professor of Christian education, as

5. E. G. Homrighausen, *Christianity in America: A Crisis* (New York: Abingdon Press, 1936); quotations on 54, 55; Samuel G. Craig, review of *Christianity in America* in *Christianity Today* 8 (July 1937): 69; Edwin E. Aubrey, review of *Christianity in America* in *Journal of Religion* 17 (July 1937): 334. For his translations of Barth, see *God's Search for Man: Sermons by Karl Barth*, trans. George W. Richards, Elmer G. Homrighausen, and Karl J. Ernst (Edinburgh: T&T Clark, 1935); and *God in Action: Theological Addresses by Karl Barth,* trans. E. G. Homrighausen and Karl J. Ernst (New York: Round Table Press, 1936).

"that of acquainting prospective ministers with the theological issues of the field, so as to impress them with their obligation to reclaim the field for theology and the Church." But even as he insisted that Christian education was not primarily a matter of humanistic technique or of a pedagogy based on the socialization of children, but rather nurture in a faith whose generation was the result of God himself, Homrighausen did not reject all that the religious education movement had achieved. "Dewey," he allowed, "has much of value in the realm of method and procedure. Many of the emphases of the 'new education,' such as pupil interest, personal effort, creative learning, individual education and growth, experience, freedom, integration of personality, development of the whole life and others, we can well study and cautiously appropriate." Homrighausen had learned too much of value during his liberal theological phase to dismiss out of hand all that the new social and psychological sciences had to contribute; or, as he put it: "We need both theology and anthropology." "Christian education," he believed, "deals with the problem of theology at its most crucial point" — the necessity "to translate (not adapt!) the meaning of that truth into terms of the contemporary age." It was at precisely this point that modern theories of sociology, psychology, and education rendered their great service.[6]

Homrighausen offered a dual legacy to Princeton's new department of practical theology, organized in 1939. First, he envisioned the field as a *theological* enterprise, not merely as a congeries of studies of techniques. Second, he believed that it needed to draw in an ancillary fashion upon the personality and social sciences. He never provided a well-articulated theory about the way in which theology could integrate into its own reflections the disciplines of education, psychology, or sociology. But he did set out the ideal that theology needed to engage these fields as it thought through its role in the modern world, and the legacy would persist at Princeton. Homrighausen himself was too much of a Socratic gadfly, who enjoyed raising many different issues, to devote all of his time working solely on one. He taught widely in the curriculum — in 1940, for example, doing the English Bible course that Charles Erdman had conducted for many years. In 1945, he taught a course in Renaissance, Reformation, and Counter Reformation. In 1954, he moved to a chair in pastoral theology. Interestingly, he chose to emphasize in his inaugural

6. Elmer G. Homrighausen, "The Task of Christian Education in a Theological Seminary," *Princeton Seminary Bulletin* 34 (1940): 3-21; quotations on 3, 9, 10, 11, 12, 13, 19.

address the necessity of the *entire* congregation creating a pastoral environment in which persons were valued, nurtured, built into community, and sent forth in mission to the world. Homrighausen also served as chair of the practical theology department from 1953 to 1960 and as dean of the seminary from 1955 to 1965. He rendered great service to the readers of *Theology Today* through his regular column "The Church in the World," which ran to nearly ninety installments between 1946 and 1973. His reports reflected not only his wide reading and numerous ecumenical contacts throughout the world but also his journeys. Homrighausen was a peripatetic intellectual and churchman, in the range of both his interests and his travels.[7]

John Sutherland Bonnell provides another instance of Princeton's effort to incorporate new scientific thinking — in Bonnell's case, psychiatry — into theological education. Bonnell is easily missed in the story of the seminary, for he was not part of the full-time faculty. But from 1938 to 1960 he was a regular visiting professor teaching a course on the cure of souls. Pastor of the Fifth Avenue Presbyterian Church in New York City, Bonnell was born on Prince Edward Island, Canada, in 1893. At about the age of 10, he started accompanying his father, superintendent of a mental hospital, on his daily rounds. When Bonnell later entered the ministry, serving first in Canada and then at Fifth Avenue from 1935 until his retirement in 1962, his experiences at his father's hospital deepened his conviction that religion, supplemented with insights from psychiatry, could help to heal psychological pain and dysfunction. He believed that ministers had an important role to play as channels of that healing and saw the task as a continuation of the tradition of pastoral conversation with the spiritually troubled. Convinced that unresolved guilt was a major source of psychological debility that appeared as neurosis or more serious mental illness, Bonnell urged ministers to listen carefully to parishioners in order to discern need and then, when appropriate, to press the individual to confess the guilt that he or she had not previously acknowledged. Confession and repentance, he believed, led not only to spiritual but also to psychic healing. Bonnell advocated a form of directive counseling that relied not only on careful listening but also on probing questions and the giving of advice. By the end of the 1950s, his writings indicated a willingness to do more listening and a bit less advising and

7. Elmer G. Homrighausen, "Toward a Pastoral Church," *Princeton Seminary Bulletin* 48 (1955): 10-19.

showed more trust in the parishioner's capacity to make an appropriate decision once counseling had helped clarify his or her situation. Bonnell's work prefigured the more clinically informed engagement with psychology and psychiatry that came to Princeton with the arrival of Seward Hiltner, James Lapsley, and James Loder in the 1960s.[8]

Samuel W. Blizzard deserves mention in this context. Although the chair in Christianity and society to which he was appointed in 1957 was located in the history department rather than in practical theology, Blizzard's interests overlapped those in the practical theology department, and he had the most thorough and rigorous training in a behavioral science of any of the faculty appointments of the Mackay era. Born in 1914 to a conservative Presbyterian family in Philadelphia, Blizzard attended Maryville College in Tennessee and spent a year at Biblical Theological Seminary in New York before completing the final two years of seminary education at Princeton and graduating with the class of 1939. Ordained into the ministry that year, he served Presbyterian churches in Roselle, New Jersey, and then in Long Green and Ashland, Maryland, through 1943. Between 1944 and 1946, Blizzard completed the Ph.D. program in rural sociology at Cornell University. Rural sociology was a logical choice for a minister interested in the sociological study of churches, for the field itself was in large measure an outgrowth of studies of rural congregations undertaken near the beginning of the twentieth century. After completing his doctorate, Blizzard taught at Wooster College for a year and then spent ten years (1947-1957) in rural sociology at Pennsylvania State University, during which time he also headed the school's social science research center. Much of his early work had to do with studies of rural churches and communities. However, when the Russell Sage Foundation asked him to direct its Training for Ministry Project (1953-1960), Blizzard's professional work then focused upon a sociological analysis of the ministry. That emphasis led to Blizzard's appointment as a visiting professor at Union Theological Seminary in New York (1953-1957), even

---

8. Compare John Sutherland Bonnell, *Pastoral Psychiatry* (New York: Harper and Brothers, 1938), with his later article, "Counseling with Divorced Persons," *Pastoral Psychology* 9 (September 1958): 11-15. For thoughtful discussions of Bonnell and his relationship to broader trends within pastoral care, see Susan E. Myers-Shirk, *Helping the Good Shepherd: Pastoral Counselors in a Psychotherapeutic Culture, 1925-1975* (Baltimore: Johns Hopkins University Press, 2009), 69, 73-75, 79-80, 83-85, 136, 209; and E. Brooks Holifield, *A History of Pastoral Care in America: From Salvation to Self-Realization* (Nashville: Abingdon Press, 1983), 230.

while he continued his work at Penn State. Then, in 1957, he took the position at Princeton Seminary, where he remained until degenerative illness forced his early retirement in 1975, only a year before his death.[9]

As a result of his project on the ministry, Blizzard was intrigued by the different roles that clergy played. He found "much confusion in contemporary usage about the role of the Protestant parish minister," for people used "similar nomenclature to describe the clergyman" but gave it different meanings. Through careful empirical research, he sought "to ferret out the various usages and connotations" and "develop a system of analysis to distinguish" among them. Blizzard arrived at a three-tiered classification of the various roles (master, integrative, and practitioner). At the level of the practice of ministry, Blizzard categorized the day-to-day functions of clergy — administrator, organizer, pastor, preacher, priest, teacher. Integrative roles described the minister's reasons for performing these activities. The integrative roles (fourteen in number) ranged from traditional ones, such as believer-saint or father-shepherd, to more contemporary roles like community problem solver or church politician. Finally, the master role designated the minister's "concept of the ministry as an occupation distinguishable from the occupational role of other persons." Through his work, Blizzard was one of the first researchers to document the fact that ministers often understood their role differently than their congregations. By the end of the tumultuous 1960s, the idea of a gap between clergy and laity would be a commonplace in the literature. Blizzard's work also provided strong evidence that clergy spent most of their time in the performance of administrative tasks and organizational responsibilities for which they had received little preparation in their seminary education.[10]

9. Gary D. Bouma, "Samuel W. Blizzard (1914-1976), Sociologist, Theological Educator and Border Broker: An Appreciative Evaluation," *Review of Religious Research* 23 (December 1981): 205-13; Edmund de S. Brunner, *The Growth of a Science: A Half Century of Rural Sociological Research in the United States* (New York: Harper and Brothers, 1957). To trace the development of his research interests, see Harriet Blizzard, comp., "The Writings of Samuel Wilson Blizzard," *Review of Religious Research* 23 (December 1983): 214-18.

10. Samuel W. Blizzard, "The Minister's Dilemma," *Christian Century* 73 (April 25, 1956): 508-10; Blizzard, "The Protestant Parish Minister's Integrating Roles," *Religious Education* 53 (July 1958): 374-80; quotation on 374; Blizzard, "The Parish Minister's Self-Image of His Master Role," *Pastoral Psychology* 9 (December 1958): 25-32; quotation on 27; Bouma, "Samuel W. Blizzard." For a bestselling work exploring the idea of a clergy-laity difference, see Jeffrey K. Hadden, *The Gathering Storm in the Churches: The Widening Gap Between Clergy and Laymen* (Garden City, NY: Doubleday, 1969).

Blizzard served, as his former student and later sociologist Gary Bouma remarked, "as a border broker between social science and theological education." He helped ease seminarians from a social science background into theological education, and he helped create the joint Master of Divinity/Master of Social Work program between the seminary and the School of Social Work at Rutgers University. His goal was not, however, to turn ministers into social workers or psychological counselors. As Bouma observes:

> He was insistent that ministers were not merely second rate clinical psychologists or social workers with a few theological assumptions, but that the ministry was a vital profession that could and should stand tall among the complement of professions common in a modern society. He viewed the abandonment of theological bases for ministry in favor of counseling competence or mere management competencies with dismay.

But clergy needed, he believed, an understanding of how the minister functioned within a web of social systems from the congregation, to the family, to the larger community. Blizzard's impact was not as great as it could have been. Because of the illness that dogged his final years, he never had the opportunity to draw his insights into a *magnum opus,* nor were his courses among the most popular on campus. "The average seminarian," Bouma remarks, "did not seem to have the time or motivation to seek the knowledge he had to offer. He seemed insufficiently pious to those who had an essentially 'spiritual' interpretation of their future role and socially active seminarians were too impatient to 'do something' to bother learning what might have been effective." Bouma also allowed that Blizzard "was a solid, but hardly charismatic lecturer."[11]

Two Major Biblical Appointments:
Bruce M. Metzger and Otto Piper

Of all the choices of faculty over which John Mackay presided in twenty-three years, probably none produced greater academic recognition for Princeton Seminary than the appointment of New Testament scholar

11. Bouma, "Samuel W. Blizzard," 210, 211.

Bruce Manning Metzger. Born in Middletown, Pennsylvania, in 1914, he attended Lebanon Valley College, studied at Princeton Seminary from 1935 to 1938, and then received a Ph.D. in classics from Princeton University in 1942. His teaching career at the seminary began even while he pursued doctoral work. Starting as an instructor in Greek in 1938 and transferring to New Testament studies the following year, he rose through the academic ranks and retired in 1984 after forty-six years of service to the seminary. Among his voluminous publications, many scholars see three of his works as most noteworthy: *The Text of the New Testament: Its Transmission, Corruption, and Restoration* (four different editions beginning in 1964, the last in 2005 with Bart D. Ehrman); *The Early Versions of the New Testament: Their Origin, Transmission, and Limitation* (1977); and *The Canon of the New Testament: Its Origin, Development, and Significance* (1987 and 1997). At the time of the appearance of *The Text of the New Testament* in 1964, no up-to-date, adequate manual to textual criticism existed in English, and Metzger's work quickly became a standard. He also participated in the international team of scholars, brought together in 1955 under the leadership of Eugene Nida of the American Bible Society, for the purpose of preparing a Greek New Testament using the best up-to-date scholarship. That work appeared in 1966.[12]

Metzger also had a passion for making the results of textual scholarship available to the average reader. He played an important role in the creation of the original Revised Standard Version of the Bible in the post–World War II era, and he headed the ecumenical team that produced the New Revised Standard Version of the Bible, including the Apocrypha, in 1990. Largely due to Metzger's influence, the NRSV committee created a study edition with copious textual notes to help the reader. Behind these efforts lay the goal that Metzger himself best explained in the editors' preface:

> The Bible carries its full message, not to those who regard it simply as a noble literary heritage of the past or who wish to use it to enhance political purposes and advance otherwise desirable goals, but to all persons and communities who read it so that they may discern and understand what God is saying to them. That

---

12. James A. Brooks, "Bruce Metzger as Textual Critic," *Princeton Seminary Bulletin* 15 (1994): 156-64; Daniel B. Wallace, "Bruce Manning Metzger," *Proceedings of the American Philosophical Society* 153 (December 2009): 489-93.

message must not be disguised in phrases that are no longer clear, or hidden under words that have changed or lost their meaning; it must be presented in language that is direct and plain and meaningful to people today.

Despite the praise that his work drew from scholars and from the churches who used these translations, some ultra-fundamentalists vilified the original RSV for its departure from the language of the King James or Authorized Version and found offensive the introduction of gender-inclusive language in the NRSV. Metzger kept in his office an urn that had been sent to the chair of the original RSV committee and then given to him when he took on leadership of the NRSV team. The urn contained the ashes of an RSV Bible that a preacher had burned in the pulpit on a Sunday morning, saying that it was the work of the devil. To a visitor, Metzger remarked puckishly: "I'm so glad to be a translator in the twentieth century. They only burn Bibles now, not the translators!"[13]

Metzger's unrivaled knowledge of the relevant languages, ancient and modern; his balanced judgment; and his painstaking attention to detail won him respect across the theological and academic spectrum. His own piety and faith in the Bible as the medium of God's revelation were evident to any who studied with him, worked with him, talked with him outside the classroom, or worshiped with him at First (later Nassau) Presbyterian Church, where he attended for many years. But Metzger did not see his primary task as a scholar to entail engaging in constructive theological work. One sensed in him a serene confidence that if the Bible could be presented with the utmost accuracy and accessibility, its message would ultimately speak for itself. The nature of Metzger's contribution was perhaps best summarized shortly before his retirement by Paul S. Minear, an emeritus professor of biblical theology at the Yale University Divinity School.

> Generations of lexicographers must do their painstaking work before dependable dictionaries of biblical languages can appear. Grammarians must sift through mountains of manuscripts to capture the variations in the use of prepositions and the subtle

---

13. *New Oxford Annotated Bible with the Apocryphal/Deuterocanonical Books,* ed. Bruce M. Metzger and Roland Murphy (New York: Oxford University Press, 1991, 1994), xiv; story of the RSV ashes recounted in Wallace, "Bruce Manning Metzger," 493.

nuances in the choice of tenses. The production of a concordance, an essential tool for any Bible student, requires patient persistence in pedestrian routines. . . . I want to voice my own appreciation for that vast army: lexicographers, grammarians, editors, collators of manuscripts, and translators of ancient texts. . . . Churches and seminaries owe them a debt which can never be paid or even calculated. More specifically, here, I want to salute as their representative, Professor Bruce M. Metzger. No living American scholar has shared more fully in pursuing these primary disciplines or in making their results accessible to the rest of us.[14]

Metzger's inaugural address as president of the Society of Biblical Literature, delivered in October 1971, provided a good example of his meticulous learning and the circumspect way in which he applied it to theological issues. He tackled the question of literary forgeries and canonical pseudepigrapha. The topic, he recognized at the outset, raised serious questions.

[H]ow far are pseudepigrapha — those inside the canon as well as those outside — to be regarded as literary forgeries? From an ethical point of view, is a pseudepigraphon [that is, a work attributed to an author other than the actual writer] compatible with honesty and candor, whether by ancient or modern moral standards? From a psychological point of view, how should one estimate an author who impersonates an ancient worthy, such as Orpheus or Enoch? Should we take him seriously, and, if we do, how does this bear on the question of his sanity? From a theological point of view, should a work that involves a fraud, whether pious or not, be regarded as incompatible with the character of a message from God?

Metzger addressed the questions with an evenhanded presentation and analysis of the views of modern scholars and supported his assessments by copious examples from antiquity. Throughout the essay, he emphasized "that a wide variety of motives prompted the production of falsely ascribed treatises," and that ancients manifested "differing degrees of

14. Paul S. Minear, "The Critic's Corner: A Scholar's Scholar," *Theology Today* 39 (January 1983): 418, 419.

sensitivity to the morality of such productions." Therefore, it was unwise to posit "a single formula that will solve all questions, whether literary, psychological, ethical, or theological." Metzger recognized that conservative biblical scholarship — including at Princeton in the nineteenth and early twentieth centuries — had defended the accuracy of ascriptions of authorship in canonical books and often treated the issue as essential to their inspiration. Metzger was uncomfortable with these global *a priori* generalizations. "Instead of beginning with declarations of what is licit and what is illicit," he suggested, "one is likely to make more progress by considering the theological problem from a historical and literary point of view." In a passage reminiscent of Charles Hodge and Benjamin Warfield's contention that inspiration employed rather than suppressed the peculiarities of the biblical writers, Metzger noted that "the inspiration of the Scriptures is consistent with any kind of form of literary composition that was in keeping with the character and habits of the speaker or writer. Whatever idiom or mode of expression he would use in ordinary speech must surely be allowed him when moved by the Holy Spirit." Metzger then pressed to his conclusion: "In short, since the use of the literary form of pseudepigraphy need not be regarded as necessarily involving fraudulent intent, it cannot be argued that the character of inspiration excludes the possibility of pseudepigraphy among the canonical writings."[15]

Metzger's painstaking scholarship stood in the line of close, textual work that had long been advocated at Old Princeton. It is perhaps not irrelevant to note that as a seminarian he had direct contact with professors who embodied that heritage. He studied theology with Caspar Wistar Hodge Jr., the last of the Hodges to teach at Princeton, and took New Testament under William Park Armstrong. Metzger, of course, was broader than that tradition, for he did not use his exegetical and historical work to become a controversialist in the manner of William Henry Green, defending the Mosaic authorship of the Pentateuch, nor did he ever issue a broadside against modern biblical scholarship, as Robert Dick Wilson did in his 1922 pamphlet *Is the Higher Criticism Scholarly?*, a query that Wilson answered on the title page with the phrase: "clearly attested facts showing that the destructive 'assured results of modern scholarship' are indefensible." Had Metzger been that sort of textual

---

15. Bruce M. Metzger, "Literary Forgeries and Canonical Pseudepigrapha," *Journal of Biblical Literature* 91 (March 1972): 3-24; quotations on 4, 19, 21, 22.

critic, it is quite certain that he would never have received the accolades of the scholarly community nor been elected president of the Society of Biblical Literature. In fact, the careful argument in his inaugural address that belief in inspiration did not preclude "the possibility of pseudepigraphy among the canonical writings" put him at odds with Old Princeton. But Metzger did manifest the style of massive erudition, close attention to detail, and careful analysis of the text to which the seminary, at its best, had always aspired.[16]

ALSO APPOINTED to the field of biblical studies as professor of New Testament in 1941, after having served as a guest professor since 1937, was Otto A. Piper. Born in Lichte, Germany, in 1891, Piper began his theological training at the Erfurt Gymnasium. He started his advanced education at Jena but, in the fashion of the day, also traveled about to other great universities — Göttingen, Heidelberg, Marburg, Munich, and Paris — where he heard the lectures of outstanding Protestant and Catholic scholars. With the outbreak of World War I, he enlisted in the German army and suffered a severe wound on the Western front. Struck under the right eye by a bullet and initially left for dead on the battlefield, he lost sight in that eye, and the capacity of the other was diminished. For the remainder of his life, damaged facial nerves and muscles made it difficult him to smile, and he used a magnifying glass to facilitate his voluminous reading. Piper's personal experience of the brutality of war turned him to pacifism and also soured him on the optimistic neo-Kantian theologies fashionable in the late nineteenth century. After completing his theological training at Göttingen in 1920, he taught there for a time and then in 1930 took the chair of theology at Münster when it was vacated by his friend Karl Barth. Outspoken in his opposition to Nazism, Piper was exiled from Germany in 1933. He, his wife, and their three young children fled to the United Kingdom, where for four years he held several temporary academic positions in England and Wales. In 1937, he came to Princeton Seminary as a guest professor, first in systematic theology. Then, when declining health forced William Park Armstrong to reduce his academic responsibilities, Piper was appointed professor of New Testament in 1941 — a position he held until his retirement in 1962. The sufferings of Piper did not end when he found a safe harbor in

16. Robert Dick Wilson, *Is the Higher Criticism Scholarly?* (London: Sunday School Times Company, 1922).

Princeton. His son Gerhard, serving in the American army, was killed on Christmas Eve 1944 at Bastogne in the Battle of the Bulge. Several years later, his first wife died of asthma. When he remarried in 1950 to a German woman whom he had first met decades earlier, he faced a prolonged wait to bring his new wife to the United States. Amid the fears generated by the Cold War, a recent federal law made immigration more difficult as a way of preventing potentially subversive aliens from entering the United States. After the Second World War, Piper, though he seldom spoke of his personal sufferings, revealed in an article for the *Christian Century* how that pain had shaped his theology. He was, he wrote of his years during the Great War, "no longer satisfied with any interpretation of the Christian faith which could not stand the test of the terrors of battle, the heartache over the loss of relatives and dearest friends, the agony of a broken body and the self-destructive fury of warring nations." In many ways, that remark described the role that suffering had played in shaping his theology throughout his life.[17]

Piper's inaugural address in 1942, which was also the same year in which he became an American citizen, gave important clues as to the approach he brought to his new position. He averred emphatically that the Bible was to be received as the Word of God, but he added that this authority did not depend exclusively on the divine origin of Scripture, "but also and above all upon the fact that it is the *viva vox evangelii,* the living voice of God by means of which He conveys to us knowledge of his saving will." Piper warned that the exegete would go astray if he sought "information concerning matters that lay outside the purpose of the several writers." Things outside their purpose included "not only secular matters" such as "facts of history, science, or philosophy, that are not connected with God's saving purpose, but also information concerning spiritual matters which God deemed good not to reveal in this life." Piper also warned scholars against being too glib in assuming that they could

17. See the perceptive essay on Piper's life and work by my colleague, C. Clifton Black, "Remembering Otto Piper," *Princeton Seminary Bulletin* 26 (2003): 320-27; also the memorial tribute, "Otto Alfred Piper, 1891-1982," *Princeton Seminary Bulletin* 4 (1983): 52-55. Otto A. Piper, "What the Bible Means to Me: Discovering the Bible," *Christian Century* 63 (February 27, 1946): 267. For other useful information on the life and thought of Piper, see Kenneth Woodrow Henke, "Otto Piper and Arthur Freeman: Biblical Theologians," *The Hinge: International Theological Dialogue for the Moravian Church* 15 (2008): 18-37. A brief discussion of Piper's life may be found in Daniel J. Theron, "Remembering Professor Otto Piper," *inSpire* 6 (Fall 2001).

reduce the results of their exegesis to readily comprehensible propositions. "[W]ould it be so bad," he asked, "if our first reaction to the revelation of the divine mysteries consisted in the confession that while they
completely overwhelmed us yet they were too great, too strange, too sublime, to be adequately apprehended by us?" He called also for a
christocentric reading of Scripture, for Christ was the "key to God's saving purpose disclosed in the Bible." Exegesis of this sort, he added, "pre-
cludes the use of isolated passages as proof-texts." Given the total range
of options in biblical interpretation, Piper leaned toward a conservative
view, but he also wanted to stand clear of the Old Princeton notion of inerrancy. Like many theological scholars of his time, he thought that the
second and third generations of Protestant theologians — the Protestant "scholastics" — had strayed from the view of the original reformers.
As he wrote in an essay fifteen years after his inaugural: "While the originators of Protestantism had cherished the Bible as a book of comfort,
admonition and encouragement since they heard Christ himself speaking through the Bible — the latter is *Deus loquens* — their followers regarded it as a collection of doctrines which were infallible, because their
writers had been inspired by the Holy Spirit in a miraculous way. As a result of that shift the truthfulness of the Christian message was tested by
its logical consistency." In Piper's view, this was an unfortunate change
that prepared the way for later rationalistic readings of Scripture. His
ideal method, by contrast, was the one that he tried to realize once he
came to Princeton: "my principal aim was to develop an exegetical
method that would enable me to interpret the New Testament writings
from within the mind of their authors, as it were, and thus as vitally concerning myself in the core of my personality. This 'existential' method
makes the study of the Bible a series of relevant discoveries and a never
ending task." Interestingly, he attributed his full realization of this
method to exposure during his time in the United Kingdom to "Bible-
loving people, who were all in some way connected with Keswick" and
who "opened my mind and heart to the Spirit's power."[18]

Beyond the circle of his students and former colleagues, Piper was
less remembered in the community of biblical scholars. He himself sup-

---

18. Otto A. Piper, "Modern Problems of New Testament Exegesis," *Princeton Seminary
Bulletin* 36 (1942): 3-14; quotations on 7, 8, 9, 11; Piper, "Biblical Theology and Systematic
Theology," *Journal of Bible and Religion* 25 (April 1957): 106; Piper, "What the Bible Means to
Me: Discovering the Bible," 268. On his view of biblical authority, see also Otto A. Piper,
"The Authority of the Bible," *Theology Today* (1949): 159-73.

plied one possible reason: "I had to endure the vitriolic attacks of fundamentalists who denounced me as a disguised modernist and the
haughty disdain of liberals who could not understand that a critical
scholar should believe that the Bible is the Word of God." An even more
important reason for the limitations of his influence in subsequent biblical scholarship lay in the fact, as C. Clifton Black has observed, that his
"publications fell between the stools of biblical interpretation and constructive theology. He published no book-length commentaries; while of
high quality, his technical exegesis was sparse." Then, too, he advocated
an understanding of God's activity in history — preeminently in his *God
and History* (1939) — that some found suspect. As one might anticipate, a
historian like Shirley Jackson Case of the University of Chicago was a bit
jaundiced toward the book because, in his opinion, Piper acted as if the
"modern methodology of the secular historian has no pertinence to the
problem of recovering more accurately the story of religious history." Joseph Haroutunian, then of Wellesley College and later a professor at
McCormick Theological Seminary, was profoundly sympathetic to many
of Piper's theological instincts and applauded his "resolute attempt to
find God in history" and to offer "a real corrective to present day sophis-
ticated views" that effectively banished God from the temporal process;
but Haroutunian was annoyed that "there is hardly a fact in Christian
history which does not exhibit God's activity according to a logic obvious
to Dr. Piper." Haroutunian found offensive — "nauseating" was his word
— the book's "pretence of knowing the logic of God's ways in detail."
Haroutunian wished for a bit more modesty in the discernment of God's
mysterious action in history.[19]

These observations should not obscure the significant contributions
that Piper made. He wrote more than twenty books in French, German,
and English as well as essays, articles, and reviews running into the hundreds. In these he dealt not only with *Heilsgeschichte* or "holy history"
but also with ethical themes such as sex, money, the morality of the
Nuremberg trials of alleged war criminals, or the meaning of the

---

19. Piper, "What the Bible Means to Me: Discovering the Bible," 268; Black, "Remembering Otto Piper," 324; Otto A. Piper, *God and History* (New York: Macmillan, 1939). For a
shorter statement of this subject, consult Otto A. Piper, "What the Bible Means to Me: The
Bible as 'Holy History,'" *Christian Century* 63 (March 20, 1946): 362-64. See the review of
God and History by Shirley Jackson Case in *Journal of Religion* 19 (July 1939): 241-44, with
quotation on 244; also the review by Joseph Haroutunian in *Journal of Bible and Religion* 7
(November 1939): 205-7.

strangely atomized yet standardized society he saw emerging in the United States by the end of the 1950s. He not only wrote about ethical themes; he embodied them as he launched his own personal relief effort for a devastated Europe in the post–World War II era. "He collected clothing from wherever he could," Daniel Theron, a doctoral student in the late 1940s, recalled. "We students were asked to help him sort and inventory every box. For years we spent many hours around the large Piper dining room table helping him. When the boxes were packed and sealed with a slip listing the contents, he would load them into his old black Dodge sedan and drive off to the post office to mail them. This went on until the mid 1950s." A major advocate for the seminary's new doctoral program, which granted its first degree in 1944, Piper advised twenty-one of the eighty-nine doctoral dissertations completed up to 1960. Moreover, Piper mentored students as he invited them to his home for Friday afternoon teas, and then he maintained correspondence with some after their graduation. In the wake of the arguments Princeton and the Presbyterian Church had been through only shortly before he came to the seminary, perhaps one of Piper's greatest contributions was to provide a model of the scholar who accepted the witness of the Bible as authoritative and drew upon the latest scholarship but did not feel the need to refight old battles over the nature of inspiration.[20]

Philosophy and Theology: Émile Cailliet and George Hendry

Émile Cailliet, the first layman to hold a professorship at the seminary, was born in 1894 at Dampierre, France. Educated as a youth in a secular environment, he claimed not to have looked at a Bible until he was 23. During his service in the French infantry during World War I, he was wounded by a dumdum bullet whose scar he bore for the remainder of his life. He recuperated in an American hospital, where he married a Scots-Irish woman whom he had met prior to the war. It was she who gave him his first Bible. As he perused its pages, he experienced a sense of Presence — "the notion of Presence," he would say in reflections dur-

20. Theron, "Remembering Otto Piper"; Black, "Remembering Otto Piper," 323. For examples of short pieces manifesting his ethical and cultural concerns, see his essays "That Strange Thing Money," *Theology Today* 16 (July 1959): 215-31; "Wholeness of Life," *Princeton Seminary Bulletin* 54 (1960): 22-27; "Vengeance and the Moral Order," *Theology Today* (1948).

ing his retirement — "that would prove crucial to my theological think-ing." He graduated from the Universities of Châlons and Nancy. He also received a Ph.D. in ethnology from the University of Montpellier in 1926 for field research he had done in Madagascar. In 1937 the University of Strasbourg awarded him a Th.D. In 1926, he and his wife moved to the United States, where he held positions at the University of Pennsylvania, Scripps College at Claremont, and Wesleyan University. In 1947, he be-came the Stuart Professor of Christian Philosophy at Princeton Sem-inary, a position he held until his retirement in 1959.[21]

In a memorial tribute to Cailliet after his death in 1981, faculty col-leagues observed that his work at Princeton focused on helping his classes "understand the modern religious mind" and on "preparing his students for the objections to their Christian thoughts which would be raised in the world 'outside.'" In so doing he drew upon cultural anthro-pology, contemporary scientific theories, and literature as well upon the thought of those commonly called "philosophers." How these diverse pieces came together is perhaps best illustrated in his book *The Christian Approach to Culture,* published six years after he began teaching at Princeton. Underlying that work was his concern that Christians needed to engage issues posed by contemporary culture. He acknowledged that "an open breach between Christianity and culture" on occasion "expresses the inevitable stand of the Christian church in the face of destructive and demonic forces," but the cost of such a stance was great both for Chris-tians and for the culture of which they were a part. The effect on believers was "to stifle any sense of responsibility in citizenship, to paralyze any ac-tive participation in the constructive tasks of society." For the larger soci-ety, it would leave "our drifting civilization" to itself without the resources of a "Christian frame of reference" that could heal its discontents. He reg-istered anxiety that the vogue of Karl Barth's theology, especially as ex-pressed by some of his disciples, was creating a mood in which creative Christian engagement with culture would be impossible. "The gist of the Barthian message," said Cailliet, "and the burden of his bulky volumes are that man is a sinner and not an image-bearer. There is not to be found in

21. Émile Cailliet, *Journey into Light* (Grand Rapids: Zondervan, 1968), 18; "Émile Cailliet, 1895-1981," *Princeton Seminary Bulletin* 5 (1984): 40-41 (the 1895 birth date in the ti-tle appears to be in error, for other sources indicate December 17, 1894, as Cailliet's date of birth); Richard J. Oman, "Émile Cailliet: Christian Centurion," *Princeton Seminary Bulletin* 5 (1984): 33-37; Frank E. Gaebelein, "Émile Cailliet (1894-1981)," *Theology Today* 40 (April 1983): 55-57.

him any likeness to God which may in any way *prepare* him to know God, or even to respond to God." While honoring the necessary theological corrective Barth had supplied, Cailliet believed that he had gone too far. In effect, Barth had consigned to philosophy "the task of analyzing scientific methods and of relating the temporary conclusion of the various branches of scientific knowledge." But any worldview that might emerge from that philosophic endeavor was irrelevant to theology. Unfortunately, said Calliet, "contemporary philosophers are quite satisfied with Barth's assignment, [and] they return his compliment 'by consigning all that he stands for to the realm of the meaningless.'"[22]

Cailliet believed there was a better way — a *Christian* way of doing philosophy that would engage culture in a meaningful fashion. It would do so knowing "that Christianity can never be identified with any specific culture." To make that equation would "amount to idolatry," he said, and "could well constitute a new aggressive form of cultural arrogance similar to that which has brought about the bankruptcy of missionary endeavor in many parts of the world today." The starting point for a true Christian engagement with culture would be an acknowledgment that all human beings have some awareness of God or some sign of God's presence in their lives, whether "in the scholar's longing for truth, the artist's quest for beauty, the plain man's craving for justice, nay, the magico-religious practices of ancient man." To make the case of the religious sensibility of the ancients, he drew upon evidence from the artifacts of prehistoric humanity and from anthropological studies of the contemporary world's so-called primitive peoples. Then he turned to the origins of Greek philosophy, especially to Socrates, the man who inspired Plato. In Socrates, Cailliet saw one for whom "true knowledge . . . consists essentially in the clarification of a life situation in the light of his call from the religious *reality* within, and not in metaphysical speculation in remote realms of intelligibility." For Socrates, the search for truth was a quest to discern the will of the *daemon* (or divinity) within, not to theorize about abstractions.[23]

With Plato and Aristotle, philosophy took a different path — what Cailliet called the "ontological deviation" — and the redirection had fate-

22. Émile Cailliet, *The Christian Approach to Culture* (New York and Nashville: Abingdon-Cokesbury Press, 1953), 24, 26, 53, 58. Cailliet quotes James H. Costen, *Christian Knowledge of God* (New York: Macmillan, 1951), 130.

23. Cailliet, *Christian Approach to Culture*, 49, 84, 126.

ful consequences for Western thought and eventually for Christian theology. In its search for clear ideas or forms, Greek philosophy became ob-
sessed with that which was unchanging, or immutable. It gave priority to
being over becoming. Had "the postulation of Ideas amounted to nothing more than a working hypothesis on the nature of reality," there would
have been no problems. But the ideas were reified into reality itself. The
result, said Cailliet, was that "Platonic man colonizes reality with abstractions," and then "these abstractions in turn have a way of standing
between him and reality." When the ideas of Plato and Aristotle were
taken into Christian theology, they created a belief that the living God of
the Scriptures was to be identified with abstract terms such as
impassibility, pure Being, pure Act, and the like. Thus in God's declaration of the divine name in Exodus 3:14, "I AM WHO I AM," Christian
thinkers put the emphasis upon the verb, defining God abstractly as pure
being. Although the Protestant reformers to a considerable degree
achieved a reinvigorated perception of the living God revealed in Scripture, their heirs soon relapsed into a scholastic theology. "The task at
hand, then," Cailliet insisted, "is to restore the true perspective which
had already been somewhat thrown out of line when Christianity began
to make its way into the world of thought." In a word, Christian thinkers
need to free themselves from the consequences of the ontological deviation and its impact upon their understanding of the faith and of culture.
They need to understand that ultimately the God of Jesus Christ, the One
who identified himself to Moses, was a Person and not some immutable
abstraction called Being itself. Or, as he put it, God was the Cosmic Self;
the subject, not the verb, of "I AM WHO I AM" needed more emphasis in
Christian philosophy and theology.[24]

Cailliet's conviction that traditional western philosophy often ob-
scured the reality of God as Person reflected his own experience of a
Presence when he first perused the Bible. The imprint of Blaise Pascal,
whom he read deeply and about whom he published a major study, was
also apparent. In *The Clue to Pascal,* Cailliet argued that Pascal had,
through his study of Scripture, recovered a Hebraic sense of God freed
from the taint of Greek philosophy and its ontological deviation. The
classic locus of Pascal's testimony in this matter was a folded parchment
found in the lining of his jacket shortly after his death. Pondering the account of Moses before the burning bush, Pascal had written of his own

24. Cailliet, *Christian Approach to Culture*, 132, 138, 157, 243.

intense experience: "FIRE: God of Abraham, God of Isaac, God of Jacob, not the God of the philosophers and the wise men."[25]

As he argued for a renewal of Pascal's vision in contemporary Christian thought, Cailliet often invoked theorists of modern science. In Max Planck and Albert Einstein, for example, he found an understanding of the universe far more dynamic than the old Newtonian science had offered, and he readily enlisted them to make his argument that ideas functioned as provisional hypotheses about reality, not the reality itself. In Charles Hartshorne, he encountered a thinker who "may very well prove to have provided for theological thought in our time the equivalent of the Planck-Einsteinian revolution in physics." Cailliet quoted Hartshorne's *The Divine Relativity* at length, only a portion of which passage is below:

> God orders the universe . . . by taking into his own life the currents of feeling in existence. He is the most irresistible of influences precisely because he is himself the most open to influence. In the depth of their hearts all creatures (even those able to "rebel" against him) defer to God because they sense him as one who alone is adequately moved by what moves them.

In short, Cailliet was deeply impressed by the thinker who spawned the theological movement known as process theology, some of whose American adherents have included, among others, John B. Cobb Jr., Schubert Ogden, Marjorie Suchocki, Rita Brock, and Catherine Keller.[26]

Since process theology is often viewed as a theologically liberal movement, one might ask whether this description fit Cailliet. He did move away from certain notions commonly associated with conservatism. He ruled out what he called a "mechanical biblicism" or any "theory of verbal inspiration." He also underscored the limitations of theological discourse. Averring that the heart of faith "is that the living God was in Christ reconciling the world unto himself," Cailliet warned against overdependence on precise theological formulation. "While the doctrinal statement of this faith should be as correct as the best-informed biblical scholarship can make it," he said, the "emphasis should never be on strict conformity with the fallible man-made language used in its in-

---

25. Émile Cailliet, *The Clue to Pascal* (Philadelphia: Westminster Press, 1943).
26. Cailliet, *Christian Approach to Culture,* 247.

firm formulation." Unlike those who saw the theological task as largely complete, nailed down as it were in the dogmatic systems of the Reformation or post-Reformation eras, Cailliet believed that the great age of theological development lay in the future. Believing that the "time is hardly ripe for the constitution of theology as a full-fledged scientific discipline," he insisted that theology was not the queen of the sciences who had been dethroned, but rather "the First-Lady-in-Waiting" whose best days lay somewhere in the future. For the moment theology was "a vigorous discipline in the making, destined to become the keystone of the edifice of human knowledge." Yet, even as he took conservatism to task, Cailliet could speak appreciative words about it, even in its fundamentalist manifestations. In an essay about a year before his retirement, he remarked that in attitude toward the Bible the fundamentalist continues "by birth and by right one of the essential aspects of the Reformation." Moreover, the zeal to bring the message of Christ to all should shame others:

> While many a sophisticated Christian feeds on an *Ersatz* diet of learned up-to-date disquisitions, Fundamentalists are out in every sort of weather ringing door bells. It is also a fact that Pentecostal sects hold the field in South America as well as on other continents where missionaries are at work. If it still be true that "by their fruit ye shall know them," what is to be the stand of many of us on the Day of Judgment?

Cailliet's appreciation of evangelical mission to those outside the Christian church led him to support Young Life, a parachurch movement that sought ways to preach the Christian message to youth outside or lapsed from the churches. In his early retirement, Cailliet wrote a deeply appreciative book about Young Life, which sometimes found itself working with and other times in tension with the churches. Cailliet was somewhat eclectic, a bit of a Christian maverick, who could in the same book cite with varying degrees of approbation passages from Charles Hartshorne's *Divine Relativity*, J. Gresham Machen's *Christianity and Liberalism,* and Harry Emerson Fosdick's *A Guide to Understanding the Bible.*[27]

27. Cailliet, *Christian Approach to Culture,* 16, 34, 36, 42, 260, 269; Émile Cailliet, "The Mind's Gravitation Back to the Familiar," *Theology Today* 15 (April 1958): 1-8; quotations on 3-4; Émile Cailliet, *Young Life* (New York: Harper and Row, 1963). "The Lady-in-waiting" im-

George Stuart Hendry (1904-1993) was born in Rayne, Aberdeen-shire, in Scotland. After completing an M.A. at the University of Aberdeen, he pursued studies in divinity at the University of Edinburgh and received the B.D. in 1927. He spent 1928-1929 in Germany, studying theology at the Universities of Berlin and Tübingen. In 1930 he assumed the pastorate of the Holy Trinity Parish Church at Bridge of Allan, near Stirling, where he served until coming to Princeton in 1949. During his years at the church, he fulfilled the ideal of the pastor-scholar. In 1935, he delivered the Hastie Lectures at the University of Glasgow on the subject of God the Creator, published in 1937 in Scotland and the following year in the United States. Although the book did not deal explicitly with Karl Barth, Hendry clearly echoed certain of Barth's themes. He criticized natural theology and stressed the kinship between traditional Scottish theology and Reformed thought on the Continent. Hendry was thus an early voice introducing Barth's ideas to Scotland — a movement that would go into high gear after World War II with the work of Thomas F. Torrance. When the first British publication in honor of Karl Barth came out in 1947 on the occasion of the Swiss theologian's sixtieth birthday, both Hendry and Torrance contributed essays to the volume. Hendry also played an important role in the preparation of a new translation of the Bible, first through his work in shepherding an overture from his presbytery (Stirling and Dunblane) to the General Assembly of the Church of Scotland in 1946 calling for a new translation of the Bible into contemporary English. Approved by the Assembly, the proposal resulted in the formation of an interchurch or interdenominational committee to oversee the project. Until he left for Princeton, Hendry served as secretary of the committee, whose labor resulted in the publication of the New Testament portion of the New English Bible in 1961 and then in 1970 the Old Testament and Apocrypha.[28]

---

age Cailliet attributed to Walter Lowrie, the Kierkegaard translator and scholar. For a more recent, perceptive essay on Young Life, consult Ronald C. White Jr., "Youth Ministry at the Center: A Case Study of Young Life," in *Re-Forming the Center: American Protestantism, 1900 to the Present,* ed. Douglas Jacobsen and William Vance Trollinger Jr. (Grand Rapids: Eerdmans, 1998), 361-80.

28. George W. Hendry, *God the Creator* (London: Hodder and Stoughton, 1937; Nashville: Abingdon, 1938); F. W. Camfield, ed., *Reformation Old and New: A Tribute to Karl Barth* (London: Lutterworth Press, 1947). See Anne-Kathrin Finke, "Karl Barth and British Theology," *Zeitschrift für Neuere Theologiegeschichte/Journal for the History of Modern Theology* 2 (January 1995): 193-224.

His nineteen years as a pastor shaped his view of his work when he came to Princeton. Hendry never forgot that his labors were on behalf of the church. Although he believed theology to be an academic discipline requiring no less thoroughness than any other, he had little patience with those who wrote in specialized or arcane jargon as if theology belonged primarily to academe. In his inaugural address at the seminary, he suggested that the "suspicion or distrust of theology as a useless intellectual game with no bearing on the real life of the church" occurred when the discipline "has attempted the impossible feat of suspending itself in midair" — that is, whenever theology has forgotten that it is "an activity of the church, by the church, for the church." "No doubt," his former student and later colleague Daniel L. Migliore has remarked, "this explains why Professor Hendry taught, preached, and wrote in a way that seminary students and pastors could understand. He had no interest in merely impressing the elite of the academy. He spoke primarily for and to the church." His lectures and sermons in chapel were studded with memorable turns of phrase. His felicity of expression often left hearers unable to imagine a better way of stating the point at hand. None of this was for the sake of ornamentation, but for clarity. On first encounter, students might mistake his personal reserve and his academic rigor for severity; but the impression would soon fade when, with a slight smile or a twinkle of the eye, he displayed a wry — and occasionally mischievous — sense of humor, though one never entirely relaxed in a seminar with him. "Hendry," one of his doctoral students reminisced, "did not allow people to take theology less seriously than he did."[29]

In his inaugural address, Hendry outlined his conception of principle and method in theology. Along with others influenced by Barth, he believed that theology had been too willing to accede to "the demands for conformity . . . thrust upon it from the side of philosophy, history, and science." "Theology is a work of faith," he insisted. "It is no part of its business to go behind faith and seek other, presumably firmer, foundations for faith." Then came one of his memorable phrases: "A man adrift on a raft in mid-ocean is not wise to jump overboard to find out the secret of

29. George S. Hendry, "Principle and Method in Theology," *Princeton Seminary Bulletin* 43 (1950): 9-13; quotation on 12; Daniel L. Migliore, "George S. Hendry: A Tribute," *Princeton Seminary Bulletin* 15 (1994): 46-51; quotation on 48; William G. Bodamer, "Reminiscences of Dr. George S. Hendry," *Princeton Seminary Bulletin* 15 (1994): 44-45. As a first-year master of divinity student in one of Hendry's classes in the fall semester of 1968, I formed impressions of him quite similar to those of Migliore and Bodamer.

its buoyancy." Theology also involved exegesis. "Theology knows the revelation of God because it knows the testimony which is borne to it in the Bible." But one did not first establish the authority of the Bible on external grounds and *then* believe what it said. "It is not the witness which authenticates the revelation," he asserted; "it is the revelation which authenticates the witness." He believed that it is "a defect of faith to identify the written record with the revelation of God and to ascribe to the record qualities which, supposedly, authenticate the witness." Moreover, true theology finds its axis in Christ, for he is the center of revelation. Christ, "as living truth, the word made flesh . . . can be apprehended only in living encounter." In that encounter, Christ "cannot be translated into propositional form and incorporated into a system." What did it mean, then, to speak of dogmatic or systematic theology? It did not mean "literal reaffirmation of the formulae in which the church has defined its understanding" of God's revelation in Christ; it meant that systematic theology "is concerned with that which these formulae sought to define." Again he offered a nautical image:

> The dogmas of the church are like buoys which mark the limits of the channel through which the living tradition of faith has flowed. Theology is dogmatic, not because it has to moor itself to these buoys, but because it has to proceed along the channel which they mark. It will take note of them; it will be grateful that they are there, and it will be advised to think twice before colliding with any of them.

The fluidity and motion suggested by his tropes recurred in the conclusion of the inaugural. Hendry noted that "theological thinking is eschatological." Revelation was not only the starting point of theology but also its goal. Living between those two frontiers, theology cannot "proceed to build up a system," fixed or immutable; it can at best be a "pilgrim theology . . . not claiming to have apprehended the truth so much as to be apprehended by it."[30]

Through several major books, Hendry embodied his understanding of what a "pilgrim theology" might look like for the late twentieth century. *The Holy Spirit in Christian Theology* (1956; revised and expanded in 1965) traced the historical development of controversies related to the

---

30. Hendry, "Principle and Method," 10, 11, 12.

Spirit. "While one may feel that little new is being said," wrote one reviewer, "the reader frequently comes to the end of a section impressed with the fact that the point under discussion is now seen in an entirely different light than before." Perhaps most noteworthy was Hendry's disagreement with Karl Barth's defense of the *filioque* as added to the Nicean formations in A.D. 589 at a council with representatives of western Christendom. The *filioque* asserted that the Spirit proceeds from the Father *and* the Son rather than simply from the Father, as the original creed said, and this addition became a bone of contention between the East and the West. Hendry also took exception to what he believed was the overstatement of the Protestant reformers in making the Holy Spirit seem to overwhelm the human spirit in regeneration. He called for "a truly evangelical conception of grace" and the Spirit's act in bringing it. He favored a notion of grace "which not only descends upon man vertically from above, reducing him to the condition of a helpless target, but which comes to meet him at his own level and engages him at the point of his freedom, which is his spirit." In *The Gospel of the Incarnation,* originally delivered as the Croall Lectures in New College, Edinburgh, in 1951 and then published seven years later after additional reflection, Hendry lamented the fragmentation of Christian thought between the Christian West and East and once again showed sympathies with the Orthodox position. In the West, Catholic and Protestant alike had given prominence to the atonement, wrought through the sacrificial death of Christ and ratified by his resurrection, as that which takes away the guilt of sin. In the East, the Orthodox stressed the fact of the incarnation itself, that God had assmed humanity in the birth of Jesus. Hendry wished to recover a more holistic emphasis upon the *entire* life of Christ. Neither his nativity alone nor his death and resurrection — nor even both ends of his life considered together — expressed the fullness of his work, not if what transpired between his birth and his death was ignored. Or, as Hendry wrote, "Salvation was not the result of something he did in entering humanity or of something he did in dying a human death; it was the work of his life and his death to relate himself freely to men and them to himself; and this relation is the core and foundation of their salvation." Although the search for the "historical Jesus" in the nineteenth century had sometimes gone astray, Hendry believed the movement gave a needed reminder to theology that the life and ministry of Christ needed to be incorporated into an understanding of the incarnation and his saving work. In a commissioned book for the southern Presbyterian Church on the contemporary theological meaning of the Westminster Confession, Hendry acknowledged the confession's "great and undoubted merits" but also called it "excessively legalistic" and believed that it exhibited "more of the character of a constitutional than a confessional document." It dared to predict "the issue of the final judgment with a confidence hardly befitting those who will be neither judge nor jury, but judged."[31]

Theology and History:
Lefferts A. Loetscher and Edward A. Dowey

Lefferts A. Loetscher represented the first appointment in history during the Mackay era. Born in 1904 in Dubuque to Frederick W. Loetscher, he moved at a young age to Princeton when his father began teaching at the seminary. Educated at the Lawrenceville School and then at Princeton University, where he graduated in 1925, Loetscher matriculated at the seminary that fall and completed his divinity studies in 1928, but stayed for an additional year of studies leading to the Th.M. Both as a student and as the son of a member of the faculty minority during the 1920s, Lefferts Loetscher was a firsthand observer of the troubles that divided the seminary and brought reorganization. Between 1929 and 1933, he served as assistant pastor at the First Presbyterian Church in Reading, Pennsylvania, and from 1933 to 1941 was pastor of the Rhawnhurst Church in Philadelphia. In 1941, he returned to Princeton Seminary as an instructor in church history, and in 1943 he received a Ph.D. from the University of Pennsylvania. Becoming a full professor in 1954, Loetscher remained at Princeton until his retirement in 1974.[32]

Lefferts Loetscher was the first professor at Princeton to specialize in American church history, and American Presbyterian history in particular. Along with Robert T. Handy of Union Theological Seminary in New York and H. Shelton Smith of Duke Divinity School, Loetscher produced the two-volume *American Christianity* (1960, 1963), which became

31. George S. Hendry, *The Holy Spirit and Christian Theology* (Philadelphia: Westminster Press, 1956), 114; Hendry, *The Gospel of the Incarnation* (Philadelphia: Westminster Press, 1958), 13; Hendry, *The Westminster Confession for Today: A Contemporary Interpretation of the Confession of Faith* (Richmond, VA: John Knox Press, 1960), 14, 15; Robert V. Smith, review of *The Holy Spirit and Christian Theology* in *Journal of Bible and Religion* 25 (January 1957): 56.

32. "Lefferts A. Loetscher," *Princeton Seminary Bulletin* 4 (1983): 50-51.

in many seminary courses throughout the land standard texts or resource books. In company with Maurice Armstrong and Charles Anderson, he produced a similar collection of Presbyterian documents, called *The Presbyterian Enterprise: Sources of American Presbyterian History.* Loetscher also wrote the posthumously published *Facing the Enlightenment and Pietism: Archibald Alexander and the Founding of Princeton Seminary.* But he is best known for *The Broadening Church* (1954), which examined the theological controversies in the Presbyterian Church from the Old School/New School reunion of 1869-1870 through the 1930s. Along with Leonard Trinterud's *The Forming of an American Tradition* (1948), which examined colonial origins, *The Broadening Church* has probably exercised the most decisive influence in the interpretation of Presbyterianism in the United States. Both books noted the varied impulses that have gone into the making of American Presbyterianism, and hence they stressed the diversity rather than the homogeneity of Presbyterianism. Or, as Loetscher observed at the beginning of his book, American Presbyterianism had contained two elements: one stressing "precise theological formulation" and "orderly and authoritarian church government," the other placing "more emphasis upon spontaneity, vital impulse, and adaptability." "It has been the good fortune and the hardship of the Presbyterian Church," Loetscher commented wryly, "to have had . . . these two elements in dialectical tension within itself from the beginning." Loetscher's interpretation actually stood closer to Charles Brigg's rendition of the denomination's past in *American Presbyterianism* than it did to Charles Hodge's *Constitutional History of the Presbyterian Church,* though Loetscher's presentation was far more nuanced and avoided the polemical tone of either of the other works. For recognition of his contributions to the profession, Loetscher served as president of the American Society of Church History for 1962, a post that his father, Frederick, had filled in 1934.[33]

---

33. H. Shelton Smith, Robert T. Handy, and Lefferts A. Loetscher, *American Christianity: An Historical Interpretation with Representative Documents,* vol. 1: *1607-1820,* vol. 2: *1820-1960* (New York: Charles Scribner's Sons, 1960, 1963); Maurice W. Armstrong, Lefferts A. Loetscher, and Charles A. Anderson, eds., *The Presbyterian Enterprise: Sources of American Presbyterian History* (Philadelphia: Westminster, 1956); Lefferts A. Loetscher, *Facing the Enlightenment and Pietism: Archibald Alexander and the Founding of Princeton Seminary* (Westport, CT: Greenwood Press, 1983); Loetscher, *The Broadening Church: A Study of Theological Issues in the Presbyterian Church since 1869* (Philadelphia: University of Pennsylvania Press, 1954), 1.

Near the close of Mackay's presidency — 1957, the same year that Samuel Blizzard was named to the position in Christianity and society — Edward A. Dowey Jr. joined the faculty with a joint appointment in both the history and theology departments. Dowey, born in 1918 in Philadelphia, was the son of a Presbyterian manse. His father served as pastor of a congregation of the United Presbyterian Church of North America, one of the smaller Presbyterian denominations in America. Dowey's childhood involved several moves as his father took subsequent pastorates in Ohio and then in Pittsburgh and eventually in Scranton, Pennsylvania, the last of these involving a transfer to the Presbyterian Church in the U.S.A. Dowey came from a quite conservative background and had aspirations for the ministry. During his time at Lafayette College, that intention had begun to wane, until a particular speaker arrived.

> It was a time of endless questioning. By my senior year I had almost decided against entering the ministry. Then President John Mackay paid a visit to Lafayette College. What he said convinced me that there were better minds among Christian thinkers than I had experienced: Kierkegaard et al. I think his visit caused me to want to get the whole story from the horse's mouth, which turned out to be Princeton Seminary.

From 1940 to 1943, Dowey pursued his studies at Princeton Seminary, where John Mackay, Josef Hromádka, and Hugh T. Kerr Jr. were the professors who most appealed to him. Hromádka, an anti-fascist émigré from Czechoslovakia after the Munich agreement sanctioned the invasion of his country by Nazi Germany, taught at Princeton Seminary for a number of years; and Dowey was impressed by both his powerful theological vision and his desire for revolutionary change. Kerr, later the long-term editor of *Theology Today,* won plaudits from Dowey because he was lively at a time when much of the teaching in theology at the seminary he found "deadly dull."[34]

34. Daniel L. Migliore, interviewer, "A Conversation with Edward A. Dowey," *Princeton Seminary Bulletin* 9 (1988): 89-103; quotation on 89-90; Elsie Anne McKee, "Edward A. Dowey, Jr.: 1918-2003," *Princeton Seminary Bulletin* 25 (2004): 99-105. On Hromádka, see Charles C. West, "Josef Lukl Hromádka," in *Sons of the Prophets: Leaders in Protestantism from Princeton Seminary,* ed. Hugh T. Kerr (Princeton: Princeton University Press, 1963), 205-23. Regarding Hugh T. ("Tim") Kerr Jr. see "In Memoriam: Hugh Thomson Kerr, 1909-1992," *Theology Today* 49 (July 1992): 147-51.

Following seminary, Dowey served as a naval chaplain in the Pacific for two years; and upon returning from the war he took an M.A. at Columbia University in New York, which also allowed him to study with Reinhold Niebuhr and Paul Tillich at Union Seminary. In 1947, he went to Zurich to investigate the possibility of doing doctoral work with Emil Brunner. Dowey thought that his interview with the Swiss theologian doomed his prospects, for the two of them had what he described as an intellectual "pitched battle." After the session, Dowey was ready to pack his bags and return home when Brunner sent him a note "urging me to stay in Zurich and write a dissertation there. He said it takes fire to make a real theologian." The dissertation became Dowey's often-cited book *The Knowledge of God in Calvin's Theology.* After returning to the United States, Dowey taught at Lafayette College and Columbia University and then at McCormick Theological Seminary before coming to Princeton. Before agreeing to come to Princeton, Dowey showed again the fire that had impressed Emil Brunner. The oath required at installation was still the one that had been taken by nineteenth-century professors, in which the professor vowed not to "teach, or insinuate any thing which shall appear to me to contradict or contravene, either directly or impliedly, any thing" asserted in the Westminster Confession. When Dowey indicated that he would not take that oath, "Dr. Mackay and Eugene Blake [then a trustee of the seminary and stated clerk of the denomination] initiated an action by which the General Assembly standardized the method of installing professors in all of the seminaries. This meant simply by reaffirming one's ordination promises."[35]

Edward Jabra Jurji and the History of Religions at Princeton

Edward Jabra Jurji, born in Latakia, Syria, in 1907, attended the American University in Beirut, Lebanon, graduating in 1928. He taught in the department of education at Mosul and Baghdad, Iraq, for two years and then at the American school in Baghdad from 1930 to 1933. He subsequently went to the United States to study at Princeton University, from which he received an M.A. in 1934 and the Ph.D. in 1936. His research concentrated on the Sufi mystical tradition in Islam and resulted in the pub-

---

35. Migliore, interviewer, "Conversation with Dowey," 95; Edward A. Dowey Jr., *The Knowledge of God in Calvin's Theology,* expanded ed. (Grand Rapids: Eerdmans, 1994).

lication of an annotated translation of a manuscript by a fifteenth-century figure. He worked primarily with Philip K. Hitti, a noted professor of Oriental studies. When he published the dissertation, Jurji also indicated indebtedness to Henry Snyder Gehman and Charles Fritsch of the seminary, whose acquaintance he had made and who had assisted him with his project. Following the receipt of the Ph.D., he stayed in Princeton as a member of the Institute for Advanced Study. In 1939, he began the bachelor of divinity (today's master of divinity) program at the seminary. After completing his studies in 1942, he stayed on as an instructor in history of religions and rose through the ranks to become full professor. He remained at Princeton Seminary until his retirement in 1977. From the 1940s to 1981, he also had a part-time pastoral relation with the Fourth Avenue Presbyterian Church (originally called the Syrian Protestant Church) in the Bay Ridge section of Brooklyn.[36]

Jurji's appointment, the first of a professor whose native country was neither the United States nor one of the European nations, represented a step toward a faculty with a more international perspective. It fit with the vision of John A. Mackay, who, it should be recalled, was not only the president of the seminary but also professor of ecumenics. Mackay taught a required course in that field in which he sought to instill a vision of the worldwide mission of the church. As part of that larger perspective, a professor teaching the history of religions — or, as it was sometimes called, comparative religion or phenomenology of religion — had an important role to play in helping future clergy understand the other faiths Christianity encountered. In Samuel Zwemer, the seminary previously had, of course, a professor with considerable missionary experience in Muslim lands and who brought that knowledge to bear in his courses on mission and history of religions. Jurji, however, represented a new level of specialization in the field — a professor with in-depth training in non-Christian religious traditions at the Ph.D. level. Since Jurji's tenure, the seminary has with subsequent appointments continued to register its commitment to the importance of having on the faculty a specialist in the history of religions, as attested by the appointment of Charles A. Ryerson and, after Ryerson's retirement, the current occupant of the position, Richard Fox Young.

36. Edward Jabra Jurji, *Illumination in Islamic Mysticism* (Princeton: Princeton University Press, 1938); see acknowledgments in the preface on an unnumbered page. See also his obituary in the *New York Times,* July 12, 1990.

Aside from the highly technical work on Sufism, Jurji generally wrote on broader themes as a historian of religions. Early in his professorship, he reflected on what he entitled "The Science of Religion: A Christian Perspective." At a time when many influenced by Karl Barth and Hendrik Kraemer hesitated to attribute any true religious knowledge — or general revelation — to non-Christian religions, Jurji argued the contrary. He found that virtually all religions gave evidence of such religious knowledge, though that knowledge had been perverted and overlaid with serious error. A year later, he speculated that it was the presence of Protestant Christian missionaries in the Middle East over roughly the previous hundred years that had helped to renew the traditional Christian churches in the region and had contributed to a revitalizing of some of the better impulses of Islamic leaders themselves. The region was, in short, "ripe for the harvest." Although his subsequent work continued to manifest unabashedly his Christian commitments, Jurji sounded less triumphalistic and more eager to find a way for the various religions to discover areas of agreement and, where possible, to make common cause for a better world order. For example, in 1955 he was speculating about the potential impact "in the councils of the nations if and when the living religions decided to speak in unison on the cardinal issue of war and peace" and likewise to make clear their united opposition to "tyranny and banditry" in international affairs. This did not mean, he insisted, "a commitment to religious syncretism nor resort to a hazy optimism regarding the equality and identity of all faiths." He envisioned an encounter of respect among religions based on their common quest for truth. He insisted that this conversation did not for one minute mean that Christians would retreat from their conviction that Christ "reveals the truth about God, that he is love, and about man that he is a sinner who can be redeemed." It did not mean the end of the missionary movement; but it did mean that "Christianity need not repudiate the elements of truth and spirituality in those religions." "To live in a state of friendly yet fierce tension with other religions," he concluded, "is the supreme challenge that comes to every living faith."[37]

In the early 1960s, Jurji wrote his own overview of the phenomenol-

37. Edward J. Jurji, "The Science of Religion: A Christian Perspective," *Theology Today* 7 (July 1950): 194-205; Jurji, "The Impact of Christianity upon the Middle East," *Theology Today* 8 (April 1951): 55-69; quotation on 57; Jurji, "The Great Religions and International Affairs," *Theology Today* 12 (July 1955): 168-79; quotations on 169, 175, 176-77.

ogy of religion. The number of issues his book treated and the sometimes difficult prose prompted reviewers to offer differing assessments, some applauding the book and others finding it muddled. Whether he succeeded or not, Jurji was attempting to lay out a framework, indebted in part to Rudolf Otto's notion of the holy or numinous, within which various faiths could be compared. Arguably the most ambitious enterprise of Jurji's academic career was to organize two conferences in Princeton, one in 1964 and the other two years later. Called the Gallahue Conferences after Edward Gallahue of Indianapolis, who provided funding, the two gatherings brought together academic representatives of major religious traditions to examine the possibilities of convergence among the religions, problems of prejudice, and areas of further fruitful conversation. While Jurji's reflections indicated something of the intellectual excitement of the encounters, they also suggested that the results were somewhat less than the glowing visions he had espied a decade earlier. In 1968 he wrote in *Numen:* "If the proceedings netted any tangible outcome at all, this was for the most part tentative and fragmentary.... If involvement in the question of religious truth were to be taken as the measure of authentic dialogue, then the conference as a whole fell short of the mark." Two years earlier he concluded somewhat acidly about the first of the Gallahue Conferences: "The parable of the Tower, with its caution against illusory utopianism, seemed to have been mastered in essence if not in form." But that awareness of illusion — and disillusion — is to move toward problems of fragmentation that figure prominently in the next chapter.[38]

38. Edward J. Jurji, *The Phenomenology of Religion* (Philadelphia: Westminster Press, 1963); Edward J. Jurji, "Interfaith and Intercultural Communication," *Numen* 15 (May 1968): 81-93; quotation on 92; Jurji, "Religious Pluralism and World Community," *Theology Today* 23 (October 1966): 346-62; quotation on 362. See, for example, the reviews of *The Phenomenology of Religion* by Harry M. Buck, *Journal of Bible and Religion* 33 (April 1965): 174-75; and Albert Rabil Jr., *Union Seminary Quarterly Review* (March 1965): 300-303.

CHAPTER SIXTEEN

Princeton and Deepening Pluralism, 1959-2004

WHEN John Mackay retired from the presidency of Princeton Seminary in 1959, the religious surge of the post–World War II era was still close to high tide. Religious affiliation in the United States had reached record levels, and so-called mainline or mainstream Protestant churches were among those continuing to experience numerical growth. In retrospect, one can see signs of a different mood beginning to take shape amid the outward tokens of religious success. Some theologians and cultural critics derided the revival for its supposed lack of theological content, for its use of religion as a tool for promoting peace of mind, achieving prosperity, or supporting the American way of life in the nation's contest with the Soviet Union. On occasion, Princeton faculty themselves raised criticisms of the revival even as they found signs of hope in aspects of it. What could scarcely have been imagined was the way in which the revival would evaporate within the next decade, or that mainline religious bodies would begin the steady downturn in membership that has continued unabated to the present.[1]

The conception that mainstream Protestants had long entertained about their place in American life also met serious challenge. If they had not always fully articulated it, they generally took for granted (much as the air they breathed) that Protestantism occupied a dominant role in setting the tone or ethos of American life. To an extent greater than often remembered, anti-Catholicism was a part of that assumption of hege-

---

1. Martin E. Marty, *Modern American Religion*, vol. 3: *Under God, Indivisible, 1941-1960* (Chicago: University of Chicago Press, 1996), 277-476.

mony. Although the crudities of Catholic-bashing nativism had largely passed away, residual suspicions still served as an occasional Protestant rallying point. For example, the National Council of Churches — the successor to the Federal Council — had barely come into existence in 1950 when President Truman's plan to name an ambassador to the Vatican prompted the new organization to damn the idea as a dangerous violation of the separation of church and state. Likewise, Protestants opposed the periodically expressed desire of Catholic prelates and some Catholic politicians for public aid to parochial schools. Yet by the early 1960s Catholicism as a negative reference point for Protestants had greatly diminished. The victorious campaign of Catholic Senator John F. Kennedy for the presidency in 1960 temporarily reignited fears in some quarters, but his conduct in office largely dissipated anti-Catholic anxieties. At the same time, the papacy of John XXIII (1958-1963) and the Second Vatican Council (1962-1965) changed both the Catholic Church and Protestants' perception of it. The warm humanity of John made the church seem less authoritarian and alien to outsiders, while the pronouncements of the Council held out an ecumenical olive branch to Protestants and also appeared to reconcile Roman Catholicism to the separation of church and state and to democracy. In short, the Catholic Church no longer seemed "un-American" to many Protestants. Moreover, the changing character of the Catholics in the pew confirmed the same point. Throughout the nineteenth century and up until Congress passed immigration restriction legislation in the 1920s, the Catholic Church's ranks had been steadily swollen by the foreign-born. But by the 1950s, Catholicism had lost much of the character of an immigrant church and thus again seemed less alien and more "American" to outsiders. While mainline Protestants generally welcomed with enthusiasm the changes within Roman Catholicism, those developments also demanded a reorientation of perspective.[2]

At the same time, the United States Supreme Court handed down decisions perceived by many Protestants as well as some Catholics as a defeat for the role of religion in public life. In 1962, the high court de-

---

2. Jay P. Dolan, *The American Catholic Experience: A History from the Colonial Times to the Present* (Garden City, NY: Doubleday, 1985), 421-54; Sydney E. Ahlstrom, "The Radical Turn in Theology and Ethics: Why It Occurred in the 1960's," *Annals of the American Academy of Political and Social Science* 387 (January 1970): 1-13; William R. Hutchison, ed., *Between the Times: The Travail of the Protestant Establishment, 1900-1960* (Cambridge and New York: Cambridge University Press, 1989).

clared unconstitutional a law providing for the recitation each morning in the public schools of state-sponsored prayer. Even though the prayer did not explicitly suggest belief in the deity of any particular religion — some wags referred to it as a prayer addressed "to whom it may concern" — the court ruled that any state sponsorship of prayer in public schools violated the "no establishment" clause of the First Amendment. The following year, a Pennsylvania law requiring the daily reading of ten verses from the Bible at the beginning of each school day was likewise deemed an impermissible establishment of religion.[3]

These symbolic changes occurred just as a series of other issues were dramatically thrust upon the nation: the civil rights struggle to end centuries of racial injustice; the escalation of American involvement in Southeast Asia into a full-blown war; and President Johnson's Great Society, with its significant expansion of social services through the establishment of Medicare and a "war on poverty." As controversy swirled about these matters, numerous campuses erupted in student protest; and among many of the so-called "baby boomers" a highly visible (though minority) counterculture wished to have done with the values and lifestyle of the "establishment." Often a new openness and freedom in sexual mores formed a part of this counterculture. By the end of the 1960s, the feminist movement had again stirred to life, and an awareness of a potential environmental crisis marked the beginnings of what one author at the time called the "greening of America." Also, in the summer of 1969, a police raid on a gay bar in the Greenwich Village area of lower Manhattan triggered angry protests that many historians see as the beginnings of the movement for gay-lesbian rights. These issues prompted virulent debate not only within the culture at large but also within many of America's churches and seminaries.

New trends roiled theological waters in the same decade. Several authors created a public stir by writing of the "death of God," which prompted *Time* magazine to run an issue with a provocative question posed in bold red letters on the cover of the April 8, 1966, issue: "Is God Dead?" The authors who used such language meant different things by it. Gabriel Vahanian, then a professor at Syracuse University and a 1958

3. For a good overview of Supreme Court decisions on matters of religion since 1960, see John F. Wilson and Donald L. Drakeman, eds., *Church and State in American History: Key Documents, Decisions, and Commentary from the Past Three Centuries,* 3rd ed. (Cambridge, MA: Westview Press, 2003), 219-411.

graduate of Princeton Seminary's doctoral program, employed the concept as a way of indicating, not atheism, but rather the collapse of puny cultural idolatries that sought to tame the transcendent God. For Thomas J. J. Altizer, influenced by Hegelian ideas, God had died in the sense that he had poured himself completely into humanity through the incarnation, transcendence emptied into immanence. Others, such as William J. Hamilton and Paul Van Buren, seemed more interested in simply bracketing ultimate theological or metaphysical issues and concentrating upon the immediate "secular" implications of Christianity. Although not a part of the "death of God" theology, young theologian Harvey Cox captured the spirit that lay behind much of it. His study book *The Secular City,* prepared for conferences organized by the National Student Christian Federation, sold over 250,000 copies and was reissued in a new edition. Eventually sales in all languages and editions reached nearly a million. At the heart of this best-seller was the affirmation that the present was pregnant with new possibilities. Cox called upon Christians to forsake the metaphysical for the practical and to throw themselves into the search for pragmatic solutions to the problems of urban civilization. His volume became, in the words of Robert S. Ellwood, "the supreme icon" of "the hopeful, secular-as-sacred expression of the early to mid-Sixties."[4]

By the end of the sixties, however, theologies often manifested a different temper, mirroring the more divided and militant mood of the second half of the decade. In 1968, for example, Mary Daly published *The Church and the Second Sex,* which offered a cogent critique of the way in which Christianity, especially Roman Catholicism, had subordinated woman and, in the name of supposedly honoring her, had denied her full humanity. In the same year, Rubem Alves received his doctorate from Princeton Seminary for the dissertation "Towards a Theology of Liberation," prefiguring later Latin American works that would seek to align the Christian church and theology with the forces making for social justice. In 1969, James H. Cone published the landmark *Black Theology and Black*

---

4. Gabriel Vahanian, *The Death of God: The Culture of Our Post-Christian Era* (New York: George Braziller, 1961); Thomas J. J. Altizer and William Hamilton, *Radical Theology and the Death of God* (Indianapolis: Bobbs-Merrill, 1966); Robert S. Ellwood, *The Sixties Spiritual Awakening: American Religion Moving from Modern to Postmodern* (New Brunswick, NJ: Rutgers University Press, 1994), 131. For a perceptive account written at the time of the movement, see F. Thomas Trotter, "Variations on the 'Death of God' Theme in Recent Theology," *Journal of Bible and Religion* 33 (January 1965): 42-48.

Power, which argued that the black experience of slavery and oppression required a special rendition of Christian theology reflecting that experience. Despite the differences among them, these works manifested an assumption that became increasingly common in the theological writings of the years ahead: the belief that context — whether it be class, gender, race, ethnicity, or whatever — made all the difference in determining the appropriate theology for a particular people in a particular place and time. This deepened concern for context was an invitation to a greater multiplicity of theologies, and these were not long in coming.[5]

These new theologies and movements were not the only ones. At least since 1942, with the organization of the National Association of Evangelicals and then the rise to national popularity of evangelist Billy Graham after 1949, persons who held views fairly similar to those of the fundamentalists were more visible on the public stage. Sometimes called neo-fundamentalists or evangelicals, these people differed from their fundamentalist forebears in the manner in which they approached those who held different views. They were far less separatist in ecclesiology, far more interested in engaging the larger culture in a positive manner, and sometimes willing to work with those of alternate theological views. A good example was the readiness of Graham and of some mainline Protestants to make common cause in support of religious revival. By the early 1970s, as some of the enthusiasms of the 1960s cooled, the media were rediscovering the phenomenon of evangelicalism — a fact helped along by the election in 1976 of a self-described "born again Christian" as president of the United States.[6]

These developments contributed to the disappearance of a single prevailing theological perspective in Protestant seminaries. In the 1950s, William Robert Miller described Neo-orthodoxy as "the normative religious outlook of the educated Protestant." Perhaps he exaggerated the extent of that theology's dominance outside of places such as Yale, Union, and Princeton. Perhaps, too, he overestimated the unity it exhib-

---

5. Mary Daly, *The Church and the Second Sex* (New York: Harper and Row, 1968); Rubem A. Alves, "Towards a Theology of Liberation: An Exploration of the Encounter between the Languages of Humanistic Messianism and Messianic Humanism" (Th.D. Dissertation, Princeton Theological Seminary, 1968); James H. Cone, *Black Theology and Black Power* (New York: Seabury, 1969).

6. Joel A. Carpenter, *Revive Us Again: The Reawakening of American Fundamentalism* (New York: Oxford University Press, 1997); Grant Wacker, "The Billy Pulpit: Graham's Career in the Mainline," *Christian Century* 120 (November 15, 2003): 20-26.

ited. Never a fully cohesive movement, it was held together from the beginning by an awareness of crisis in western culture, a sense of the inadequacy of liberalism, and a willingness to look seriously at classic Christian doctrines. Once the immediate sense of crisis faded and liberalism — at least in its more exuberant nineteenth-century forms — had passed from the scene, much of the common focus of the movement also disappeared. By the close of the 1950s, discerning critics were already suggesting that the term's utility was gone; and certainly by the end of the 1960s no one could doubt that Neo-orthodoxy had passed, at least as the regnant perspective. Too many voices were speaking for a single one to claim dominance; and even after the tumult of the sixties had subsided, the decade left immense diversity in its wake. In the half-century after John Mackay retired, Princeton Seminary would be doing theology in an educational and religious environment more radically pluralistic than ever before. The presidents who would lead the school into that new world were James I. McCord and Thomas W. Gillespie.[7]

James I. McCord

James Iley McCord, who succeeded Mackay in 1959, guided Princeton through the tumult of the 1960s and beyond, retiring in 1983. A native of Texas born in 1919, he received his undergraduate training at Austin College and then went on for his basic theological education at Union Theological Seminary in Richmond, with further advanced work at Harvard University and the University of Geneva. In 1942, he was ordained to the Presbyterian ministry and served as interim pastor of the Westminster Presbyterian Church in Manchester, New Hampshire, until 1944, when he became pastor of the University Presbyterian Church in Austin as well as dean and professor of systematic theology at Austin Presbyterian Seminary. When he assumed the presidency of Princeton Seminary in 1959, he was only 40 years old.[8]

---

7. William R. Miller, ed., *Contemporary American Protestant Thought: 1900-1970* (Indianapolis: Bobbs-Merrill Co., 1973), lxvi; Sydney E. Ahlstrom, "Neo-Orthodoxy Demythologized," *Christian Century* 74 (May 22, 1957): 649-51.

8. *Biographical Catalogue of Princeton Theological Seminary*, comp. Arthur M. Byers Jr. (Princeton: Princeton Theological Seminary, 1977), xxi; *New York Times*, February 21, 1990; Thomas W. Gillespie, "A Memorial Tribute to the Rev. Dr. James Iley McCord," *Princeton Seminary Bulletin* 11 (1990): 121-27.

McCord demonstrated adroitness as a churchman and as an administrator. He continued the commitment to the ecumenical movement that both Ross Stevenson and John Mackay had exhibited. Serving as president of the World Alliance of Reformed Churches and as chair of the Consultation on Christian Union, which sought to achieve the union of ten major American Protestant denominations, McCord also participated extensively in the activities of the National Council of Churches and the World Council of Churches and sought to form relationships with Christian leaders around the world. By any institutional measure, the seminary prospered on his watch. The seminary's endowment increased from $11 million to $150 million, the number of students more than doubled, and a major complex for housing married students was purchased. In these endeavors, McCord was aided not only by his own considerable prowess in fundraising but also by trustee Sir John Templeton, whose management of the seminary's portfolio in the latter portion of McCord's presidency and in the first part of Thomas Gillespie's enhanced the seminary's investments dramatically. During the time of campus upheavals in the late 1960s and early 1970s, McCord managed to steer a course that allowed for the expression of student frustrations without resulting in a major paralysis of the campus. The closest Princeton came to such an event was the barricading of the trustees in the board room for a short time in the spring of 1970 in protest over the United States invasion of Cambodia. When one compares that incident to the disruptions at universities such as Columbia, the seminary's difficulties were minor indeed.[9]

By his own assessment, however, and by that of those who knew him, James McCord viewed institutional achievements as secondary to his primary mission: to promote first-rate theological learning and reflection. In his opening convocation address in 1959, he described his vision of what the school should ideally be. He argued that Princeton Seminary "must remain in a dialectical relationship to the Church, since she is the servant both of the Church and of the Church's Head. This means that a theological faculty must be free to perform a prophetic function and must not be subjected to any pressure that will hinder its faithfulness to the truth." The notion that the seminary must be free *for* the church, not from the church, remained an abiding theme for McCord over the years. He expressed his concern in the opening address that Presbyterian semi-

9. Gillespie, "Memorial Tribute"; *New York Times*, May 25, 1983.

naries, like most American seminaries, had frequently defaulted on their responsibility to do critical theology for the church. "We have not yet faced up," he charged, "to many of the issues raised by the nineteenth century, to the questions posed by the new sciences, and to the Church's obligation to do her theological task for every generation. The result is that theology has become largely irrelevant in many quarters and often incredibly dull." Just as the Academy in Calvin's Geneva had incorporated the latest humanist learning into its instruction, "we, standing in the same tradition, must take seriously the new tools of today, such as the social sciences, the insights of sociology, anthropology, and psychology." Rejoicing in "the long and deep ties between Princeton University and Princeton Seminary," he voiced his conviction that "the best theological education" took place in "the intellectual climate that a university and seminary together provide." McCord also worried that Princeton, part of a bourgeois church, needed to immerse itself more in a world where colonialism was dissolving and revolutions were ignited. "It is our task from the beginning of our junior year to be involved in the world's thought and in the world's need." Reiterating many of these themes in his inaugural address some months later, McCord seemed to be calling for a radical rethinking of the curriculum:

> We cannot go on expecting each student to achieve a synthesis on his own when we as a faculty cannot do it. . . . It can only come if there is free and open communication among disciplines, a willingness to cross or ignore traditional lines, and an openness to new materials, new ideas, and new sciences. Inevitably this will result in more inter-departmental work and in the older disciplines beginning to accept responsibility for the foundations of all areas that have to do with the church's ministry to the world. This will mean that the endless proliferation of courses will come to an end.[10]

But even as McCord proposed to incorporate new learning into theological education, he wished to do so for purposes highly tradi-

10. James I. McCord, "The Idea of a Reformed Seminary," *Princeton Seminary Bulletin* 53 (1960): 5-9; McCord, "The Seminary and the Theological Mission," *Princeton Seminary Bulletin* 54 (1960): 52-58. McCord reiterated the "freedom for" notion in his remarks at his successor's inauguration; see McCord, "The Charge to the New President," *Princeton Seminary Bulletin* 5 (1984): 96.

tional. For example, he titled his 1960 opening convocation address, "The Theological Dilemma of the Protestant Minister." Alluding to a recent study entitled *The Ministry in Historical Perspectives,* he noted that H. Richard Niebuhr, one of the editors, had proposed for the minister a new role model: the pastor-director. McCord was deeply troubled by the apparent displacement of the office of minister of the Word. McCord then proceeded to analyze why he thought this traditionally central function appeared problematic. He mentioned Karl Barth, whom he admired greatly, as having inadvertently contributed to the problem. The movement the Swiss theologian inaugurated has discovered that "its very success . . . has been its weakness. It has tended toward Biblicism, has often ignored both the issues raised and the tools produced by the nineteenth century, and has had little influence on contemporary culture." In short, the words the Barthian had to speak were deemed irrelevant by many. Then, too, he added, through the mass media a general "debasement of words" had occurred. But whatever the sources of suspicion of the function, McCord remained convinced that the ministry of the Word was the central task of the ministry, even for the new forms of ministry arising at the beginning of the 1960s. McCord observed:

> The counselor, the chaplain, and the other types of ministries that have emerged in our time have to do with the Word, spoken sometimes to groups and communicated at other times from person to person. No matter what variety of ministry may be our lot, we shall have to do with the Word of God and shall be negligent to the point of impiety if we fail to acquire the most thorough competence in it.

Within his first couple of years as president, McCord had sounded themes that would reverberate throughout his tenure: the importance of innovative theological reflection, an eagerness to encounter new forms of learning offered by the university, and a willingness to rethink the implications of the gospel in light of revolutionary developments in the world. Yet this was always in service to what he understood as the core of theological education: rigorous thought about God's liberating work through Jesus Christ. Out of that dialectic emerged McCord's understanding of the seminary's mission. Depending upon circumstances, one side of the dialectic or the other might be dominant in his thought at a given moment; but both need to be taken into account if one is to understand what McCord was about.[11]

McCord could speak of humanity's coming of age along with the more radical theologians who borrowed the phrase from Dietrich Bonhoeffer, martyred by the Nazis in 1945, whose writings — especially the sometimes enigmatic *Letters and Papers from Prison* — were enjoying a considerable theological vogue. Avant-garde thinkers often employed "man come of age" to argue that the notion of God was now untenable, but McCord's usage of the phrase was more nuanced. He, too, appreciated Bonhoeffer, and he observed that the man come of age "should be approached in his strength and not in his weakness." This man "should not be blackmailed into the Church. . . . [T]he Church of tomorrow must be something more than a refuge for those unwilling to face the future." Bonhoeffer, as McCord evaluated him, understood that the theological renewal represented by Barth and others "had enabled us to recover the living center of the Gospel" — God's self-revelation — but now it was necessary "to establish a point of contact with humanity." What Bonhoeffer saw in his prison cell when he wrote of man come of age was "a clue to the point of contact with the new man. It lies in a humanity that is common to all and involves a humanism that is truly Christian." McCord could even see a silver lining in the cultural disestablishment of Protestantism that appeared to be taking place in America. He suggested "that precisely because the Church is losing her privileged position and being shorn of her old securities, that precisely because the spirit of contemporary culture is increasingly inimical to the Gospel, the Church may be freer than she has been at any time in the modern age to be the Church." McCord pointed to "ministers in Little Rock [Arkansas] who responded to the challenge of integration and who discovered, some of them for the first time, the reality of the Church as a reconciled and reconciling fellowship of men."[12]

McCord offered his most uncritical embrace of the spirit of the 1960s in his opening convocation address on September 16, 1969. He began in a historical vein, observing how conceptions of the ministry had developed in the United States. In the nineteenth century, clergy aspired to be

11. James I. McCord, "The Theological Dilemma of the Protestant Minister," *Princeton Seminary Bulletin* 54 (1960): 3-10.

12. James I. McCord, "The New Man in the New Age," *Princeton Seminary Bulletin* 55 (1961): 15; McCord, "The Four Dimensions of Mission," *Princeton Seminary Bulletin* 55 (1962): 5.

pulpit princes. More recently, after the struggle against Nazism in Germany, many took as their model the theological professor. Remembering what Barth and others did to preserve the integrity of the Christian message, how they "had rescued the church during the ideological struggle by calling it back to its living center, Jesus Christ," would-be clergy aspired to turn their congregations into mini-seminaries where theology would be central. Believing that the "minister is a teacher . . . and a minister without theology is like a ship without a rudder," McCord had a deep commitment to this view, but he recognized that it, too, might ossify. "Theology," he warned, "can become doctrinaire and congregations can become enclaves, while the world moves on into a new age with all of its agonizing problems and amazing prospects." The proposal of H. Richard Niebuhr for the pastor-director still did not enamor McCord. He found it too tame, for it lacked the element of the prophetic — a slight variation of his earlier criticism that it ignored the ministry of the Word. McCord suggested that perhaps one might think in 1969 of the "pastor as missioner." By this he meant that the pastor would be "an agent of change who wants to be related to a congregation of people who will be agents of change." In fact, he professed to "know few ministers today who do not feel that they are taking part in this exodus, moving out from behind stained glass curtains to inspire and lead increasing numbers in their congregations in the mission of Christ to human need." This exodus was taking place in a world moving beyond old ideologies. The communist world was fracturing into Russian, Chinese, and Yugoslavian variants that mocked the old notion of one monolithic "specter haunting the world." Moreover, hints of a possible Christian-Marxist dialogue held "out the hope of better mutual understanding and of relations that will go beyond mere coexistence." Furthermore, he suggested considering how the struggle between the United States and the U.S.S.R. looked from the perspective of "almost any underdeveloped country in, say, southeast Asia." From that vantage point "the two super-powers are like two giants locked in an ideological struggle; [both] are Western, by Asian standards both are rich, and both are colonial powers." From the standpoint of "the world of undeveloped nations . . . and that includes not only Asians, Africans, and Latin Americans, but also those disinherited and dispossessed in our own land," the ideological conflict between the two superpowers seemed irrelevant. And within western lands themselves there was a deep alienation between generations, which signified, McCord believed, a *kairos,* "a fulfilled time, or transparent time, the revealing of a vision. . . .

I believe such a vision has come to this generation. It is a vision of the unity of mankind in which old barriers have been broken down and walls of separation have been razed." And who better than the church to lead an exodus into this new world? The church's Bible was the story of one exodus after another — Abraham being led out from Ur, Israel liberated from bondage in Egypt, and Jesus himself, "the Chief Pilgrim, . . . through his death and resurrection leading mankind in an exodus from death and bondage into life and freedom." With its nearly millennial vision of a new world where the old lines of conflict would be abolished and the church would be part of the vanguard, McCord's address bears comparison to the spirit of a popular movie released about ten months before his convocation remarks: *The Shoes of the Fisherman,* in which a fictional Russian pope, portrayed by Anthony Quinn, points the way to a world beyond east-west rivalry and toward an order in which the disinherited may expect better things.[13]

Even at the height of his enthusiasm for the possibilities of the times, McCord maintained a measure of distance from it. For example, in the 1969 address he saw the polarization between the right and the left growing "ever more strident," with both sides indulging "in non-negotiable demands," and he warned pastors to avoid succumbing to the divisions. "Resolve now," he urged, "never to draw a circle that excludes anyone from the range of your pastoral concern. Others may draw circles to exclude you, but never reciprocate." He also warned that advocates of change needed "the constant reminder that the Gospel of Jesus Christ is a permanent *metanoia,* or conversion. No human institution, no human system, no human construct is free from the judgment of God." Even at the point of his greatest hopes for the spirit of the age, McCord never forgot that no age ever fully embodies the kingdom of God. By the early 1970s and beyond, McCord's criticisms of the age appeared to have mounted as he implied that the excesses of the age often exceeded its benefits. In his farewell remarks to the class of 1971, he warned: "We live in a world that has become one-dimensional, that is content to live only on the surface, and modern man is left bereft of any clue to meaning or purpose."[14]

13. James I. McCord, "Ministry in a Revolutionary Time," *Princeton Seminary Bulletin* 62 (1969): 12-20. *The Shoes of the Fisherman,* based on the novel of the same name by Morris L. West published in 1963, was released in November 1968.

14. McCord, "Ministry in a Revolutionary Time"; McCord, "The Frontier of the Spirit," *Princeton Seminary Bulletin* 64 (1971): 76.

His farewell remarks to the class of 1975 adopted an introspective approach as he began with haunting lines from Greek poet C. P. Cavafy, which offered "the best description I know of the mood of the church and the nation today." Cavafy's "Waiting for the Barbarians," read in greater detail by McCord, included the lines:

What are we waiting for, assembled in the forum?
  The barbarians are due here today.

Why isn't anything happening in the senate?
Why do the senators sit there without legislating?

  Because the barbarians are coming today,
  What laws can the senators make now?
  Once the barbarians are here, they'll do the legislating.

And then a bit later in the lines quoted by McCord:

Why this sudden restlessness, this confusion?
(How serious people's faces have become.)
Why are the streets and squares emptying so rapidly,
everyone going home so lost in thought?

  Because night has fallen and the barbarians have not come.
  And some who have just returned from the border say
  there are no barbarians any longer.

And now, what's going to happen to us without barbarians?
They were, those people, a kind of solution.

McCord noted how American Christians had for at least a generation found their problems in various barbarians: "A few years ago it was the frightened and reactionary right that we feared, the Joe McCarthy's, and more recently it has been the romantic and radical left. . . . Now there is the great moral morass on the Potomac [the Watergate scandal that had driven President Nixon from office a year earlier]." McCord went on to note that the church in 1975 faced no ideological intrusion from a powerful state as it did with the Third Reich; "there is no compelling philosophy that is an alternative to the Christian faith," and "no dominant world

470

view that offers a substitute for Christ." In other words, those "just in from the border tell us there are no barbarians any longer." McCord concluded, "let me suggest that we do as Socrates did centuries ago, cease looking for a solution from without and begin to look within."[15]

This pensive mood indicated a growing tendency in the latter portion of McCord's presidency to place more emphasis upon rigorous reflection on the core of the Christian message and to say less about the alternate pole of his dialectic for theological education — the encounter with "secular" disciplines and with the concerns of the contemporary world. He thundered a warning to the class of 1975. ("Thundered" is the appropriate word, as all who ever heard his voice, best described as something between raspy and booming, will attest.)

> We are painfully aware of how we baptize pop psychology with religious patter and peddle it, or we borrow Marxist rhetoric to assuage our guilt, and dispense it as the Gospel. Is there any wonder that no one takes our ministry seriously? . . . Your generation will be responsible for recovering the living center of the Gospel that will help the Church transcend a fuzzy pluralism and the offering of cheap grace.

In 1980, he offered an assessment of where the theological enterprise stood, lamenting among seminary professors "a sense of helplessness and futility, a suspicion that the tradition has little to say to the contemporary world." He suspected that this sense of uselessness might "account for the recent tendency of theologians to get caught up in the themes of someone else's creation: liberation, ecology, and a host of others, using them as interpretative clues for the substance of theology." While McCord affirmed that those matters were "important in their own right," he felt that theological understanding "is not significantly enhanced simply by a flirtation with particular problems as they are presently understood." He renewed a suggestion that he had raised from time to time over the years — namely, that theological reflection on the tradition should be *catholic,* in the sense that it takes seriously the religious

15. James I. McCord, "On Getting and Keeping a Sense of Humor: Farewell Remarks to Graduating Class 1973," *Princeton Seminary Bulletin* 67 (1975): 49-50; C. P. Cavafy, *Collected Poems,* trans. Edmund Keeley and Philip Sherrard, ed. George Savidis, rev. ed. (Princeton: Princeton University Press, 1992).

experience of the wider community of faith. For McCord that wider community stretched from the patristic witness so valued by Orthodoxy, to Roman Catholicism, to the historic Protestant traditions, but also to newer phenomena such as fundamentalism and Pentecostalism. Only as *all* these Christian traditions came to appreciate the mutual riches they shared, only as they reflected deeply on that broad heritage, would they have a word to say to the contemporary world. "At the present moment in history," he wrote, "our perception of the tradition in its essential dimensions is so dwarfed that it has less and less to say to the human condition. The rectification of this situation is the scholarly task upon which we should be launched." To make his own contribution in this regard, McCord was instrumental in creating the Center of Theological Inquiry, which was located in Princeton and of which he became the first chancellor upon leaving his post at the seminary.[16]

Thomas W. Gillespie

Upon the retirement of James McCord, the seminary tapped Thomas William Gillespie, a native Californian born in 1928, to be the school's fifth president, serving from 1983 until his retirement in 2004. In choosing him, the trustees were turning to a veteran pastor of the Presbyterian Church. With twenty-nine years of service in two different congregations — first in Garden Grove as the organizing pastor and then in Burlingame, California — his pastoral experience far exceeded that of any of his predecessors. After serving in the United States Marine Corps and then pursuing his undergraduate education at Pepperdine University, he took the basic theological degree at Princeton Seminary between 1951 and 1954. During his years of congregational service, he continued advanced studies at the University of Southern California and received a Ph.D. in New Testament at Claremont in 1964, thus providing a modern instance of the venerable ideal of the scholar-pastor. In addition to his congregational responsibilities, he took on major assignments for the Presbyterian Church. He served as a member of the Presbyterian delega-

---

16. James I. McCord, "Priorities for Ministry," *Princeton Seminary Bulletin* 3 (1982): 309; McCord, "The Seminary: An Appraisal," *Theological Education* 17 (Autumn 1980): 53-58. For his comments on the purpose of the Center of Theological Inquiry, see the version of "The Seminary: An Appraisal" that appeared in *Theology Today* 38 (October 1981): 286.

tion to the Consultation on Christian Union and was on the General Assembly task force that wrestled with the question of homosexuality and the church and delivered its report in 1978.[17]

Like McCord's tenure, Gillespie's years as president were marked by significant institutional growth. The library expanded significantly with the addition of the new Luce Library to supplement Speer; other building projects included the construction of the Witherspoon Apartments, a thoroughgoing renovation of Stuart Hall, and the addition of Templeton Hall, which served as a new office and speech building. Moreover, Scheide Hall, a building largely serving as a musical annex to Miller Chapel, was added. The growth of the endowment increased manyfold as it had under McCord, and the number of faculty positions increased. Gillespie also introduced a more informal style of leadership and oversaw the creation of a faculty manual, which began the regularization of faculty procedure.[18]

As one looks at Gillespie's comments about seminary education, one detects themes somewhat different from McCord's, especially those in the early years of the latter's presidency. McCord had urged that "the best theological education" takes place "in the intellectual climate that a university and seminary together provide." Gillespie approached the university more warily. In his own inaugural address in 1984, he noted how universities, with which theological education had originally been associated and after which it often patterned itself, had changed. Originally intended to be a place in which a community of scholars discovered the unity of truth, the university had become in the modern era a place in which "knowledge is fractured into myriad disciplines and sciences, many of which cannot communicate with each other for lack of a common medium of discourse. The *uni*versity has become a *multi*versity." Quoting Russell Kirk, he saw the modern university as too often afflicted with "purposelessness," "intellectual disorder," and an impersonal size that created "The Lonely Crowd on the campus of Behemoth University." It was not that Gillespie failed to appreciate the importance of what the modern university had to offer. In 1996, at an interreligious service commemorating the two hundred fiftieth anniversary of Princeton Uni-

---

17. William O. Harris, "Thomas William Gillespie: A Biographical Essay," in *Theology in the Service of the Church: Essays in Honor of Thomas W. Gillespie,* ed. Wallace M. Alston Jr. (Grand Rapids: Eerdmans, 2000), 1-11; *New York Times,* May 30, 2004.

18. Harris, "Thomas William Gillespie"; *New York Times,* May 30, 2004.

versity's founding, he declared: "Under the aegis of the modern university, the human adventure of intellectual inquiry has been both breathtakingly exciting and unbelievably productive." Yet in the same address he expressed his concern that the modern university, a product of the "Enlightenment . . . with its confidence in a universal reason that was alleged to be constant for all people at all times in all places" and the joining of that confidence "to the emerging empirical sciences," created in the modern university a world in which the only thing that "counted now as knowledge — in contradistinction to opinion or belief, not to mention superstition — were the demonstrable results of the so-called hard sciences." As a result, he observed, "perhaps the humanities have suffered the greatest loss of status in the modern university — with the exception of theology, once the queen of the sciences, which has been banished to the university divinity school or redefined and reassigned to religious-studies programs." And now something called postmodernity had come into vogue. Gillespie puckishly quoted Ernest Gellner's description of postmodernism: "It is strong and fashionable. Over and above this, it is not altogether clear what the devil it is." Gillespie then went on to note sagely that it appeared to be "more a mood than a movement — . . . a mood that compels more and more people to exercise a 'hermeneutics of suspicion'" with regard to the modern claim of a universal truth or reason unconditioned "by gender, race, and ethnicity, as well as by historical and social location." That relativizing of truth troubled Gillespie, but he also saw grounds for hope in it. "It seems clear to me that knowledge will be redefined in terms of a new humility." Perhaps even the insight of Michael Polanyi might find a hearing — "that all knowledge is personal in character, that it is constructed by the interplay between the subjective and objective, and, most important, that it entails 'belief' in the sense of undemonstrated and undemonstrable assumptions." Should this come to pass, Gillespie wondered if "perhaps even theology will be invited back to the academic conversation as a representative of knowledge rather than mere faith." In short, Gillespie admired the accomplishments of the modern university but was ambivalent about its implications for theological education.[19]

His remark about theology being "redefined and reassigned to religious-studies programs" pinpointed an issue that particularly trou-

---

19. Thomas W. Gillespie, "The Seminary as Servant," *Princeton Seminary Bulletin* 5 (1984): 87-95; Gillespie, "Wisdom in a Motto," *Princeton Seminary Bulletin* 18 (1997): 1-8.

bled him — and not only him but many others engaged in theological education. The story of religious studies programs and their dramatic growth in the 1960s unfolded according to different subplots in various places, but certain general trends were common. As these programs sought to establish their credibility within the university, especially within state schools or large private universities, their proponents contended, as Conrad Cherry notes, that their method was scholarly objectivity aimed at "teaching *about* religion, instead of instructing *in* religion." Moreover, like other disciplines in the university, religious studies adopted "the strategies of specialization from their desire to establish a bona fide university discipline." This specialization meant, in part, that the departments added to the traditional list of topics they covered. No longer content to deal primarily with subjects such as Bible or the history of Christian thought and institutions, they added studies on all manner of religious phenomena. The growth of these departments in turn had an impact upon the universities that minted the Ph.D.s hired to staff the programs. Before 1960, most Ph.D.s from university divinity schools found teaching positions in seminaries, in other divinity schools, or in church-related colleges, where a Christian (usually Protestant) ethos prevailed. But as the market shifted toward new religious studies programs, the divinity schools then experienced pressure to produce Ph.D. candidates reflecting the needs of that clientele — a pressure made more extreme after 1970, when the dramatic expansion of higher education during the 1960s slowed and the competition among Ph.D. candidates for entry-level academic jobs grew more fierce. In short, by the time Gillespie was voicing his concerns about the relation of universities to theological training, the ecology of higher education had changed significantly from the days when McCord had enthusiastically called for cooperation.[20]

Gillespie said, partly in humor and also with a bit of sadness, that Princeton's unabashedly theological commitment was on occasion portrayed as a "circle the wagons" mentality. This perception was something

20. Conrad Cherry, *Hurrying Toward Zion: Universities, Divinity Schools, and American Protestantism* (Bloomington: Indiana University Press, 1995), esp. 87-123. For an exploration of Gillespie's concerns about the religious studies paradigm for theological education, see his final opening convocation address as president, "Why a Theological Education?" *Princeton Seminary Bulletin* 25 (2004): 1-11. For a broader account of the role of universities and religion in American life, see George M. Marsden, *The Soul of the American University: From Protestant Establishment to Established Nonbelief* (New York: Oxford University Press, 1994).

of a caricature of Gillespie's position and of the seminary's actual practice. Gillespie was not calling for a monolithic mentality within the school and certainly not for uncritical indoctrination. Theological education, he insisted in one address,

> does not spare its students from the necessity of distancing ourselves, if not from God, then at least from ourselves — our important but limited experiences, our formational but particular traditions, and even our sincere but unexamined convictions. Theological reflection requires us to hear a story about the church that is greater than our own story or that of our faith community. It mandates that we listen to questions and answers that we have never heard before and often wish we did not have to hear now. In our theological education, we must even learn to live with questions for which there are no answers — at least none that are available to us. Our imagination is stretched, our reasoning is pushed, and our tolerance of ambiguity is taxed.[21]

As one looks at the faculty appointments and program of the Gillespie years and those of the previous McCord era, one does *not* have a sense that wagons were being circled. During those years, one sees continuing evidence of creative engagement with the changing face of the church, the academy, and the world.

Biblical Theology: Bernhard Anderson and J. Christiaan Beker

During the Neo-orthodox era, one of the chief efforts to recover unity within the field of biblical studies was the so-called biblical theology that flourished among Presbyterian scholars in the 1940s and 1950s. Whether biblical theology ever constituted anything as unified as a movement is a subject of scholarly debate; but many Presbyterians — among them G. E. Wright, Floyd V. Filson, Otto Piper, and James Smart — approached the Scriptures in a way transcending the polarity between modernists and fundamentalists. They believed, in the words of W. Eugene March, that it was "possible to draw together the results of critical scholarship in such

---

21. Gillespie, "Why a Theological Education?" 2; Gillespie, "Becoming Theologians," *Princeton Seminary Bulletin* 18 (1997): 4-5.

a way that fully honored scientific objectivity while at the same time presenting the Bible in a manner appropriate to its status as Canon." They readily acknowledged that historical criticism had demolished many traditional views of the Bible; but having wrought its destructive work, scholarship could now enter a positive stage, offering a new synthesis friendly to faith. Critical study, they believed, had established the distinctiveness separating biblical religion from other ancient Near Eastern faiths. Moreover, they assumed that the Bible, despite the admitted diversities of its writers and their conditions, exhibited a thematic unity. This unity did not reside, as conservative exegetes had once supposed, in the fact that the Bible presented a single body of doctrinal propositions. The unity of the Bible was dynamic, based upon the action of a God revealing himself to men and women in particular historical events as he worked out a saving purpose culminating in Jesus Christ.[22]

One of the persons sometimes associated with the Old Testament phase of that movement was Bernhard Anderson, whose book *Understanding the Old Testament* was one of the most popular texts of its day, setting a record in sales and in translation into other languages. Anderson, a United Methodist who had served as dean of the divinity school at Drew University, came to Princeton Seminary in 1968 and spent the remainder of his career there until his retirement in 1983. Well-versed in biblical archaeology and the latest trends in historical and exegetical work, he understood the difficulties of rendering the Old Testament into a single narrative readily accessible to contemporary Christians. Yet that goal always remained a central one of his career; he wanted to show how, despite its different genres and contexts, the Old Testament could be read as a Christian book, that is, as part of the one redemptive story reaching its culmination in Jesus Christ. In his inaugural address at Princeton, he suggested that the final possibility of such a reading came from regarding Scripture as a drama and having "an awareness of who the Director of the drama is, . . . and above all the givenness of the plot of the biblical story." Then it becomes possible "to present the biblical drama as 'the story of our life' and the medium of God continuing to speak to his people." As one of his Old Testament successors at Prince-

---

22. W. Eugene March, "'Biblical Theology,' Authority, and the Presbyterians," *Journal of Presbyterian History* 59 (Summer 1981): 113-30; Brevard Childs, *Biblical Theology in Crisis* (Philadelphia: Westminster Press, 1970); James D. Smart, *The Past, Present, and Future of Biblical Theology* (Philadelphia: Westminster Press, 1979).

ton, Dennis Olson, remarked of a later "experiment in Old Testament theology" by Anderson, the latter was attempting "to hold together in some balance the insights of historical criticism and the literary shape of the final form of the text."[23]

Another powerful teacher and scholar of biblical theology — in his case, with the emphasis on New Testament — was J. Christiaan ("Chris") Beker, appointed to the New Testament faculty in 1964. Born in 1924 in a small village in the Netherlands, where his father was pastor of a Dutch Reformed church, Beker experienced a nightmare when the Nazis overran the Netherlands in May 1940, the month he turned 16. He hid himself so that he would not be forced to work in a German labor camp; but then, fearing that his action might bring punishment upon his family, he turned himself in to the Nazis and was sent to work in a factory near Berlin. Sick with typhus and shattered by the fear of Allied bombing by day and by night, he was sent back to his family. Upon recovery from the typhus, he went into hiding out of concern that he might be betrayed and forced to go back with the Germans. As a result of these horrific experiences, he suffered for the remainder of his life from manic-depressive or bipolar disorder. Yet out of his existential agony came the decision to study theology. After studying at Utrecht at the close of the war and being awarded a fellowship that allowed him to study at the University of Chicago, where he received a Ph.D. in 1955, he taught at Union Seminary in New York and the Pacific School of Religion in Berkeley, California, before going to Princeton. Although he was well versed in the technical tools of exegesis and textual criticism, his passion was to bring forth from the New Testament its message of hope in the midst of despair. He wrote ten different books, one of the most discussed being *Paul's Apocalyptic Gospel* (1982). He was an immensely popular teacher, alternately compassionate and profane, as he sought to share what his colleague Daniel Migliore described as his "profound grasp of the dialectic of suffering and hope, etched deep in his soul by his study of the biblical witness and his own life experience."[24]

23. Bernhard W. Anderson, "The Contemporaneity of the Bible," *Princeton Seminary Bulletin* 62 (1969): 50; Dennis T. Olson, "Bernhard W. Anderson, *Contours of Old Testament Biblical Theology* and James Barr, *The Concept of Biblical Theology:* A Review Essay," *Princeton Seminary Bulletin* 21 (2000): 350.

24. Daniel L. Migliore, "J. Christiaan Beker: A Tribute (1924-1999)," *Princeton Seminary Bulletin* 21 (2000): 96-98; quotation on 97. See also Ben C. Ollenburger, "Suffering and Hope: The Story Behind the Book," *Theology Today* 44 (1987): 350-59.

Of course, it must be remembered that Bruce Metzger, who continued teaching until 1983, was still providing not so much a biblical theology per se as the tools for minute textual analysis. One of the great strengths of the Princeton program in biblical studies was that it had room for both the approach of a Beker and a Metzger.

Theology, the Behavioral Sciences, and Ministry: Seward Hiltner and James E. Loder

The appointment in 1961 of Seward Hiltner as professor marked a major step in placing Princeton in the front rank of the field of pastoral theology. Born in 1909 at Tyrone, Pennsylvania, Hiltner graduated from Lafayette College in 1931 and went on to study at the University of Chicago Divinity School. Skipping the basic theological degree, he went straight into a Ph.D. program. Anton T. Boisen, who had become chaplain at a state hospital near Chicago and who pioneered in providing clinical training for ministerial students, enlisted Hiltner in a summer program. Partly as a result of several psychotic episodes that he himself suffered and analyzed, Boisen taught ministerial students to regard the hospital patients as "living human documents" who could teach them about religious experience and mental illness. After initial work with Boisen, Hiltner continued his hospital studies under other early leaders of the clinical movement, and he was won over to Boisen's view that theological insight could be gained from close observation of psychological conflicts. Ordained to the Presbyterian ministry in 1935, Hiltner delayed the completion of his Ph.D. by moving to New York to become the second executive secretary of the Council for the Clinical Training of Theological Students. In 1938, he assumed the post of executive secretary of the commission on religion and health of the Federal Council of Churches. In 1944, he organized the first national conference on clinical training and edited the proceedings in an influential volume, *Clinical Pastoral Training* (1945). During World War II, he brought together an influential discussion group of social scientists, theologians, and psychotherapists, including such important figures as Ruth Benedict, Erich Fromm, Rollo May, Carl Rogers, and Paul Tillich. In 1949, he published *Pastoral Counseling,* which soon became a classic in the field. Then, having already established himself as a commanding figure in the field, he went back to Chicago, joined the divinity school faculty, and finally finished his dissertation. In 1958, he published what many consider his most significant work, *Preface to Pastoral Theology.*[25]

As a pastoral counselor, Hiltner helped to define a burgeoning field. Various forms of psychotherapy, having grown between the World Wars, accelerated even more dramatically after 1945. The vogue of pastoral counseling in part reflected the larger therapeutic culture in which, for some, psychology replaced religion as a way of giving meaning to life and the therapist supplanted the minister as the appropriate guide. At its best, however, the clinical pastoral education movement and the new emphasis upon pastoral counseling did not represent an effort, as James McCord put it in 1975, to "baptize pop psychology with religious patter and peddle it." And in 1961, when he came to Princeton, Hiltner embodied the field at its best. As a counselor, he was influenced by Freudian theories of the personality; but he did not think the average minister had the qualifications to perform classic psychoanalysis and regarded such practice as lying beyond the clerical métier. He preferred a style of counseling similar to that of Carl Rogers in which the minister adopted a largely non-directive stance, listened carefully to the parishioner, mirrored back to him or her what was being said, and in the process created an environment in which the counselee felt accepted and thus potentially freed to gain insight. Pastoral counseling was not, for Hiltner, a matter of giving advice or problem solving — acts that he regarded as almost certain evidence that the counselor had failed. "Insight," Hiltner wrote, "cannot be given; what the counselor does is to set up the conditions so that there is a chance that it may come." Hiltner was acknowledging, in therapeutic language, a classic theological insight: "The wind bloweth where it listeth."[26]

25. "Seward Hiltner, 1909-1984," *Princeton Seminary Bulletin* 7 (1986): 76-78; E. Brooks Holifield, *A History of Pastoral Care in America: From Salvation to Self-Realization* (Nashville: Abingdon Press, 1983). For what follows on Seward Hiltner and James Loder, I am indebted to Gordon Mikoski and Richard Osmer, *With Piety and Learning: The History of Practical Theology at Princeton Theological Seminary, 1812-2012* (Zurich: Lit Verlag, 2011), 139-63. See also Anton T. Boisen, *Out of the Depths: An Autobiographical Study of Mental Disorder and Religious Experience* (New York: Harper, 1960).

26. Susan E. Myers-Shirk, *Helping the Good Shepherd: Pastoral Counselors in a Psychotherapeutic Culture, 1925-1975* (Baltimore: Johns Hopkins University Press, 2009), esp. 86-101; Hiltner quotation on 101; Holifield, *History of Pastoral Care in America*, 269-356. On the larger issue of therapeutic culture, see the classic work by Philip Rieff, *The Triumph of the Therapeutic: Uses of Faith after Freud* (New York: Harper and Row, 1966); for more recent helpful accounts, see Eva S. Moskowitz, *In Therapy We Trust: America's Obsession with Self-*

Although many have regarded Hiltner exclusively as a pastoral counselor, his concern was broader. He had a vision of practical theology as a whole; his major work was, it should be remembered, *Preface to Pastoral Theology,* not his introduction to pastoral counseling. In fact, in the early 1960s he expressed anxiety over efforts to create a specialized field of pastoral counseling, for he feared the breakup of the professional unity of the ministry and the isolation of the counselor from the church. One of his major contributions in *Preface to Pastoral Theology* was conceptualizing ministerial practice in terms of three perspectives: shepherding, communicating, and organizing. The word "perspective" requires emphasis, for Hiltner was not identifying sharply demarcated offices or roles that the minister fulfilled on clearly separate occasions. Rather, he was speaking of dimensions that, to greater or lesser degree, existed in every act of ministry. In employing this analytic framework, Hiltner was inviting the clergy to form a holistic vision of their work and urging greater reflection upon the acts of ministry they performed. "Which perspective best illuminates," the minister might ask, "what I am trying to accomplish in this sermon, meeting, hospital visit, or whatever? And why does this perspective seem most appropriate?" Not only did Hiltner's model encourage a holistic conception of ministry; it also broke free of the older paradigm that implied that the classic disciplines — Bible, theology, and history — provided all that the minister needed to know theologically and that the practical theology department merely offered "how to" instruction in the application of that knowledge. Hiltner — and subsequent scholars in the practical theology department — understood themselves to be engaged in theological reflection, not in purveying mere technique. One of Hiltner's major efforts to push this vision of theological education was Princeton's Doctor of Ministry program, of which he was arguably the chief architect.[27]

Another major contributor to rethinking the way in which the behavioral sciences and theology could be meaningfully related was James E. Loder. A native of Nebraska born in 1931, Loder came from a non-churchgoing family; but when he began to attend church on his own

---

Fulfillment (Baltimore: Johns Hopkins University Press, 2001); and Andrew Joseph Polsky, *The Rise of the Therapeutic State* (Princeton: Princeton University Press, 1991).

27. Rodney Hunter, "A Perspectival Pastoral Theology," in *Turning Points in Pastoral Care: The Legacy of Anton Boisen and Seward Hiltner,* ed. LeRoy Aden and Harold Ellens (Grand Rapids: Baker Book House, 1990), pp. 53-79.

at about the age of 8, his parents supported the decision. After graduating from Carlton College in Minnesota in 1953, Loder came to Princeton Seminary and finished his studies in 1957. At Princeton he could on occasion be feisty. For example, as Dana Wright reported on the basis of an interview he had with Loder not long before the latter's death in 2001, Loder "and several other students refused to take D. Campbell Wyckoff's course in Christian education because it supposedly lacked philosophical depth." Instead of pulling professorial rank on the students, Wyckoff allowed them to create their own course at a level they deemed appropriate as long as it met the academic requirements. Loder also faced deep grief during seminary. His father died during his second year, and he experienced months of depression while also suffering from mononucleosis. He later remembered crying out to God in despair and receiving an overwhelming sense of the divine presence and that all was well with his father. After this experience, he read a seminary text, Emil Brunner's *The Scandal of Christianity,* which helped him understand what he had experienced. A professor recommended that Loder read Kierkegaard, who remained a significant influence for the remainder of Loder's life. He went on to Harvard, where he received a Th.M. and Ph.D. While working on his dissertation, he received a fellowship that allowed him to go to the Menninger Clinic in Topeka, Kansas, where he met Seward Hiltner. In 1962, Loder was invited back to Princeton Seminary to teach Christian education. Campbell Wyckoff, despite his earlier set-to with Loder, recognized talent when he saw it and supported the appointment. Beginning as instructor, Loder eventually became the Synnott Professor of the Philosophy of Education in 1982.[28]

A turning point in his intellectual and personal pilgrimage came in 1970 on the New York State Throughway. En route with his family to Toronto, Loder saw an elderly couple at the side of the highway and stopped to help. Another motorist, having fallen asleep, rammed into Loder's car, flipped it over, and dragged it for some yards, and left Loder trapped under the vehicle. Although death seemed certain, Loder had a powerful sense of the presence of God, and he survived. Describing this event later in his book *The Transforming Moment,* Loder indicated that it forced him "to reenvision the spiritual center of my vocation." Although

28. Freda A. Gardner, "James Edwin Loder, Jr.: A Tribute," *Princeton Seminary Bulletin* 23 (2002): 188-94; Dana R. Wright, "Ruination unto Redemption in the Spirit: A Short Biography of a Reformed 'Wise Guy,'" *Princeton Seminary Bulletin* 23 (2002): 77.

this experience bore parallels to his earlier sense of the presence of God after the death of his father, the experience on the New York Throughway brought a more fundamental intellectual reorientation of his work. "Before 1970," he said in an interview, "I was doing all of my teaching within a basic psychoanalytic model. . . . After 1970 I realized it was the Spirit of God who creates the problem and guides us into truth." It was not that Loder abandoned what he had learned from the personality sciences; rather, he sought to arrive at a paradigm that would do justice to the agency of the human psyche, the reality of human systems of interaction, *and* the prevenience of the divine spirit. As he sought to work through these ideas, he ranged far and deeply. For example, in *The Knight's Move: The Relational Logic of the Spirit in Theology and Science,* a book he co-authored with his friend Jim Neidhardt, who was a physicist at the New Jersey Institute of Technology, the two managed to reach across a spectrum of thinkers, including Niels Bohr, Albert Einstein, and Søren Kierkegaard. In his final book, *The Logic of the Spirit: Human Development in Theological Perspective,* Loder sought to correlate theories of human development by psychologists such as Sigmund Freud, Erik Erikson, and Jean Piaget with theologians such as Kierkegaard (always Kierkegaard for Loder!), Karl Barth, Wolfhart Pannenberg, and Thomas F. Torrance.[29]

As his colleague Professor Freda Gardner observed,

No student who ever came to Jim for help at whatever level failed to be impressed, and many confounded, by the intricate diagrams of his thought and hypotheses scribbled on his office chalkboard. Many, given a "tour" of Jim's thinking and gaining a sense that they understood what he was explaining, realized, almost before reaching the outer door, that they had been witnesses to something powerful and promising but without any certainty about what that was.

29. James Loder, *The Transforming Moment: Understanding Convictional Experiences* (San Francisco: Harper and Row, 1981), 6; Dana R. Wright with John D. Kuentzel, "Are You There?" in *Redemptive Transformation in Practical Theology: Essays in Honor of James E. Loder Jr.,* ed. Dana R. Wright and John D. Kuentzel (Grand Rapids: Eerdmans, 2004), 15-16; W. Jim Neidhardt and James E. Loder, *The Knight's Move: The Relational Logic of the Spirit in Theology and Science* (Colorado Springs: Helmers and Howard, 1992); James E. Loder, *The Logic of the Spirit: Human Development in Theological Perspective* (San Francisco: Jossey-Bass, 1998).

But the passion with which he expressed his ideas and the fervor with which he expected others to engage them (whether they agreed with him or not) made Loder a compelling teacher who regularly drew packed classrooms for non-required courses. He also maintained a rather full schedule of appointments with students who sought his counsel on matters psychological, spiritual, and vocational. When one thinks of the drama of Jim Loder's personal gaze into the Void and the "transforming moment" that followed, perhaps the closest similar recorded crisis in the previous history of the seminary was that of the young Archibald Alexander, striving to make spiritual sense of the topsy-turvy religious world of late-eighteenth-century Virginia.[30]

History, Ecumenics, and Sociology

One of the early appointments in the field of history was James Hastings Nichols, named to the newly defined position in modern European church history in 1962. Nichols was born in Auburn, New York, in 1915. He was the son of Robert Hastings Nichols, who had served as the principal author of the Auburn Affirmation of 1924, whose call for greater theological inclusivity had set on edge the teeth of Princeton Seminary's ultra-conservative faculty majority. James Nichols studied at Yale and Harvard, receiving a Ph.D. from Yale, and then served as assistant professor at Macalester College in Minnesota from 1940 to 1943. From 1943 to 1962, he taught at the University of Chicago, then he answered the call to Princeton Seminary. One of Nichols's major studies, *Romanticism in American Theology,* ironically, was a painstaking historical reconstruction of the Mercersburg Theology of John Williamson Nevin and Philip Schaff, who, in Nichols's well-argued judgment, had gotten the better of Charles Hodge in their ongoing argument over the proper Reformed doctrines of the church and sacraments. In addition to producing a major interpretation of Christianity in the modern era, he also wrote on the ecumenical movement and served as an observer on behalf of the World Alliance of Reformed Churches at the Second Vatican Council in Rome. He served in the 1970s as academic dean of the seminary, where he was noted for his quiet, no-nonsense insistence on scholarly excellence. In one memorable address to incoming students in September 1970, when

---

30. Gardner, "James Edwin Loder, Jr.," 189-90.

the cry had peaked that theological education must be "relevant" to social change, he declared:

> The primary task [of the ministry] is to help men to recognize and respond to the actuality of God. This normally involves social and political action. But no social or political cause *as such* is the same thing as the knowledge and service of God. No cause, whether the movement for a new congress — which I support — or the movement for withdrawal from Vietnam — which I support, or that for full rights for minorities — which I support — can be made the substitute for or equivalent of, obedience to God, without idolatry.

Tragically, Nichols took early retirement due to the early signs of Alzheimer's — a story movingly recounted by his daughter, the novelist Sue Miller.[31]

Other departmental appointments also injected new energy and sometimes new directions into the life of the seminary. In 1968, Karlfried Froehlich, a 38-year-old native of Germany educated at Göttingen and Basel, who had taught church history at Drew University in Madison, New Jersey, joined the history department as professor of early and medieval church history and infused the entire department with his infectious energy. (After 1979, Froehlich turned over the responsibility for the early church to Professor Kathleen McVey, an expert in Syriac Christianity and the first Roman Catholic to be appointed to the seminary faculty.) From 1974 to 1981, before assuming the presidency of Louisville Presbyterian Theological Seminary, John M. Mulder held the post in American church history previously occupied by Lefferts Loetscher. Mulder's research into the impact of religion on the development of Woodrow Wilson added a new cultural and political dimension to the teaching of American church history. Later, some years after the retirement of Nichols, the appointment of James Deming to the post of European church history brought the insights of social history to the department. In 1985, Jane Dempsey Douglass, who had worked on Cal-

---

31. Charles C. West, "Memorial Minute: James Hastings Nichols," *Princeton Seminary Bulletin* 12 (1991): 327-30; James H. Nichols, "Theological Education at Princeton," *Princeton Seminary Bulletin* 63 (1970): 42-43; Sue Miller, *The Story of My Father: A Memoir* (New York: Alfred A. Knopf, 2003).

vin's notion of women and freedom and had served as president of the American Society of Church History, joined the department; during part of her tenure she was also president of the World Alliance of Reformed Churches — the same position that John A. Mackay had once held. After the retirements of Edward Dowey and Karlfried Froehlich, Elsie A. McKee and Paul Rorem, both Ph.D. graduates of the seminary, returned to take up faculty positions. McKee expanded her expertise in Calvin to include the history of worship as part of her academic portfolio, and Rorem, an expert on the pseudo-Dionysian corpus, also created important new courses. In a word, the varieties of academic method and expertise increased significantly during the McCord-Gillespie years.

Ultimately the most controversial appointment in the department occurred with the election of M. Richard Shaull to the position of mission and ecumenics in 1962. Born in Pennsylvania in 1919, Shaull attended Elizabethtown College and then Princeton Seminary from 1938 to 1941. After a brief pastorate in the United States, he entered missionary service in Latin America, serving in Colombia. He returned to the United States to write a Th.D. dissertation at Princeton Seminary, "The Power of God in the Life of Man: A Study of Protestant and Catholic Concepts of New Life in Christ," submitted in 1959. He subsequently went to Brazil to teach at the Presbyterian Seminary in Campinas. Forced out of the country when a military junta came to power, Shaull was invited to assume the position at Princeton Seminary. During this period of revolutionary political change, Shaull himself was considerably radicalized and wished to align Christianity with the forces calling for a new social order. In an era of many Princeton seminarians themselves looking for revolutionary change, the classes of Dick Shaull often drew massive attendance by those who considered him something of a guru. It was a designation Shaull would have rejected for himself, however, for he was not interested in establishing his own authority over students but in empowering them. He did not hesitate to confront authority, including the authority of the institution where he was teaching. Perhaps it was that feeling of discomfort with the authority of the school that prompted him to leave Princeton in 1980.[32]

Subsequent appointments to the Luce Professorship of Ecumenics

32. Mark L. Taylor, "M. Richard Shaull: A Tribute," *Princeton Seminary Bulletin* 24 (2003): 343-47.

and Missions held by Shaull brought significant variations. Samuel Hugh Moffett, a missionary to China and to Korea as well as son of the American Presbyterian minister often credited with starting Protestant missionary work in Korea, held the post for roughly five years. Alan P. Neely, who had served as a missionary in Colombia and as professor of missiology in the Southeastern (Baptist) Theological Seminary in North Carolina, filled the Luce chair from 1988 until his retirement in 1996. A committed Baptist, Neely knew at first hand the pain created by the battles within the Southern Baptist Convention and by the takeover of the denomination by fundamentalists. He resisted that coup as a perversion of a heritage that he loved deeply, and he was one of the founders of the Alliance of Baptists, a national organization of progressive Baptists. Yet despite events that would have left many embittered, Neely continued to exhibit an irenic and generous spirit that refused to be confined by ecclesiastical partisanship. At the heart of his ministry was a desire to build relationships among people of different cultures and traditions. During a fairly lengthy interim between Luce professors, Andrew F. Walls, the distinguished Scottish missiologist, filled in as a guest professor of world Christianity until the Luce chair was split into two appointments: one in missional theology occupied by Darrell F. Guder and the other in history held by Luis N. Rivera-Pagán. To enumerate these appointments is to realize that there was no single mold into which Princeton missiologists were cast in the McCord-Gillespie years.[33]

The same thing might be said of the appointments made to the chair in Christianity and society. When Samuel Blizzard was forced to take early retirement, he was replaced in 1976 by Gibson Winter, an ordained Episcopal priest who had achieved notoriety with several books, most notably *The Suburban Captivity of the Churches,* while he was teaching at the University of Chicago. Winter had first broached the idea of the book in an article for the *Christian Century* in the late 1950s. The gist of his argument was that the integrity of American Christianity had been compromised by the enthrallment of denominations to creating new congregations in the burgeoning suburbs while urban churches were dying. A credible Christian witness required the linking of suburban and urban churches in the sharing of funds and in planning common ministry. As this thumbnail sketch suggests, Winter, while having sociological knowl-

33. For a sketch about Neely, see my "Alan Preston Neely: A Tribute," *Princeton Seminary Bulletin* 25 (2004): 106-8.

edge, was really more of a social ethicist than a sociologist in the tradition of Sam Blizzard. With the retirement of Winter in 1985, the seminary filled the post with sociologist Richard K. Fenn, who came from the University of Maine. Likewise an Episcopal priest, Fenn, who has recently retired from the seminary, made the chair once again unambiguously a post in sociology, though in his case it was far more in the tradition of theoretical sociology than the empirical "number crunching" manner of Sam Blizzard. A post successively occupied by men as different as Blizzard, Winter, and Fenn was scarcely monolithically defined.

Developments in Theology and Ethics

As one looks at the appointments in theology during the McCord-Gillespie years, no single person can fully summarize the breadth of concerns and emphases there manifested, but arguably the one who best epitomized the diversities within the department and certainly had the longest period of service was Daniel L. Migliore. A native of Pittsburgh born to a Presbyterian manse in 1935, Migliore majored in history as an undergraduate at Westminster College in New Wilmington, Pennsylvania, then took his basic theological study at Princeton Seminary during the last three years of John Mackay's presidency. He received his Ph.D. from Princeton University in 1964 and spent an additional year of advanced study at Tübingen in 1965-1966. He was appointed to the seminary faculty as an instructor in New Testament in 1962 and was transferred to the field of theology in 1966. He retired as the Charles Hodge Professor of Systematic Theology in 2009. Migliore's life and career at Princeton thus stretched from his student days under Mackay, to faculty appointment early in the McCord era, service through all of the Gillespie years, and retirement during the administration of the current president, Iain R. Torrance. Seldom has any member of the faculty enjoyed a period of service of comparable length since the tenures of Charles Hodge and William Henry Green in the nineteenth century or William Park Armstrong in the early twentieth. Since the 1950s, the only person to exceed Migliore in years of service has been James Franklin Armstrong, who graduated with the class of 1954, began teaching Old Testament at the seminary in 1956, and over the years served as registrar, director of admissions, the James Lenox Librarian, and the dean of academic affairs, retiring in 2005.

Migliore not only lived through a considerable portion of the seminary's history; he served as a bridge, mediating the concerns of the so-called Neo-orthodox era of theology with some of the newer themes that have emerged since the 1960s. For example, his *Called to Freedom* (1980) employed classic theological figures such as Calvin and Barth to show the resources that they might bring to the project of human liberation. Particularly notable was Migliore's conviction that liberation theology spoke not only to those whom Franz Fanon had called the wretched of the earth, but also to relatively comfortable North Americans, people who had not known economic oppression or want and yet needed to be freed of the bourgeois distortions of the gospel. Among these was the middle-class propensity to make the gospel a private affair or to take refuge in a biblicism that actually denied the living Christ to whom Scripture witnesses. Some reviewers wished that "the author had listened more to the voice of the poor and exploited in black America and the Third World, and less to Calvin, Barth, Luther, and Jüngel." But the criticism missed the deeper point that Migliore was making — namely, that classical theology had much to offer to theologies of liberation as well as the other way around. One sees the same desire to clarify and, where possible, to find grounds of agreement in Migliore's *Faith Seeking Understanding: An Introduction to Christian Theology* (1991), a book that, as one writer rightly described it in a cover blurb, "manages to be at once deeply traditional and freshly contemporary." Of particular delight were the imaginary theological dialogues that he created between figures such as Barth, Bultmann, Reinhold Niebuhr, and advocates of feminist and liberationist theologies. The dialogues managed to convey considerable insight and wit at the same time. In these and his other books, one sees in Daniel Migliore what his colleagues and many classes of students have found: a man passionate about Reformed theology, uncommonly lucid in its presentation, eager to bring it into dialogue with the broader Christian tradition, and scrupulously fair in his presentations of alternative views.[34]

During the McCord years, Princeton Seminary theologians also made a significant contribution to the rethinking of the confessional

---

34. Daniel L. Migliore, *Called to Freedom: Liberation Theology and the Future of Christian Doctrine* (Philadelphia: Westminster Press, 1980); review of *Called to Freedom* by Noel Leo Erskine, in *Journal of the American Academy of Religion* 49 (September 1981): 532; Daniel L. Migliore, *Faith Seeking Understanding: An Introduction to Christian Theology* (Grand Rapids: Eerdmans, 1991). The cover blurb was from Cornelius Plantinga Jr.

standards of the United Presbyterian Church in the U.S.A. — a new denomination formed by the merger in 1958 of the Presbyterian Church in the U.S.A. with the smaller United Presbyterian Church of North America. The first General Assembly of the new denomination charged a committee with the task of preparing a "brief contemporary statement of faith." The committee's chair was Princeton's Edward A. Dowey; and before the committee's completion of its work, others appointed to the committee from the seminary faculty included George Hendry and Charles West.

Charles West, the newest of the three to Princeton, was an early faculty appointee of the McCord years. In 1961, he became associate professor of ethics, and two years later he assumed the Stephen Colwell Chair of Christian Ethics. (The name of the chair was a fitting memorial to Stephen Colwell, a trustee of the seminary from 1843 to 1871, who, despite his success as a northern industrialist, had serious reservations about the moral implications of market capitalism and has been seen by some scholars as a forerunner of the Social Gospel.) Born in Plainfield, New Jersey, in 1921, West attended Columbia University, graduating in 1942. By the end of college, he recalled, "I broke down in sheer exhaustion from the effort of trying to promote all good causes and stand for all good things." Realizing in his weariness "that there is an overwhelming and forgiving love of God which reaches into my life and which upholds me," West decided to attend Union Seminary in New York. Four years later, after completing his B.D. at Union and taking an extra year of study in ethics at Yale Divinity School, he was ordained to the Presbyterian ministry, and he and his wife Ruth were off to China as missionaries. Following several years in China, during which time the communist government came to power, West went to Germany, where he served as a fraternal worker in Berlin under the World Council of Churches. From 1956 to 1961, he was associate director of the Ecumenical Institute at Bossey. He later expressed his interest in the study of ethics in these terms: "Not truth in itself but true understanding of human relations with each other and with God . . . this has been the object of my search." West was convinced that true Christian ethics had to be missionary and ecumenical in character. Communities, he observed, "that close in on themselves become pockets of enmity toward other communities." He saw the church as the "one community that depends finally not on the good-will or the affections of a particular group of people, but on the love of Christ which binds us all, which forgives us all, which gives the whole world new life."

Hence, the ecumenical, missionary, and ethical tasks of Christianity ultimately belonged together.[35]

Although the General Assembly's committee for the preparation of a new statement of faith did not achieve unanimity on all matters, there was a broad consensus that reflected both the themes of the Neo-orthodox era and some of the new concerns emerging in the 1960s. After initial study, Dowey's committee requested and received a mandate to make a broader review of the Reformed confessional heritage. In 1965 the group proposed a *Book of Confessions;* and two years later, after some changes suggested by a committee of review, it was officially adopted by the denomination. In the *Book of Confessions* were included not only a contemporary statement (the "Confession of 1967") but also documents from various periods of church history. Although most discussion during the revision process focused upon C-67, as it was often popularly called, one must underscore the significance of the entire book. The fact that the denomination now had a multiple confessional base, composed of documents with somewhat different emphases and reflecting diverse historical settings, stood as an implicit reminder that no one creed could capture the faith in its fullness and that every creed is at least in part a creature of its own time and place.[36]

C-67 took as its central theme: "In Jesus Christ, God was reconciling the world to himself." Explicating that motif, the confession echoed many of the themes of the theological renaissance of the previous thirty

35. Stewart Davenport, *Friends of the Unrighteous Mammon: Northern Christians and Market Capitalism, 1815-1860* (Chicago: University of Chicago Press, 2008), 107-21; Bruce Morgan, "Stephen Colwell," in *Sons of the Prophets: Leaders in Protestantism from Princeton Seminary,* ed. Hugh T. Kerr (Princeton: Princeton University Press, 1962), 123-47. See the very informative dialogue between Charles West and his wife Ruth in Ruth C. West, "An Ecumenical Journey: A Conversation between Ruth and Charles West," *Princeton Seminary Bulletin* 12 (1991): 119-33; quotations on 119, 120, 123. For illustrations of West's desire to build dialogue across barriers, see Charles C. West, *Communism and the Theologians: Study of an Encounter* (Philadelphia: Westminster Press, 1958); and West, *Outside the Camp: The Christian and the World* (Garden City, NY: Doubleday, 1959); and his inaugural address, "The Missionary Context of Christian Ethics," *Princeton Seminary Bulletin* 58 (1964): 20-33.

36. In this and the next several paragraphs, I draw on insights first developed in my "Redefining Confessionalism: American Presbyterians in the Twentieth Century," in *The Confessional Mosaic: Presbyterians and Twentieth-Century Theology,* ed. Milton J Coalter, John M. Mulder, and Louis B. Weeks (Louisville: Westminster/John Knox Press, 1990), 59-83, esp. 66-70.

years: the priority of God's activity in redemption, the radical sinfulness of humankind, the christocentric nature of revelation, and the role of the Holy Spirit in bringing God's work in Christ to fulfillment. The last two themes shaped the confession's much-discussed treatment of Scripture. To avoid any hint of bibliolatry, C-67 subordinated the Bible to Christ: "The one sufficient revelation of God is Jesus Christ, the Word of God incarnate." The central theme of Scripture was its witness to that living Word — a witness that could be made efficacious only by "the illumination of the Holy Spirit." Although the Bible remained the indispensable "witness without parallel," and although the church received it "as the word of God written," the confession deliberately rendered the "w" in *word* in lowercase to avoid any suggestion of inerrancy and to prevent the notion that one could somehow establish the authority of Scripture without reference to its christocentric focus or independent of the work of the Holy Spirit. This emphasis freed the confession to acknowledge the fully human character of the Scriptures; and, for the first time in a creedal statement, American Presbyterians endorsed modern biblical scholarship: "The Scriptures, given under the guidance of the Holy Spirit, are nevertheless the words of men, conditioned by the language, thought forms, and literary fashions of the places and times at which they were written. . . . The church, therefore, has an obligation to approach the Scriptures with literary and historical understanding."

To confess was not primarily to affirm certain beliefs (though the act entailed these), but rather to bear "a present witness to God's grace in Jesus Christ." That witness was decisively oriented toward the world. As God was in Christ reconciling the world to himself, Christians were summoned to a ministry of reconciliation. All of the church's words and actions were to be evaluated in light of this mission; and all of its ordinances and polity were to be instruments to that end. Or, as C-67 succinctly summarized: "To be reconciled to God is to be sent into the world as his reconciling community." The responsibility of the church to be a reconciling agent was not left in the abstract. C-67 listed four examples of concerns to which the church should address itself: (1) racial and ethnic discrimination; (2) the dangers of nationalism in the achievement of peace, justice, and freedom; (3) the prevalence of "enslaving poverty" throughout the world; and (4) "anarchy in sexual relationships." To a degree unprecedented in a confessional document, political, social, and economic issues emerged as matters of theological import. Equally important was the tone of the statements, which implied a new commitment to prophetic judgment of existing inequities within society and which appeared to cast the church in the role of social critic. And the point to be underscored in this context is that scholars from Princeton Theological Seminary were in the forefront of shaping and stating this Presbyterian theological consensus. Given the conflicting currents then at work within American religion, 1967 was about the last moment when a confessional accord of this length and depth could have been reached.

When, roughly a decade and a half later, the United Presbyterian Church (the "northern" church) and the Presbyterian Church in the U.S. (the "southern" church) reunited in 1983 to form the PC(USA), the task of preparing a new confessional statement was again placed before the church. Princeton seminary faculty again played an important role. Jane Dempsey Douglass, professor of historical theology; Clarice Martin, assistant professor of New Testament; and E. David Willis, professor of systematic theology, all served on the committee charged with drafting a new statement. In the years between the adoption of the *Book of Confessions* and the reunion of 1983, Protestant theology had become more relentlessly plural and contextual. Various theologies — feminist, black, liberationist, womanist, and resurgent evangelical, to name only a few of the options — competed; but none succeeded in dominating the voice of mainstream Protestantism in general or Presbyterianism in particular. The makeup of the drafting committee was instructive. The committee that wrote C-67 had only one woman and one African American member; the remainder were white males who, with one or two exceptions, would have been considered Neo-orthodox. (And one of these resigned, complaining of Neo-orthodox domination of the committee.) The committee appointed after the 1983 reunion included a significant number of women as well as men, persons holding a wide variety of theological views, and members of various ethnic constituencies. The committee also sought to hear the diversity of opinions within the church at large. It held forums at various locations and circulated an early draft of the statement for comment by the church, receiving over 15,000 written communications in response. Many of the concerns received by the committee were incorporated in the final version of the statement. While longer than the Apostles' or Nicene creeds, the resulting "A Brief Statement of Faith" was much shorter than any other document in the *Book of Confessions.* It consisted of just over 550 words set in broken line format, designed for use in worship and instruction. The document deftly affirmed traditional Trinitarian views, kept the christocentric emphasis of

C-67, spoke of the fall and redemption of humanity, but also incorporated phrases and themes of particular resonance for those deeply committed to feminist, liberationist, and environmentalist theologies. The genius of "A Brief Statement" was that it took contemporary concerns and grounded them in the traditional Trinitarian faith of the church catholic. At the time, some observers marveled that people of very diverse theological views were able to achieve this unity, but they also suspected that agreement might dissolve if the members of the committee — or of the church at large — began to spell out what they meant by the brief generalizations they had adopted.[37]

Princeton and Pluralism in the McCord-Gillespie Years

As diversity increased within mainstream Protestantism and within the Presbyterian Church, it did so at Princeton as well, though not as rapidly as in many other places. While the faculty has members with liberationist and feminist sympathies, these are not so pronounced as they have been at many other theological schools.

Princeton did begin to accommodate gender and ethnic diversity. For example, in terms of faculty composition, it hired its first permanent black teacher in the person of Geddes Hanson, appointed as an instructor in pastoral theology in 1969 and then rising through the ranks until his recent retirement. Hanson concentrated mainly on theories of church organization and administration and was one of the stalwart workshop leaders of the Doctor of Ministry program. In 1971, Edler Garnet Hawkins accepted the seminary's appointment to serve as professor of practical theology and coordinator of black studies at Princeton Seminary. Born in the Bronx in 1908, Hawkins went to high school there, then took undergraduate training at Bloomfield College in New Jersey, and subsequently studied for the ministry at Union Seminary in New York, graduating in 1938. President Henry Sloan Coffin was a trusted counselor, and faculty members Reinhold Niebuhr, Paul Tillich, and Harry Ward heavily influenced Hawkins. Invited to become the organizing pastor of St. Augustine Presbyterian Church, which was "a new church development in a racially changing neighborhood," Hawkins had relative

---

37. For further discussion of "A Brief Statement of Faith," see my "Presbyterians Confess Their Faith Anew," *Christian Century* 107 (July 11-18, 1990): 676-80.

freedom to determine how his ministry could best be developed. Not so much a lone ranger as the inspirer of a group of committed women and men in his congregation, he encouraged the church to attack what was called the "Bronx slave market," where unemployed black women would gather to await being picked up for a day's work as domestics, often for wages as low as fifteen cents per hour. He encouraged his people to secure revision of Bronx housing codes that were used to exploit black residents, and he was also instrumental in fighting the local political machine that helped perpetuate these injustices. In addition to these activities, he served on a variety of presbytery committees, represented the Presbyterian Church at the National Council of Churches, helped to bring a black caucus into existence within his denomination, and was elected the first African American moderator of the United Presbyterian General Assembly in 1964.[38]

Later, other African American scholars would join the faculty, most in the Gillespie era but a few (in a time of more limited availability of positions due to the economic downturn) in the Torrance era as well. Clarice Martin served for a period as untenured professor in New Testament. Peter J. Paris, a distinguished social ethicist who probed the social teachings of the black churches and served as president of the American Academy of Religion, taught for more than twenty years at Princeton Seminary. Cleophus J. LaRue has brought homiletic expertise, especially in the topic of preaching in African American traditions. Luke Powery's interests in preaching involve performance studies, especially as related to the African diaspora. Yolanda Pierce joined the history department as professor of African American religion and liaison with the Princeton University Center of African American Studies. Professor Pierce, the first Pentecostal appointment to the faculty, has researched eighteenth- and nineteenth-century African American spiritual and slave narratives, memoirs and autobiographies, as well as other religious writing and has a major interest in contemporary black church traditions.[39]

Sang Hyun Lee, appointed in the 1980s and only recently retired from Princeton, became the first Asian American to teach in the theology department. His simultaneous interests in the colonial New England theo-

---

38. "Edler Garnett Hawkins — Urban Pastor," *Journal of Presbyterian History* 51 (Winter 1973): 373-75.

39. The enumerations and computations in the paragraphs that follow are based chiefly on various editions of the *Princeton Seminary Catalogue.*

logian Jonathan Edwards and work on theological topics relating to Korean Americans made him a unique cross-cultural theological bridge, a role that he fulfilled not only in his courses but also as director of the Program for Asian American Theology and Ministry. Choon-Leong Seow, professor of Old Testament with interests in wisdom literature and the history of Israelite religion, now serves as interim director of the Asian American Theology and Ministry program. Bo Karen Lee teaches spirituality and historical theology.

Also created in the Gillespie years was the John A. Mackay Professorship, which has brought for short-term appointment a long list of men and women from Latin America, Asia, and Europe — scholars who usually serve either a semester or a year, their rotating presences enriching the seminary community's appreciation of the varieties within world Christianity.

The first continuing appointment of a woman professor to the faculty came in 1961 with the appointment of Freda A. Gardner as assistant professor of Christian education. She eventually attained promotion to associate professor in 1977 — much longer, it should be noted, than would ordinarily have been the case in such promotions. In fact, as Chris Beker noted at his retirement dinner in 1994, Freda Gardner came to the seminary at a time when "women students were sequestered in Tennent Hall, and their voices were scarcely heard in classroom sessions," and when "she had, until the situation was corrected much later, the dubious distinction of being a 'permanent assistant professor.'" After becoming one of the most influential Christian educators in the Presbyterian Church, she retired as full professor in 1992, and subsequently was elected as moderator of the Presbyterian General Assembly. She was the only woman with faculty rank until joined in 1970 by instructors Elizabeth Edwards and Katharine Doob Sakenfeld. Professor Sakenfeld has spent her entire career at Princeton Seminary, along the way winning election to the presidency of the Society of Biblical Literature, serving as director of Ph.D. studies, and doing much creative work on feminist biblical hermeneutics. It should perhaps also be noted that the first woman to occupy a faculty post at the rank of full professor was Jane Dempsey Douglass, former president of the American Society of Church History, who joined the history department as professor of historical theology in 1985.[40]

This account should also take into account the various programs

40. J. Christiaan Beker, "Farewell Remarks," *Princeton Seminary Bulletin* 16 (1995): 36.

and offices begun in recent decades to address diversity: for example, Women's Studies, the Hispanic/Latina(o) Leadership Program, the Office of Multicultural Relations, the Hispanic Theological Initiative, the Program for Asian American Theology and Ministry, as well as the Program for African American Studies in Ministry. All of these programs and faculty appointments — and, of course, the rising number of women and the greater number of ethnic groups represented in the student body — are all causes for rejoicing. These changes represent the direction in which Princeton Seminary is committed to move even further, for progress has been slower than most leaders of the seminary would wish. Yet, on balance, the McCord-Gillespie years did experience a growth of new intellectual specialties and perspectives within the faculty and greater diversity with regard to gender, race, and ethnicity.

A Postscript on Diversity at Princeton

It can be misleading, of course, to enumerate faculty appointments, new programs, and rising numbers of women and non-Anglo students as evidence of smooth and uninterrupted growth in diversity. The increased presence of women on campus over the last few decades provides an illustration of the pains and difficulties of change. By Samuel Miller's account, "pious females" raised money for the seminary in its first years, and women probably cooked for students in the refectory. They ran eating clubs for students by the end of the nineteenth century, one of which (the Benham Club) was named for Anna Benham, in whose home it met. Yet for most of its history Princeton Seminary was overwhelmingly a bastion of male dominance. The school's leaders assumed, as did most (male) Protestants of the time, that the Bible placed sharp limits upon the things women could do within the church. Thus in 1919, when the nation debated whether to give suffrage to women through a constitutional amendment and when the Presbyterian Church was experiencing rumbles of discontent about the limited role of women in the denomination, Benjamin Warfield wrote an article insisting that Paul's "prohibition of speaking in the church to women is precise, absolute, and all-inclusive." To claim otherwise was to deny the authority of God's revelation. Moreover, he suggested that the underlying assumptions of modern feminism and those of the apostle Paul were "rooted in a fundamental difference" about "the constitution of the human race." "To the feminist movement," he noted, "the human race is made up of individuals; a woman is just another individual by the side of the man; and it can see no reason for any differences in dealing with the two." But for the apostle "the human race is made up of families, and every several organism, the church included, is composed of families, united together by this or that bond. The relation of the sexes in the family follows it therefore into the church." In short, the family as headed by the husband and father was the model for church and society.[41]

Such rigidity began to soften after 1930 within the Presbyterian Church in the U.S.A. Although the denomination voted down the ordination of female clergy in 1930, almost 40 percent of the presbyteries endorsed the change, and the denomination approved the election of women as ruling elders. Then, in 1938, the church officially recognized the position of Certified Church Worker, a designation chiefly for women functioning as Christian educators. Several years later, in response to a General Assembly suggestion that Presbyterian colleges or schools of Christian education affiliate with seminaries, the Tennent School moved to Princeton under the aegis of Princeton Theological Seminary. In 1956 the General Assembly finally gave approval to the ordination of female clergy. Yet none of these changes suggested that a tidal wave of egalitarian inclusivity had rolled across the denomination. Even when the path to ordained ministry had been theoretically opened to all, relatively few women went to seminary in the first ten to fifteen years after the 1956 decision; and many of them went to become Christian educators, not clergy. As late as 1969, when seminaries reported an uptick of women students — numbers that would grow dramatically within the next couple of decades — the actual total of ordained women among nearly 13,000 Presbyterian clergy was only 69. This undoubtedly had much to do with the culture of seminaries. As Lois Boyd and R. Douglas Brackenridge have observed:

> Oral accounts indicate that women assumed seminary would provide a gender-inclusive environment; instead they encountered passive opposition from male colleagues, professors, and administrators. They not uncommonly were counseled to seek

41. Benjamin B. Warfield, "Paul on Women Speaking in the Church," *The Presbyterian* (October 30, 1919): 9; *The Benham Club of Princeton, New Jersey* (Princeton: Privately printed, 1912).

unordained positions. Moreover, women complained of professors referring to class members as "men," using masculine pronouns in reference to God, and producing syllabi devoid of subjects of special interest to women.[42]

Princeton Seminary was not immune to these problems. Professor Freda A. Gardner, now emerita, has recalled a story told to her by Harriet Pritchard, one of the women who held a temporary position in Christian education prior to Gardner's appointment. On one occasion, according to Pritchard, John Mackay visited the women in Tennent Hall and "basically asked us all to become 'courageous spinsters.'" As Pritchard interpreted his remarks, Mackay was concerned that women had come to seminary primarily to find husbands and that they might well distract male students from their ministerial preparation. After Gardner moved into an apartment in Tennent Hall in 1961, she heard additional stories of Mackay having visited the women's residence to scold them for "stealing my men from their calls to ministry." Concern about the implications of women in the School of Christian Education also appeared in a memo to the administration drafted by the two senior professors in Christian education during the first year that the Tennent School was in Princeton:

> It now seems that marital mortality is a serious problem. This is not undesirable, but it does affect our policy on admissions.... We must not allow the marriage problem to become a joke.... Our objectives will be realized even though marriage takes place, if we can make the students aware of their responsibility to the church that educated them and conscious of their vocations even though married.... We cannot prevent marriage, nor do we desire to do so.... We need to stress the obligation of those trained in our School to become educational leaders.

The memo expressed slightly different concerns than Mackay's remarks to the women. The memo voiced fears that women might marry and abandon their vocations, Mackay that the men themselves might be sto-

42. Lois A. Boyd and R. Douglas Brackenridge, *Presbyterian Women in America: Two Centuries of a Quest for Status,* 2nd ed. (Westport, CT: Greenwood Press, 1996), 122-23, 128, 136. See also Margaret Bendroth, "An Understated Tale of Epic Social Change: Women's Ordination 50 Years Ago and Now," *Journal of Presbyterian History* 83 (Fall/Winter 2005): 105-17.

len "from their calls to ministry" by female students. Yet both came down to the same anxiety: women were viewed as a potentially disruptive presence within a theological world that still thought of itself as male. Under these circumstances, it is not surprising that women might wonder how, or if, they had a place in the community. One female student from the 1970s, who has subsequently gone on to a distinguished career in ministry, observed: "The men took themselves for granted. They asked women 'Why are you here?'"[43]

Even as professors, women often heard the same question. In one of Freda Gardner's classes, all male, a student referred to the church's Women's Association as the "stitch and bitch" club — a comment that prompted laughter from the entire class and no rebuttals from fellow students. (To their credit, many of these men later came back to campus as alumni and, with a "raised" consciousness about gender stereotypes, sought out Professor Gardner and apologized for their earlier insensitivity.) When Karl Barth came to Princeton in the early 1960s to deliver the Annie Kinkead Warfield Lectures, James McCord introduced him to Gardner as one of the newest faculty appointments. Incredulous, the venerable Swiss theologian asked: "Vat? A voman?" Of her own experience in preparing for ministry and then coming to Princeton, Professor Katharine Doob Sakenfeld has observed:

> In all my years before arriving at PTS I had encountered not one female minister or even a trained female Christian educator: not in home congregations in three states, not in college in Ohio, not while I was in seminary or Ph.D. studies. When I was ordained in 1970 I knew no other ordained woman minister (though there were a few, even in the Presbyterian Church). Furthermore, through all my advanced studies in the 1960s I never had a female teacher nor heard the word "feminism". . . . Being the first of anything casts a certain aura about you — sometimes an aura of blessing but more often an aura of "odd."

Especially in her early years of teaching at Princeton, Sakenfeld, in company with other women faculty as well as the female students they were

---

43. Freda A. Gardner and Katharine Doob Sakenfeld, "In the Beginning Male and Female: Then *She* Came to Seminary," Frederick Neumann Lecture delivered at Princeton Theological Seminary, October 27, 2011.

teaching, encountered "on the part of many, serious questioning about whether women were called [to ministry] in the same way that men claimed to be." Even today, in a theologically diverse student body, some of whom come from backgrounds in which they have never met a clergywoman, the question still arises from time to time. Princeton's adjustment to diversity — whether in matters of gender, ethnicity, or race — is not a completed chapter in the seminary's life but an ongoing process.[44]

44. Gardner and Sakenfeld, "In the Beginning Male and Female."

Princeton in the Twenty-First Century

O N SEPTEMBER 14, 2004, Iain R. Torrance addressed the first opening convocation of his presidency at Princeton Seminary. He proposed "to say a little about how I see the world, how the world has changed, and how I believe this seminary may fit in and make a difference." With a few broad evocative strokes drawn partly from the work of Jonathan Sacks, Chief Rabbi of the United Hebrew Congregations of the Commonwealth, and partly from Alasdair MacIntyre, Torrance noted that "we are now living amidst the fragments of the morality of the past" and "have lost confidence in grand metanarratives." Yet various religions continue to abide, to prosper, and sometimes to speak in strident voices. The problem is the need to exorcise "Plato's ghost" — the notion "that truth is unreachable but objective, and it follows that if I am right, then you are wrong." (Perhaps there is here a hint of Émile Cailliet's plea to abandon the "ontological deviation" that had marred western philosophy since Plato?) In any event, Torrance followed Sacks in asserting that what the current situation demands is not so much the affirmation of universals upon which everyone can agree — these tend in the present era to be rather watery and insubstantial. Rather, we need to allow a realm within which the ultimate commitments of each religion or persuasion can be honored — a "space to grant dignity to one another's absolutes." While affirming what Sacks had said, Torrance suggested that something more than space — as important as that might be — was also needed. "But as a Christian," the new president noted, "I would add that we are also called not to be afraid. Where God is, I believe there is an absence of fear, an increase of love, and increased dissatisfaction with the way things are." A remarkable ideal was being set forth. It was emphatically *not* a call to syncretism — the blending of religions into something like an overcooked stew in which all distinctive flavors are lost. Rather, it was a call for Christians to explore and reaffirm their traditions in a spirit free from fear and enlivened by a charity that allows Christian believers and adherents of other faiths to learn from each other while respecting, in Sacks's phrase, the dignity of their differences.[1]

Six months later, in his inaugural address, Torrance suggested how the reading of Scripture might inform the theological task. He began with an arresting quotation from Stanley Hauerwas: "No task is more important than for the Church to take the Bible out of the hands of individual Christians in North America. North American Christians are trained to believe that they are capable of reading the Bible without spiritual and moral transformation." What especially troubled Torrance was that "we are now in a context in which our tradition, the Christian tradition, has reached virtual deadlock over a whole series of issues, a zero-sum game in which if there are winners there are losers also." He found part of the problem to lie in the prevailing assumption that individual Christians, faced with disputed questions, could pick up the Bible and find there ready answers to the queries they had posed. In fact, their approach reflected "a cultural narcissism" in which they often simply projected their own assumptions into the Bible. Hence, the title of the inaugural address: "Beyond Solipsism." Torrance noted how Scripture often does not directly answer the questions we may pose to it. Jesus, for example, "evaded the question" when asked, "Is it lawful for a man to divorce his wife?" He "instead reached back to a fundamental vision or awareness for humankind," saying: "In the beginning it was not so." In his closing paragraphs, which in a coded way also invited consideration of "Princetonian exceptionalism," Torrance called for a theological education intended

to feed the imagination of our students and to wean it from the cultural narcissism to which I have referred. We can pay critical

1. Iain R. Torrance, "More than Regent's Park?" *Princeton Seminary Bulletin* 25 (2004): 240-47; quotations on 241, 243, 245; Jonathan Sacks, *The Dignity of Difference: How to Avoid the Clash of Civilizations*, rev. ed. (London and New York: Continuum, 2003). For a thoughtful commentary on the questions posed by other religions, see Richard Fox Young, "Interreligious Literacy and Hermeneutical Responsibility: Can There Be a Theological Learning from Other Religions, or Only a Phenomenological-Historical Learning from Them?" *Theology Today* 66 (October 2009): 330-45.

attention to our curriculum so as to prepare people who do not fear or demonize difference; we can provide a context within which that which is controversial may be safely debated. We can teach about the indirectness of truth.

As a way of modeling that style of education, Torrance had included within the inaugural activities a symposium that brought together diverse participants: David Ford, Regius Professor of Divinity at the University of Cambridge, and Setri Nyomi, general secretary of the World Alliance of Reformed Churches; but also Peter Ochs, professor of modern Judaic studies at the University of Virginia, and Libyan Muslim scholar Aref Ali Nayed, then a visiting fellow at Cambridge and, as of this writing, one of those deeply involved in the struggle for a new post-Qaddafi order in his native land. At the symposium, these scholars of the Abrahamic faiths focused upon the interpretation of the scriptures of their traditions with a view, as the new president said, toward allowing "the notion of scriptural reading to question our practices, institutions, and curricula."[2]

A native of Scotland, Iain Richard Torrance came from a family of distinguished theological scholars. He pursued his higher education at the Universities of Edinburgh, St. Andrews, and Oxford. Ordained to the ministry of the Church of Scotland in 1982, he served for several years as pastor of a parish in the Shetland Islands, where he and his wife Morag had their two children. In 1985, he assumed a post as lecturer in New Testament at Queen's College in Birmingham and then taught patristics and New Testament at the University of Birmingham. In 1993, he went to the University of Aberdeen and eventually was appointed dean of the faculty of arts and divinity. He served for many years as a reservist military chaplain and was appointed as a chaplain to Queen Elizabeth II in Scotland. He also engaged in various ecumenical conversations. Moderator of the General Assembly of the Church of Scotland in 2003-2004, he visited China, Sudan, and Eritrea on behalf of the church and also the British military units stationed in Iraq. The extreme poverty that he saw in Sudan and the aftermath of the war in Eritrea made a powerful and lasting impression. His various scholarly and ministerial activities throughout the United Kingdom as well as his travels gave him a deepened awareness of ethnic and religious diversity as these forces were changing the face of Europe.

2. Iain R. Torrance, "Beyond Solipsism," *Princeton Seminary Bulletin* 26 (2005): 59-66; quotations on 59, 63, 65-66.

The Deepening Pluralism of the United States and Its Religions

When Iain Torrance assumed the presidency of the seminary along with a professorship in patristics in 2004, he came to a United States that likewise was becoming pluralistic far beyond what previous generations had known. To be sure, the United States has always been peopled by immigrants of many nations; but initially the diversity was chiefly Protestant and primarily of European origin. As we have seen, the identification of the United States as a Protestant, even a generically Christian, nation grew increasingly problematic in the twentieth century, especially after 1960. But now the pluralism of America has accelerated well beyond what had been apparent in the 1960s, when James McCord occupied the president's residence in Springdale. In fact, as the seminary stands poised to enter its third century of preparing candidates for Christian ministry, the society it faces is one scarcely imaginable even a half-century ago. Will Herberg's classic description of American religion in 1955 as a triple melting pot that he called *Protestant-Catholic-Jew* now seems quaintly out of date. One of the triggers of this change was the enactment in 1965 of an immigration reform law that, in the midst of the escalating Vietnam War and the flurry of other "Great Society" legislation, received relatively little notice at the time. In retrospect, one can see that it was as revolutionary as the various civil rights laws or the creation of Medicare. The law ended the old discriminatory quota system of 1924 that heavily favored immigrants from northern and western Europe. Diana Eck has given but one example of the impact of this law by noting the new connectedness between the United States and the Indian subcontinent.

> The immigration of the past forty years, since the passage of the 1965 Immigration and Nationalities Act, has created a living bridge between India and America with constant two-way traffic. South Indian Tamil and Telugu Americans consecrate temples in suburban Nashville and Kansas City, import sacred images from the artisan workshops of Mahabalipuram, and fly home to Chennai for a family wedding. Indian scientists in the Silicon Valley check the cricket scores on their cell phones. Gujaratis hold their *garbhas* in rented VFW halls. Bengalis order up Durga Puja images from Calcutta and erect huge altars to the goddess in suburban high school gymnasiums. During the Diwali season in India, American Hindus create new versions of Diwali in Salt Lake

City and Cleveland. The Hindu American Foundation lobbies the federal government to issue a Diwali postage stamp in recognition of America's Hindu community. It also keeps a watchful eye on Hindu civil rights, just as the Sikh Coalition documents discrimination against Sikhs and meets with the National Transportation Safety Board about travel restrictions relating to turbans and *kirpans.*[3]

The demographic changes wrought by immigration are extraordinary. According to the 2004 *Statistical Abstract of the U.S.,* over 7,000,000 people from Asia immigrated to the United States between 1971 and 2002, over 800,000 from Africa, and well over 10,000,000 from Latin America. With regard to the Latin American presence, Luis Rivera-Pagán rightly observed in 2000 "that when John Mackay was President of Princeton Theological Seminary, Latin America began at the Río Grande; now, it begins on the frontier with Canada." One may take the seminary's location — Princeton, New Jersey — as an illustration of the changes. A vibrant Hispanic community has taken shape. A few miles north of town on Route 1 stands the Islamic Society of Central New Jersey, and barely outside the township on Route 27 in Kingston is located the Durga Mandir, where the goddess Durga is honored as well as Shiva, Ganesh, Hanuman, and Vishnu among other Hindu deities.[4]

These demographics mean more than the fact that Christianity now shares the stage of American life with other religious traditions. The shift has occurred at roughly the same time that the axis of world Christianity has moved from Europe and North America to the so-called global south. Whatever the relative political and economic strengths of these two broad regions may be in the future, it seems clear that the growing world majority of Christians in the South will have considerably more to say in defining the nature of the Christian movement in the twenty-first century. Their impact will affect the understanding of Christianity in the United States not only from outside but also from within. If current pat-

3. Will Herberg, *Protestant-Catholic-Jew: An Essay in American Religious Sociology* (Garden City: Doubleday, 1955); Diana L. Eck, "Prospects for Pluralism: Voice and Vision for the Study of Religion," *Journal of the American Academy of Religion* 75 (December 2007): 747-48.

4. *Statistical Abstract of the U.S.* 2004 (Table 8); Luis Rivera-Pagán, "Myth, Utopia, and Faith: Theology and Culture in Latin America," *Princeton Seminary Bulletin* 21 (2000): 159-60.

terns of immigration continue to bring large numbers of Latin Americans, Asians, and Africans to these shores, many of the newcomers will be — as they already are — Christians who will put their own stamp upon the faith just as surely as the English Puritans shaped colonial New England or the Scots-Irish Presbyterians made their mark in the eighteenth century upon places such as Pennsylvania, Maryland, Virginia, and Delaware.[5]

These developments have taken place amid changing attitudes toward ecclesiastical forms that American Christians have taken for granted. The denomination, long assumed to be the basic structure through which one expressed one's adherence to the faith, has come into question. By the late 1980s, Robert Wuthnow was writing of "the declining significance of denominationalism." Increasingly, he noted, Christians placed less stock in their denominational allegiances and often moved through a series of affiliations. As various organizations devoted to particular causes or issues formed within them, denominations often appeared to be functioning as holding companies for special interest groups. More recently, Wuthnow has observed that younger Americans — those in their 20s or 30s, sometimes referred to as "the millennials" because they have come of age with the dawn of the new millennium — frequently engage in spiritual *bricolage* or tinkering in which they piece together whatever works for them in giving meaning to their lives. America's increasing religious diversity, from mosques or temples down the street, to new age literature or self-help books at Barnes and Noble, as well as the almost infinite types and amounts of information available through the Internet provide an extraordinary number of bits and pieces with which the tinkers can work. What form or forms of corporate religious life will emerge from this tinkering is unclear.[6]

As it faces a future of uncertain contours, the seminary continues to affirm basic commitments that it has held from the beginning, but it speaks also in new tones with new emphases. The first sentence of the school's current mission statement reads: "Princeton Theological Sem-

5. For relatively recent statistics on the shift to the global South, see, for example, *The World Christian Database: Center for the Study of World Christianity* at http://www.world christiandatabase.org/wcd. Accessed on September 22, 2011.

6. Robert Wuthnow, *The Restructuring of American Religion: Society and Faith since World War II* (Princeton: Princeton University Press, 1988), 71-99, 127; Wuthnow, *After the Baby Boomers: How Twenty- and Thirty-Somethings Are Shaping the Future of American Religion* (Princeton: Princeton University Press, 2007), esp. 12-19.

inary prepares women and men to serve Jesus Christ in ministries marked by faith, integrity, scholarship, competence, compassion, and joy, equipping them for leadership worldwide in congregations and the larger church, in classrooms and the academy, and in the public arena." The statement blends faith and scholarship — or piety and learning, as did the original Plan — and it recognizes that the school's first task is to prepare people for Christian ministry. Ministry in congregations is given precedence, but other forms of ministry are recognized as well. The assumption of the original Plan, that ordained ministry was limited to males, was so taken for granted by the founders that they did not even bother to state it. Princeton Seminary now emphatically affirms that both women and men are called to ministry. Like the original Plan, the current statement recognizes that Princeton is affiliated with the Presbyterian Church and "stands within the Reformed tradition," but it places that relationship within the context of the larger "unity of Christ's servant church throughout the world." From its outset, Princeton welcomed non-Presbyterian students. However, the ecumenical dimension that has steadily expanded since the days of Ross Stevenson and John Mackay receives a deeper and broader definition: "In response to Christ's call for the unity of the church, the Seminary embraces in its life and work a rich racial and ethnic diversity and the breadth of communions represented in the worldwide church." And all of this leads to the final sentence, which reads in part: "To these ends, the Seminary provides a residential community of worship and learning where a sense of calling is tested and defined, where Scripture and the Christian tradition are appropriated critically, where faith and intellect mature and lifelong friendships begin. . . ."[7]

It is in light of these goals that one must interpret several institutional initiatives begun during the Torrance years. First, the administration, faculty, student representatives, and trustees, drawing on the input of previous students, have engaged in a curricular reassessment and revision. The school has committed itself to a more self-conscious process of setting its goals and of engaging in ongoing assessment of whether the desired outcomes have been attained. Second, the building of a new library to replace the outdated Speer Library — the adjoining Luce Library dedicated in 1994 will remain — is designed to enable the seminary to make many of its holdings more readily available not only to those in

7. *Princeton Theological Seminary: 2011-2012 Catalogue* 35 (Princeton: Princeton Theological Seminary, 2011), 25.

residence but also to the worldwide church through digitization already begun. Third, the rebuilding of the Charlotte Rachel Wilson apartment complex in West Windsor Township attests the seminary's continuing dedication to the value of a residential community where women and men of various communities of Christian faith and of diverse racial and ethnic backgrounds may get to know one another as friends and to respect the dignity of difference that exists even among Christians.

As Princeton moves into its third century of training people for ministry in a world very different from and far more diverse than the one Archibald Alexander, Samuel Miller, and Charles Hodge knew, it is useful to draw on some reflections of Andrew F. Walls, guest professor and deeply appreciated colleague from a few years back. In his thoughtful essay "The Ephesian Moment," Walls ponders the meaning of the ever-changing history of the Christian movement in light of the incarnation of Christ and of the church as the body of Christ in whom he becomes complete and thereby completes all things. "The understanding of Christ — knowing the 'full stature' — thus arises," says Walls, "from the coming together of the fragmented understandings that occur within the diverse culture-specific segments of humanity where he becomes known." Walls recognizes that the coming together of these fragmentary understandings can be painful, for all of us are tempted to draw back from that which challenges our own understanding of Christianity. Thus, says Walls,

> There are two dangers. One lies in an instinctive desire to protect our own version of Christian faith, or even to seek to establish it as the standard, normative one. The other, and perhaps the more seductive in the present condition of Western Christianity, is the postmodern option: to decide that each of the expressions and versions is equally valid and authentic, and that we are therefore at liberty to enjoy our own in isolation from all the others.

But neither of these alternatives is acceptable, for as Walls concludes, "None of us can reach Christ's completeness on our own. We need each other's vision to correct, enlarge, and focus our own; only together are we complete in Christ." It is in that faith and hope that Princeton Seminary enters its third century.[8]

---

8. Andrew F. Walls, *The Cross-Cultural Process in Christian History* (Maryknoll, NY: Orbis Books, 2002), 78-79.

Index

philosophy and rational Christianity, 67-69, 96, 316; New England trip (1801), 38-40; and Old School/New School differences, 135-40, 141; *Outlines of Moral Science*, 67-68; and Philadelphia Presbyterianism, 41-44; and piety, 35, 77-80; and Plan of Union (1801), 38-39, 122, 139; and Posey household, 30-34; *Practical Sermons*, 78, 80; as president of Hampden-Sydney College, 37-38, 40-41; as professor of didactic and polemical divinity, xvi-xviii, xix-xx, 26, 64-65, 198; and Puritanism, 35; on religion in contrast to melancholy and depression, 79; Sabbath Conferences, 77-80; on Scripture, xvi-xviii, xix-xx; and slavery, 41-44, 87, 153, 154-56; on theological education, xvi-xviii, xix-xx, 77-80; *Thoughts on Religious Experience*, 78; and Turretin's elenctic theology, 68-69, 96; and women writers on theology, 166-67

Alexander, Charles Beatty, 332-33

Alexander, Ersbell, 29

Alexander, James W., 42, 115, 137; on father Archibald Alexander, 69, 78, 90, 142; on Princeton students' diversity and educational experiences, 88; on the Sabbath Conferences, 78

Alexander, Janetta Waddel, 40, 42-43, 105

Alexander, Joseph Addison, 104-15; biblical scholarship, 110-15; early precocity and education, 105-6; facility with languages, 104, 105, 237; and German biblical criticism, 108-9, 110-15; and Caspar Wistar Hodge, 108, 116, 225; literary masks, 106; and mentor Hengstenberg, 108-9, 112; *Princeton Review* essays and articles, 104, 109, 110; professionalization and specialization, 91, 104-5, 115, 116; protégé William Henry Green, 236, 237; seminary

teaching career, 109-10, 115, 116, 237; spiritual turmoil, 106-8

Alexander, William, 29-30

Alexander Hall, 83, 187

Alianza Popular Revolucionaria Americana (APRA) (Peru), 385-86

Alison, Francis, 5-6, 45

Allen, Ethan, 20

Allen, Richard, 43

Alliance of Baptists, 487

Alliance of Reformed Churches Throughout the World Holding the Presbyterian System, 269

Allis, Oswald, 367, 368, 424

Alt, Albrecht, 114

Altizer, Thomas J. J., 461

Alves, Rubem, 461

American Academy of Political and Social Sciences, 189-90

American Academy of Religion, 495

American and Foreign Antislavery Society, 85

American Anti-Slavery Society (AAS), 85, 86, 128-29, 157, 169

American Bible Society, 121, 433

American Board of Commissioners for Foreign Missions, 81, 121

American Colonization Society (ACS), 84-85, 153, 155

American Council of United Churches, 349-50, 355

American Education Society (AES), 121, 130, 133-34

American Home Missionary Society, 121, 130, 133

American Journal of Theology, 279

American Missionary Association, 191

American Society of Church History, 313, 452, 486, 496

American University (Lebanon), 454

Anderson, Bernhard, 476-78; *Understanding the Old Testament*, 477

Anderson, Carolina Still, 188

Anderson, Charles, 452

Anderson, Matthew, 185-89, 195-96;

Index

Ellinwood, Frank F., 301, 303, 304-5, 310

Ellwood, Robert S., 461

Ely, Ezra Stiles, 124-25; *A Contrast Between Calvinism and Hopkinsianism,* 124-25

Emancipation Proclamation, 177, 192-93

Emmanuel Movement, 276

Emmons, Nathanael, 39, 40, 122-23, 206, 213

Encyclopedia Britannica, W. R. Smith's articles in, 243

Enlightenment: Illuminati movement, 81; influences on North American colleges, 8-9; and Miller, 55-56; and original Plan of the seminary, xx; Scottish, 216-17

Environmental movement and the "greening of America," 460

Episcopalians: Miller's defense of Presbyterianism against Hobart and, 57-59, 133; and Tractarianism, 212; Trinity Episcopal (New York City), 49, 57-58

Erdman, Charles Rosenbury, 311, 323-29; appointment as professor of practical theology, 311-12, 323-29, 330; background and education, 324; and beginnings of fundamentalist-modernist conflict, 362-63; and the Board of Foreign Missions, 396; and curriculum controversies, 311, 323-24, 327-28; family involvement in premillennial and holiness movements, 324-25, 327; and First Presbyterian Church, 326, 362; and General Assembly plan authorizing overtures to other denominations, 348; inaugural address, 311; and Machen, 362-63; and Mackay, 376-77, 398; nomination to be moderator of General Assembly, 363; popularity with colleagues, 326, 377; retirement, 422; *The Spirit of Christ: Devotional Studies in the Doctrine of the Holy Spirit,* 325

Erdman, Mary Estelle Pardee, 324

Erdman, William Jacob, 324-25

Erikson, Erik, 483

Erskine, Ebenezer, 284

Establishment clause of the First Amendment, 460

Ethics, Christian: Greene and, 285-88; West's study of, 490-91

Ethnology (American school of anthropology), 218-20

Evangelical Alliance, 222-23

Evangelical Protestantism: "born again" Christianity, 462; Cailliet and, 446; evangelical fundamentalism, 271, 278, 446, 462; healing movement, 275-78; holiness movements, 273-75, 280, 318-20, 324-25, 327; Jacksonian Democrats and Whig party of 1830s, 148; in Latin America, 380, 407, 412-13, 446; Pentecostalism, 276-78, 380, 407, 412-13, 446; Warfield and, 271-79, 280. *See also* Premillennialism

"Evangelical Society" and Philadelphia Presbyterians, 43-44

Evangelische Kirchenzeitung, 102

"Evangelization" and premillennialism, 272-73, 305-7

Evolutionary theory. *See* Darwinism (evolutionary theory)

Ewald, Heinrich, 238

Existential approaches: and Homrighausen, 426-27; Piper's existential exegetical method, 439

Fagg's Manor, 10

Fanon, Franz, 489

Federal Council of Churches: adoption of "Social Creed of the Churches," 287; Delaware Conference (1942), 402-3, 416; ecumenical ventures, 348-49, 401, 402-3; and Hiltner, 479

Federalists, 19-20, 48, 143n

Female Association for the Relief of

519

Move, 483; *The Logic of the Spirit,* 483; as teacher, 483-84; *The Transforming Moment,* 482-83

Loetscher, Frederick, 336, 422, 451; and curricular reform decision, 338; on John D. Davis, 296, 297-98; and the fundamentalist-modernist controversy, 367, 369; inaugural address ("Church History as a Science and Theological Disciplines"), 336

Loetscher, Lefferts, 451-52; *American Christianity* (co-editor), 451-52; and American church history, 451-52, 485; on Archibald Alexander, 34-35; *The Broadening Church,* 452; *Facing the Enlightenment and Pietism,* 452; on the fundamentalist-modernist controversy and 1929 reorganization, 365-66, 368, 451; on Machen's ecclesiology, 358; *The Presbyterian Enterprise* (co-editor), 452; as Princeton student, 451

Log College and New Side Presbyterians, 5-6, 10-11

Longfellow, Henry Wadsworth, 99-101, 108

Longfield, Bradley, 325, 353, 360

Louisville Presbyterian Theological Seminary, 485

Lovejoy, Elijah Parish, 86-87

Lowrie, Walter M., 377

Luce Library, 508-9

Luthardt, Christoph Ernst, 256; *Apologetic Lectures on the Fundamental Truths of Christianity,* 256

Lyell, Charles, *Principles of Geology,* 221

Macalester College (Minnesota), 484

Macartney, Clarence, 356, 363, 364, 424

Machen, Arthur, 350-51

Machen, J. Gresham, 196, 232, 350-63; anti-liberal polemics, 337, 350, 354, 356-59, 361; attack on Presbyterian Board of Foreign Missions, 395-97; on changes in theological education, 334, 354-55; *Christianity and Liberalism,*

350, 356-59, 361, 446; classical education, 351-52; and curricular reform decision, 338; ecclesiology of, 357-60; and Erdman, 362-63; First Presbyterian Church temporary post, 362; and fundamentalist-modernist controversy, 350-63, 367-68, 395-97; and General Assembly plan authorizing overtures to other denominations, 349-50, 355; and German biblical scholarship, 353-54; and Herrmann, 353-54; inauguration as professor of New Testament literature and exegesis, 337, 354; libertarian view of government, 358-59; as New Testament instructor, 323, 354; and Old South traditions, 350-52, 358, 360; *The Origin of Paul's Religion,* 350; and Orthodox Presbyterian Church, 396; and Prohibition, 358; and racial segregation, 255; as seminary student, 352-53; and Southern Presbyterianism, 350-51, 354, 358-60; and Stevenson's appointment as president, 334; and Westminster Theological Seminary, 368, 369, 395

Machen, Mary ("Minnie") Gresham, 351

MacIntyre, Alasdair, 502

Mackay, Duncan, 373

Mackay, Isabella Macdonald, 373

Mackay, Jane Logan Wells, 379-80, 385, 386, 414

Mackay, John A., 370-421; and Barth, 372, 391-93; and Brunner, 205, 372, 392, 423; on the church and social justice, 405-6, 412-14; and church response to communism, 371, 406, 408-12; early life, family, and education (Scotland), 373-77; ecumenical gatherings and conferences, 402-3, 416; and Erdman, 376-77, 398; and European theologians, 372, 391-93; and Free Church, 373-76, 379-80,

159; students from slaveholding states, 155-56; Thirteenth Amendment ending, 177, 183; Warfield on legacy of, 253-55. *See also* Abolitionism; Colonization movement

Sloan, Douglas, 6

Smart, James, 476

Smith, Elihu Hubbard, 51

Smith, Gerald Birney, 279-80

Smith, H. Shelton, 451

Smith, Hannah Whittall, 273-74

Smith, Henry Boynton, 182, 238, 298-99

Smith, Henry Preserved, 267, 281

Smith, J. Ritchie, 336-37, 367; "Augustine as an Exegete," 336-37; *The Teaching of the Gospel of John,* 337

Smith, Joseph, 163

Smith, Robert Pearsall, 273-74

Smith, Samuel Stanhope, 17-22, 24, 29-30; and Common Sense philosophy, 18; *Essay on the Causes of the Variety of Complexion and Figure in the Human Species,* 18; and General Assembly, 18, 37; and Ashbel Green, 21-22, 26, 61, 95; opposition from trustees, 18-22, 61; as president of College of New Jersey, 17-22, 26

Smith, William Robertson, 243-45; *The Old Testament in the Jewish Church,* 243, 244; *The Prophets of Israel,* 243

Social Gospel movement, 286-89, 307-8, 317-18, 335; emergence of, 286-89; Federal Council of Churches and the "Social Creed of the Churches," 287; and Greene, 286-89, 307-8; and Mcfarland, 286, 307-8; and new fields of social work and sociology, 318; and Presbyterian Church in the U.S.A., 286; and Stevenson, 335; urban outreach congregations, 317-18

Social sciences and theology: Blizzard's sociological analysis of the ministry/clergy, 430-32; curriculum changes and students' demand for courses in sociology, 327, 331; faculty appoint-

ments in Christianity and society, 487-88; Greene's concern with Christian ethics and sociology, 285-88; the Master of Divinity/Master of Social Work program, 432; Progressive era reforms and new fields of social work and sociology, 318; rural sociology, 430

Society for Improvement in Biblical Literature, 97

Society for the Promotion of Agriculture, Arts, and Manufactures, 49

Society of Biblical Literature (SBL), 313, 435-36, 496

Society of Friends (Philadelphia), 42

Society of Inquiry on Missions and the General State of Religion, 81-82, 88, 301

Southeastern (Baptist) Theological Seminary (North Carolina), 487

Southern Baptist Convention, 487

Southern Presbyterians: Cumberland Church, 193-94, 254-55; and Machen, 350-51, 354, 358-60; Presbyterian Church in the Confederate States of America, 176, 181; reunion with Northern denomination, 193-94, 254-55, 348; slavery question, 172-73, 174, 181, 195; spirituality of the church and *jure divino* Presbyterianism, 173-74, 360; split from Old School Northern denomination, 172-76, 181, 198, 360; and Thornwell, 173-74, 351, 359-60. *See also* Old School–Southern Presbyterian split (Civil War–era)

Soviet Union, 408, 468

Spain: Franco regime, 404-5; Hispanic Christianity, 378-79; Mackay's studies in, 378-79; the Residencia de Estudiantes, 378

Sparks, Jared, 70

Speer, Robert E.: and foreign missions, 301, 302-3, 376, 380, 393-94, 396-97; and the fundamentalist-